Fourth Edition

Racial and Ethnic Relations

Joe R. Feagin
University of Florida

Clairece Booher Feagin

PRENTICE HALL, *Englewood Cliffs, New Jersey, 07632*

Library of Congress Cataloging-in-Publication Data

Feagin, Joe R.
    Racial and ethnic relations / Joe R. Feagin, Clairece Booher
Feagin. -- 4th ed.
      p.   cm.
    Includes bibliographical references and index.
    ISBN 0-13-751140-X
    1. Minorities--United States. 2. United States--Race relations.
3. United States--Ethnic relations.   I. Feagin, Clairece Booher.
II. Title.
E184.A1F38   1993
305.8'00973--dc20
                                             92-25736
                                              CIP

Acquisitions Editor: NANCY ROBERTS
Editorial/production supervision,
   interior design, and pagemakeup: ELIZABETH BEST
Copy Editor: BRUCE FULTON
Cover Designer: JOE DIDOMENICO
Prepress Buyer: KELLY BEHR
Manufacturing Buyer: MARY ANN GLORIANDE
Editorial Assistant: PATRICIA NATURALE

©1993, 1989, 1984, 1978 by Prentice-Hall, Inc.
A Simon & Schuster Company
Englewood Cliffs, New Jersey 07632

Printed in the United States of America
10 9 8 7 6 5 4 3 2 1

0-13-751140-X

Prentice-Hall International (UK) Limited, *London*
Prentice-Hall of Australia Pty. Limited, *Sydney*
Prentice-Hall Canada, Inc., *Toronto*
Prentice-Hall Hispanoamericana, S.A., *Mexico*
Prentice-Hall of India Private Limited, *New Delhi*
Prentice-Hall of Japan, Inc., *Tokyo*
Simon & Schuster Asia Pte. Ltd., *Singapore*
Editora Prentice-Hall do Brasil, Ltda., *Rio de Janiero*

Contents

Preface

During the late 1970s and much of the 1980s the interest of many Americans in racial and ethnic issues seemed to be declining. However, by the late 1980s and early 1990s this decline was sharply reversed, and there was much discussion and debate about racial and ethnic cultures and conflict in the United States. This discussion signaled a renewed recognition that racial and ethnic divisions and discrimination still create serious problems for countries such as the United States. In addition, by the early 1990s many Americans were becoming aware that racial and ethnic conflicts in other countries, from the Republic of South Africa and Lebanon to Yugoslavia and the former Soviet Union, were extraordinarily important in the modern world and had the potential to tear apart even a modern industrialized nation.

One result of this reinvigorated discussion of racial and ethnic matters is the creation in recent years of college and university courses focusing on cultural diversity and multiculturalism in the United States. We have revised this edition of *Racial and Ethnic Relations* with this renewed interest in U.S. racial and ethnic heritages and conflicts in mind. This book is designed both for social science courses titled Race Relations, Racial and Ethnic Relations, other Minority Groups, and Minority Relations, and for the various courses on cultural diversity, multiculturalism, and racial and ethnic groups offered in college, university, and other corporate settings.

Our purpose is to provide the reader with access to much of the important literature on racial and ethnic groups in the United States. We have drawn on a broad array of sources, including articles, books, and other data analyses by sociologists, political scientists, social psychologists, anthropologists, historians, economists, journalists, and legal scholars. We have focused on a modest number of major racial and ethnic groups, preferring to accent depth rather than breadth in our contribution to the social science literature. We have chosen to concentrate on groups that are important in the United States, rather than to compare racial and ethnic relations around the globe. In recent decades social science analyses of the United States have begun to dig deeper into the "what," "why," and "how" of racial and ethnic relations here, particularly relations involving such little-studied groups as Italian Americans, recent Asian American immigrants, Cuban Americans, and Puerto Ricans. But that research still has a long way to go before one can view it as complete. Until we have that comprehensive analysis, it is difficult to systematically compare the racial and ethnic situation in the United States with that in other countries. Thus we have set ourselves this difficult task: an exploration of the diversity, depth, and significance of racial and ethnic relations in one country—the United States.

The introduction to Part I accents the racial and ethnic mosaic that is the United States and briefly traces the study of racial and ethnic relations. It serves as an introduction to Chapters 1 and 2, which discuss major concepts and theories in the study of racial and ethnic relations in the United States. The introduction to Part II sketches the political and economic history of the United States to provide the context for understanding the adaptation and oppression of certain immigrant groups that, voluntarily or involuntarily, came to these shores. Only one major group, Native Americans ("Indians"), cannot be viewed as immigrants; indeed, they as the original inhabitants were the victims of the stream of immigrants from Europe.

This edition of *Racial and Ethnic Relations* is thoroughly revised and updated, incorporating the research literature of the late 1980s and early 1990s. Chapters 1 and 2 include new concepts, such as oppositional culture and symbolic racism, and new or reworked theories of racial and ethnic relations, such as the racial formation theory. The remaining chapters include new research data on specific racial and ethnic groups. (As of summer 1992 most 1990 census data on racial and ethnic groups are not yet available.) We have tried where the research is available to make clearer the role of women in a particular group's adaptation and development and where possible to note more fully the cultural resources a group utilized in the process of adaptation and resistance.

This edition has been carefully copyedited for clarity and readability, in line with helpful suggestions from numerous students, teachers, editors, and reviewers. We are indebted to many insightful readers and colleagues whose advice and suggestions have made this a better book: Anthony Orum, James Button, Edward Múrguía, Leslie Inniss, S. Dale McLemore, Louis Schneider, Nestor Rodríguez, Gilberto Cardenas, David Roth, John S. Butler, Andrew M. Greeley, Joseph Lopreato, Graham Kinloch, Eric Woodrum, Lester Hill, Edna Bonacich, Chad Oliver, Marcia A. Herndon, Rogelio Nunez, Tom Walls, Samuel Heilman, Phylis Cancilla Martinelli, José Limon, Devon Peña, Diana Kendall, Robena Jackson, Mark Chesler, David O'Brien, and Bradley Stewart. I would also like to thank the Prentice-Hall reviewers: Brenda L. Moore, SUNY at Buffalo, Curtis Jones, Grand Valley States University, MI, Andrew Greeley, University of Chicago, Esther Ngn-ling Chow, The American University, Mark Chesler, University of Michigan, Richard Alba, SUNY at Albany, Satoshi Ito, College of William and Mary, Lewis Killian, University of West Florida, Bruce Chadwick, Brigham Young University, Russell Thornton, University of California, Berkeley, Elizabeth Higginbotham, Memphis State University, Sharon Collins, University of Illinois, Nestor Rodriguez, University of Houston, and John Liu, University of California, Irvine. We are indebted to Nikitah Imani and Debi Van Ausdale for research assistance on this fourth edition.

We hope you find this edition informative and intellectually stimulating. We welcome suggestions and corrections for future editions. Please write to us at the Department of Sociology, University of Florida, Gainesville, FL, 32611-2036.

Joe R. Feagin
Clairece Booher Feagin

Part 1

The Racial
and Ethnic Mosaic

More than two hundred years ago the new United States severed its colonial ties with Europe. Born in revolution, this new nation was portrayed as centrally dedicated to freedom and equality. Over the next two centuries a vigorous nation would emerge, with great racial and ethnic diversity. Yet the new society had its seamy side. Racial and ethnic oppression and conflict—these too were imbedded in the founding period and in the history of the new republic. By the end of the seventeenth century the enslavement of Africans and African Americans was fundamental to the economy of the North American colonies, and slave resistance and revolt were recurring problems for white slaveholders. In succeeding centuries other non-European peoples, such as Japanese and Mexican Americans, would suffer serious yokes of oppression. But non-Europeans were not the only ones to face oppressive conditions. Discrimination against later white immigrant groups was part of the sometimes forgotten history of both the pre- and postrevolutionary periods.

In the earliest period the colonial population on the prospering Atlantic coast was predominantly English in its origins and basic social institutions. Because of England's huge appetite for raw materials and new markets, English authorities encouraged non-English immigration to the colonies. Yet there was popular opposition, verbal and violent, to the long line of new white immigrants. "Foreigners" soon became a negative category for the colonists. "Despite the need for new settlers English colonials had mixed feelings about foreign arrivals. Anglo-Saxon mobs attacked Huguenots in Frenchtown, Rhode Island, and destroyed a Scotch-Irish frontier settlement in Worcester, Massachusetts."[1] In the 1700s colonies such as Virginia, Pennsylvania, and Rhode Island attempted to block or restrict non-British immigrants.[2]

The basic documents of the new republic reflect its patterns of racial relations and racial subordination, and some of the republic's first laws were aimed at hampering groups of non-English origin. The otherwise radical Declaration of Independence, prepared mostly by Thomas Jefferson, had originally contained language accusing King George of pursuing slavery, of waging "cruel war against human nature itself, violating its most sacred rights of life and liberty in the persons of a distant people who never offended him, captivating them and carrying them into slavery in another hemisphere, or to incur miserable death in the transportation thither."[3] Jefferson further noted that the English king had not attempted to prohibit the slave trade and had encouraged the slaves to "rise in arms" against white colonists. But because of pressure from white slaveholding interests in the South and white slave-trading interests in New England, this critique of slavery was omitted from the final version of the Declaration. Even in this revolutionary period the doctrines of freedom and equality could not be extended to the African American population, for criticism of King George on the issue of slavery was in fact criticism of the North American social and economic system. Jefferson himself was a slaveholder whose wealth was tied to an oppressive, slaveholding agricultural system.

The Constitution explicitly recognized racial subordination in three places. First, as a result of a famous compromise between northern and southern representatives to the Constitutional Convention, Article I originally stipulated that three-fifths of a given state's slave population was to be counted among the total in apportioning the state's legislative representation and taxes—that is, each slave was officially viewed as three-fifths of a person. Interestingly, in this case southern slaveowners pressed for full inclusion of the slaves in the population count, while northern interests were opposed.

In addition, a section was added to Article I permitting the slave trade to continue until 1808. The Constitution also incorporated a fugitive-slave provision requiring the return of runaway slaves to their owners, a provision opposed by few whites at the time.[4] Neither the statement in the Declaration of Independence that "all men are created equal" nor the Constitution's Bill of Rights was seen as applying to what was a large proportion of the U.S. population at that time—people of African descent. Slavery, ironically, would last much longer in the new democratic republic than in aristocratic Britain.[5]

African Americans were not the only group to suffer from government action. Numerous other non-English groups continued to find themselves less than equal under the law. Anti-immigrant legislation in the late 1700s and early 1800s included the Alien, Sedition, and Naturalization acts.[6] Irish, German, and French immigrants were growing in number by the late eighteenth century, and concern with the liberal political sentiments of the new immigrants was great. The Naturalization Act stiffened residency requirements for citizenship from five to fourteen years; the Alien Act gave the president the power to expel foreigners. President John Adams was pressed to issue orders deporting immigrants under the Alien Act, and did so in two cases. Shiploads of foreign immigrants left the country out of fear of exclusion.

Inequality in life chances along racial and ethnic lines was a fundamental fact of the new nation's institutions. At first liberty and justice were for British males only. This situation did not go unchallenged. By the late eighteenth century many Irish and German immigrants had come into the colonies. Indeed, a significant proportion of the four million persons enumerated in the first United States census were of non-English origins.

Over the next two centuries English domination was modified by the ascendance of other northern Europeans. These groups in turn were challenged by southern and eastern European and non-European groups trying to move up in the social, economic, and political systems. Gradually the new nation became an unprecedented mixing of diverse peoples.

Most in the non-British immigrant groups eventually came to adopt the English language and adjust to English institutions, seen by most as the core society and culture. Most entering groups adapted to the dominant culture and ways, with some, especially white groups, gaining substantial power and status in the process. Yet other groups, non-Europeans in particular, remained subordinate politically and economically. Racial and ethnic diversity and inequality were and continue to be part of the foundation of this society. Intergroup relations were not always peaceful, nor was the principle of equality always the basis for such relations.

Today, as in the past, issues of immigration, adaptation, inequality, and hierarchy are very much at the heart of the sociological study of racial and ethnic relations in the United States. In the two chapters of Part I we will define basic terms used by social scientists and examine these concepts from a critical perspective. Chapter 1 examines terms such as *race, racism, ethnic group,* and *prejudice.* Chapter 2 reviews major conceptual frameworks, including assimilation theories and power–conflict theories, for interpreting the complex structure and long-term development of racial and ethnic relations in the United States.

NOTES

1. Leonard Dinnerstein and Frederic C. Jaher, "Introduction," in *The Aliens,* ed. Leonard Dinnerstein and Frederic C. Jaher (New York: Appleton-Century-Crofts, 1970), p. 4.
2. Leonard Dinnerstein and Frederic C. Jaher, "The Colonial Era," in *The Aliens,* ed. Dinnerstein and Jahr, p. 17.
3. Quoted in Peter M. Bergman, *The Chronological History of the Negro in America* (New York: Harper & Row, Pub., 1969), p. 52.
4. John Hope Franklin, *From Slavery to Freedom,* 2nd ed. (New York: Knopf, 1963), pp. 141–43.
5. Ibid., p. 143.
6. Samuel E. Morison, *The Oxford History of the American People* (New York: Oxford University Press, 1965), p. 353.

Chapter 1

Basic Concepts
in the Study
of Racial
and Ethnic Relations

Statue of Liberty, New York Harbor, New York, N.Y.
Photo by Laimute E. Druskis

In the 1980s Susie Guillory Phipps, the wife of a white businessperson in Sulphur, Louisiana, went to court to try to get the racial designation on her birth certificate at the Louisiana Bureau of Vital Records changed from "colored" to "white." A 1970 Louisiana "blood" law required that persons with one-thirty-second or more "Negro blood" (ancestry) were to be designated as "colored" on birth records; prior to 1970 "any traceable amount" of black ancestry had been used to define a person as colored. The white-skinned Phipps was the descendant of an eighteenth-century white plantation owner and an African American slave, and her small amount of African ancestry was enough to get her classified as colored on her official Louisiana birth certificate. Because other records supported the designation, Phipps lost her case against the state of Louisiana.[1]

This controversy raises the basic question of how a person comes to be defined as *white* or *black* in U.S. society. It is only under racist assumptions that having one black ancestor makes one black while having one white ancestor does *not* make one white. If the latter were the law in Louisiana, of course, many *black* residents there, those who have at least one white ancestor (often a slaveholder), would be classified as *white*! This sad story of legal racism illustrates the way in which racial categories are defined socially and politically, and not scientifically.

A logical place to start making sense out of this definitional controversy is with basic terms and concepts. People have often used such terms as *racial groups* and *prejudice* without specifying their meaning. Since these are basic concepts in the study of intergroup relations, we will analyze them in detail.

ISSUES OF RACE

Both *racial group* and the more common term *race* have been used in a number of senses in social science and popular writings. *Human race, Jewish race, Negro race*—such terms in the literature suggest a range of meanings. *Race* in sixteenth- and seventeenth-century Europe referred to descendants of a common ancestor, emphasizing kinship linkages rather than physical characteristics such as skin color. It was only in the late eighteenth century that the term race came to mean a distinct category of human beings with physical characteristics transmitted by descent.[2]

In the 1600s François Bernier was one of the first Europeans to sort out human beings into distinct categories, relying heavily on facial characteristics and skin color. Soon a hierarchy of physically distinct groups (but not yet termed *races*) came to be accepted, not surprisingly with white Europeans at the top. Africans were relegated by European observers to the bottom, in part because of (black) Africans' color and allegedly "primitive" culture, but also because Africans were often known to Europeans as slaves. Economic and political subordination resulted in a low position in the white classification system.[3]

Immanuel Kant's use of the German phrase for "races of mankind" in the 1770s was one of the first explicit uses of the term in the sense of biologically distinct categories of human beings. The use of *race* by biologists and physical anthropologists in the late eighteenth and nineteenth centuries retained this biological meaning. Basic to this increasingly prevalent view was the idea of a set number of genetic groups with differing physical characteristics, together with the idea that these characteristics made for a natural hierarchy of groups. By the late nineteenth century numerous European and U.S. writers were systematically downgrading all peoples not of northern European origin, especially southern Europeans, as inferior "races."[4]

Ideological Racism

It was in this context that ideological racism emerged. We can define *ideological* racism specifically as *an ideology that considers a group's unchangeable physical characteristics to be linked in a direct, causal way to psychological or intellectual characteristics, and that on this basis distinguishes between superior and inferior racial groups.*[5] The "scientific racism" of such European writers as Count de Gobineau in the mid-nineteenth century was used to justify the spread of European colonialism in Asia, Africa, and the Americas. A long line of racist theorists followed in de Gobineau's footsteps, including Nazi leaders such as Adolf Hitler. They broadly applied the ideology of racial inferiority to culturally distinct white European groups, such as Jewish Europeans. In a racist ideology real or alleged physical characteristics are linked to cultural traits that are considered undesirable.

Ideological racism has long been common in the United States. For example, in 1935 an influential white University of Virginia professor wrote that

> the size of the brain in the Black Race is below the medium both of the Whites and the Yellow-Browns, frequently with relatively more simple convolutions. The frontal lobes are often low and narrow. The parietal lobes voluminous, the occipital protruding. The psychic activities of the Black Race are a careless, jolly vivacity, emotions and passions of short duration, and a strong and somewhat irrational egoism. Idealism, ambition, and the co-operative faculties are weak. They love amusement and sport but have little initiative and adventurous spirit.[6]

We see in this crude ideological racism a linking of physical and personality characteristics. Although this type of racist portrait often passed for science prior to World War II—and in today's white supremacy organizations (for example, the Ku Klux Klan) some of it still does—it is in fact pseudoscience. Ideological racists have simply accepted as true the stereotyped characteristics traditionally applied by whites to African Americans or other minority groups.

Modern biologists and anthropologists have demonstrated the wild-eyed irrationality of this racist mythology. The basic tenet of racist thinking is that physical differences such as skin color or nose shape are intrinsically tied to meaningful differentials in intelligence or culture. Yet no scientific support for this assumed linkage exists. Indeed, given the constant blending and interbreeding of human groups over the centuries and in the present, it is impossible to sort human beings into unambiguously distinct groups on physical grounds. Modern biologists and anthropologists have made it clear that few groups have been isolated enough to have genetic homogeneity. The diversity of traits within groups alleged to be distinct is usually as great as the differences between those groups. As a result, most physical and social scientists reject attempts at constructing typologies of racial groups.[7]

However, the lack of scientific support has not lessened the tremendous popularity of racist ideologies. The scholar Ashley Montagu has noted the extreme danger of ideological racism, a view shaped in part by his observation of the consequence of the German Nazi ideology, according to which there were physically distinct Aryan and Jewish races.[8] That racist ideology lay behind the killing of millions of European Jews during the 1930s and 1940s.

Racial Group

Social scientists focus on the *social* definition of race and racial groups. Oliver Cox, one of the first to underscore this perspective, defined a race as "any people who are distinguished, or consider themselves distinguished, in social relations with other peoples, by their physical characteristics."[9] From the social-definition perspective, characteristics such as skin color have *no self-evident meaning*; rather, they primarily have *social meaning*. Similarly, a racial group has been defined by Pierre van den Berghe as a "human group that defines itself and/or is defined by other groups as different from other groups by virtue of innate and immutable physical characteristics."[10]

A racial group is not something naturally generated as part of the self-evident order of the universe. A person's race is typically determined by and important to certain outsiders, although a group's self-definition can also be important. In this book we will define a *racial group* as a *social group that persons inside or outside the group have decided is important to single out as inferior or superior, typically on the basis of real or alleged physical characteristics subjectively selected.*

In the United States a number of groups would fit this definition. Asian Americans, African Americans, Native Americans ("Indians"), and Mexican Americans have had their physical characteristics, such as skin color and eye shape, singled out by white Americans as badges of social and racial inferiority. Some groups once defined as racial groups—and as physically and mentally inferior groups at that—are no longer defined that way. In later chapters we will see that Irish and Italian Americans were once defined as inferior *racial* groups by Anglo-Protestant Americans. Later, social definition as a racial group was replaced by definition as an *ethnic group,* a term to be examined shortly.

Why are some physical characteristics, such as skin color, selected as a basis for distinguishing human groups, whereas other characteristics, such as eye color, seldom are? These questions cannot be answered in biological terms. They require historical and sociological analysis. Such characteristics as skin color are, as Banton has argued, "easily observed and ordered in the mind."[11] But they become highlighted in group interaction. More important than ease of observation is the way in which economic or political subordination and exploitation often lead to the need to identify the powerless group in a certain way. In justifying exploitation the exploiting group often views the real (or alleged) physical characteristics singled out to typify the exploited group as inferior racial characteristics. Technological differences in military firepower, for example, between European and African peoples facilitated the subordination of Africans as slaves in the English and other European colonies. In turn, the darker skin of the Africans and their descendants came to be used by white groups as an indicator of subordinate status. Skin-color characteristics have no inherent meaning; in group interaction they became important because they can be used to classify members of the dominant and subordinate groups.

Knowledge of one's relatives sometimes affects one's assignment to a racial group, particularly for those who lack the obvious physical characteristics. People have been distinguished not only on the basis of their own physical characteristics but also on the basis of a socially determined "rule of descent."[12] Descent is *not* determined scientifically; rather it is based on social perception of a person's ancestry. With regard to African Americans, for example, as the clear-cut color characteristic accented in the early colonial period became more problematical over time, the ancestry aspect became more critical in the identification process. Pettigrew has noted that "black" Americans in the United States today "evidence an unusually wide range of physical traits. Their skin color extends from ebony to a shade paler than many 'whites.'"[13] In some communities in the southern United States this *social* aspect of the defining process becomes obvious when a light-skinned person without any of the physical traits whites usually associate with black Americans is treated as a black person because one of his or her ancestors or relatives is known to have been of African ancestry.

ETHNIC GROUP AND MINORITY GROUP

Ethnic Group

The term *ethnic group* has been used by social scientists in two different senses, one narrow and one broad. Some definitions of the term are broad enough to include socially defined racial groups. For example, in Gordon's broad definition an ethnic group is a social group distinguished "by race, religion, or national origin."[14] Like the definition of racial group, this definition contains the notion of set-apartness. But here the distinctive characteristics can be physical or cultural, and language and religion are seen as critical signs of ethnicity even where there is no physical distinctiveness. Glazer has given this inclusive definition of ethnic groups:

> A single family of social identities—a family which, in addition to races and ethnic groups, includes religions (as in Holland), language groups (as in Belgium), and all of which can be included in the most general term, ethnic groups, groups defined by descent, real or mythical, and sharing a common history and experience.[15]

Today many scholars, such as Thomas Sowell in his *Ethnic America* and Werner Sollors in an introduction to *The Invention of Ethnicity*, still view religious, national origin, and racial groups as falling under the umbrella term ethnic group.[16]

Other scholars prefer a narrower definition of ethnic group, one that omits groups defined *primarily* in terms of real or alleged physical characteristics (those called racial groups) and is limited to groups distinguished *primarily* on the basis of cultural or nationality characteristics. Indeed, the word *ethnic* comes from the Greek *ethnos*, originally meaning "nation." In its earliest English usage, about A.D. 1470, the word referred to culturally different "heathen" nations (those not Christian or Jewish). Apparently the first usage of ethnic group in terms of national origin developed in the period of heavy immigration from southern and eastern European nations to the United States in the early twentieth century. Since the 1930s and 1940s a number of prominent social scientists have suggested that the narrower definition of ethnic group, more in line with the original Greek meaning of nationality, makes the term more useful.[17]

Social scientist W. Lloyd Warner, who was perhaps the first to use the term *ethnicity*, distinguished between ethnic groups, which he saw as characterized by cultural differences, and racial groups, characterized by physical differences. In his view, moreover, the greater the cultural and racial differences between a group and the core society, the slower that group's assimilation into the core society.[18] More recent scholars have also preferred the narrower usage. In van den Berghe's view, for example, ethnic groups are "socially defined but on the basis of cultural criteria."[19] In this book, the usual meaning of *ethnic group* will be the narrower one—*a group socially distinguished or set apart, by others or by itself, primarily on the basis of cultural or nationality characteristics.*

The definitions of ethnic group vary because of different underlying assumptions. Those who prefer the broader definition tend to argue that the experiences of people defined as nonwhite or non-European are essentially similar to the experiences of white groups.* Some have argued that in the United States the situation and experiences of non-European groups such as African Americans are in broad ways similar to those of white immigrants from Europe. Often a further assumption is that the experiences of both white and nonwhite groups are adequately explained by the same theoretical framework—usually an assimilationist framework.[20] Researchers who prefer the narrower definition, who see ethnic groups as a category separate from racial groups, usually have different underlying assumptions. These include the view that the experiences of non-European racial groups have been distinctively different from those of European groups.[21] Scholars such as Philomena Essed argue that the increasing public and scholarly use of the umbrella term *ethnic group* for all groups, including racial groups, in the last decade or two has political overtones: "Indeed, the substitution of 'ethnicity' for 'race' as a basis of categorization is accompanied by increasing unwillingness among the dominant group to accept responsibility for the problems of racism."[22] This point will become clearer when we discuss theories of race and ethnicity in the next chapter.

Whether ethnic group is defined in a narrow or a broad sense, ancestry is very important. Perception of common ancestry, both real and mythical, has been important both to outsiders' definitions and to ethnic groups' self-definitions. German sociologist Max Weber saw ethnic groups broadly as "human groups that entertain a subjective belief in their common descent—because of similarities of physical type or of customs or both, or because of memories of colonization or migration—in such a way that this belief is important for the continuation of the nonkinship communal relationships."[23] Collective memory and consciousness of one's own kind are accented.

Definitions of *racial group* and *ethnic group* that emphasize their social meaning and construction move us away from a biological determinism according to which such groups are self-evident with unchanging physical or mental characteristics. People themselves, both outside and inside racial and ethnic groups, determine when certain physical or cultural characteristics are important enough to single out a group for social purposes, whether for good or for ill.

A given social group may be viewed by different outsiders or at different times as a racial or an ethnic group. And some groups have been defined by the same outsiders as important on the basis of both physical and cultural criteria. During the 1930s Jewish Germans, for example, were spoken of as a "race" in Nazi Germany, in part because of alleged differences from other Germans in physical characteristics. However, in Nazi Germany, identification of Jewish Germans for persecution by Nazi bureaucrats and storm troopers was based more on ethnic characteristics—on cultural characteristics such as

---

*In this book the term *nonwhite* will ordinarily refer to groups that are, or are seen as, substantially of non-European origin, such as African Americans. The term *white* will be used for groups basically of European origin and often will encompass different nationality and religious groups.

religion or language and on genealogical ties to known Jewish ancestors—than on physical characteristics.

Moreover, St. Clair Drake's research on early black African contacts with Europeans and lighter-skinned North Africans has shown that in the first centuries of contact, during the Egyptian, Greek, and Roman periods, the culture and nationality of black Africans were far more important than their physical characteristics in shaping reactions to them. Before the sixteenth century "neither White Racism nor *racial slavery* existed."[24] Similarly, Frank Snowden has demonstrated that the early encounters between African blacks and Mediterranean whites led to a generally favorable image of African blacks among whites and to friendships and intermarriage—much different from black–white relations in modern race-conscious societies. While some whites in these periods did express negative views of Africans' color, these views never developed into an acute color consciousness, an ideological racism that regarded African blacks as an inferior species with severe cognitive deficits. The argument is that virulent color prejudice, or ideological racism, emerged in the modern world, probably with the imperial expansion into Africa and the Americas by European nations between the 1400s and the 1700s.[25]

Minority Group

Other terms have been used for racial and ethnic groups. Prominent among these has been the term *minority group.*[26] Louis Wirth explicitly defined a minority group in terms of subordinate position, as "a group of people who, because of their physical or cultural characteristics, are singled out from others in the society in which they live for differential and unequal treatment and who therefore regard themselves as objects of collective discrimination."[27]

The term *minority group* implies the existence of a "majority group," a dominant group with superior resources and rights. This points up differences in *power* among groups and underscores racial and ethnic *stratification,* a hierarchy of more and less powerful groups. It is perhaps more accurate to use the term *dominant group* for a majority group, as well as *subordinate group* for a minority group, since the "majority group" can be numerically a minority, as was the case with the ruling white Europeans in a number of colonial societies.

PREJUDICE AND STEREOTYPING

Another important term is *prejudice,* which in popular discourse is tied mostly to negative attitudes about members of selected racial and ethnic groups. An understanding of how and why negative attitudes develop is best achieved by first defining *ethnocentrism,* which was long ago described by Sumner as the "view of things in which one's own group is the center of everything, and all others are scaled and rated with reference to it."[28] Members of social groups develop, on the one hand, *positive ethnocentrism,* a loyalty to the values, beliefs, and members of one's own group. This kind of ethnocentrism often becomes linked with negative views of outgroups, views manifested in prejudices and stereotypes. Such negative views, which seem to grow out of a constant evaluating of outgroups in terms of ingroup values and ways, are linked to social, economic, and political interaction among groups.[29]

Prejudice has been defined by Gordon Allport as "thinking ill of others without sufficient warrant."[30] The term comes from the Latin word *praejudicium,* or a judgment made on the basis of prior experience. In English the word evolved from meaning "hasty judgment" to the present connotation of unfavorableness that goes with the meaning of an unsupported or biased judgment. Although prejudice can theoretically apply to pre-judgments in favor of a group, its current meaning in both popular usage and social science analysis is almost exclusively in terms of negative views. *Prejudice* can be defined more precisely, to closely paraphrase Allport, as *an antipathy based upon a faulty generalization. It may be felt or expressed. It may be directed toward a group as a whole, or toward an individual because he or she is a member of that group.*[31] Prejudice is here viewed as involving a negative feeling or attitude toward the outgroup and an inaccurate belief as well; it has both emotional and cognitive aspects. An example might be "I as a white person hate black and Latino people, because black and Latino people always smell worse than whites." The first part of the sentence expresses the negative feeling (the hatred), the last part an inaccurate generalization. This latter cognitive aspect has been termed a *stereotype*—that is, *an overgeneralization associated with a racial or ethnic category that goes beyond existing evidence.*

Why do some people stereotype others? Why have Irish Americans been stereo-typed as lazy drunkards, African Americans as indolent or oversexed, Italian Americans as criminals with "Mafia" ties, Asian Americans as "treacherous Orientals"? Such questions encourage us to examine the role that prejudices and stereotypes play in the history and daily lives of individuals and groups. Sociologically oriented analysts of stereotyping emphasize group pressures on individuals for conformity or rationalization, while psychological analysts stress individual irrationality or personality defectiveness.

Much research has underscored the expressive function of prejudice for the individual. Frustration-aggression theories, psychoanalytic theories, and authoritar-ian-personality perspectives focus on the *externalization* function of prejudice—the transfer of an individual's internal psychological problem onto an external object as a solution to that problem. Many psychologically oriented interpretations stress "sick" or "abnormal" individuals whose race or ethnic prejudice is intimately linked to special emotional problems, such as a deep hatred of their fathers.[32]

In a classic study of prejudice and personality, *The Authoritarian Personality,* Adorno and his colleagues argue that people who hate Jewish Americans or black Americans typically differ from tolerant persons in central personality traits—specif-ically, that they exhibit "authoritarian personalities."[33] Those with authoritarian personalities differ from others in their greater submission to authority, tendency to stereotype, superstition, and great concern for social status. They view the world as sinister and threatening, a view easily linked to intolerant views of outgroups occupying subordinate positions in the social world around them.

Some scholars have raised serious questions about this stress on the expressive function of prejudice. Williams and Pettigrew have suggested that *conformity* may be a much more important factor.[34] Most people accept their own social situation as given and hold the prejudices taught at home and at school. Conformity to the prejudices of relatives and friends is a major source of individual prejudice. Most prejudices are not the result of deep psychological pathologies, but rather reflect shared social definitions of outgroups. This is the social-adjustment function of prejudice. Most of us can think of situations where we or our acquaintances have adjusted to new racial beliefs while moving from one region or setting to another. As Schermerhorn notes, "prejudice is a product of *situations*," not "a little demon that emerges in people simply because they are depraved."[35]

An additional function of stereotyping is that it helps rationalize a subordinate group's position. Whereas prejudice is deeply rooted in human history, stereotyping in the form of a fully developed racist ideology may be relatively recent, perhaps developing, as we have noted, with the European colonization of peoples of color around the world. Modern prejudice, Cox argues, "is a divisive attitude seeking to alienate dominant group sympathy from an 'inferior' race, a whole people, for the purpose of facilitating its exploitation."[36] When peoples are subordinated, as in the cases of the white enslavement of black Africans in the American colonies and the restrictive quotas for Jewish Americans in some colleges in the 1920s and 1930s, those in power—here Anglo-Protestant whites—gradually develop views that rationalize the exploitation and oppression of others.

A few scholars have argued that discrimination may also be motivated by a desire to protect one's own privileges. Some people discriminate because by doing so they gain economically or politically. Such people strive to maintain their privileges, whether or not they rationalize the striving in terms of prejudice. Wellman has argued that much discrimination is a "rational response to struggles over scarce resources." Such struggles involve a system of racial inequality in which the dominant racial group benefits economically, politically, and psychologically—and acts to keep it that way. However, in the everyday world of discrimination it is very likely that the desire to protect privilege will be accompanied by negative views of the group targeted for discrimination.[37]

Several researchers have examined changes in racial prejudices and stereotypes in the United States in recent decades. Sears and McConahay have studied what they term *symbolic* or *modern racism*—that is, white beliefs that there is no such thing as serious antiblack discrimination and that black Americans are making illegitimate demands for social changes. These social psychologists have found that among whites, "old-fashioned racism" favoring rigid segregation and extreme antiblack stereotypes has largely been replaced by this modern racism whose proponents accept modest desegregation but resist the large-scale changes necessary for full racial integration of the society.[38] Similarly, Lawrence Bobo has suggested that whites have an "ideology of bounded racial change." That is, whites' support for changes in discrimination ends when such changes seriously endanger their standard of living. Bobo suggests that many whites display "a loosely coherent set of attitudes and beliefs that, among other things, attributes patterns of black–white inequality to the dispositional shortcomings of black Americans."[39]

Thomas Pettigrew has suggested that what he calls the "ultimate attribution error" on the part of whites includes not only blaming black victims for their failures but also discounting black successes by attributing the latter to luck or unfair advantages rather than to intelligence and hard work.[40] Research on modern racism has mostly examined white attitudes toward black Americans, but many of the new concepts can be used to interpret white prejudices and stereotypes directed at other minority groups.

DISCRIMINATION

Distinguishing Dimensions

Public discussions of discrimination and of government programs to eradicate it are often confusing because the dimensions of discrimination are not distinguished. As a first step in sorting out the confusion, we suggest the diagram in Figure 1–1. The dimensions of discrimination include (a) motivation, (b) discriminatory actions, (c) effects, (d) the relation between motivation and actions, (e) the relation between actions and effects, (f) the immediate institutional context, and (g) the larger societal context.[41] A given set of discriminatory acts—such as the exclusion of Jewish American applicants to Ivy League colleges in the 1920s or the exclusion of African American children from all-white public schools in the 1950s—can be looked at in terms of these dimensions. One can ask what the motivation was for this discrimination. Was it prejudice, stereotyping, or what? One can also ask what form the exclusionary practices actually took. In the case of segregated public schools in the South, principals refused black children entrance into their buildings. Also of importance are the effects of these practices. One effect was the poorer school facilities most black children encountered. But these practices were often not the actions of isolated white principals. Rather, they were part of an institutionalized pattern of segregated education in the South, the effects of which are still present in U.S. society. Finally, such legalized patterns of school discrimination were part of a larger social context of general racial subordination of black Americans across many institutional areas in the South. Discrimination remains a multidimensional problem encompassing all institutional areas of U.S. society.

FIGURE 1–1   The Dimensions of Discrimination

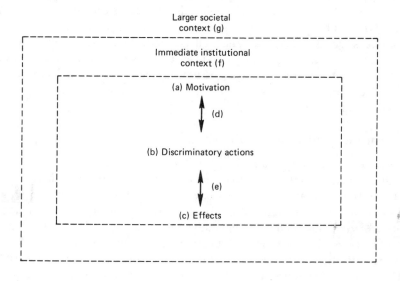

Research on Prejudice and Discrimination

Much research on discrimination has focused on one type of motivation (*a* in Figure 1–1)—prejudice. Many analysts emphasize the relation between prejudice and discrimination (*d* in Figure 1–1), viewing prejudice as the critical cause of discriminatory treatment of a singled-out group. Allport suggested that few prejudiced people keep their prejudices entirely to themselves; instead they act out their feelings in various ways.[42] In his classic study *An American Dilemma* (1944), Gunnar Myrdal saw race prejudice as "the whole complex of valuations and beliefs which are behind discriminatory behavior on the part of the majority group."[43] A few years later Robert K. Merton argued that for some people discrimination is motivated not by their own prejudices but by fear of the prejudices of others in the dominant group.[44]

Some experimental studies by social psychologists have focused on the relationship between prejudice and expressed discrimination. These researchers have examined whether prejudiced people do in fact discriminate, and if so, how that prejudice is linked to discrimination. Such studies have generally found a low positive correlation between expressed prejudice (for example, on questionnaires) and the measured discriminatory behavior. That is, knowing how prejudiced a subject is does not necessarily help predict his or her actions. Some experimenters have tried to develop new, more subtle measures of discrimination, often focused on white attitudes and actions. One such measure involved setting up an experimental situation in which whites encountered a black or white person (a confederate of the researcher) who needed help making a phone call at a public telephone. The researcher then observed if the race of the person needing help affected white responses. Public opinion surveys of white attitudes toward blacks have shown a significant decline in old-fashioned racist attitudes since the 1940s, and some of these experimental researchers have asked whether the whites responding to such surveys are concealing racial prejudices. Reviewing experimental studies that have used the less obvious measures of discrimination, such as the phone call experiment, Faye Crosby and her associates found that white discrimination actually varies with the situation. It is more likely in anonymous situations than in face-to-face encounters whites have with blacks. The researchers also noted that experimental studies have found much more antiblack discrimination than they should have if the unprejudiced views that whites openly express in public opinion surveys were used to predict white behavior toward black Americans in experimental or research settings. Many whites seem to hide their racial feelings when responding to pollsters.[45]

Institutional and Individual Discrimination

The emphasis on individual prejudice and on bigoted individuals in many assessments of discrimination has led some to accent the institutionalization of discrimination. For example, Hamilton and Carmichael have developed the concepts of *individual racism*, exemplified by the actions of white terrorists bombing a black church, and *institutional racism*, illustrated by accumulating institutional practices that lead to large numbers of black children suffering constantly because of inadequate food and medical facilities in many cities.[46] Their book *Black Power* is an attempt to move beyond a focus on individual bigots. Institutional racism can involve actions in which people have "no intention of subordinating others because of color, or are totally unaware of doing so."[47] In his analysis of racism and mental health, Pettigrew has distinguished between *direct* and *indirect* racial discrimination, applying the latter term to restrictions in one area (such as screening out job applicants because they do not have a college degree) that are shaped by racial discrimination in yet another area (historical exclusion of black Americans from many white universities in the South prior to the 1960s).[48]

Recent conceptual work on discrimination accents the point that the individual ("micro") and institutional ("macro") dimensions are so closely intertwined that they must be viewed as two aspects of the same phenomenon. Social psychologist Essed has underscored the "mutual interdependence of the macro and micro dimensions" of white racism. From the macro perspective racism is "a system of structural inequalities and a historical process." From a micro perspective racism involves discriminators whose specific actions are racist "only when they activate existing structural racial inequalities in the system." The routine actions of discriminators both reinforce and are shaped by a hierarchical system of racial dominance and inequality.[49]

The working definition of *discrimination* we use in this book is as follows: *actions carried out by members of dominant groups, or their representatives, that have a differential and harmful impact on members of subordinate groups.* The dominant and subordinate groups here are racial and ethnic groups. Thus discrimination involves actions, as well as one or more discriminators and one or more victims. A further distinction between *intentional* (motivated by prejudice or intent to harm) and *unintentional* (not motivated by prejudice or intent to harm) is useful for distinguishing different types of racial and ethnic discrimination.[50]

Drawing on these two dimensions of scale and intention, we suggest four major types of discrimination: Type A, *isolate discrimination,* is harmful action taken intentionally by a member of a dominant racial or ethnic group against members of a subordinate group, without the support of other members of the dominant group in the immediate social or community context. An example would be a white police officer who implements antiblack hostility by beating up black prisoners at every opportunity, even though the majority of fellow officers and department regulations specifically oppose such actions. (If the majority of officers in that department behaved in this fashion, the beatings would fall under the heading of type C discrimination.) The term *isolate* should not be taken to mean that type A discrimination is rare, for it is indeed commonplace.

Type B, *small-group discrimination,* is harmful action taken intentionally by a small number of dominant-group individuals acting in concert against members of subordinate racial and ethnic groups, without the support of the norms and of most other dominant-group members in the immediate social or community context. The bombing of Irish Catholic churches in the 1800s by small groups of British Americans or of the homes of black families by small Ku Klux Klan–type groups in recent decades are likely examples.

Type C, *direct institutionalized discrimination,* is organizationally prescribed or community-prescribed action that by intention has a differential and negative impact on members of subordinate racial and ethnic groups. Typically, these actions are not sporadic, but are routinely carried out by a large number of dominant-group individuals guided by the legal or informal norms of the immediate organizational or community context.

Historical examples include the intentional exclusion of African Americans and Jewish Americans from certain residential neighborhoods and jobs. Type C discrimination can be seen today in the actions of real estate agents who steer black homebuyers away from white housing areas. They are acting in accord with informal norms shared by many whites in their communities.[51]

Type D, *indirect institutionalized discrimination*, consists of dominant-group practices having a harmful impact on members of subordinate race and ethnic groups even though the organizationally or community-prescribed norms or regulations guiding those actions have been established with no intent to harm. For example, intentional discrimination institutionalized in the schooling of subordinate-group members such as black and Latino Americans—resulting in inadequate educations for many of them—has often handicapped their attempts to compete with dominant-group members in the employment sphere, where hiring and promotion standards incorporate educational requirements. In addition, the impact of past discrimination often lingers on in the present: current generations of groups once severely subordinated may enjoy less in the way of inherited wealth and other resources.

The Sites and Range of Discrimination

Discrimination includes a spatial dimension. For instance, in a white-dominated society a nonwhite person's vulnerability to discrimination usually varies from the most private to the most public sites. If a minority person is in a relatively protected site, such as with friends at home, then the probability of experiencing racial or ethnic hostility and discrimination is low. In contrast, if that same person is in a moderately protected site, such as a professor in a departmental setting within a predominantly white university, the probability of experiencing hostility and discrimination may increase, although the professional status of the professor offers some protection. The probability of hostility and discrimination may increase further as a nonwhite person moves from work and school settings into such public accommodations as hotels, restaurants, and stores, or into public spaces such as city streets, although weak social constraints on discriminatory behavior may still exist there. As we will see in the chapters that follow, those members of subordinate racial and ethnic groups who have ventured the most into settings once reserved for members of dominant groups, either in the past or in the present, are likely to face overt discrimination and hostility.[52]

In his classic study *The Nature of Prejudice* Allport notes that discrimination by members of a dominant group against those in a subordinate group ranges from antilocution (speaking against), to avoidance, to exclusion, to physical attack, to extermination.[53] For example, a dominant-group member, such as an English American, may try to exclude a Jewish American from his or her university or club. Or a white American may hurl a racist epithet against an Asian or African American.

One can also distinguish covert and subtle categories of discrimination from the more blatant forms. *Subtle discrimination* can be defined as unequal and harmful treatment of members of subordinate racial and ethnic groups that is obvious to the victim but not as overt as traditional, door-slamming varieties of discrimination. In modern bureaucratic settings such as corporate workplaces many white employers and employees have internalized inclinations to subtle discriminatory behavior that they consider normal and acceptable. This type of discrimination often goes unnoticed by non-discriminating members of the dominant group.[54]

For instance, in research on black managers who have secured entry-level positions in corporations, Ed Jones has found a predisposition among whites, both co-workers and bosses, to assume the best about persons of their own color and the worst about (black) people different from themselves in evaluating job performance. Like Pettigrew's "ultimate attribution error," this predisposition, which can be conscious or subconscious, can result in discrimination in promotions (or in such matters as socializing over lunch) that is more subtle than the blatant discrimination of exclusion. The black managers interviewed by Jones and other researchers report that their achievements are often given less attention than their failures, while the failures of comparable white managers are more likely to be excused in terms of situational factors or even overlooked. This negative feedback on a black worker's performance makes it more difficult for him or her to perform successfully in the future.[55]

Covert discrimination, in contrast, is harmful treatment of members of subordinate racial and ethnic groups that is hidden and difficult to document and prove. Covert discrimination includes tokenism and sabotage. For example, in one research study a black female mail carrier reported that white male co-workers were hiding some of her mail, so that when she returned from her route, there was still mail waiting to be delivered. Because of this sabotage her white manager blamed her and gave her a less desirable route.[56] Moreover, nonwhite employees, such as Asian or Latino Americans, are sometimes hired as "tokens" or "window dressing": they are placed in conspicuous positions just to make an organization look good, instead of being evaluated honestly in terms of their abilities for higher-level employment. Some employers hire a few nonwhite employees for "front" positions to reduce pressures to expand the number of nonwhite employees to more representative numbers. Tokenism thus becomes an intentional barrier to minority advancement.

Various combinations of blatant, covert, and subtle forms of discrimination can coexist in a given organization or community. The patterns of discrimination cutting across political, economic, and social organizations in our society can be termed *systemic discrimination.* Related to systemic discrimination is the *cumulative* impact of discrimination on its victims. Particular instances of racial or ethnic discrimination may seem minor to outside observers if considered in isolation. But when blatant actions, such as verbal harassment or physical attack, combine with subtle and covert slights, such as sabotage, the cumulative impact of all this discrimination over months, years, and lifetimes is more than the sum of the individual instances. Racial and ethnic oppression is typically both systemic and cumulative.

Responding to Discrimination

The responses of subordinate-group members to discrimination can range from deference or withdrawal, to verbal confrontation and physical confrontation, to legal action. Even where dominant-group members expect acquiescence in discrimination, some subordinate-group members may not oblige. Victims often fight back, especially if they are among those subordinate-group members with some money or legal resources.

Discrimination that begins as one-way action may become two-way negotiation, often to the surprise of the discriminators.

Consider this example from research by Feagin and Sikes, in which a black woman manager in a major U.S. corporation describes a meeting with her white boss about her job performance:

> We had a five scale rating, starting with outstanding, then very good, then good, then fair, and then less than satisfactory. I had gone into my evaluation interview anticipating that he would give me a "VG" (very good), feeling that I deserved an "outstanding" and prepared to fight for my outstanding rating. Knowing, you know, my past experience with him, and more his way toward females. But even beyond female, I happened to be the only black in my position within my branch. So the racial issue would also come into play. And he and I had had some very frank discussions about race specifically. About females, but more about race when he and I talked. So I certainly knew that he had a lot of prejudices in terms of blacks. And [he] had some very strong feelings based on his upbringing about the abilities of blacks. He said to me on numerous occasions that he considered me to be an exception, that I certainly was not what he felt the abilities of an average black person [were]. While I was of course appalled and made it perfectly clear to him.... But, when I went into the evaluation interview, he gave me glowing comments that cited numerous achievements and accomplishments for me during the year, and then concluded it with, "so I've given you a G." You know, which of course just floored me.... [I] maintained my emotions and basically just said, as unemotionally as I possibly could, that I found that unacceptable, I thought it was inconsistent with his remarks in terms of my performance, and I would not accept it. I think I kind of shocked him, because he sort of said, "well I don't know what that means," you know, when I said I wouldn't accept it. I said, I'm not signing the evaluation. And at that point, here again knowing that the best way to deal with most issues is with facts and specifics, I had already come in prepared.... I had my list of objectives for the year where I was able to show him that I had achieved every objective and I exceeded all of them. I also had...my sales performance: the dollar amount, the products...both in total dollar sales and also a product mix. I sold every product in the line that we offered to our customers. I had exceeded all of my sales objectives. You know, as far as I was concerned, it was outstanding performance.... So he basically said, "well, we don't have to agree to agree," and that was the end of the session. I got up and left. Fifteen minutes later he called me back in and said, "I've thought about what you said, and you're right, you do have an O." So it's interesting how in fifteen minutes I went from a G to an O. But the interesting point is had I not fought it, had I just accepted it, I would have gotten a G rating for that year, which has many implications.[57]

This example of a blatant attempt at discrimination illustrates a number of points we have made in this chapter. Because of certain physical characteristics this woman is viewed by her white boss as a member of a racial group he stereotypes as generally incapable. He discriminates by downplaying her accomplishments with a low evaluation. In this case she did not acquiesce to his negative rating. Because of prior experience with his racist and sexist attitudes this black woman came to the encounter with some expectation of having to counter his actions. The one-way action probably expected by the boss soon became two-way negotiation. This black woman made tactical use of her middle-class resources to win a concession and a changed evaluation.

Over the last two decades there has been an increase in the number of middle-class black and other nonwhite Americans having the resources to contest blatant discrimination more directly and, sometimes, successfully. Thus microlevel discrimination may be the first stage in a two-way encounter. The initial discrimination, the counter, and the discriminator's response, as well as the resources and perceptions of those involved, can constitute a broader process of interactive negotiation.

SUMMARY

In this chapter we have examined the key terms *race, racial group, racism, ethnic group, minority (subordinate) group, majority (dominant) group, prejudice, stereotyping, discrimination, individual* and *institutional discrimination, subtle* and *covert discrimination,* and *systemic* and *cumulative discrimination.* These critical concepts loom large in discussions of race and ethnic issues. More than a century of discussion of these concepts lies behind the voyage we have set out on here and in the following chapters. We must carefully think through the meaning of such terms as *race* and *racial group,* because such concepts have themselves been used in the shaping of ethnic and race relations.

Ideas about race and racial groups have been dangerous for human beings, playing an active role in the triggering, or the convenient rationalizing, of societal processes costing millions of lives. Ideas can have an impact. The sharp cutting edge of race, as in "racial inferiority" theorizing, can be seen in the enslavement by white Europeans of black Africans between the seventeenth and nineteenth centuries and in Nazi actions taken against European Jews in the 1930s and 1940s. Sometimes it is easy to consider words and concepts as harmless abstractions. However, some reflection on both recent and distant Western history gives the lie to this naive view. The concept may not be "mightier than the sword," to adapt an old cliché, but it is indeed mighty.

NOTES

1. Frances F. Marcus, "Louisiana Repeals Black Blood Law," *New York Times,* July 6, 1983, p. A10.
2. Wilton M. Krogman, "The Concept of Race," in *The Science of Man in the World Crisis,* ed. Ralph Linton (New York: Columbia University Press, 1945) p. 38.
3. Winthrop D. Jordan, *White over Black* (Baltimore: Penguin, 1969), p. 217.
4. Peter I. Rose, *The Subject Is Race* (New York: Oxford University Press, 1968), pp. 32–33; Thomas F. Gossett, *Race* (New York: Schocken Books, 1965), p. 3.
5. See Pierre L. van den Berghe, *Race and Racism* (New York: John Wiley, 1967), p. 11.
6. Robert Bennett Bean, *The Races of Man* (New York: University Society, 1935), pp. 94–96, quoted in *In Their Place: White America Defines Her Minorities, 1850–1950,* ed. Lewis H. Carlson and George A. Colburn (New York: John Wiley, 1972), p. 106.
7. Michael Banton and Jonathan Harwood, *The Race Concept* (New York: Praeger, 1975), pp. 13–50.
8. Ashley Montagu, *Race, Science and Humanity* (Princeton, N.J.: D. Van Nostrand, 1963).
9. Oliver C. Cox, *Caste, Class, and Race* (Garden City, N.Y.: Doubleday, 1948), p. 402.
10. Van den Berghe, *Race and Racism,* p. 9.
11. Michael Banton, *Race Relations* (New York: Basic Books, 1967), p. 57; see also p. 58.
12. Charles Wagley and Marvin Harris, *Minorities in the New World* (New York: Columbia University Press, 1958), p. 7.
13. Thomas F. Pettigrew, *A Profile of the Negro American* (Princeton, N.J.: D. Van Nostrand, 1964), p. 69.
14. Milton M. Gordon, *Assimilation in American Life* (New York: Oxford University Press, 1964), p. 27.
15. Nathan Glazer, "Blacks and Ethnic Groups: The Difference, and the Political Difference It Makes," *Social Problems* 18 (Spring 1971): 447. See also Nathan Glazer and Daniel P. Moynihan, "Introduction," in *Ethnicity,* ed. Nathan Glazer and Daniel P. Moynihan (Cambridge: Harvard University Press, 1975), p. 4.
16. Werner Sollors, *The Invention of Ethnicity* (New York: Oxford University Press, 1989); Thomas Sowell, *Ethnic America* (New York: Basic Books, 1981).
17. William M. Newman, *American Pluralism* (New York: Harper & Row, Pub., 1973), p. 19.
18. W. Lloyd Warner and Leo Srole, *The Social Systems of American Ethnic Groups* (New Haven: Yale University Press, 1945), pp. 284–86.
19. Van den Berghe, *Race and Racism,* p. 10.
20. See Glazer, "Blacks and Ethnic Groups."

21. D. John Grove, *The Race vs. Ethnic Debate: A Cross-National Analysis of Two Theoretical Approaches* (Denver: Center on International Race Relations, University of Denver, 1974); Robert Blauner, *Racial Oppression in America* (New York: Harper & Row, Pub., 1972).

22. Philomena Essed, *Understanding Everyday Racism* (Newbury Park, Calif.: Sage Publications, Inc., 1991), p. 28.

23. Max Weber, "Ethnic Groups," in *Theories of Society,* ed. Talcott Parsons et al. (Glencoe, Ill.: Free Press, 1961), 1:306.

24. St. Clair Drake, *Black Folk Here and There* (Los Angeles: UCLA Center for Afro-American Studies, 1987), 1: xxiii. See also vol. 2 of this work.

25. Frank Snowden, *Color Prejudice* (Cambridge: Harvard University Press, 1983), pp. 3–4, 107–8.

26. This term was suggested by Donald M. Young in *American Minority Peoples* (New York: Harper, 1932), p. xviii.

27. Louis Wirth, "The Problem of Minority Groups," in *The Science of Man in the World Crisis,* ed. Linton, p. 347.

28. William G. Sumner, *Folkways* (New York: Mentor Books, 1960), pp. 27–28.

29. Robin M. Williams, Jr., *Strangers Next Door* (Englewood Cliffs, N.J.: Prentice-Hall, 1964), pp. 22–25.

30. Gordon Allport, *The Nature of Prejudice,* abridged ed. (New York: Doubleday, Anchor Books, 1958), p. 7 (italics omitted); see also pp. 6–7.

31. Ibid., p. 10 (italics added).

32. See Thomas F. Pettigrew, *Racially Separate or Together?* (New York: McGraw-Hill, 1971), pp. 134–35.

33. T. W. Adorno et al., *The Authoritarian Personality* (New York: Harper, 1950), pp. 248–79.

34. Williams, *Strangers Next Door,* pp. 110–13; Pettigrew, *Racially Separate or Together?* p. 131.

35. R. A. Schermerhorn, *Comparative Ethnic Relations* (New York: Random House, 1970), p. 6.

36. Cox, *Caste, Class, and Race,* p. 400.

37. David M. Wellman, *Portraits of White Racism* (Cambridge: Cambridge University Press, 1977).

38. David O. Sears, "Symbolic Racism," in *Eliminating Racism,* ed. Phyllis A. Katz and Dalmas A. Taylor (New York: Plenum, 1988), pp. 55–58; John B. McConahay, "Modern Racism," in *Prejudice, Discrimination and Racism,* ed. John F. Dovidio and Samuel L. Gaertner (Orlando, Fla.: Academic Press, 1986).

39. Lawrence Bobo, "Group Conflict, Prejudice, and the Paradox of Contemporary Racial Attitudes," in *Eliminating Racism,* ed. Katz and Taylor, pp. 99–101.

40. Marylee Taylor and Thomas Pettigrew, "Prejudice," in *Encyclopedia of Sociology,* ed. Edgar F. Borgatta and Marie L. Borgatta (New York: Macmillan, 1992), p. 1538.

41. Figure 1–1 and portions of this discussion are adapted from Joe R. Feagin, "Affirmative Action in an Era of Reaction," in *Consultations on the Affirmative Action Statement of the U.S. Commission on Civil Rights* (Washington, 1982), pp. 46–48.

42. Allport, *The Nature of Prejudice,* p. 14.

43. Gunnar Myrdal, *An American Dilemma* (New York: McGraw-Hill Paperback, 1964; originally published 1944), 1:52.

44. Robert K. Merton, "Discrimination and the American Creed," in *Discrimination and National Welfare,* ed. Robert MacIver (New York: Harper, 1949), pp. 103ff. See also Graham C. Kinloch, *The Dynamics of Race Relations* (New York: McGraw-Hill, 1974), p. 54.

45. Faye Crosby, Stephanie Bromley, and Leonard Saxe, "Recent Unobtrusive Studies of Black and White Discrimination and Prejudice," *Psychological Bulletin* 87 (1980): 546–63. See also Lester Hill, "Prejudice and Discrimination" (Ph.D. diss., University of Texas, 1978). This paragraph also draws on Joe R. Feagin and Douglas L. Eckberg, "Discrimination: Motivation, Action, Effects, and Context," in *Annual Review of Sociology,* ed. Alex Inkeles, Neil J. Smelser, and Ralph H. Turner (Palo Alto, Calif.: Annual Reviews, 1980), pp. 3–4.

46. Charles Hamilton and Stokely Carmichael, *Black Power* (New York: Random House Vintage Books, 1967), p. 4. See also Louis L. Knowles and Kenneth Prewitt, eds., *Institutional Racism in America* (Englewood Cliffs, N.J.: Prentice-Hall, 1969), p. 5.

47. Anthony Downs, *Racism in America and How to Combat It* (Washington, D.C.: U.S. Commission on Civil Rights, 1970), pp. 5, 7.

48. Thomas F. Pettigrew, "Racism and the Mental Health of White Americans: A Social Psychological View," in *Racism and Mental Health,* ed. Charles V. Willie, Bernard M. Kramer, and Bertram S. Brown (Pittsburgh: University of Pittsburgh Press, 1973), p. 271.

49. Essed, *Understanding Everyday Racism,* p. 39.

50. Joe R. Feagin, "Indirect Institutionalized Discrimination," *American Politics Quarterly* 5 (April 1977): 177–200.

51. Diana M. Pearce, "Black, White, and Many Shades of Gray: Real Estate Brokers and Their Racial Practices" (Ph.D. diss., University of Michigan, 1976); Diana Kendall, "Square Pegs in Round Holes: Nontraditional Students in Medical Schools" (Ph.D. diss., University of Texas, 1980).

52. Joe R. Feagin, "The Continuing Significance of Race: Antiblack Discrimination in Public Places, " *American Sociological Review* 56 (February 1991): 101–16.

53. Allport, *The Nature of Prejudice,* pp. 14–15.

54. Nijole V. Benokraitis and Joe R. Feagin, *Modern Sexism* (Englewood Cliffs, N.J.: Prentice-Hall, 1986), pp. 30–33.

55. Ed Jones, "What It's Like to Be a Black Manager," *Harvard Business Review* 64 (May/June 1986): 84–93; Thomas Pettigrew and Joanne Martin, "Shaping the Organizational Context for Black American Inclusion," *Journal of Social Issues* 43 (Spring 1987): 41–78; Joe R. Feagin and Melvin Sikes, *Modern Racism: On Being Black and Middle Class* (New Haven: Yale University Press, forthcoming).

56. Cited in Benokraitis and Feagin, *Modern Sexism,* p. 109.

57. Quoted in Feagin and Sikes, *Modern Racism,* Chap. 5.

Chapter 2

Adaptation and Conflict:
Racial and Ethnic Relations
in Theoretical Perspective

Immigrants to Ellis Island, New York, N.Y.
Photo courtesy of The Library of Congress

RACIAL AND ETHNIC HIERARCHIES

How do racial and ethnic groups develop? How do they come into contact with one another in the first place? How do they adjust to one another beyond the initial contact? There are a number of social science theories of how intergroup contact leads to initial patterns of racial and ethnic interaction and stratification. Various other theories explore the persistence of racial and ethnic patterns. Group domination and stratification, as well as intergroup conflict, are critical issues in these racial and ethnic theories.

U.S. society is made up of a diversity of racial and ethnic groups. As in the 1790s, so in the 1990s the number of racial and ethnic groups in North America remains impressive, although the exact mix of groups is different. Racial and ethnic diversity is basic in the history of this society.

Yet diversity, as the common terms *majority group* and *minority group* suggest, has often been linked to a racial and ethnic *hierarchy,* to stratification and substantial inequality among groups. Human beings organize themselves in a number of different ways—for example, for earning a living, for conducting religious rituals, and for governing. Among the important features of social organization are ranking systems. Such systems rank *categories* of people, not just individuals. In this and other societies several social ranking systems coexist, some systems classifying people by their racial or ethnic group or gender group, others ranking people by their handicapped status or social class position. Each ranking system has distinct social categories, and rewards, privileges, and power vary with a group's position in the system. Some categories, such as English Americans in the U.S. racial/ethnic system, have generally had much greater power and resources than certain others, such as African Americans. Such power and resource inequality often persists from one generation to the next. In racial/ethnic ranking systems, certain *ascribed* (that is, attributed, not achieved) characteristics— such as one group's racial characteristics as perceived by another group—become the criteria for unequal social positions and social rewards.[1]

The image of a ladder will make the concept of racial and ethnic stratification clearer. In Figure 2–1 the positions of five selected racial and ethnic groups at a specific time are diagramed on a ladder. Some groups are higher than others, suggesting that they have greater privileges than the lower groups. The privileges can be thought of as social, economic, and political. A group substantially higher than another on an important dimension is viewed as a dominant group; one substantially lower than another is seen as a subordinate group. The more groups in a society, the more complex the image, with middle groups standing in a relation of dominance to some groups and in a relation of subordination to others.

Take the United States in 1790, about the time of its founding. For that year one might roughly diagram the five groups in Figure 2–1 in terms of such factors as overall economic power or social status, so that the top group would be English Americans, with Scottish Americans a bit down the ladder. A little farther down might be the Irish immigrants, a group at the time composed mostly of poor farmers and indentured servants. At the bottom in terms of power and resources would be African Americans, most of whom were in slavery in the South. Those Native American ("Indian") groups and individuals within

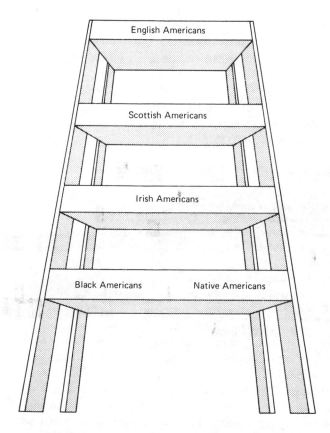

FIGURE 2-1 A Ladder of Dominance: The United States as of 1790

the boundaries of the new nation—many others were still outside it—were also at the bottom of the racial/ethnic hierarchy in terms of economic and political power and resources. The new nation encompassed a racial–ethnic hierarchy from its beginning.[2]

Some Basic Questions

A number of social science theories have been developed to explain this diversity and stratification and the intergroup adaptation that creates them. In some contexts *theory* means vague speculation, but in the social sciences the term refers to a conceptual framework used to interpret or explain some aspect of our everyday existence. The social theorists Barth and Noel have summarized some major questions raised in the analysis of racial and ethnic relations:

1. How does one explain the origin and emergence of racial and ethnic diversity and stratification?
2. How does one explain the continuation of racial and ethnic diversity and stratification?
3. How does one interpret internal adaptive changes within systems of racial and ethnic diversity and stratification?
4. How does one explain major changes in systems of racial and ethnic diversity and stratification?[3]

MIGRATION AND GROUP CONTACT

The origin of race and ethnic relations and stratification systems lies in intergroup contact. Different groups, often with no common ancestry, come into each other's spheres of influence. Contact can be between an established or native people and a migrating people (group A → land of group B) or between migrating groups moving into a previously uninhabited area (group A → new land ← group B). The movement of the English colonists into the lands of Native Americans in the 1600s is an example of the first case.

Migration has been viewed by Charles Tilly in terms of:

1. the actual migrating units (for example, families);
2. the situation at the point of origin (for example, the home country);
3. the situation at the destination (for example, a U. S. city);
4. the socioeconomic and political framework within which the migration occurs (for example, modern capitalism).[4]

Certain characteristics of the precontact situation shape both the migration and the outcome of the contact generated by the migration. The resources and characteristics of the migrating group (such as its wealth or language) and of the receiving group (such as its receptiveness to newcomers) are critical. Push factors generating migration stem from what is happening in the home country of the immigrants. The technological level of each group, such as its industrial skills or firepower, can be an important factor in the initial contact situation. Technological development has played a major role in giving advantage to certain groups. Some argue, for example, that Native Americans lost out to European settlers mostly because of their less developed weaponry. Critical too may be the economic (for example, the job) or religious situation at the point of origin of the migrants. A depressed economy or painful religious conflict in the sending countries has generated major migrations to the United States. Pull factors are also important. Immigrants to a country may be attracted by the portrayal, accurate or inaccurate, of better conditions— such as "lots of jobs"—at the destination.[5]

Types of Migration

In his pioneering book *Comparative Ethnic Relations* Schermerhorn suggested four major types of migration that generate racial and ethnic relations. These can be seen as a continuum from involuntary to completely voluntary migration:

1. movements of forced labor;
2. contract-labor movement;
3. movement of displaced persons and refugees;
4. voluntary migration.[6]

Movements of forced labor would include the forcible removal of Africans to North America; *contract-labor* transfer includes the migration of indentured Irish servants to the English colonies and of Chinese laborers to western North America. The *displaced persons* category is exemplified in the streams of refugees produced by war, such as Jewish immigrants from Europe in the 1930s and Vietnamese refugees more recently.

Voluntary migration covers the great migration of southern and eastern European groups to the United States in the early twentieth century and of several Asian groups in the late twentieth century.

Another important type of migration often precedes the types just listed—the voluntary migration of powerful colonizers sometimes termed *colonization migration.* Colonization migration can be seen in the English trading companies whose employees founded the first North American colonies, a development that led to the dispersal or destruction of Native American groups already inhabiting the continent.[7] We will return to this issue of colonialism later.

PATTERNS OF RACIAL AND ETHNIC ADAPTATION

The Initial Contact

What happens once different human groups come into contact as the result of migration? A close look at racial and ethnic contact reveals a variety of outcomes. In the initial stage the range of outcomes includes:

1. exclusion or genocidal destruction;
2. egalitarian symbiosis;
3. a hierarchy or stratification system.

Genocide is the killing off of one group by another—a common outcome of contacts between European settlers and Native Americans on the Atlantic coast of North America. *Egalitarian symbiosis* consists of peaceful coexistence and a rough economic and political equality between two groups. A few examples of this outcome can be found in the history of world migrations, but they are rare, especially in North America. Some authors argue that by the early nineteenth century Scottish Americans were approaching equality with English Americans in many areas. A more common result of migration and contact is hierarchy, or stratification. Lieberson has listed two hierarchies that can result from intergroup contact. *Migrant superordination* occurs when the migrating group imposes its will on indigenous groups, usually through superior weapons and organization. The Native American populations of the United States and Canada were subordinated in this fashion. *Indigenous superordination* occurs when groups immigrating into a new society become subordinate to groups already there, as was the case for Africans forcibly brought to North and South America by Europeans.[8]

Later Adaptation Patterns

Beyond the initial period of contact between two groups, the range of possible outcomes of intergroup contact includes:

1. continuing attempts at genocide;
2. continuing egalitarian symbiosis;
3. replacement of stratification by inclusion along "core-conformity" lines;
4. replacement of stratification by inclusion along cultural pluralism lines;
5. continuing subordination, ranging from moderate to extreme, of a racial/ethnic group.

One type of outcome can be a continuing thrust by the dominant group to kill off the subordinate group. Attempts by European Americans to exterminate some Native American groups continued until the early twentieth century. Alternatively, an egalitarian symbiosis can continue beyond initial peaceful interaction. Another outcome is for an initial hierarchy, a sharp inequality of power and resources, to be modified in the direction of extensive assimilation of the incoming group within the core culture and society. This can take two forms. In the first, inclusion is along core-conformity lines, with the incoming group mostly conforming to the dominant group. Here greater acceptance and resource equality are attained by surrender of most of the immigrant groups's cultural heritage. Some have argued that many non-English European immigrant groups, such as Scottish and Scandinavian groups, eventually gained rough equality with the English Americans in this way.

A second possibility is cultural pluralism—substantial economic and political assimilation and greater equality along with substantial persistence of subcultural (e.g., religious) distinctiveness. According to this view, substantial assimilation of the immigrant group to the host group is primarily economic and political, with cultural distinctiveness continuing in certain major respects. Interaction between certain white immigrant groups, such as Irish Catholic Americans and the host group, might be cited as an example.

A fifth outcome of continuing intergroup contact is persisting, and substantial, racial or ethnic stratification. The extent and inequality of the stratification can vary, but for many non-European groups, such as Native Americans and Mexican Americans, political and economic inequality has remained so great as to constitute *internal colonialism*. Even in this case, partial acculturation usually occurs in terms of adaptation to the core culture (for instance, to the English language).

Types of Theories

In the United States, explanatory theories of racial and ethnic relations have been concerned with migration, adaptation, exploitation, stratification, and conflict. Most such theories can be roughly classified as either *order* theories or *power–conflict* theories, depending on their principle concerns. *Order theories* tend to accent patterns of inclusion, of the orderly integration and assimilation of particular racial and ethnic groups to a core culture and society, as in the third and fourth of the outcomes just described. The central focus is on progressive adaptation to the dominant culture and on stability in intergroup relations. *Power–conflict* theories give more attention to the first and fifth outcomes—to genocide and continuing hierarchy—and to the persisting inequality of the power and resource distribution associated with racial or ethnic subordination. In the United States most assimilation theories are examples of order theories. Internal colonialism theories and class-oriented neo-Marxist viewpoints are examples of power–conflict theories. There is considerable variation within these broad categories, but they do provide a starting point for our analysis.

ASSIMILATION AND OTHER ORDER PERSPECTIVES

In the United States much social theorizing has emphasized assimilation, the more or less orderly adaptation of a migrating group to the ways and institutions of an established host group. Hirschman has noted that "the assimilation perspective, broadly defined, continues to be the primary theoretical framework for sociological research on racial and ethnic inequality." The reason for this dominance, he suggests, is the "lack of convincing alternatives."[9] The English word *assimilate* comes from the Latin *assimulare,* "to make similar."

Robert E. Park

Robert E. Park, a major sociological theorist, argued that European out-migration was a major catalyst for societal reorganization around the globe. In his view intergroup contacts regularly go through stages of a *race relations cycle.* Fundamental social forces such as out-migration lead to recurring cycles in intergroup history: "The race relations cycle which takes the form, to state it abstractly, of *contacts, competition, accommodation* and eventual *assimilation,* is apparently progressive and irreversible."[10] In the contact stage migration and exploration bring peoples together, which in turn leads to economic competition and thus to new social organization. Competition and conflict flow from the contacts between host peoples and the migrating groups. Accommodation, an unstable condition in the race relations cycle, often takes place rapidly. It involves a forced adjustment by a migrating group to a new social situation. Park seems to have viewed accommodation as involving a stabilization of relations, including the possibility of permanent caste systems. Sometimes he spoke of the race relations cycle as inevitably leading from contact to assimilation. At other times, however, he recognized that the assimilation of a migrant group might involve major barriers and take a substantial period of time to complete.

Nonetheless, Park and most scholars working in this tradition have argued that there is a long-term trend toward assimilation of racial and ethnic minorities in modern societies. "Assimilation is a process of interpenetration and fusion in which persons and groups acquire the memories, sentiments, and attitudes of other persons or groups, and, by sharing their experience and history, are incorporated with them in a common cultural life."[11] Even racially subordinate groups are expected to assimilate.[12]

Stages of Assimilation: Milton Gordon

Since Park's pioneering analysis in the 1920s, many U.S. theorists of racial and ethnic relations and numerous textbook writers have adopted an assimilationist perspective, although most have departed from Park's framework in a number of important ways. Milton Gordon, author of the influential *Assimilation in American Life*, distinguishes a variety of initial encounters between race and ethnic groups and an array of possible assimilation outcomes. While Gordon presents three competing images of assimilation—the melting pot, cultural pluralism, and Anglo-conformity— he focuses on Anglo-conformity as the descriptive reality. That is, immigrant groups in the United States, in Gordon's view, have typically tended to give up much of their heritage for the dominant, preexisting Anglo-Saxon core culture and society. The touchstone of adjustment is viewed thus: "If there is anything in American life which can be described as an overall American culture which serves as a reference point for immigrants and their children, it can best be described, it seems to us, as the middle-class cultural patterns of, largely, white Protestant, Anglo-Saxon origins, leaving aside for the moment the question of minor reciprocal influences on this culture exercised by the cultures of later entry into the United States."[13]

Gordon notes that Anglo-conformity has been substantially achieved for most immigrant groups in the United States, especially in regard to cultural assimilation. Most groups following the English have adapted to the Anglo core culture. Gordon distinguishes seven dimensions of adaptation:

1. *cultural assimilation*: change of cultural patterns to those of the core society;
2. *structural assimilation*: penetration of cliques and associations of the core society at the primary-group level;
3. *marital assimilation*: significant intermarriage;
4. *identification assimilation*: development of a sense of identity linked to the core society;
5. *attitude-receptional assimilation*: absence of prejudice and stereotyping;
6. *behavior-receptional assimilation*: absence of intentional discrimination;
7. *civic assimilation*: absence of value and power conflict.[14]

Whereas Park believed structural assimilation, including primary-group ties such as intergroup friendships, flowed from cultural assimilation, Gordon stresses that these are separate stages of assimilation and may take place at different rates.

Gordon conceptualizes structural assimilation as relating to primary-group cliques and relations. Significantly, he does not highlight as a separate type of structural assimilation the movement of a new immigrant group into the *secondary groups* of the host society—that is, into the employing organizations, such as corporations or public bureaucracies, and the critical educational and political institutions. The omission of secondary–structural assimilation is a major flaw in Gordon's theory. Looking at U.S. history, one would conclude that assimilating into the core society's secondary groups does *not necessarily* mean entering the dominant group's friendship cliques. In addition, the dimension Gordon calls *civic assimilation* is confusing since he includes in it "values," which are really part of cultural assimilation, and "power," which is a central aspect of structural assimilation at the secondary-group level.

Gordon's assimilation theory has influenced a generation of researchers. For example, Silvia Pedraza made significant use of Gordon's conceptual framework in her research on Cuban and Mexican immigration, and Richard Alba contrasted his view of the loss of strong ethnic identities among white ethnic Americans with Gordon's idea of identificational assimilation. And in a recent examination of Gordon's seven dimensions of assimilation, J. Allen Williams and Suzanne Ortega drew on interviews with a midwestern sample to substantiate that cultural assimilation was not necessarily the first type of assimilation to occur. For example, the Mexican Americans in the sample were found to be less culturally assimilated than African Americans, yet were more assimilated structurally. Those of Swiss and Swedish backgrounds ranked about the same on the study's measure of cultural assimilation, but the Swedish Americans were less assimilated structurally. Williams and Ortega conclude that assimilation varies considerably from one group to another and that Gordon's seven types can be grouped into three more general categories of structural, cultural, and receptional assimilation.[15]

In a later book, *Human Nature, Class, and Ethnicity* (1978), Gordon has recognized that his assimilation theory neglects power issues and proposed bringing these into his model, but so far he has provided only a brief and inadequate analysis. Gordon mentions in passing the different resources available to competing racial groups and refers briefly to black–white conflict, but gives little attention to the impact of economic power, inequalities in material resources, or capitalistic economic history on U.S. racial and ethnic relations.[16]

Focused on the millions of white European immigrants and their adjustments, Gordon's model emphasizes *generational* changes within immigrant groups over time. Substantial acculturation to the Anglo-Protestant core culture has often been completed by the second or third generation for many European immigrant groups. The partially acculturated first generation formed protective communities and associations, but the children of those immigrants were considerably more exposed to Anglo-conformity pressures in the mass media and in schools.[17] Gordon also suggests that substantial assimilation along certain other dimensions, such as the civic, behavior-receptional, and attitude-receptional ones, has occurred for numerous European groups. Most white groups have also made considerable progress toward equality at the secondary–structural levels of employment and politics, although the dimensions of this assimilation are neither named nor discussed in any detail by Gordon.

For many white groups, particularly non-Protestant ones, structural assimilation at the primary-group level is underway, yet far from complete. Gordon suggests that substantially complete cultural assimilation (for example, adoption of the English language) along with structural (primary-group) pluralism form a characteristic pattern of adaptation for many white ethnic groups. Even these relatively acculturated groups tend to limit their informal friendships and marriage ties either to their immediate ethnic groups or to *similar* groups that are part of their general religious community. Following Will Herberg, who argued that there are three great community "melting pots" in the United States—Jews, Protestants, and Catholics—Gordon suggests that primary-group ties beyond one's own group are often developed within one's broad socioreligious community, whether that be Protestant, Catholic, or Jewish.[18]

In his influential books and articles Gordon recognizes that structural assimilation has been retarded by racial prejudice and discrimination, but he seems to suggest that non-European Americans, including African Americans, will eventually be absorbed into the core culture and society. He gives the most attention to the gradual assimilation of middle-class non-Europeans. In regard to blacks he argues, optimistically, that the United States has "moved decisively down the road toward implementing the implications of the American creed [of equality and justice] for race relations"—as in employment and housing. This perceived tremendous progress for black Americans has created a policy dilemma for the government: should it adopt a traditional political liberalism that ignores race, or a "corporate liberalism" that recognizes group rights along racial lines? Gordon includes under corporate liberalism government programs of affirmative action, which he rejects.[19] The optimism of many assimilation analysts about the eventual implementation of the American creed of equality for black and certain other non-European Americans is problematical, as we will see in Chapter 8.

Some assimilation-oriented analysts such as Gordon and Alba have argued that the once prominent ethnic identities, especially of European American groups, are fading over time. Alba suggests that there is still an ethnic identity of consequence for non-Latino whites, but declares that "a new ethnic group is forming—one based on a vague *ancestry* from anywhere on the European continent."[20] In other words, such distinct ethnic identities as English American and Irish American are gradually becoming only a vague identification as "European American," although Alba emphasizes this as a trend, not a fact. Interestingly, research on intermarriages between members of different white ethnic groups has revealed that large proportions of the children of such marriages see themselves as having multiple ethnic identities, while others choose one of their heritages, or simply "American," as their ethnic identity.[21]

Ethnogenesis and Ethnic Pluralism

Some theorists working in the assimilation tradition reject the argument that most European American groups have become substantially assimilated to a generic Anglo-Protestant or Euro-American identity and way of life. A few have explored models of adjustment that depart from Anglo-conformity in the direction of ethnic or cultural pluralism. Most analysts of pluralism accept some Anglo-conformity as inevitable, if not desirable. In *Beyond the Melting Pot,* Glazer and Moynihan agree that the original customs and home-country ways of European immigrants were mostly lost by the third generation. But this did not mean the decline of ethnicity. The European immigrant groups usually remained distinct in terms of name, identity, and, for the most part, primary-group ties.[22]

Andrew Greeley has developed the interesting concept of *ethnogenesis* and applied it to white immigrant groups, those set off by nationality and religion. Greeley is critical of the traditional assimilation perspective because it assumes "that the strain toward homogenization in a modern industrial society is so great as to be virtually irresistible."[23] Traditionally, the direction of this assimilation in the United States is assumed to be toward the Anglo-Protestant core culture. But from the ethnogenesis perspective, adaptation has meant more than this one-way conformity. The traditional assimilation model does not explain the persistence of ethnicity in the United States—the emphasis among immigrants on ethnicity as a way of becoming American and, in recent decades, the self-conscious attempts to create ethnic identity and manipulate ethnic symbols.[24]

The complex ethnogenesis model of intergroup adaptation proposed by Greeley is illustrated in Figure 2–2. Greeley suggests, as shown in the left-hand box (host/common/immigrant), that in many cases host and immigrant groups had a somewhat similar *cultural* inheritance. For example, some later European immigrant groups had a cultural background initially similar to that of earlier English settlers. As a result of interaction in schools and the influence of the media (signaled by the long arrows in the center of the figure), over several generations the number of cultural traits common to the host and immigrant groups often grew. Yet, as is illustrated in the right-hand boxes, late in the adaptive process certain aspects of the heritage of the home country remained very important to the character of the immigrant–ethnic group. From this perspective, ethnic groups share traits with the host group *and* retain major nationality character-istics as well. A modern ethnic group is one part home-country heritage and one part common culture, mixed together in a distinctive way because of a unique history of development within the North American crucible.[25]

A number of research studies have documented the persistence of distinctive white ethnic groups such as Italian Americans and Jewish Americans in U.S. cities, not just in New York and Chicago but in San Francisco, New Orleans, and Tucson as well. Yancey

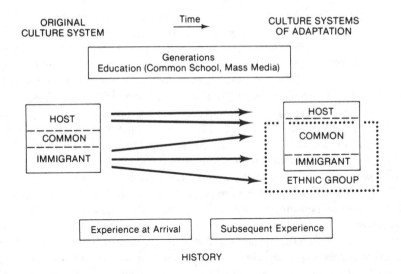

ORIGINAL   Time   CULTURE SYSTEMS
CULTURE SYSTEM   ────►   OF ADAPTATION

Generations
Education (Common School, Mass Media)

HOST

HOST

COMMON

COMMON

IMMIGRANT

IMMIGRANT

ETHNIC GROUP

Experience at Arrival   Subsequent Experience

HISTORY

Source: Andrew M. Greeley, *Ethnicity in the United States* (New York: John Wiley, 1974), p. 309.

FIGURE 2–2   The Ethnogenesis Perspective

and his associates have suggested that ethnicity is an "emergent phenomenon"—that its importance varies in cities and that its character and strength depend on the specific historical conditions in which it emerges and grows.[26]

Some Problems with Assimilation Theories

Most assimilation theorists take as their examples of ethnic adaptation white European groups migrating more or less voluntarily to the United States. But what of the adaptation and assimilation of non-European groups beyond the stage of initial contact? Some analysts of assimilation include nonwhite groups in their theories, despite the problems that arise from such an inclusion. Some analysts have argued that assimilation, cultural and structural, is the necessary, if long-term, answer to the racial problem in the United States. One prominent analyst of U.S. race relations, Gunnar Myrdal, argued that as a practical matter it is "to the advantage of American Negroes as individuals and as a group to become assimilated into American culture, to acquire the traits held in esteem by the dominant white Americans."[27] In Myrdal's view there is an ethical contradiction in the United States between the democratic principles of the Declaration of Independence and institutionalized discrimination against black Americans. For Myrdal this represents a "lag of public morals," a problem solved in principle but still being worked out in an ongoing assimilation process that may or may not be completed.

More optimistic analysts have emphasized progressive inclusion, which will eventually provide black Americans and other minority groups with full citizenship, in fact as well as in principle. For that reason, they expect ethnic and racial conflict to disappear as various groups become fully assimilated into the core culture and society. Nathan Glazer,

Milton Gordon, and Talcott Parsons have stressed the egalitarianism of U.S. institutions and what they view as the progressive emancipation of non-European groups. Gordon and others have underscored the gradual assimilation of middle-class black Americans over the last several decades. Full membership for black Americans seems inevitable, notes Parsons, for "the only tolerable solution to the enormous [racial] tensions lies in constituting a single societal community with full membership for all."[28] The importance of racial, as well as ethnic, stratification is expected to decline as powerful, universalistic societal forces wipe out the vestiges of earlier ethnocentric value systems. White immigrants have desired substantial assimilation, and most have been absorbed. The same is expected to happen eventually for non-European groups.

Assimilation theories have been criticized as having an "establishment" bias, as not distinguishing carefully enough between what *has* happened to a given group and what the establishment at some point felt *should have* happened. For example, a number of Asian American scholars and leaders have reacted vigorously to the application of the concept of assimilation to Asian Americans, arguing that the very concept originated in a period (1870–1925) of intense attacks by white Americans on Asian Americans. The term was thus tainted from the beginning by its association with the dominant European American group's ideology that the only "good groups" were those that assimilated (or could assimilate) in Anglo-conformity fashion.

Unlike Park, who paid substantial attention to the historical and world-economy context of migration, many of today's assimilation theorists do not analyze sufficiently the historical background and development of a particular racial or ethnic group within a national or world context. In addition, assimilation analysts such as Gordon tend to neglect the power imbalance and inequality in racial and ethnic relations, which are seen most clearly in the cases of non-European Americans. As Geschwender has noted, "they seem to have forgotten that exploitation is the driving force that gives meaning to the study of racial and ethnic relations."[29]

Biosocial Perspectives

Some U.S. theorists, including assimilationists, now accent a biosocial perspective on racial and ethnic relations. The idea of race and ethnicity being deeply rooted in the biological makeup of human beings is an old European and American notion that has received renewed attention from a few social scientists and biologists in the United States since the 1970s. In *Human Nature, Class, and Ethnicity,* for example, Gordon suggests that ethnic ties are rooted in the "biological organism of man." Ethnicity is a fundamental part of the physiological as well as the psychological self. Ethnicity "cannot be shed by social mobility, as for instance social class background can, since society insists on its inalienable ascription from cradle to grave." What Gordon seems to have in mind is not the old racist notion of the unchanging biological character and separateness of racial groups, but rather the rootedness of intergroup relations, including racial and ethnic relations, in the everyday realities of kinship and other socially constructed group boundaries. Gordon goes further, however, emphasizing that human beings tend to be "selfish, narcissistic and perpetually poised on the edge of aggression." And it is these selfish tendencies that lie behind racial and ethnic tensions.[30] Gordon is here adopting a Hobbesian (dog-eat-dog) view of human nature.

Critics of this biosocial view have suggested that it reads back into funda-mental "human nature" what are in reality only the specific characteristics of an individualistic value system that has evolved under modern capitalism. That is, under capitalism selfishness and narcissism are *learned* rather than rooted deeply in the human biological makeup.

Although decidedly different from the earlier biological theories, the modern biosocial analysis remains problematical. The exact linkages between the deep genetic underpinnings of human nature and concrete racial or ethnic behavior are not spelled out beyond some vague analysis of kin selection and selfish behavior. A more convincing sociobiological analysis might attempt to show more exactly how the "desires" of the human genes are changed, through several specified levels or techniques, into social phenomena such as slavery or language assimilation. As yet, this important task has not been done.

Another difficulty with the biosocial approach is that in the everyday world, racial and ethnic relations are *immediately social* rather than biological. As Edna Bonacich has pointed out, many racial and ethnic groups have mixed biological ancestry. Jewish Americans, for example, have a very mixed ancestry: as a group, they share no distinct biological characteristics. Biologically diverse Italian immigrants from different regions of Italy gained a sense of being Italian American (even Italian) in the United States. The bonds holding Jewish Americans together and Italian Americans together were not genetically based or biologically primordial, but rather the result of real *historical* experiences as these groups settled into the United States. Moreover, if ethnicity is primordial in a biological sense, it should always be a prominent force in human affairs. Sometimes ethnicity leads to recurring conflict, as in the case of Jews and Gentiles in the United States; in other cases, as with Scottish and English Americans, it quietly disappears in the assimilation process. Sentiments based on common ancestry are important, but they are activated primarily in the concrete experiences and histories of specific migrating and host groups.[31]

Emphasizing Migration: Competition Theory

A contemporary example of the exploration of migration issues in the Robert Park tradition is *competition theory*. Park emphasized the role of the migration of peoples in the creation of ethnic relations. This migration led in turn to competition for scarce resources, then to accommodation and assimilation. Competition theorists have explored the contact and competition parts of this "race relations cycle." Unlike some order-oriented theorists, they do address questions of protest and conflict, although they do not give much attention to power, exploitation, or inequality issues. The *human ecology* tradition in sociological thought draws on the ideas of Park and other ecologists and emphasizes the "struggle of human groups for survival" within their physical environments. This tradition, which highlights demographic trends such as the migration of groups and population concentration in cities, has been adopted by competition analysts researching racial and ethnic groups.[32]

Competition theorists such as Susan Olzak and Joane Nagel view ethnicity as a social phenomenon distinguished by boundaries of language, skin color, and culture. They consider the tradition of human ecology valuable because it emphasizes the stability of ethnic population boundaries over time, as well as the impact of shifts in these boundaries resulting from migration; ethnic group membership often coincides with the creation of a distinctive group niche in the labor force. Competition occurs when two or more ethnic groups attempt to secure the same resources, such as jobs or housing. Competition theorists have accented the ways in which ethnic group competition and the accompanying ethnic solidarity lead to collective action, mobilization, and protest.[33]

According to competition theorists, collective action is fostered by immigration across borders and by the expansion of once-segregated minorities into the same labor and housing markets to which other ethnic groups have access. A central argument of these theorists is that collective attacks on a subordinate ethnic group—immigrant and black workers, for instance—increase at the local city level when the group moves up and out of segregated jobs and challenges other groups and not, as one might expect, in cities where ethnic groups are locked into residential segregation and poverty. For example, empirical data presented by Olzak in an article on ethnic and racial violence in the late nineteenth century support the view that ethnic collective action, such as Anglo-Protestant crowds attacking European immigrants coming into the United States, increases when immigration expands and economic recessions occur. Olzak uses such data to argue that the ethnic boundary of the native-born, those already in certain city areas, was mobilized against immigrant and black workers "when ethnic competition was activated by a rising supply of low wage labor and tight labor markets. In this case the ethnic groups that mobilized were not fully assimilated, but had retained aspects of their traditional identity and drew on that for mobilization against other groups."[34]

Competition theorists explicitly contrast their analyses with the power–conflict views we will discuss in the next section, perspectives that emphasize the role of capitalism, economic subordination, and institutionalized discrimination. Competition theorists write about urban ethnic worlds as though institutionalized racism and capitalism-generated exploitation of workers are not major forces in recurring ethnic and racial competition in cities. As we have seen, they emphasize migration and population concentration, as well as other demographic factors.

As we will see shortly, a power–conflict theorist might counter this emphasis by noting that the competition theorists are studying markets and interethnic competition in cities without a clear historical sense of the great inequality that is the foundation of urban job and housing markets in capitalist countries such as the United States. Missing from competition theory is a fundamental and systematic concern with the issues of inequality, power, exploitation, and discrimination accented by power–conflict theories.

POWER–CONFLICT THEORIES

The last few decades have witnessed the development of power–conflict frameworks explaining U.S. racial and ethnic relations, perspectives that place much greater emphasis on economic stratification and power issues than one finds in assimilation and competition theories. Within this broad category of power–conflict theories are a number of subcategories, including the caste perspective, the internal colonialism viewpoint, and a variety of class-based and neo-Marxist theories.

The Caste School

One early exception to the assimilation perspective was the *caste school* of race relations, which developed in the 1940s under W. Lloyd Warner and Allison Davis.[35] Focusing on black–white relations in the South, these researchers viewed the position of black Americans as distinctively different from that of other racial and ethnic groups. After the Civil War a new social system, a caste system, replaced the old slavery system of the South. The white and black castes were separated by a total prohibition of intermarriage as well as by economic and social inequality. Warner and his associates were critical of the emphasis in most social science analysis on prejudiced attitudes and feelings. Instead, they emphasized *institutionalized discrimination* as the foundation of a castelike system of U.S. apartheid.[36]

Early Class Theories of Race Relations

William E. B. Du Bois, one of the first sociological theorists in the United States, was an African American civil rights activist who had experienced the brutality of racism firsthand. Drawing on Marxist class analysis in his writings from the early 1900s to his death in 1963, Du Bois was perhaps the first theorist to emphasize that racial oppression and capitalist-class oppression were inextricably tied together in the United States. In his view the interplay of racism and capitalism explained why there has never been democracy for people of all races and creeds in the United States. In a 1948 article titled "Is Man Free?" he argued that both black workers and white workers were prevented from exercising full democratic rights because of the control of the small capitalist class (for example, the owners of workplaces) over the economy and politics. He believed that a truly democratic U.S. society must include not only equality for black Americans but also full control of workplaces by workers. Du Bois's Marxist ideas are still fresh and provocative but have been ignored in most social science analysis of racial issues.[37]

An early power–conflict analyst who did draw on Du Bois and on class analysis was Oliver C. Cox, a black scholar whose work has also been neglected, in part because of its Marxist approach. Cox emphasized the role of the capitalist class in racial exploitation; he analyzed the economic dimensions of the forced slave migration from Africa and the oppressiveness of later conditions for African American slaves. Slave trade was "a way of recruiting labor for the purpose of exploiting the great natural resources of America." The color of Africans was not important: they were chosen "simply because they were the best workers to be found for the heavy labor in the mines and plantations across the Atlantic." A search for cheap labor by a profit-oriented capitalist class led to a system of racial subordination. Racial prejudice developed later as an ideology rationalizing this subordination of African Americans.[38]

Internal Colonialism

Analysts of internal colonialism prefer to see the racial stratification and the class stratification of U.S. capitalism as *separate but related* systems of oppression. Neither should be reduced in social science theories to the other. An emphasis on power and resource inequalities, particularly white–minority inequalities, is at the heart of the internal colonialism model.

The framework of internal colonialism is built in part upon the work of analysts of *external colonialism*—the worldwide imperialism of certain capitalist nations, including the United States and European nations.[39] For example, Balandier has noted that capitalist expansion has affected non-European peoples since the fifteenth century: "Until very recently the greater part of the world's population, not belonging to the white race (if we exclude China and Japan), knew only a status of dependency on one or another of the European colonial powers."[40] External colonialism involves the running of a country's economy and politics by an outside colonial power. Many colonies eventually became independent of their colonizers, such as Britain or France, but continued to have their economies directed by the capitalists and corporations of the colonial powers. This system of continuing dependency has been called *neocolonialism*. Neocolonialism is common today where there are few white settlers in the colonized country. Colonies experiencing a large in-migration of white settlers often show a different pattern. In such cases external colonialism becomes *internal colonialism* when the control and exploitation of non-European groups in the colonized country passes from whites in the home country to white immigrant groups within the newly independent country.[41]

Non-European groups entering later, such as African slaves and Mexican farm workers in the United States, can also be viewed in terms of internal colonialism. Internal colonialism here emerged out of classical European colonialism and imperialism and took on a life of its own. The origin and initial stabilization of internal colonialism in North America predate the Revolutionary War. The systematic subordination of non-Europeans began with "genocidal attempts by colonizing settlers to uproot native populations and force them into other regions."[42] Native Americans were killed or driven off desirable lands. Slaves from Africa were a cheap source of labor for capital accumulation before and after the Revolution. Later, Asians and Pacific peoples were imported as contract workers or annexed in an expansionist period of U.S. development. Robert Blauner, a colonialism theorist, notes that agriculture in the South depended on black labor; in the Southwest, Mexican agricultural development was forcibly taken over by European settlers, and later agricultural development was based substantially on cheap Mexican labor coming into what was once northern Mexico.[43]

In exploiting the labor of non-European peoples, who were made slaves or were paid low wages, white agricultural and industrial capitalists reaped enormous profits. From the internal colonialism perspective, contemporary racial and ethnic inequality is grounded in the economic *interests* of whites in low-wage labor—the underpinning of capitalistic economic exploitation. Non-European groups were subordinated to European American desires for *labor* and *land*. Internal colonialism theorists have recognized the central role of *government* support of the exploitation of minorities. The colonial and U.S. governments played an important role in legitimating slavery in the sixteenth through the nineteenth centuries and in providing the government soldiers who subordinated Native Americans across the nation and Mexicans in the Southwest.

Most internal colonialism theorists are not concerned primarily with white immigrant groups, many of which entered the United States after non-European groups were subordinated. Instead, they wish to analyze the establishment of racial stratification and the control processes that maintain persisting white dominance and ideological racism.

Stokely Carmichael and Charles Hamilton, who in their writings in the 1960s were among the first to use the term *internal colonialism,* accented institutional racism—discrimination by the white community against blacks as a group (see Chapter 1).[44] From this perspective African Americans are still a "colony" in the United States in regard to education, economics, and politics.

A Neo-Marxist Emphasis on Class

Analysts of racial and ethnic relations have combined an internal colonialism perspective with an emphasis on class stratification that draws on the Marxist research pioneered by Du Bois and Cox. Mario Barrera, for example, has suggested that the heart of current internal colonialism is an interactive structure of class *and* race stratification that divides our society. Class, in the economic-exploitation sense of that term, needs to be central to a colonialism perspective. Basic to the U.S. system of internal colonialism are four classes that have developed in U.S. capitalism:

1. *capitalists*: that small group of people who control capital investments and the means of production and who buy the labor of many others;
2. *managers*: that modest-sized group of people who work as administrators for the capitalists and have been granted control over the work of others;
3. *petit bourgeoisie*: that small group of merchants who control their own businesses and do most of their work themselves, buying little labor power from others;
4. *working class*: that huge group of blue-collar and white-collar workers who sell their labor to employers in return for wages and salaries.

The dominant class in the U.S. political-economic system is the capitalist class, which in the workplace subordinates working people, both nonwhite and white, to its profit and investment needs. And it is the capitalists who decide whether and where to create jobs. They are responsible for the flight of capital and jobs from many central cities to the suburbs and overseas.

Barrera argues that each of these classes contains important segments that are set off in terms of race and ethnicity. Figure 2–3 suggests how this works. Each of the major classes is crosscut by a line of racial segmentation that separates those suffering institutionalized discrimination, such as black Americans and Mexican Americans, from those who do not. Take the example of the working class. Although black, Latino, and other minority workers share a similar *class* position with white workers, in that they

FIGURE 2–3   The Class and Race Structure of Internal Colonialism

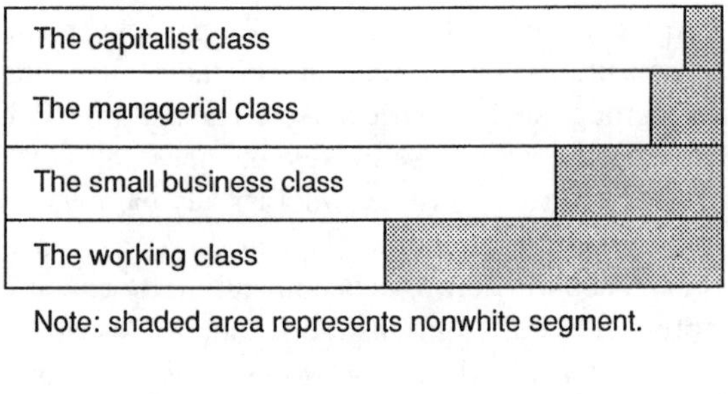

Note: shaded area represents nonwhite segment.

are struggling against capitalist employers for better wages and working conditions, they are *also* in a subordinate position because of structural discrimination along racial lines within that working class. Barrera notes that the dimensions of this discrimination often include lower wages for many minority workers, as well as their concentration in lower-status occupations. Minority Americans suffer from both class exploitation (as wage workers) and racial exploitation (as workers of color).[45]

Ideology and Oppositional Culture

Internal colonialism theorists have studied the role of cultural stereotyping and ideology in limiting the opportunities of subordinate groups of color. A racist ideology dominates an internal colonialist society, intellectually dehumanizing the colonized. Stereotyping and prejudice, seen in many traditional assimilation theories as more or less temporary problems, are viewed by colonialism analysts as a way of rationalizing exploitation over a very long period, if not permanently. Discrimination is a question not of individual bigots but rather of a system of racial exploitation rationalized by prejudice.[46]

In his book on the English colonization of Ireland, Michael Hechter has developed a theory of internal colonialism that emphasizes how the subordinate group utilizes its own culture to *resist* subordination. Hechter argues that in a system of internal colonialism, cultural as well as racial markers are used to set off subordinate groups such as African Americans in the United States and the Irish in the United Kingdom. Resistance to the dominant group by the subordinate group often takes the form of cultural solidarity in opposition to the dominant culture. This solidarity can become the basis for protest movements by the subordinated group.[47]

Beginning in the 1960s, a number of power–conflict scholars and activists have further developed this idea of *oppositional culture* as a basis for understanding the resistance of non-European groups to the Euro-American core culture. Bonnie Mitchell and Joe Feagin have built on the idea of oppositional culture suggested in the work of Hechter and Blauner.[48] They note that in the centuries of contact before the creation of the United States, Mexico, and Canada, North America was populated by a diverse mixture of European, African, and Native American cultures. The U.S. nation created in the late 1700s encompassed African enslavement and the genocide of Native Americans. Faced with oppression, these and other victims of internal colonialism have long drawn on their own cultural resources, as well as their distinctive knowledge of Euro-American culture and society, to resist oppression in every way possible.

The cultures of those oppressed by European Americans have not only provided a source of individual, family, and community resistance to racial oppression and colonialism but have also infused, albeit often in unheralded ways, some significant elements into the evolving cultural mix that constitutes the core culture of the United States. The oppositional cultures of colonized groups such as African Americans, Latino Americans, and Native Americans have helped preserve several key elements of U.S. society, including its tradition of civil rights and social justice. Another key element, ironically enough given the usual white image of minority families, is the value of extended kinship relations. The tendency toward extended kin networks is both culturally encouraged and economically beneficial for oppressed minority groups. For example, research on black and Latino communities has found extensive kinship networks to be the basis of social and economic support in difficult times. Native American groups have also been known for their communalism and extended family networks.[49]

Partly as a result of shared histories of oppression and partly as a result of commitment to values different from Euro-American norms, majorities in these non-European groups have developed strong and highly complex kin ties that bind their communities together and create the conditions for survival in the face of discrimination and oppression. This reality contrasts with the exaggerated stereotype of endemic family pathology in these groups. Internal colonialism theories accent both the oppression of minority Americans and the oppositional cultures that enable minority groups not only to survive but also to resist oppression, passively and actively.

Criticism of Internal Colonialism Theories

British social scientist Robert Miles has criticized those using the internal colonialism and institutional racism concepts for neglecting class divisions among dominant group whites. In his view the racist attitudes of white workers come from their *powerlessness*, not from their power as whites in the racial hierarchy. Miles argues that not all black Americans are subordinate to all whites; some occupy middle-class positions and have power over some poorer whites and blacks.[50] However, Miles does not understand how racial subordination works in the United States. Every black person, at every class level, can be a racial target of, for example, a white police officer intent on racial harassment or a white supremacy group intent on a racial murder (see Chapter 8). In this sense the "power" of even middle-class black Americans has significant racial limits. Although internal colonialism analysts recognize the importance of class distinctions, as we saw in the case of Barrera, they accent an ingrained system of racial subordination cutting across class levels.

Joan Moore has criticized the term *neocolonialism*. As we have noted, a neocolonial situation is one in which a Third World country (for example, an African country) has separated itself politically from a European colonial power but continues to be dependent on that country. The former colony needs "foreign experts." It has a class of indigenous leaders who help the former colonial power exploit the local population. It has a distinct territorial boundary. Moore suggests that this neocolonialism model does not apply very well to subordinate nonwhite groups in the United States, in that these groups are not generally confined to a specific bounded territory, nor do they contain the exploitative intermediary elite of Third World neocolonialism. This space-centered critique has been repeated by Omi and Winant, who argue that the social and spatial intermixing of white and nonwhite groups in the United States casts serious doubt on the internal colonialism argument about territorially bounded colonization.[51]

However, most internal colonialism researchers have recognized the differences between internal colonial and neocolonial oppression. These theorists note that the situations of minority groups in the United States are different from those of, for instance, Africans in a newly independent nation still dependent on a European country. In response to Moore's critique, internal colonialism analysts might argue that there are many aspects of colonialism evident in U.S. racial and ethnic relations; they might emphasize that non-European groups in the United States (1) are usually residentially segregated, (2) are typically "superexploited" in employment and deficient in other material conditions when compared with white immigrants, (3) are culturally stigmatized, and (4) have had some of their leaders co-opted by whites. While these conditions in the United States are not defined as precisely as they are in the case of Third World neocolonialism, they are similar enough to allow the use of the idea of colonialism to assess racial and ethnic relations in the United States.

The Split Labor Market View: Another Class-Based Theory

Colonialism analysts such as Blauner are, as Miles suggests, sometimes unclear about whether all classes of whites benefit from the colonization of nonwhites, or just the dominant class of capitalist employers. A power–conflict perspective that helps in assessing this question is the *split labor market* view, which treats class in the sense of position in the "means of production." This viewpoint has been defended by Edna Bonacich. She argues that in U.S. society the majority-group (white) workers do not share the interests of the dominant political and economic class, the capitalists. Yet both the dominant employer class and the white part of the working class discriminate against the nonwhite part of the working class.[52]

Using a Marxist class analysis of racial subordination, Oliver Cox argued that the capitalist class, motivated by a desire for profit and cheap labor, sought African labor for the slave system in the United States. Ever since, this employer class has helped keep African Americans in a subordinate economic position in U.S. society. Al Szymanski argues that since employers have not created enough jobs for all those wishing to work, black and white workers are pitted against each other for too few jobs, often to the broad advantage of employers as a class. Employers benefit from the lower wages of black workers and from the divisions created between black and white workers (see the preceding discussion of Barrera's work), divisions reducing the likelihood of large working-class unions and class-based mobilization.[53]

In contrast, Bonacich emphasizes that discrimination against minority workers by ordinary white workers seeking to protect their own privileges, however limited these may be, is important. Capitalists bring in nonwhite laborers to decrease labor costs, but white workers resist because they fear job displacement or lower wages. For example, over the last century white workers' unions have restricted the access of black workers to many job ladders, thus splitting the labor market and reducing black incomes. Research on unions in Alabama by Stanley Greenberg provides historical evidence for this argument. Greenberg concludes that from the 1880s to the 1960s the industrial unions in Alabama "helped forge a labor framework" that created and perpetuated rigidly segregated white and black jobs.[54] White workers gain and lose from this structural racism. They gain in the short run, because there is less competition for privileged job categories from the nonwhites they have excluded. But they lose in the long run because employers can use this cordoned-off sector of nonwhites to undercut them.[55]

"Middleman" Minorities and Ethnic Enclaves

Drawing on insights of earlier scholars, Bonacich has explored the in-between position, in terms of power and resources, that certain racial and ethnic groups have occupied in stratified societies. These groups find their economic niche serving elites and workers as small-business people positioned between producers and consumers. Some ethnic and racial groups become small-scale traders and merchants doing jobs that dominant groups are not eager to do. For example, many first-generation Jewish and Japanese Americans, excluded from mainstream employment by white Protestants, became small-scale merchants, tailors, restaurant operators, or gardeners. These groups have held "a distinctive class position that is of special use to the ruling class." They "act as a go-between to this society's more subordinate groups."[56]

Bonacich and Modell have found that Japanese Americans fit the middleman minority model. Before World War II Japanese Americans resided in highly organized communities. Their local economies were based on self-employment, including gardening and truck farming, and on other nonindustrial family businesses. The group solidarity of the first generation of Japanese Americans helped them establish successful small businesses. However, they faced hostility from the surrounding society, and in fact were driven into the businesses they developed because they were denied other employment opportunities. By the second generation there was some breakdown in the middleman position of Japanese Americans, for many of that generation moved into professional occupations outside the niche economy.[57]

Some middleman minorities, such as Jewish and Korean American merchants in central cities, have become targets of hostility from less well off groups, such as poor African Americans. In addition, strong ethnic bonds can make the middleman group an effective competitor, and even Anglo-Protestant capitalists may become hostile toward an immigrant middleman minority that competes too effectively. Thus Jewish Americans have been viewed negatively by better-off Anglo-Protestant merchants, who have the power to discriminate against them, as well as by poor black renters and customers with whom Jews deal as middleman landlords and merchants. Some scholars of racial and ethnic relations have criticized the application of middleman minority theory to Asian Americans, arguing that Japanese Americans and Chinese Americans, although substantially involved in trade, have rarely been a *middle* group of entrepreneurs situated between a poor nonwhite group and a richer white group. More generally, the middleman minority perspective does not deal adequately with the movement of large numbers of the middleman minority into the majority group.

A somewhat similar perspective, *enclave theory,* examines secondary–structural incorporation into the economy, especially the ways in which certain non-European immigrant groups have created social and economic enclaves in cities. Both the middleman and the enclave perspectives give more emphasis to economic inequality and discrimination than assimilation perspectives, and they stress the incorporation of certain groups, such as Asians and Cubans, into the United States through the means of small businesses and specialized ethnic economies. The major differences between the two viewpoints seem to stem from the examples emphasized. Groups accented by enclave theorists, such as Cuban Americans, have created ethnic enclaves that are more than merchant or trading economies—they often include manufacturing enterprises, for example. In addition, ethnic enclaves usually compete with established Anglo-Protestant business elites. In contrast, the middleman minorities develop trading economies and are likely to fill an economic niche that *complements* that of established white elites. However, the aforementioned research of Bonacich on Jewish Americans suggests that there is little difference between the real-world experiences of those described as middleman minorities and those described as enclave minorities.

An example of the ethnic enclave perspective can be seen in the work of Portes and Manning, who examined the enclave communities and economies of the Cubans in Miami and the Koreans in Los Angeles, groups that have developed many small businesses catering to customers inside and outside their own ethnic communities. Enclave economies require an immigrant group with entrepreneurial talents, business experience, available capital, and a pool of low-wage labor. These characteristics enabled Cuban Americans in Miami to build a strong ethnic economy. Ethnic enclaves, unlike the "colonies" of internal colonialism, typically do not relegate newcomers to a permanent position of inferiority. Portes and Manning criticize the internal colonialism and split labor market viewpoints for trying to encompass all non-European minorities, although they agree that the situations of African Americans, Mexican Americans, and Native Americans can be explained as internal colonialism. Enclave analysts have so far paid insufficient attention to the exploitation that goes on in the enclave economy, such as the exploitation of low-wage immigrant labor by the ethnic-immigrant (e.g., Cuban American) employers. They also neglect the surrounding political and economic system—in the Cuban and Korean cases, multinational capitalism—which shapes the initial migration as well as the character of enclave economies. In some ways, then, ethnic enclave theorists straddle the fence between the order and power–conflict theories.[58]

Women and Gendered Racism: New Perspectives

Most theories of racial and ethnic relations have neglected gender stratification, the hierarchy in which men as a group dominate women as a group in terms of power and resources. In recent years a number of scholars have researched the situations of women within racial and ethnic groups in the United States. Their analyses assess the ways in which male supremacy, or a patriarchal system, interacts with and operates within a system of racial and ethnic stratification. Discussing racial and ethnic cultures around the globe, Adrienne Rich has defined a *patriarchal system* as "a familial-social, ideological, political system in which men—by force, direct pressure, or through ritual, tradition, law and language, customs, etiquette, education, and the division of labor—determine what part women shall or shall not play, and in which the female is everywhere subsumed under the male."[59]

Asking whether racism or patriarchy has been the primary source of oppression, social psychologist Philomena Essed examined black women in the United States and the Netherlands.[60] She found racism and sexism interacting regularly. The oppression of black women can be seen as *gendered racism*. For example, under slavery African American women were exploited not only for labor but also as sex objects for white men. And after slavery they were excluded from most job categories available to white men and white women; major employment changes came only with the civil rights movement of the 1960s. Today racism has many gendered forms. In the U.S. mass media the white female is the standard for female beauty. Minority women are often stereotyped as matriarchs in female-headed families and are found disproportionately in lower-status "female jobs," such as typists. Some women of color are closely bound in their social relations with those who oppress them in such areas as domestic employment ("maids") and other low-paid service work.[61]

In her book *Black Feminist Thought* Patricia Hill Collins argues that a black feminist theoretical framework can help highlight and analyze the negative stereotypes of black women in white society—the stereotypes of the docile mammy, the domineering matriarch, the promiscuous whore, and the irresponsible welfare mother. These severely negative images persist among many whites because they undergird white discrimination against black women in the United States.[62]

Scholars assessing the situations of other women of color, including Native American, Asian, and Latino women, have similarly emphasized the cumulative and interactive character of racial and gender oppression and the necessity of liberating these women from white stereotypes and discrimination. For example, Denise Segura has examined labor-force data on Mexican American women and developed the concept of "triple oppression," the mutually reinforcing and interactive set of race, class, and gender forces whose cumulative effects "place women of color in a subordinate social and economic position relative to men of color and the majority white population."[63]

Class, the State, and Racial Formation

Looking at the important role of governments in creating racial and ethnic designations and institutionalizing discrimination, Michael Omi and Howard Winant have developed a theory of *racial formation.* Racial tensions and oppression, in their view, cannot be explained solely in terms of class or nationalism. Racial and ethnic relations are substantially defined by the actions of governments, ranging from the passing of legislation, such as restrictive immigration laws, to the imprisonment of groups defined as a threat (for example, Japanese Americans in World War II). Although the internal colonialism viewpoint gives some emphasis to the state's role in the exploitation of nonwhite minorities, it has not developed this argument sufficiently.

Omi and Winant note that the U.S. government has shaped the politics of race: the U.S. Constitution and a lengthy series of laws openly defined racial groups and interracial relationships (for example, slavery) in racist terms. The U.S. Constitution counted each African American slave as three-fifths of a person, and the Naturalization Law of 1790 explicitly declared that only *white* immigrants could qualify for naturalization. Many non-Europeans, including Africans and Asians, were prevented from becoming citizens. Japanese and other Asian immigrants, for example, were until the 1950s banned by law from becoming citizens. In 1854 the California Supreme Court ruled that Chinese immigrants should be classified as "Indians"(!), therefore denying them the political rights available to white Americans.[64]

For centuries, the U.S. government officially favored northern European immigrant groups over non-Europeans and southern European groups such as Italians. For example, the Immigration Act of 1924 was used to exclude Asian immigrants and most immigrants from southern and eastern Europe, whom political leaders in Congress saw as racially inferior and as a threat to their control of the society. North European Americans working through the government thereby shaped the subsequent racial and ethnic mix that is the United States.

Another idea accented recently by Omi and Winant is that of *social rearticulation,* the recurring historical process of rupturing and reconstructing the understandings of race in this country. The social protest movements of various racial and ethnic groups periodically challenge the government's definition of racial realities, as well as individual definitions of those realities. The 1960s civil rights movement, for instance, rearticulated traditional cultural and political ideas about race in the United States, and in the process changed the U.S. government and broadened the involvement of minority Americans in the politics of that government. New social movements regularly emerge, sometimes bringing new identities and political norms.[65]

Resistance to the Dominant Group

Recent research has highlighted the many ways in which powerless groups fight back against the powerful. One power–conflict theorist who has made an important contribution to our understanding of how the oppressed react to oppression is James Scott. Influenced by the work of scholars such as John Gaventa on the many "faces of power" Scott has shown that at the heart of much interaction between the powerless and the powerful is intentional deception.[66] For example, African American slaves were not free to speak their minds to their white masters, but they did create a crucial discourse among themselves that was critical of their white oppressors. Scott cites a proverb of African slaves on the Caribbean island of Jamaica: "Play fool, to catch wise." Looking closely at the lives of slaves and the poor everywhere, Scott has developed the idea of a backstage discourse by the oppressed that includes views that cannot be discussed in public for fear of retaliation. In addition to secret ideological resistance on the part of slaves and other poor people, a variety of other resistance tactics are used, including foot-dragging, pilfering, dissimulation, and flight. Scott cites Afro-Christianity as an example of how African American slaves resisted the "ideological hegemony" (attempts to brainwash) of white slavemasters. In public religious services African American slaves controlled their gestures and facial expressions and pretended to accept Christian preaching about meekness and obedience. Backstage, where no whites were present, Afro-Christianity emphasized "themes of deliverance and redemption, Moses and the Promised Land, the Egyptian captivity, and emancipation."[67] For slaves the Promised Land meant the North and freedom, and the afterlife was often viewed as a place where the slaves' enemies would be severely punished.

Historian Sterling Stuckey has noted that slave spirituals, although obviously affected by Christianity, "take on an altogether new coloration when one looks at slave religion on the plantations where most slaves were found and where African religion, contrary to the accepted scholarly wisdom, was practiced." The religion of African Americans mixed African and European elements from the beginning. Yet at its core the expressive, often protest-inclined African values prevailed over the European values.[68] Stuckey has shown that African culture and religion were major sources of the slaves' inclination to rebellion. The work of Scott and Stuckey can be linked to the analyses of Hechter and Mitchell and Feagin that we cited previously, for they too have accented the role of an oppositional culture in providing the foundation of resistance to racial oppression.

We can conclude this discussion of the most important critical power–conflict theories by underscoring certain recurring themes:

1. a central concern for racial and ethnic inequalities in economic position, power, and resources;
2. an emphasis on the links of racial inequalities to the economic institutions of capitalism and to the subordination of women under patriarchal systems;

3. an emphasis on the role of the government in legalizing exploitation and segregation and in defining racial and ethnic relations;
4. an emphasis on resistance to domination and oppression by those oppressed.

SUMMARY

This chapter has reviewed some of the major theories of migration and subsequent patterns of intergroup adaptation. Migration—varying from the movement of conquerors to slave importation to voluntary immigration—creates intergroup contact and thus racial and ethnic relations. Adaptation can have different outcomes in the period of initial contact, ranging from extreme genocide to peaceful symbiosis to some type of hierarchy and inequality. Further adaptation may lead not only to further genocide or symbiosis but also to Anglo-conformity, to some type of cultural pluralism, or to continuing inequality and hierarchy.

Generally speaking, assimilation theories focus on voluntary immigrant groups and emphasize Anglo-conformity or cultural pluralism outcomes. Power–conflict theories focus on involuntary immigration or colonial oppression and thus accent substantial power/resource inequality and hierarchy. Both types of theories offer insights into the character and development of racial and ethnic relations. Assimilation analysts have pointed out the different dimensions of intergroup adaptation, such as acculturation and marital assimilation, and have accented the role of value consensus in holding a racial and ethnic system together. Power–conflict analysts have stressed the forced character of much cultural and economic adaptation, particularly for non-European groups, and have underscored the role of coercion, segregation, colonization, and institutionalized discrimination in keeping groups on the bottom rungs of the societal ladder. They have also accented the role of government in racial oppression and the importance of oppositional cultures in providing the foundations for group resistance to oppression.

Power–conflict theorists have emphasized the importance of examining racial and ethnic relations in the context of the historical development of capitalism and patriarchy. In the introduction to Part II we will explore the utility of such an approach in evaluating the broad contours of racial and ethnic relations over three and a half centuries of American history.

NOTES

1. See Tamotsu Shibutani and Kian M. Kwan, *Ethnic Stratification* (New York: Macmillan, 1965), pp. 28–33; and Donald L. Noel, "A Theory of the Origin of Ethnic Stratification," in *Majority and Minority*. ed. Norman R. Yetman and C. Hoy Steele (Boston: Allyn & Bacon, 1971), p. 32.
2. William M. Newman, *American Pluralism* (New York: Harper & Row, Pub., 1973), pp. 30–38.
3. Ernest A. T. Barth and Donald L. Noel, "Conceptual Frameworks for the Analysis of Race Relations: An Evaluation," *Social Forces* 50 (March 1972): 336.
4. Charles Tilly, *Migration to an American City* (Wilmington: University of Delaware Agricultural Experiment Station, 1965).
5. Barth and Noel, "Conceptual Frameworks," pp. 337–39.
6. R. A. Schermerhorn, *Comparative Ethnic Relations* (New York: Random House, 1970), p. 98.
7. Ibid., p. 99.
8. Stanley Lieberson, "A Societal Theory of Racial and Ethnic Relations," *American Sociological Review* 29 (December 1961): 902–10.
9. Charles Hirschman, "America's Melting Pot Reconsidered," *Annual Review of Sociology* 9 (1983): 397–423.
10. Robert E. Park, *Race and Culture* (Glencoe, Ill.: Free Press, 1950), p. 150 (italics added).
11. Robert E. Park and Ernest W. Burgess, *Introduction to the Science of Society* (Chicago: University of Chicago Press, 1924), p. 735.

12. Janice R. Hullum, "Robert E. Park's Theory of Race Relations" (M.A. thesis, University of Texas, 1973), pp. 81–88; Park and Burgess, *Introduction to the Science of Society*, p. 760.
13. Milton M. Gordon, *Assimilation in American Life* (New York: Oxford University Press, 1964), pp. 72–73.
14. Ibid., p. 71.
15. Silvia Pedraza, *Political and Economic Migrants in America: Cubans and Mexicans* (Austin: University of Texas Press, 1985), pp. 5–7; Richard Alba, *Ethnic Identity: The Transformation of White America* (New Haven: Yale University Press, 1990), p. 311; J. Allen Williams and Suzanne T. Ortega, "Dimensions of Assimilation," *Social Science Quarterly* 71 (1990): 697-709.
16. Milton M. Gordon, *Human Nature, Class, and Ethnicity* (New York: Oxford University Press, 1978), pp. 67–89.
17. Gordon, *Assimilation in American Life*, pp. 78–108.
18. See Will Herberg, *Protestant—Catholic—Jew*, rev. ed. (Garden City, N.Y.: Doubleday, Anchor Books, 1960).
19. Milton M. Gordon, "Models of Pluralism: The New American Dilemma," *Annals of the American Academy of Political and Social Science* 454 (1981): 178–88.
20. Alba, *Ethnic Identity*, p. 3
21. Stanley Lieberson and Mary Waters, "Ethnic Mixtures in the United States," *Sociology and Social Research* 70 (1985): 43–53; Cookie White Stephan and Walter Stephan, "After Intermarriage," *Journal of Marriage and the Family* 51 (May 1989): 507–19.
22. Nathan Glazer and Daniel P. Moynihan, *Beyond the Melting Pot* (Cambridge: M.I.T. Press and Harvard University Press, 1963).
23. Andrew M. Greeley, *Ethnicity in the United States* (New York: John Wiley, 1974), p. 293.
24. Ibid., pp. 295–301.
25. Ibid., p. 309.
26. William L. Yancey, D. P. Ericksen, and R. N. Juliani, "Emergent Ethnicity: A Review and Reformulation," *American Sociological Review* 41 (June 1976): 391–93. See also Greeley, *Ethnicity in the United States*, pp. 290–317.
27. Gunnar Myrdal, *An American Dilemma* (New York: McGraw-Hill, 1964), 2:929.
28. Talcott Parsons, "Full Citizenship for the Negro American? A Sociological Problem," in *The Negro American*, ed. Talcott Parsons and Kenneth B. Clark (Boston: Houghton Mifflin, 1965–66), p. 740.
29. James Geschwender, *Racial Stratification in America* (Dubuque, Iowa: Wm. C. Brown, 1978), p. 58.
30. Gordon, *Human Nature, Class, and Ethnicity*, pp. 73–78. See also Clifford Geertz, "The Integrative Revolution," in *Old Societies and New States*, ed. Clifford Geertz (New York: Free Press, 1963), p. 109.
31. Edna Bonacich, "Class Approaches to Ethnicity and Race," *Insurgent Sociologist* 10 (Fall 1980): 11.
32. Frederik Barth, "Introduction," in *Ethnic Groups and Boundaries: The Social Organization of Culture Difference* (Oslo: Universitets Forlaget, 1969), pp. 10–17.
33. Susan Olzak, "A Competition Model of Collective Action in American Cities," in *Competitive Ethnic Relations*, ed. Susan Olzak and Joane Nagel (Orlando, Fla.: Academic Press, 1986), pp. 17–46.
34. Susan Olzak, "Have the Causes of Ethnic Collective Action Changed over a Hundred Years?" (technical report, Department of Sociology, Cornell University, 1987), p. 18.
35. W. Lloyd Warner, "Introduction," in Allison Davis et al., *Deep South* (Chicago: University of Chicago Press, 1941), pp. 4–6; W. Lloyd Warner and Leo Srole, *The Social Systems of American Ethnic Groups* (New Haven: Yale University Press, 1945), pp. 295–96.
36. Compare Robert Blauner, *Racial Oppression in America* (New York: Harper & Row, Pub., 1972), p. 7.
37. William E. B. Du Bois, "Is Man Free?" *Scientific Monthly* 66 (May 1948): 432–34. See also Manning Marable, *How Capitalism Underdeveloped Black America* (Boston: South End Press, 1983), pp. 3–15.
38. Oliver C. Cox, *Caste, Class, and Race* (Garden City, N.Y.: Doubleday, 1948), p. 332.
39. Ronald Bailey and Guillermo Flores, "Internal Colonialism and Racial Minorities in the U.S.: An Overview," in *Structures of Dependency*, ed. Frank Bonilla and Robert Girling (Stanford, Calif.: privately published by a Stanford faculty–student seminar, 1973), pp. 151–53.
40. G. Balandier, "The Colonial Situation: A Theoretical Approach," in *Social Change*, ed. Immanuel Wallerstein (New York: John Wiley, 1966), p. 35.
41. Pablo Gonzalez-Casanova, "Internal Colonialism and National Development," in *Latin American Radicalism*, ed. Irving L. Horowitz et al. (New York: Random House, 1969), p. 130; Bailey and Flores, "Internal Colonialism," p. 156.
42. Bailey and Flores, "Internal Colonialism," p. 156.
43. Blauner, *Racial Oppression in America*, p. 55. Our analysis of internal colonialism draws throughout on Blauner's provocative discussion.
44. Stokely Carmichael and Charles Hamilton, *Black Power* (New York: Random House, Vintage Books, 1967), pp. 2–7.
45. Mario Barrera, *Race and Class in the Southwest* (Notre Dame, Ind.: University of Notre Dame Press, 1979), pp. 214–17.
46. Guillermo B. Flores, "Race and Culture in the Internal Colony: Keeping the Chicano in His Place," in *Structures of Dependency*, ed. Bonilla and Girling, p. 192.
47. Michael Hechter, *Internal Colonialism* (Berkeley: University of California Press, 1975), pp. 9–12; Michael Hechter, "Group Formation and the Cultural Division of Labor," *American Journal of Sociology* 84 (1978): 293–318; Michael Hechter, Debra Friedman, and Malka Appelbaum, "A Theory of Ethnic Collective Action," *International Migration Review* 16 (1982): 412–34. See also Geschwender, *Racial Stratification in America*, p. 87.
48. Joe Feagin and Bonnie Mitchell, "America's Non-European Cultures: The Myth of the Melting Pot," in *The Inclusive University: Multicultural Perspectives in Higher Education*, ed. Benjamin Bowser, Gale Auletta, and Terry Jones (forthcoming).
49. Carol B. Stack, "Sex Roles and Survival Strategies in an Urban Black Community," in *Woman, Culture and Society*, ed. Michelle Zimbalist Rosaldo and Louise Lamphere (Stanford, Calif.: Stanford University Press, 1974), p. 128; Ronald Angel

and Marta Tienda, "Determinants of Extended Household Structure: Cultural Pattern or Economic Need?" *American Journal of Sociology* 87 (1981–82): 1360-83.

50. Robert Miles, *Racism* (London: Routledge, 1989), pp. 53–57.
51. Joan W. Moore, "American Minorities and 'New Nation' Perspectives," *Pacific Sociological Review* 19 (October 1976): 448–55; Michael Omi and Howard Winant, *Racial Formation in the United States* (New York: Routledge & Kegan Paul, 1986), pp. 47–49.
52. Bonacich, "Class Approaches to Ethnicity and Race," p. 14.
53. Cox, *Caste, Class, and Race*; Al Szymanski, *Class Structure* (New York: Praeger, 1983), pp. 420–40; Al Szymanski, "Racial Discrimination and White Gain," *American Sociological Review* 41 (1976): 403–14.
54. Stanley B. Greenberg, *Race and State in Capitalist Development* (New Haven: Yale University Press, 1980), p. 349.
55. Barrera, *Race and Class in the Southwest*, pp. 201–3; Bonacich, "Class Approaches to Ethnicity and Race," p. 14.
56. Bonacich, "Class Approaches to Ethnicity and Race," pp. 14–15.
57. Edna Bonacich and John Modell, *The Economic Basis of Ethnic Solidarity* (Berkeley: University of California Press, 1980), pp. 1–37. For a critique, see Eugene Wong, "Asian American Middleman Minority Theory: The Framework of an American Myth," *Journal of Ethnic Studies* 13 (Spring 1985): 51–87.
58. Alejandro Portes and Robert D. Manning, "The Immigrant Enclave: Theory and Empirical Examples," in *Competitive Ethnic Relations*, ed. Olzak and Nagel, pp. 47–68.
59. Quoted in Michael Albert et al., *Liberating Theory* (Boston: South End Press, 1986), p. 35.
60. Philomena Essed, *Understanding Everyday Racism* (Newbury Park, Calif.: Sage Publications, Inc., 1991), pp. 30–32.
61. Ibid., p. 32
62. Patricia Hill Collins, *Black Feminist Thought: Knowledge, Consciousness, and the Politics of Empowerment* (Boston: Unwin Hyman, 1990), pp. 40–48.
63. Denise A. Segura, "Chicanas and Triple Oppression in the Labor Force," in *Chicana Voices: Intersections of Class, Race and Gender*, ed. Teresa Cordova et al. (Austin, Tex.: Center for Mexican American Studies, 1986), p. 48.
64. Omi and Winant, *Racial Formation in the United States*, pp. 75–76.
65. Howard Winant, "Racial Formation Theory and Contemporary U.S. Politics," in *Exploitation and Exclusion*, ed. Abebe Zegeye, Leonard Harris, and Julia Maxted (London: Hans Zell, 1991), pp. 130–40.
66. James C. Scott, *Domination and the Arts of Resistance* (New Haven: Yale University Press, 1990); John Gaventa, *Power and Powerlessness* (Urbana, Ill.: University of Illinois Press, 1980).
67. Scott, *Domination and the Arts of Resistance*, p. 116.
68. Sterling Stuckey, *Slave Culture* (New York: Oxford University Press, 1987), pp. 27, 42–46.

Part II

A Nation of Immigrants: An Overview of the Economic and Political Conditions of Specific Racial and Ethnic Groups

In the chapters that follow we examine a number of important racial and ethnic groups in U.S. society. For each we will look at many aspects of its history and analyze its current situation in terms of the theories of racial and ethnic relations reviewed in Chapter 2. Before examining these groups in detail, we will set them in the historical context of nearly four centuries of U.S. economic and political development. We accent two important dimensions of U.S. society in this overview: the changing capitalistic economy and the expanding political and governmental framework. Within these broad frameworks each group worked out its own cultural patterns in the mosaic nation called the United States.

IMMIGRATION, THE ECONOMY, AND GOVERNMENT

American economic development has proceeded through several stages: mercantilism, a plantation economy, competitive industrial capitalism, and multinational (oligopoly) capitalism. Economic institutions and developments have shaped the character of all waves of immigration and the subsequent patterns of immigrant adjustment.

Table II–1 briefly lists most of the immigrant groups discussed in this book. Each group entered North America under particular historical circumstances. Many started in slavery, low-wage jobs, or small businesses. Political and economic conditions at the time of entry were very important. For example, some groups entered when low-wage jobs were plentiful on farms or in cities; others entered when fewer jobs were available. The extent of racial and ethnic discrimination and oppression has varied considerably. Also important were the economic and

TABLE II-1 Selected Immigrant Groups: An Overview

Immigrant Group	Time of Entry	Economic Conditions in North America	Government Conditions and Actions
Phase One: Commercial Capitalism and the Slave Society: 1600–1865			
1. English	1600s–1800s	Mercantilism; land taken from Native Americans; English entrepreneurs and yeoman farmers; commercial capitalism emerges.	English state creates land companies; colonial governments define individualized property and protect property.
2. Africans	1600s–1800s	Enslaved as property; became major source of labor for plantation capitalism.	Colonial governments establish slave codes; U.S. Constitution legitimates slave trade; U.S. government controlled by plantation oligarchy.
3. Irish Catholics	1830s–1860s	Driven out of Ireland by famine; labor recruited for low-wage jobs in transport, construction.	U.S. government opens up western lands; Irish take urban political machines from British Americans.
Phase Two: Industrial Capitalism: 1865–1920			
4. Chinese	1850s–1870s	Contract labor and low-wage work in mining, railroads, construction; menial service work for white settlers.	Local governments help recruit Chinese labor; later, anti-Chinese laws passed in California; 1882 Exclusion Act.
5. Italians	1880s–1910s	Moved as peasants into industrial capitalism; overseas recruitment for low-wage industrial and construction jobs in the cities.	Government backing for labor recruitment; U.S. treaties with Europe; intervention in European affairs (World War I); numbers reduced by 1924 Immigration Act.

6.	Eastern European Jews	1880s–1910s	Industrial capitalism utilized their skilled and unskilled labor; small entrepreneurs re-established themselves; much anti-Semitic discrimination.	Government backing for labor recruitment; U.S. treaties with Europe; numbers reduced by 1924 Immigration Act.
7.	Japanese	1880s–1900s	Recruited as agricultural laborers for Hawaii; later migrated to West Coast as laborers, served in domestic work; created small businesses.	Government backing for labor recruiting; U.S. imperialism in Asia; conquest of Philippines and Hawaii; government laws exclude Asians.

Phase Three: Advanced Industrial (Multinational) Capitalism: 1920s–1990s

8.	Mexicans	1910s–1990s	With Asian/European labor cut off, Mexicans recruited for farms and industry; low-wage jobs in construction.	U.S. government provides labor recruitment programs and fosters U.S. agribusiness in Mexico, stimulating out-migration; U.S. Border Patrol monitors immigration.
9.	Puerto Ricans	1940s–1990s	Early farm labor migration; U.S. corporations recruit labor; blue-collar work in service economy.	Conquest of Puerto Rico in 1898; U.S. government–supported agribusiness takes over economy, creates surplus labor, stimulates migration to U.S.
10.	Recent Asian and Caribbean Groups	1960s–1990s	Many political and economic refugees; create economic niches; make use of expanding service economy.	U.S. intervention in Asia from 1853 to 1990s; government action in South Korea, Vietnam, Taiwan, Philippines stimulates out-migration; Cubans and Haitians flee political repression.

*Note: Pilipino is now the preferred term for the group often called Filipino (see Chapter 12).

other resources brought by the immigrant groups. Those immigrants who came voluntarily and with a little capital, some education, or entrepreneurial experience often had access to better jobs or developed small businesses—opportunities not available to immigrants with less in the way of resources.

Note too that Native Americans (not listed here) were the original inhabitants of the land to which the English and subsequent immigrants migrated; many lost lives and lands as a result of the European invasion and conquest. They, of course, do not celebrate the European "discovery of America."

COMMERCIAL CAPITALISM AND THE SLAVE SOCIETY: 1607–1865

Colonial Society and Slave Labor

The colonial society that grew up on the east coast of North America during the 1600s was tied closely to England and the expansionist policies of the English political and economic elites. The early economic system in these colonies was a combination of state enterprises under the English king and enterprises developed by independent entrepreneurs, including by the eighteenth century the slave plantation owners in the South and the merchants in the North. As was the case with other European colonial powers, the objective of English colonization was to secure raw materials and markets for English goods. The first joint-stock companies were formed by merchants under the auspices of James I of England. Employees of the Southern Company settled Jamestown; this was the English colony that bought enslaved Africans from a Dutch ship in 1619.

English merchants and entrepreneurs invested capital in the extraction of raw materials for home industries. The colonies served the empire as a source of raw materials and as a dumping ground for the surplus workers and peasants displaced by the expansion of capitalism in Europe. Production for profit was not the only important economic dimension, for the colonies also became home to many English and other northern European immigrants—people displaced from the land—seeking to become small farmers. In the colonies there were two major modes of production, the household mode and the capitalist (slave plantation and merchant) mode.[1] The North American colonies had so much free land that it was difficult for English entrepreneurs to secure enough European labor, particularly for large-scale agriculture. They tried using white indentured servants, but these immigrants worked off their terms of servitude and went into farming for themselves.

In the 1600s African slaves became the forced labor used by white merchant and agricultural capitalists in the colonies. After 1790 the emergence of cotton and sugar as international commodities produced by the slave plantations created a strong demand for slaves. The number of slaves increased from 59,000 in 1714 to 3.9 million in 1860. The forced labor of African and African American slaves built up profits (capital) not only for further slave owner investments in expanding plantations and allied enterprises, but also for the white merchants, shippers, and industrialists of the North and South.

There is some debate over whether slave plantation agriculture was fully capitalist, but Bonacich's evaluation seems convincing:

> Although colonial producers of raw materials came to depend upon coerced labor, their orientation was essentially capitalist. They were involved in the investment of capital in the enterprise whose purpose was the production of commodities for a market, while profits were created by the extraction of surplus from labor by having the slaves work longer hours than was necessary for their own subsistence. The oppression of African Americans, past and present, is rooted in the requirements of early capitalism.[2]

Civil War: The Southern Plantation Oligarchy versus Northern Entrepreneurs

By the late 1700s the slave mode of production was generally profitable; the South was the most prosperous and powerful region in the country from the late 1700s to the 1850s. Southerners owned much of the productive land, much of the agricultural produce for export, many processing mills and other valuable equipment, and the slave laborers. They dominated U.S. politics, as most presidents between Washington and Lincoln were either slaveholders or very sympathetic to slavery; for decades few major decisions made by the federal legislative and judicial branches went against the interests of the slaveholding oligarchy. The U.S. Civil War was largely a struggle for economic and political power between northern industrialists and small farmers on the one hand and the southern plantation oligarchy on the other. The victory of the North marked the arrival of northern industrialists as the dominant force in the U.S. economy and government.[3]

Immigrant Laborers in the North

During the 1800s in the northern states the growing industrial working class and the class of small farmers were peopled with immigrants from Ireland, Germany, and Scandinavia. Immigrant labor often became the labor for the growing number of industrial enterprises—the textile mills, railroad shops, and foundries. The pull factors motivating millions of Irish Catholic immigrants to cross the Atlantic after 1820 were the same as those that have attracted European immigrants for centuries to a United States portrayed by industrial recruiters as the land of opportunity. There were major push factors as well. In Ireland a potato disease created severe food shortages; this crisis plus political and economic oppression by England generated the migration of 1.6 million Irish to the United States over several decades. Many small farmers and artisans from Ireland sold their labor to U.S. employers; they became domestic servants, railroad laborers, miners, and industrial workers in cities.

The arrival of large numbers of white immigrants from northern Europe laid the foundation for new patterns of racial conflict. African Americans became a smaller percentage of urbanites in the North. Free black workers were used by industrial entrepreneurs in the North as low-wage labor, sometimes as strikebreakers—actions that increased the hostility of white immigrant workers toward black Americans. By the 1840s some free black workers in the North were being displaced from jobs by white immigrants, including Irish American workers.

Western Expansion: Native Americans and Mexican Americans

Fostered by U.S. governmental decrees and military protection, the great westward expansion in the nineteenth century brought not only Native Americans but also a new group—the Mexicans—into the orbit of exploitation by white European American entrepreneurs, soldiers, and settlers. The racist ideology of the "white man's civilizing responsibility" for non-European groups guided white expansionists and justified for them the taking of Mexican and Native American lands in the West. Expansionists believed the "Mexican race" and the "Indian race" should become subordinate to the "Anglo-Saxon race." The first Mexican citizens, long residents of the Southwest, did not migrate; they and their land were brought into the United States by force as the result of the Mexican-American War of the 1840s.

INDUSTRIAL CAPITALISM: 1865–1920

Industrial Capitalism and Government Expansion Overseas

The Civil War was followed not only by westward expansion but also by an industrial boom. An economy dominated by competitive capitalism, by small and medium-sized businesses, gradually became one that was dominated by large enterprises. The growth of these enterprises was dramatic, and the United States soon surpassed Great Britain in numerous production categories. The proportion of workers engaged in agriculture declined between the 1860s and the 1920s while the proportion in manufacturing doubled. By the last two decades of the nineteenth century many corporations were growing through mergers and acquisitions.

Leading industrialists expanded corporate investments and activities in numerous countries overseas, often backed by a U.S. government beginning to grow in size and military power. The movement of U.S. Navy ships, as well as private merchants and missionaries, into Asian countries such as China, Japan, and the Philippines disrupted the rural economies of these countries, often increasing the surplus of farm workers and urban migration there. U.S. military and economic power pressured Asian workers and elites to submit to U.S. influence. Labor recruiters enticed many Asian workers to Hawaii and the West Coast of the United States. More than 200,000 Chinese laborers came to the United States between 1848 and 1882 to undertake the "dirty work" along the West Coast, including mining, railroad, and service jobs. After the Chinese were excluded by a racist law, Japanese immigrants were recruited for similar low-wage jobs. Japan sent many thousands of emigrants to the United States, a migration triggered by Western influence and by labor recruiting by U.S. employers.[4]

The U.S. victory in the Spanish-American War of the 1890s resulted in the annexation of Puerto Rico and the Philippines by the expansionist U.S. government and the effective domination of Cuba. When the United States took over Puerto Rico much of that island was owned by smaller farmers, but soon U.S. companies were monopolizing production. Puerto Rico, the Philippines, and Cuba would later send large numbers of emigrants to the U.S. mainland.[5]

African Americans: Exclusion from Western Lands

The second half of the nineteenth century was a period of major governmental growth and bureaucratization in the United States. Government action had a major influence on racial and ethnic relations. One of the first actions of Abraham Lincoln and the new Republican legislators in the early 1860s was to pass the Homestead Act, an "affirmative action" program for the many white immigrant families seeking land, including the Germans, Scandinavians, and Irish. A European American family wishing to farm was given 160 to 320 acres of land if it would develop it. After the Civil War the U.S. Land Office ruled that most black Americans were ineligible for these land grants because they were not citizens when the act was passed. Some land was made available in portions of the former slave states, but black families for the most part did not have the great opportunity to build up the landed wealth that many white families had.[6]

In the late 1800s and early 1900s southern black workers were one possible source of labor for northern industries, but the white oligarchy in the South, after the brief Reconstruction period, took control of the South's economy and its local and state governments and saw to it that most freed slaves and their children remained in the South as low-wage labor. There was little distribution of slave plantation land to the black men and women who had made that land fruitful. Most freed slaves found themselves in new forms of subordination to white agricultural entrepreneurs, including sharecropping and tenant farming.

Southern and Eastern European Immigrants

Unable to use southern black labor, or preferring not to use it, northern industrialists turned to Europe. The majority of the 20.7 million immigrants to the United States between 1881 and 1920 were from southern and eastern Europe. Labor shortages and increasing wages for native white workers encouraged U.S. industrialists to seek immigrant labor. A 1910 survey of twenty major manufacturing and mining industries found that six out of every ten workers were foreign-born. Without this immigrant labor the great industrial expansion of the United States would not have been possible.[7] In some cases these new workers displaced native-born white workers. Anti-immigrant hostility among the workers in older European American groups increased as a result.[8]

European Immigrants and Black Americans

Irving Kristol has argued that "The Negro Today Is Like the Immigrant of Yesterday." His argument illustrates the view that the experience of black Americans moving to the industrial cities is not significantly different from that of recent white immigrant groups, that African Americans should eventually move up just as those immigrants did.[9] This argument overlooks important differences between the experiences of white and black immigrants. Group mobility was possible for European immigrants because

1. most arrived at a time when urban jobs were available, when U.S. capitalism was expanding and opportunities were relatively abundant;
2. many had technical or other skills or a little capital—resources available to few black Americans;
3. most faced far less severe employment and housing discrimination than black workers;
4. most found housing, however inadequate, reasonably near the workplace;
5. in key cities the political system was changing from Anglo-Protestant business dominance to shared power by business elites and political machines oriented to white immigrant voters.[10]

In the critical periods of European immigration, cities such as New York, Philadelphia, Boston, and Chicago were expanding centers of manufacturing. Blue-collar jobs were frequently available, if not plentiful. In the mid-nineteenth century Irish and German immigrants were attracted to rural areas and to the cities, where most found industrial, service, or government jobs. From 1890 to 1930 southern and eastern Europeans came in large numbers to the cities. One study notes that "the Italian concentration in construction and the Polish in steel were related to the expansion of these industries as the groups arrived."[11] Many workers migrated as a result of labor recruiting by U.S. employers in Europe.

Among the immigrants in the 1880–1920 period were large numbers of Jewish immigrants fleeing oppression in Europe. Although poverty-stricken, many Jewish immigrants were part of an urban industrial proletariat and came with some experience in skilled trades. One study found that two-thirds of the Jewish immigrants were skilled workers, whereas other southern and eastern European immigrants were primarily peasant farmers or farm workers. When Jewish immigrants entered in large numbers around 1900, the clothing industry was moving to mass production and offered jobs for tailors and seamstresses, as well as unskilled jobs, and there were also chances for small-scale entrepreneurs in a number of areas.

The situation for the African Americans who began to move to the northern cities after 1910 was different. Black workers who migrated from the South had no access to government jobs and were regularly displaced by the new white immigrant groups, who forced them out of job after job, such as construction and transport jobs, and into marginal, low-paying jobs. Lieberson has explored why southern and eastern European immigrants have done well in northern cities, compared with black Americans. Among his conclusions are that (l) black migrants were the victims of more severe racial discrimination over a longer period than were white immigrant groups, and (2) economic competition between whites and the growing group of black workers in the urban North led to extensive hostility and institutionalized discrimination by whites.[12]

ADVANCED INDUSTRIAL (MULTINATIONAL) CAPITALISM: 1920s–1990s

Other Non-European Immigrants

With the industrialization accompanying World War I came a sharp decline in the number of laborers available for agricultural work. The need was filled in part by Mexican labor, recruited with substantial help from the federal government. Mexican laborer and family migrations increased significantly in the 1920s. Agencies in Los Angeles and San Antonio recruited Mexican workers for agriculture and for some low-skilled jobs in the steel, auto, and other urban industries. Blauner has captured the contrast between the nonwhite and the white immigrant workers of this period and later: "America has used African, Asian, Mexican, and, to a lesser degree, Indian workers for the cheapest labor, concentrating people of color in the most unskilled jobs, the least advanced sectors of the economy, and the most industrially backward regions of the nation."[13]

Large Corporations and the U.S. Business Cycle

Since the 1920s large corporations, many with an international orientation, have come to dominate the U.S. economy and politics. By the 1920s a large number of Americans, including recent immigrant workers, were working in the auto industry or in related industries such as steel. Aggressive competition among auto firms in the 1920s resulted in the production of more cars than were needed in the economy. This overproduction, a chronic problem in a capitalist economy, resulted in major cutbacks in employment in many areas, thus helping to trigger the Great Depression of the 1930s, which hit especially hard among recent black and Latino migrants to cities. Unemployed whites, including recent immigrants and their children, even took over the lower-paying jobs previously held by nonwhite Americans. The federal government grew as political and business leaders tried to develop economic and social programs to save the foundering capitalist system. However, racial discrimination was continued in the dramatic New Deal relief programs of the 1930s: typically black workers received lower wages than whites, were employed only as unskilled laborers, and were employed after whites.[14]

The Postwar Era: The United States and the World

For three decades after World War II the U.S. government, the U.S. military, and American multinational corporations substantially dominated the world economy, in large part because industrial societies elsewhere, such as Germany and Japan, had been destroyed by the war. Since World War II it has become easier for corporations to move capital investments from the central city to the suburbs, from northern to southern cities, and from U.S. cities to cities overseas. Much of this "capital flight" has resulted in economically abandoned central cities, such as in Detroit and Newark. The federal government has facilitated this outward expansion of investment and jobs by funding home mortgage programs and highway systems built in accord with the needs of companies developing plants and of white workers living outside central cities. As a result, after World War II many white Americans—the children and grandchildren of European immigrants—followed the new industrial plants and allied workplaces to the suburbs.

Into the central cities came more non-European workers and their families—African Americans, Puerto Ricans, Mexicans and Mexican Americans, Native Americans, and Asian Americans. After World War II these immigrants to northern and western cities inhabited areas increasingly abandoned by industry and by the children of European immigrants. Among these more recent immigrants were the Puerto Ricans, many of whom were recruited for low-wage city jobs in the 1950s and 1960s. U.S. industrial and agribusiness development in Puerto Rico helped to stimulate a large out-migration. Although many older cities have seen an increase in black and Latino political and governmental influence in recent years, these city governments often face severe economic troubles.

Government Involvement Overseas and Asian Immigration

Until the mid-1960s U.S. immigration legislation was so restrictive that most Asians desiring to emigrate could not enter. By the mid-1960s the discriminatory quotas for Asians had been lifted, and since then there has been a great increase in Asian immigrants, especially the Chinese, Koreans, Filipinos, Asian Indians, and Vietnamese. U.S. support for South Korea during and after its war with North Korea built strong ties between the two countries. A succession of dictators in South Korea drove out some dissenters, who migrated to the United States; other Koreans came for economic or educational reasons. The immigration of the Chinese (especially from Taiwan), the Filipinos, and the Vietnamese has also been related to the involvement of the U.S. government and U.S. businesses overseas. The U.S. arming and political support of the Philippine government and the Chinese government on Taiwan and U.S. participation in the war in South Vietnam played a role in generating large groups of Filipinos, Chinese, and Vietnamese dependent on or oriented to the United States. As with earlier immigrant groups, many of these people migrated to the United States seeking better opportunities for themselves and their families.

Latin American Immigration and the Sunbelt Boom

Caribbean immigrants to the United States since the 1960s have included Cubans and Haitians moving to Florida. The U.S. government long supported a dictatorship in Cuba, which was overthrown by a guerrilla movement led by Fidel Castro. Many Cuban business people and professionals fled in the first waves of emigration after Castro took power. Often having economic and educational resources, these Cubans established a major economic niche and great political influence in south Florida. After 1980 a significant number of poorer Cubans migrated to the United States, some of them expelled as alleged "undesirables" by the Castro government. Most Cuban immigrants have been welcomed by the U.S. government as political refugees from a Communist government, and hundreds of millions of dollars in federal subsidies have been provided to facilitate their adjustment to a new country. In contrast, Haitians fleeing politically repressive governments on their Caribbean island have for the most part not been welcomed by the U.S. government. Many have been forced to return, and most of those allowed to stay have not been provided with the same level of government support as the Cuban immigrants. A major reason for this differential treatment seems to be that the repressive government in Cuba is seen as a political opponent of the United States, whereas the repressive governments in Haiti have generally been viewed as political allies of the United States.

In recent decades much investment capital and federal government aid have shifted to Sunbelt states and cities. The growing economies in the Sunbelt have created a demand for low-wage workers in sectors such as construction and agriculture. Many people have immigrated from Mexico and Central America for economic reasons. Others, like earlier European groups, have come fleeing political oppression. Mexican immigrants make up a significant portion of the undocumented immigrants. They are attracted by the possibility of jobs, and many are pushed by economic problems in their home country. U.S. corporations operating in Mexico have played a role in generating Mexican out-migration. For example, some U.S. agribusiness firms have stimulated the development of export-oriented agriculture in Mexico, taking over large amounts of land for that purpose and driving off many Mexican peasants who farmed the land to feed their families.

Immigration Restrictions

European immigrants made up more than half of all those coming to the United States during the decade of the 1950s. Their proportion dropped to one-third in the 1960s, to 18 percent in the 1970s, and fell to only 10 percent during the 1980s. The change is the result of the abolition of discriminatory national-origin quotas by the 1965 Immigration Act. The many Asian and Latino immigrants coming to the United States since the 1960s have come to be seen as a "problem" by Americans of European ancestry. The major 1986 Immigration Reform and Control Act and more recent immigration acts have been passed with a number of provisions specifically limiting this mostly non-European immigration to the United States. Many native-born workers and leading politicians are concerned that the United States cannot absorb so many new immigrants, even though the ratio of immigrants to the native-born population was much higher earlier in the twentieth century than it is today. The percentage of foreign-born in the U.S. population today is smaller than that of many other nations, including several in Europe. Implicit in many discussions of the new immigrants is a concern that most are from Asia and Latin America—that is, they are not white and European.[15]

SUMMARY

In this introduction we have briefly reviewed the economic and governmental contexts within which particular groups have immigrated and adjusted. We have seen that the time of entry for particular groups and the resources they bring affect their economic and political success. A complete understanding of the streams of migration to the United States requires an analysis of immigration in light of the economic and political contexts of entry and upward mobility. Capitalist development and expansion, as well as related U.S. political involvement overseas and domestic governmental expansion and legislative action, have not only shaped the context and character of U.S. immigration and the patterns of race and ethnic relations in North America for several centuries, but have also provided crucibles within which the family patterns, distinctive cultures, and political resistance of specific groups have developed.

NOTES

1. Edna Bonacich, "United States Capitalist Development: A Background to Asian Immigration," in *Labor Immigration under Capitalism,* ed. Lucie Cheng and Edna Bonacich (Berkeley: University of California Press, 1984), p. 82.
2. Ibid., p. 81.
3. Herbert Aptheker, lectures on American history, University of Minnesota, 1984.
4. Lucie Cheng and Edna Bonacich, "Imperialism, Distorted Development, and Asian Emigration to the United States," in *Labor Immigration under Capitalism,* ed. Cheng and Bonacich, pp. 214-17.
5. Bonacich, "United States Capitalist Development," pp. 99-110.
6. Coretta Scott King, "It's a Bit Late to Protest Preferential Treatment," *Detroit Free Press,* December 13, 1985, p. 9A.
7. Stephen Steinberg, *The Ethnic Myth* (New York: Atheneum, 1981). p. 36.
8. Bonacich, "United States Capitalist Development," pp. 112-15.
9. Irving Kristol, "The Negro Today Is Like the Immigrant of Yesterday," *New York Times Magazine,* September 11, 1966, pp. 50-51, 124-42.
10. Theodore Hershberg et al., "A Tale of Three Cities: Blacks, Immigrants, and Opportunity in Philadelphia: 1850–1880, 1930, 1970," in *Philadelphia,* ed. Theodore Hershberg (New York: Oxford University Press, 1981), pp. 462-64.
11. William Yancey, E. P. Ericksen, and R. N. Juliani, "Emergent Ethnicity," *American Sociological Review* 41 (June 1976): 393.
12. Stanley Lieberson, *A Piece of the Pie* (Berkeley: University of California Press, 1980), pp. 377-83.
13. Robert Blauner, *Racial Oppression in America* (New York: Harper & Row, Pub., 1972), p. 62.
14. H. Sitkoff, *A New Deal for Blacks* (New York: Oxford University Press, 1978), pp. 37–38; C. G. Wye, "The New Deal and the Negro Community," *Journal of American History* 59 (December 1972): 634.
15. Charles B. Keeley, "Population and Immigration Policy: State and Federal Roles," in *Mexican American and Central American Population Issues and U.S. Policy,* ed. Frank D. Bean, Jurgen Schmandt, and Sidney Weintraub (Austin, Tex.: Center for Mexican American Studies, 1988).

Chapter 3

English Americans
and the Anglo
Core Culture

U.S. President George Bush, The Oval Office, Washington, D.C.
Photo by David Valdez, The White House, Washington, D.C.

Cleveland Amory tells a story about prominent English American families in Massachusetts. A Chicago banking firm wrote a Boston investment company for a letter of recommendation for a young Bostonian. Eloquently praising the young man's virtues, the company's letter pointed out that his mother was a member of the Lowell family, his father a member of the Cabot family, and his other relatives members of other prominent New England families. The bank wrote back, thanking the company but noting that this was not the type of letter of recommendation they had in mind: "We were not contemplating using Mr. _____ for breeding purposes."[1] Apocryphal or not, this story illustrates the elite status of the "proper Bostonians" and suggests their wealth and prominence in the history of New England.

The story also underscores the importance of inbreeding, descent, and interlocking family ties over generations. Ethnicity involves cultural or nationality characteristics that are distinguished by the group itself or by important outgroups, but lines of descent are the channels for passing along ethnic characteristics to later generations.

Who are these English Americans? They are the single largest ethnic group in the United States. If all Americans claiming some English ancestry are counted, the number is about 50 million, larger than the current population of England.[2] The phrase *English Americans* itself may sound a bit strange. We hear discussions of Mexican Americans, African Americans, even Irish Catholics, but few speak of English Americans. One reason for this is that other labels are used to designate the group. Perhaps the most common are the inaccurate terms *Anglo-Saxon* and *white Anglo-Saxon Protestant.* Although in-depth analyses of this ethnic group are rare, numerous authors have commented on its central importance. A prominent historian of immigration sums up its impact: "Our American culture, our speech, our laws are basically Anglo-Saxon in origin."[3]

Sociologist Milton Gordon's view of the shaping impact of this first large group of European immigrants on the core culture of the United States has already been noted: "If there is anything in American life which can be described as an overall American culture which serves as a reference point for immigrants and their children, it can best be described...as the middle-class cultural patterns of, largely, white Protestant, Anglo-Saxon origins."[4] This comment suggests the importance of the core culture in the adaptation process faced by later immigrant groups. To take another example, Herberg has noted the influence of this group on the self-image of Americans: "It is the *Mayflower,* John Smith, Davy Crockett, George Washington, and Abraham Lincoln that define the American's self-image, and this is true whether the American in question is a descendant of the Pilgrims or the grandson of an immigrant from southeastern Europe."[5] This is the result of an essentially one-way cultural assimilation, whereby everyone adapts to the Anglo core culture.

Two troubling problems come to mind here. One is that no social science analyst has ever undertaken a comprehensive analysis of these English Americans, an immigrant group of paramount importance in U.S. history. Why has this group been so neglected? The answer seems to be that many scholars have taken them for granted as the ancient core of U.S. society and culture. A second question concerns the term *Anglo-Saxon.* Numerous sources use the term loosely for persons or institutions of English extraction. Yet Anglo-Saxon is an inadequate designation for the immigrants from England and their descendants. The term derives from the names for the Germanic tribes, the Angles and the Saxons, that came to the area now called England in the fifth and sixth centuries A.D. But there were other people there already—the Celts—and the Germanic tribes were followed by the Normans from France. The English settlers of the American colonies already embodied several centuries of the blending and fusion of several nationality types.[6] So, at best, the term *Anglo-Saxon* is a misleading shorthand for a complex heritage.

Some authors use *Anglo-Saxon* and related terms such as the ethnocentric "old-stock Americans" in even broader senses. The terms are sometimes used in a loose way to include British groups other than the English—the Scots and the Welsh. Certain other north European groups that have substantially assimilated to the Anglo core culture— particularly Scandinavian and German Protestants—are sometimes included in the terms *Anglo-Saxon* and *Anglo-Protestant.* In any event, when the terms *Anglo-Saxon, Anglo-Protestant,* and *British* are used by authors, English Americans and the core culture they generated are at the heart of the discussion.

Americans of English and British descent have, on occasion, publicly expressed a sense of superiority and of prominence in the nation. In the late 1780s, John Jay, the first chief justice of the U.S. Supreme Court, wrote in *The Federalist, "Providence has been pleased to give this one connected country to one united people—a people descended from the same ancestors, speaking the same language, professing the same religion, attached to the same principles of government, very similar in their manners and customs. "*[7] This very inaccurate and greatly ethnocentric perspective has been a central problem for non-English groups ever since.

THE ENGLISH MIGRATIONS

Some Basic Data

What was the origin of those English Americans whose company now numbers in the tens of millions? As every schoolchild should know, it was migration. Although the English were not the first to come to North America, they were the first to colonize it in large numbers. By the early eighteenth century there were approximately 350,000 English and Welsh colonists in North America. At the time of the Revolution this number had increased to between one and two million.[8]

Migration to the American colonies was very heavily English until 1700. Then the English migration receded to modest levels until well into the nineteenth century.[9] Nearly three million English migrated to the United States between 1820 and 1950, with the years 1880–1900 seeing the heaviest flow. The English migration to the colonies, and later to the United States, was one of the largest population flows to the United States; these immigrants continued to be an important part of U.S. migration until World War I.[10]

The First Colonial Settlements

The migration of the English settlers in the seventeenth century, together with the establishment of settlements, was different from later European migration streams.

This movement can be viewed as *colonization migration,* a concept we explored in Chapter 2. Colonization, unlike other types of migration, involves the subordination of native people. Unlike the French and Spanish, who also explored North America, the English had come to establish permanent colonies. The colonies developed under the auspices of the English king and his merchants and were viewed as an extension of the mother country.[11]

Why did the English Crown become interested in North American colonies? Various explanations for colonial development were put forth by English advocates in the colonial period. Commercial objectives were often mentioned; much attention was given to the need for trading posts and for new sources of raw materials, as well as for new markets for English goods.[12] Other colonial advocates emphasized Protestant missionary objectives, the search for a passage to Asia, the need to stop Spanish and French expansion, and the need for a place for England's surplus population. Nonetheless, the central objective of colonization was economic gain: "What England primarily looked for in colonies was neither expansion of territory *per se* nor overseas aggregations of Englishmen, but goods and markets."[13]

The English colonization was a case of Lieberson's migrant superordination (see Chapter 2). It had dire consequences for Native American ("Indian") tribes. Geographical expansion proceeded rapidly. Native Americans were perceived as a threat. The French were interested in the fur trade, but the English wanted land for economic colonization and farming.[14] At first, some tribes were treated in a friendly fashion, if only because the settlers depended on Native American food and advice for survival. The settlers soon gained numerical superiority over the native population, forcing them back into frontier areas or slaughtering them.[15] Few settlers seemed concerned over the genocidal consequences of their colonialism. In Massachusetts a plague had wiped out many Native Americans prior to the *Mayflower's* landing. The famous minister Cotton Mather commented, "The woods were almost cleared of those pernicious creatures, to make room for a better growth."[16]

The English established large settlements in North America. The first joint-stock companies were formed by merchants under the auspices of James I of England in the early 1600s. Employees of the Southern Company settled Jamestown, a colony where the primary goal was economic. Initially planning to develop the colony with poor white labor, the leaders at Jamestown soon perceived a labor shortage and bought Africans from a Dutch ship in 1619, laying the foundation for the oppressive institution of slavery. The northern colony of Plymouth was settled in 1620 under the auspices of another royal company. The Plymouth settlers—the famous Pilgrims—had seceded from the Anglican church.[17] Both settlements nearly expired in their early years because of disease and starvation. The Plymouth colony managed to survive with the aid of friendly Native Americans. By 1640 there were thousands of English colonists in the New England area; it was these colonists who first regarded themselves as English *Americans.*[18]

What was the racial and ethnic mix of this colonial population? The American Historical Association has developed rough estimates of the "national stocks" of the white population in 1790 based on a surname analysis:[19]

English	60.1%
Scotch, Scotch-Irish	14.0
German	8.6
Irish (Free State)	3.6
Dutch	3.1
French, Swedish	3.0
Other	7.6
Total	100.0%

These estimates give the English the primary position among whites, with other British groups accounting for significant proportions. In addition, it is important to note that African Americans, mostly slaves, made up one-fifth of the total population in revolutionary America.[20]

Later Migration

There was a modest flow of immigrants from the British Isles and the rest of Europe between the Revolution and 1820, but the century following 1820 saw the greatest Atlantic migration in history. The English and other British contributions to this nineteenth-century migration have been neglected.[21] This neglect underscores the ease with which the later English immigrants blended in. As we have noted, nearly 3 million came between 1820 and 1950. By the 1910s English migration had declined significantly.[22]

Economic motives were paramount for the nineteenth-century immigrants. Depressions were numerous, causing widespread unemployment in the textile industry, the largest employer in Britain. Emigration came to be seen as one solution to unemployment.[23] The skills of textile workers facilitated their mobility. As with their predecessors, this immigrant group attained a relatively successful position in a country just beginning to industrialize. English immigrants moved in large numbers from manufacturing and mining industries at home to comparable positions in U.S. industry, their skills spurring the dramatic industrialization of nineteenth-century America.[24] When English American workers were eventually displaced by machines or later immigrant groups, they often moved up into managerial and technical positions. With their help, U.S. industry surpassed the industry of the mother industrial society.[25]

Was adaptation to the core culture difficult for these English immigrants? The ease with which many moved into industry indicates the swiftness of their assimilation at the level of secondary organizations. Their skills kept most from the poverty that usually faced other immigrants. Larger numbers moved into clerical and professional jobs than was the case with most other white immigrant groups. Acculturation was easy for the English immigrants. They would be more readily hired where the ability to speak English was important. These English immigrants avoided most of the anti-immigrant agitation others faced. Indeed, new English immigrants often shared the ethnocentric or racist views held by previous English settlers, including the stereotyping of Jews, hostility towards blacks, and hatred of southern Europeans. Structural assimilation in the primary-relations sphere, to use the concept developed by Milton Gordon, was rapid for them. Marriage with citizens was common. Kinship and friendship ties were easily developed. Enforced residential segregation did not develop for these immigrants.[26]

Ties to the homeland were not immediately severed. The monarch was widely revered. British taverns flourished in American cities. Although English newspapers were published for immigrants, they seldom lasted more than a year or two. Organizations such as the St. George's Society were created to aid destitute English settlers, and there were also social clubs. However, the organizations for preserving English culture were fewer and less exclusive than similar organizations among other immigrant groups, and many children of English immigrants soon left these organizations. Berthoff quotes a son of an English immigrant, who was reviewing the Revolutionary War for his father: "You had the King's army, and we were only a lot of farmers, but we thrashed you!"[27] Here the pinnacle of identificational assimilation has been reached as early as the second generation; the son's identity is clearly English *American.*

Smaller numbers of English immigrants have come to the United States since 1910, generally less than a few thousand each year. In the 1930s, indeed, more people returned to England than came in as immigrants. One distinctive aspect of English migration since the 1950s has been a "brain drain": a significant proportion of the immigrants in this period have been managerial, professional, and technical workers, including physicians and college professors. Although relatively few compared with the numbers in earlier decades, these immigrants generated controversy in Great Britain over the costly loss of highly educated workers.[28]

The modest migration since 1910, coupled with dramatic increases in immigration from outside England, has had a dramatic demographic effect. Of the major white ethnic groups in the United States in 1790, only the British groups have declined sharply as a proportion of the total U.S. population. Whereas in 1790 the English were 60 percent of the white population, by 1980 only 27 percent of white Americans reported English ancestry.[29]

Other Protestant Immigrants

The terms *Anglo-Saxon* and *Anglo-Protestant* have sometimes been used by researchers to include not only the English but also the Scots, the Welsh, and even Scandinavians and Germans. The Welsh entered the colonies in relatively small numbers, beginning in the early 1600s. The total number who came has been estimated at just over 100,000, with many going into industrial jobs or farming. The first generations retained their customs, language, and distinctive communities, but they were soon assimilated to the white Anglo-Protestant mainstream.[30]

In terms of power the Scots were perhaps the closest to the dominant English group from the first century onward, although they would feel Anglo-conformity pressures. Scottish Highlanders and Lowlanders, as well as Scottish emigrants to Ireland, came to the new nation in the 1600s and 1700s. By the late eighteenth century there were perhaps 250,000 Scots, a number to be supplemented over the next century by three-quarters of a million migrants. In the colonial period many were merchants, clerks, soldiers, and middle-income farmers, although the majority probably were servants, laborers, and poor farmers. Assimilation to the English core culture accompanied inclusion in the economic system, so that by the early 1800s the Scots had probably moved up to near parity with the English. They too became an important segment of the white Anglo-Protestant mainstream.

German immigrants made up the largest non-British group. Germans were nearly a tenth of the colonists in the eighteenth century; in the century after 1820 several million would come to the United States. Some were Catholics and Jews, but the largest proportion was Protestant. Many became farmers, merchants, and, later, industrial workers. Over several generations much, but by no means all, of the German culture was reshaped by the well-established Anglo-American patterns. Cultural assimilation, together with substantial mobility in the economic and political spheres, came in a few generations for these Protestants. Yet some distinctiveness did persist, in the form of German customs and residential concentrations.

Scandinavian immigrants, such as Swedes and Norwegians, did not enter in large numbers until the 1870s and 1880s. In all perhaps two million came. Many immigrants entered as farmers and laborers, but the next generation moved into skilled blue-collar and white-collar positions. Here too substantial assimilation to the British American core culture came in a few generations. Still, some distinctiveness in customs and residential concentration persists today.

These white Protestant groups from northern Europe assimilated relatively rapidly to the core culture, particularly in the cultural, economic, and political spheres. However, this assimilation was not always peaceful. In the period of early contact even some of these groups suffered physical attacks and cultural pressures from the English American group. This, however, did not last long. Within a generation or so English Americans were marrying with other British Americans, and sometimes with Scandinavians and Germans. By the early twentieth century the designations *white Anglo-Saxon Protestant* and *white Anglo-Protestant* increasingly came to blur the distinction between the English and those later north European groups that had substantially assimilated to the English core culture and its institutions.

REACTIONS TO LATER IMMIGRANTS

Not all immigrant groups have had the easy reception enjoyed by the nineteenth-century English immigrants. Established English Americans, themselves descendants of earlier immigrants, were often hostile to the new immigrant groups. Anti-immigration agitation, or *nativism,* goes far back in American history, but the term was apparently first used in the 1840s and 1850s. Nativists were nationalists who saw themselves as the only true Americans. Higham notes three main themes in reactions to immigrants: anti-Catholicism, xenophobia, and racism (Anglo-Saxonism).[31]

In the earliest period, concern was centered in religious and moral desirability. Certain religious groups (such as Catholics), paupers, and convicts were discouraged by English American Protestants from entering the colonies. Antiforeign sentiment was directed primarily at non-English immigrant groups. French Huguenot refugees are one example. Virginia tried to prohibit their immigration, and other colonies placed restrictions on them. At least one Huguenot community was attacked.[32]

The Huguenots were joined as targets by other immigrants. As Jordan notes, "in the early years Englishmen treated the increasingly numerous settlers from other European countries, especially Scottish and Irish servants, with condescension and frequently with exploitative brutality."[33] Many resented the intrusion of new peoples onto what was seen as English soil. In Virginia and Maryland discriminatory duties were placed on non-English servants coming into the colonies. Catholics among the Irish were "doubly damned as foreign and Papist."[34]

There was some ambivalence about the new immigrants. On the one hand, immigrants provided needed labor, ship captains profited from immigration, and new immigrants were encouraged to settle in frontier areas to increase colonial security. On the other hand, immigrants were often seen as a threat, and English American mobs occasionally tried to prevent their landing.[35]

More Fear of Immigrants

Anti-foreign sentiment took legal form in the late 1700s after the Federalist party became concerned about political radicalism among new immigrants and about the growing support among non-British immigrants for the Jeffersonian Republicans. The 1798 Alien Act empowered the English American president to deport immigrants considered a threat to the new nation. The period of residence required for citizenship was raised from two to five years in 1795 and to fourteen years in 1798. Attempts were also made to set an exorbitant fee for naturalization. These strategies were designed to limit the political power of the new non-English immigrants.[36]

Numerous attempts were made to reduce the influence of new immigrants by pressuring them to assimilate to the English core institutions. When Benjamin Franklin set up a Pennsylvania school in the 1740s, he was concerned about the many non-English immigrants who did not know the language and customs.[37] Franklin exhibited strong ethnic prejudices about the German immigrants in his region, fearing that they would "shortly be so numerous as to Germanize us instead of us Anglifying them."[38] Ethnic homogeneity was the goal of the English founding fathers and prominent educators of the eighteenth century. George Washington believed in a homogeneous citizenry. Thomas Jefferson and Benjamin Rush expected those who were educated to fit into a culturally homogeneous mass of citizens. But such unity could be had only by the subordination of other ethnic identities to that of the core society.[39]

Anti-Catholic sentiment was at the core of much nativist agitation, especially in the nineteenth century. Irish and German immigrants entering during the 1840s and 1850s generated a burst of agitation and a variety of secret societies, sometimes termed the Know-Nothing movement, that sought to fight both immigration and Catholicism. (When questioned, members of these societies would supposedly say, "I don't know nothing.") During the 1850s the ethnocentric Know-Nothings were elected to state legislatures, Congress, and state executive offices. They also precipitated numerous violent attacks against immigrants and Catholics.[40]

Race-oriented nativism developed in the mid-nineteenth century, with other north European Protestants now joining the English Americans. From their perspective U.S. development was the perfect example of what could be accomplished by the "Anglo-Saxon race." This Anglo-Saxonism was picked up by the expansionists who lusted after Mexican land in California and Texas. The vigorous thrust into those areas was seen as directed and legitimated by a racial mandate to colonize the inferior races. One expansionist commented that "the Mexican race now see in the fate of the aborigines of the north, their own inevitable destiny. They must amalgamate or be lost in the superior vigor of the Anglo-Saxon race, or they must utterly perish."[41] Anglo-Saxonism was to play an important role in racist thought after the Civil War, for it provided the rationalization for U.S. imperialist military and business expansion overseas, in places such as the Philippines.

The upper classes in the United States became a stronghold of this nativism after the Civil War. They were influenced in part by "scientific" historians in England, who argued for the superiority of the supposed Anglo-Saxon background of England's greatness. There was an Anglo-Saxon school among U.S. social scientists; its guiding idea was that democratic institutions in this country had come from England, whose institutions had in turn derived in part from early Germanic tribes.[42] These social scientists ignored the Norman (French) impact on English culture, convinced that English institutions were the most civilized in the world. U.S. intellectual thought also came under the influence of social Darwinism, which extended Charles Darwin's thought into the social realm. This perspective contained notions of racism based on a social "survival of the fittest." One prominent advocate of biological evolution, John Fiske, celebrated the superiority of English civilization and claimed it was the destiny of the English people to populate all the world's empty spaces.[43] Even more influential were popular writers such as Josiah Strong, a Congregationalist minister whose book *Our Country* (1885) sold thousands of copies. Strong was a vigorous advocate of Anglo-Saxon myths in combination with attacks on Catholics and other non-British immigrants. The English peoples were rapidly multiplying, he argued, and the United States was destined to be the seat of an "Anglo-Saxon race" whose numbers would approach (by the 1980s, he predicted) a billion strong. Survival of the fittest, he argued, dictated the ultimate superiority of the "Anglo-Saxon race" throughout the world.[44]

Racism and Nativism since 1890

The increase in immigration from southern and eastern Europe and from Asia around the turn of the twentieth century focused anti-immigration sentiment on these groups. For example, Henry Cabot Lodge, an English American aristocrat from New England and a powerful political figure, was fiercely determined to defend the English "race" against immigrant threats in the 1890s. English Americans in Boston formed the Immigration League to fight the increasing southern and eastern European immigration. The league worked diligently for a literacy test, which passed Congress, and associated itself with the eugenics movement started by Sir Francis Galton, a prominent English Darwinist. The U.S. eugenicists argued that heredity shaped moral as well as biological characteristics, and that allowing "unfit" immigrants to enter and procreate would destroy the "superior race" of north Europeans. The unfit should be excluded or even eliminated.[45]

Perhaps the most prominent American to contribute to the development of racial nativism was Madison Grant, an American of English extraction who fused various racist ideas in his influential book *The Passing of the Great Race* (1916). Particularly worried about the influence of newer groups from southern and eastern Europe, Grant claimed that interbreeding these various "races" would lead to mongrelization. The northern Europeans, the "Nordic race," were the superior "race."[46] Such "scientific" racism resulted in the 1920s in immigration legislation that discriminated against non-British white groups. Various "national origin" quotas were spelled out to restrict immigration from southern and eastern Europe. Britons, in contrast, were allowed to constitute nearly half of all immigration.

The 1920s and 1930s saw an outpouring of racial nativism on many fronts. Journalists such as Kenneth L. Roberts continued to write wildly about the racial "mongrelization" caused by the new white immigrants.[47] Nativist organizations such as the revived Ku Klux Klan provided a social outlet for those who wished to subordinate African, Catholic, and Jewish Americans and preserve the so-called Anglo-Saxon race. Opposition to foreign immigration resurfaced after World War II, when various members of Congress and (northern) European American organizations opposed legislation permitting displaced persons, such as European Jews and Catholics, to migrate to the United States.

In recent decades nativism on the part of British and other north European Americans has persisted, if in more subtle forms. Sometimes it has taken the form of stereotyping and harassing those not of north European ancestry. In recent presidential campaigns, for example, Democratic party candidates have been targeted because of their south European ancestry. In the 1984 election the Italian ancestry of the Democratic vice-presidential candidate, Geraldine Ferraro, was attacked. Among other things, Republicans (many of north European ancestry) alleged that she and her Italian American husband had connections with organized crime. In the 1988 election country-music personalities and other supporters of Republican candidate George Bush, an English American, poked fun at the Greek ancestry and name of Democratic candidate Michael Dukakis. The same joking confronted Greek American Paul Tsongas in his campaign for the Democratic party nomination in 1992.[48] Some white Americans of south European ancestry are still viewed by northern Europeans, if often jokingly, as somehow not fully "American."

Another form of nativism can be seen in the various anti-immigration organizations that have flourished in the last decade or two. Like their predecessors in the early twentieth century, these organizations have opposed and stereotyped recent immigrants, in this case those coming from Asia and Latin America since the 1960s. Some of these nativists have focused on the languages of the immigrants, an issue we consider in the next section. In addition, some white supremacy groups, including the Ku Klux Klan, have regularly held rallies across the United States and put out literature attacking non-European groups as a threat to "American" jobs and the Anglo core culture. These groups, it should be noted, include not only significant representations of northern European Americans, but also some whites with southern and eastern European ancestries.

THE ENGLISH CORE CULTURE AND MAJOR U.S. INSTITUTIONS

Most analysts of the U.S. racial and ethnic scene have assumed that the core culture and society are English or Anglo-Protestant. During the first century of colonial settlement along the East Coast, an English heritage integrated most of the colonies. Political, legal, and economic institutions were generally based on English models. U.S. institutions were not identical to the English, however. The dominant Anglican church in the colonies soon gave way to religious liberty, and there was also no hereditary ruling class. The availability of land—the basis of wealth—guaranteed greater democracy in the colonies. Traditional English ways were modified under new conditions.[49]

Language

The United States has no official language, but English is the dominant language in most areas of the society. The lasting dominance of the English language makes conspicuous the impact of early English settlers and their descendants. When Europeans first came there were perhaps a thousand Native American languages and dialects were spoken, and several hundred are still being spoken. But today the number of Americans speaking these original languages and dialects is far smaller than those speaking the languages of the European conquerors—English, Spanish, and French. The principal U.S. language over the last two centuries has not been a simple blend of Native American and early immigrant languages, but an English language that has incorporated words from both European and U.S. sources. Warner and Srole conclude that "our customary way of life is most like the English, and our language is but one of the several English dialects."[50] Historically, assimilation pressures on non-English-speaking immigrants have first taken the form of language pressure.

As early as the 1740s, native-born Americans of British background attacked later immigrants for their alleged mongrelization of the core culture. From then to the present the dominance of the English language has been a major concern of nativists. As we noted earlier, Benjamin Franklin, an English American, viewed German-speakers as ignorant and a threat to the English language and core culture.[51]

Today about 25 million Americans live in homes where a language other than English is spoken. Since the 1980s this relatively small group of non-English-speakers has been attacked as un-American by organized nativists, who worry that many newcomers, especially Latino and Asian immigrants, have not accepted English as their primary language. They are especially concerned that Spanish, spoken by 7–8 percent of Americans at home, is challenging the dominance of English. One result of lobbying by new nativist organizations has been the introduction of legislation to make English the official language. In 1986 California passed a ballot proposition (by 73 percent of the vote) that declared English to be the official language of this most populous state in the Union. By 1992 such legislation had been passed in seventeen states. In addition, in 1981 an English Language Amendment to the U.S. Constitution was introduced in Congress; it has been reintroduced in subsequent sessions of Congress but as of late 1992 had not been voted upon.[52]

Today nativist organizations such as the California English Campaign and the national group U.S. English, with its 350,000 members and $7 million annual budget, argue that they are not trying to discriminate against immigrants, but that they wish immigrants to quickly become part of the mainstream by adopting English as their primary language. However, until 1988 U.S. English was a project of U.S. Inc., a nonprofit organization that supports a variety of groups pressing for significant immigration restrictions. Leaders of Latino civil rights groups have pointed out that pro-English advocates favor discrimination in the form of prohibiting Spanish as a language in government agencies and cutting off expenditures for bilingual programs in schools and for bilingual ballots in states with Latino voters. A number of studies have shown that minority children who are "denied the right to view the world through their language and culture, are made to feel inferior," and may react in such negative ways as dropping out of school or engaging in drugs or crime—outcomes that cost not only themselves but the greater society dearly.[53] The implementation of English-only laws can have other effects, including the prohibition of testimony by non-English-speakers in court and the abolition of language interpreters in government agencies, including police departments.

Nativist campaigns to promote the English language underscore the traditional dominance of that language—and the uneasiness that descendants of earlier immigrants to the United States still feel in the presence of the languages and cultures brought by newcomers to this "nation of immigrants."[54] As legal scholar Juan Perea notes, their "first myth is that our national unity somehow depends solely on the English language, ergo we must protect the language through constitutional amendment or legislation. A corollary is that the only language of true American identity is the English language."[55]

What is ironic about these English-only movements is that most immigrants not only recognize that English is the language of social and economic discourse in the United States, but also strive hard to learn the language. English, as we have noted, is in fact the dominant language. In a recent year, for example, no less than 40,000 immigrants were turned away or were on waiting lists for adult English classes in the city of Los Angeles alone. A study by Veltman has shown that three-quarters of Latino immigrants speak English every day. It is also unfortunate that the lack of knowledge of languages other than English cripples most Americans who go abroad to conduct business or to deal politically with people in other nations. This parochialism will continue to hurt the United States in its operations in a linguistically diverse world.[56]

Religion and Basic Values

The English religious influence on the United States has been of great importance. For the first two hundred years English churches, or derivatives thereof, dominated the American scene. The Anglican church received some government support, but this privileged position was lost in the Revolution. The disproportionate number of Anglican and Congregational churches was obvious at the time of the Revolution, although Baptist and Presbyterian churches were by then becoming more numerous. In the century after 1776, English dominance of U.S. religious institutions decreased as Catholic, Jewish, and other religious groups grew with immigration.[57]

Herberg argues, however, that the Catholic and Jewish faiths, as well as non-British Protestantism, have been greatly shaped by the "American way of life," his phrase for the Anglo-Protestant core culture.[58] One important study of Judaism has shown the substantial impact of Protestant institutions on eastern European Judaism. The immigrant synagogues made major changes over time in response to the core culture. For example, religious schools adapted to Protestant American scheduling and formats. Among Reform Jews, English came to be the language of worship, and the worship itself was modified with the introduction of Friday-night services.[59] The impact of the core culture on the non-Protestant religions of later immigrants has been mixed; the immigrant has been expected to adapt in many areas, but some religious heritage has been preserved. "Cultural pluralism" has some descriptive accuracy for U.S. religious patterns.

Also important is the impact of British Protestant values on later immigrants. The importance of the ascetic Protestantism that many of the early English settlers brought to the colonies cannot be underestimated. Puritanism was important in establishing the so-called Protestant work ethic at the center of the value system—the idea of hard work as a duty of every individual. Richard Baxter, an important English Puritan minister, exemplified this important perspective, advocating not only hard work but also abstinence from personal pleasures.[60] "Continuous work was seen as a major defense against the sinful temptations of the flesh; the primary objective of work was to glorify God. Idleness was regarded as sin."[61]

This is the work ethic that has become so distinctive and dominant in the United States. The emerging capitalistic system in the late 1700s and the 1800s was pervaded by "pursuit of profit, and forever *renewed* profit, by means of continuous, rational, capitalistic enterprise."[62] Benjamin Franklin personified this spirit of capitalism with his famous maxims about time being money, about punctuality, and about the virtues of hard work.

The English influence on American culture in general has been similarly extensive. To cite only a few examples: Major musical and artistic developments in the earliest period were linked to the English (and later British) religious traditions. The first book published in the New England colonies was the *Bay Psalm Book* (1640), which drew on the English tradition. "Yankee Doodle" was probably an English tune, the original lyrics satirizing ragtag colonial soldiers. Only when the Revolution began did American soldiers take it over from the British. Before, during, and after the Revolution, English melodies were the basis of most popular and political songs.[63] The national anthem, "The Star-Spangled Banner," draws on an English drinking song for its melody.

Interestingly, over the next two centuries the English influence on U.S. popular music has receded dramatically before the pervasive influence of African American music (for example, ragtime, jazz, and rock and roll), Irish American (so-called Scotch-Irish) country music, and the Mexican American music of the Southwest. Today popular music is one major area of U.S. culture where English influence has almost disappeared.

Education

English and other British Americans took advantage of what few educational opportunities were available in the colonial period; better-off parents sent their children to private schools established before 1800. With the public school movement, which began in earnest in the first decades of the nineteenth century, British dominance of public schools became a fact of life. British Americans took advantage of schools. Urban schools were seen as a means of socializing non-British immigrants into Anglo-Protestant values and the values of the U.S. industrial system. British American industrialists and educators established most public schools, shaped curricula and teaching, and supervised operations. Although some, such as John Dewey, believed education gave greater opportunity to poor immigrants, many educators emphasized the social-control aspects of schools. Americanization pressures on immigrant children were often intense. Whether children were Irish, Jewish, or Italian, Anglicization was designed to ferret out non-Anglo-Protestant ways, to assimilate the children in terms of Anglo-Protestant manners, work habits, and values.[64]

As we will see in later chapters, the social-control function of schools and the British American influence on their structure and operation are still evident today. Later immigrants, such as Asians and Latinos, have faced Anglo-conformity pressures similar to those experienced by earlier Irish and Italian immigrants. Indeed, the schools are a major battleground for those concerned with making English the government-sanctioned language.

Political and Legal Institutions

The political and legal institutions affecting all Americans have been shaped, and are still being shaped, by the English political heritage in two basic ways: laws and traditions inherited from the English and their application by English immigrants and their descendants. Given the near monopoly of English settlers in colonial society on the eastern seaboard, English legal institutions became dominant. Concern for the rule of law and for the "rights of Englishmen" was manifest. The famous Mayflower Compact, a political framework theoretically providing for equality under the law, has been praised. New England, with its Puritan institutions, provided the model for later U.S. political and legal developments.[65]

Huntington has argued that the North American colonies took on a distinctive set of political institutions—those characteristic of sixteenth-century England. Although many of these constitutional features were being *abandoned* in England, they became part of the original political structure on this side of the Atlantic. The basic ideas include unity of government and society, subordination of government to law, a balance of power between the legislature (Parliament in England) and the executive (the king in England), and heavy reliance on local governments.[66] American political and legal institutions, including the U.S. Constitution, have reflected these ideas ever since. Authority and power were centralized in England, but here they were separated into three branches— the executive, judicial, and legislative. The position of the U.S. president is unusual: the United States, unlike almost every other modern political system, does not distinguish between the head of government and the chief of state. The Watergate scandal of the Nixon administration in the 1970s and the "Contragate" scandal of the Reagan administration in the 1980s showed how powerful the executive was relative to Congress. The United States was a new society, but an "old" political state.

Another important English influence can be seen in the representative assemblies in the colonies and, later, the United States. The British Crown established these assemblies in the colonies almost from their start, based on the parliamentary model.[67] Gradually these assemblies grew in power vis-à-vis the London government. Crown infringements on them helped generate the Revolution.

The U.S. legal framework reflects much English influence. Prior to the Revolution, English common law was asserted to be "the measure of rights of Americans."[68] The colonies had similar legal frameworks, but negative feeling arose over English common law because of the tension between the new nation and mother England. Some wanted a new U.S. legal code, "but," as Pound notes, "most lawyers sought to reshape or add to the existing stock of authoritative legal materials."[69] Although there was variation in how English statutes were incorporated into the U.S. legal system, their implementation was thoroughgoing: "the use of English statutes was provided for at an early stage in twenty-six of the twenty-eight jurisdictions organized between 1776 and 1836."[70] Although the U.S. legal system has been patched many times, the basic cloth today is still English common law.[71]

Officeholding

In addition to their fundamental impact on U.S. political institutions, English Americans have had a major impact on the operation of those institutions. The first president of the United States, George Washington, was of English ancestry, as was the forty-first president, George Bush, two centuries later. English Americans have filled many major offices in various political contexts throughout U.S. history.

There have been relatively few studies of English, or British, influence on the U.S. political structure. Davie notes that "the colonial assemblies were almost exclusively English in makeup."[72] The Declaration of Independence was signed by fifty-six European American males, thirty-eight of whom were English by background or birth; nine were Scottish or "Scotch-Irish," three Irish, five Welsh, and one Swedish.[73] A majority of the members of the Constitutional Convention were also English, and the Constitution was framed around their concerns not only for democratic institutions reminiscent of English institutions but also for the protection of property and wealth. As a result, most people of wealth in the new nation—merchants, financiers, shippers, wealthy farmers, and their allies—supported the Constitution out of economic self-interest. Slaves, indentured servants, poor farmers, laborers, and women had no say in the framing of the U.S. Constitution. The framers of the Constitution perpetuated social class lines similar to those in England.[74]

Studies of U.S. presidents, Supreme Court justices, and members of Congress have revealed a distinctive pattern persisting to the present. Presidents and presidential candidates have been "required" to possess ancestry qualifications, preferably British American or northern European ancestry. Of the forty-one presidents from Washington to Bush, about two-thirds had English ancestry and all the rest had north European (mostly British) backgrounds.[75] No southern Europeans, Jewish Americans, Latino Americans, Asian Americans, or African Americans have been president. A study of the origins of Supreme Court justices from 1789 to 1957 found that over half were also English or Welsh. In all periods, including the present, British Americans and other north Europeans have dominated the nation's highest court.[76] An analysis of 162 prominent political leaders (including presidents, representatives, senators, and Supreme Court justices) of the period 1901–10 found that over half were of English or Welsh origin.[77]

Baltzell has traced the rise of English American leaders such as Robert Todd Lincoln, the son of Abraham Lincoln, at the turn of the twentieth century. Lincoln was educated at Phillips Academy and Harvard and became a millionaire lawyer at the heart of the U.S. ruling class. In 1901, the year of Queen Victoria's death, Lincoln was part of the British and British American establishments that dominated much of the world. A northwestern European Protestant, Theodore Roosevelt, occupied the White House, and J. P. Morgan, a leader in the (Protestant) Episcopal church, had just put together the first billion-dollar corporation. The Senate of the United States was a north European Protestant millionaires' club.[78]

Even when new immigrant groups managed to break into politics, as in the case of Irish and Italian Americans, they were usually subservient to Anglo-Protestant leaders. The newer immigrants and their children did gain significant political power in the first decades of the twentieth century in a few cities, but not at the national level. There has been only one Catholic president, Irish American John F. Kennedy (1961–63). His presidency marked only a brief shift from a homogeneous political establishment, for Kennedy was followed by more men of north European Protestant stock.[79]

What of the English American impact on local governments? A study of New Haven up to 1960 illustrates English political dominance in New England. For many decades a patrician elite there "completely dominated the political system. They were of one common stock and one religion, cohesive in their uniformly conservative outlook on all matters, substantially unchallenged in their authority, successful in pushing through their own policies, and in full control of such critical institutions as the established religion, the educational system (including not only all the schools but Yale as well), and even business enterprise."[80] Moreover, a study of the mayors of Cleveland in the 1836–1901 period found that most were part of an Anglo-Protestant elite with strong ties to New England. Their political framework was guided by what was termed the "New England creed," proposition one of which was "The good society is white and Protestant."[81]

For several decades Americans of British ancestry have had to compete with more recent immigrants for power in local politics, and today the ethnic mix in local political institutions varies. The large cities of the Midwest and East have seen the rise to political power of Irish, Italian, and, most recently, African and Latino Americans. Still, British Americans continue to exercise great influence in local politics, especially in suburban politics, although they receive little mass media attention.

Economic Institutions

The English heritage is reflected in U.S. economic institutions—in the values that shape those institutions and in the actual dominance of English American individuals. Just as the U.S. legal system incorporated portions of the English legal system, the economic system developed under the mercantile capitalism that dominated much of Europe during colonial times. Then, as we have seen, the British Crown wished to increase the raw materials and the markets available to the mother country. To this end, the first English colonies were set up by state-chartered trading companies, or were proprietary colonies established by men of wealth.

Mercantile capitalism, which still existed in the colonies at the time of the Revolution, was a state-directed capitalism linked to English nationalism. The American Revolution was basically a clash between English and British American commercial interests, a clash that unified the colonies and brought a political break between similar economic systems.[82]

Industrial capitalism developed several decades later, again with intimate connections to the English system. The basic ideas for U.S. industrial development arrived through English channels, and English capitalists and skilled workers provided much knowhow for U.S. economic development. After the Revolution, as before, Britain and the United States formed a single Atlantic economy, so close and important were their economic connections.[83]

Direct Participation in the Economy

English and British Americans have influenced the operation of the U.S. economy through direct control of critical positions. In the beginning they established most of the colonies and controlled much of the land and wealth. In the early period control of the colonies lay primarily in the hands of English and other British American landowners and merchants.[84] Morison has argued, however, that those who eventually came to dominate many colonies in the late prerevolutionary period were yeoman farmers.[85] The founders of the colonies had included English aristocrats, but they had died or returned to England by the mid-1650s. Whatever their background, those with land and wealth needed labor. Because there was no surplus population in the colonies, labor from Europe and Africa was imported. By the 1730s a substantial Irish migration had begun. A large proportion of these immigrants were indentured servants. The African slave trade eventually supplanted the trade in white servants.[86]

As we move toward the Civil War period and then into the twentieth century, we again find few studies on the dominance of the economy by English or British Americans. A study of the wealth of males living in 1860 concludes only that the wealth of "native-born males," doubtless mostly British Americans, was about twice that of "foreign-born males."[87] U.S. industrialization in the nineteenth century was partially fueled by English and Dutch capital.

U.S. business elites have long been dominated by Americans of British or other north European descent. In the nineteenth century the most famous of these were the industrialists and financiers, many of whom have been regarded as "robber barons." They included John D. Rockefeller, Leland Stanford, J. P. Morgan, Jay Gould, and Jim Fisk, all men of great wealth and power. Their ethnic heritages were typically English, with a few other northern Europeans mixed in. Many of these men, or their associates or family members, became senators, representatives, and governors.[88]

A study of top executives and entrepreneurs in the late-nineteenth-century iron and steel industry found that few came from recent immigrant families; most were native-born and had fathers with capitalist or professional backgrounds. Most did not fit the image of a poor immigrant "making good," as did the steel magnate Andrew Carnegie, who came to America as a poor boy. Over half were of English or Welsh ancestry; most of the rest were either Scottish or Irish.[89] A study of wealthy manufacturers, bankers, and merchants in the first decades of the twentieth century found that the backgrounds of about half were English; a significant percentage of the rest were Scottish or Irish. A survey of two hundred major executives serving the largest companies from 1901 to 1910 found that 53 percent were of English or Welsh origin, 7 percent were Scottish, 14 percent were Irish, and 8 percent were Canadian or British (unspecified).[90]

A few studies have also made clear the extent of British American dominance in local economies. Burlington, Vermont, was dominated in the 1930s by "Old Americans"—those who had been in the United States for four generations, probably heavily English and English Canadian. They controlled banking and manufacturing, and they constituted a disproportionate number of professional and political officials. Anderson underscores the racist dimension of this dominance: "Traditions of family and name, of power and influence, in the financial and civil life of the community, of race-consciousness, plus a very deep conviction that the Protestant traditions of their forefathers are basically important to the development of free institutions in America, set the Old Americans apart as a group distinct from other people."[91]

A few studies of the economically influential have been done since the 1930s. The "proper Philadelphians" about whom the sociologist Baltzell has written typically had English or British backgrounds. This is suggested by the decided dominance of Episcopalians and Presbyterians in the Philadelphia *Social Register* for the year 1940.[92] These Philadelphians were persons of great power and influence in the 1940s, particularly in banking, law, engineering, and business.[93] In an analysis of the 1950s and 1960s, Baltzell underscored the continuing dominance of British Americans at the national level. Although non-British groups had significantly penetrated the economic and political systems by that point in our history, they had not been as successful in the executive suites of large corporations, where the leadership was "still mainly composed of managers of Anglo-Protestant background."[94]

Contemporary Elites

A 1970s study by Dye of the top decision makers in the United States identified four thousand people in the top positions in corporations (industry, communication, banking), government, and the public sector (education, mass media, law). Dye concluded that "great power in America is concentrated in a tiny handful of men. A few thousand individuals out of 200 million Americans decide about war and peace, wages and prices, consumption and investment, employment and production, law and justice, taxes and benefits, education and learning, health and welfare, advertising and communication, life and leisure."[95]

Decisions of importance are reached at the middle and lower levels of the society, but it is the few thousand people in these top positions who make the most critical decisions—those affecting the lives of members of all racial and ethnic groups. Dye's research revealed that the social origins of the four thousand were not typical. They were generally affluent, white, Anglo-Protestant males. There were only a few African Americans and virtually no Mexican Americans, Native Americans, or Asian Americans. Dye has estimated that these elites were "at least 90 percent Anglo-Protestant" and noted that "there were very few recognizable Irish, Italian, or Jewish names" in the group.[96]

In the late 1980s and the early 1990s popular magazines such as *U.S. News & World Report* have proclaimed that there is a different makeup to those in the media, politics, and the universities who most influence American life. Elites "today represent a real break with their predecessors. Almost none of them are WASP's; fewer still are in the *Social Register*."[97] This view of an integrated elite has grown with the more conservative political thinking in the 1980s and early 1990s. But much of it is inaccurate. One must be careful to distinguish social and economic realities from rags-to-riches myths. By the 1990s the upper reaches of U.S. institutions had broadened to include not only the British Americans but also those with other northern European ancestry, particularly German, "Scotch-Irish," and Scandinavian Americans. And by the 1990s a handful of Catholic and Jewish Americans were beginning to penetrate elite bastions of economic power. Yet Catholic and Jewish Americans are still not proportionately represented at the very top of the economic and political pyramids of power. And almost no non-Europeans can be found at the top.

Research studies by Dye and others in the 1980s and 1990s have found a continuing pattern of disproportionately white and north European Protestant dominance at the top levels of U.S. industrial, public interest, and governmental organizations. One 1980s study found that 57 percent of business leaders were Anglo-Protestants, much higher than their proportion in the population. When other white Protestants were added in, the percentage rose to 79 percent.[98]

Catholic critics such as Michael Novak have been outspoken about the persisting influence of Anglo-Protestants:

> In the country clubs, as city executives, established families, industrialists, owners, lawyers, masters of etiquette, college presidents, dominators of the military, fundraisers, members of blue ribbon committees, realtors, brokers, deans, sheriffs—it is the cumulative power and distinctive styles of WASPs that the rest of us have had to learn in order to survive. WASPs never had to celebrate Columbus Day or march down Fifth Avenue wearing green. Every day has been their day in America.[99]

It is important to note the caustic character of this assessment of the economic power of the so-called Anglo-Saxon Protestants. In recent decades the term *WASP,* originally shorthand for *White Anglo-Saxon Protestant,* has been widely used in a derogatory way, particularly by writers of southern and eastern European heritage. Another example is Schrag's book *The Decline of the WASP.*[100] One significance of this greater derogatory use of *WASP,* and of the stereotyping associated with the term, is that English and other British Americans have increasingly been challenged for political and economic dominance by Americans from southern and eastern Europe.

English Americans as a Group: U.S. Census Data

Some English Americans have done well in the higher echelons of U.S. society. What about the 50 million or so ordinary English Americans? U.S. Census Bureau data for 1950 and 1970 on these English Americans are not very useful for estimating the general social and economic position of the group in U.S. society, because they are limited only to recent immigrants and their children. But in the 1980 census (1990 data are not yet available) a general question on national ancestry was asked, a question that provides a picture of a larger group of English Americans. By supplementing these more recent data with the earlier figures we can evaluate the position of English Americans in regard to education, income, and occupation.

In the years 1950 and 1970 the native-born children of (then) recent English immigrants to the United States had a median level of educational attainment higher than that for all persons twenty-five and over. The 1980 data are available for a larger group, those who identified themselves as English in reply to a question on ancestry. In 1980 the median number of years of school completed for those reporting English ancestry was 12.5, a figure virtually identical to the medians for all men (12.6) and all women (12.4).[101]

Family income data are available for 1969 and 1979. In 1969 the median income of second-generation English American families and unrelated individuals (those living alone in households) was $11,374; the figure for all families and unrelated individuals in the United States was lower—$9,590. In the late 1960s these children of recent English immigrants were doing better in terms of income than the typical household. However, 1980 census figures for Americans of English ancestry, a much larger group, show a different pattern. Those with English ancestry reported a median family income of $19,807 for the year 1979; the median income for all U.S. families was $19,917. In 1980 English American families had a median income close to that of the typical family.[102]

Occupational data show a somewhat similar pattern. An examination of the occupational distribution of second-generation English Americans for 1950 and 1970 reveals that these children of immigrants were more likely to be found in the better-paying professional, technical, managerial, and crafts jobs than the employed population as a whole. They were less likely to be found in less skilled blue-collar positions. However, the 1980 occupational distribution for those of English ancestry is similar to that of the general population. There was a slightly smaller proportion of English Americans in professional and technical occupations (12.8 percent) than in the population as a whole (15.4), but the proportion of managers and officials was larger (14.7 percent) than for the population as a whole (10.4 percent). Taken together, these two categories of better-paying, white-collar jobs accounted for a bit more than one quarter of English American workers and about one quarter of the U.S. population as a whole. The proportions of English Americans in the clerical/sales, skilled-blue-collar, unskilled-blue-collar, and service categories were similar to the corresponding proportions for the population in general. It is important to note that the disproportionate influence of English Americans in corporate America and in U.S. political institutions and the impact of English culture on the U.S. core culture do not mean that most of those with English American ancestry are better off today in terms of education, income, and occupational position than white Americans in general.[103]

ASSIMILATION: BLENDING WITHIN BRITISH PROTESTANT AMERICA

Although they constitute the group whose culture and institutions have been the standard for whether or not other immigrants have assimilated, English Americans are rarely written about or researched in the United States. One 1992 survey of a large data bank with thousands of articles and stories in hundreds of U.S. magazines, newspapers, newsletters, journals, and other publications appearing between 1978 and 1992 found not one serious article focusing on Americans of English or British ancestry. In this fourteen-year period it was very rare for journalists or editors even to mention English Americans in any context. This neglect of such a powerful ethnic group suggests just how much the English have blended into, or become, the sociocultural background of this society.[104]

A few recent studies of white ethnic Americans have found that there is indeed a large English American group, made up of some 50 million or so Americans who in censuses have claimed partial or total English ancestry. There is still some tendency for those of English descent to marry others with the same background. In an analysis of the most recent data available Lieberson and Waters found that 56 percent of women with English ancestry had mates partly or wholly of English ancestry. However, dispersal has also been characteristic of the English Americans and other north European Americans. A study by Alba in New York State found that those respondents with English ancestry had dispersed throughout the New York region: their ancestors had immigrated to the area in the seventeenth and eighteenth centuries, and the descendants had much time to move around. Residential dispersion, in fact, is one reason that so little attention is paid to this ethnic group. In addition, 95 percent of those whites with English or Dutch ancestry reported mixed ethnic backgrounds: when asked, they might list two or three countries from which their ancestors came. And 40 to 50 percent of those with British backgrounds said that their ethnic identity had no importance to them. Alba cautions that this latter response may mean that many have come to see their "English or British American" identity as synonymous with a "truly American" identity. Their English or British identity may be so integrated in their minds with what is American that they see no need to identify assertively with their country of origin. In contrast, more recent immigrant groups (for example, south European Catholics) were much more likely to strongly identify with their national heritage.[105]

The largest white ethnic group in the South is Americans of English descent. Those of English ancestry exceed those of African ancestry by a significant margin.[106] Yet researchers have not closely examined the diverse ethnic origins of white southerners. In analyzing this group, Killian refers to English Americans and other white ethnic groups as *white southerners,* and occasionally as *white Anglo-Saxon Protestants.* Part of the southern white population is descended from early Irish immigrants, those often called "Scotch-Irish." There are also large proportions of French, Spanish, or German descent. Killian notes that English and other British Americans have become submerged in a larger and ethnically diverse white population that has emphasized whiteness above all else: "For a southerner, the salient fact was and is whether he was white or black; all else was secondary."[107]

Although white southerners of English descent remain influential in southern politics and the southern economy, they are not examined as a group by scholars or journalists. Killian's book is important in that it leads us to think about regional diversity, the ethnic diversity of the South, and the role of English Americans among white southerners. Unfortunately, Killian provides little data on the last item. A specific book-length analysis of English Americans in the South (or the North) has yet to be written.

As we have noted before, the theoretical frameworks of U.S. assimilation analysts generally take the English (or British) Americans as the starting point for the analysis of assimilation in the United States. Milton Gordon's important seven-stage framework, discussed in detail in Chapter 2, assumes Anglo-conformity as the general trend of adaptation by subsequent immigrant groups in the American colonies and, later, in the United States. Eventual inclusion of later groups is accented.

Looking at English Americans, other theorists of U.S. racial and ethnic relations accent the ways in which the English colonization process began the establishment of hierarchies and stratification systems. The subordination of Native Americans by English settlers is a clear example of what Lieberson has called *migrant superordination,* which takes place when a migrating group imposes its will on a native group. The entry of later groups of immigrants in a subordinate position in the American system, such as in the case of African slaves, is an example of Lieberson's concept of *indigenous superordination.* Lieberson's concepts give attention to critical social hierarchies, with unequal power and resources, developing in U.S. racial and ethnic history. The importance of these will become clear in later chapters.

SUMMARY

The purpose of this chapter has been to examine one of the most neglected of all white ethnic groups, English Americans. Their blending into the background makes it difficult to assess the power, location, and achievements of these first immigrants and their millions of descendants. Those of English ancestry still make up a little more than a quarter of the white population, and there is still some tendency for them to marry others of the same ancestry.

It was the English who first colonized on a large scale the area that became the eastern United States. We have detailed what the original English colonization and migrations meant for U.S. institutions, past and present. *Dominance* is the appropriate term for English influence on U.S. religious, economic, and political institutions. The colonization migration of the English created a dominant culture and social structure to which subsequent immigrant groups were required to adapt. The study of assimilation in the United States can begin with the English. For centuries English migrants and their millions of descendants have been disproportionately represented in key social, economic, and political positions in this society. Between the mid-1800s and the 1990s they have been joined in their dominant position by certain other Protestant groups. The result is a more diverse Anglo-Protestant group, but one that still has disproportionately great power.

The tremendous impact of Anglo-Protestant Americans on the culture and institutions does not mean that substantial segments have not stayed working-class or poor. There have long been significant regional and denominational differences within English and British American groups. Episcopalians are a bit different from Congregationalists, and southerners are different from New Englanders.

In recent decades English and British Protestant dominance has been challenged by Catholic Americans and Jewish Americans, as well as by some non-European groups. Some analysts have argued that Anglo-Protestant influence is on the wane. Schrag, for instance, has argued that Anglo-Saxon Protestants are on the road to cultural decline. In this view, white Anglo-Saxon Protestant domination in areas such as music and the arts came to an end sometime after World War II; the "decline of the WASP" is to be seen in the increasing non-Anglo-Saxon dominance of music, literature, and art. But even Schrag presents a different conclusion for the economic sphere: the Anglo-Protestant "elite still controls its own corporate offices, its board rooms, its banks and foundations."[108] Thus analyses arguing for the decline of whites of English and British ancestry as a force in this society, as the data in this chapter suggest, are at the least premature.

NOTES

1. Cleveland Amory, *The Proper Bostonians* (New York: Dutton, 1947), p. 11.
2. Thomas Sowell, *Ethnic America* (New York: Basic Books, 1981), p. 4.
3. Carl Wittke, "Preface to the Revised Edition," in *We Who Built America*, rev. ed. (Cleveland: Case Western Reserve University Press, 1967).
4. Milton M. Gordon, *Assimilation in American Life* (New York: Oxford University Press, 1964), p. 72.
5. Will Herberg, *Protestant—Catholic—Jew*, rev. ed. (Garden City, N.Y.: Doubleday, Anchor Books, 1960), p. 21.
6. Rowland T. Berthoff, *British Immigrants in Industrial America* (Chicago: University of Chicago Press, 1953), p. 1.
7. John Jay, Alexander Hamilton, and James Madison, *The Federalist* (London: Penguin Classics, 1987 [1788]), p. 91.
8. Wilbur S. Shepperson, *British Emigration to North America* (Oxford: Basil Blackwell, 1957), p. 3.
9. Conrad Taeuber and Irene B. Taeuber, "Immigration to the United States," in *Population and Society*, ed. Charles B. Nam (Boston: Houghton Mifflin, 1968), p. 316.
10. Immigration and Naturalization Service, *1975 Annual Report* (Washington, 1975), pp. 62–64.

11. Alice Marriott and Carol K. Rachlin, *American Epic* (New York: Mentor Books, 1969), p. 105.
12. Samuel Eliot Morison, *The Oxford History of the American People* (New York: Oxford University Press, 1965), pp. 48–49.
13. Klaus E. Knorr, *British Colonial Theories, 1570–1850* (Toronto: University of Toronto Press, 1944), p. 126.
14. Marriott and Rachlin, *American Epic*, p. 106.
15. Ibid., pp. 104–6; Winthrop D. Jordan, *White over Black* (Baltimore: Penguin, 1969), p. 89.
16. Quoted in John Collier, *Indians of the Americas*, abridged ed. (New York: Mentor Books, 1947), p. 115.
17. The remainder of this paragraph and the following paragraph draw on Morison, *Oxford History of the American People*, pp. 50–154; and Maldwyn A. Jones, *American Immigration* (Chicago: University of Chicago Press, 1960), pp. 10–38.
18. Morison, *Oxford History of the American People*, p. 74.
19. *Proceedings of the American Historical Association*, vol. 1 of *Annual Report of the American Historical Association* (Washington, 1932), p. 124.
20. Jones, *American Immigration*, pp. 34–35.
21. Berthoff, *British Immigrants in Industrial America*, p. vii.
22. Ibid., p. 5.
23. Shepperson, *British Emigration to North America*, p. 20.
24. Berthoff, *British Immigrants in Industrial America*, pp. 28–29; Charlotte Erickson, "English," in *Harvard Encyclopedia of American Ethnic Groups*, ed. Stephan Thernstrom (Cambridge: Harvard University Press, 1980), pp. 324–32.
25. Shepperson, *British Emigration to North America*, pp. 27–32, 84; Berthoff, *British Immigrants in Industrial America*, pp. 46–87, 122; Charlotte Erickson, "Agrarian Myths of English Immigrants," in *In the Trek of the Immigrants*, ed. O. Fritiof Ander (Rock Island, Ill.: Augustana Library Publications, 1964), pp. 59–64.
26. Berthoff, *British Immigrants in Industrial America*, p. 125.
27. Ibid., p. 210; see also pp. 143–83.
28. Erickson, "English," pp. 335–36.
29. Stanley Lieberson and Mary C. Waters, *From Many Strands* (New York: Russell Sage, 1988), pp. 40–41.
30. This section draws heavily on Charles H. Anderson, *White Protestant Americans* (Englewood Cliffs, N.J.: Prentice-Hall, 1970), pp. 28–71, 79–87. See also Ian C. Graham, *Colonists from Scotland* (Ithaca, N.Y.: Cornell University Press, 1956); and Albert B. Faust, *The German Element in the United States* (New York: Steuben Society, 1927).
31. John Higham, *Strangers in the Land* (New York: Atheneum, 1963), p. 4.
32. Henry P. Fairchild, *Immigration* (New York: Macmillan, 1920), p. 47; Jones, *American Immigration*, p. 44.
33. Jordan, *White over Black*, p. 86.
34. Ibid., p. 87.
35. Jones, *American Immigration*, pp. 41–46.
36. Fairchild, *Immigration*, pp. 57–58.
37. Michael Kammen, *People of Paradox* (New York: Knopf, 1972), p. 66.
38. Quoted in Nancy F. Conklin and Margaret A. Lourie, *A Host of Tongues* (New York: Free Press, 1983), p. 69.
39. Kammen, *People of Paradox*, p. 74; Jordan, *White over Black*, p. 339.
40. Higham, *Strangers in the Land*, p. 6; Marcus L. Hansen, *The Immigrant in American History* (New York: Harper Torchbooks, 1964), pp. 111–36; Wittke, *We Who Built America*, p. 505.
41. Quoted in Richard Hofstadter, *Social Darwinism in American Thought*, rev. ed. (Boston: Beacon Press, 1955), pp. 171–72.
42. Higham, *Strangers in the Land*, p. 32; Hofstadter, *Social Darwinism in American Thought*, pp. 173–74.
43. Higham, *Strangers in the Land*, p. 33.
44. Hofstadter, *Social Darwinism in American Thought*, pp. 178–79; Lewis H. Carlson and George A. Colburn, *In Their Place* (New York: John Wiley, 1972), pp. 305–8. Carlson and Colburn provide excerpts from the writings of Strong.
45. Higham, *Strangers in the Land*, pp. 96–152.
46. E. Digby Baltzell, *The Protestant Establishment* (New York: Random House, Vintage Books, 1966), pp. 96–98; Higham, *Strangers in the Land*, pp. 148–57.
47. See, for example, the excerpt from Roberts's *Why Europe Leaves Home* in *In Their Place*, ed. Carlson and Colburn, p. 312.
48. Richard Alba, *Ethnic Identity: The Transformation of White America* (New Haven: Yale University Press, 1990), p. 365.
49. Jones, *American Immigration*, pp. 36–38.
50. W. Lloyd Warner and Leo Srole, *The Social Systems of American Ethnic Groups* (New Haven: Yale University Press, 1945), p. 287.
51. Quoted in Juan F. Perea, "Demography and Distrust: An Essay on American Languages, Cultural Pluralism and Official English," *Minnesota Law Review* 77 (1992): in press.
52. Susanna McBee, "A War over Words," *U.S. News & World Report*, October 6, 1986, p. 64.
53. Bill Piatt, *Only English? Law and Language Policy in the United States* (Albuquerque: University of New Mexico Press, 1990), p. 159.
54. Amado Padilla et al., "The English-Only Movement," *American Psychologist* 46 (February 1991): 120–30; National Education Association, *Official English/English Only* (Washington, D.C.: National Education Association, 1988), pp. 5–7.
55. Perea, "Demography and Distrust."
56. National Education Association, *Official English/English Only*, p. 7; Carl J. Veltman, *Language Shift in the United States* (Berlin: Mouton, 1983).
57. Edwin S. Gaustad, *Historical Atlas of Religion in America* (New York: Harper & Row, Pub., 1962), pp. 1–20.
58. Herberg, *Protestant—Catholic—Jew*, p. 82.
59. Marshall Sklare, *Conservative Judaism* (Glencoe, Ill.: Free Press, 1955), pp. 31–117.
60. Cited in Max Weber, *The Protestant Ethic and the Spirit of Capitalism*, trans. Talcott Parsons (New York: Scribner's, 1958), pp. 158–60.
61. Joe R. Feagin, *Subordinating the Poor* (Englewood Cliffs, N.J.: Prentice-Hall, 1975), p. 22.

62. Weber, *The Protestant Ethic*, p. 17; see also p. 50.
63. David Ewen, *History of Popular Music* (New York: Barnes & Noble, 1961), pp. 1–10.
64. See Samuel Bowles and Herbert Gintis, *Schooling in Capitalist America* (New York: Basic Books, 1976).
65. Morison, *Oxford History of the American People*, p. 55.
66. Samuel P. Huntington, "Political Modernization: America versus Europe," *World Politics* 18 (April 1966): 147–48.
67. Jack P. Greene, *The Quest for Power* (Chapel Hill: University of North Carolina Press, 1963), pp. 1ff.
68. Roscoe Pound, *The Formative Era of American Law* (Boston: Little, Brown, 1938), pp. 7–8.
69. Ibid., p. 12.
70. Elizabeth G. Brown and William W. Blume, *British Statutes in American Law, 1776–1836* (Ann Arbor: University of Michigan Law School, 1964), p. 44. See also Lawrence M. Friedman, *A History of American Law* (New York: Simon & Schuster, 1973), pp. 96ff.
71. Pound, *The Formative Era of American Law*, p. 81.
72. Maurice R. Davie, *World Immigration* (New York: Macmillan, 1939), p. 36.
73. Henry J. Ford, *The Scotch-Irish in America* (Princeton, N.J.: Princeton University Press, 1915), p. 491.
74. Charles A. Beard, *An Economic Interpretation of the Constitution of the United States* (New York: Macmillan, 1947), p. 17.
75. Joseph N. Kane, *Facts about the Presidents*, 3rd ed. (New York: Wilson, 1974).
76. John R. Schmidhauser, "The Justices of the Supreme Court: A Collective Portrait," *Midwest Journal of Political Science* 3 (February 1959): 1–57.
77. William Miller, "American Historians and the Business Elite," *Journal of Economic History* 9 (November 1949): 202–3.
78. Baltzell, *The Protestant Establishment*, pp. 10–12.
79. On Protestant presidents before Kennedy, see ibid., p. 21.
80. Robert A. Dahl, *Who Governs?* (New Haven: Yale University Press, 1961), pp. 15–16.
81. Matthew Holden, Jr., "Ethnic Accommodation in a Historical Case," *Comparative Studies in Society and History* 8 (January 1966): 172.
82. Rowland Berthoff, *An Unsettled People* (New York: Harper & Row, Pub., 1971), p. 13; Oliver C. Cox, *Caste, Class, and Race* (Garden City, N.Y.: Doubleday, 1948), pp. 338–39; Barrington Moore, Jr., *Social Origins of Dictatorship and Democracy* (Boston: Beacon Press, 1966), pp. 112–13.
83. Frank Thistlewaite, *The Anglo-American Connection in the Early Nineteenth Century* (Philadelphia: University of Pennsylvania Press, 1959), pp. 5–11.
84. Jesse Lemisch, "The American Revolution Seen from the Bottom Up," in *Toward a New Past*, ed. Barton J. Bernstein (New York: Random House, 1968), p. 8; J. O. Lindsay, ed., *The Old Regime*, vol. 7 of *The New Cambridge Modern History* (Cambridge: Cambridge University Press, 1957), pp. 509–11.
85. Morison, *Oxford History of the American People*, p. 89.
86. Abbot E. Smith, *Colonists in Bondage* (Chapel Hill: University of North Carolina Press, 1947), pp. 25, 336; Jordan, *White over Black*, p. 47; Howard Zinn, *The Politics of History* (Boston: Beacon Press, 1970), p. 68.
87. Lee Soltow, *Men and Wealth in the United States, 1850–1870* (New Haven: Yale University Press, 1975), p. 149.
88. Matthew Josephson, *The Robber Barons* (New York: Harcourt, Brace & World, 1934), pp. 32–35, 315–452.
89. John N. Ingham, *The Iron Barons* (Westport, Conn.: Greenwood Press, 1978), pp. 14–16.
90. Miller, "American Historians and the Business Elite," p. 202.
91. Elin L. Anderson, *We Americans* (Cambridge: Harvard University Press, 1937), p. 137; see also pp. 21–247.
92. E. Digby Baltzell, *An American Business Aristocracy* (New York: Collier Books, 1962), p. 267.
93. Ibid., p. 431.
94. Baltzell, *The Protestant Establishment*, p. 321.
95. Thomas R. Dye, *Who's Running America?* (Englewood Cliffs, N.J.: Prentice-Hall, 1976), pp. 3–8, 150–53. See also Thomas R. Dye, *Who's Running America? The Carter Years* (Englewood Cliffs, N.J.: Prentice-Hall, 1979), pp. 171–77.
96. Thomas R. Dye, letter to author, April 11, 1977.
97. Julia Reed, "The New American Establishment," *U.S. News & World Report*, February 8, 1988, p. 38.
98. Richard D. Alba and Gwen Moore, "Ethnicity in the American Elite," *American Sociological Review* 47 (June 1982); see also Thomas R. Dye, *Who's Running America? The Conservative Years* (Englewood Cliffs, N.J.: Prentice-Hall, 1986), pp. 185–99.
99. Michael Novak, "The Nordic Jungle: Inferiority in America," in *Divided Society*, ed. Colin Greer (New York: Basic Books, 1974), p. 134.
100. Peter Schrag, *The Decline of the WASP* (New York: Simon & Schuster, 1971).
101. U.S. Bureau of the Census, *U.S. Census of Population, 1980: General Social and Economic Characteristics*, PC 80-1-C1 (Washington, 1983), pp. 21, 172.
102. U.S. Bureau of the Census, *U.S. Census of Population, 1970: Subject Reports—National Origin and Language*, PC(2)-1A (Washington, 1973), p. 368; U.S. Bureau of the Census, *Census of Population, 1980*, pp. 51, 177.
103. U.S. Bureau of the Census, *U.S. Census of Population, 1950: Special Reports—Nativity and Parentage*, P-E No. 3A (Washington, 1954), p. 137; U.S. Bureau of the Census, *U.S. Census of Population, 1970*, p. 125; U.S. Bureau of the Census, *U.S. Census of Population, 1980*, p. 174.
104. Joe R. Feagin, "A Preliminary Analysis of Media Treatment of Ethnicity and Race" (research paper, University of Florida, 1992). The analysis used Mead Data Central's Nexis database.
105. Lieberson and Waters, *From Many Strands*, p. 173; Alba, *Ethnic Identity*, pp. 49–82.
106. Lieberson and Waters, *From Many Strands*, pp. 53–56.
107. Lewis M. Killian, *White Southerners* (New York: Random House, 1970), p. 16.
108. Schrag, *The Decline of the WASP*, p. 164.

Chapter 4

Irish Americans

Annual St. Patrick's Day Parade, New York, N.Y.
Photo by Marc Anderson, United Press International

Numerous discussions of ethnicity have focused on the *white ethnics*, a term sometimes used for European Catholic and Jewish Americans. Anglo-Protestant Americans have, on occasion, blamed these groups for corruption and racial discrimination in U.S. cities. They have spoken of white ethnic "hardhats" as though they were uneducated buffoons with a corrupt or authoritarian bent. Not surprisingly, white ethnics have counterattacked, arguing that hypocritical Anglo-Protestants have little awareness of the experiences of white Catholic and Jewish Americans. It is the purpose of this chapter on the Irish Americans, and the following chapters on Italian and Jewish Americans, to analyze the neglected experiences of the non-British white Americans who helped build the United States.

The Irish Americans are one of the major groups that come to mind when white ethnic groups, especially those in the cities, are mentioned. The traditional view of the Irish contains images of parading leprechauns in funny suits, shamrocks, Saint Patrick's Day, and big-city political machines. The Irish, furthermore, are said by some to be among the more conservative and racist of white Americans, with greater alcoholism problems than other Americans. This superficial imagery is an inaccurate portrayal of the realities of the Irish American experience. The Irish American contribution to the development of the United States has been major.

How did the Irish come to these shores in the first place? What was their immigration experience? What proportions were Protestant and what Catholic? What conflicts have occurred? How does the assimilation model fit the Irish experience? How successful have the Irish been? Let us turn now to these questions.

IRISH IMMIGRATION: AN OVERVIEW

On the migration continuum from slave importation to voluntary immigration, the Irish migration to North America would be toward the voluntary end. Even so, this movement was less voluntary than the migrations of some other European groups, for there was great economic and political pressure to leave Ireland. Yet there was a choice in the points of destination. There has been great variation in the numbers. Perhaps 200,000 to 400,000 Irish left for the colonies prior to 1787; between 1787 and the 1820s approximately 100,000 migrated.[1] The period 1841–60 saw the heaviest migration, with about 1.6 million immigrants. Migration peaked again in the 1880s and the 1890s, but then dropped off sharply in subsequent decades. From 1961 to 1990 the total number of immigrants was less than 80,000.[2]

The Eighteenth-Century Migration

The first Irish came prior to 1700, in small numbers. In the 1650s Captain John Vernon supplied 550 persons from southern Ireland as servants and workers for the English colonists and entrepreneurs in New England, and by 1700 a few Irish Catholic families had settled in Maryland.[3] Not until the 1700s did large numbers of Irish arrive on North American shores. A significant proportion of these were from northern Ireland (Ulster) and had some Scottish ancestry, but many were from southern Ireland and could trace their ancestry back into ancient Irish history.

There were both push and pull factors. The image of North America as a land of opportunity was for most immigrants a major pull factor, but domestic pressures were also important. In the 1100s Ireland was conquered by the English. By the 1600s, Scots, in increasing numbers, were being encouraged to migrate across the channel to Ireland and to develop lands given to English and Scottish landowners by the king of England. Subsequently the English oppressors drove many of the native Irish people off the land.[4]

As a result of this English colonizing of Ireland, the Ulster (northern) Irish who migrated to North America contained a significant number of persons of Scottish ancestry. Yet the latter were the fourth or fifth generation of Scots in Ireland. They had become Irish.[5] There is some debate among scholars as to how much the Scottish settlers blended with the Irish, but it is clear that some intermixture, cultural and marital, did occur. Their primary nationality, as they themselves would say, was not Scottish but Irish.

To what extent were the migrants from northern Ireland in the 1700s joined by those from southern areas? To what extent were these migrants Celtic* or Catholic? These questions are debated by scholars. The traditional view has been that virtually all the immigrants before 1800 were "Scotch-Irish," Protestants from northern Ireland. Ford and Leyburn claim that the immigrants were generally persons from the North with Presbyterian backgrounds.[6] Other authors have provided evidence of a large southern (and thus Catholic) component to this migration. O'Brien cites "unquestionable proof that every part of Ireland contributed to the enormous emigration of its people, and while there are no official statistics now available—for none were kept—to indicate the numerical strength of those Irish immigrants, abundant proof of this assertion is found in authentic records."[7]

For example, tens of thousands of people with old Celtic names appear in various records. Evidence of the significant quantity of non-Ulster immigrants is also suggested by data on passenger ships. Of 318 such ships sailing between 1767 and 1769, 60 percent neither came from nor returned to northern Irish ports; in the period 1771–74, the figure was 57 percent of 576 ships. Such evidence is only suggestive, however, since an unknown number of ships from northern Ireland stopping in southern ports for provisions gave the latter as their points of departure. In addition, some scholars have argued that the Scottish population in Ulster was not nearly as large as the eighteenth-century Irish migration. Greeley concludes that it is possible that most in the early stream of Irish immigrants were Catholic at least in their remote origins.[8]

O'Brien argues that southern Irish immigrants gave up the traditional faith in part because there were few Catholic churches in the colonies, in part because the extremely hostile Protestant environment in many areas of Ireland and the colonies made it dangerous to practice the Catholic faith.[9] Local laws often required children to be baptized Protestant, and great antagonism was directed at "papists." Conversion of the Catholic Irish to Protestantism was common in the early migration. One Episcopalian clergyman wrote to a missionary society that "there were many Irish Papists in Pennsylvania who turn Quakers and get into places as well as Germans."[10] Some scholars have suggested that these early immigrants represented the less devout agricultural proletariat and thus found it relatively easy to sever their weak identification with the Catholic church once they arrived in their new homeland.[11]

The northern Irish in the first streams of immigration regarded themselves as Irish rather than Scotch-Irish. In the first two centuries of Irish presence the term *Scotch-Irish* was seldom used. The new migrants gave Irish names to their settlements and joined

---

Celtic refers to those inhabitants of Ireland whose ancestry dates back far before the Roman and English invasions of the island.

organizations such as the Friendly Sons of Saint Patrick rather than Scottish American societies.[12] The term *Scotch-Irish* came into heavy use only after 1850, when some older Irish Protestant immigrants and their British friends sought to distinguish themselves from the recent Irish Catholic immigrants who were at that time the focus of much discrimination.[13] The issue of the "Scotch-Irish race" and its impact had become heated by the late nineteenth century. Prominent politicians engaged in blatant racism when they praised the members of the "Scotch-Irish race" as great pioneers and democrats while damning the "Catholic Irish race." Consider Henry Cabot Lodge's remarks in an 1891 issue of *Century Magazine*: "I classified the Irish and the Scotch-Irish as two distinct race-stocks, and I believe the distinction to be a sound one historically and scientifically."[14]

In his book, *The Winning of the West*, Theodore Roosevelt dramatized the contributions of the Scotch-Irish frontier people. We had not understood, Roosevelt argued, the important part "played by that stern and virile people," the brave "Puritans" of the West.[15] In the early 1900s other U.S. scholars argued, inaccurately, that the Scotch-Irish were not really Irish, that they saw themselves as Scots resident in Ireland, a distinct and superior racial type with a different "type of frame and physiognomy."[16]

The view that the Scotch-Irish were part of the Anglo-Saxon or Teutonic "race" was so vigorously argued that it reached the absurd point of denying any Celtic (i.e., Catholic) part in the mixture: "Whatever blood may be in the veins of the genuine Scotch-Irishman, one thing is certain, and that is that there is not mingled with it one drop of the blood of the old Irish or Kelt."[17] The data showing large numbers of Celtic Irish in the early migration pose serious questions for this racist glorification of the Protestant Irish.

Early Life

What was life like for the early Irish settlers in an English-dominated society? Perhaps half became indentured servants; others became farmers or farm workers, often in frontier areas. The English treated Irish servants as lowly subordinates, even to the point of brutality. Discriminatory import duties and longer indenture terms were placed on Irish servants.[18] Irish Catholic servants suffered because of their nationality and their religion. As early as 1704 heavy taxes were placed on Irish Catholic immigrants. Laws were passed excluding them or discouraging their importation.[19] With times as hard as this, significant numbers of the Irish gave up their Catholicism. Not all converted, however. Irish immigrants in some Pennsylvania counties were predominantly Catholic. Pressing for religious tolerance, several prominent Irish Catholics wrote President Washington in the late 1700s asking that the full religious rights of Catholics be protected.[20]

Pennsylvania and New England received the first groups of Ulster Irish, in the decades before 1740. After 1740 many migrated to the valleys of Virginia and the Carolinas. Many of these also were indentured servants; others became farmers. Immigrants' letters to Ireland reveal that America was considered a land of hope.[21] Many eighteenth-century Irish immigrants, encouraged to settle in frontier areas as a barrier against the Native Americans, came into conflict with the latter, as well as with British American landowners on whose land they sometimes squatted.[22]

By 1790 almost 10 percent of the white United States population of 3.2 million was Irish. The Ulster Irish constituted large proportions of the Georgia, Pennsylvania, and South Carolina populations; those from the southern areas of Ireland were most substantially represented in Maryland, Virginia, Delaware, and North Carolina. The Irish were a large nationality group at the time of the new nation's birth.[23]

The pull factors motivating millions of Irish Catholics to cross the Atlantic after 1830 were the same as those that attracted European immigrants for centuries to North America, which was portrayed, often in exaggerated terms, as the land of golden opportunity. Push factors loomed even larger. The famine that came to Ireland in the 1840s spurred emigration to the United States. Irish peasants relied heavily on potatoes for food. The potato blight caused a massive failure of that crop, and many people starved to death or died from diseases such as hunger typhus. During these famine years Ireland actually produced more than twice the food, including corn and cattle, that was needed to feed the hungry. The dominant English landlords saw to it that these foodstuffs were exported to England and elsewhere or consumed by those in Ireland with money. The Irish were right when they said that "God sent the blight, but the English landlord sent the famine."

In addition, English leaders advocated emigration to the United States and elsewhere as the proper solution for the poor Irish. Many Irish who emigrated to the United States mourned their departure with a sad, all-night farewell ceremony called the "American wake"; they saw their new land as a place of involuntary exile, a condition Kerby Miller sees as the foundation of Irish American homesickness and nationalism. The long history of English conquest and oppression of the Irish lies behind the persisting conflict between the two peoples, in places such as Northern Ireland, in the late twentieth century.[24]

The Atlantic crossing was dangerous. Few ships arrived that had not lost a number of their poorly accommodated passengers to starvation or disease. The survivors usually chose urban destinations. New York became a major center, eventually housing more Irish than Dublin. Like most urban migrants, the new immigrants went where relatives or fellow villagers had settled. Residential segregation for Irish Americans in the nineteenth century had a distinctive form. Huge ghetto communities, such as black and Latino Americans now live in, were not the rule. The Irish newcomers found housing wherever they could, usually in the little houses and shanties on the side streets or in the alleys beside or behind the fashionable homes of affluent Anglo-Protestant urbanites. As blue-collar workers, they often lived within walking distance of manufacturing jobs. They clustered in smaller, more dispersed settlements than would be the case for later immigrant groups.[25]

These scattered settlements were reinforced by a second large stream of immigrants from Ireland between 1870 and 1900, and by significant but declining numbers of immigrants from 1900 to 1925. These later immigrants were forced out not by famine, but primarily by poverty and the hope for a better life. In New York, Boston, and Philadelphia, poor housing with its attendant disease was frequently their lot. An analysis of New York revealed that the 1877 death rate for the Irish-born was high, as was the mortality rate for their American-born children. Whole families were consigned to a single room in crowded apartment houses called *rookeries*. The Irish were overrepresented in the almshouses of some cities. Irish crime rates, high for some categories of minor offenses, were exaggerated by Anglo nativists; the rate of serious offenses was low. The poverty of Irish immigrants had several causes. Many of the immigrants had few skills, but more important reasons were hard jobs, low wages, and direct institutionalized discrimination against those of Irish descent.[26]

From the beginning, Irish women have been central to the establishment of strong Irish American communities. One distinctive aspect of the Irish immigration was the presence of large numbers of young single women. These women decided that Ireland held no hope for them and that America was the land of opportunity. More women than men migrated to the United States, and foreign-born women outnumbered men in the Irish American communities. Once in the U. S. these women did not subscribe to the cult of womanhood, which emphasized that the woman's place was only in the home. Most did not live lives of sheltered domesticity but rather became self-sufficient persons with distinctive work histories. They made important contributions to the mobility of Irish Americans into middle-income America.

The famine in Ireland destroyed many Irish families, and for six decades young, unmarried women came to the United States to avoid the terrible life awaiting them in Ireland. In contrast with male Irish immigrants and female immigrants from many other countries, these women were willing to postpone or forego marriage and to work in the homes of native-born Americans as domestic servants. Many also supported families in the old country. Their values, expressed in the decisions they made about work, were fundamental life-choice values that have persisted into the late twentieth century. Among them was a strong commitment to their Irish heritage and to personal independence. Interestingly, the daughters of these women often became schoolteachers or clerical workers.[27]

STEREOTYPING

The resistance of English Americans to the Irish immigration dates back to the seventeenth and eighteenth centuries. "Papists" were the targets of open hatred. Protestant and Catholic Irish Americans suffered from nativistic concern over their political persuasions, as in the conflicts in the 1790s between the Federalists and the Jeffersonians. Yet it was the nineteenth-century Irish, poor Catholics from the famine-ridden Emerald Isle, who were attacked the most.

In a study of Civil War public literature on the Irish, Dale Knobel found what he terms the Paddy stereotype, a view of the Irish that experienced gradual change from the 1820s to the Civil War. From the 1820s to the mid-1840s this stereotype of the Catholic Irish emphasized their morality, style, and lack of intelligence. Alleged character faults such as ingratitude, wickedness, and ignorance were accented in this early stereotype. With the surge in Irish migration in the late 1840s and early 1850s the image in the literature came to emphasize conflict, hostility, and emotionality. Words such as *temperamental, dangerous, quarrelsome, idle*, and *reckless*—characteristics emphasizing conduct as much as character—came into use after 1845. The Anglo-American image of the Irish had hardened and become less tolerant as the numbers of Irish immigrants grew. During the following decades various phrases that were derogatory to the Irish, such as *Irish buggy* for wheelbarrow, *Irish promotion* for demotion, and *paddy wagon* for a vehicle used by the police to transport criminals, came into use.[28]

Attacks on Irish Catholics took the form of cartoons that stereotyped the Irish by means of outrageous symbols—an apelike face, a fighting stance, a jug of whisky, a shillelagh. The influential caricaturist Thomas Nast published cartoons of this type in *Harper's Weekly* and other magazines. One of his caricatures shows a stereotyped southern black man and a nasty, apelike Irishman, both portrayed as ignorant voters and a threat to orderly politics. "New York's leading cartoonists of the 1870s and 1880s," notes Curtis, "certainly did not refrain from simianizing Irish-American Paddies who epitomized the tens of thousands of working-class immigrants and their children caught up in urban poverty and slum conditions after their flight from rural poverty and famine in Ireland."[29]

The Ape Image

Not surprisingly, the apelike image of the Irish was imported from England. With the rise of debates over evolution in England, the poor Irish came to be regarded by many in England and the U.S. as the "missing link" between the gorilla and the human race. With the constant threat of Irish rebellion on the one hand and the press of Darwinism on the other, "it was comforting for some Englishmen to believe—on the basis of the best scientific authority in the Anthropological Society of London—that their own facial angles and orthognathous features were as far removed from those of apes, Irishmen, and Negroes as was humanly possible."[30] In rationalizing the exploitation of the Irish and black Africans, racists on both sides of the Atlantic developed dehumanizing stereotypes.

Notice the comparable position of black and Irish Americans in this mythology. Greeley has underscored the parallels in prejudice and stereotyping:

> Practically every accusation that has been made against the American blacks was also made against the Irish: Their family life was inferior, they had no ambition, they did not keep up their homes, they drank too much, they were not responsible, they had no morals, it was not safe to walk through their neighborhoods at night, they voted the way crooked politicians told them to vote, they were not willing to pull themselves up by their bootstraps, they were not capable of education, they could not think for themselves, and they would always remain social problems for the rest of the country.[31]

Early stage shows made fun of the Irish by using these stereotypes, just as they did with black Americans. In the nineteenth century the Catholic Irish were often socially defined by those in dominant groups as physically different, and thus as a "race." In the twentieth century, the emphasis on this alleged physical distinctiveness would disappear.

Recent Decades

In 1932 white students at Princeton University were given a list of eighty-four positive and negative traits and asked to identify those they associated with ten racial and ethnic groups, including Irish Americans. Fifty years later, a similar questionnaire was given to a predominantly white sample of students at Arizona State University. In 1932 the Princeton students rated the following among the top ten traits of Irish Americans: "pugnacious," "quick-tempered," "quarrelsome," "aggressive," and "stubborn." This rather negative stereotype accented images of aggression and fighting on the part of the Irish. This imagery decreased significantly in the 1982 sample, for the Arizona State students listed only "quick-tempered" and "stubborn" in their top ten traits for the Irish; more positive traits appeared in the top ten, including "intelligent" and "loyal to family ties." Moreover, in neither sample did the Irish receive the most negative stereotypes available to the students—the traits of "treacherous" and "sly," which groups such as the

Jewish, Japanese, and black Americans received. These results suggest a reduction since the 1930s in the traditional stereotyping of Irish Americans and signal substantial attitude-receptional assimilation, to use Milton Gordon's conceptual term.[32] In a recent study of white ethnic groups in a large metropolitan area of upper New York State, about one-fifth of those with Irish ancestry reported encountering stereotypes of Irish Americans as politicians and police officers, heavy drinkers, or poets. They also encountered stereotypes of Irish women as "long-suffering."[33]

Irish Catholic Americans have been seen by some analysts as a particularly anti-black group of white Americans. Compared with some other white Americans, though, Irish Catholics have been found to be relatively liberal. A review of 1970s' opinion polls came to this conclusion:

> Surveys in the 1970s revealed that in the North Irish Catholics were more sympathetic to integrated neighborhoods, integrated schools, and interracial marriages than other white Catholics and white Protestants. Among whites only Jews are more liberal on racial issues than Irish Catholics.[34]

Irish Catholics in the North are more likely than most other white groups to live in racially integrated neighborhoods. Nonetheless, Irish Catholics in major cities, like other whites, have played a significant role in discrimination against nonwhite Americans.

PROTEST AND CONFLICT

From their first decades in North America, Irish Americans suffered not only verbal abuse and stereotyping but also intentional discrimination and violent attacks. Irish Americans have on occasion retaliated, even to the point of violence. In other situations they have inaugurated conflict. As noted in Chapter 2, ethnic conflict means a struggle over resources and can be generated by inequality. Conflict can take both nonviolent and violent forms, and it often involves groups with differing power and resources.

Assimilation theorists have usually neglected the conflict that has characterized inter-ethnic and interracial relations. Indeed, some views of U.S. history embody a myth of peaceful progress. In this view the members of each white ethnic group have advanced higher on the social ladder by pulling themselves up by their bootstraps—by hard work and diligent effort, not by active protest and collective violence. This image is incorrect. As with other white groups, the Irish Americans have struggled for their "place in the sun" with many groups, from established Anglo-Protestants to Native Americans. They have been involved in conflict with groups above and below them in the racial and ethnic hierarchy.

Early Conflict

The first major conflict was with the established groups that controlled the major institutions in the North American colonies at the time of the initial Irish immigration. A few eighteenth-century Irish settlements were damaged or destroyed by attacks. British Americans attacked and destroyed an Irish community in Worcester, Massachusetts, in the eighteenth century. There was a great deal of vigorous opposition from the colonists to both Catholic and Protestant Irish migrants.[35] Conflict arose between the Irish Protestant farmers in the frontier areas and the British plantation gentry in the coastal areas of the colonies. In the early period, the backcountry Irish Americans were seen as crude frontier people. Settling in frontier areas, the Irish sometimes defied laws made by eastern interests and engaged in aggressive protest, such as the Whisky Rebellion and the Regulation movement—to extend their control where it suited their ends.[36]

Conflict with Native Americans was also part of the Irish American experience. The Irish were encouraged to settle the frontier areas of the colonies so that the dominant eastern interests would be protected from Native Americans. The bloody practice of scalping was institutionalized by English and Irish settlers determined to exterminate Native Americans. Placing bounties on the scalps of Native American men and women became common in New England and the middle colonies. Conflict between Irish Americans who were taking Native American lands and Native Americans who were protecting their way of life became widespread in Virginia and the Carolinas.[37]

In the 1790s there were violent attacks on Irish Catholics. In 1798 a disturbance known as the Federal Riot took place at Saint Mary's Church in Philadelphia: Irish opponents of a new anti-alien law who had come to the church with a petition for the congregation to sign were beaten up by a group of Federalist rioters.[38] Although the Irish had a valid reputation for aggressiveness, much of the rioting after 1800 was directed against them because they were immigrants and Roman Catholics. Most "Irish riots" were triggered by anti-Irish incidents, often by anti-Catholic acts. An 1806 riot in New York was generated by Protestant attempts to break up a Catholic religious service. Catholic churches were destroyed in several cities.[39] By 1850 most large cities had seen anti-Catholic demonstrations and riots. Philadelphia became a center for anti–Irish Catholic violence. There, in 1844, two major riots "resulted in the burning of two Catholic churches...; the destruction of dozens of Catholic homes; and sixteen deaths."[40] In the 1850s Protestant nativist groups such as the Know-Nothings played a major role in attacks on Irish Americans.[41]

Group Conflict

Conflict in the mining areas was a major feature of the Irish American experience in the latter half of the nineteenth century. Irish workers and better-paid English workers often did not get along. Old feuds were renewed. In the early days of copper mining in Michigan, English and Irish miners competed for jobs.[42] Similar struggles characterized the coal-mining areas of Pennsylvania, where the Irish played a major role in developing the anthracite coal mines. Here they found English and Welsh mining capitalists and English workers in control of skilled work.[43] Conditions were oppressive. Pay rates were low, perhaps $20 to $30 a month. Often pay was in the form of a "bobtail check": money owed the company for groceries and rent equaled one's wages, a situation of wage slavery.[44] Such oppression and poverty led to violent conflict between predominantly British Protestant owners and superintendents and Irish Catholic miners.

As early as the Civil War, trouble between Irish Americans and the older groups flared up in Pennsylvania. Irish workers who saw the Civil War as "a rich man's war" opposed the Union cause and the draft. Many feared freed black slaves would come north and take their jobs. The use of troops against Irish American groups protesting the war was narrowly avoided.[45]

The major coal strike of 1875, called the Long Strike, forced many miners to the brink of starvation. The mine owners broke the strike and crushed attempts at unionization.[46] In response, secret Irish organizations linked to the Ancient Order of the Hibernians (AOH) sometimes resorted to assassination and sabotage. The owners reacted with violence against the AOH groups. The Anglo-Protestant establishment engineered numerous shootings of workers, and the miners replied with armed defense and guerrilla warfare.[47] Although called Molly Maguires (an older organization in Ireland), the protesting miners were not part of that secret organization. Instead, they were members of miners' organizations who went underground when moderate protests failed to improve their poor living and working conditions.

Rather than yield to the reasonable requests of the miners for better wages, British American and other mine owners hired an army of private detectives to put down the workers' rebellion. One detective, sent into the fields to spy, gathered information to be used in court cases; twenty Irish miners were publicly hanged for engaging in protest. The owners' counterattack in the courts was reinforced by nativist portrayals of the Irish members of the secret societies as undisciplined and violent. This nativism was evident in the trials of the miners, whose convictions were influenced by Irish stereotypes in the minds of non-Irish authorities.[48]

Violence and Conflict

Irish Americans have found themselves competing economically with groups lower on the socioeconomic ladder, as we have seen in the case of the Irish Protestants and Native Americans in conflict on the frontier. As early as the 1840s, Irish competition with black Americans in northern cities engendered substantial distrust and hostility between the two groups. Between the 1840s and the 1860s Irish workers attacked black workers in several cities in the North. During the Civil War Irish hostility toward black Americans increased, for the two groups were competitors in the struggle for the low-paying jobs at the bottom of the employment pyramid. Irish opposition to black workers was basically but not totally economic: "they feared the competition of the hordes of freed slaves who might invade the North, and valued the security that came from the existence in the country of at least one social class below them."[49]

Excluded from unions, black workers sometimes were used by white employers as strikebreakers. The use of black strikebreakers helped to spur the 1863 Irish riot, usually termed the Draft Riot, the most serious riot in U.S. history. Perhaps four hundred white rioters were killed in the streets, together with some free blacks and some white police officers and soldiers. Rioters attacked "Yankees," the police, and blacks.[50] At the front of the rioters were Irish American workers upset at the use of black strikebreakers on the waterfront and at the Civil War draft. This black–Irish tension has persisted for more than a century in several cities. Irish and other white ethnic frustration at black civil rights gains from the 1960s to the 1990s has been a familiar topic in the mass media. Many Irish Americans have felt that black Americans receive a disproportional share of government benefits, including affirmative action, more than urban white ethnics receive. Today there are still serious tensions between the black and Irish residents of major cities such as Boston and Chicago.

On the West Coast Irish American workers fought to maintain their economic position in the mid-nineteenth century. Competition from Chinese American laborers led to anti-Chinese attacks in Irish American papers, as well as to meetings and parades demanding prohibition of further Chinese immigration. Anti-Chinese protest was led by Irish immigrants and their descendants.[51] By 1900 the new immigrants from southern and eastern Europe were confronting Irish Americans in the Midwest and on the East Coast. In Chicago and Boston, Irish control of the church and of political parties was a major source of friction with these new immigrant groups; the new immigrants resented Irish control of city governments and jobs.

In the 1930s Father Charles Coughlin and his organization, the Christian Front, spread anti-Jewish views among Irish and other Gentile Americans. In 1938 Coughlin serialized an anti-Semitic document, the Protocols of the Elders of Zion, a well-known forgery accusing Jews of conspiracy, in his magazine. The Christian Front went so far as to make a list of non-Jewish merchants who promised not to hire Jewish workers or to deal with Jewish businesses.[52]

POLITICS AND POLITICAL INSTITUTIONS

When the Irish began arriving in the seventeenth century, much of the general political framework had already been fashioned by the English. Those Irish immigrants who came in the eighteenth century played a modest role in shaping the nation's initial institutions. Some were among the founding fathers. There were a number among the signers of the Declaration of Independence—altogether eight of the fifty-six, five from the north and three from the south of Ireland. Only four men born in Ireland were members of the Constitutional Convention, together with three other men of Irish descent. At least two Irish Americans were members of the first U.S. Senate, and two were members of the first U.S. House. Before 1800 a few could also be found participating in state and local government as governors of territories and states and as mayors.[53]

Most of the Irish migrating after the Revolutionary War settled in eastern cities, where they became involved in politics. Irish Americans, not unexpectedly, were anti-Federalist and supported the democratic faction of Thomas Jefferson. Here again was interethnic competition. The Federalist-sponsored Alien and Sedition Acts of 1798 were directed in part against Irish immigrants. Irish immigrants taking offense at such actions led to the downfall of the Federalists. They turned out en masse to help elect Jefferson as president. A few decades later the same Irish American vote would play an important role in electing the first Irish (Protestant) president, Andrew Jackson.[54]

Political Organization in the Cities

Traditionally discussion of Irish Americans in politics has focused on the Irish Catholics. The common terms used are *boss* and *machine*. The theme of corrupt urban machines has been tied to hostile views of Catholic immigrants. Protestant views have tended to be pious: "In general, the Irish Catholic political machines in the United States have been notoriously and flamboyantly corrupt—a disgrace to Catholicism, to American democracy, and to the Irish people."[55] Commenting on the Irish machine in New York, William Adams argued that "the 'horrible example' of New York politics combined with a rapid increase of pauper immigrants to check the advance of liberal ideas."[56] The tone of such analyses is that the Irish Americans were more unscrupulous and corrupt in their political activities than other white ethnic groups. In fact the Irish entered a political system that already had many weaknesses, including no secret ballot and much corruption. Machines existed before the Irish Americans controlled them. Anglo-Protestant political organizations by which those in power secured their poor constituents jobs, housing, and food were already the rule in numerous cities.

Why the strong Irish involvement in local politics? Politics was a means to social mobility, a means of achieving power in the face of great Anglo-Protestant opposition. The dominant Anglo-Protestant perspective on government in the nineteenth and early twentieth centuries tended toward a hands-off view, with government staying out of economic affairs as much as possible. It was against this do-nothing background that desperate urban residents, plagued with unemployment, low income, and poor housing, joined large urban political organizations. Taking control of local party organizations, immigrant leaders shaped government programs benefiting the poor. Providing jobs—for example, in real estate and transportation construction—was one of the machines' critical functions.[57]

One of the first great political machines was New York City's Tammany Society. In 1817 a group of Irish Americans, incensed at discrimination at the hands of this Protestant machine, broke into one of its meetings and demanded the nomination of an Irish American for Congress. Although they were driven away this time, a few decades later Irish Americans penetrated the New York political organization. Irish political power brought new leadership to Tammany Hall in the 1860s and 1870s.

One later figure in Tammany Hall, William M. "Boss" Tweed, has long been cursed for his alleged greed and corruption. Numerous articles and textbooks have heralded this image of Boss Tweed. Yet this image is grossly exaggerated. In reality, Tweed was a political leader who represented the underdog, including Irish and Jewish Americans, in nineteenth-century New York. He was tolerant of religious beliefs, a family man, and ambitious. He identified with New York's poor immigrants and worked to build schools and hospitals. He was hated by Anglo-Protestant Republicans because of his identification with immigrants. Yet Tweed's own ethnic background remains unclear; he was apparently of Scottish or Irish descent. Because of growing Irish political power, Tweed became a powerful leader and rewarded Irish and other immigrant constituents with jobs, schools, and social services. Research on Tweed indicates that he may well have been less corrupt than many of the Anglo-Protestant politicians who dominated urban politics before and after his era.[58]

With the election of New York City's first Irish American mayor in the 1880s, Irish Americans began to play a major role in New York politics. They held many elective posts and gained heavy representation in appointed public jobs. They also moved into important positions in the governments of numerous other cities with large Catholic populations. In vigorous fights with English and other British Americans, the Irish gradually won a place in the political sun in Boston, Brooklyn, Philadelphia, New Haven, and Chicago.[59] By the 1960s these Irish political organizations were gone except in Chicago, where the paramount Irish boss, Mayor Richard J. Daley, maintained great power into the 1970s. Although Irish Americans constituted only 10 to 15 percent of Chicago's population in the 1960s, a quarter of Chicago's fifty aldermen, its mayor, and 42 percent of its ward committee members were Irish. Chicago's political machine was characterized by many complexities. It was responsible for tremendous urban development and renewal. At the same time, city construction contracts were awarded in questionable ways to friends of the political machine.[60]

By the 1980s, Daley was dead, and Chicago's Irish-dominated political machine was weakened to the extent that a black mayor, Harold Washington, was elected against the machine's wishes. In New York City the number of Irish Americans in political office has declined steadily over the past few decades. Indeed, there were so few Irish Americans in New York City government by the late 1980s that the mayor found it difficult to assemble a contingent of top officials of Irish descent to march in the Saint Patrick's Day Parade. However, as was documented in a recent study of the four-county metropolitan region around New York State's capital city (Albany), Irish Catholic politicians, concentrated in the Democratic party, still exercise significant political influence in some U.S. urban areas.[61]

Pragmatism in Politics

For Irish Americans, politics is an honorable profession. Family and friends often provide the important networks for entry into political positions. Irish Americans have developed a political style based on concern for individuals and personal loyalty to leaders. Individual charity is a major feature. One Irish official is quoted by Levine: "When a man is ill in government and without enough time for retirement or health benefits, an efficient man fires him. Yet the Irish administrator says, 'What the hell, he has two kids,' and keeps him on. He knows this is a risky thing, letting him come in at ten and leave at two. So what happens? He gets a little more work out of the others to make it up."[62]

In recent decades Irish politicians have been influenced by reform movements to clean up blatant corruption. Some Irish politicians have been reformers themselves, playing a major role in bringing down the corrupt leaders of political machines in New York and other cities. Yet the personal, pragmatic, nonideological style of Irish American politics remains.[63]

Pragmatic politics, with its coalition and compromise themes, is a major Irish contribution to U.S. politics. One principle is that a city is a mosaic of racial and ethnic groups and the political machine is a broker, balancing these groups so that a coalition can hang together. The leaders believe in balanced tickets, for they know that people vote along ethnic lines: they are aware of the hopes and fears of the rank-and-file voters. Such politicians are also aware of the tendency in these same groups toward trust, rationality, and sympathy for humanistic reforms.[64] Irish American politicians have been critical to urban coalition building. Irish organizations have also made a major contribution to the bricks-and-mortar development of cities. Without the Irish contractors tied to the machines, who would have met the need for public buildings, streets, and subways in many cities?[65]

With suburbanization and intermarriage, this Irish political style has begun to fade, but it has by no means disappeared. A study of fifty-one cities by Clark found that those with large Irish American populations were more likely than other cities to have a local government (often Irish-dominated) that provided a high level of public services for city residents. There was more responsiveness to poor groups, including black residents, in these Irish-populated cities than in other cities. Irish political machines may be fading, but their humane, services-oriented, patronage approach to government often persists. Some analysts have attempted to link the upward mobility of Irish Americans to a growing "conservatism," noting that in the 1960s and 1970s Irish electorates in New York and Connecticut tended to prefer more conservative political candidates in mayoral, guber-natorial, and senatorial races. Elsewhere, however, they have continued to vote for liberal and moderate Democrats in such races.[66]

Taken as a whole, Irish Americans are generally more liberal than numerous other white Gentile groups. In general, Irish Catholic Americans have had a progressive political tradition. Today they are substantially Democratic, with a large proportion of liberal Democrats among them. And they have been central figures in labor unions fighting for workers' rights.

National and International Politics

After 1840 the Irish American electorate was increasingly sought by presidential and congressional candidates. Grant, the Republican presidential candidate in 1868, wooed Irish voters; after he was elected he made a few Irish appointments to his administration. In most succeeding elections the Irish vote has been sought by presidential candidates of both parties.[67]

One study of the 1901–10 period found that 13 percent of 162 prominent political leaders, including presidents, senators, representatives, and Supreme Court justices, were Irish, compared with 56 percent who were English or Welsh.[68] However, Irish Catholic influence at the national level was weak. In a letter to Theodore Roosevelt, Finley Peter Dunne, a prominent Irish writer, commented on the lack of Irish influence: "As for the point about Irishmen holding office, I simply wanted to emphasize the fact that Irishmen are the most unsuccessful politicians in the country. Although they are about all there is to politics in the North between elections, there is not, with one exception, a single representative Irish man in any important cabinet, diplomatic, judicial or administrative office that I know about."[69] Penetration at the city level did not necessarily lead to important positions in the federal executive or judicial branches for Irish Catholics.

Most literature on Irish Americans in politics at the national level, as well as at the local level, focuses on Irish Catholics. Millions of Irish American Protestants, many of whom live in the rural South, have received little attention in analyses of politics. One Irish Protestant who has received attention was the Scotch-Irish president Woodrow Wilson, who held office at a crucial time in the history of Ireland. Because Wilson was not sympathetic to Irish national consciousness or Irish Catholic causes and did not support the Irish fight against England, he was opposed by the Irish Catholic press. Many Irish Americans, primarily Catholics, have reacted strongly to the oppression of their brothers and sisters in Ireland. In the late 1800s and early 1900s numerous Irish nationalist groups came to public attention. Through the years they have attempted to shift U.S. foreign policy away from its generally pro-English stance.[70]

After World War I, the stand of Wilson and many other Protestants on the question of Northern Ireland's independence was a critical issue for Irish Catholic Americans. In 1918 the British had arrested several dozen Irish representatives to the British Parliament after they had met separately and set up an Irish Republic. The rebellion by the Irish

Republican Army (IRA), which had been organized to resist British rule, was brutally suppressed and IRA leaders were executed. The Anglo-Irish Treaty of 1921 established an Irish Free State in southern Ireland, but Northern Ireland was kept under British rule. The brutality and other issues surrounding independence racked Irish American communities and lead to protest meetings.[71] In subsequent decades the issue of an independent, united Ireland has remained important and has continued to generate financial and political support among Irish Americans. Irish American senator Edward Kennedy of Massachusetts once introduced a U.S. Senate resolution asking for the removal of British soldiers from Northern Ireland.

More recently IRA fugitive Joe Doherty, convicted in absentia in Belfast, Ireland, for his part in the 1980 killing of a British military officer and held in U.S. prisons from 1983 until he was extradited to Britain in 1992, became a rallying point for Irish American opposition to British rule of Northern Ireland. During the more than eight years he was held in the United States, Doherty wrote a popular weekly column in the New York newspaper *Irish People* supporting the IRA's cause and received visits from more than one hundred members of Congress as well as New York's Cardinal O'Connor in support of his request for political asylum. He was named honorary Grand Marshall of the Saint Patrick's Day parade in ten major U.S. cities. In early 1992, following the U.S. Supreme Court's decision to deny Doherty political refugee status and extradite him, Irish American supporters protested on the Manhattan street corner that was named in his honor.[72]

The controversy over Northern Ireland's independence from Britain not only illustrates the interethnic struggle that continues to the present, in this case over foreign policy within the traditional political arena, but also shows how events in the country of origin of a segment of the population can long affect ethnic relations within the United States. This theme will reappear in the chapters that follow, as, for example, in the effect of events in Italy on Italian Americans and in Japan on Japanese Americans. The *world* is still the context of interethnic and interracial relations in the United States.

An Irish Catholic President

Alfred E. Smith, who became the Democratic candidate for president in 1928, was the first Irish Catholic to carve out an important role in presidential politics. But his Catholic religion, his calls for modification of Prohibition, and his lack of knowledge of much of the non-eastern United States counted against him in this first Irish Catholic presidential campaign. Although he lost the election, he managed to equal or exceed the Republican vote in eleven of the nation's twelve largest cities, pulling the new urban immigrants into a national voting bloc in the Democratic party for the first time. No candidate could again ignore the growing importance of the non-Protestant vote in the cities.[73]

In 1930, with the exception of one Supreme Court justice, there were still no Irish Catholics holding major positions in the judicial and executive branches of the federal government. Franklin Roosevelt was the first president to appoint Irish Catholics to important positions, which included ambassador to Great Britain, postmaster general, and attorney general. Many Irish Catholics were sent to Congress for the first time in Roosevelt's New Deal electoral landslides. Roosevelt, and subsequently Truman, appointed far more Irish Catholic judges and executive officers than previous presidents.[74]

Not until 1960, more than three hundred years after the first few Irish Catholics had come to the United States and more than a century after sizable Irish American Catholic communities had been established, was the first (and only) Irish Catholic president elected. Six of the thirty-six presidents from Washington to Nixon had Irish backgrounds, but except for John Kennedy all of these were Protestant Irish, as was a more recent president, Ronald Reagan.

President Kennedy was a descendant of Irish Catholic politicians in Boston; he was elected on the "backs of three generations of district leaders and county chairmen."[75] His grandfather had been mayor of Boston; his father was the first Irish Catholic to serve as ambassador to Great Britain. John Kennedy came from the small, wealthy elite. Yet he was a pragmatic politician. Day-to-day problems of food and shelter were critical issues to him. In the 1960 presidential election Irish Catholic votes in New England, New York, and Pennsylvania helped to create Kennedy's victory. Nationwide he received an estimated 75 percent of the Irish vote, but only 50.1 percent of the total vote. As president, Kennedy acted to some extent on behalf of America's newer and emergent urban groups, appointing the first Italian American and the first Polish American to a presidential cabinet and the first black American to head an independent government agency.[76]

THE IRISH IN THE ECONOMY

As we noted in Chapter 2, one type of structural assimilation involves large-scale movement by members of an immigrant group into the secondary-organization levels of a society, such as into positions in governmental agencies. Another critical movement is into the economic organizations—the farms and factories—of the core society. The majority of Irish immigrants started out at the bottom of the economic pyramid, filling the hard, dirty, laboring jobs on farms and in cities. The eighteenth-century Irish immigrants contributed significantly to the economic development of the colonies and the new nation. In New England and other northern states they were important in commerce; they worked as weavers for textile industries and laborers for road and canal systems. In the South they became farm laborers, farmers, and owners of small businesses. Few data are available on the mobility patterns of these Irish immigrants or their descendants over the next century or two. Many moved from indentured service to their own farms. Most seem to have moved up the economic ladder over the next few generations, sometimes at the expense of later immigrants.[77]

Male and Female Work: The Irish after 1830

Irish Catholic labor was critical to industrial and commercial development in the United States. Irish immigrants after 1830 typically became urban workers, miners, or transportation workers. Hard, low-paying work was the lot of most immigrants. They had migrated looking for work. Irish men found it in unskilled jobs, on the docks and in the factories of large cities; Irish women found it as servants in Anglo-Protestant homes. Many Irish immigrants were single females unattached to family groups. Impoverished and alone in an alien land, these women moved into domestic work where they could live with a family. In the 1855 census of New York

City three-quarters of the domestics (maids and other servants) were Irish, although the Irish were only one-quarter of the population. Later immigrant women, such as Italian and Jewish immigrants, were not as likely to go into domestic work. This had little to do with differences in cultural backgrounds but reflected the different character of later migration: Jewish and Italian women generally came with their families. Irish women who came alone did so not by choice but because of the adverse economic conditions in Ireland under English rule.[78]

Male Irish immigrants became farm laborers, railroad laborers, miners, and textile workers. Many died helping build transportation systems, as the old saying "There's an Irishman buried under every railroad tie" indicates. As late as 1876, half of Irish-born Americans were still in the worst-paid, dirtiest jobs, compared with 10 to 20 percent of other white groups.[79]

Irish Catholics encountered direct institutionalized discrimination in employment. Stereotyped as unskilled or rowdy, Irish men and women were denied jobs by Protestant employers. Few capitalists would hire them except for unskilled positions. By the 1840s Boston newspapers were carrying anti-Irish advertisements with the phrase "None need apply but Americans."[80] The Irish in Boston were relegated to the least-skilled occupations.

Numerous observers have blamed these Irish immigrants for the emergence of urban poverty. Against the contributions of such immigrants, argues Adams, "must be set certain intangible social burdens on the whole community and some definite expenditures, of which poor relief through almshouses, hospitals, and dispensaries was most costly."[81] Many among the Irish became dependent on charity or public aid. But local and state governments in that period actually provided rather little in the way of support for the poor—the majority of whom were *not* Irish Americans.

Few among the millions of immigrants and their children moved from rags to riches. Many did save some money, and many sent significant sums back to Ireland. This charitable impulse reduced their own chances for mobility in the United States. A study of Newburyport, Massachusetts, revealed that Irish working-class families were more likely to have accumulated some property (housing) than was commonly thought. But one price of accumulating property was a spartan life and the early employment of children, reducing the education of the younger generation. Economic advance in one generation did not necessarily mean upward mobility for subsequent generations. In addition, building a separate church and parochial school system meant some drain on family resources.[82]

Even with these burdens, Irish Catholics began to move up the socioeconomic ladder after the Civil War. One of the earliest Irish communities to achieve structural movement upward in the economy was a small group in Newburyport. By the decade after the Civil War, Philadelphia had become a major eastern center for manufacturing and transportation, and the Irish Americans concentrated in unskilled labor there began to gain semiskilled and skilled positions. Economic gains were reflected in the erection of churches, parochial schools, and charitable institutions. A significant number of the Irish in Philadelphia began to move into better housing in middle-income residential areas, although many still found themselves in segregated, inferior housing.[83]

Significant numbers of Catholic Irish became upwardly mobile near the turn of the twentieth century. These were immigrants who entered the U.S. economy when expanding industries needed large numbers of low-wage workers. New cities emerged as capitalists centered new types of manufacturing in the industrial heartland, from Pittsburgh to Chicago and Detroit. Powerful urban political machines facilitated mobility by providing some economic resources—menial jobs at the least—for the start of the upward trek. Machines channeled money into building projects, facilitating the emergence of an Irish business elite. By the end of the nineteenth century the Irish in Philadelphia could boast of twice the proportion of contractors and builders that other immigrant groups had. The growing number of worker organizations also aided Irish mobility. The Irish controlled a few labor organizations in Massachusetts and New York as early as the 1850s. By the early 1900s unions had emerged among dockworkers, construction workers, and miners, with some providing the base for protest. To the present day, Irish Americans have been prominent in important labor organizations, including the AFL–CIO.[84]

Irish Americans, especially Irish Protestants, had begun to penetrate business and professional areas by the middle of the nineteenth century; the 1890 census showed 1.7 percent of foreign-born Irish males in professional positions. A small number of Irish Protestants became wealthy entrepreneurs. Among the handful of native-born U.S. millionaires in the 1761–1924 period, 8 percent were Irish, apparently Protestant Irish, a proportion considerably smaller than the English and Scottish contingent.[85]

Although some progress was obvious for rank-and-file Irish Catholics by the turn of the century, discrimination and poverty still had an impact. One study of Irish-born immigrants in 1890 Boston revealed an occupational distribution of 0 percent in the professions, 10 percent in other white-collar jobs, and 65 percent in low-skilled jobs. This employment situation contrasted greatly with that of the native-born Boston residents, mostly non-Irish, 47 percent of whom had white-collar jobs. The second-generation Irish Americans fared better, although not nearly as well as the non-Irish.[86]

Mobility in the Twentieth Century

A study of Philadelphia's Irish population in 1900 found evidence of slow movement up the social and economic ladder. Although a large majority, 70 percent, worked in manufacturing, laboring, and domestic service jobs, some held political office in the urban political organizations; there was a small but growing middle-income group; and a few had become prosperous in business, mining, and construction. Interestingly, the middle-income group grew to the point of being stereotyped as "lace curtain" Irish, based on the prosperity that enabled this group to afford lace window curtains. However, fewer than 10 percent of employed men and women held professional or managerial jobs; a majority were still rather poor.[87]

Information available on mobility among Irish Americans after 1900 suggests increasing economic security for a growing segment. Apparently the mostly Protestant descendants of pre-1840 immigrants were still disproportionately concentrated in farming areas, in towns, and in southern and border states. In the late nineteenth and early twentieth centuries, and probably in later decades as well, a significant proportion became relatively prosperous farmers, owners of small businesses, and skilled blue-collar workers, as well as part of the growing clerical-job category. Many blended into the Anglo-Protestant mainstream. Whether the overwhelming majority were moving up the socioeconomic ladder is unclear, for many remained poor in rural areas.

Some concrete data are available on the Irish Catholics. By the 1930s they still had not blended into the Anglo-Protestant mainstream. In their study of Newburyport in the 1930s Warner and Srole found Irish Americans moving closer to native Yankee residents in socioeconomic status. No Irish, however, could be found at the top. The Depression hit the Irish hard, postponing for a decade the major economic breakthrough just within their reach. Baltzell's study of Philadelphians in 1940 revealed that few people of wealth and influence were Catholic; white Protestants still dominated at the top.[88]

Business leadership in the 1950s and 1960s continued to be British American. In those decades Irish Catholics were less conspicuous in the ranks of leading scientists and industrialists than might have been expected. This may be in part because their ancestors brought little scientific or management experience from the homeland. Some have suggested that modest representation in scientific fields may be due to Catholic education, with its classical emphasis. But it was also because of anti-Catholic discrimination at higher levels in business and industry.[89]

Recent Successes

As we have noted, government employment has been central for Irish Catholics, many of whom have been employed in politics, in police, fire, and public works departments, in the courts, and in schools and colleges. Recruitment patterns for government jobs based on patronage and kinship networks have created a "one big family" style work force in some cities. Such a situation in Boston was challenged by affirmative action suits beginning in the 1970s and has contributed to tensions between blacks and Latinos on the one side, and Boston's Irish on the other.[90]

Since the 1940s Irish Catholics have moved up economically. By the early 1970s 66 percent of younger-generation Irish Catholic males held white-collar positions compared with 38 percent of their fathers. Both generations were more likely to be found in better-paying white-collar jobs than their counterparts in most other Catholic groups. The 1970 census showed that median income was higher for second-generation Irish American families than for the typical U.S. household. Data from the 1980 census, which included all Americans of Irish ancestry, reported a similar pattern: Irish American families as a group had a somewhat higher median income than the typical U.S. family. At the beginning of the 1990s the occupational distribution for Irish Americans as a group closely paralleled that of all whites in the United States.[91]

In an analysis of the economic status of Irish Catholics and Irish Protestants, using combined data from opinion surveys for the years 1972–87, Greeley demonstrates that Irish Catholics are now one of the most prosperous of the white ethnic groups; Irish Protestants appear to be among the least successful. "There is a nice irony: the first immigration [most of whom were Protestant or became Protestant after immigration] was from peasant field to peasant field, in the latter case your own field, and was—once the Atlantic had been crossed—probably an easier migration; but the descendants of the immigrants ended up in a backwater of the changing nation. The second immigration [Irish Catholics] was from field to factory; but the descendants of this immigration were to ride the main stream of American expansion to great success." The following grouped 1972–87 survey data bear out this observation:[92]

	Irish Catholics	Irish Protestants	All Whites
Percentage in Professional Jobs	34	14	24
Percentage in White-Collar Jobs	68	50	51

Compared with the average white American and also with Irish Protestants, Irish Catholics were more likely to be employed in a professional or white-collar job. The percentage of Irish Protestants in white-collar jobs was very near that of the total white population, but Irish Protestant representation in the professions was far lower than that of all whites.

To control for any advantage in achieving success that one religious group might have achieved because of a longer period of residence in the United States, Greeley made an additional comparison between fourth-generation Irish Catholics and Protestants and other fourth-generation white Americans:

	Irish Catholics	Irish Protestants	All Whites
Percentage in Professional Jobs	38	20	27
Percentage in White Collar Jobs	71	51	51

Notice that fourth-generation members of each group perform better than their group as a whole except for the percentage of the total white population in white collar jobs. The differences between Irish Catholics and the other categories remain, and the income differential between Irish Catholics and all whites increases. Fourth-generation Irish Protestants have achieved parity with the fourth-generation white population in white-collar employment and narrowed the gap in the percentage of professionals.

The mass media symbols of success of Irish Americans have typically been athletes, entertainers, politicians, or a few entrepreneurs such as Joseph Kennedy. Another group of Irish heroes has received little notice—the growing group of Irish Ph.D.s and academics. Catholics make up one-fourth of faculty members in top state colleges and universities, and about half of these are Irish. Irish Catholics are heavily represented in humanities departments. Moreover, many graduate-trained Irish Catholics have moved into local, state, and federal government as lawyers, administrators, researchers, and elected officials. Daniel Patrick Moynihan, Irish American U.S. senator from New York, has noted, "So many Irish-Americans have succeeded in various fields that their prominence no longer is noteworthy."[93]

EDUCATION

Organized education on a significant scale for Irish Protestants began after the Civil War. In the South, public schools spread in the Reconstruction period, and by the early twentieth century many of the Protestant Irish had taken advantage of them.

The Catholic Irish, in contrast, relied on parochial and public schools in urban areas of the North for organized education. Because of the heated anti-Catholicism of the period, no Catholic schools of any kind existed in 1790. It was not until the 1820–40 period that numerous parochial schools were established. In cities some Irish Catholic children were beginning to receive public education, although the intense Americanization pressures in the public schools gave strong impetus to the development of separate, church-related schools as a means of retaining ethnic identity. By the late 1800s and early 1900s the center of the Irish Catholic community in numerous cities was a church and parochial school system, attached to which were hospitals and charitable organizations.[94]

By 1960 nearly 13,000 elementary and secondary Catholic schools had an enrollment of five million children. Irish Catholic Americans were at the center of this immense network, which was by then a subject of controversy in the United States. Financed by Catholic Americans, these private schools had gradually come to receive some public aid as well, bringing extensive opposition from Protestant and Jewish groups and not a few court cases.[95]

Even in the 1920s Irish Catholics were going to college in large numbers, above the national average for all whites. By that decade the educational achievements of Irish Catholic Americans were impressive, with Catholic colleges being built and college attendance for Irish Catholics on the increase. The Presbyterian Irish had earlier made important contributions in the area of education, including the establishment of institutions such as Princeton to provide an educated ministry for local Presbyterian churches.[96]

Greeley's recent analysis of grouped 1972–87 survey data on Irish Americans found a pattern in educational achievement similar to that in economic success.[97]

	Irish Catholics	Irish Protestants	All Whites
Attended College	45%	29%	28%
College Graduate	22%	11%	16%

Compared with the average white American and also with Irish Protestants, Irish Catholics are more likely to have attended college and to be college graduates. Irish Protestants are close to the total white population in percentage attending college but fall below the larger group in the percentage of graduates. A comparison of the fourth generation of each group revealed a similar pattern:[98]

	Irish Catholics	Irish Protestants	All Whites
Attended College	53%	31%	38%
College Graduate	24%	13%	16%

For both Irish groups, educational achievement was greater for members of the fourth generation than for all generations taken together. Irish Catholics remain well ahead of both other categories at both levels of education. Fourth-generation Irish Protestants narrowed the gap in percentage of college graduates between themselves and the total fourth-generation white population but fell below the larger group in percentage attending college.

RELIGION

In the political and economic spheres Irish Americans were pressured to assimilate, nonreciprocally, to the established Anglo-Protestant core society and culture. In the religious sphere, the earliest Irish immigrants, whether Catholic or Ulster Presbyterian, largely blended into various Protestant denominations. However, later groups of Irish Catholic immigrants played a major role in firmly establishing what may well be the single most important non-Protestant institution in the United States—the Roman Catholic church. The strong ties of loyalty between these Irish immigrants and the Catholic church grew in part out of longtime English oppression in Ireland. Although the Catholic church has had to adapt to some extent to the preexisting Protestant system, its impact has been to accent the issue of separation of church and state in the United States and to reinforce the right of all Americans to choose any faith.

Irish Catholics fought intense anti-Catholic prejudice and discrimination to root the Catholic church in Anglo-Protestant soil. New churches sprang up wherever Catholic workers went. Priests had long suffered with the poor in Ireland and in the United States, so the church was respected. In addition to church organizations, related benevolent and charitable community organizations were of great consequence. The Ancient Order of Hibernians is one major example.[99]

The Catholic church's hierarchy in the United States has long been disproportionately Irish American. One analysis of Catholic bishops from 1789 to 1935 revealed that 58 percent were Irish. In the 1970s a third of the priests and half of the upper hierarchy were Irish compared with 17 percent of the total Catholic population. In the 1990s Irish Americans still account for a disproportionate number of Catholic priests, but do not generate a disproportionate number of Catholic bishops in the United States.[100]

In northern cities many Irish American neighborhoods were built around the parish church. Local politics has often blended with church and school, as have local stores and taverns:

> Among Irish Americans, that particular part of the urban turf with which you are identified and in which live most of the people on whom you have a special claim...is virtually indistinguishable from the parish; when asked where they are from, Irish Catholics in many cities give not the community's name but the name of the parish—Christ the King, St. Barnabas, All Saints...and so forth.[101]

In the last few decades many central city churches have been closed or merged, as Irish Americans have moved to the suburbs. Today in the suburbs of many cities the Irish Catholic parish survives. Loyalty to the church remains strong: one 1990 survey by the National Opinion Research Center (NORC) found that more than half of Irish Catholics go to services every week, a much higher proportion than among other whites in the survey.[102]

Irish Catholic priests have shaped the U.S. church in a number of distinctive ways, some conservative and some progressive. Irish American archbishops and cardinals have often been conservative, but many priests and bishops have led progressive struggles. For example, the former president of Notre Dame University, Father Theodore M. Hesburgh, symbolizes the liberalism in Irish Catholicism. For many years, including those he spent on the U.S. Commission on Civil Rights, Father Hesburgh has been outspoken in his support for civil rights laws, antisegregation action, and affirmative action benefiting African Americans.[103]

ASSIMILATION THEORIES AND THE IRISH

Now we can examine how the theories and concepts discussed in Chapter 2 help illuminate the experiences of Irish Americans. As we have seen, some power-conflict analysts (such as students of internal colonialism) specifically omit immigrant groups such as the "white ethnics" from their analyses, preferring to focus on nonwhite groups because most of these have endured much greater violence and repression while being subordinated in the North American colonies and the United States.

The assimilation theories of Gordon and Greeley seem the most relevant for analysis of groups such as Irish, Italian, and Jewish Americans. Yet in looking at these groups from the assimilation perspective we must keep in mind something many assimilationists tend to forget—the substantial conflict and ethnic stratification that has characterized the experiences of these white ethnic Americans.

Compared with many other ethnic and racial groups, Irish Americans are several steps higher on the ladder of economic success and dominance. Among Irish Americans each generation became more incorporated in the core institutions than prior generations. The eighteenth-century Irish moved up the social and economic ladders quietly but surely; they were typically Protestants. Substantial assimilation on a number of dimensions apparently came by the late nineteenth century for many of the descendants of these Irish. One observer argues that this group blended in rather quickly, for "their social and political activities have mixed freely and spread freely through the general mass of American citizenship."[104] The Scotch-Irish propagandists have exaggerated the rapidity of this cultural and structural assimilation, but there is doubtless truth to the view that the early Irish immigrants and their descendants assimilated relatively rapidly at the level of culture, slowly but surely at the level of structural integration into the economy and the polity, and gradually into more intimate social ties and even identification with English and other British American families. Sometime in the last century many Scotch-Irish became a difficult-to-distinguish part of what can be viewed as the Anglo-Protestant mainstream.

Assimilation came more slowly for Irish Catholics, who entered in increasing numbers after 1840. Rapid adaptation to the core culture, particularly in learning the language and certain basic values, is necessary to movement within U.S. institutions. In this regard, assimilation had come early for most Irish immigrants. Clark argues that the Irish Catholic adjustments were not as difficult as some have believed. U.S. cities offered hope for escape from the oppressive conditions of Ireland. The expanding industrial environment meant a greater chance for mobility. Ireland's customs and U.S. customs had some similarities. While assimilation at all levels took several generations, much cultural assimilation took place in the first decades.[105]

Religion was an exception. Most of these Irish Catholic immigrants did not become Protestants. In new Irish communities external hostility and a common background reinforced a protective separatist reaction. Conflict with the nativists intensified Irish American commitment to the Catholic church. The core culture eventually came to accommodate Protestant, Catholic, and Jewish religious communities. At the same time, the Catholic community made adjustments to the English-dominated milieu in such areas as language and restructured church organizations. Such adaptation made the

Catholic church and school system an important medium within which new immigrants began their acculturation and even some structural assimilation (for example, priests helped in securing employment).[106]

Did commitment to the Catholic religion decline in later generations of Irish Catholics? Some analysts have claimed this, arguing that cultural assimilation will thus soon be complete. Some recent studies have not found this to be the case, however. As a group, Irish Americans are among the most likely to attend mass of all the Catholic groups studied. Greeley has presented information on Irish Catholics that indicates an increase in religious devotion over the last few decades. And a 1990 opinion survey by NORC, noted previously in this chapter, found that Irish Catholics were much more likely to attend church services often than white Americans as a whole.[107]

In regard to the dimensions Milton Gordon calls behavior-receptional assimilation and attitude-receptional assimilation—in effect, discrimination and prejudice—there have been substantial changes since the mid-nineteenth century for the Catholic Irish. Stereotyping has declined substantially since the days of the apelike image, although negative feelings directed against Irish Catholicism and urban machine politics have persisted. Discrimination has declined significantly, although it is still felt at the very highest levels of the U.S. economy and government. Thus the United States has had only one Irish Catholic president.

Patterns of Structural Assimilation

At the structural-assimilation (secondary-group) levels Irish Americans have made slow but significant movement into the Anglo-Protestant core society. We have seen the steady movement of the Irish from unskilled work into white-collar occupations and the relatively high occupational levels of the Irish Catholics in recent decades. Housing upgrading has paralleled these developments, although some self-segregation persists in some cities in the East and Midwest. After a century of struggle in the political sphere, Irish Catholics are now substantially integrated at local and state levels; in the last two or three decades they have moved significantly into the judicial, legislative, and executive branches of the federal government, if not yet in representative numbers to the top. At the local level, Irish Americans have shaped urban politics in a number of cities.

In the mid-1900s some argued that the higher status accompanying economic assimilation caused Irish Americans to move away from the Democratic party. Looking at the period between the 1940s and the 1960s, Glazer and Moynihan argued that the "mass of the Irish have left the working class, and in considerable measure the Democratic party as well."[108] Yet voting data for roughly that same period suggested continuing Irish American loyalty to the Democratic party. Urban politicians, particularly Democrats, gave great attention to the Irish community, and many liberal Democratic leaders were Irish. Greeley's analysis found that 61 percent of Irish Catholics and 54 percent of Irish Protestants identified themselves as Democrats; 28 percent of Irish Catholics and 22 percent of Irish Protestants labeled themselves as liberal. This suggests that one assimilation theory of ethnic politics—that economic mobility weakens traditional ethnic voting patterns—is not necessarily correct. Absorption into the Republicanism of Anglo-Protestants has not happened for the majority of either Irish Catholics or Irish Protestants.[109]

As for structural incorporation at the level of primary-group ties, data on informal groups and voluntary associations point up some interesting trends. Ethnic clubs and organizations, since World War II if not before, have apparently declined in importance for the Irish Catholics. Benevolent societies have declined in numbers; so have the great fund drives to support Irish causes. This indicates increasing integration into the voluntary associations of the larger society. Irish attendance at Catholic parochial schools has also declined, which may mean that Irish children are making more friendships across ethnic lines than ever before.[110]

Intermarriage may be the ultimate indicator of adaptation at the primary-group level. Abramson's study points up an increasing intermarriage rate for Irish Catholics. One national survey in the 1960s reported substantial endogamy for Irish Catholics: 65 percent of respondents with Irish fathers also had Irish mothers and 43 percent of married men had a wife with an Irish father. Over half the respondents to the national survey had a non-Irish spouse. Moreover, a more recent survey of a large metropolitan area in upper New York State found that 82 percent of Irish Americans there had mixed ethnic ancestry.[111]

Is There an Irish American Identity Today?

Among the final stages of assimilation is what Gordon and Greeley have seen as identificational adaptation. Ultimately, this type of adaptation would mean a loss of a sense of Irishness and the development of a sense of peoplehood that is solely American or Anglo-Protestant American. One's sense of identity would no longer be Irish. This may have happened for many Irish Protestants, but most Irish Catholics still have a feeling of Irishness, although for some it may be a vague sense.

Some Irish Catholic writers, such as Daniel P. Moynihan, have argued that Irish Americans are losing their ethnic identity because of the decline in immigration from Ireland. Marjorie Fallows has argued that the American Irish are fully acculturated to the core culture; even Irish Catholicism has become generally "Americanized" and fully compatible with the Protestant ethic. In her view distinctive ethnic traits that are culturally significant are rare among the American Irish today, except in isolated ethnic enclaves. Fallows and others have argued that even though there are still a few ethnically distinct Irish Catholic communities in northern cities, this does not mean that most Irish Catholics live in such communities. Indeed, they assert that cultural and structural (primary-group) assimilation are all but complete for those Irish Catholics living outside ethnic neighborhoods.[112]

Richard Alba interviewed respondents in eight white ethnic groups in a metropolitan area in upper New York State. He found ethnic identity declining somewhat in significance among Irish Americans, especially in fourth and later generations. However, those with pure Irish ancestry had a stronger sense of their ethnic identity than most of the other groups examined. Those with mixed Irish ancestry were also loyal to their Irish heritage. They were three times as likely to identify solely as Irish as they were to choose another ethnicity from their mixed background. And the Irish were less likely than other ethnic groups to attach no importance to their ethnic identity.[113]

The Irish Catholic group has changed over generations of contact with the public school system and the mass media, but it has retained enough distinctiveness to persist as an ethnic group into the last decade of the twentieth century. The theory of ethnogenesis discussed in Chapter 2 seems appropriate to Irish Catholic Americans. This ethnic group has been more than a European nationality group. The Irish who came in large numbers after 1840 forged, over several generations, a distinctive U.S. ethnic group. Ethnicity was an important way for the Irish Catholics to attach themselves to the new scene, a way of asserting their own identity in a buzzing confusion of diverse nationality groups. For Irish Catholics, because of nativistic attacks and discrimination, ethnic identity was less voluntary in the first few decades than it was to become later. In the beginning Irish Americans had a cultural heritage that was distinctly different from that of the British American host culture. Over several generations of sometimes conflictual interaction the Irish adapted substantially to the host society. This process created a distinctive Irish American ethnic group that reflected elements both of its nationality background and of the host culture.

The persistence of Irish American ethnicity and its positive and negative functions is in evidence in the desegregation struggle that took place in South Boston between the 1970s and the 1980s. Boston's predominantly Irish working-class community's vigorous, sometimes violent, opposition to a judge's 1974 school desegregation plan for the area involved more than a legal desegregation struggle. The controversy reflected different views of schooling and of urban communities; the South Boston Irish have seen the central-city schools as a socializing force, reinforcing local and traditional family and community values, whereas many black Bostonians and some suburban whites have viewed desegregated schools primarily as avenues of upward mobility for black Americans. Irish American resistance to racial desegregation of central-city neighborhoods and schools has been based in part on racial prejudice. But it has also been partly based on the desire of Irish Americans to protect their ethnic community institutions against all intruders, whoever they may be. Historian Ronald Formisano writes that the court-ordered school desegregation "was at one level an attempt by mobile professionals and elites to impose their liberal, cosmopolitan, middle-class values on working- and lower-middle-class people who embraced the values of localism and personalism. The residents of defended neighborhoods certainly saw desegregation in part as an attempt by elite outsiders to change them and their way of life."[114]

In his analysis of grouped 1972–87 opinion poll data the Irish American sociologist Andrew Greeley examined four survey questions that tap what he views as traditional Irish Catholic cultural traits: gregariousness, gathering in a public house, religious intensity, and activity in religious organizations. None of these has been eliminated from the Irish American culture; on all four survey questions Irish Catholics ranked higher in social activity than did the national sample as a whole.[115] Greeley has concluded that Irish Catholic distinctiveness persists, particularly in certain northern cities:

> On the basis of the evidence available to us, the Irish-American subculture is likely to persist indefinitely. The Irish Catholic Americans will continue to be different in their religion, their family life, their political style, their world view, their drinking behavior, and their personalities....The Irish will continue to be affluent and probably will become even more affluent as they settle down securely amidst the upper crusts of the middle class with a firm foothold in the nation's economic and political, if not intellectual and artistic, elites.[116]

Greeley even sees evidence of a return to higher levels of self-conscious identification among young Irish Americans. Whether this trend will continue remains to be seen. Whatever happens, however, it is clear that the impact of the Irish background on Irish American behavior remains strong.[117]

SUMMARY

The Irish began moving to North America quite early, with indentured servants and farmers entering in the 1700s. The earlier immigration apparently included more southern, or Celtic, Irish than exaggerated accounts about the Scotch-Irish have suggested. The majority of the descendants of these early migrants were, or became, Protestants, settling disproportionately in the rural South and in frontier areas. Many of the descendants of these early settlers became part of the Anglo-Protestant mainstream over the next several generations. However, a significant proportion remained poor. The Protestant Irish in particular have received little attention from scholars in recent decades.

After the 1830s large numbers of Irish Catholic immigrants settled in the cities of the North, where many suffered violence at the hands of Catholic-hating nativists and discrimination by Anglo-American employers. Poverty-stricken Irish Catholics slowly began moving toward economic equality with older groups. Conflict, sometimes violent, marked their climb. Political innovators, the Irish Catholics shaped the political organizations of major cities to facilitate their integration into core political and economic institutions.

Economic mobility since 1860 has been so dramatic that by the early 1990s Irish Catholics ranked above the national average for all whites on a number of important socio-economic dimensions. In contrast, those still identifying themselves as Irish Protestants generally lagged behind both Irish Catholics and all whites in attainments. Nevertheless, both of these Irish groups constitute major segments of Middle America today.

NOTES

1. U.S. Department of Justice, Immigration and Naturalization Service, *Annual Report* (Washington, 1973), pp. 53–55. The figures for 1820–67 represent "alien passengers arrived"; for later periods they represent immigrants arrived or admitted.
2. Cited in William Peterson, *Population*, 2nd ed. (New York: Macmillan, 1969), p. 260; U.S. Bureau of the Census, *Statistical Abstract of the United States: 1991* (Washington, 1991), p. 10.
3. Philip H. Bagenal, *The American Irish* (London: Kegan Paul, Trench & Co., 1882), pp. 4–5.
4. Henry Jones Ford, *The Scotch-Irish in America* (Princeton, N.J.: Princeton University Press, 1915), pp. 125–28.
5. James G. Leyburn, *The Scotch-Irish* (Chapel Hill: University of North Carolina Press, 1962), pp. 142–43.
6. Ford, *The Scotch-Irish in America*, pp. 183–86; Leyburn, *The Scotch-Irish*, pp. 160ff.
7. Michael J. O'Brien, *A Hidden Phase of American History* (New York: Devin-Adair Co., 1919), p. 249; see also pp. 287–88.
8. See Robert J. Dickson, *Ulster Immigration to Colonial America, 1718–1773* (London: Routledge & Kegan Paul, 1966), pp. 66–68; Grady McWhiney, *Cracker Culture* (Tuscaloosa: University of Alabama Press, 1988), pp. 3–4, 15–18; Andrew M. Greeley, "The Success and Assimilation of Irish Protestants and Irish Catholics in the United States," *Sociology and Social Research*, 72, no. 4 (July 1988): 231.
9. O'Brien, *A Hidden Phase of American History*, p. 267.
10. Quoted in ibid., p. 254.
11. McWhiney, *Cracker Culture*, pp. 5, 188; Emmet Larkin, "The Devotional Revolution in Ireland, 1850–1875," *American Historical Review*, 77 (1972): 623–52; S.J. Connolly, *Priest and People in Pre-Famine Ireland* (Dublin: Gill & Macmillan, 1982), cited in Greeley, "Success and Assimilation," pp. 229–30.
12. Thomas D'Arcy McGee, *A History of Irish Settlers in North America* (Boston: Office of American Celt, 1851), pp. 25–34.
13. Leyburn, *The Scotch-Irish*, pp. 331–32.
14. Quoted in Ford, *The Scotch-Irish in America*, pp. 520–21.
15. Theodore Roosevelt, *The Winning of the West* (New York: Review of Reviews Co., 1904), 1:123–25.
16. Ford, *The Scotch-Irish in America*, pp. 522, 539.
17. John W. Dinsmore, *The Scotch-Irish in America* (Chicago: Winona Publishing Co., 1906), p. 7.
18. Winthrop D. Jordan, *White over Black* (Baltimore: Penguin, 1969), pp. 86–88.
19. Edwin S. Gaustad, *Historical Atlas of Religion in America* (New York: Harper & Row, 1962), pp. 34–35; Dennis Clark, *The Irish in Philadelphia* (Philadelphia: Temple University Press, 1973), p. 8.
20. Quoted in McGee, *A History of Irish Settlers in North America*, p. 79.
21. Ford, *The Scotch-Irish in America*, pp. 180–240; E. R. R. Green, "Ulster Immigrants' Letters," in *Essays in Scotch-Irish History*, ed. E. R. R. Green (London: Routledge & Kegan Paul, 1969), pp. 100–102.

22. Leyburn, *The Scotch-Irish*, pp. 262–69.
23. American Historical Association, *Annual Report* (Washington: U.S. Government Printing Office, 1932), 1:255–70.
24. Arnold Shrier, *Ireland and the American Emigration, 1850–1900* (Minneapolis: University of Minnesota Press, 1958), pp. 13–16; T. A. Jackson, *Ireland Her Own* (New York: International Publishers, 1970), pp. 243–45; Kerby A. Miller, *Emigrants and Exiles* (New York: Oxford University Press, 1985), p. 556.
25. Carl Wittke, *The Irish in America* (Baton Rouge: Louisiana State University Press, 1956), pp. 24–27; Theodore Hershberg et al., "A Tale of Three Cities," in *Majority and Minority*, 3rd ed., ed. Norman Y. Yetman and C. Hoy Steele (Boston: Allyn & Bacon, 1982), pp. 184–85.
26. Bagenal, *The American Irish*, p. 72 (the statistics on crime and poverty are found on pp. 70–71); Wittke, *The Irish in America*, p. 46.
27. Hasia R. Diner, *Erin's Daughters in America* (Baltimore: Johns Hopkins, 1983), pp. xiii–xv.
28. Dale T. Knobel, *Paddy and the Republic* (Middletown, Conn.: Wesleyan University Press, 1986), pp. 24–27; Bill Bryson, *The Mother Tongue: English and How It Got That Way* (New York: Morrow, 1990).
29. Lewis P. Curtis, Jr., *Apes and Angels: The Irish in Victorian Caricature* (Washington, D.C.: Smithsonian Institution Press, 1971), p. 59.
30. Ibid., p. 103.
31. Andrew M. Greeley, *That Most Distressful Nation* (Chicago: Quadrangle, 1972), pp. 119–20.
32. Leonard Gordon, "Racial and Ethnic Stereotypes of American College Students over a Half Century" (paper presented at meetings of the Society for the Study of Social Problems, Washington, D.C., August 1985), pp. 14–15.
33. Richard D. Alba, *Ethnic Identity: The Transformation of White America* (New Haven: Yale University Press, 1990), p. 156.
34. Andrew M. Greeley, *The Irish Americans* (New York: Harper & Row, 1981), p. 167.
35. Leonard Dinnerstein and Frederic C. Jaher, "Introduction," in *The Aliens*, ed. Leonard Dinnerstein and Frederic C. Jaher (New York: Appleton-Century-Crofts, 1970), p. 4.
36. Leyburn, *The Scotch-Irish*, pp. 234, 301–16.
37. Ford, *The Scotch-Irish in America*, pp. 291–324; Leyburn, *The Scotch-Irish*, pp. 225–30.
38. Nathan Glazer and Daniel P. Moynihan, *Beyond the Melting Pot* (Cambridge: M.I.T. Press and Harvard University Press, 1963), p. 220; McGee, *A History of Irish Settlers in North America*, p. 88.
39. Wittke, *The Irish in America*, pp. 47ff, 119; Wayne G. Broehl, Jr., *The Molly Maguires* (Cambridge: Harvard University Press, 1964), p. 75.
40. Clark, *The Irish in Philadelphia*, p. 21.
41. Wittke, *The Irish in America*, p. 120.
42. Rowland T. Berthoff, *British Immigrants in Industrial America* (Cambridge: Harvard University Press, 1953), pp. 187, 190–93.
43. Broehl, *The Molly Maguires*, p. 85.
44. Leonard P. O. Wibberly, *The Coming of the Green* (New York: Henry Holt & Co. 1958), pp. 101–3.
45. Broehl, *The Molly Maguires*, pp. 87–90.
46. Ibid., pp. 198–99.
47. Anthony Bimba, *The Molly Maguires* (New York: International Publishers, 1932), pp. 70–73.
48. Broehl, *The Molly Maguires*, pp. vi, 359–61.
49. Oscar Handlin, *Boston's Immigrants, 1790–1865* (Cambridge: Harvard University Press, 1941), p. 137.
50. See James McCague, *The Second Rebellion* (New York: Dial Press, 1968).
51. Wittke, *The Irish in America*, pp. 191–92.
52. Richard Polenberg, *One Nation Divisible* (New York: Penguin, 1980), pp. 40–41.
53. Ford, *The Scotch-Irish in America*, pp. 246, 462, 491; McGee, *A History of Irish Settlers in North America*, p. 71; Shane Leslie, *The Irish Issue in Its American Aspect* (New York: Scribner's, 1919), p. 8.
54. Maldwyn A. Jones, "Ulster Emigration, 1783–1815," in *Essays in Scotch-Irish History*, ed. Green, p. 67.
55. Paul Blanshard, *The Irish and Catholic Power* (Boston: Beacon Press, 1953), p. 282.
56. William F. Adams, *Ireland and Irish Emigration to the New World* (New Haven: Yale University Press, 1932), p. 377.
57. Wittke, *The Irish in America*, p. 104; Edward M. Levine, *The Irish and Irish Politicians* (Notre Dame, Ind.: University of Notre Dame Press, 1966), pp. 6–9.
58. Leo Hershkowitz, *Tweed's New York* (New York: Doubleday, Anchor Books, 1987), pp. xiii–xx.
59. Glazer and Moynihan, *Beyond the Melting Pot*, pp. 218–62; Robert A. Dahl, *Who Governs?* (New Haven: Yale University Press, 1963), p. 41.
60. Levine, *The Irish and Irish Politicians*, p. 146.
61. Mike Royko, *Boss: Richard J. Daley of Chicago* (New York: Dutton, 1971); Sam Roberts, "In Search of Irish, or the Greening of the Suburbs," *New York Times*, March 17, 1988, p. B1; Alba, *Ethnic Identity*, p. 156.
62. Levine, *The Irish and Irish Politicians*, pp. 145–55, quotation on p. 174.
63. Wittke, *The Irish in America*, pp. 110–12.
64. Greeley, *That Most Distressful Nation*, pp. 206–9.
65. Dennis J. Clark, "The Philadelphia Irish," in *The Peoples of Philadelphia*, ed. Allen F. Davis and Mark H. Haller (Philadelphia: Temple University Press, 1973), p. 145.
66. Terry N. Clark, "The Irish Ethnic and the Spirit of Patronage," *Ethnicity* 2 (1975): 305–59; Mark R. Levy and Michael S. Kramer, *The Ethnic Factor* (New York: Simon & Schuster, 1972), pp. 130–35; Greeley, *The Irish Americans*, pp. 168–69.
67. Maldwyn Jones, *American Immigration* (Chicago: University of Chicago Press, 1960), p. 236.
68. William Miller, "American Historians and the Business Elite," *Journal of Economic History* 9 (November 1949): 202–3.
69. Quoted in Elmer Ellis, *Mr. Dooley's America* (New York: Knopf, 1941), p. 208.

70. Donald H. Akenson, *The United States and Ireland* (Cambridge: Harvard University Press, 1973), pp. 40–42.
71. Wittke, *The Irish in America*, pp. 281–91.
72. Linda Greenhouse, "Supreme Court Ruling Clears Way for Deportation of an I.R.A. Man," *New York Times*, January 16, 1992, p. A1; "O'Connor Seeks Aid for I.R.A. Fugitive," *New York Times*, February 1, 1992, sec. 1, p. 25; Cal McCrystal, "Notebook: A Tug-of-War for America's Irish Soul," *Independent*, February 2, 1992, p. 23.
73. William V. Shannon, *The American Irish* (New York: Macmillan, 1963), pp. 151–81.
74. Ibid., pp. 332–52; Samuel Lubell, *The Future of American Politics*, 2nd rev. ed. (New York: Doubleday, Anchor Books, 1955), pp. 83–84.
75. Glazer and Moynihan, *Beyond the Melting Pot*, p. 287.
76. Ibid; Shannon, *The American Irish*, pp. 395–411; Levy and Kramer, *The Ethnic Factor*, pp. 126–27. Compare John R. Schmidhauser, "The Justices of the Supreme Court: A Collective Portrait," *Midwest Journal of Social Science* 3 (February 1950): 1–57.
77. Leyburn, *The Scotch–Irish*, p. 322 and elsewhere.
78. Stephen Steinberg, *The Ethnic Myth* (New York: Atheneum, 1981), pp. 160–64.
79. Bagenal, *The American Irish*, p. 69.
80. Handlin, *Boston's Immigrants*, p. 67.
81. Adams, *Ireland and Irish Emigration to the New World*, p. 358.
82. Stephan Thernstrom, *Poverty and Progress* (Cambridge: Harvard University Press, 1964), pp. 154–58.
83. Ibid., p. 184; Clark, *The Irish in Philadelphia*, pp. 59, 167–75.
84. Greeley, *That Most Distressful Nation*, p. 120; Clark, "The Philadelphia Irish," p. 143; Wittke, *The Irish in America*, pp. 217–27.
85. Pitirim Sorokin, "American Millionaires and Multi-Millionaires," *Social Forces* 3 (May 1925): 634–35. Data are based on father's ancestry.
86. Stephan Thernstrom, *The Other Bostonians* (Cambridge: Harvard University Press, 1973), p. 131; Berthoff, *British Immigrants in Industrial America*.
87. Hershberg et al., "A Tale of Three Cities," p. 190.
88. Lloyd Warner and Leo Srole, *The Social Systems of American Ethnic Groups* (New Haven: Yale University Press, 1945), pp. 93–95; E. Digby Baltzell, *An American Business Aristocracy* (New York: Collier Books, 1962), pp. 267–431; E. Digby Baltzell, *The Protestant Establishment* (New York: Random House, Vintage Books, 1966), pp. 320–21.
89. Shannon, *The American Irish*, pp. 436–37.
90. Ronald P. Formisano, *Boston against Busing: Race, Class, and Ethnicity in the 1960s and 1970s* (Chapel Hill: University of North Carolina Press, 1991), p. 15.
91. Harold J. Abramson, *Ethnic Diversity in Catholic America* (New York: John Wiley, 1973), pp. 41–44; Levy and Kramer, *The Ethnic Factor*, p. 125. See also Greeley, *The Irish Americans*, p. 111; U.S. Bureau of the Census, *U.S. Census of Population, 1970: Subject Report—National Origin and Language*, PC(2)-1a (Washington, 1973), p. 152; U.S. Bureau of the Census, *U.S. Census of Population, 1980: General Social and Economic Characteristics*, PC80-1-C1 (Washington, 1983), pp. 21, 51, 177.
92. Greeley, "Success and Assimilation," pp. 231–36. The percent "professional" in Greeley's survey data is much higher than in comparable census data. By grouping the 1972–87 samples Greeley accumulated enough Irish for analysis.
93. Quoted in Roberts, "In Search of Irish," p. B1.
94. John T. Ellis, *American Catholicism* (Garden City, N.Y.: Doubleday, Image Books, 1965), p. 62; Clark, *The Irish in Philadelphia*, p. 123.
95. David O. Moberg, *The Church as a Social Institution* (Englewood Cliffs, N.J.: Prentice-Hall, 1962), p. 193.
96. Andrew M. Greeley, *Ethnicity, Denomination and Inequality* (Beverly Hills, Calif.: Sage Publications, Inc., 1976), pp. 45–53.
97. Greeley, "Success and Assimilation," pp. 231–36.
98. Ibid.
99. Wittke, *The Irish in America*, pp. 52–61, 205.
100. Owen B. Corrigan, "Chronology of the Catholic Hierarchy of the United States," *Catholic Historical Review* 1 (January 1916): 267–389; Gaustad, *Historical Atlas of Religion in America*, p. 103; Ellis, *American Catholicism*, p. 56; Wittke, *The Irish in America*, p. 91; Greeley, *That Most Distressful Nation*, p. 93; correspondence between Andrew Greeley and the authors.
101. Greeley, *The Irish Americans*, p. 145.
102. National Opinion Research Center, 1990 General Social Survey. Tabulations by authors.
103. Greeley, *The Irish Americans*, pp. 130–32.
104. Ford, *The Scotch-Irish in America*, p. 538.
105. Clark, *The Philadelphia Irish*, p. 178.
106. Thernstrom, *Poverty and Progress*, p. 179.
107. Abramson, *Ethnic Diversity in Catholic America*, p. 111; Greeley, *The Irish Americans*, pp. 149–51.
108. Glazer and Moynihan, *Beyond the Melting Pot*, p. 219.
109. Raymond E. Wolfinger, "The Development and Persistence of Ethnic Voting," *American Political Science Review* 60 (1965): 907; Greeley, "Success and Assimilation," p. 236.
110. Joseph P. O'Grady, *How the Irish Became American* (New York: Twayne, 1973), p. 141; Marjorie R. Fallows, *Irish Americans: Identity and Assimilation* (Englewood Cliffs, N.J.: Prentice-Hall, 1979), p. 147.
111. Abramson, *Ethnic Diversity in Catholic America*, p. 53; Alba, *Ethnic Identity*, p. 47.
112. Fallows, *Irish Americans*, pp. 148–49. See also Richard D. Alba, "Social Assimilation among American Catholic National-Origin Groups," *American Sociological Review* 41 (December 1976): 1032.

113. Alba, *Ethnic Identity*, pp. 55, 61.
114. Formisano, *Boston Against Busing*, pp. 220–21.
115. Greeley, "Success and Assimilation," p. 233.
116. Greeley, *The Irish Americans*, p. 206.
117. Ibid. See also Andrew M. Greeley, *Ethnicity in the United States* (New York: John Wiley, 1974), p. 311.

Chapter 5

Italian Americans

Little Italy: Grand Street, New York, N.Y.
Photo Courtesy of New York Convention and Visitors Bureau, New York, N.Y.

For many decades Italian Americans have found themselves to be the targets of Anglo-Protestant hostility. This mostly Catholic group was attacked by Anglo-Americans for being especially prejudiced against black Americans, for being unsophisticated, superpatriotic hardhats with connections to the "Mafia." In the 1960s and 1970s a counterattack developed. Many white ethnic leaders, including Italian Americans, came to view Anglo-Protestant intellectuals and officials very critically: "The ethnic American is sick of being stereotyped as a racist and a dullard by phony white liberals, pseudo black militants and patronizing bureaucrats.... He pays the bill for every major governmental program and gets nothing or little in the way of return."[1] Richard Gambino, an Italian American scholar, noted that "the white elite has shown little understanding of Italian-American history, culture, or problems and less empathy with them."[2]

The militant defense of things Italian and the achievements of Italian Americans had by the 1980s and 1990s brought this group greater acceptance among other Americans, including many Anglo-Protestant voters. Clear signals of the rising prominence of Italian Americans in the United States could be seen in the selection of Geraldine Ferraro, an Italian American member of Congress, as the Democratic party's vice-presidential candidate in 1984 and the substantial national support for New York governor Mario Cuomo as a possible Democratic presidential nominee in 1992.

ITALIAN IMMIGRATION

Italian explorers, including Cristoforo Colombo (Christopher Columbus), played a major role in opening the Americas to European exploration and exploitation. An Italian navigator, Amerigo Vespucci, made a number of voyages to the Americas shortly after Colombo's voyages. Because of his early maps the continents even came to be named after him.[3]

Numbers of Immigrants

Small numbers of Italians migrated to the colonies prior to the 1800s. Schiavo notes that "in Virginia, a small group of Italians settled with Filippo Mazzei in 1774 in order to introduce wine making and Italian agricultural methods."[4] Thomas Jefferson was influenced by Mazzei's intellectual talents and subsequently invited other Italian agricultural experts and crafts workers to Virginia. Jefferson was also responsible for bringing an Italian architect to design his home at Monticello, Italian artists to create sculptures, bas-reliefs, and frescoes to decorate the U.S. Capitol, and Italian musicians to form the first U.S. Marine Corps band.[5]

Since 1820 more than five million Italians have migrated to the United States. Until 1860 the migration was quite small. Between 1861 and 1880 migration picked up a little, totaling 67,500. In the next four decades, Italian immigration became heavy, with more than four million recorded immigrants. Prior to 1880 most immigrants were from northern Italy; now they came in very large numbers from the south. The heavy migration of poor farmers and laborers had begun just three decades after the formerly independent regions of Italy were unified into one state.[6]

Certain factors are relevant to the study of this migration: the point of origin, the destination, the migrating units, and the larger context. As with the Irish, land and agricultural problems triggered much of the Italian out-migration. National unification under a government controlled by northern Italians had brought heavy taxes to southern Italy. Low incomes, poor soil and weather, poor health conditions, a feudal land system, unreasonable taxes, and corruption in government were important push factors at the point of origin. Areas with a large and militant working-class population sent fewer migrants in spite of their poverty. Agricultural organization and labor militancy in Italy significantly lowered out-migration rates.[7]

The often exaggerated image of the United States as a place of expanding economic opportunity was a major pull factor. Some came to stay, but for the majority of the early immigrants the United States was seen as a temporary workplace, not a permanent new home. They came with the idea of accruing capital for enterprises back home; of these, some returned but others remained. Most who came were poor. A considerable portion of the immigration was stimulated by aggressively expanding industrial capitalism in the United States; many came as a direct result of labor recruiting in Italy.[8]

Migration along family and kinship networks, typical for poor and working-class migrants from most European countries, lessened the pain of resettlement. Italians came in large numbers from the same villages, with men often migrating first. Chains of kin migration across the Atlantic linked areas in Italy and America. Most immigrants headed for urban points; like the Irish, most had had enough of farm life. Industrialized East Coast cities, such as Boston, New York, and Philadelphia, were popular destinations. In larger cities immigrants went to "Little Italies," where fellow villagers from Italy resided.[9] Remigration for Italians was well above that of other groups. Approximately 1.3 million returned to the homeland between 1902 and 1914. In some years returnees equalled 60 to 70 percent of new immigrants; in 1908, 245,000 went back while only 71,000 arrived. Some returned with savings sufficient to buy land and start a new life in Italy.[10]

Beginning in 1897, nativist agitation resulted in numerous legislative attempts to restrict immigration. Between 1924 and 1965 immigration quotas sharply curtailed Italian immigration. The Immigration Act of 1924 established a small, discriminatory quota for Italians. By 1929 the annual quota for Italians was only 5,802, compared with 65,721 for Great Britain and 25,957 for Germany. These quotas were only slightly altered by the 1952 Walter-McCarran Act. The quota system was based on Protestant nativists' belief that those countries that had furnished the most "good American citizens"—that is, immigrants prior to 1880—should receive the largest quotas. The British, Germans, Irish, and Scandinavians were given 76 percent of the total, although the demand from those countries had slackened considerably by that time.[11]

Pressure on Italy's small quota had produced a backlog of 250,000 applicants by the time the 1965 Immigration Act replaced the national-origin quota system. The first stage of the 1965 act allowed the unfilled quotas of some countries to supplement the filled quotas of certain other countries. As a result, the number of Italian entrants increased significantly. In 1966 some 26,447 Italian immigrants were admitted; in 1967, 28,487. However, the 1965 act set an annual limit of 20,000 for each country beginning in 1968, and the backlog of Italian applicants again increased. Italian migration continued at a high level in the early 1970s; 1972 and 1973 saw twice as many entrants from Italy as from any other European country. By the late 1970s the backlog was exhausted, and since that time the annual number of Italian immigrants has dropped significantly.

Life for the Immigrants

What was life like for the large numbers of Italians who immigrated in the peak 1880–1920 period? Most worked as unskilled laborers on transportation systems such as canals and railroads and on city water and sewer systems. Pay was typically low, and individuals as well as families were poor. Segregated in "Little Italy" ghettos within cities, Italian immigrants and their children faced economic, political, and social discrimination. There is irony here, since *ghetto* is thought to be an Italian (Venetian) word first applied to the practice of segregating Jews in Italy in the sixteenth century. In the United States it was the Italian Catholics who found themselves in ghettos. In many cities Italian Americans replaced earlier groups as part of an invasion-succession process. Yet other groups would follow on their heels.[12]

Some analysts have viewed working-class communities in cities as disorganized "slum" areas with little positive social life. This was not true for such Italian American communities. As with the Irish before them, Italians developed their own extensive friendship and kinship circles, political clubs, avenues for mobility, and community celebrations. Central to Italian American communities were indigenous organizations and festivals, including clubs and mutual-benefit societies—societies whose members made small monthly payments to ensure a proper funeral and a decent burial upon their demise. In 1927 Chicago had two hundred mutual-aid societies and many other clubs and lodges. Legal agencies developed; Italian newspapers flourished.[13]

Italian American communities, such as the North End of Boston, were laid on the bedrock of kinship networks, with extended-family members living near one another. As a result, and contrary to nativist propaganda, few among first-generation Italian Americans ended up in almshouses. As in Italy, Italian immigrant families in the United States tended to be patriarchal, and kinship solidarity was emphasized. Home ownership was highly valued. The community was a critical factor in cementing Italian Americans to certain northern and midwestern cities.[14]

STEREOTYPES

Nativist images of Irish Americans had been harsh, but by the end of the nineteenth century the stereotype of the apelike Irish was giving way to harsh stereotypes of southern and eastern Europeans. Italian Catholics were one target of stereotyping. The stereotype was strong and frequently absurd:

> It is urged that the Italian race stock is inferior and degraded; that it will not assimilate naturally or readily with the prevailing "Anglo-Saxon" race stock of this country; that intermixture, if practicable, will be detrimental; that servility, filthy habits of life, and a hopelessly degraded standard of needs and ambitions have been ingrained in Italians by centuries of oppression and abject poverty.[15]

Such indictments appeared in national magazines. In the 1888 *North American Review*, labor activist T. V. Powderly alleged that southern and eastern Europeans were an inferior stock that lived immoral lives centered in liquor.[16] The new immigrants were often condemned by nativists as "dagos" or "wops," the latter term probably coming from the letters WOP, used to identify immigrants "without papers" at Ellis Island.

Myths of Biological Inferiority

Popular writers, scholars, and members of Congress warned of the peril of allowing inferior stocks from Europe into the United States. Kenneth L. Roberts, a prominent journalist, wrote of the dangers of the newer immigrants making Americans a mongrel race: "Races can not be cross-bred without mongrelization, any more than breeds of dogs can be cross-bred without mongrelization. The American nation was founded and developed by the Nordic race, but if a few more million members of the Alpine, Mediterranean and Semitic races are poured among us, the result must inevitably be a hybrid race of people as worthless and futile as the good-for-nothing mongrels of Central America and southeastern Europe."[17] The "Alpine, Mediterranean, and Semitic races" generally covered countries of heavy emigration other than those of northern Europe; the Italians and European Jews were thought by such writers to be examples.

Half-truths about disease and illiteracy were circulated about the southern and eastern European immigrants. It was true in some years between 1880 and 1920 that half the adult Italian immigrants could not read and write, but in other years the overwhelming majority were literate. In no year were the charges of total illiteracy leveled at Italian Americans by the press and politicians accurate.[18] Particularly hostile was the leap from the proportions illiterate to assumptions of low intelligence.

In the first three decades of the twentieth century stereotypes of intellectual inferiority were based in part on misreadings of the results of new psychological tests inaccurately labeled intelligence (IQ) tests. The term *intelligence test* is inaccurate because the tests measured selected, learned verbal and quantitative skills, not a broad or basic intelligence. In 1912 Henry Goddard gave Binet's diagnostic test and related tests to a large number of immigrants from southern and eastern Europe. His data supposedly showed that 83 percent of Jewish and 79 percent of Italian immigrants were "feeble-minded," a category naively defined in terms of low scores on the new tests.[19]

With the coming of World War I some prominent psychologists developed verbal and performance tests for large-scale testing of draftees. Although the results were not used for military purposes, detailed analyses were published in the 1920s and gained public and congressional attention because of the racial-inferiority interpretation some psychologists placed on the test results of the southern and eastern Europeans among the draftees.[20]

In 1923 Carl Brigham, a Princeton psychologist who would later play a role in developing today's college entrance tests, wrote a detailed analysis of the alleged intellectual inferiority of immigrant groups, including Italian Americans, drawing on data from army tests. The average scores for foreign-born draftees ranged from highs of 14.87 for English and 14.34 for Scotch draftees, to an average of 13.77 for all white draftees, to lows of 10.74 for Polish and 11.01 for Italian draftees. The low test scores for such groups as the Italian Americans were boldly explained in racial terms; those groups were considered inferior "racial stocks." These results were used by psychologists such as Brigham to support the prevalent ideology of "Nordic" intellectual superiority being espoused by racist theorists such as Madison Grant. Brigham went on to argue that the sharp increases in southern and eastern European immigration had lowered the general level of American intelligence.[21]

The political implications of Brigham's analysis were proclaimed: immigration limits were necessary. Political means should be developed within the United States to prevent the continued "propagation" of "defective strains" in the population.[22] Here was pseudoscientific support for such government action as passage of the 1924 Immigration Act, which would soon restrict Italian and other southern European immigration.

An important aspect of this stereotyping of Italian and other European immigrants is the role of the government, a point underscored by Omi and Winant in their racial formation theory (see Chapter 2). The definition of these immigrants as undesirable ethnic groups was stimulated by social psychologists working with and for state agencies, in this case the U.S. armed forces, and their research was used by another branch of government, the Congress, to restrict immigration.

The "intelligence" differences measured by psychological tests were assumed to reflect the inferior or superior genetic background of European "racial" stocks. In those decades few seriously considered the possibility that the linguistic (English), cultural (northern European–American), and educational bias in the tests and in interpretive procedures could account for the differences. These debates over the inferiority of European "racial" groups are now a historical curiosity. No social scientists today would advance arguments of white ethnic inferiority on the basis of paper-and-pencil test data.[23]

Some immigrant leaders developed strategies for dealing with concern over "blood" lineage. One prominent Italian American leader, Fiorello La Guardia, suffered personal attacks that incorporated stereotypes. For his criticism of officials such as President Herbert Hoover he received letters such as the following: "You should go back where you belong and advise Mussolini how to make good honest citizens in Italy. The Italians are preponderantly our murderers and boot-leggers."[24] La Guardia's countertactic was often biting humor. When asked to provide material on his family background for the *New York World*, he saw the ghost of "blood" inferiority behind the request and commented: "I have no family tree. The only member of my family who has one is my dog Yank. He is the son of Doughboy, who was the son of Siegfried, who was the son of Tannhäuser, who was the son of Wotan. A distinguished family tree, to be sure—but after all he's only a son of a bitch."[25] Humor has been a useful response to hostile ethnic stereotyping.

The Mafia Myth

Even into the 1990s the most persistent of Italian American stereotypes has been the criminality image. As early as the 1870s Italians were depicted as lawless, knife-wielding thugs looking for a fight. A report of the influential United States Immigration Commission argued that certain types of criminality were "inherent in the Italian race."[26] Yet the validity of the criminality stereotype is disputed by official government data from the early decades of this century. For example, the arrest rate for drunkenness and disorderly conduct for the Italian foreign-born in 1910 was quite low—158 per 100,000 people, compared with 202 for American-born whites. The arrest rate for prostitution was very low, and the imprisonment rate in 1910 was much lower than public stereotypes would suggest: 527 prisoners per 100,000 for the Italian-born, 727 for English and Welsh foreign-born, and 371 for the white American-born population.[27]

While noting that some persons involved in organized crime in Italy did immigrate to the United States, di Franco points out the outrage that most Italian immigrants felt at being associated with those criminals who actually victimized them. Small-scale crime fostered in part by poverty and discrimination was a problem in Italian American communities, but it did not involve a sinister conspiracy. Prohibition catapulted Italian Americans into organized crime, which at that time was controlled mostly by Irish and Jewish Americans. For many immigrant groups crime has been an avenue of mobility. Increasingly in the twentieth century, the Sicilian term *Mafia* has been used to describe these gangsters, many of whom have been neither Sicilian nor Italian. Indeed, Italian Americans had low crime rates in the 1920s and 1930s. What data are available suggest that foreign-born Italian Americans had crime rates close to those for all native-born Americans.[28]

The image of Italian criminality has taken on a widespread mythological character; the stereotype of the Italian American as a Mafia hoodlum committed to crime and violence persists. Into the early 1990s Italian names for criminals in TV series and movies clearly signaled ties to the so-called "Mafia." Without exception, every non-Italian respondent in Waters's 1986–87 study of white ethnics in California and Pennsylvania used the Mafia and gangsters to characterize Italian Americans; most said their ideas were based on media images.[29]

That organized crime continues as a major enterprise cannot be disputed. That a small proportion of Italian Americans play a role in it is not disputed. That these Italian Americans control a nationwide crime syndicate with no help from other racial and ethnic groups can be disputed; that the Italian (Sicilian) term *Mafia* should be used to describe such a syndicate can be rejected. Organized crime is a multi-ethnic enterprise drawing from most racial and ethnic groups; Italian Americans are a small percentage of such criminals today. FBI statistics show that only 4 percent of the 500,000 Americans estimated to be involved in organized crime belong to Italian American crime networks; of these 20,000 only 1,700 are actually Italian Americans. In addition, reports in the early 1990s indicated that except in New York City and Chicago's suburbs the power of Italian American crime families had declined significantly; more recent immigrant groups, such as those from Asia and Latin America, had taken over much organized crime.[30]

Stereotypes and Discrimination

A study of the portrayal of Italian Americans on prime-time television examined a sample of 263 programs for one season in the 1980s. The study found that negative images of Italian Americans outnumbered positive images by two to one. Most of the ninety-six Italian characters in the shows studied were males with low-status jobs. A significant percentage were portrayed as criminals, and many were pictured as "lovable or laughable dimwits who worked in jobs that offered little pay and less prestige." The majority of Italian Americans portrayed on television made grammatical errors, misunderstood English words, or spoke broken English.[31]

An Italian American in a northern California city described his experience with ethnic slurs: "When I joined the office in the new location I became a member of the Rotary Club, and of course there were very few Italian members. So the minute I came on board, they started referring to me as the Godfather of the country." He went on to say that he found this humor very degrading, since he seemed always to have to explain that he had no ties to the so-called "Mafia." Numerous other Italian Americans have reported similar experiences, including discrimination in corporations and much barbed Mafia joking.[32]

The Mafia myth had a negative impact on the 1984 presidential election. A smear campaign aimed at Democratic vice-presidential candidate Geraldine Ferraro, an Italian American, accused her husband of "mob connections." Recalling the first time her son had been called a "wop," when he was six or seven years old, Ferraro indicated that encounters with anti-Italian attitudes were common. The problem of the Mafia myth has also plagued the presidential aspirations of New York governor Mario Cuomo since the mid-1980s. One of the reasons he gave for not running for president in 1992 was that anti-Italian prejudice would hurt his candidacy: "People who didn't know me said years ago that they would not vote for me because I was apt to have Mafia connections." One prominent political figure running for the 1992 Democratic nomination admitted stating privately that in his opinion Cuomo acted as though he had Mafia connections.[33]

The Mafia image is not the only negative stereotype to which Italian Americans are subjected. Among all the European ancestry groups included in Alba's 1984–85 study of white ethnics in a large metropolitan area of upper New York State, the Italian American respondents reported encountering the greatest number of stereotypes. Images referred to physical appearance (big noses), mannerisms (talking with their hands), family life (being family-oriented and good with children), as well as Mafia connections ("they all have something to do with organized crime"). Similarly, Waters's non-Italian white respondents in California and Pennsylvania held both negative and positive stereotypes of Italian Americans. Some described Italians as dirty, loud, temperamental, selfish, unambitious, combative, and not very bright; others listed characteristics such as having excellent food, doing well in business, being affectionate, family-oriented, fun at parties, and exceptionally clean housekeepers.[34]

CONFLICT

The myth of peaceful progress is again dispelled by the history of struggles of Italian Americans with Anglo-Protestant nativists, Irish Catholics, and black Americans. Irish and Italian Americans had fought on the streets of Boston by the 1860s, and Italian parents accompanied their children to school for protection. In the 1870s Irish workers on strike in New York attacked Italian strikebreakers; four Italians were killed in Pennsylvania in a clash with striking Irish miners.

By the 1880s nativists had initiated attempts to control immigrants from southern Italy, sometimes under the guise of "legal action" to prevent alleged crime, sometimes in the form of vigilante action. In the 1880s in Buffalo, New York, more than three hundred Italians—most of the local Italian population—were detained by police after an incident in which one Italian had killed another; only two of the three hundred were found holding weapons. The Italian American community protested to the Italian government. Replying to the governor of New York, the police chief of Buffalo explained that he thought Italian Americans as a rule carried concealed weapons and were a threat to social order.[35]

In addition to violent incidents in northern areas, several dozen Italian Americans were killed by mobs in numerous places in the South. Attacks in the South were motivated by a variety of reasons, including labor competition and a desire to maintain racial lines. Italian Americans were viewed as a threat to white solidarity in the South because they were more likely than other whites to support black political rights. They worked alongside blacks as laborers or sold to them as small shopkeepers. In one town five Sicilian shopkeepers were lynched for this reason.[36] One well-publicized attack occurred in New Orleans after the 1891 murder of a white police superintendent who was investigating crime among Italian Americans. A number of Italian Americans were jailed for the murder, and the police refused to intervene when a large group led by prominent citizens stormed the jail and killed eleven of them. Newspapers and major political figures praised the deed, using the incident to advance the stereotypical theme of criminality. Theodore Roosevelt made negative comments about Italian Americans, calling the 1891 lynchings in New Orleans "a rather good thing."[37]

More Legalized Killings

Italian Americans were fired on and forced to leave Marksville, Louisiana, for violating southern racial taboos. Two hundred were driven out of Altoona, Pennsylvania, in 1894. In some areas, they counterattacked. In 1899 an Italian agricultural community in Arkansas suffered vandalism, and its schoolhouse was burned by whites. Groups of Italian citizens armed themselves and patrolled their area, effectively ending the attacks.[38]

Some killings were legalized. One of the most famous murder trials of all time was that of Nicola Sacco and Bartolomeo Vanzetti, Italian-born workers who were tried for robbery and murder in Massachusetts. Numerous witnesses testified that the defendants were elsewhere at the time of the crime, but the testimony of Italian-born witnesses was ignored by the court. Anti-Italian prejudice was evident in the trial and in the presiding judge. The two men clearly did not receive a fair trial. As suspected political radicals, they were executed in 1927 in the midst of hysteria over left-wing, un-American activities. In recent years several books have reassessed the prosecution's case presenting new evidence that has brought into question its most important points.[39]

Conflict with Black Americans

Since the 1930s conflict between Italian Americans and groups lower on the socioeconomic ladder has been part of the urban scene. "Law and order," school desegregation, and busing have been major issues in the northern metropolitan areas. In the 1960s and 1970s Italian American leaders sometimes complained that blacks were the "darlings" of the white Protestant liberals and received disproportionate press coverage and federal aid. Italian Americans in some areas of such cities as Newark and Philadelphia have found themselves surrounded by large numbers of black Americans migrating from other regions. With these poor immigrants have come increased crime and drug problems. Realistic fears about urban crime have been coupled with exaggerated views of the black role in that crime, much like Anglo-Protestant fears exaggerating the Italian role in urban crime.[40]

In the spring of 1990 a group of Italian American youths attacked and killed a black youth, Yusuf Hawkins, in the predominantly Italian Bensonhurst area of New York City. The attackers believed that the victim was on his way to date an Italian American girl.

Actually, Hawkins had gone to Bensonhurst to inquire about buying a used car. Members of the Federation of Italian American Organizations actively sought to calm racial tensions, calling the attention of Italian residents to their own history of discrimination. Some residents, though, noted that this incident was not unique. One woman told of two of her Brazilian friends who had been abducted, stabbed, and brutally beaten by a group of Italian American youths in the fall of 1988. The victims survived and gave descriptions of their assailants to the police, yet no arrests were ever made; the community ignored that racial incident.[41]

A number of surveys in the late 1960s and early 1970s showed significant antiblack prejudice and strong opposition to neighborhood desegregation among Italian Americans. One survey found that 70 percent of Italians would object if a black family moved into their area, a figure higher than for whites in general.[42] By the 1990s, however, Italian American attitudes had liberalized. Sixty percent of Italian Americans, compared with 55 percent of all whites, said they would work for improved racial relations and 85 percent of Italian Americans, compared with 79 percent of all whites, said they would vote for a qualified black presidential candidate. On several other opinion poll items, such as a question asking if they would object to sending their children to a school that was half black, Italian Americans were somewhat more likely to be opposed than whites as a group (19 percent compared with 16 percent).[43] On the whole, Italian Americans are less negative in their views of black Americans than they were in the past. Yet a sizeable minority among Italian Americans, as among other white groups, remain openly racist in their attitudes toward black Americans, a situation that has on occasion fueled antiblack violence such as the Bensonhurst incidents.

POLITICS

The first major Italian influence on U.S. politics was that of Filippo Mazzei, a friend of Thomas Jefferson who, as we have seen, came to the colonies to help with agricultural development. Mazzei also helped Jefferson bring legal reforms to Virginia. Mazzei's writings speak vigorously of freedom and equality and include phrases similar to those Jefferson later used in the Declaration of Independence—for example, "All men are by nature created free and independent."[44]

City Politics

During and after the great migration of 1880–1920, Irish Americans recruited Italian Americans into the Democratic party. In Chicago, Italian Americans benefited from the political patronage system; many were employed by the city in the 1890s, mostly in menial positions such as street sweeping. Italian Americans had elected an alderman there by 1892, and by the mid-1890s they had a few representatives in the Illinois legislature. Italians had begun to enter elected offices in New York by 1900, and by 1920 they were central to city politics—for example, in passing out life-sustaining job favors.[45]

The political participation of Italian immigrants suffered a setback during the 1919–22 Red Scare. The infamous raids conducted by Attorney General Palmer in this period were aimed largely at immigrant families, often Italian, thought to be radical or subversive. Many aliens were illegally detained or arrested, and some were deported as a result.[46] Such activities had a major dampening effect on political participation.

By the late 1930s a few cities, such as New York, San Francisco, and New Orleans, had Italian mayors. Nonetheless, the typical urban picture was of Italian American communities governed by non-Italian politicians. Substantial political gains were made in the next few decades. A number of smaller cities, particularly in New Jersey, elected Italian mayors, and by 1947 Italian Americans had gained great influence in New York City politics. Irish American control of New Haven's local government kept Italian Americans from moving up for a number of decades, and it was not until the late 1950s that Italian Americans were well represented in city government positions there. Over the next two decades, the number of Italian Americans serving as mayor or city-council member became conspicuous in many northern cities.[47] Prominent Italian American mayors in recent decades have included Anthony Celebrezze (Cleveland), Joseph Alioto (San Francisco), George Moscone (San Francisco), and Frank Rizzo (Philadelphia). Of those who have served as chief executives in major cities, most have been liberal Democrats.

As they did with the Irish, Anglo-Protestant urban reform movements often reduced the benefits going to the Italian working class. These movements were aimed at ridding urban politics of machine bosses and corruption. But defeating the machine meant decreasing the political power of working-class ethnics.[48] Reform in the guise of urban renewal and urban redevelopment has hurt Italian communities. For example, the West End of Boston once contained a large, viable, Italian working-class community. In the late 1950s the area, which had relatively little political clout, was officially designated a "slum" by the politically powerful city fathers and razed for urban renewal. New apartment buildings were built, development that was expected to improve the tax base of the central city. But several thousand Italians were forced to relocate, a move that brought them great pain.[49]

State and National Politics

Very few Italians served in state and national legislatures in the North prior to 1900. One was Francis Spinola, a brigadier general in the Union army, a member of the New York legislature, and a member of the U.S. House of Representatives. After 1900 the few successes at state and national levels were based on the concentration of voters in urban communities. Prior to 1950 New York had had only six Italian American representatives in Congress. The most famous was Fiorello La Guardia, a man proud of his heritage. In Congress he became the most vigorous supporter of Italian immigration, attacking nativism and the anti-Italian quota system it had fostered. He was the first Italian American to rise through ethnic politics in New York City, where he was elected mayor in 1934. La Guardia showed that Italian Americans and other white ethnics could support reform movements aimed at urban machines, in this case Tammany Hall, and promote honest government.[50]

International politics affected Italian American political activities, just as the Ireland–Britain struggle has affected Irish Americans. During the Great Depression Mussolini became a hero for many Italian Americans, as well as for many non-Italian Americans, although antifascist activity was also a significant force in many Italian communities. During World War II Italian Americans suffered some discrimination. Italian American subversion was widely alleged, but not proven, and the use of the Italian language was prohibited on the radio in New York and Boston. Several thousand Italians were arrested, and nearly two hundred aliens were placed in internment camps after the United States declared war. However, the action taken against Italian Americans was far less substantial than that against Japanese Americans.[51]

Richard Alba has argued that the war contributed to eventual Italian American mobility and assimilation, particularly after 1945. The solidarity with other Americans that was generated by the struggle against fascism in Germany and Japan helped the Italian immigrants and their children assimilate more rapidly to the core culture and institutions. Italian Americans enlisted in the armed forces and served in ethnically integrated units. (In contrast, African Americans and Japanese Americans served in segregated units.) Novels and films about the armed forces celebrated the ethnic diversity of U.S. soldiers. The war contributed to what Alba terms "a different vision of America, which included ethnic Americans, or more precisely those who were white, in the magic circle of full citizenship."[52]

Since the Great Depression Italian Americans have slowly moved into the middle levels of state and federal government, including the judicial system. Franklin Roosevelt appointed the first Italian American judge to the federal courts; President Harry Truman appointed the second and third. Only one Italian American (a current Justice, Antonin Scalia) has ever served on the Supreme Court. Progress in congressional representation has been more substantial. By the late 1940s eight Italian Americans held seats in Congress. By the 1950s ever larger numbers of Italian Americans were serving in state legislatures. John Pastore of Rhode Island became the first Italian American governor (1946) and the first senator shortly thereafter. In 1962 Anthony Celebrezze became the first Italian American ever to serve in a presidential cabinet.[53]

During the 1970s and 1980s the numbers of Italian American cabinet members, governors, and state legislators grew. Mario Cuomo, governor of New York in the 1980s and early 1990s, was considered a contender for the Democratic party's presidential nomination in 1992. Cuomo was a keynote speaker at the 1984 Democratic party convention that nominated Geraldine Ferraro as its vice-presidential candidate. It was a source of great pride for many Italian Americans that the first woman ever nominated for vice-president of the United States was an Italian American. In the early 1990s twenty-eight Italian Americans representing fourteen states were members of the U.S. House of Representatives, and four Italian Americans representing New York, Arizona, New Mexico, and Vermont served in the U.S. Senate.

In the late 1960s Republican strategists began a concerted effort to attract the white ethnic vote, including the Italian American vote, away from the Democratic party. Fears about black civil rights actions fueled white ethnic discontent. Although this strategy produced notable success in the 1972 presidential election, survey data for the late 1970s showed Italian Americans leaning strongly toward the Democratic party. Only 22 percent called themselves Republicans at that time; in most contests Italian Americans continued to vote for the Democratic party. During the 1980s many moved their political allegiance to the Republican party. In the early 1990s opinion poll data found 49 percent of Italian Americans calling themselves Republicans compared with 39 percent calling themselves Democrats; 53 percent voted for the Republican presidential candidate in 1988.[54]

Nationwide Italian American organizations have achieved some political success. In the mid-1960s the 130 chapters of the American Committee on Italian Immigration held rallies and lobbied successfully in support of the 1965 Immigration Act, which brought change to racist U.S. immigration laws. Since its creation in 1976 the National Italian American Foundation, headquartered in Washington, D.C., has operated as a clearinghouse of information on Italian politicians and political issues of importance to Italian Americans.[55]

THE ECONOMY

Structural adaptation by immigrant groups includes their movement into secondary-organization levels of the core society—into the economic as well as the political and educational organizations. Economic mobility entails the penetration of higher levels of employment and the attendant economic benefits. Italian Americans began at the bottom of the ladder. The small number of immigrants prior to 1880 were mostly artisans, street sellers, and political exiles, primarily from northern Italy. The southern Italian immigrants, who came after 1880, were economically oppressed; they responded to the tremendous U.S. demand for unskilled labor that existed in the late nineteenth century.[56]

Large numbers came to the United States with the aid of *padroni*, labor bosses who linked the new immigrants to employment, food, and housing. Some claim this system was imported from Italy, but others have argued that it was a normal part of U.S. industrialization, which virtually devoured immigrant workers. The padroni acted primarily as agents who secured cheap labor for transportation, construction, and manufacturing enterprises within the United States. Exploitation often resulted from the padrone system. Exorbitant prices were charged by the labor bosses for housing and food; labor abuses were heaped on workers isolated in camps. By 1909, because of legislation passed in several states, contractors and other business operators had begun to change from the extralegal padroni to legitimate agents.[57]

Early Poverty and Discrimination

Urban poverty coupled with dangerous working conditions was the lot of most immigrants. Stella sums this up: "The Italian immigrant may be maimed and killed in his industrial occupation without a cry and without indemnity. He may die from the 'bends' working in the caissons under the river, without protest; he can be slowly asphyxiated in crowded tenements, smothered in dangerous trades and occupations (which only the ignorant immigrant pursues, not the native American); he can contract tuberculosis in unsanitary factories and sweatshops."[58] A number of studies documented poor community conditions—overcrowding and exorbitant rents in run-down housing, as well as inadequate water and sewage facilities. In big cities such as New York, death rates from infectious diseases were often high.[59]

Lack of skills affected the first generation of immigrants. Some who came were skilled workers, but overall this group had the highest percentage of unskilled laborers among major immigrant groups in this period. One study found that of the immigrants entering around 1900, 0.2 percent were professional workers, 12.7 percent trade or industrial workers, and 64.9 percent farmers or farm workers, with the rest being women (working in the home) and children. Poor farmers and their families made up the majority. However, a study of

Italian-born males in the United States found few of those immigrants employed in agriculture, but a high proportion employed as unskilled workers—miners, laborers, and fishermen. Many replaced Irish Americans in building roads and railroads. Few were in clerical fields or the professions. Those in the domestic and personal service areas were mostly barbers and restaurant workers. Italian women were employed primarily in trade.[60]

Background handicaps such as a poor command of English and lack of vocational skills were not the only restrictions on occupational opportunity. Discrimination played an important role. Isolate, small-group, and direct and indirect institutionalized discrimination—all four types outlined in Chapter 1—held Italians back. Higham asserts that from the first years of heavy migration the new Italian residents were "abused in public and isolated in private, cuffed in the works and pelted on the streets, fined and imprisoned on the smallest pretext, cheated of their wages, and crowded by the score into converted barns and tumble-down shanties that served as boarding houses."[61] Discrimination was well institutionalized; discrimination in wages was often blatant, as in an 1895 ad for laborers to build a New York City reservoir that listed daily wages as $1.30 to $1.50 for "whites" and $1.15 to $1.25 for "Italians."[62] Just as important was indirect discrimination in the form of recruitment practices with a built-in bias. Informal social networks were then as now the major means of circulating job information. Anglo-Protestant and Irish American sponsors were important in most urban job networks, protecting their own kind and often discriminating against Italian Americans.[63]

Unions

One additional factor operating against Italian Americans, at least in the beginning, was discrimination by worker organizations, which kept them from moving into many blue-collar jobs. Some became strikebreakers as a result of that exclusion and also because their poverty-stricken condition led them to be hired as "scabs" by employers seeking to destroy unions. In their first decades in the cities Italian immigrants were not as active in unions as native-born whites.

However, some later immigrants who brought radical working-class ideas with them from Italy became very active in labor unions. Some were union leaders and took part in major strikes, such as that in Lawrence, Massachusetts, in 1912. Joseph Ettor, Italian American organizer of the Industrial Workers of the World (IWW), was asked to assist textile factory workers, including Italian American women. The workers had gone on strike over reduced wages after the woolen company in Lawrence refused arbitration. The strike was sometimes violent. The state militia, made up of native-born white-collar workers, was called in, and one woman striker was killed in clashes between the militia and 25,000 strikers. The 7,000 Italian Americans were the largest nationality group among the strikers and included prominent union leaders. By the early 1900s Italian Americans were extensively involved in the union rank and file and leadership. Italian Americans have for decades been among the strongest union members.[64]

Upward Mobility

Progress for most Italian Americans came slowly but steadily. An early study of Italian workers found that as late as 1916 half were laborers, but fifteen years later only 31 percent were. Data on occupation show a decline from 33 percent in unskilled positions in 1916 to 11 percent in 1931. Small-business and skilled blue-collar positions were more common by 1931.[65]

Mobility was evident, but so was the persisting economic differential between Italian Americans and other whites. A study in Newburyport, Massachusetts, in the early 1930s revealed that Italians there were lower than other whites on the "prestige" ladder and somewhat lower on the occupational ladder. The Great Depression slowed advancement, but did not stop it. By 1939 Italian Americans had begun to supplant Jewish Americans as the major group in a number of important unions of skilled workers. They had become numerous in the garment industry and in building trades. Italian Americans paralleled the economic pattern of the Irish, moving up from unskilled to skilled blue-collar positions in a few generations.[66]

Since the 1920s organized crime has provided better-paying jobs for a few Italian Americans in northern cities, although the so-called "good citizens" of the cities, both Italians and non-Italians, were the ones who kept bootlegging, prostitution, and gambling operations going with their patronage.[67] Later, money from organized crime would flow to legitimate enterprises, just as it had earlier for other ethnic groups. Members of families successful in organized crime would move out of illegitimate enterprises altogether. This trend, according to Ianni, supports "the thesis that for Italian Americans, as for other ethnic groups, organized crime has been a way station on the road to ultimately respectable roles in American society."[68] But only a few Italian Americans ever made it up this way. The line between legitimate and illegitimate business, moreover, has often been fuzzy in this society, and not just in the case of white ethnics in organized crime. The early Anglo-Protestant "heroes of industry" were often involved in a variety of questionable economic and political activities, including illegal ones.[69]

A few Italian Americans became nationally prominent entrepreneurs and scientists. Amadeo Giannini, founder of the Bank of America, made his fortune in California financing generations of small businesses and ranches; he permitted his depositors a voice in bank management. Italian Americans such as Di Giorgio and Gallo began to play major roles in restaurant, agricultural, and contracting businesses. Scientists Enrico Fermi and Salvador Luria won Nobel Prizes. As with groups before and after them, Italian Americans also found upward mobility in sports, as is indicated by the careers of such men as Rocky Marciano and Joe DiMaggio.[70]

Recent Decades

By the 1950s further advances for Italian Americans had become evident, although not to the level of major white Protestant groups. One urban study in the 1950s suggested that second-generation Italian Catholics had yet to equal white Protestants in the proportion possessing higher-level white-collar jobs. An examination of the occupational distribution of all second-generation Italian Americans in the 1950 and 1970 censuses reveals that these children of immigrants were less likely to be found in professional and technical jobs and clerical or sales positions than the employed population as a whole. They were, however, more likely than the general population of workers to be employed as managers or officials. They were also more likely than the general population to be found in skilled blue-collar jobs.[71]

Survey data at the beginning of the 1990s showed significant mobility in the occupational distribution for Americans of Italian ancestry. A slightly smaller proportion of Italian Americans were in professional and technical occupations (17 percent) than in the white population as a whole (21 percent), but the proportion in managerial jobs was significantly larger (20 percent compared with 14 percent). The proportions of Italian Americans in white-collar, blue-collar, and service jobs were very similar to those of the white population as a whole. Although Italian Americans are still underrepresented among top corporate officials, the National Italian American Foundation reported that in 1991 some 150 Italian Americans held top- or second-ranking positions in major American companies. "Our feeling here is that Italian Americans are making a substantial impact— after a very slow century—on American corporate life." Lee Iacocca, head of Chrysler Corporation, is the best known among these.[72]

By the end of the 1960s the income level for Italian Americans was higher than that of the typical U.S. household. The 1980 census figures and survey data for the early 1990s have shown a similar pattern; Italian American families, taken as a group, had a median income somewhat higher than that of the typical American family.[73]

Some Persisting Problems

Over the last two decades discrimination against Italian Americans has some-times been a problem at the highest levels of this society. One study in the mid-1970s in northeastern cities found that Italian Americans were heavily represented among rank-and-file workers in police, fire, and sanitation departments and in public utilities but generally had weak representation in higher-level administrative positions in city departments.[74] Discrimination against Italian Americans at the City University of New York (CUNY) was documented in a 1970s study of CUNY's higher-level positions that concluded: "In decision-making positions of Dean, Director and Chair-man of the system's 18 colleges, there are only 20 Italian Americans out of a total of 504 positions."[75] A small percentage of the faculty were Italian Americans, and these tended to be at the lowest ranks. In 1975 an affirmative action program for Italian American faculty was put into place, but fifteen years later the percentage of Italian American faculty had not increased. Between the 1970s and the 1990s there was little change. At the beginning of the 1990s, Italian Americans still constituted fewer than 6 percent of CUNY's faculty in contrast with much larger percentages of the faculties at private universities in New York City. At that time CUNY's student body was about 17 percent Italian American. In the summer of 1990 CUNY professors protested discrimination in the hiring of Italian Americans in a class action complaint to the U.S. Department of Labor. In addition, CUNY's Italian Studies Advisory Council report-edly encountered discrimination when it submitted a proposal to establish a Ph.D. program in Italian that would link the study of the Italian language with the language actually spoken by Italian Americans and that would offer courses in literature written by Italian Americans. Although the council had found independent funding for the proposed program, the relevant CUNY administrators refused to read the proposal.[76]

Some exclusive residential areas and top business clubs still discriminate against Italian Americans, if subtly. Into the 1980s and 1990s some important private clubs barred Italian Americans. Italian Americans are underrepresented in the very top positions of major corporations. In certain areas, especially those with large numbers of new immigrants, poverty remains a problem. In the 1970s a few Italian American urban communities saw a growing number of poverty-stricken residents. One 1975 report found poverty rates from 15 to 18 percent among families in those New York City census tracts with 50 percent or more foreign-born Italians. Some of these poor were aged immigrants who came in the first two decades of the twentieth century; others were among the thousands who came in the late 1960s and 1970s, after earlier immigration restrictions were removed. Another example involves older Italian Americans in Boston's North End. By the 1980s this once vigorous Italian American community of 10,000 had become home to growing numbers of young non-Italian professionals who found the North End a chic place to live. Many of the older Italian residents had been forced out by gentrification and condo expansion. Economic pressures undercut the quality of life of those who remained, and many longtime community residents fell into poverty.[77]

Yet we must put these problems of poverty and discrimination in perspective. The overall picture of recent occupational and income mobility for Italian Americans, a white ethnic group oppressed on a large scale just a few decades ago, is quite impressive. At least two among them, Mario Cuomo and Lee Iacocca, have been touted as presidential candidates for the Democratic party. The majority of Italian Americans have made strides up the socioeconomic ladder, so much so that on many socioeconomic indexes they are at least at parity with Anglo-Protestants taken as a group.

EDUCATION

Organized education for Italian Americans began toward the end of the nineteenth century. Many immigrants came from areas in Italy where the poor were provided with little schooling. Half could not read or write. Like many immigrants to the United States they adopted a pragmatic approach to education, valuing it but asking, "What is the practical value of this for jobs, for later life?" Many poor families made sacrifices to get their first child through elementary school, then expected this child to help, with a job, to get later children through school.

From the start, the Protestant establishment imposed a serious obstacle for the educational advancement of Italian immigrants. As they had been with the Irish, Protestant educators were very concerned about the alleged corruption and cultural inferiority of Italian Americans. Many schools became pressure cookers of Americanization in which educators sought to teach Italian immigrants Anglo-Protestant ways as quickly as possible. Anglo-Protestant norms about health, dress, work, and language were pressed on immigrants and their children. Discrimination was a fact of life. These pressures were especially strong for second-generation children, most of whom went to public schools. (Conflict with the Irish, as well as economic problems, kept many Italian parents from sending their children to parochial schools.) Public schools were Procrustean beds shaped in Anglo-centric form. Rather than give in to hostile pressures, some children left school.[78]

In spite of such obstacles, Italian Americans made dramatic progress in educational attainment. For example, between 1950 and 1970 the median years of education completed for the native-born children of Italian immigrants rose by 1.5 years. In both 1950 and 1970 these children of immigrants had median levels of educational attainment higher than those for all persons in the United States twenty-five and over. Data from the 1980 census include all those who identified their ancestry as Italian, both the native-born and the foreign-born. In 1980 the median number of years of school completed for all adults reporting Italian ancestry was 12.3 years, compared with 12.5 years for all U.S. adults. Survey data for 1990 show a median education level of 12.5 years for Italian Americans compared with 12.4 years for all U.S. adults. Educational parity had been achieved.[79]

One analysis of survey data found that by the late 1970s only 19 percent of first- and second-generation Italian Americans had a year or more of college training compared with 42 percent of third- and fourth-generation Italian Americans. The gender imbalance in college attendance was significant: among these later generations 29 percent of the men but only 13 percent of the women were college graduates. In addition, survey data for 1990 indicated that 15 percent of all Italian Americans, men and women taken together, were college graduates.[80]

RELIGION

The Catholic church has been important in the lives of Italian Americans. In southern Italy the church was associated with an oppressive landlord system. Male peasants attended mass infrequently, primarily on ceremonial occasions; older women were the most active church members. In the United States, Protestant opposition to Catholicism presented an obstacle to the free practice of religion. Anglo-Protestant social workers in settlement houses attempted to Americanize the new Catholic population, which consisted of immigrants from southern and eastern Europe. One Protestant minister argued that "public schools, mission schools and churches will do the work to evangelize the immigrants. And it must be done, business pleads for it, patriotism demands it, social considerations require it."[81]

Many Irish Catholic churches were overwhelmed by the number of Italian immigrants. For the Italians, the Irish were too orthodox. Religion was not an intimate part of political identity for the Italian immigrant, as it was for the Irish immigrant, whose religious expression was tied to a nationalist heritage of anti-English agitation. Saints were important to Italian immigrants and their children, as were the religious festivals that played an important role in cementing the Italian community.[82]

Irish American pastors often saw the new parishioners in a negative light. They were not considered to be as serious as the Irish. Sometimes this tension escalated. Once ethnic parishes for Italian Americans had developed, they were warned away, on occasion forcefully, from Irish American parishes. Italian Americans reciprocated. Many first-generation Italian Americans preferred to send their children to public schools rather than to the Irish-dominated parochial schools, a reaction that would not be as vigorous in later generations.[83]

Gradually, Italian Catholicism, with its festivals and ceremonies, took its place alongside Irish Catholicism. By 1900 there were fourteen Italian parishes in New York, by 1924 fifty-three, and by 1961 seventy-four. The first Italian American cardinal, a second-generation Italian American, became head of the archdiocese of Chicago in 1983.[84]

A 1960s study of Italian and Irish Catholics in New York City suggested the controversial conclusion that third-generation Italians were becoming more "Irishized" in their religious practices; the data showed less emphasis on the Virgin Mary, fewer masses said for deceased relatives, and more emphasis on generous contributions to the church than in earlier generations. Tardi's late 1980s study of Italian American Catholics in New Jersey found that only about 40 percent were practicing Catholics, although the percentage was higher for the second generation than for the first or third generation. The incompatibility of the Catholic church's doctrines with real-life issues was cited as a major reason for withdrawing from the church. Among all respondents, the influence of religion in their lives was ranked as significantly weaker than the influence of the family. Catholicism today seems less central for Italian Americans than it is for Irish Americans.[85]

ASSIMILATION OR ETHNOGENESIS?

Acculturation pressures came early for southern and eastern European immigrants. Unlike the British before them, they spoke no English, nor were they familiar with the customs of Anglo-Protestant society. Often concentrated in so-called "Little Italies," Italian immigrants learned Italian dialects other than their own, and most picked up some English. Cultural adaptation was slowed by factors other than language and community: poverty, the intention of some to return home, and anti-immigrant hostility in the new environment.[86]

The first-generation family was in transition, cross-pressured between the old Italian and the new American ways. Families became less patriarchal and kin solidarity often weakened somewhat, as did ties to religion. Children were more on their own. Speaking Italian at home was sometimes a point of intergenerational conflict, since the younger members felt school pressures to speak only English.[87]

A second point of intergenerational conflict was marriage. First-generation parents saw it as a family matter, while the children tended to see it as an individual matter. Given this tension, it is not surprising that second-generation families adapted in different ways. One type abandoned the old ways, changing the Italian name and moving out of an Italian residential area. This was rare. A second type rejected the old ways in part, perhaps by moving out of Italian communities but remaining near enough to maintain close ties to the first generation. This was the largest group. A third type stayed in the old community and retained many of the old ways.[88] By the 1980s the third and fourth generations were coming into their own, and many were moving into the white multi-ethnic suburbs. At the beginning of the 1990s Italian Americans were still concentrated in the Northeast; they constituted about one-sixth of the population in several northeastern states such as New York. No longer a predominantly central-city group, they were about as likely to reside in suburbs as the average white American.

Structural Assimilation

Structural assimilation can be seen as movement into the secondary organizations—the businesses and bureaucracies—of the larger society, as well as into its primary social networks: social clubs, neighborhoods, and friendship circles. Structural movement by

Italian Americans over the first several decades came with considerable violence and resistance from earlier groups. Positioning at the lower socioeconomic levels was a fact of life for a time.

In recent decades Italian Americans have made impressive gains in employment, income, and education and advances in politics. Alba has noted that this upward educational and occupational mobility has contributed to assimilation in other areas, since Italian Americans had equal-status contact with members of other white groups in the workplace, the suburbs, and the colleges, contacts that have in turn created cross-ethnic friendship networks.[89]

The success of Italian Americans and other white ethnic groups is sometimes compared with the relative lack of success of other groups, such as black Americans. Why were the Italian Americans so successful in assimilating to core-society institutions and organizations? The answer to this question lies not just in the hard work and sacrifice of several generations of Italian Americans, for those factors are also characteristic of nonwhite Americans. It lies also in the timing of Italian immigrants' entry into the United States: jobs and housing near jobs were available to the masses of Italians who arrived in the last decades of the nineteenth century and the first decades of the twentieth century. The second and third generations emerged with enough economic support from their parents to get the education they needed for the better-paying jobs opening up during and after World War II. Expansion of jobs on the middle rungs of the occupational ladder made possible the upward mobility of many white ethnic Americans. The poverty and ethnic discrimination faced by these immigrants, although very serious, was never as thorough-going as the extreme poverty and institutionalized racial discrimination faced by such groups as black Americans.

World War II helped in another respect as well. Wartime solidarity hastened the convergence of white ethnics, including Italian Americans, in core institutions, such as the ethnically integrated units of the armed forces. In contrast, nonwhite minorities, such as black Americans and Japanese Americans, were kept in segregated units. After the war many Italian Americans took advantage of the G.I. grant programs to get educations at colleges across the U. S. At that time, black Americans were still excluded from the same white colleges.

Many Italian American families, both in the suburbs and in central cities, have remained enmeshed in kinship and friendship networks composed at least partially of other Italian Americans. Research studies have revealed the persisting importance of these networks, particularly in working-class communities. In his classic 1962 study Gans wrote about an "urban village" in Boston, a blue-collar Italian American community with intimate ties between relatives and friends. A 1975 study of Italian Americans in the Bridgeport, Connecticut, metropolitan area found a continuation of close kinship ties, particularly among the first and second generations; later generations were more likely to have non-Italian friends. However, even for the younger generations, about 80 percent of friends were Catholic.[90]

Recent research shows similarly strong informal networks. A 1985 study of Italian Americans in another northeastern city found strong family systems persisting among the several hundred people interviewed. Inmarried Italian Americans were more family-centered than those who had intermarried and than those in a sample of white Protestants.

Older Italian Americans were more likely than non-Italians to have younger relatives nearby; parents and their children had strong bonds. Although most Italian Americans in this study had non-Italian friends and co-workers, they spent much of their time with close relatives. Ninety-two percent of the inmarried respondents reported seeing parents daily or weekly, compared with 81 percent of the outmarried Italians and 71 percent of the non-Italian Protestants. Sixty-three percent saw siblings daily, compared with 32 percent of the outmarried respondents and 12 percent of the non-Italians. Ties to Italian relatives, including parents, were weaker among the intermarrieds than among the inmarrieds, but most still lived near relatives. The researcher predicted that increasing intermarriage would result in a diminishing family orientation among Italian Americans. Alba's 1984–85 study in a large metropolitan area of upstate New York found that Italian Americans were one of the most residentially concentrated of white ethnic groups. They were also more likely to name a relative as a close friend and had one of the highest rates of intraethnic friendships. And among three generations of Italian Americans in Tardi's late 1980s New Jersey study, sharing problems and needs with family members was the daily norm. Her respondents defined their Italian American ethnicity in terms of a warm and cohesive family structure that they perceived as distinctive among white ethnic groups.[91]

While kinship and primary-group ties remain strong among Italian Americans, suburbanization has shrunk formerly large ethnic enclaves. Yet even among the third and fourth generations in suburbia, Italian Americans still prefer residential clustering. A recent analysis of census tracts in New York City, Long Island, and adjacent areas of New Jersey and lower New York State found that the 2.1 million Italian Americans living there—more than one-fourth of whom were of mixed ancestry—lived in predominantly Italian American neighborhoods. These data suggest that structural assimilation at the primary level has not yet occurred for these Italian Americans.[92]

Studies of marriages in New Haven in 1870 and Chicago in 1920 found high rates of inmarriage for Italians: 94 to 98 percent of all marriages were endogamous. In subsequent decades inmarriage decreased: the New Haven figure was 77 percent by 1950. Twenty-five years later in the Bridgeport study, 84 percent of the respondents reported both of their parents were of Italian ancestry. Only 44 percent were themselves married to Italian Americans, although the rate of religious endogamy was high: most marriages outside the Italian group were with persons raised as Catholics. Exogamous marriages were more likely for those with higher-status educational and occupational achievements. By 1980, according to census data, fewer than half of Italian Americans had endogamous marriages; those under thirty with unmixed Italian ancestry had an outmarriage rate of nearly 80 percent. Even with this decline, Italian Americans in the twenty-five-to-thirty-four age group in California and Pennsylvania in 1986–87 were eight times more likely to have endogamous marriages than were non-Italian whites.[93]

Alba argues that while ethnicity is still important for the first and second generations, a transition is under way for later generations. He sees ethnicity receding for the third and fourth generations as Italian Americans become more structurally integrated into the mainstream of white America. To support his case, Alba cites the growing incidence of mixed ancestry among the younger generation: 54 percent of all Italian American respondents in his mid-1980s upstate New York study reported ethnically unmixed ancestry. Yet for those born after 1940 the proportion dropped to only one-third. Alba predicts that a much more assimilated Italian American group will emerge as the younger generations succeed the earlier ones.[94]

Across-the-board assimilation of Italian Americans is progressing although they still encounter significant stereotyping and discrimination in the larger society. Italian Americans remain underrepresented at the highest economic and political levels of U.S. society. Even Alba, who has written about the "twilight of ethnicity" among Italian Americans, has noted, "Because networks of sponsorship tend to perpetuate the ethnic patterns of the past, elite levels register only slowly the ethnic changes at lower levels, and the Italian-American gap in representation is unlikely to close anytime soon."[95]

An Italian Identity?

Identificational assimilation involves giving up one's ethnic identity for that of the core culture. For many Italian Americans this has not happened. Ethnic ties and accents are greater in older generations and among all generations in the persisting ethnic enclaves. In distinctively Italian American neighborhoods in northern cities, large numbers of older Italian Americans and new Italian immigrants of the last few decades are helping to keep alive visible cultural characteristics. Monte Carmelo, the pseudonym used in LaRuffa's study of an Italian American community in the Bronx, is an example of the durability of an Italian American enclave. Once a 100-square-block community of 28,000 Italian Americans, it is now a multi-ethnic community whose population is only one-third Italian American. Yet Monte Carmelo's vitality makes it a symbol of ethnicity far beyond the community's boundaries and a magnet for Italian Americans, including many former residents of the area, who come there to shop, socialize, hear mass in Italian, celebrate festivals, and participate in various organizations. Many of Monte Carmelo's merchants and leaders of civic and social organizations are Italian Americans who live outside the enclave yet maintain a strong commitment to preserving its ethnic identity.[96]

A sense of ethnic identity has also been found outside the ethnic enclave. Martinelli's study of first-, second-, and third-generation Italian Americans in Scottsdale, Arizona, in 1982–83 found that rather than losing their cultural identity, these respondents, almost half of whom had lived in Arizona six or fewer years, were developing a uniquely Italian American culture. Almost one-quarter reported a strong ethnic identity, and over half had a moderate ethnic identity. Sixty percent maintained daily or weekly contact with relatives locally, and a large percentage of friendships were with other Italian Americans. In the New York State study cited earlier, Italian Americans, even those of mixed ancestry, were the most likely of the various white ethnic groups to feel a sense of ethnic identity and to consider their ethnic identity as very important. Among those of mixed ancestry who identified ethnically, almost three-quarters described themselves solely as Italian American.[97]

A prominent historian of immigration, Marcus Lee Hansen, once argued that there is inevitably an increase in ethnic awareness in the third generation of an immigrant group; this substantially assimilated generation vigorously searches out its roots. Some studies of Italian Americans in the early 1970s did find greater pride in ethnicity expressed among third-generation respondents compared with earlier generations. Younger Italian Americans faced less discrimination and stereotyping than the older generations did; the assimilation of older Italian Americans made it possible for younger generations to openly express their ethnicity. However, in her New Jersey study in the late 1980s, Tardi found a strong pride in ethnic identity among Italian Americans of the first, second, *and* third generations. By that time, the structural factors associated with greater freedom to express ethnic pride, such as diminishing overt discrimination against Italian Americans and increasing numbers of prestigious and highly visible Italian Americans in public life, appear to have been affecting all generations.[98]

Micaela di Leonardo sees ethnicity as a variable, stronger in some areas than in others. Her study of Italian Americans in California found a relationship between the strength of ethnic networks and identity and the work an individual does. Most working-class Italian Americans in California no longer worked with large numbers of other Italian Americans and therefore expressed their ethnic identity differently from shopkeepers and independent professionals, who were free to stress their ethnicity in their work, often in serving an ethnic clientele. The latter groups were more likely than the former to participate in Italian American voluntary organizations and to accent the continuing cohesiveness of the Italian American community. Participation in the economy may or may not destroy ethnic identity, depending on the character of one's participation and on where one works.[99]

The ethnogenesis model of Andrew Greeley (see Chapter 2) seems to fit the Italian experience. Italians came to the United States with significant differences from the dominant British American group, but they shared some historical background and a Christian tradition with that group. Through interaction in public schools and the influence of mass media, the gap narrowed substantially, but by no means completely. Italian Americans became similar in some ways to the host culture, but in other ways they retained their distinctiveness. Because of their heritage, together with segregation and strong community and kinship networks, a distinctive U.S. ethnic group developed over time. It is no longer an Italy-centered group dominated by that heritage, nor has it simply become British Protestant American or even simply "American." It remains *Italian* and *American*. Substantial adaptation without complete assimilation currently characterizes Italian Americans.

SUMMARY

Today many descendants of the Italian immigrants who entered around the turn of the century are clustered in several northeastern states. Most remain Catholic, although many are not active in the church. These Americans have played an important role in the culture, politics, and economy of the United States. We have focused primarily on the descendants of the 1880–1920 and earlier streams of migration, examining the beginnings of this important migration and tracing its dramatic impact. Poverty and difficult working conditions greeted these immigrants. They were not prepared for the intense nativist attacks from Anglo-Protestants, who falsely stereotyped Italian Americans as an inferior, immoral, and corrupt people. Much nativist activity was aimed at proving their inferiority. The widespread Mafia myth further stigmatized Italian American communities. Even violent attacks from other white Americans were endured in many immigrant communities.

Political avenues were closed for a time; the economy consigned Italian Americans to low-paying jobs; schools tried to make carbon-copy Anglo-Protestants out of them. Yet in spite of these problems the immigrants and their descendants persevered and prospered. After World War II they began to make their mark in politics, the economy, and education. Their economic and political mobility has made them another U.S. success story, although a considerable price was often exacted for that success. Today, Italian Americans are one of the major groups in the great American drama of blending and pluralism. As a group, they have retained a significant degree of ethnic distinctiveness, ethnicity that is likely to persist for the foreseeable future.

NOTES

1. From the *New York Times*, June 17, 1970, p. 31. © 1970 by the New York Times Company. Reprinted by permission.
2. Richard Gambino, *Blood of My Blood* (Garden City, N.Y.: Doubleday, Anchor Books, 1975), p. 344.
3. Giovanni Schiavo, *The Italians in America before the Civil War* (New York: Vigo Press, 1934), pp. 55–180.
4. Ibid., p. 135.
5. Philip di Franco, *The Italian American Experience* (New York: Tom Doherty Associates, 1988), pp. 45–47.
6. U.S. Department of Justice, Immigration and Naturalization Service, *Annual Report* (Washington, 1973), pp. 52–54 (figures for 1820 to 1867 represent alien passengers arrived; for 1868–91 and 1895–97, immigrant aliens arrived; for 1892–94 and 1898–1973, immigrant aliens admitted); Schiavo, *The Italians in America*, p. 204; Carl Wittke, *We Who Built America*, rev. ed. (Cleveland: Case Western Reserve University Press, 1964), p. 441; Humbert S. Nelli, *The Italians in Chicago, 1880–1930* (New York: Oxford University Press, 1970), p. 5; Grazia Dore, "Some Social and Historical Aspects of Italian Emigration to America," in *The Italians*, ed. Francesco Cordasco and Eugene Bucchioni (Clifton, N.J.: Augustus M. Kelley, 1974), p. 7.
7. Joseph Lopreato, *Italian Americans* (New York: Random House, 1970), pp. 23–27; John S. MacDonald, "Agricultural Organization, Migration, and Labor Militancy in Rural Italy," *Economic History Review*, 2d ser., 16 (1963–64): 61–75. We are indebted to Phyllis Cancilla Martinelli for her useful suggestions concerning the sections that follow. We draw on her suggestions in this paragraph and in the rest of this chapter.
8. Luciano J. Iorizzo and Salvatore Mondello, *The Italian-Americans* (New York: Twayne, 1971), pp. 57–59; Michael La Sorte, *La Merica* (Philadelphia: Temple University Press, 1985), pp. 1–13, 189–202.
9. Antonia Stella, *Some Aspects of Italian Immigration to the United States*, reprint ed. (San Francisco: R & E Associates, 1970), p. 33; Rudolph J. Vecoli, "Contadini in Chicago," in *Divided Society*, ed. Colin Greer (New York: Basic Books, 1974), p. 220.
10. William Petersen, *Population*, 2d ed. (New York: Macmillan, 1969), p. 260; La Sorte, *La Merica*, pp. 189–202.
11. John Higham, *Strangers in the Land*, rev. ed. (New York: Atheneum, 1975), pp. 312–24.
12. Stanley Lieberson, *Ethnic Patterns in American Cities* (Glencoe, Ill.: Free Press, 1963), pp. 209–18; La Sorte, *La Merica*, pp. 61–158.
13. William F. Whyte, *Street Corner Society*, 2d ed. (Chicago: University of Chicago Press, 1955), pp. 272–73; Walter Firey, *Land Use in Central Boston* (Cambridge: Harvard University Press, 1947), pp. 187–88; Wittke, *We Who Built America*, p. 446.
14. Firey, *Land Use in Central Boston*, p. 193; Paul J. Campisi, "Ethnic Family Patterns: The Italian Family in the United States," in *The Italians*, ed. Cordasco and Bucchioni, pp. 311–14; Lopreato, *Italian Americans*, pp. 51–53; Whyte, *Street Corner Society*, p. 274.
15. Eliot Lord, John J. D. Trenor, and Samuel J. Barrows, *The Italian in America*, reprint ed. (San Francisco: R & E Associates, 1970), pp. 17–18.
16. Quoted in Iorizzo and Mondello, *The Italian-Americans*, p. 64.
17. Kenneth L. Roberts, *Why Europe Leaves Home*, excerpted in "Kenneth L. Roberts and the Threat of Mongrelization in America, 1922," in *In Their Place*, ed. Lewis H. Carlson and George A. Colburn (New York: John Wiley, 1972), p. 312.
18. Mary F. Matthews, "The Role of the Public School in the Assimilation of the Italian Immigrant Child in New York City, 1900–1914," in *The Italian Experience in the United States*, ed. Silvano Tomasi and M. H. Engel (New York: Center for Migration Studies, 1970), p. 127; Stella, *Some Aspects of Italian Immigration*, pp. 38, 54.
19. Cited in Leon J. Kamin, *The Science and Politics of I.Q.* (New York: John Wiley, 1974), pp. 15–16.
20. Ibid., pp. 16–19.
21. Carl C. Brigham, *A Study of American Intelligence* (Princeton, N.J.: Princeton University Press, 1923), especially pp. 124–25 and 177–210. Later Brigham recanted.
22. See Roberts, *Why Europe Leaves Home*; for earlier views see Woodrow Wilson, *A History of the American People* (New York: Harper, 1902), 5:212–14.
23. See Kamin, *The Science and Politics of I.Q.*, p. 30.
24. Quoted in E. Digby Baltzell, *The Protestant Establishment* (New York: Random House, Vintage Books, 1966), p. 30.
25. Quoted in ibid.
26. Iorizzo and Mondello, *The Italian-Americans*, pp. 35–36; quotation cited in Nelli, *The Italians in Chicago*, p. 126.

27. Stella, *Some Aspects of Italian Immigration*, pp. 60–61, 73.
28. di Franco, *The Italian American Experience*, pp. 84–86; Gambino, *Blood of My Blood*, pp. 293–98; Lopreato, *Italian Americans*, p. 126; Nelli, *The Italians in Chicago*, pp. 154–55.
29. Mary C. Waters, *Ethnic Options: Choosing Identities in America* (Berkeley: University of California Press, 1990), pp. 142–43.
30. Gambino, *Blood of My Blood*, pp. 300–301; Selwyn Raab, "The Mob in Decline," *New York Times*, October 22, 1990, p. A1.
31. Robert Lichter and Linda Lichter, "Italian-American Characters in Television Entertainment" (report prepared for the Commission for Social Justice, Order of Sons of Italy, May 1982).
32. Quotation cited in Micaela di Leonardo, *The Varieties of Ethnic Experience* (Ithaca, N.Y.: Cornell University Press, 1984), pp. 160–61; Susanna Tardi, *Family and Society: The Case of the Italians in New Jersey* (Ann Arbor, Mich.: UMI Dissertation Service, 1991), p. 189.
33. Donna Haupt, Jan Mason, and Penny Ward Moser, "The Embattled Queen of Queens," *Time*, October 1, 1984, p. 34; Vivienne Walt, "Cuomo: Hurt by Prejudice toward Italians," *Newsday*, July 23, 1991, p. 19; Vivienne Walt, "Local Pols Still Wild about Bill," *Newsday*, January 30, 1992, p. 8.
34. Richard D. Alba, *Ethnic Identity* (New Haven: Yale University Press, 1990), pp. 141–42; Waters, *Ethnic Options*, pp. 142–43.
35. William F. Whyte, "Race Conflicts in the North End of Boston," *New England Quarterly* 12 (December 1939): 626; Iorizzo and Mondello, *The Italian-Americans*, pp. 35, 66.
36. Luciano J. Iorizzo, "The Padrone and Immigrant Distribution," in *The Italian Experience in the United States*, ed. Tomasi and Engel, pp. 49–51; Gambino, *Blood of My Blood*, p. 119; Higham, *Strangers in the Land*, p. 169.
37. di Franco, *The Italian American Experience*, p. 85; Gambino, *Blood of My Blood*, pp. 118, 280–81; quotation cited in Gambino, *Blood of My Blood*, p. 118.
38. Gambino, *Blood of My Blood*, pp. 104, 119; Higham, *Strangers in the Land*, p. 90. See also Andrew F. Rolle, *The American Italian* (Belmont, Calif.: Wadsworth, 1972).
39. See, for example, William Young and David E. Kaiser, *Postmortem* (Amherst: University of Massachusetts Press, 1985). See also a work from the 1970s, Gambino, *Blood of My Blood*, pp. 120–21.
40. Iorizzo and Mondello, *The Italian-Americans*, p. 207; Gerald D. Suttles, *The Social Order of the Slum* (Chicago: University of Chicago Press, 1968), pp. 102–3; Richard Krickus, *Pursuing the American Dream* (Garden City, N.Y.: Doubleday, Anchor Books, 1976), p. 280.
41. Curtis Rist, "Prosecutor: Race Riot in Bensonhurst," *Newsday*, April 17, 1990, p. 4.
42. Cited in Mark R. Levy and Michael S. Kramer, *The Ethnic Factor* (New York: Simon & Schuster, 1972), p. 174.
43. National Opinion Research Center, General Social Surveys, 1989 and 1990. Tabulations by authors.
44. Schiavo, *The Italians in America before the Civil War*, pp. 163–66.
45. Nelli, *The Italians in Chicago*, pp. 75–76; Wittke, *We Who Built America*, p. 447; Lopreato, *Italian Americans* 4, pp. 113–17; Giovanni Schiavo, *Italian American History* (New York: Vigo Press, 1947), 1:499–504.
46. See Gambino, *Blood of My Blood*, p. 117.
47. Rolle, *The American Italian*, p. 85; William F. Whyte, *Street Corner Society*, p. 276; Samuel Lubell, *The Future of American Politics*, 2d ed. (Garden City, N.Y.: Doubleday, Anchor Books, 1955), p. 70; Lopreato, *Italian Americans*, p. 114; di Franco, *The Italian American Experience*, pp. 139–59.
48. Joel H. Spring, *Education and the Rise of the Corporate State* (Boston: Beacon Press, 1972), pp. 86–87.
49. Herbert J. Gans, *The Urban Villagers* (Glencoe, Ill.: Free Press, 1962), pp. 285–87.
50. di Franco, *The Italian American Experience*, pp. 146–47; Salvatore J. LaGumina, "Case Studies of Ethnicity and Italo-American Politicians," in *The Italian Experience in the United States*, ed. Tomasi and Engel, p. 147; Krickus, *Pursuing the American Dream*, pp. 174–81.
51. Wittke, *We Who Built America*, p. 450; Iorizzo and Mondello, *The Italian-Americans*, pp. 200–205, 208; Gambino, *Blood of My Blood*, p. 316.
52. Richard Alba, *Italian Americans* (Englewood Cliffs, N.J.: Prentice-Hall, 1985), pp. 78–81.
53. Lubell, *The Future of American Politics*, pp. 70, 83–84; LaGumina, "Case Studies of Ethnicity and Italo-American Politics," p. 145.
54. Alba, *Italian Americans*, p. 143; General Social Surveys, 1989 and 1990. See also Andrew M. Greeley, *Ethnicity in the United States* (New York: John Wiley, 1974), pp. 94–101.
55. Krickus, *Pursuing the American Dream*, p. 92; Sylvia Pellini Macphee, *Changing Perspectives of Italian Americans* (Cambridge, Mass.: Center for Community Economic Development, 1974), pp. 10–15.
56. Iorizzo, "The Padrone and Immigrant Distribution," p. 43.
57. di Franco, *The Italian American Experience*, pp. 139–41; Nelli, *The Italians in Chicago*, pp. 56–60, 64–66; anonymous, "The Philanthropists' View of the Italian in America," in *The Italian in America: The Progressive View*, ed. Lydio F. Tomasi (New York: Center for Migration Studies, 1972), p. 79 (this article is reprinted by Tomasi from *Charities*, an early journal of social and settlement workers); Iorizzo and Mondello, *The Italian-Americans*, pp. 138–58.
58. Stella, *Some Aspects of Italian Immigration*, p. 94.
59. Nelli, *The Italians in Chicago*, pp. 13–14; Antonio Stella, "Tuberculosis and the Italians in the United States," in *The Italians*, ed. Cordasco and Bucchioni, pp. 449ff.
60. Gambino, *Blood of My Blood*, p. 85; Leonard Covello, "The Influence of Southern Italian Family Mores upon the School Situation in America," in *The Italians*, ed. Cordasco and Bucchioni, p. 513; Lord, Trenor, and Barrows, *The Italian in America*, pp. 16–19; E. P. Hutchinson, *Immigrants and Their Children, 1850–1950* (New York: John Wiley, 1956), pp. 137–38.
61. Higham, *Strangers in the Land*, p. 48.

62. Gambino, *Blood of My Blood*, p. 77.
63. Stephan Thernstrom, *The Other Bostonians* (Cambridge: Harvard University Press, 1973), p. 161.
64. Elizabeth Gurley Flynn, "The Lawrence Textile Strike," in *America's Working Women*, ed. R. Baxandall, L. Gordon, and S. Reverby (New York: Random House, Vintage Books, 1976), pp. 194–99; Nelli, *The Italians in Chicago*, pp. 78–85; Gambino, *Blood of My Blood*, pp. 115–17.
65. John J. d'Alesandre, "Occupational Trends of Italians in New York City," *Italy-America Monthly* 2 (February 1935): 11–21.
66. W. Lloyd Warner and Leo Srole, *The Social Systems of American Ethnic Groups* (New Haven: Yale University Press, 1945), pp. 96–97; Gambino, *Blood of My Blood*, p. 101; Wittke, *We Who Built America*, p. 443.
67. Nelli, *The Italians in Chicago*, pp. 211–14; Smith, *The Mafia Mystique*, p. 322.
68. Ianni, *A Family Business*, p. 193.
69. Smith, *The Mafia Mystique*, p. 323.
70. Rolle, *The American Italians*, pp. 89–93.
71. Thernstrom, *The Other Bostonians*, p. 171; U.S. Bureau of the Census, *U.S. Census of Population, 1950: Special Reports—Nativity and Parentage*, P–E No. 3A (Washington, 1954), p. 155; U.S. Bureau of the Census, *U.S. Census of Population, 1970: Subject Reports—National Origin and Language*, PC(2)-1A (Washington, 1973), p. 166.
72. General Social Surveys, 1989 and 1990; personal correspondence with Dr. Alfred Rotondaro, executive director of the National Italian American Foundation, June 12, 1991. The percent "professional" runs higher in survey than census data.
73. U.S. Bureau of the Census, *U.S. Census of Population, 1970: Subject Reports—National Origin and Language*, p. 167; U.S. Bureau of the Census, *U.S. Census of Population, 1970: General Social and Economic Characteristics*, Final Report PC(1)-C1, United States Summary (Washington, 1972), pp. 177, 368; General Social Surveys, 1989 and 1990.
74. Gambino, *Blood of My Blood*, p. 89.
75. *National Center for Urban Ethnic Affairs Newsletter 1*, no. 5 (1976): 8.
76. Robert Viscusi, "Giving the Boot to Italians," *Newsday*, May 30, 1991, p. 74.
77. Congress of Italian-American Organizations, *A Portrait of the Italian-American Community in New York City* (New York, 1975), pp. 7–10, 49–51; "Ferraro's Mixed Blessing," *Newsweek*, October 1, 1984, p. 12.
78. Lawrence A. Cremin, *The Transformation of the School* (New York: Knopf, 1961), pp. 67–68; Colin Greer, *The Great School Legend* (New York: Basic Books, 1972), pp. 3–6.
79. U.S. Bureau of the Census, *U.S. Census of Population, 1950: Special Reports—Nativity and Parentage*, p. 155; U.S. Bureau of the Census, *U.S. Census of Population, 1950: Vol. II, Characteristics of the Population*, Part 1, United States Summary (Washington, 1953), p. 96; U.S. Bureau of the Census, *U.S. Census of Population, 1970: Subject Reports—National Origin and Language*, p. 165; U.S. Bureau of the Census, *U.S. Census of Population, 1970: General Social and Economic Characteristics*, p. 368; U.S. Bureau of the Census, *U.S. Census of Population, 1980: General Social and Economic Characteristics*, PC 80-1-C1 (Washington, 1983), pp. 21, 172; General Social Surveys, 1989 and 1990. The 1950 ancestry figures are for persons fourteen and older.
80. Alba, *Italian Americans*, pp. 120–21; General Social Surveys, 1989 and 1990.
81. Quoted in Silvano M. Tomasi, "The Ethnic Church and the Integration of Italian Immigrants in the United States," in *The Italian Experience in the United States*, ed. Tomasi and Engel, p. 168.
82. Rudolph J. Vecoli, "Contadini in Chicago: A Critique of the Uprooted," in *The Aliens*, ed. Leonard Dinnerstein and Frederic C. Jaher (New York: Appleton-Century-Crofts, 1970), p. 226; Harold J. Abramson, *Ethnic Diversity in Catholic America* (New York: John Wiley, 1973), pp. 136–39.
83. Tomasi, "The Ethnic Church," p. 167.
84. Ibid., pp. 187–88; Nelli, *The Italians in Chicago*, p. 195; di Franco, *The Italian American Experience*, pp. 269–70.
85. Nicholas J. Russo, "Three Generations of Italians in New York City: Their Religious Acculturation," in *The Italian Experience in the United States*, ed. Tomasi and Engel, pp. 200–206; Tardi, *Family and Society*, pp. 145–53.
86. Covello, "The Influence of Southern Italian Family Mores," p. 515.
87. Paul J. Campisi, "Ethnic Family Patterns: The Italian Family in the United States," *American Journal of Sociology* 53 (May 1948): 443–49; Covello, "The Influence of Southern Italian Family Mores," pp. 525–30.
88. Irvin L. Child, *Italian or American?* (New Haven: Yale University Press, 1943) (an important excerpt from this book can be found in *The Italians*, ed. Cordasco and Bucchioni, pp. 321–36); Alba, *Italian Americans*, p. 114.
89. Alba, *Italian Americans*, p. 166.
90. Herbert Gans, *The Urban Villagers*, rev. ed. (New York: Free Press, 1982), pp. 412–13; Greeley, *Why Can't They Be Like Us?* (New York: Dutton, 1971), p. 77. See also Phyllis Cancilla Martinelli, "Beneath the Surface: Ethnic Communities in Phoenix, Arizona" (paper, Arizona State University, 1980); James A. Crispino, *The Assimilation of Ethnic Groups: The Italian Case* (New York: Center for Migration Studies, 1980), pp. 80–86.
91. Colleen L. Johnson, *Growing Up and Growing Old in Italian American Families* (New Brunswick, N.J.: Rutgers University Press, 1985), pp. 221–28; Richard D. Alba, *Ethnic Identity* (New Haven: Yale University Press, 1990), pp. 47–48, 59–61, 70–71, 224–26; Tardi, *Family and Society*, pp. 179–92.
92. Anthony L. LaRuffa, *Monte Carmelo: An Italian-American Community in the Bronx* (New York: Gordon & Breach, 1988), pp. 135–39.
93. Francis X. Femminella and Jill S. Quadagno, "The Italian American Family," in *Ethnic Families in America*, ed. Charles H. Mindel and Robert W. Habenstein (New York: Elsevier, 1976), pp. 74–75; Ruby Jo Reeves Kennedy, "Single or Triple Melting Pot? Intermarriage in New Haven, 1870–1950," *American Journal of Sociology* 58 (July 1952): 56–59; Nelli, *The Italians in Chicago*, p. 196; Crispino, *The Assimilation of Ethnic Groups*, p. 105; Alba, *Italian Americans*, pp. 146–47; Waters, *Ethnic Options*, p. 104.
94. Alba, *Italian Americans*, pp. 159–62; Alba, *Ethnic Identity*, p. 47.
95. Alba, *Italian Americans*, p. 162.
96. LaRuffa, *Monte Carmelo*, pp. 17–28.

97. Phyllis Cancilla Martinelli, *Ethnicity in the Sunbelt* (New York: AMS Press, 1989), pp. 234–58; Alba, *Ethnic Identity*, pp. 59–60, 70.

98. Marcus Lee Hansen, "The Third Generation," in *Children of the Uprooted*, ed. Oscar Handlin (New York: Harper & Row, 1966), pp. 255–71; P.J. Gallo, *Ethnic Alienation* (Rutherford, N.J.: Fairleigh Dickinson University Press, 1974), p. 194; John M. Goering, "The Emergence of Ethnic Interests," *Social Forces* 49 (March 1971): 381–82; Tardi, *Family and Society*, pp. 179–92.

99. di Leonardo, *The Varieties of Ethnic Experience*, p. 156.

Chapter 6

Jewish Americans

Lighting of the candles for Chanukah
Photo by Pinnex ©1972. Courtesy of Monkmeyer Press Photo Service

Jews have been scapegoats for the hatreds of dominant peoples around the globe for thousands of years. From the Egyptian and Roman persecutions in ancient times, to the massacres and expulsions in Spain in the late 1400s, to the brutal pogroms of the Russian czar in the 1880s, to the German Nazi massacres, Jews might be regarded as the most consistently and widely persecuted ethnic group in world history. Residing in many lands, the continually harassed ancestors of Jewish Americans forged distinctive traditions. Indeed, the intellectual pillars of modern civilization—Karl Marx, Sigmund Freud, and Albert Einstein—were Jewish.

Jewish Americans have contributed much to the success of this nation—as pioneers in trade and commerce, workers in industry, professionals, government officials, and entertainers. They have benefited from a political structure that separates church and state and prohibits religious qualifications for holding public office. Jewish immigrants have come from countries in which they were clearly outsiders, prohibited from owning land and subjected to government-sponsored persecutions and mass murder. In the United States, Alan Dershowitz points out in his book, *Chutzpah,* "the Jews did not have to evaluate every single event by reference to their own survival."[1] For the most part U.S. law never became the enemy of the Jews. Still, more than any other white ethnic group, Jewish Americans have often been treated as outsiders in the United States.

By tradition, Jewish ethnicity is based on matrilineal ancestry: a Jew is a person whose mother is Jewish. In the contemporary United States many Jewish writers define Jews as those who identify themselves as Jews. Some Jewish Americans have focused their identity primarily on their religion; others have defined their Jewishness primarily in terms of group membership. Given the many changes experienced by Jewish Americans over the past quarter century, a major question among many Jewish writers today is if, and if so on what basis, Jewish identity will survive in the United States.[2]

MIGRATION

From 1500 to World War II

The earliest Jewish settlers came as individuals to the Atlantic Coast colonies in the 1600s seeking economic opportunities denied to them in their European countries of origin. The first Jewish community in North America dates from the arrival in 1654 of twenty-three Jews fleeing the Catholic Inquisition in Portuguese-controlled Brazil. Most of these were Sephardic Jews, those whose background was the Jewish subculture of Spain. Having been refused entry at their intended destination, the Spanish-controlled Caribbean islands, these refugees faced resistance in New Amsterdam on the grounds that they would present unwelcomed economic competition. They were grudgingly allowed to settle and later given the right to own land and engage in trade.[3]

Over the next hundred years small numbers of descendants of Marranos—Jews who had been forced to publicly convert to Christianity during the Spanish Inquisition under threat of death but who privately maintained allegiance to Judaism—came to the colonies. These were mostly urbane and cosmopolitan merchants and traders whose lives prior to immigration had not been confined to Jewish ghettos. In port cities from New York to Georgia they established small Jewish American communities organized around Orthodox synagogues, but their life outside the communities was characterized by substantial cultural assimilation—in language, dress, and manners. Occasionally they even married with other white ethnic Americans.[4]

Immigration of the more traditional Ashkenazi Jews (those from England, Germany, and Poland) began in the early 1700s, and soon this group outnumbered Sephardic Jews. Many were attracted by reports of economic prosperity in the United States. For the most part the new immigrants integrated into the Sephardic communities and adopted their acculturated practices. Estimates of the American Jewish population at the time of the American Revolution range from 1,000 to 2,500—a very small percentage of the total population of the colonies.[5]

After 1820 immigration of central European Jews increased dramatically in response to declining economic conditions and increased anti-Semitism in Europe and economic expansion in the United States. These immigrants have often been called "German Jews," although their countries of origin included Bohemia and Moravia as well as Germany. Hertzberg notes that the typical Jewish immigrant in the 1830s and later was a single male, the poorly educated younger son of a cattle dealer or peddler who had no prospects in the impoverished, overpopulated regions of central Europe where the number of Jewish households was not allowed to increase. This stream of immigrants included peddlers, merchants, and craft workers from small towns. Many settled in the Midwest, Far West, and South, and by 1860 Jewish American communities and synagogues had been established in many cities. Such geographic mobility facilitated acculturation. By 1880 most Jewish Americans were of central European descent. The size of the Jewish population grew from 15,000 in the early 1840s to about 170,000 by 1870.[6]

Eastern European Jews, the third and largest group of Jewish immigrants, began to arrive in 1870. These immigrants are often called the "Russian Jews" because the overwhelming majority came from Russia or Russian-controlled areas, where overpopulation, poverty, and lack of economic opportunities were the major push factors. In Russia in the 1880s, government-sponsored massacres, called *pogroms,* affected all social classes of Jews and contributed to an increase in emigration. The poor and the less well educated were the most likely to leave for America. German Jews, who were largely acculturated by the time the eastern European immigrants began to arrive, often felt their position in mainstream society threatened by the newcomers. Still, during the 1903–1905 Russian pogroms German Jews in the United States provided assistance for the large numbers of new immigrants and fought against immigration restrictions.[7]

Jewish immigration from 1881 to the mid-1920s totaled approximately 2.5 million, with most coming between 1890 and 1914 and in the five years following World War I. By 1914 there were ten times as many Jewish Americans of eastern European descent as there were of German descent. By the mid-1920s Jewish Americans composed 3.5 percent of the U.S. population. Unlike earlier Jewish immigrants, eastern European Jews constituted a large proportion of all immigrants during this period. And unlike some non-Jewish European immigrants of this period, almost none of the eastern European Jews returned home. Most settled in large East Coast cities. As peddlers, street vendors, and unskilled workers they became part of the growing urban communities. These new immigrants brought with them a distinctive language and culture (both Yiddish), a strong sense of Jewish identity, some Orthodox religious observances, and a determination to succeed in their new homeland.[8]

After the restrictive 1924 Immigration Act, an act aimed at limiting eastern and southern European immigration, the numbers of Jewish newcomers declined rapidly. Between 1921 and 1936 fewer than 400,000 Jewish immigrants entered the country. During the Great Depression the number of immigrants from all parts of the globe was sharply reduced. President Franklin Roosevelt's administration did permit some increase in Jewish refugees from Germany after the Nazi persecution became known, yet Roosevelt, and particularly his State Department, did much less than they could have to allow Jews to flee to the United States. The obstacles to Jewish immigration were a disgrace: the U.S. State Department adopted the callous policy of requiring affidavits of financial solvency and good character and used visa regulations to slow the flow of refugees fleeing the threat of Adolf Hitler's death camps. In June 1940 the State Department put an end to most immigration from Germany and central Europe. Because of these actions more than 400,000 slots within U.S. immigration quotas for refugees from countries under Nazi control were left unused between 1933 and 1943. These unfilled quotas may represent lives lost to extermination by the Nazis because of U.S. immigration policy.[9]

The 150,000 refugees who did manage to enter between 1935 and the early 1940s included many highly talented people. One-fifth were professionals, and many of the rest had trade skills. They set up businesses from New York to San Francisco; contrary to the prevailing stereotype, they were no burden on their new homeland. Among these refugees were some of the world's most able scientists and artists—among the former were Albert Einstein, Leo Szilard, and Edward Teller, all of whom played a critical role in the U.S. nuclear research program—and scholars such as Eric Fromm, Herbert Marcuse, and Bruno Bettelheim.

World War II to the Present

After the arrival of thousands of postwar refugees, Jewish migration again tapered off significantly to an estimated 8,000 annually in the 1950s and 1960s. By the 1970s a significant number of Israelis—estimated at 100,000 or more—had come to the United States. Large numbers were "illegals." Between 1966 and 1982 nearly 250,000 Soviet Jews left their country. Prior to 1975 most went to Israel, but by the late 1970s most were coming to the United States. By 1980 nearly 100,000 had entered. The cost of helping the immigrants was borne largely by the American Jewish community. In a survey of these immigrants, most said they were proud of their Jewish heritage and had left the Soviet Union because of fear of anti-Semitism.[10]

Since World War II many Jewish Americans have participated in the migration from cities to suburbs, and the proportions living in the South and West have about doubled. For example, a late 1980s survey of the Rhode Island Jewish community revealed the impact of migration from the Northeast. The population in the largest urban area, Greater Providence, had dropped about a fifth since the early 1960s, and the state's Jewish population had also declined. The average age for Rhode Island's Jewish population had risen because of declining birthrates and out-migration of the young.[11]

In 1990 the National Jewish Population Survey (NJPS) estimated the American Jewish population at more than 6.8 million—half the world's Jewish population. This figure included 5.5 million religious and secular Jews and 1.3 million (mostly the children of mixed-ethnic marriages) with some Jewish ancestry. More than 90 percent of the American Jewish population were born in the United States. Forty percent lived in the Northeast, about one-quarter each in the South and the West, and the rest in the Midwest. Just under half the adults were of Ashkenazi origin, and 8 percent were of Sephardic origin; most of the rest were unsure of their background. Although the American Jewish community has declined as a percentage of the total population since the peak year of 1937, Glazer suggests that its "institutions are on the whole more extensive and stronger than in the 1930s, and Jewish political strength is substantially greater."[12]

STEREOTYPING AND PREJUDICE

Jewish Americans have been socially defined by outsiders on the basis of both real or alleged physical and cultural characteristics. In the early 1900s, in the 1930s and 1940s, and even to the present, they have been considered by some non-Jews to be a biologically inferior "race."[13] No white group in history has suffered under a broader range of stereotypes for a longer period than have the Jews. For centuries, Jews have been targets for intensely held prejudices, hostile attitudes, and discriminatory behavior, collectively known as *anti-Semitism*. For almost two thousand years the writings and liturgies of Christendom have been rife with anti-Semitism. Many Christians have held Jews as a group culpable for the death of their Christ; Jews have been cursed and killed as "Christ killers." (Ironically, Jesus himself was a Jew.) From the earliest colonial period, Christian groups in North America brought the "Christ killers" view with them. Many Christian ministers and priests passed along these views to each new generation.[14]

Anti-Semitism has accented a number of other themes. One cliché is that many Jews are examples of economic deviousness. Unlike African Americans and Native Americans, who are frequently stereotyped by whites as unintelligent, Jewish Americans have been seen as too hardworking, too intelligent, and too crafty. McWilliams has suggested that this "devious" stereotype developed to rationalize the American Jews' relative success as "middleman" merchants and brokers.[15]

Although some early political leaders, such as John Adams, wrote tributes to the achievements of Jewish Americans, positive comments did not predominate in the next few generations. Even Adams's grandson, the intellectual Henry Adams, upset with the rapidly industrializing United States, was anti-Semitic. For him the Jewish American was a symbol of the materialistic world he disliked; Jewish Americans became the scapegoats for angry members of the old-money Protestant elite whose social position, based on ancestry, had been taken over by the newly wealthy (and non-Jewish) captains of industry.[16]

The crude stereotype of Jewish Americans as social climbers became the subject of frequent parodies in the media, including vaudeville, after the Civil War. Clumsy Jewish figures speaking inflected English were depicted in high-society positions. By the 1880s newspaper and magazine cartoons were caricaturing Jewish Americans as long-nosed, garishly dressed merchants speaking broken English. It was also during this period that Jews began to be excluded from many areas of life. In 1877 a prominent Jewish American banker was denied accommodation in a major hotel. The following year a Jewish American was excluded from the New York City Bar Association, and New York's City College banned Jewish Americans from Greek-letter fraternities. In a growing number of contexts, Jewish Americans were officially classified as outsiders.[17]

In subsequent decades stereotypes of Jewish Americans as radicals or "Communist" sympathizers appeared in political cartoons in the mass media. A common allegation was that "Jews were taking over the government." By 1941 hatred of Jewish Americans had risen to a fever pitch. They were falsely accused by members of Congress, the press, and prominent citizens of bringing the United States into war with Germany. A World War II social science study reported in the book *The Authoritarian Personality* found substantial support among samples of non-Jewish Californians for crude stereotypes of Jews as revolutionary, clannish, and parasitic. After World War II a *Fortune* magazine poll found that three-quarters of non-Jewish Americans who felt some groups had more power than was good for the country's economy cited the Jews.[18]

Much evidence confirms the persistence of anti-Semitism today among non-Jewish Americans. The president of a major Baptist organization publicly stated that God does not hear the prayers of Jews, and a leader of the conservative Moral Majority group repeated the age-old stereotype that Jews had a "supernatural" ability to make money. Gary Tobin has reported that interviews with Jewish Americans in a number of metropolitan areas at various times in the 1980s revealed a significant incidence of anti-Semitism, typically encounters with negative references or remarks. Between 17 and 28 percent of the respondents reported such experiences during the year prior to their interview. The rate was much higher for young adults: over half of those in Kansas City and Atlantic City, 40 percent in St. Louis, and 46 percent in Washington, D.C.[19]

Some older Jewish Americans who experienced hostility, discrimination, and exclusion during the early decades of this century feel that the relatively better current situation is proof that anti-Semitism is no longer a significant problem. Charles Silberman points to the many successes of Jewish Americans and the access they have to most areas of this society. Others, particularly members of the younger generation, are more skeptical. Dershowitz discusses a number of social phenomena that constitute a new variety of anti-Semitism. The "new strains of the old virus" include anti-Zionism and the application of higher standards of moral and political conduct for Israel and Jews in general than for other nations or ethnic groups.[20] More than two-thirds of all respondents to the previously cited 1990 NJPS considered anti-Semitism to be a serious and continuing problem in the United States. Respondents identifying as religious felt anti-Semitism the most keenly.[21]

OPPRESSION AND CONFLICT

The pogroms and various acts of discrimination and exclusion experienced by Jewish immigrants in their European homelands led to what has been called an "oppression mentality" for many Jewish Americans, the acute awareness that anti-Jewish oppression "can always happen again." And indeed violent anti-Semitism has occurred in the United States. In the 1880s Jewish American merchants in the South suffered violent attacks from non-Jewish farmers who blamed them for economic crises. In the 1890s the farms and homes of Jewish

American landlords and merchants were burned in Mississippi. In the early 1900s riots erupted against Jewish American workers brought into factories in New Jersey. Just before World War I in Georgia, Leo Frank, the Jewish part-owner of a pencil factory, was convicted of killing a girl employee, though evidence pointed elsewhere. After being beaten up in prison, he was taken from the prison hospital and lynched by an angry white mob.[22]

Southern demagogues such as Tom Watson used the Frank case to fuel the flames of anti-Semitism for political purposes. About this time the Ku Klux Klan was revived; it proceeded to wage violence against black, Jewish, and Catholic Americans. In the 1920s and 1930s crosses were burned on Jewish property; synagogues were desecrated and vandalized. On occasion, the victims fought back. In the 1920s Jewish and Catholic immigrants attacked parades and gatherings of the Ku Klux Klan in Ohio and New Jersey.[23]

Organized Anti-Semitism

Between 1932 and 1941 the number of openly anti-Semitic regional and nationwide organizations grew from only one to well over a hundred. Two dozen were large-scale operations holding numerous anti-Semitic rallies, some drawing thousands. Millions of anti-Semitic leaflets, pamphlets, and newspapers were distributed. Among the more prominent groups were the German-American Bund and the Silver Shirts. Father Charles Coughlin's organizations, the National Union for Social Justice and the Christian Front, became active in anti-Jewish agitation in the 1930s.[24] Early in 1940 the FBI arrested more than a dozen members of a Christian Front group reportedly intending to kill "Jews and Communists, 'to knock off about a dozen Congressmen,' and to seize post offices, the Customs House, and armories in New York. In the homes of the group were found 18 cans of cordite, 18 rifles, and 5,000 rounds of ammunition."[25] Coughlin himself did not openly advocate violence, but he defended those who did.

Increased anti-Semitism in Nazi Germany was an important factor in the rising number of neo-Nazi attacks against Jewish Americans in the United States. German Gentiles had long portrayed their Jewish neighbors in terms of negative stereotypes. The Nazi Holocaust began with restrictions on Jewish communities in the Nazi sphere, soon to be followed by deportation to forced-labor camps and extermination by starvation and mass killings. An estimated six million European Jews were killed. Extermination and forced migration reduced the Jewish population in countries such as Poland and Germany to 10 percent of their former numbers. In the United States the sense of oppression among Jewish Americans was reinforced not only by newspaper reports of European refugees but also by the growing knowledge that the U.S. government was aiding these actions in Germany, at first by continuing normal economic and diplomatic relations and later by turning its back on thousands of refugees.[26]

Violent attacks on Jewish Americans, their property, and their synagogues were common after World War II. More than forty major incidents were reported in 1945–46 in the United States, and there have been numerous attacks each year since. The Anti-Defamation League (ADL) publishes an annual report on anti-Semitic incidents. Only the most blatant instances of anti-Semitism are reported to the ADL; personal experiences of discrimination are usually not reported. The ADL's first survey (1979) included 129 reported cases of vandalism, such as attempted arson and the painting of swastikas on tombstones or synagogues. Between 1979 and 1984 a total of 3,694 incidents was reported. The numbers increased in the late 1980s and early 1990s. A record 1,897 incidents were reported for 1991—up 11 percent over 1990. The 1991 incidents included 950 attacks on individuals and 49 acts of vandalism against Jewish-owned property (arson, bombings, and cemetery desecrations). Among these incidents, 101 occurred at sixty college campuses. Several state legislatures have passed laws making these religious desecrations special crimes, and dozens of people have been arrested for such attacks.[27]

Attacks on black and Jewish Americans by the Ku Klux Klan and neo-Nazi organizations have reappeared in recent years. One neo-Nazi group, The Order, was formed in Idaho in 1983 to conduct a war against the "Zionist Occupation Government." Members of the group machine-gunned a Jewish American talk-show host in Denver, committed armed robberies, counterfeited money, set fire to a synagogue, and killed police officers trying to capture them. "Hate crimes" by groups of skinheads (young, white neo-Nazis who shave their heads) have been significant in recent years.[28]

Religious Discrimination and Conflict

A number of federal court cases have involved religious discrimination against Jewish Americans. In the 1950s and 1960s Orthodox Jewish business owners fought local Sunday "blue laws" requiring businesses to close on Sunday, the Christian holy day; they argued that such laws violated their First Amendment right not to be penalized for their religious practices. The Supreme Court rejected their case and upheld the blue laws. In addition, Christian religious observances, such as reciting the Lord's Prayer, were once standard in public schools. The imposition of these practices on Jewish American children was opposed in courts from New York to California. In the 1960s the Supreme Court ruled against these officially sanctioned religious practices in the public schools.[29] Although in the mid-1980s a more conservative Supreme Court upheld the practice of daily prayers in state legislatures and the local government practice of constructing Christian nativity scenes on public property as part of an official Christmas celebration, the Court reaffirmed the principle of the separation of church and state in a 1992 decision, Lee v. Weisman, which involved prayer at a junior high school graduation.[30]

In other cases where individual claims to religious liberty, especially by non-Christians, are made against the government, the same conservative Court has ruled in favor of government bans on religious expression. In a five-to-four decision the Court ruled in 1986 that the U.S. Air Force could require an Orthodox rabbi employed as a chaplain to remove his small religious cap, the yarmulke, when working indoors. Since childhood Rabbi S. Simcha Goldman, an Orthodox Jew, had observed the Orthodox tradition of keeping his head covered, a tradition designed to remind individuals of God's omnipresence. The Pentagon decided to spend a large amount of money in court defending its position of preventing Orthodox Jews from wearing the yarmulke while in uniform. Several dissenting justices asked why military authorities had the right to limit religious freedom when civil authorities did not. The impact of these recent cases is to give court sanction to government decisions on which religious expressions are permissible within the government sphere and which are not.[31]

Jewish Americans Fight Back

Fear of street crime led to the formation of several militant self-protective associations beginning in the late 1960s. In 1968 Rabbi Kahane in New York City organized the Jewish Defense League (JDL) to deal with threats against Jewish American communities in the cities. The JDL's goals included not only the reinvigoration of ethnic pride but also the physical defense of citizens wherever threatened. The JDL organized armed citizen patrols in New York and other cities specifically to protect communities from street crime. During the 1980s JDL members protesting the treatment of Jews in the Soviet Union disrupted Soviet diplomatic activities and even tried to assassinate high-level Soviet diplomats. Strober argues that the JDL has touched a "middle-class nerve" and that for many Jewish Americans the traditional organizations have appeared unwilling to vigorously defend Jewish interests.[32] Although most Jewish Americans have disapproved of the JDL's violent tactics, often vigorously, many have supported some of its defensive aims. In 1990 Rabbi Kahane was assassinated; an Egyptian-born Muslim was charged with his murder but was acquitted by a New York City jury. The assassination did not end the JDL's activities, and the league's controversial new leader, Irv Rubin, has continued to pursue the goal of aggressive defense of Jewish American communities.

Black–Jewish Relations

Black Americans and Jewish Americans share a long history. During World War II black soldiers were allowed to serve only in all-black units. One of these units, the 761st Tank Battalion, led General George Patton's Third Army and was the first of the groups that liberated the Jews in the concentration camps at Dachau and Buchenwald. Even though they were denied equality at home, these black troops risked their lives to free the Jewish victims of Nazism.[33] Later, during the 1960s, Jewish Americans gave much support to the black civil rights movement in the South. Some died there fighting for black rights.

However, there has been conflict between Jewish Americans and African Americans since the black ghetto riots of the 1960s. In the 1960s rebellions—and again in similar 1980s and 1990s rebellions—black rioters attacked some Jewish American businesses that they saw as exploitative. This and other developments generated a backlash among many Jewish Americans. Moreover, in some areas black street criminals have been seen as responsible for destroying the peace of Jewish neighborhoods. Much controversy between black and Jewish Americans has centered in certain areas of New York City. In the early 1990s there was great tension between Hasidic Jews and blacks in Brooklyn. The Hasidic community in the Williamsburg area of Brooklyn even set up its own crime patrols to police the area against nonwhite criminals living nearby. The patrols harassed and beat some black and Latino residents from nearby areas who ventured into the Hasidic community. In the nearby area of Crown Heights a Hasidic driver ran over a black child, setting off anti-Jewish rioting by angry groups of black residents in which a young rabbinical student was murdered. The traffic death, rioting, and murder greatly increased the tensions between the black and Jewish residents of New York City.[34]

Since the 1960s black anti-Semitism and criticism of Zionism have also alienated a significant number of Jewish Americans from active participation in black–Jewish coalitions. At a time of declining anti-Semitism among whites, anti-Semitism, particularly among younger, better-educated black Americans, appears to have increased. Antiblack sentiments are not unknown among Jewish Americans. However, the pattern here is reversed: Jewish leaders, the young, and the better educated are less antiblack in their views than older, less well educated, rank-and-file Jewish Americans.[35]

That economic advancement has been more available to Jewish than to black Americans is one source of black antagonism. In the 1970s some black leaders broadcast anti-Semitic statements aimed at the Jewish merchants and landlords they believed were exploiting their ghettoized brothers and sisters. A few black leaders seized upon the "abstract idea of the conspiratorial Jew,"[36] as when they falsely blamed Jewish American leaders for President Jimmy Carter's firing of Andrew Young from his post as U.N. ambassador in 1979. Also troubling has been the appearance of political anti-Semitism, illustrated during Jesse Jackson's 1984 campaign for the Democratic presidential nomination. Jackson referred to New York City as "Hymietown" and to Zionism as the "poison weed" of Judaism. Jackson subsequently apologized, but both he and a large number of the black delegates to the Democratic convention refused to disavow the comments of one of his supporters, Louis Farrakhan, whose anti-Semitic utterances included a reference to Judaism as a "gutter religion."[37]

In her book *Deborah, Golda, and Me: Being Female and Jewish in America*, Letty Pogrebin discusses some reasons for the current tensions between black and Jewish Americans: "The differences between blacks and Jews are rarely more obvious than when each group speaks about its own 'survival,' a word that both use frequently but with quite dissimilar meanings.... Blacks worry about their actual conditions and fear for the present; Jews worry about their history and fear for the future." Pogrebin argues that each group fears the other for different reasons: Jewish Americans fear the greater numbers of blacks in the cities and a few black leaders such as Farrakhan who have made strongly anti-Semitic remarks. Black Americans, in contrast, fear Jewish Americans because they are affluent, powerful, and white.[38]

The tensions between black and Jewish Americans that can be seen in some urban communities have not substantially affected Jewish American commitments to civil rights and antidiscrimination legislation. Among the major white socioreligious groups in the United States, Jewish Americans are still the most liberal on racial issues. One study of National Opinion Research Center polls from 1980 to 1990 found that Jewish American views on racial matters were far more liberal than those of white Protestants and white Catholics, and were close to those of black respondents.[39]

Jewish American individuals and organizations continue to support black civil rights causes and black communities. For example, even though some Jewish businesses were burned during the 1992 Los Angeles riot, thirty synagogues and Hillel centers (campus organizations for Jewish students), as well as the antihunger organization Mazon, provided large amounts of clothing and food to black churches offering relief to black families in the riot areas. The Los Angeles riot also provoked a number of Jewish American leaders to call for an expansion of Jewish American action in the "noble tradition of compassion for the stranger."[40]

POLITICS

From their first arrival in the colonies, Jewish Americans insisted on maintaining important aspects of their culture. As a result they were treated as outsiders to the political system. Members of the first Jewish community in New Amsterdam were specifically barred from holding public office, and in general, voting and officeholding in the colonies were limited to Christians. Jewish Americans made substantial contributions to the American Revolution, and the new government to which the Revolution gave birth brought important benefits to Jewish citizens by establishing the separation of church and state. The Constitution's prohibition of religious qualifications for public office and the Bill of Rights' protection of speech and religious choice granted political freedom at the federal level. However, political enfranchisement was slower to come at the state level. Only five states had removed voting and officeholding restrictions by 1790; six others carried Christians-only provisions for political participation as late as 1876. Until the Civil War, rabbis were prohibited from serving as army chaplains. Still, "anti-Semitism never became rooted in the political tradition of American society," notes Chaim Waxman, as it had in the European political systems from which the immigrants had come. Will Herberg has written: "In America, religious pluralism is...not merely a historical and political fact, it is...the primordial condition of things, an essential aspect of the American Way of Life."[41]

In the first years of the new republic the anti-Jewish practices of some Federalist officials, combined with Federalist support for the Alien and Sedition Laws, guaranteed that Jewish Americans would support the liberal Jeffersonian political party, later to become the Democratic party. A few Jewish Americans, mostly Democrats, were elected to local, state, and national offices prior to the Civil War. Although Jews supported Democrats for decades, some voters gravitated to the antislavery Republican party in the 1850s, especially Abraham Lincoln's admirers in the Midwest.[42]

The voting power of Jewish Americans increased as they became more concentrated in northern cities at the beginning of the twentieth century. While some Socialist party candidates received strong support, many Jewish Americans remained Republicans or supported the Irish-dominated Democratic machines, which provided jobs and shelter to needy immigrants.[43] Eastern European Jews became famous for exercising the franchise and undertaking volunteer political activity. Whereas in the early twentieth century Irish Americans used ethnic politics to advance their interests—to create jobs and patronage—Jewish Americans, although concerned with the same bread-and-butter matters, were more issue-oriented, particularly in the matter of civil rights.[44]

Jewish Americans and the Democratic Party

In spite of their conscientious activity, by the 1910s few Jewish Americans had been able to win electoral office; few had been appointed to high-level positions. An occasional city-council member, one or two state legislators, a judge—this was the extent of their success. At the national level the impact was modest as well. Many Jewish Americans still voted for Republicans. The appearance of an internationalist Democratic candidate, Woodrow Wilson, brought a majority of Jewish voters to the

Democrats for the first time in decades. Wilson appointed a few Jewish Americans to important positions, including Louis Brandeis to the Supreme Court.[45]

After Wilson, Jewish American voters generally supported Republican presidential candidates until the late 1920s, although they were shifting to Democratic candidates at the local, state, and congressional levels. In 1920 there were eleven Jewish members of Congress, ten of them Republicans, but by 1922 most were Democratic. New York governor Al Smith, of poor Irish background, attracted a lot of Jewish Americans to the Democratic party and received substantial support in his 1928 bid for the presidency.[46]

Although Jewish Americans have become increasingly more suburban and middle-income since the 1920s, their vote has not shifted heavily back to the Republican party. Franklin Roosevelt brought Jewish Americans firmly into the Democratic fold in 1932. Roosevelt's anti-Nazi rhetoric and his support of social security and union organization won over many Jewish voters. Until Roosevelt, few Jewish Americans had served in the executive or judicial branches of the federal government. Benjamin Cohen, Felix Frankfurter, and Louis Brandeis served as advisers to Roosevelt, and Roosevelt appointed Henry Morgenthau, Jr., secretary of the Treasury.[47] Yet Roosevelt's strong regard among Jewish Americans did not lead him to take dynamic political action on behalf of the refugees from Nazi-dominated Europe. One reason for this was his fear of the intense anti-Semitism prevailing in the United States during the 1930s and 1940s. Anti-Jewish discrimination was then quite common in politics, social affairs, education, employment, jury selection in certain states, and residential restrictions.[48]

Since Roosevelt the proportion of the Jewish American vote going to Democratic presidential candidates has remained substantial. In 1948 three-quarters of Jewish voters supported Harry Truman. Three-quarters voted for Adlai Stevenson during the Eisenhower landslides, and more than three-quarters supported John Kennedy in 1960. Considerably more than three-quarters voted for Lyndon Johnson in 1964 and for Hubert Humphrey in 1968. In 1976 Democrat Jimmy Carter received 70 percent of the Jewish vote. In 1980, however, Carter received only 45 percent of the Jewish vote in his second bid for the presidency, according to one poll, with the rest split between Ronald Reagan and an independent candidate. This, the lowest percentage given to a Democratic presidential candidate since Franklin Roosevelt, was said to have reflected Jewish concern over Carter's attempts to build bridges to the Arab world. Jewish Americans feared that Israel's security might be jeopardized by Carter's peace initiatives in the Middle East.

But in 1984, according to a *Times*/CBS report, Jewish Americans were the only major white group to give a majority of their votes (66 percent) to the Democratic candidate, Walter Mondale. One reason for this large anti-Reagan vote among Jewish Americans was Reagan's close ties to the religious right, including fundamentalist Christian ministers. Some of these preachers made anti-Semitic remarks and asserted the dominance of Protestant Christian values over those of other religious traditions. A 1984 poll found that 57 percent of Jewish respondents identified themselves as Democrats, 31 percent as independents, and only 12 percent as Republicans.[49] In addition, liberals outnumbered conservatives among Jewish respondents to the 1990 National Jewish Population Survey, although a significant portion identified themselves as middle-of-the-road politically. The survey also found that most Jewish Americans were registered to vote.[50]

Historically, Jewish Americans have been underrepresented among elected and appointed officials. Barely a hundred Jewish Americans have ever been a U.S. senator, House member, or governor. Recent years have seen improvement. In the early 1990s Jewish Americans were represented by thirty-three members of the House and eight senators. So far, only half a dozen Jewish Americans have served on the United States Supreme Court, although perhaps a fifth of the nation's lawyers in recent decades have been Jewish. The first Jewish American in a presidential cabinet was Oscar Straus, appointed by Theodore Roosevelt in 1906. Fewer than two dozen have served in cabinets since that time. Jewish Americans have served in significant (although less than representative) numbers in local and state executive and legislative offices. It was not until 1974 that a Jewish American (Abraham Beame) became mayor of New York City. Also in the 1970s, Dianne Feinstein became the first Jewish woman chosen mayor of a major city, San Francisco.[51]

While these numbers are impressive compared with the limited political power of nonwhite groups, discrimination still plays a role in limiting the number of Jewish Americans who occupy the political front lines. The proportion of Jewish Americans in elected office is low given their high proportion among political activists. Isaacs has stressed that although there are more Jews than Presbyterians or Episcopalians in the United States, in recent years Jewish Americans have not held nearly as many congressional offices as have these powerful Protestant groups.[52]

Unions and Community Organizations

Eastern European Jewish immigrants actively protested oppressive working conditions in the 1890s, organizing to fight long hours, low pay, and unsafe working conditions. Tens of thousands of workers struck the New York garment industry in 1910 and inspired union militants elsewhere.[53] New York City data for the 1930s show large numbers of Jewish Americans in food, entertainment, clothing, and jewelry unions. Jewish union leaders went beyond the problems of wages and working conditions to grapple with broader issues, developing health, pension, and educational programs that would be imitated by all unions. Jewish workers also played an important role in the growth of the American Socialist party between 1905 and 1912 and other subsequent labor-liberal parties.[54]

The organized Jewish American community has long been impressive. One important aspect of this "civic Judaism," to use Woocher's term, is the North American Jewish federation movement, made up of more than two hundred local community federations and many social service and educational agencies representing and serving Jewish Americans. The federation movement originally emphasized philanthropy and Jewish immigrant adjustment, but more recently has stressed social activism and political survival.[55]

By the 1930s several civic and civil rights organizations had been established whose importance would persist: the Anti-Defamation League, the American Jewish Congress, the American Jewish Committee, and the United Jewish Appeal. Since 1906 the American Jewish Committee has vigorously fought anti-Semitic prejudice and discrimination in the United States. The American Jewish Congress, established in the 1910s by eastern European Jews, has also fought for the civil rights of Jewish Americans. Both are large organizations with large budgets. The Anti-Defamation League, established in 1913 as a branch of the fraternal organization B'nai B'rith, has carried out a vigorous civil rights campaign, attempting to root out anti-Semitism. The United Jewish Appeal, established in 1939, has been a successful fund-raising organization aiding a variety of causes, including war refugees and the state of Israel.[56]

The founding and survival of Israel have been concerns of major Jewish American organizations in the post–World War II period. During the Eisenhower administration Jewish American pressure to support Israel often went unheeded, but by the 1960s U.S. support for Israel sharply increased. Since the 1960s Jewish American pressure has been mobilized for numerous other political causes, such as support for Jews in the (former) Soviet Union and opposition to political candidates taking a tolerant position toward Arab nations hostile to Israel.[57] In addition to combating anti-Semitism, some organizations have broadened their focus and worked to eliminate all racial prejudice and discrimination and to ensure the continued separation of church and state. Jewish American commitment to expanded civil rights for African Americans has been strong since the 1800s. Numerous Jewish congregations and their rabbis were active in the black civil rights protests of the 1950s and 1960s. Jewish Americans were also active in the antiwar movement of the 1960s and 1970s.[58] These three decades were the period one author describes as the Jews' "golden age," when many Jewish Americans committed their efforts to the rights of the "real underdogs."[59]

In recent years some Jewish Americans have accused the well-off board members of the American Jewish Committee, the American Jewish Congress, the United Jewish Appeal, and the Anti-Defamation League of being more sympathetic to the needs of employers than to traditional concerns for workers, the poor, and discrimination against blacks and other nonwhites. This criticism may be somewhat unfair, but it does point up a dilemma faced by Jewish Americans today. As the most affluent of "white ethnic" groups, Jewish Americans might be expected to develop the generally conservative orientation of other high-income white groups.[60] Yet, given their Jewish past and the periodic recurrence of anti-Semitism in the United States, most Jewish Americans remain more liberal, politically and economically, than non-Jewish whites.

THE ECONOMY

From their earliest presence in colonial communities Jewish immigrants contributed to the prosperity of America. One Jewish immigrant from Poland, Haym Salomon, played a critical role in financing the American Revolution with a loan to the struggling revolutionary government.[61] The opening of commerce in the Americas presented a golden opportunity for European Jews, who had centuries of experience as a "middleman" trading minority in Europe, where they were excluded from landownership and skilled-worker guilds. Their success in commercial pursuits made them an accessible scapegoat for the non-Jewish poor, who saw them as exploiters, and for the non-Jewish rich, who viewed them as a political threat. The often marginal nature of their businesses, as well as outside white hostility, fostered the growth of an ethnic economy in which Jewish Americans provided economic aid to one another in order to maintain their enterprises and communities.[62]

Establishing an Economic Niche: A "Middleman Minority"?

The rate of penetration of a new immigrant group into the core society depends on its own economic background as well as the economic conditions at the point of destination. Most central European Jews came to the United States poor. But they arrived at a time when frontier development and industrial growth were exploding, and they found that their experience in buying and selling was in demand. As peddlers they roamed city streets and the countryside in the South and West. Many started as poor peddlers and became prosperous shopkeepers, and a few became bankers, retailers, and industrialists.[63]

By the late nineteenth century, census figures showed, 58 percent of employed Jewish Americans were in trading or financial occupations, 20 percent were office workers, and 6 percent were professionals. The remaining 16 percent were blue-collar workers or farmers. Jewish American entrepreneurs were concentrated in clothing, jewelry, meat, and leather businesses. By the 1890s a majority of the German and other central European Jews seemed to be moving up the economic ladder. Although they had prospered by the second generation, they were still unable to enter the top positions in an economy whose central industrial enterprises were firmly controlled by British Americans.[64]

Coming in next, the Jewish immigrants from eastern Europe entered the expanding U.S. industrial economy at an opportune time. Most were poor and poorly educated; nearly half the women were illiterate. But their considerable experience in coping with oppression provided them a cultural heritage replete with strategies for finding economic niches in which they could survive. Most settled in the industrial cities, and large numbers found employment in the expanding garment industry. As some moved out of the manual occupations, new Jewish immigrants filled their places at the bottom rungs of the mobility ladder—until discriminatory quotas curtailed immigration in the 1920s. Men, women, and children—whole families—engaged in low-wage manufacturing work. The long hours and poor conditions of the sweatshops of industrial capitalism led to many reform and union movements.[65]

Many who had been small merchants in eastern Europe continued as such in the United States. In the early 1900s more than one-third of the eastern European immigrants were employed in the garment industry, one-quarter were in building trades, and one-fifth were in retail trade. Many wage earners set their sights on a business career. Some moved up the economic ladder from junk peddler to owner of a scrap-metal yard, or from needleworker to clothing entrepreneur. But those in the second generation were encouraged to seek clerical and sales work. A few eventually worked their way to the head of clothing firms; by 1905 a significant proportion of the clothing industry in New York City was under eastern European Jewish management. A number went into the professions; by 1905 eastern European Jews had a toehold in law, medicine, and dentistry in New York.[66]

Jewish women contributed significantly to family incomes. A Philadelphia study in this early period found that one in three Jewish American households had a woman working outside the home. Most unmarried Jewish American women worked. Because of the low wages of both male and female workers, families needed the wages women earned outside the home or from taking in sewing or laundry in the home. Wives joined their husbands in the small retail shops that supplied many Jewish neighborhoods. Many women were left to raise their children alone when their husbands died or deserted the family. At least one-quarter of immigrant fathers left their families, because of economic (for example, job search) and other reasons. A National Desertion Bureau was established in 1911, which contributed to the support of a hundred thousand deserted families in this early period.[67]

From the Depression to 1950

About one-quarter of Jewish Americans in Detroit and Pittsburgh in the mid-1930s were owners or managers, compared with about 9 percent of the total population. A study in Newburyport, Massachusetts, estimated that just under half of the Jewish Americans there had moved into the middle-income range. As in the case of Japanese Americans (see Chapter 11), the solidarity of the Jewish American community and its heavy involvement in small and medium-sized businesses were sources of community survival during the Great Depression. Whenever possible, Jewish American businesses dealt with one another and hired unemployed relatives. Crime, including organized crime, was a way out of poverty for a small proportion of first- and second-generation Jewish Americans in the early decades, but it declined significantly as a force with the movement of large numbers out of the working class and the central-city neighborhoods following World War II.[68]

The ethnic economy provided a fallback position for those who faced anti-Jewish discrimination in the 1930s. One of the goals of anti-Semitic organizations was to reduce the number of Jewish Americans in private and public employment. Non-Jewish whites in the teaching, banking, medical, legal, and engineering professions sought to prohibit Jewish Americans from employment in their sectors. In many cities securing skilled blue-collar jobs and clerical jobs was difficult. The Great Depression accentuated the problem. "No Jews need apply" signs were common, particularly in larger businesses and professional institutions. Placement agencies throughout the Midwest, to take just one area, reported that from two-thirds to 95 percent of job listings excluded Jewish Americans from consideration. Jews faced discrimination in the teaching profession, particularly in smaller cities and at colleges. Discrimination from 1900 to the 1950s was rife in housing; real estate agents from Philadelphia to Boston to Chicago discriminated against Jewish Americans, while neighbors made life miserable for those who managed to pioneer in desegregating an area. Later, even those who managed to move into the suburbs in significant numbers often found Protestant-oriented organizations and recreational facilities off limits to them.[69]

One of the fears of anti-Semites has been the alleged Jewish dominance of banking. Yet a *Fortune* magazine survey in 1936 found very few Jewish Americans in banking and finance, and a later survey found that only 600 of the 93,000 banking officials in the United States were Jewish Americans. Nor were they very numerous in heavy industries such as steel or automobiles or in public utilities. Their representation was small in the press and in radio. The *Fortune* survey found that the only sectors Jewish Americans dominated were clothing, textiles, and the movies. Even in law and medicine Jews had little representation in the powerful positions. The author of the 1936 *Fortune* article seemed puzzled at the clustering in certain industrial and business areas and explained the situation in the stereotypical terms of Jewish American clannishness.[70]

Such patterns were by no means mysterious; they reflected the extent to which Jewish Americans had to work outside mainstream industries and businesses because of blatant institutionalized discrimination. As McWilliams noted in *A Mask for Privilege,*

discrimination forced Jewish Americans to become "the ragpickers of American industry." They were channeled by discrimination into higher-risk economic spheres marginal
to the mainstream economy.[71]

After World War II, extensive employment discrimination continued to be directed
at Jewish Americans. Job advertising included restrictions, and many employment agencies required applicants to list their religion or ethnicity, which in turn was used to
discriminate among them. In spite of this, many Jewish Americans were able to share in
postwar prosperity, particularly in the new and more risky industries such as television
and plastics. For Jewish Americans the postwar economic pyramid had a modest working-class base and no significant wealthy elite at the top. Jewish Americans remained
concentrated primarily in trade, clothing, and jewelry manufacturing; commerce; mer-
chandising; certain light industries; mass communications; and certain professions.[72]
The 1957 Current Population Survey found that three-quarters of Jewish American men
were employed in white-collar jobs, compared with 38 percent of white Protestants. Over
half were in professional and managerial jobs, twice the percentage for white Protestants.
Less than a quarter were in blue-collar positions.[73] Research on business executives,
presidents, and board chairmen indicates that in 1900 just under 2 percent were Jews; in
1925 and 1950 the figure was between 2 and 3 percent. Given the preponderance of Jewish
Americans in commercial and business employment, these proportions are much lower
than they would be if there had been no anti-Jewish discrimination. A very large
proportion of the Jewish American executives—just under half—made it to the top in
Jewish businesses within the ethnic economy.[74]

From the 1950s to the 1990s

Data from the 1950s show a sizable proportion (30 percent) of Jewish household
heads with incomes above $7,500, compared with 13 percent of the total population.
This advantaged economic position has continued in each succeeding decade,
although a significant minority, mostly elderly (an estimated 15 percent in the
mid-1980s) live in poverty. In a 1987 survey in Rhode Island, over half the Jewish
American households responding to a question about family income earned more than
$40,000 per year; 22 percent earned more than $75,000. However, more than half of
those sixty-five and above had annual household incomes below $25,000; one-third
of these received less than $15,000.[75]

The 1990 National Jewish Population Survey (NJPS) estimated the 1989 median
annual income for all Jewish American households (families and individuals) to be
$39,000. In the same year, the median income for all U.S. households was $28,906, and
for all white households $30,406. Fourteen percent of Jewish multi-person households
were classified as low-income (that is, with incomes under $20,000 a year). No direct
comparison is available for the general population. However, 18 percent of all U.S.
households had incomes below $25,000 in that year.[76]

Occupational Mobility

Continuing occupational mobility has characterized Jewish Americans since the
1960s. In that decade an estimated one-quarter of male Jewish workers in New York City
were in blue-collar occupations. The blue-collar proportions in studies of other cities were

lower. Occupational data for New York, Providence, Milwaukee, Detroit, and Boston showed that 20 to 32 percent of Jewish American males were in professional positions and 28 to 54 percent were in managerial–official positions. Over half of all Jewish American workers in each city were in these two categories, while most of the rest were in other clerical or sales positions. In comparison, the majority of the total employed populations in those cities were in blue-collar positions. Recent research has confirmed this trend toward white-collar employment. More than one-third of the respondents in the 1987 Rhode Island survey were in professional occupations; most of the rest were in white-collar occupations. The 1990 NJPS also revealed that most Jewish Americans held salaried white-collar positions; 16 percent were self-employed.[77]

Contrary to the stereotype, in recent decades Jewish American executives have not controlled banking in any area of the United States. Excluding one New York bank (31 percent of whose top managers were Jewish), in 1976 only 2.5 percent of executives in commercial banks nationwide were Jewish. Among the primary areas of Jewish American population concentration, New York (25 percent Jewish) had the lowest proportion of Jewish executives (2.7 percent) and San Francisco (10 percent Jewish population) had the highest proportion (4.96 percent). A decade later Korman found that only 3.4 percent of the executives in ten of the nation's largest corporate banks were Jewish American.[78]

An early 1980s study of Jewish Americans in the corporate elite found that most were in Jewish-founded corporations or occupied lower managerial positions in other corporations. Those who have cracked the top of the corporate establishment, such as Irving Shapiro, formerly chief executive officer of du Pont, have usually been brought in from the outside (Shapiro was brought in from government). They have rarely been given the chance to start at the bottom of the corporate hierarchy and work up in the usual way. "They are not even remotely close to being the dominant force they are tragically and mistakenly thought to be by anti-Semites."[79]

In the mid-1980s, an estimated 6 to 8 percent of senior executives in U.S. corporations were Jewish Americans. Studying the distribution of Jewish American executives in corporate America, Korman found that the major (Fortune 500) industries he analyzed fell into three significant groups. Group A, those industries in which Jewish Americans constituted less than 5 percent of senior executives (below the overall corporate percentage of Jewish executives), included many of the largest and most powerful corporations in terms of annual sales and number of employees. Of the thirteen diverse industries in this group, the petroleum industry had the lowest percentage of senior executives who were Jewish Americans. Group B included seven industries with proportions of Jewish senior executives (5 to 8 percent) at or near the overall corporate percentage. In only three industries was the level of Jewish senior executives above the nationwide figure: publishing and printing (9.5 percent), textiles and vinyl flooring (9.9 percent), and apparel (26.7 percent). Among service industries in the Fortune Service 500, Jewish Americans constituted approximately 2 percent of senior executives in utilities and transportation and just under 5 percent in life insurance. The service industries in which percentages of Jewish executives were highest were retailing and supermarket chains.[80]

In interviews with management consultants and corporate managers Korman found that the "outsider" status of Jewish managers was taken for granted; all found the absence of significant numbers of Jewish Americans in high-level executive positions to be predictable. All agreed that in order to succeed in the corporate hierarchy, Jewish Americans must divest themselves of all visible Jewish identity. Some of the Jewish respondents cited specific anti-Jewish actions that had blocked their career advancement; some were denied titles appropriate to their actual duties. Like Asian Americans (see Chapters 11 and 12), many found they could hold professional or staff positions but would never be seriously considered for higher executive positions.[81]

Perhaps because of the greater freedom to excel, many of the nation's writers, scholars, and professors are Jewish American. Jewish Americans are well represented among distinguished scholars at major universities and among top literary figures. They include Nobel laureate Saul Bellow and prominent intellectuals such as Irving Howe and Seymour Martin Lipset. They have been the backbone of literary and critical magazines such as the *Partisan Review, Dissent, Commentary,* and the *New York Review of Books.*

The effects of anti-Semitism keep many Jewish Americans in the "gilded ghetto," where they find themselves economically successful but frequently denied the social recognition and political power that success should have brought. Ghetto-ization has been subtle, and progress toward inclusion slow. In 1983 New York City introduced a law banning discrimination, including anti-Jewish discrimination, in private clubs; the law did not pass until 1985, and only then after the minimum club membership covered was increased from 100 to 400. In May 1992 a bill banning race and gender discrimination in large private country clubs made its way to the floor of the New York state senate after being blocked for ten years by its white Protestant opponents. In March of the same year a similar bill banning discrimination in private clubs finally passed the Florida legislature. The American Jewish Congress headed up a coalition of civil rights groups that worked together to get the bill passed. Still, in the 1990s Florida is one of only a few states with strong laws prohibiting discrimination in private clubs. Experts estimate that three-quarters of the nation's private golf and country clubs have no black members, and many take either no female or Jewish members or only token numbers. Much discrimination has been hidden by secrecy at the higher socioeconomic levels of this society. Exclusion from private social clubs and private schools, where much important information is exchanged, creates economic and political disabilities in other spheres—a clear example of the indirect discrimination discussed in Chapter 1.[82]

EDUCATION

Education, secular or religious, was not as high a priority for the earliest groups of Jewish immigrants as it was for later groups; the earlier arrivals focused on success in business rather than on entering a profession or preserving the European tradition of religious scholarship. Significant participation in public schools came with the surge of eastern European immigrants, for whom secular education was a means of becoming American. Parents pushed their children to succeed in school so that they could prosper economically and socially. College was especially valued as a door to a career for the young. Adults, too, were eager to learn the customs of their new country; thousands studied English at evening schools established by philanthropic organizations, many of which were operated by the already acculturated German Jews. Because eastern European immigrants felt it important for their U.S.-born children to retain their Jewish identity, they established numerous Jewish schools that taught Hebrew, Jewish history, and religious rituals and practices.[83]

Educational mobility for second- and third-generation Jewish Americans came swiftly. Large numbers of students graduated from high schools in northern cities, and a significant number pursued college educations. By 1910 one-fourth of all students in U.S. medical schools were Jewish Americans, and by 1920 the proportion of Jewish students in New York City colleges and universities was estimated to be greater than the Jewish proportion of the general population. By the late 1930s almost half of Jewish students in New York City managed to complete high school, compared with only one-quarter of other students. Nine percent of the nation's 1.1 million college students were Jewish Americans, although they constituted only 3.7 percent of the total population.[84]

Discriminatory Quotas for Jewish Students

Restrictive quotas for Jewish American students were imposed at numerous colleges and universities from the 1920s to the 1950s. In 1918 Dean Frederick Jones of Yale called for a ban on Jewish students because they were winning most of Yale's scholarships and Gentile students were said to be discouraged by their success. In 1922 Harvard University president A. L. Lowell also called for discriminatory quotas on Jewish students. Covert methods of limiting Jewish admissions, such as "character" tests and requirements for "geographic balance" among an entering class were employed at many schools. Columbia's Jewish enrollment dropped from 40 percent to 15 percent and Harvard's from 21 percent to 10 percent. In the 1920s, three-quarters of Gentile students applying to a major medical school in New York were admitted; the percentage of Jewish students admitted peaked at half but eventually dropped to one-fifth. In the same decade restrictions were placed on Jewish admissions to law schools and to the bar in various states. Fraternities and sororities, institutions that groomed students from the "right" racial and ethnic backgrounds for success, excluded Jewish Americans from membership.[85]

Jewish Americans were also excluded from teaching positions in higher education. Between the 1920s and the 1940s Jewish Ph.D.s, however distinguished, found it difficult to get appointments at Anglo-Protestant-dominated universities. In 1940 fewer than two in every one hundred of the nation's college and university faculty members were Jewish. The sudden increase in college enrollments following World War II created a demand for teachers; by the end of the 1960s the proportion of Jewish faculty members in U.S. institutions of higher education had risen to 9 percent and in elite colleges the figure was 20 percent.[86]

Affirmative Action Programs

Affirmative action programs, seeking to improve educational opportunities and job chances for black and other non-European groups, have become a political issue for many Jewish Americans since the late 1960s. Some have objected to the use of affirmative action goals to benefit these groups. Jewish Americans have long been among the most vigorous supporters of the principle of merit, because of the quota restrictions that denied them access to higher education and jobs from the 1920s to the 1950s. Moreover, some have opposed recent affirmative action programs, such as those in college admissions, because of Jewish Americans' heavy commitment to higher education, a commitment that reflects the past exclusion of Jewish Americans from many sectors of the academic and business worlds. The admissions preferences for non-Jewish minorities can disproportionately affect Jewish Americans' access to college degrees and perpetuate the effects of anti-Jewish discrimination in the past.[87]

However, voicing support for affirmative action, Harvard law professor Dershowitz notes the "real difference between the institutional impact and intensity of the hurt suffered as part of an invidious pattern of racial *subordination* and as part of a benevolent pattern of racial *equalization*." He points out the bias of admission programs, such as those in Ivy League colleges, that hold fairly constant the number of students admitted from certain white Anglo-Protestant pools (descendants and relatives of alumni and those admitted to achieve "geographic balance"), yet at the same time make room for certain affirmative action applicants (Latinos and blacks) by reducing the number of other minorities (Jewish and Asian Americans) who are admitted. He argues that it would be much more equitable for those white Anglo-Protestant groups that have long benefited from the exclusion of all minorities to bear a heavier share of the burden of this equalization.[88]

Achievements in Education

Severe discrimination declined after World War II, and large numbers of Jewish American veterans took advantage of free college and graduate school tuition under the GI bill. Since that time the educational attainment of Jewish Americans has reached ever higher levels. A 1987 survey of the Rhode Island Jewish community found that most respondents were college graduates and that one-quarter of the younger adults had received advanced degrees. The 1990 NJPS estimated that only about 6 percent of Jewish adults twenty-five and older had less than a high school education, compared with almost one-quarter of all white adults in the United States. Approximately half of adult females and almost 60 percent of adult males were college graduates, compared with 17 percent of all white adult females and 24 percent of all white adult males. Almost one-quarter of Jewish females and one-third of Jewish males held advanced degrees, compared with 6 percent of all white females and 11 percent of all white males.[89]

Schooling in Jewish religion and culture also persists. The proportion of second-generation eastern European Jews who received instruction in religious schools was small considering the heavy emphasis traditionally placed on Jewish education in Europe. In New York City the proportion did not exceed one-quarter during the early decades of the twentieth century. Yet surveys in recent decades have found strong support among parents for some type of Jewish education for their children, and large percentages of both adults and children have reported receiving such education. More than 86 percent of the adult respondents in the 1987 Rhode Island study, and 80 percent of the children in their households, had received at least some Jewish education. The 1990 NJPS estimated that approximately half of all Jewish adults nationwide had received some Jewish education. In that year, approximately 400,000 Jewish American children were enrolled in some form of religious education. The renewed emphasis on formal learning of one's heritage and religion in the lower grades has carried over to colleges and universities. In the 1960s there were more than five dozen faculty positions in Jewish studies; by the 1980s there were more than three hundred.[90]

RELIGION AND ZIONISM

Religious services for members of the first Jewish community in New Amsterdam were restricted to their homes. In the British colonies religious freedom was variable, but most restricted Jewish American participation in colonial life. The anti-Jewish bias of other settlers sustained a vigorous oppositional culture, the base for much Jewish protest against religious and political oppression from then to the present. Support for maximizing religious freedom increased after 1790, particularly among Thomas Jefferson and his followers. While the new nation remained fundamentally Christian, religious freedom gradually became law in each of the new states, in most by 1850.

Until the 1790s, the Sephardic tradition prevailed in the synagogues. As the numbers of German and other central European Jews increased, some broke away from Sephardic congregations and developed the practice of founding multiple synagogues in a community, each following the traditions of its members. The two hundred synagogues founded by the new immigrants served as an antidote to loneliness as well as a center for religious observances. All but one of these were Orthodox, although during the 1850s and 1860s most congregations Americanized their religious practices to achieve greater respectability in the eyes of non-Jews. This Reform movement became organized in the Union of American Hebrew Congregations in the 1870s. The new Reform temples had shorter services, organ music, and English prayers. The changes taking place in U.S. Judaism were articulated by Isaac Mayer Wise, the spiritual leader of German Jewish immigrants in the mid-1800s, who advocated a more optimistic faith that could celebrate democracy in its "temples without tears." He was dedicated to maintaining the separation of religion from civic life and ensuring that Jewish Americans were "absolutely at home as equals in America."[91]

In the 1820s a number of independent Jewish organizations emerged as some philanthropic societies broke away from the synagogues that had founded them. Some service organizations founded over the next few decades had greater memberships than synagogues. Although festivals and rites of passage continued to be celebrated in the synagogue, these independent societies and organizations came to replace the synagogue as the center of life in the Jewish community.[92]

The role of Judaism, the Jewish religion, in Jewish identity was a point of conflict between the German Jews and the new eastern European immigrants. The German Jews saw themselves as Americans whose religion happened to be Judaism. They endeavored to be inconspicuous in order to be accepted as true Americans. In contrast, the new immigrants had a strong desire to maintain their old ethnic identity. Most were Orthodox, observing the Sabbath and kosher dietary laws insofar as the conditions of poverty that defined immigrant life would permit. Theirs was a grassroots adaptation of Orthodoxy that focused on family and group feeling and stressed charitable acts, support of Jews abroad, and selective observance of rituals. They were eager neither to totally re-create their past nor to abandon it.[93]

Conservative Judaism, which began in the late 1880s as a modified traditionalism in reaction to Reform groups, was especially appealing to the U.S.-born generation of eastern European Jews. The Conservative synagogues observed many Orthodox rituals and traditions, although they discontinued the separation of men and women at worship services as well as certain traditional religious practices, such as strict dress and grooming codes.[94]

By the 1920s there were more than three thousand Reform, Orthodox, and Conservative congregations. By 1935 Orthodox synagogues had about one million members, Conservative synagogues 300,000, and Reform temples 200,000. The authority of the rabbi, as well as the traditional ritual and theology, became less important as one moved from Orthodox to Conservative to Reform congregations. Many of the synagogues built in the new middle-class neighborhoods in the 1920s were designed as community centers as well as religious centers. However, membership and attendance were low: by the 1930s only one-quarter of Jewish American families were formally affiliated with a synagogue. The thoroughly Jewish atmosphere of highly concentrated neighborhoods provided a strong sense of ethnic identity; most apparently felt little need to ensure the survival of Jewishness through formal affiliations or extensive religious education for their children. During this period some second-generation eastern European Jews turned away from all branches of Judaism; secularism, socialism, labor radicalism, and Zionism became the new "religions" of many younger Jewish Americans during the crises of the Depression and World War II.[95]

Trends in Religious Practice and Identity

Expanding suburbanization after World War II brought an increase in the number of congregations in the rings around central cities. As a small minority in suburbia, Jewish American families sought a public symbol to affirm their Jewishness and a means to ensure the Jewishness of their children. Synagogue membership and ritual observances, especially the more child-centered Hanukkah and Passover celebrations, saw marked increases. Silberman suggests that "the new suburbanites desperately wanted to be full members of American society, but it was not until that desire began to be realized that they discovered how much they wanted to remain Jews as well."[96]

Jewish American religion currently reflects a substantial interest in the traditional heritage, maintenance of the synagogue as a community center, and home religious practices. Although lighting Hanukkah candles was the only religious ritual always practiced by a majority of the respondents to the 1987 Rhode Island survey, more than half lit Sabbath candles and had a Passover Seder at least sometimes, and two-thirds fasted on Yom Kippur. Most parents felt it was important for their children to know about Jewish customs and beliefs, to become Bar/Bat Mitzvah, to give charity, to have Jewish friends and marry a Jew, and to read prayers in synagogue services. The two most important issues defining Jewishness for these respondents were having close family ties and remembering well the European Holocaust.[97]

According to the 1990 NJPS, 62 percent of Americans of Jewish ancestry identified themselves as religious. However, less than 5 percent felt that their Jewish identity was based solely on religious group membership. Even among the religious Jews "cultural group" and "ethnic group" were named the most frequently as basies of Jewish identity. The survey also noted a general movement away from traditional Judaism. One-quarter of religious Jews were raised Orthodox, but fewer than 7 percent identified as Orthodox in 1990. The direction of change was reversed for Reform Jews: 28 percent of religious Jews were raised Reform but 43 percent identified as Reform in 1990. The overall percentage of religious Jews who were raised Conservative and the percentage identifying as Conservative in the 1990 survey were the same. Significantly, 43 percent of those identifying as non-religious Jews reported that they had been raised as Orthodox, Conservative, or Reform.[98]

Active membership is not a majority phenomenon. According to the national survey, only 41 percent of entirely Jewish households and 13 percent of mixed households were affiliated with a synagogue or temple in 1990. Among the affiliated, Conservative congregations had the largest proportion of households (43 percent). The relatively larger household size of those who are affiliated suggests that families with children are the most likely to be active.[99] Rituals remain important. Well over half of religious Jews and approximately one-tenth of secular Jews reported fasting on Yom Kippur and attending synagogue on high holidays. More than three-quarters of entirely Jewish households and approximately 60 percent of mixed Jewish-Gentile households reported that they attended Passover Seder at least sometimes and lit Hanukkah candles.[100]

Judaism has become one of the major U.S. religious traditions. Blau has suggested that much of Jewish American religion has been flexible. Modern Judaism is a "voluntary" faith: Jewish Americans can reject it or accept it to varying degrees. Some call this Judaism a "cardiac" religion, emphasizing the heart or one's morals rather than rigid ritual and doctrine. The tolerance that has developed for different "denominations" within Judaism is similar to that of Protestantism.[101] Blau's analysis has some validity for Reform and Conservative branches of Judaism, but it does not apply to Orthodox Judaism, which bases Jewish identity on heredity (descent from a Jewish mother) and involves ritual observance with fewer adaptations to the values of the secular world. In contrast, Reform Judaism accepts Jewish heredity through either a Jewish father or mother and emphasizes universal humanitarian Jewish principles rather than ritual. It defines Jewishness as a religious preference rather than an all-encompassing identity. Conservative Judaism represents a middle path between Orthodoxy's tradition and Reform's assimilationism. Conservatives are willing to adapt to the core culture yet wish to retain much of the form and content of the Jewish tradition.[102]

Zionism

At the heart of modern Jewish consciousness is a concern for the survival and prosperity of the Middle-Eastern nation of Israel. For many Jewish Americans "Israel represents Jewry's positive response to centuries of anti-Semitism in general and to Hitler's attempted genocide in particular."[103] Whether active in religious Judaism or not, many Jewish Americans share the commitment to Zionism—the right of Jews everywhere to have a secure national homeland. Some commentators have suggested that Zionism is like a religion in its fervor. This commitment to Israel has affected not only Jewish voting patterns and black–Jewish relations (because of pro-Arab sentiments among some black leaders) but also Jewish American philanthropy. Jewish American financial support has been critical to Israel's survival in the face of hostility from many nearby Arab governments.

In the last decade debate has increased among Jewish Americans over certain actions of the government of Israel, such as the 1982 invasion of Lebanon and the 1988 suppression of Palestinian protests in the occupied West Bank areas. Almost all the respondents in the 1987 survey of the Rhode Island Jewish community reported that the state of Israel was important to them; nearly half had visited Israel. In the 1990 NJPS, 83 percent of religious Jews and almost half of secular Jews felt an attachment to Israel.[104]

Yet many Jewish Americans have raised questions about the direction of Israel's development and the wisdom of Israeli leaders. One-quarter of the respondents and most Jewish leaders in the American Jewish Committee's 1989 survey agreed that Israel's continued occupation of territories it has captured since 1967 would "erode Israel's democratic and humanitarian character." Most favored "territorial compromise for credible guarantees of peace" and peace negotiations between Israel and the Palestine Liberation Organization (PLO) if the latter organization recognized the state of Israel and renounced terrorism.[105]

ASSIMILATION OR PLURALISM?

Two different theoretical perspectives have been used to explain the experiences of Jewish Americans—Anglo-conformity perspectives and cultural pluralism approaches. Most scholarly analyses of Jewish Americans have reflected some type of assimilation viewpoint. The dominant perspective among Jewish Americans themselves has been at least partially assimilationist: the view that some adaptation to the surrounding culture is critical to achieving economic success and avoiding anti-Semitic prejudice and discrimination.[106]

An alternative to the traditional theory of Anglo-conformity assimilation, cultural pluralism can be seen in the views of certain Jewish leaders since the early 1800s. It was a Jewish American of Polish and Latvian origin who best formulated this perspective. Horace Kallen (1882–1974) argued that membership in ethnic–cultural groups was not a membership one could readily abandon. Writing in the *Nation* in 1915, he argued that ethnic groups had a right to exist on their own terms; that is, democracy applied to ethnic groups. He argued against the ruthless Americanization advocated by many white Anglo-Protestant nativists. By the 1920s he had given the name *cultural pluralism* to the view that each ethnic group has the democratic right to retain its own heritage. However, some scholars have argued that Kallen's cultural pluralism is not a useful perspective for understanding the adaptive history of Jewish Americans, since massive acculturation and much other assimilation have been facts of life for most.[107]

Patterns of Assimilation

Partial cultural assimilation came relatively quickly for each of the three major streams of Jewish immigrants and their children. Most Sephardic and German Jews rapidly adapted to their environment, picking up English and basic values, but they maintained a commitment to Judaism. They came in small numbers into a rapidly expanding United States with a vast frontier. Then came the large numbers of eastern Europeans. German Jews pressed the new immigrants to Americanize rapidly. In New York City German social workers came "downtown" to help assimilate the new eastern Europeans. Yet for the most part the two groups remained separate. Most new arrivals were committed to retaining their distinctiveness and their sense of Jewish peoplehood. Their Yiddish culture, which became in part an oppositional culture, played a crucial role in perpetuating the Jewish heritage and in resisting anti-Semitism. The immigrants had no illusions that they would cease to be outsiders in a predominantly non-Jewish society, yet they eagerly embraced the opportunities for jobs, for citizenship, and for an education for their children.[108]

Second-generation eastern European Jews were more affected by assimilation pressures and rapidly picked up the language and values pressed on them in the media and the public school system. Like the young Italian Americans discussed in the last chapter, they were caught between the culture of their parents and the core culture, a situation guaranteed to create family tensions. The proportion speaking Yiddish declined substantially. Their Judaism, particularly the Reform and Conservative variants, was Americanized. Moreover, many members of the third east European generation moved out of predominantly Jewish neighborhoods. Still, they too were eager to accent their Jewishness in a combination of religious and secular practices.[109]

In the sphere of structural assimilation at the secondary level of the economy and politics, the central and eastern Europeans advanced quickly. A large portion of German Jews and some eastern European Jews achieved substantial economic success in the first generation. And as a group the eastern Europeans moved from a blue-collar concentration to a white-collar concentration in three generations. The initial concentration in certain blue-collar and entrepreneurial categories reflected discrimination as well as the skills that the immigrants brought with them. For many, the ethnic niche economy was critical; often concentrated in middleman positions, many prospered. Hard work and mastery of the core culture's educational system facilitated upward movement over several generations. However, even today the occupational distribution of Jewish Americans underscores the point that even the prosperous among them are not yet fully integrated in the upper reaches of this society. The absence of Jewish Americans at the very top in many spheres of the economy and politics is indicative of continuing discrimination.

Jewish Americans have, over a few generations, moved well up the economic ladder in the United States. Most came in poor; most today are part of middle-income America. Why were they able to move up the ladder so successfully? Some have explained this in terms of certain basic values and religious traditions. Nathan Glazer has argued that "Judaism emphasizes the traits that businessmen and intellectuals require, and has done so at least 1,500 years before Calvinism.... The strong emphasis on learning and study can be traced that far back, too. The Jewish habits of foresight, care, moderation probably arose early."[110]

Others have argued that this image of success growing out of traditional religious values is greatly exaggerated if not mythological. Jewish American success had less to do with religious factors than with historical and structural factors. Although the eastern European immigrants were among the poorest, least educated European Jews, they were not illiterate peasants lacking urban experience. In the period 1880–1920 most came from urban areas of eastern Europe, where they had worked in a variety of urban occupations, such as manufacturing, craftwork, and small-scale commerce. Some had experience as small merchants. Others were textile workers. Compared with the literacy level of most other immigrants at this time, theirs was high. European Jews migrated to the United States at a time of expanding manufacturing and trade. Their urban backgrounds and skills fit in well with the needs of U.S. capitalism, especially in the textile industry. Steinberg concludes that, contrary to what Glazer has argued, Jewish immigrants did not need to rely only on their traditional religious values; they came in with "occupational skills that gave them a decisive advantage over other immigrants." The fit between Jewish American skills and economic circumstances at a critical time was better than it would be for later nonwhite migrants (such as black Americans and Puerto Ricans) to the big cities.[111]

Hertzberg takes another tack and attributes the immigrants' success largely to their "'Jewish head'...the heritage of siege mentality, of centuries of being an embattled bastion in a hostile 'exile,' and of having only one tool for survival, the use of one's wits." This is a type of oppositional culture that facilitates survival under anti-Semitic oppression. Hertzberg also notes the unique relationship of the eastern Europeans to their countries of origin, places in which Jewish life had ceased to be viable. They had an overwhelming need to succeed in the United States; returning to Europe was not an option.[112]

Although American Jews have shown greater geographic mobility than many other groups in recent years, the majority have not achieved full structural assimilation at the informal level. Decreasing residential concentration has not eliminated the informal social cohesion of Jewish Americans. Goldscheider notes that geographic mobility for this group is based on the same factors as geographic mobility for other Americans: housing markets, family life cycle, and economic constraints. "It is no longer the case," he claims, "that the greater the residential dispersal and integration, the weaker the informal ties to the Jewish community.... The evidence from Jewish communities...shows that there are few long-term effects of migration on ethnic cohesion."[113]

Thus in the early 1980s informal social ties were found to be strong in Los Angeles's large Jewish American community, even though the housing pattern there was dispersed; "the picture that emerges...is of a vibrant people whose closest personal associations are with other Jews in the family, friendship, and occupational groupings."[114] In 1987 only a quarter of Rhode Island's Jews lived in neighborhoods that were half Jewish or more, yet three-quarters reported that two or more of their closest friends were Jewish. Even among the young, two-thirds reported having mostly Jewish friends. About one-quarter of all the respondents, and a larger proportion of the young, expressed the desire to have more Jewish families living in their neighborhoods.[115] Nationally the figures on friendship are not as high. In the 1990 NJPS, 45 percent of religious Jews, but only 12 percent of secular Jews, reported that most or all of their friends were Jewish.[116]

Intentional discrimination played a major role in frustrating the rise of first-generation Sephardic, German, and eastern European Jews. Even the acculturated children and grandchildren of these immigrants have faced anti-Semitic barriers that have stalled structural assimilation in some areas. Discrimination channeled the first eastern Europeans into familiar ghetto communities. In the World War II period many Jewish Americans even changed their names. In Los Angeles following World War II, for example, just under half of all those petitioning for name changes were Jewish, although Jewish residents made up only about 6 percent of the population. This may seem like a final rejection of Jewish identity. For most, however, a name change was simply instrumental in securing a job and in facilitating structural mobility. In spite of the affluence of later generations, some economic and social discrimination persists. Milton Gordon has argued that while Jewish Americans have experienced partial assimilation at the behavior-receptional level (that is, discrimination has declined), less assimilation has occurred at the attitude-receptional level because of the persistence of anti-Semitism.[117]

Intermarriage

Opposed by some on the grounds that it threatens the solidarity and survival of the Jewish American community, intermarriage has generally increased generation by generation, reflecting the decline of negative mutual images, desires to assimilate, and greater acceptance of ethnic diversity in the United States. Outmarriage has been more common for those Jews who are geographically separated from large Jewish communities. Since the 1960s the proportion of interfaith marriages has risen steadily—from 11 percent for those who married prior to 1965, to 31 percent in the period 1965–74, to 57 percent for those who married in the late 1980s. This trend has led some observers to predict the disappearance of the American Jewish community within a few decades. However, Judaism's increasing acceptance of mixed marriages has since 1980 resulted in a growing percentage of intermarried couples who along with their children embrace Judaism and identify themselves as Jewish.[118]

For example, in Rhode Island the percentage of marriages in which both partners were Jewish-born declined from 98 percent before 1960 to 62 percent in the period 1980–87. However, in this latter period 12 percent of the Jewish-born partners married a convert. The Jewish partners in these marriages were almost equally divided between husband and wife; a quarter century earlier almost all intermarriages involved a Jewish-born husband. Moreover, 70 percent of the Rhode Island respondents said they would accept a child's intermarriage; about half said they would encourage the non-Jewish spouse to convert. The major concern over intermarriage, expressed by 60 percent of these respondents, was the future of the American Jewish community.[119] In addition, in the 1990 NJPS fewer than half the respondents stated that they would support marriage between their child and a non-Jewish person, although only 22 percent of religious Jews and between 3 and 6 percent of other Jews would openly oppose such a marriage.[120]

Assessing the implications of the growing number of intermarriages, Goldscheider argues against Gordon's view that they can be regarded as an unambiguous measure of assimilation to the Anglo-Protestant society. "Strong communal bonds and networks link the intermarried to the community.... There is evidence as well that an increasing proportion of American Jews are accepting the intermarried within the community."[121]

Recent Immigrants: Strong Jewish Identity

The social and economic adjustment of recent Jewish immigrants raises some interesting issues about assimilation and U.S. culture. In one opinion survey of 900 émigrés from the former Soviet Union, most reported that they had left the country because of the anti-Semitism there. The immigrants were asked to compare their lives in the United States with life in their home country. Most reported having trouble with English and with initially finding a job but rated their life as Jews, as well as their housing, income, and overall standard of living, better than that in the former Soviet Union. Other answers were more surprising. Most considered their cultural environment worse in the United States, and large percentages felt their friendship, social status, and work atmosphere was worse in the United States. They liked the freedom and creativity of the United States, but disliked the vulgarity and "low" cultural tastes.

Thismostlywelleducated group of immigrants appears to be assimilating satisfactorily to the U.S. economy and to material conditions but is having trouble with certain social and cultural adjustments.[122]

Steven Gold has examined adaptation among a more diverse group of refugees from the former Soviet Union in two recently established immigrant communities in Los Angeles and San Francisco. In both communities the Jewish population was geographically concentrated; residents of the full-faceted Los Angeles community could lead an active life without any knowledge of English. Many had little contact with other Jewish Americans because of differences in language and culture. However, some, particularly the younger ones with a good education, found desirable jobs and moved into the middle class. Many middle-aged émigrés whose job skills were not transferable or who were unwilling to take a lower-prestige job than they had held in their native country had more difficulty adapting and often remained isolated from fellow émigrés out of a sense of shame. Older émigrés were the least likely to adapt. Few voluntary support organizations had been formed in either California city, a phenomenon Gold attributes to the coercive nature of the autocratic system they left behind. Most support came from their extended families. The strong sense of Jewish identity of these new immigrants is yet another factor reinforcing Jewish ethnicity in the United States.[123]

Contemporary Jewish Identity and the Future of the American Jewish Community

What does it mean to be Jewish American in the 1990s? Asked to specify the basis of Jewish identity, 90 percent of the respondents to the 1990 NJPS cited cultural or ethnic group membership; this was true for both religious and secular Jews. Fewer than 5 percent of all respondents defined Jewishness *only* as religious group membership.[124] Significantly, Israel has been a major focus of this Jewish American identity and consciousness, a focus reducing the possibility of identificational assimilation. In the 1990 NJPS most religious Jews reported a great emotional attachment to Israel, and just under half of secular Jews also reported such an attachment.[125]

The size of the American Jewish population has remained stable since 1970. The NJPS estimate of the core Jewish population in 1970 was 5.4 million; by 1990 it had risen slightly, to 5.5 million. However, low birthrates and marital assimilation are seen by some as threats to the continuation of Jewish ethnicity. Most entirely Jewish households are small, averaging 2.2 persons. This reflects the older age of the group as well as the small number of children per family. Jewish American families have fewer children than the population as a whole, and the core population has almost one-third more elderly persons than the total U.S. population. However, the 1990 NJPS found that virtually all children of Jewish parents were being raised as Jewish. Significantly, even though only a small percentage of non-Jewish-born spouses in mixed marriages have converted to Judaism, an estimated 28 percent of their children were being raised as Jewish.[126] Commitment to passing on Jewish culture and a sense of Jewish identity to succeeding generations remains very strong.

Andrew Greeley's *ethnogenesis* perspective, which we discussed in Chapter 2, recognizes the reality of cultural differences among contemporary ethnic groups (in the tradition of Kallen's cultural pluralism) and seems to fit the Jewish experience. Jewish

Americans are more than a single European nationality group. They are a composite group of Sephardic, central European, and eastern European origin. In the United States Jewish immigrants and their descendants have forged a distinctive ethnic group, shaped partially by the European cultural heritage and partially by adaptation to the Anglo-Protestant core culture. Despite substantial adaptive changes, Jewish American ethnic and cultural distinctiveness remains. Persisting anti-Semitism, and especially respect for an ancient heritage and the socialization of children by parents in this heritage, continue to shape the behavior and beliefs of Jewish Americans.

How strong is Jewish identity? Is it, as Herbert Gans argues, only a "symbolic ethnicity," without much deep and lasting significance? In the view of Gans, and of Richard Alba, ethnicity for many white ethnic Americans is today little more than a desire to maintain some feeling for ethnic background without strong commitments to ethnic behavior or strong social ties.[127] Some Jewish scholars, such as Arthur Hertzberg, have argued that the weakening of religious ties among Jewish Americans signals that Jewish ethnicity is increasingly symbolic, that "it is well on its way to becoming memory."[128] Yet Hertzberg, who wishes for a revival of true Judaism among Jewish Americans, recognizes that Jewish ethnicity will probably last a few more generations. And Alba recognizes that Jewish Americans are different from other white ethnic Americans because of their extensive social networks, especially those rooted in religious congregations and schools, and because of their "centuries old tradition of survival as a minority in Gentile-dominated societies."[129]

Thinking along different lines, Silberman suggests that the greater acceptance of Jewish Americans in a largely non-Jewish society today compared with fifty years ago makes Jewish Americans less likely to abandon their Jewishness, since their identity has ceased to be the focal point of widespread discrimination and instead has become a badge of pride linked to a worldwide Jewish struggle such as that of Israel.[130] Thus a sense of Jewishness is likely to remain strong for the majority of Jewish Americans for the foreseeable future.

SUMMARY

Jewish Americans, most of whom are descendants of central and eastern Europeans, have become substantially assimilated in the cultural arena. An economically prosperous ethnic group that has made dramatic progress up the mobility ladder, Jewish Americans have struggled against great prejudice and discrimination and not a little violence. Theirs is a success story. But as we have seen, a price has been paid for that success. Moreover, significant anti-Semitism persists today, often limiting movement to the very top in the economy and in politics. Coupled with the substantial vertical progress over the decades has been horizontal mobility in the form of suburbanization. The first-generation eastern European Jews were concentrated in central-city ghettos; subsequent generations began moving in large numbers into suburban areas.

Central to an adequate understanding of Jewish Americans today is an understanding of their ties to Israel. The creation of Israel and periodic Arab–Israeli conflicts have generated a strong commitment to Israel, philosophically and financially. Israel continues to be seen among Jewish Americans as a critical place of refuge for a people that has survived the Roman persecution, the Spanish Inquisition, Russian pogroms, and the Nazi Holocaust. Related to this commitment has been the flow of thousands of Jewish Americans to the work camps, towns, and cities of Israel. Yet recent decades have also seen a significant number of Israeli and Soviet Jewish immigrants escaping the threat of war or seeking new economic and political opportunities. Many Jewish immigrants from the (former) Soviet Union have settled in the United States—40,000 in 1990 alone. They provide a contemporary reminder of the sojourner character of much Jewish experience.

Perhaps most important, we have demonstrated in this chapter just how diverse the U.S. melting pot is—a diversity that makes for great vitality and creativity. The Jewish American presence and participation in U.S. institutions mean that this nation is not by definition a Christian country; it is a nation of many religious groups, including Protestants, Catholics, Jews, and Muslims. One of the contributions of Jewish Americans has been their stand for the Jewish religious and cultural heritage in spite of nativist discrimination and other opposition—and thereby the expansion of religious liberty for all citizens.

Jewish Americans have contributed substantially to the emphasis on education in the United States, to high achievement in the arts and sciences, and to the values of justice, tolerance, and fairness. Jewish Americans have not been passive victims of anti-Semitic prejudice and discrimination; they and their organizations have occupied the forefront of the fight against the broader prejudice and racism that continue to plague U.S. society.

NOTES

1. Alan Dershowitz, *Chutzpah* (Boston: Little, Brown, 1991), p. 202.
2. Ibid., pp. 198–99, 206, 343–54; Arthur Hertzberg, *The Jews in America* (New York: Simon & Schuster, 1989), pp. 377–88.
3. Hertzberg, *The Jews in America*, pp. 13–28.
4. Charles E. Silberman, *A Certain People* (New York: Summit Books, 1985), pp. 40–42; Chaim I. Waxman, *America's Jews in Transition* (Philadelphia: Temple University Press, 1983), pp. 5–6.
5. Silberman, *A Certain People*, pp. 42–45; Waxman, *America's Jews in Transition*, pp. 6–8.
6. Silberman, *A Certain People*, pp. 42–49; Hertzberg, *The Jews in America*, pp. 102–4.
7. Hertzberg, *The Jews in America*, pp. 152–54, 185; Silberman, *A Certain People*, p. 49; Waxman, *America's Jews in Transition*, p. 43.
8. Hertzberg, *The Jews in America*, pp. 160–76, 224; Silberman, *A Certain People*, pp. 49–51.
9. Milton Meltzer, Never to Forget: The Jews of the Holocaust (New York: Harper & Row, Pub., 1976), p. 45.
10. Maurice J. Karpf, *Jewish Community Organization in the United States* (New York: Arno, 1971), p. 33; Sidney Goldstein, "American Jewry: A Demographic Analysis," in *The Future of the Jewish Community in America*, ed. David Sidorsky (New York: Basic Books, 1973), p. 71; Alvin Chenkin, "Jewish Population in the United States," in *American Jewish Yearbook, 1973* (New York: American Jewish Committee, 1973), pp. 307–9; Arthur A. Goren, "Jews," in *Harvard Encyclopedia of American Ethnic Groups* (Cambridge: Harvard University Press, 1980), pp. 591–92; Rita J. Simon and Julian L. Simon, "Social and Economic Adjustment," in *New Lives*, ed. Rita J. Simon (Lexington, Mass.: Heath, Lexington Books, 1985), pp. 26–41.
11. Calvin Goldscheider and Sidney Goldstein, *The Jewish Community of Rhode Island* (Providence: Jewish Federation of Rhode Island, 1988), pp. 3–35.
12. Barry A. Kosmin et al., *Highlights of the CJF 1990 National Jewish Population Survey* (New York: Council of Jewish Federations, 1991), pp. 3–6, 10, 20–22, 25–26; Nathan Glazer, *New Perspectives in American Jewish Sociology* (New York: American Jewish Committee, 1987), p. 8.
13. See David Sidorsky, "Introduction," in *The Future of the Jewish Community in America*, ed. Sidorsky, pp. xix–xxv; and Stephen D. Isaacs, *Jews and American Politics* (Garden City, N.Y.: Doubleday, 1974), pp. ix–x.
14. Charles Y. Glock and Rodney Stark, *Christian Beliefs and Anti-Semitism* (New York: Harper & Row, Pub., 1966), p. 64 et passim.
15. Carey McWilliams, *A Mask for Privilege* (Boston: Little, Brown, 1948), pp. 164–65, 170–73; John Higham, "Social Discrimination against Jews in America, 1830–1930," *Publication of the American Jewish Historical Society* 47 (September 1957): 5.
16. Silberman, *A Certain People*, p. 48; Hertzberg, *The Jews in America*, pp. 86–87, 188–89; Higham, "Social Discrimination against Jews in America," pp. 9–10.
17. Silberman, *A Certain People*, p. 47.

18. Gustavus Meyers, *History of Bigotry in the United States*, rev. ed. (New York: Capricorn Books, 1960), pp. 277–313; McWilliams, *A Mask for Privilege*, pp. 110–11; T. W. Adorno et al., *The Authoritarian Personality* (New York: Harper, 1950), pp. 69–79; Isaacs, *Jews and American Politics*, pp. 51, 98.

19. Gary A. Tobin, *Jewish Perceptions of Antisemitism* (New York: Plenum, 1988), pp. 106–12.

20. Silberman, *A Certain People*, pp. 22–27, 335–37, 360–66; Dershowitz, *Chutzpah*, pp. 116–29.

21. Kosmin et al., *Highlights of the CJF 1990 National Jewish Population Survey*, p. 29.

22. Henry L. Feingold, *Zion in America* (New York: Twayne, 1974), pp. 143–44; C. Vann Woodward, *Tom Watson* (New York: Oxford University Press, 1963), pp. 435–45.

23. Rufus Learski, *The Jews in America* (New York: KTAV Publishing House, 1972), pp. 290–91; John Higham, *Strangers in the Land* (New York: Atheneum, 1975), pp. 298–99; Woodward, *Tom Watson*.

24. Milton R. Konvitz, "Inter-group Relations," in *The American Jew*, ed. O. I. Janowsky (Philadelphia: Jewish Publication Society of America, 1964), pp. 78–79; Donald S. Strong, *Organized Anti-Semitism in America* (Washington, D.C.: American Council on Public Affairs, 1941), pp. 14–20.

25. Strong, *Organized Anti-Semitism in America*, p. 67.

26. Lucy S. Dawidowicz, *The War against the Jews: 1933–1945* (New York: Holt, Rinehart & Winston), p. 148; see also pp. 164 and 403.

27. Lewis H. Carlson and George A. Colburn, "The Jewish Refugee Problem," in *In Their Place*, ed. Lewis H. Carlson and George A. Colburn (New York: John Wiley, 1972), pp. 290–91; Stephanie Chavez, "Anti-Semitic Incidents Reported Rising," *Los Angeles Times*, February 7, 1992, p. A3.

28. Lenni Brenner, *Jews in America Today* (Secaucus, N.J.: Lyle Stuart, 1986), p. 209; See discussion of "hate crimes" in Chapter 12.

29. Konvitz, "Inter-group Relations," pp. 85–95.

30. Dershowitz, *Chutzpah*, p. 326; Linda Greenhouse, "Justices Affirm Ban on Prayers in Public School," *New York Times*, June 25, 1992, p. A1.

31. Robert F. Drinan, "The Supreme Court, Religious Freedom and the Yarmulke," *America*, June 12, 1986, pp. 9–11.

32. Gerald S. Strober, *American Jews* (Garden City, N.Y.: Doubleday, 1974), pp. 149–76.

33. "Laurel and Kareem Abdul-Jabbar Acquire Television Movie Rights," *Business Wire*, May 4, 1992, n.p.

34. "Two Deaths Ignite Racial Clash in Tense Brooklyn Neighborhood," *New York Times*, August 21, 1991, p. A1; Scott Minerbrook and Miriam Horn, "Side by Side, Apart," *U.S. News & World Report*, November 4, 1991, p. 44.

35. Silberman, *A Certain People*, p. 340.

36. Ibid., p. 41.

37. Ibid., pp. 333, 339–43; Dershowitz, *Chutzpah*, pp. 241, 301–2.

38. Letty Cottin Pogrebin, *Deborah, Golda, and Me: Being Female and Jewish in America* (New York: Crown Publishers, 1991).

39. Joe R. Feagin and Leslie Inniss, "Racial Attitudes in Four Socio-Religious Groups" (research paper, University of Florida, 1992).

40. Tom Tugend, "L.A. Jews Step Up Aid to Riot-Hit Areas," *Jerusalem Post*, May 12, 1992, n.p.

41. Waxman, *America's Jews in Transition*, pp. 5–10, quotation from p. 10; Hertzberg, *The Jews in America*, pp. 62–69; Lawrence H. Fuchs, *The Political Behavior of American Jews* (Glencoe, Ill.: Free Press, 1956), pp. 23–25; Silberman, *A Certain People*, p. 44; Will Herberg, *Protestant—Catholic—Jew*, rev. ed. (New York: Doubleday, Anchor Books, 1960), pp. 98–99.

42. Hertzberg, *The Jews in America*, pp. 108–9; Mark R. Levy and Michael S. Kramer, *The Ethnic Factor* (New York: Simon & Schuster, 1972), p. 101; William R. Heitzmann, *American Jewish Voting Behavior* (San Francisco: R & E Research Associates, 1975), pp. 27–28.

43. Irving Howe, *World of Our Fathers* (New York: Simon & Schuster, 1976), pp. 362–64; Emanuel Hertz, "Politics: New York," in *The Russian Jew in the United States*, ed. Charles S. Bernheimer (Philadelphia: John Winston and Co., 1905), pp. 256–65.

44. Edward M. Levine, *The Irish and Irish Politicians* (Notre Dame, Ind.: University of Notre Dame Press, 1966); Isaacs, *Jews and American Politics*, pp. 23–24; Feingold, *Zion in America*, p. 321.

45. Hertz, "Politics," pp. 265–67; Heitzmann, *American Jewish Voting Behavior*, p. 37; Fuchs, *The Political Behavior of American Jews*, pp. 57–58.

46. Levy and Kramer, *The Ethnic Factor*, pp. 102–3; Howe, *World of Our Fathers*, pp. 381–88.

47. Hertzberg, *The Jews in America*, pp. 282–83.

48. Heitzmann, *American Jewish Voting Behavior*, p. 49; Fuchs, *The Political Behavior of American Jews*, pp. 99–100.

49. Isaacs, *Jews and American Politics*, pp. 6, 152; Heitzmann, *American Jewish Voting Behavior*, pp. 56–58; Strober, *American Jews*, pp. 186–88; Levy and Kramer, *The Ethnic Factor*, p. 103; Milton Plesur, *Jewish Life in Twentieth Century America* (Chicago: Nelson Hall, 1982), pp. 134–52; William Schneider, "The Jewish Vote in 1984," *Public Opinion* 7 (December/January 1985): 58; Brenner, *Jews in America Today*, pp. 37, 128–31.

50. Kosmin et al., *Highlights of the CJF 1990 National Jewish Population Survey*, pp. 30–35.

51. Isaacs, *Jews and American Politics*, pp. 23, 201; Levy and Kramer, *The Ethnic Factor*, p. 118; Plesur, *Jewish Life in Twentieth Century America*, pp. 143–45.

52. Isaacs, *Jews and American Politics*, pp. 12, 118–19.

53. Bernard Cohen, *Sociocultural Changes in American Jewish Life as Reflected in Selected Jewish Literature* (Rutherford, N.J.: Fairleigh Dickinson University Press, 1972), pp. 183–85; Learski, *The Jews in America*, pp. 158–59; Rudolf Glanz, *The Jewish Woman in America*, vol. 1, *The Eastern European Jewish Woman* (New York: KTAV Publishing House, 1976), pp. 48–57.

54. Nathan Reich, "Economic Status," in *The American Jew*, ed. Janowsky, pp. 70–71; Karpf, *Jewish Community Organization in the United States*, pp. 11–12; Howe, *World of Our Fathers*, pp. 391–93; Feingold, *Zion in America*, pp. 235–36.

55. Jonathan S. Woocher, *Sacred Survival* (Bloomington: Indiana University Press, 1986), pp. vii–viii.
56. Karpf, *Jewish Community Organization in the United States*, pp. 62–65; Naomi Cohen, *Not Free to Desist* (Philadelphia: Jewish Publication Society of America, 1972), pp. 3–18, 37–80, 433–52.
57. Arnold Foster and Benjamin R. Epstein, *The New Anti-Semitism* (New York: McGraw-Hill, 1974), pp. 155–284; Strober, *American Jews*, pp. 7–42.
58. Wolfe Kelman, "The Synagogue in America," in *The Future of the Jewish Community in America*, ed. Sidorsky, pp. 171–73.
59. Dershowitz, *Chutzpah*, p. 49. See also Hertzberg, *The Jews in America*, pp. 350–51.
60. Brenner, *Jews in America Today*, p. 10.
61. Hertzberg, *The Jews in America*, pp. 17–28, 63.
62. Feingold, *Zion in America*, p. 12; McWilliams, *Brothers under the Skin*, pp. 305–6.
63. Wittke, *We Who Built America*, p. 325; George Cohen, *The Jews in the Making of America* (Boston: Stratford Co., 1924), pp. 120–22; Silberman, *A Certain People*, pp. 44–45; Waxman, *America's Jews in Transition*, pp. 22–24.
64. Jacob Lestchinsky, "Economic and Social Development of American Jewry," in *The Jewish People* (New York: Jewish Encyclopedic Handbooks, 1955) 4:78.
65. Nathan Goldberg, *Occupational Patterns of American Jewry* (New York: Jewish Teachers Seminary Press, 1947), pp. 15–17; Marshall Sklare, *America's Jews* (New York: Random House, 1971), p. 61; Isaac M. Rubinow, "Economic and Industrial Conditions: New York," in *The Russian Jew in the United States*, ed. Bernheimer, pp. 110–11.
66. Lestchinsky, "Economic and Social Development of American Jewry," pp. 74–77; Rubinow, "Economic and Industrial Conditions," pp. 103–7; Waxman, *America's Jews in Transition*, p. 58; Hertzberg, *The Jews in America*, p. 198.
67. Charlotte Baum, Paula Hyman, and Sonya Michel, *The Jewish Woman in America* (New York: Dial Press, 1976), p. 98; Hertzberg, *The Jews in America*, pp. 198–201.
68. Karpf, *Jewish Community Organization in the United States*, pp. 9–14; Lestchinsky, "Economic and Social Development of American Jewry," pp. 91–92; W. Lloyd Warner and Leo Srole, *The Social Systems of American Ethnic Groups* (New Haven: Yale University Press, 1945), p. 112; Silberman, *A Certain People*, pp. 127–30.
69. McWilliams, *A Mask for Privilege*, pp. 38, 40–41; Karpf, *Jewish Community Organization in the United States*, pp. 20–21; Higham, "Social Discrimination against Jews in America," pp. 18–19.
70. For the February 1936 *Fortune* survey, see Karpf, *Jewish Community Organization in the United States*, pp. 9–11.
71. McWilliams, *A Mask for Privilege*, pp. 143–50. See also Lestchinsky, "Economic and Social Development of American Jewry," p. 81.
72. Lestchinsky, "Economic and Social Development of American Jewry," pp. 71, 87; McWilliams, *A Mask for Privilege*, p. 159; Reich, "Economic Status," pp. 63–65; Dershowitz, *Chutzpah*, p. 74.
73. Cited in Barry R. Chiswick, "The Labor Market Status of American Jews," in *American Jewish Handbook*, ed. M. Himmelfarb and D. Singer (New York: American Jewish Committee, 1984), p. 137.
74. Mabel Newcomer, *The Big Business Executive* (New York: Columbia University Press, 1955), pp. 46–48.
75. Donald J. Bogue, *The Population of the United States* (Glencoe, Ill.: Free Press, 1959), p. 706; Silberman, *A Certain People*, pp. 117–18; Goldscheider and Goldstein, *The Jewish Community of Rhode Island*, p. 12.
76. Kosmin et al., *Highlights of the CJF 1990 National Jewish Population Survey*, p. 19; U.S. Bureau of the Census, *Statistical Abstract of the United States: 1991* (Washington, 1991), p. 450. Median household income is lower than median family income in census data.
77. Goren, "Jews," p. 593; Sklare, *America's Jews*, pp. 61–62; Goldscheider and Goldstein, *The Jewish Community of Rhode Island*, pp. 11–12; Kosmin et al., *Highlights of the CJF 1990 National Jewish Population Survey*, p. 12.
78. Abraham K. Korman, *The Outsiders: Jews and Corporate America* (Lexington, Mass.: Heath, Lexington Books, 1988), pp. 79–82.
79. Richard L. Zweigenhaft and G. William Domhoff, *Jews in the Protestant Establishment* (New York: Praeger, 1982), p. 46.
80. Korman, *The Outsiders*, pp. 66–88.
81. Ibid., pp. 35–41.
82. "Florida Legislature Passes Bill," PR Newswire, March 13, 1992, n.p; Sklare, *America's Jews*, p. 65; McWilliams, *Brothers under the Skin*, pp. 310–11.
83. Hertzberg, *The Jews in America*, pp. 50, 273; Silberman, *A Certain People*, p. 51; Waxman, *America's Jews in Transition*, p. 53.
84. J. K. Paulding, "Educational Influences: New York," in *The Russian Jew in the United States*, ed. Bernheimer, pp. 186–97; Cohen, *The Jews in the Making of America*, pp. 140–41; Karpf, *Jewish Community Organization in the United States*, p. 57; Hertzberg, *The Jews in America*, p. 200; Waxman, *America's Jews in Transition*, p. 137.
85. Silberman, *A Certain People*, pp. 52–55; Hertzberg, *The Jews in America*, pp. 246–47; Higham, "Social Discrimination against Jews in America," p. 22; Karpf, *Jewish Community Organization in the United States*, p. 19; McWilliams, *A Mask for Privilege*, pp. 128–29.
86. Silberman, *A Certain People*, pp. 98–100; Hertzberg, *The Jews in America*, p. 309; Dershowitz, *Chutzpah*, pp. 73–74.
87. Strober, *American Jews*, pp. 120–30; Maurice R. Berube and Marilyn Gittell, "The Struggle for Community Control," in *Confrontation at Ocean Hill–Brownsville*, ed. Maurice R. Berube and Marilyn Gittell (New York: Praeger, 1969), pp. 3–12 and elsewhere; Joe R. Feagin and Harlan Hahn, *Ghetto Revolts* (New York: Macmillan, 1973), pp. 327–28; Nathan Glazer, *Affirmative Discrimination* (New York: Basic Books, 1975), pp. 33–76, 196–221.
88. Dershowitz, *Chutzpah*, pp. 75–79, quotation from pp. 78–79.
89. Hertzberg, *The Jews in America*, p. 309; Goldscheider and Goldstein, *The Jewish Community of Rhode Island*, pp. 11, 25–28; Kosmin et al., *Highlights of the CJF 1990 National Jewish Population Survey*, pp. 10–11.
90. Silberman, *A Certain People*, pp. 171–72; Goldscheider and Goldstein, *The Jewish Community of Rhode Island*, pp. 11, 25–28; Kosmin et al., *Highlights of the CJF 1990 National Jewish Population Survey*, pp. 10–11; Robert Alter, "What Jewish Studies Can Do," *Commentary* 58 (October 1974): 71–74.
91. Waxman, *America's Jews in Transition*, p. 10; Hertzberg, *The Jews in America*, pp. 117–23, 146–47, 254–62, quotation from p. 120. See also Silberman, *A Certain People*, p. 46.

92. Waxman, *America's Jews in Transition,* p. 10; Hertzberg, *The Jews in America,* pp. 113–16.
93. Hertzberg, *The Jews in America,* pp. 159–61, 167–68, 195, 214–36.
94. Ibid., pp. 277–79; Waxman, *America's Jews in Transition,* p. 17.
95. Kelman, "The Synagogue in America," pp. 157–58; Louis Lipsky, "Religious Activity: New York," in *The Russian Jew in the United States,* ed. Bernheimer, pp. 152–54; Silberman, *A Certain People,* pp. 170–77; Hertzberg, *The Jews in America,* pp. 277–79.
96. Silberman, *A Certain People,* pp. 176–81, quotation from p. 179.
97. Goldscheider and Goldstein, *The Jewish Community of Rhode Island,* pp. 18–25.
98. Kosmin et al., *Highlights of the CJF 1990 National Jewish Population Survey,* pp. 6, 28, 32–33.
99. Ibid., pp. 36–37.
100. Ibid., pp. 35–36.
101. J. L. Blau, *Judaism in America* (Chicago: University of Chicago Press, 1976), as summarized in Samuel C. Heilman, "The Sociology of American Jewry," in *Annual Review of Sociology,* ed. Ralph Turner, vol. 8 (Palo Alto, Calif.: Annual Reviews, 1982), p. 147.
102. Michael Greenstein, *The American Jew: A Contradiction in Terms* (New York: Gefen Publishing House, 1990), pp. 1–5.
103. Dershowitz, *Chutzpah,* p. 209.
104. Goldscheider and Goldstein, *The Jewish Community of Rhode Island,* p. 22; Monty Noam Penkower, *At the Crossroads: American Jewry and the State of Israel* (Haifa, Israel: University of Haifa, 1990), p. 26; Kosmin et al., *Highlights of the CJF 1990 National Jewish Population Survey,* pp. 29, 35.
105. Penkower, *At the Crossroads,* p. 27.
106. Howe, *World of Our Fathers,* p. 645; Karpf, *Jewish Community Organization in the United States,* pp. 37–39, 49–50; Tobin, *Jewish Perceptions of Antisemitism,* p. 84.
107. Milton R. Konvitz, "Horace Meyer Kallen (1882–1974)," in *American Jewish Yearbook, 1974–1975* (New York: American Jewish Committee, 1974), pp. 65–67; Milton Gordon, *Assimilation in American Life* (New York: Oxford University Press, 1964), pp. 142–59.
108. Hertzberg, *The Jews in America,* pp. 102–30, 167–76, 195.
109. Sidney Goldstein and Calvin Goldscheider, *Jewish Americans* (Englewood Cliffs, N.J.: Prentice-Hall, 1968), p. 226; Silberman, *A Certain People,* pp. 173–81.
110. Nathan Glazer, "The American Jew and the Attainment of Middle-class Rank: Some Trends and Explanations," in *The Jews,* ed. M. Sklare (Glencoe, Ill.: Free Press, 1958), p. 143, quoted in Stephen Steinberg, *The Ethnic Myth* (New York: Atheneum, 1981), p. 93.
111. Steinberg, *The Ethnic Myth,* pp. 94–102.
112. Hertzberg, *The Jews in America,* pp. 167–71, 195, 254–55, quotation from p. 171. Waxman, *America's Jews in Transition,* pp. 55–58.
113. Calvin Goldscheider, *Jewish Continuity and Change* (Atlanta: Scholars Press, 1986), pp. 17–18, quotation from p. 17.
114. Quoted in Sidney Goldstein, "Jews in the United States: Perspectives from Demography," in *American Jewish Yearbook, 1981* (New York: American Jewish Committee, 1980–81), p. 28.
115. Goldscheider and Goldstein, *The Jewish Community of Rhode Island,* p. 28.
116. Kosmin et al., *Highlights of the CJF 1990 National Jewish Population Survey,* p. 35.
117. Gordon, *Assimilation in American Life,* pp. 76–77.
118. Paul R. Spickard, *Mixed Blood* (Madison: University of Wisconsin Press, 1989), pp. 180–228; Kosmin et al., *Highlights of the CJF 1990 National Jewish Population Survey,* p. 14.
119. Goldscheider and Goldstein, *The Jewish Community of Rhode Island,* pp. 13–15.
120. Kosmin et al., *Highlights of the CJF 1990 National Jewish Population Survey,* p. 29.
121. Goldscheider, *Jewish Continuity and Change,* pp. 15–19, quotation from p. 16.
122. Simon and Simon, "Social and Economic Adjustment," pp. 27–38.
123. Steven J. Gold, *Refugee Communities* (Newbury Park, Calif.: Sage Publications, Inc. 1992), pp. 39–44, 67–89.
124. Kosmin et al., *Highlights of the CJF 1990 National Jewish Population Survey,* p. 28.
125. Ibid., p. 29.
126. Ibid., pp. 3–6, 14–17.
127. Herbert J. Gans, "Symbolic Ethnicity," *Ethnic and Racial Studies* 2 (1979): 1–20; Richard Alba, *Ethnic Identity: The Transformation of White America* (New Haven: Yale University Press, 1990), p. 306.
128. Hertzberg, *The Jews in America,* p. 386.
129. Alba, *Ethnic Identity,* p. 310.
130. Silberman, *A Certain People,* pp. 25, 159–324.

Chapter 7

Native Americans

Native Americans
Photo Courtesy of M. B. Duda/Photo Researchers, Inc.

During 1991 and 1992 Native American groups across the nation held protests as the year-long celebration of the 500th anniversary of Columbus's 1492 voyage to the Americas began. In Washington, D.C., two protesters spray-painted "500 years of genocide" on a statue of Columbus, and a third read a list of human rights violations while pouring blood into the statue's outstretched hands. In Tuscon students and representatives of the Apache Survival Coalition held a "drum-in" to protest both the Columbus Quincentenary and the construction of the Columbus telescope on top of a sacred Apache mountain. In Minneapolis protesters held a sunrise ceremony to remember the Native American nations that were destroyed by European immigrants and to celebrate those that survived. Seven hundred protesters organized by the American Indian Movement confronted a Columbus Day celebration in Denver, calling it "a commemoration of centuries of racism in the Americas." In these and many other cities Native Americans were joined by members of African American, Puerto Rican, Mexican American, and other organizations.[1] Native American activist Suzan Shown Harjo explained the Native American position regarding the Columbus Quincentenary: "As Native American peoples…we have no reason to celebrate an invasion that caused the demise of so many of our people and is still causing destruction today. The Europeans stole our land and killed our people."[2]

With this chapter we begin to consider several groups of non-European ("nonwhite") ancestry who were subordinated by European colonization and expansion. The term *white* as a self-designation for Europeans developed in the context of contact with the darker-skinned peoples of both Africa and the Americas, whom Europeans often called *black* and *red* respectively.[3] As colonizers, white Europeans achieved dominance and became a numerical majority. People of color, often collectively termed *nonwhites,* became subordinated minorities. In this and subsequent chapters we will see critical differences in the past and present experiences of these European and non-European Americans. We will also discover the relevance of power–conflict theories in interpreting the past and present of these subordinated groups.

The first victims of European colonization of this continent were the Native Americans—members of the hundreds of nations and smaller groups who were present at the time of the Europeans' entry. Called collectively, and erroneously, "Indians" by their European conquerors, Native Americans have suffered from a variety of stereotypes, from the wooden cigar-store figure to the bloodthirsty savage of the movies to the noble primitive of novels. Distorted images of tomahawks, scalping, feathered headdresses, and warriors on wild ponies have been impressed on the Euro-American mind by sensationalism in magazines, newspapers, and movies and on television.

Coupled with stereotypes and distortions has been a tendency to ignore the past and present reality of Native American life. Reflect for a moment on the notion of Europeans "discovering" America. In fact, the fifteenth-century European explorers were latecomers, for the continent they happened upon was already peopled by several million inhabitants. The ancestors of these peoples had discovered the continent at least twenty thousand years earlier—when, most scholars believe, they had migrated across the land bridge from Asia to Alaska. Reflect too on the name Native Americans have had to bear ever since, the "Indians" (*los Indios*), a name bestowed by their conquerors that reflects a colossal geographical error, the assumption that the early expeditions had found the Asian Indies they were seeking.

CONQUEST BY EUROPEANS AND EURO-AMERICANS

As we explained in Chapter 2, migration varies from voluntary movement to forced slave importation and typically involves a dominant racial or ethnic group that is already established within certain boundaries and is incorporating the new immigrant group. In the case of Native Americans, however, it is the dominant group itself that migrated; that is, the Europeans moved into the territories of Native American groups. This process may be called *colonization migration.* Unlike other types of migration, colonization migration involves the conquest and domination of a preexisting geographical group by outsiders. Such migration also illustrates what some call *classical colonialism.*

How many Native Americans were there at the time Europeans came into North American history? Early on, some analysts estimated the native population of North America in 1500 at between 900,000 and 1,150,000 persons. In recent decades, however, the estimate has been revised upward sharply. A considered estimate by Kirkpatrick Sale puts the number in North America at fifteen million at the time of conquest, with tens of millions in Central and South America as well. Based on an extremely thorough assessment by Henry Dobyns and on suggestions from Russell Thornton, this figure is undoubtedly more accurate than earlier estimates, whose low figures have often been used for the purpose of legitimating the European conquest of an allegedly unoccupied land.[4]

European diseases and firepower sharply reduced the number of Native Americans in North America to approximately 250,000 by 1890. The population remained below 300,000 until the 1930s, when it began to grow. The 1990 census counted almost 1.9 million people who listed their background as American Indian. Today Native Americans live on 250 reservations, in other rural areas, and in cities; most live west of the Mississippi.[5]

The term *Indian* and most names of major groups are terms of convenience applied by European American settlers. In most history books not one of the major tribes is recorded under its own name. For example, the "Navaho" call themselves *Dine*, meaning "The People."[6] The renaming of Native American nations by outsiders is a result of their subordination and suggests one difference between colonized groups and European immigrants: colonized peoples have had less control over the naming process.

Native American Societies: Are They Tribes?

Although many people today think of them as a single category, Native Americans have for centuries been a diverse collection of societies, with dramatic differences in population, language, economy, polity, and customs. Some define the common term *tribe* as a group of relatives with their own language and customs who occupy a definite territory. Yet such a definition obscures the great variety in size and complexity of Native American groups, which have ranged from very small hunting and gathering societies to large, well-organized groups. Although it is difficult to avoid the term *tribe* for all Native American groups, we will also use the term *society* in order to suggest that not all groups were well organized with definite territories.

There were hundreds of distinct groups at the time of the European invasion. Traditionally, Native American societies have been grouped by geographical area as follows: (1) the societies of the East, who hunted, farmed, and fished, and whose first encounters with whites were with English settlers; (2) the Great Plains hunters and agriculturalists, whose first encounters were with the Spaniards; (3) the fishing societies in the Northwest; (4) the seed gatherers of California and neighboring areas; (5) the Navaho shepherds and Pueblo farmers in the Arizona–New Mexico area; (6) the desert societies of southern Arizona and New Mexico; and (7) the Alaskan groups, including the Eskimo.[7] In this chapter we will sometimes be speaking of the hundreds of past and present Native American societies as though they were one group; at other times we will be speaking of one specific group within this larger category.

Forced migration at gunpoint was the lot of some native groups after they had been defeated. Tribes in the West, such as the Navaho, were rounded up after military engagements and forced to migrate to barren reservations. Perhaps the most famous forced march was that of thousands of Cherokees, Creeks, Chickasaws, Choctaws, and Seminoles from their eastern lands to Indian Territory, the eastern half of present-day Oklahoma. *Internal migration* in the twentieth century has involved relocation from rural areas to the cities. During the 1950s, under President Eisenhower's secretary of the interior, an urban relocation program was expanded to cover many Native American groups and numerous cities; a Bureau of Indian Affairs (BIA) branch was set up to oversee relocation services. The scale of this internal migration can be seen in the fact that more than 200,000 Native Americans moved to the cities between the late 1950s and the 1980s, settling for the most part in poverty-stricken areas.[8]

Why have Native Americans moved to the cities? The reasons vary. Many GIs and nurses returning after World War II felt estranged from their former lifestyle on reservations. In addition, poverty and unemployment on reservations led many Native Americans to seek the expanding economic opportunities of cities.[9]

The Colonial Period

Various strategies were developed by the Europeans for dealing with those Native Americans whose land they coveted. These ranged from honest treaty making with equals, to deceptive treaty making, to attempts to exterminate the "Indian menace," to enslavement like that of Africans, to confinement in barren prison camps called reservations.[10]

In the 1600s the Dutch established several communities on the East Coast displacing or wiping out native societies. A Dutch governor was one of the first to offer a government bounty for Native American scalps, to be used as proof of death; Europeans played a major role in spreading this bloody practice conventionally attributed only to Native Americans.[11] English settlers gained superiority over the Native Americans, forcing them into the frontier areas or killing them off.[12] Few whites seemed concerned about the genocidal consequences of their expansion. It is often noted that some English settlers relied on friendly Native Americans to survive the first devastating years, but the new settlers soon turned on their neighbors. A war with the Pequots in 1637 ended when whites massacred several hundred inhabitants of a Native American village and sent the survivors into slavery. The 1675–76 King Philip's War with the Wampanoag tribe and its allies, precipitated by the oppressive tactics of the New England settlers, resulted in substantial losses on both sides. English retaliation was brutal. Hagan notes that the Native American leader, Metacom (known by the English as King Philip), was "captured, drawn, and quartered: his skull remained on view on a pole in Plymouth as late as 1700."[13] Survivors were sold as slaves.

Few people today are aware that Native Americans were enslaved by the European settlers. A 1708 report mentioned 1,400 Native American slaves in the Carolina area. By the mid-eighteenth century between 5 and 10 percent of slaves were Native Americans. As late as the 1790 census, 200 of the 6,000 slaves in Massachusetts were Native Americans. Native Americans were replaced by Africans in part because escape was a constant problem with the former.[14]

The English defeat of the French after a ten-year war resulted in the French withdrawal from the continent in the mid-1700s. This move brought many Native American societies into contact with the less sophisticated and generally more brutal policy of the English.[15]

Treaties, Reservations, and Genocide

With the founding of the United States, Native Americans found themselves in a strange political position. The U.S. Constitution only briefly mentions Native Americans in giving Congress the power to regulate commerce with the tribes. And the 1787 Northwest Ordinance made the following solemn promises:

> The utmost good faith shall always be observed towards the Indians; their land and property shall never be taken from them without their consent; and in their property, rights, and liberty, they shall never be invaded or disturbed, unless in justified and lawful wars authorized by Congress; but laws founded in justice and humanity shall from time to time be made, for preventing wrongs being done to them, and for preserving peace and friendship with them.[16]

Washington's secretary of war, whose department had responsibility for "Indians," adopted a policy of peaceful adjustment. Supreme Court decisions in the early 1800s laid out principles that Native American societies had a right to their lands and that they were nations with a right to self-government. Chief Justice John Marshall argued that the U.S. government must take seriously its treaties with Native Americans. By the late 1700s the executive and legislative branches had become actively involved. In 1790 an act licensing "Indian traders" was passed. A treaty was signed with the Senecas in 1794, and in 1796 government stores were established to provide Native Americans with supplies on credit.[17]

Federal officials, by action or inaction, supported the recurrent theft of Native American lands. In practice, they approved of ignoring boundary rights wherever necessary.[18] A French observer of the 1830s noted the hypocrisy of high-sounding U.S. treaties: "this virtuous and high-minded policy [of treaty making] has not been followed. The rapacity of the settlers is usually backed by the tyranny of the government."[19] The procedure was often not one of immediate expropriation of land, but rather of constant encroachment by European settlers, a process sanctioned after the fact by the government and legitimated by treaties.

The subordination of Native Americans was encouraged by Andrew Jackson, a president critical of treaty making, who even encouraged the states to defy Supreme Court rulings concerning Native Americans. Gradual displacement gave way to brutally oppressive marches over hundreds of miles at gunpoint, a policy of genocide explicitly designed to rid entire regions of those stereotyped by Euro-Americans as "savages." Congress passed the Indian Removal Act in 1830, and within a decade many of the tribes of the East had migrated voluntarily or at gunpoint to lands west of the Mississippi under the auspices of "negotiated" treaties. Atlantic and Gulf Coast tribes, such as the Cherokees, as well as midwestern tribes, such as the Ottawas and Shawnees, were forcibly removed to the Indian Territory in a migration known as the Trail of Tears. Large numbers died in the forced march, and the relocated peoples faced problems in the new lands, where unfamiliar agricultural techniques were required and there was different game to learn how to hunt.[20]

Westward-moving settlers precipitated struggles with the Plains societies, many of whom had by that time given up agriculture for a nomadic hunting and raiding lifestyle. Most Native American groups in this region had participated in intergroup raiding, but the genocidal actions of federal troops and white settlers were a new experience. It was the nomadic, horse-oriented Plains peoples who forever came to symbolize "the Indian" in the white imagination. Mass media presentations have severely distorted the reality of the Plains wars, which usually did *not* involve chiefs in warbonnets on stallions facing a brave collection of U.S. Army officers backed by heroic men on a sun-swept plain.[21]

Myths about Conflict

Movies and television have portrayed the 1840–60 era of white overlanders as one of constant conflict with western societies. The movies and television have created many unforgettable, often racist images of the West—wagon trains moving across the West, wagons in a circle, whooping Indians on ponies, thousands of dead settlers and Indians, and treacherous "red men." However, histories by John D. Unruh and others have made clear that these images are largely mythological. Between 1840 and 60 approximately 250,000 white settlers made the long journey across the plains to the West Coast; far less than 1 percent of those migrants died at the hands of the native inhabitants. Indeed, between 1840 and 1860 a total of *only 362 white settlers and 426 Native Americans* died in *all* the recorded battles between the two groups along wagon train routes. There is only *one* documented attack by Native Americans on a wagon train in which there were as many as two dozen casualties for the white settlers. Most of the accounts of massacres of whites by "wild Indians" are either fictions or great exaggerations of minor encounters.[22]

Unruh's research also highlights the cooperation between Native Americans and the new settlers. Native Americans often provided food and horses for weary white travelers. Some served as guides. Moreover, Unruh and other historians make clear the crucial role of the federal government and of federal troops in attacking and oppressing the native tribes. By the 1850s an army of federal agents, from the famous "Indian agents" to surveyors, road builders, and treaty agents, was facilitating the westward migration of whites.

A recurring pattern emerged in the growing conflict between whites and natives. Settlers would move onto native lands to farm. The federal government, by means of a treaty involving threat or coercion, would provide land for the resettlement of the Native American group affected. More white settlers, prospectors, and hunters moving along migratory paths from the East would gradually intrude on these new tribal lands. This land theft would then be legitimated by yet another treaty, and the process might begin again. Or perhaps a treaty promise of supplies or money to those Native Americans living in a restricted area would not be kept, and some Native American men would leave the area seeking food or revenge. The U.S. Army would then take repressive action, sometimes intentionally punishing an innocent group and thus precipitating further uprisings by Native Americans.

The treaties, part of U.S. law, were often masterpieces of fraud; consent was gained by deception or threat. Three hundred treaties with Native American tribes were made between 1790 and the Civil War. Most were not honored in full. As time passed, treaties established regulations governing tribal behavior and provided for restricted areas called reservations. Tribes became dependent on the federal Bureau of Indian Affairs and on Congress, which by the Civil War could change treaties without the consent of Native Americans. This treaty process was abandoned by the U.S. government by 1871.[23]

Massacres of Native Americans

Serious treaty violations often led to conflict. For example, in an 1862 uprising in Minnesota the eastern Sioux killed some settlers after losing much of their land to settlers and suffering at the hands of white Indian agents. Delays in payment of promised supplies resulted in warriors burning and killing throughout the Minnesota Valley; massive white retaliation followed. About the same time, conflict occurred in Colorado between local tribes and a state militia left in charge when the U.S. Army was withdrawn to fight the Civil War. The guerrilla warfare of the tribes was met by savage retaliation. In 1864 Colonel John Chivington, a minister, and his Colorado volunteers massacred nearly two hundred Native Americans in a peace-seeking band at Sand Creek.[24] The massacre was one of the most savage in western history: "Children carrying white flags were slaughtered and pregnant women were cut open. The slaughter and mutilation continued into the late afternoon over many miles of the bleak prairie."[25]

After the Civil War, large railroad corporations gobbled up millions of acres in the West. Buffalo were slaughtered by the millions, and the economy of the Plains tribes was destroyed. In the late 1860s a federal peace commission met with numerous tribes at Medicine Lodge Creek in Kansas. Reservations were worked out for all the Plains tribes, but it was only after two more decades of battles that all bands agreed to settle in the areas designated by the U.S. government.[26]

Settlers, miners, and the army violated treaties with the Sioux and moved into the Dakota Territory. Controversy over the white invasion escalated; troops were sent in to force Sioux bands onto a smaller reservation, even though the bands were already on what the government regarded as "unceded Indian territory." In this force was Colonel George A. Custer. The most widely known battle of the Plains struggle occurred at the Little Big Horn in 1876 when Custer and his soldiers were wiped out by a group of Sioux and allied tribes that had refused to settle on the reservation.

One of the last engagements was the massacre at Wounded Knee Creek fourteen years later. Attempting to round up the last few Sioux bands, the U.S. Army intercepted one group near the Dakota Badlands and forced them to camp. The colonel in command ordered a disarming of the camp, which was carried out in ruthless fashion. One young Sioux shot into a line of soldiers; the troops replied by shooting at close range with rifles and machine guns. Perhaps three hundred Native Americans, many of them old men, women, and children, were killed on the spot or while running from the camp.[27]

In the Southwest, Native American resistance was, on occasion, substantial. Even after the United States took over the region by military conquest in the 1840s, slave raids on the Navaho by New Mexican settlers continued for a decade or two. Military expeditions were conducted in the Southwest against the scattered Navaho and Apache communities in an attempt to hem them in. Colonel Kit Carson succeeded in getting the Mescalero Apaches to agree to reside on a reservation. Establishing headquarters in Navaho territory, Carson began a scorched-earth program, destroying Navaho fields and herds. He then herded his captives three hundred miles to a reservation—the famous Long Walk central to Navaho history. By 1890 virtually all the remnants of Native American tribes had been forced onto reservations.[28]

Early Cultural Borrowing

The cultures of the Native American peoples encountered by European colonizers in the Western Hemisphere were in many ways more highly developed than European cultures. These peoples built great cities and roads, developed advanced agricultural systems, and created calendars and numerical systems superior to those of Europeans. Significantly, the European invaders borrowed heavily from Native American agriculture and pharmacology. Indeed, Weatherford has estimated that 60 percent of the foods (for example, potatoes, corn, peanuts, and many grains) eaten by people around the globe today were first developed by Native Americans in the Western Hemisphere. Many medicinal plants and their derivatives (for example, quinine) were taken from Native Americans in what is now North, Central, and South America. In addition, European Americans such as Benjamin Franklin and Thomas Jefferson admired the democratic political institutions of major North American tribes.[29]

STEREOTYPING AND RACIST IMAGES

Soon after the arrival of European settlers in the Americas, stereotypes of Native Americans as lazy and wild and of Europeans as provident and steady, along with classification by skin color, served to distinguish the colonizers from the colonized. Thus self-identified "hardworking whites" legitimated the dispossession and attempted enslavement of "lazy red savages." Another early myth, that of the "child of nature" or "noble savage," was a mixture of appreciation and prejudice. French philosophers such as Jean Jacques Rousseau who had read of European contacts with Native Americans utilized scanty data to argue for a golden age of human existence when there was only the unsophisticated "primitive" unspoiled by European civilization. The "child of nature" image, with its emphasis on *child* as well as *nature*, played an important role in the expectations of missionaries bringing Christianity to the Native Americans.[30]

European settlers were shocked by the unwillingness of the native residents to submit to the "civilizing" pressures of missionaries and landseeking farmers. Any violent resistance reinforced new stereotypes of the "bloodthirsty savage." This image became common after the first battles with Native Americans resisting the seizure of their lands. By the mid-1600s Europeans in New England and Virginia were writing that the Native Americans were wild beasts who should be hunted down like other animals. Puritan leaders such as Cotton Mather even saw them as agents of the Devil.[31]

It was the era of westward expansion that imprinted on the public mind, in dime novels and later in movies and TV programs, the image of cruel Native American warriors attacking helpless settlers. Yet the much more significant savagery of the settlers has seldom been accented in the mass media. Carlson and Coburn have commented on the staggering number of Native Americans killed in the mass media: "The Indian, who had been all but eliminated with real bullets, now had to be resurrected to be killed off again with printer's ink."[32] The distorted image of Native Americans as savages can still be found in many textbooks in U.S. schools.

Another erroneous but persisting image is that of the "primitive hunter" who made little use of the land. Most tribes that were forced off lands or killed off were composed *not* of nomadic hunters but of part-time or full-time farmers. Groups such as the Cherokee had by the removal period of the 1830s developed their own mills and other enterprises. Even Alexis de Tocqueville, an astute French observer of American life in the 1830s, accepted the myth, writing that it would be difficult to "civilize" the "Indians" without settling them down as agriculturalists.[33]

Two paradoxical stereotypes were applied to Native American women by European Americans, both based on the woman's relationship with white men: a Princess who saves the white man from her own barbarous people and a Squaw who becomes the white man's sexual partner. Rayna Green documents how the image of the esteemed Princess, portrayed as only slightly darker-skinned than Europeans and with distinctly European features, became a symbol of the New World in Europe, a many-faceted "Mother figure—exotic, powerful, dangerous, and beautiful."[34] The Squaw, portrayed by white racists as darker, fatter, and cruder than the Princess, shared the negative traits of drunkenness, stupidity, and thievery attributed by whites to Native American men, and her destruction was thereby justified as necessary to the progress of "white civilization."

Studies of elementary, high school, and college social science textbooks have found stereotypes about Native Americans. Most school texts deal briefly with Native Americans, almost always in the past tense, with a few references to pioneer days and occasional use of derogatory terms such as *squaw* and *buck*. Numerous children's books on the market today, including story books, picture books, and coloring books, portray Native Americans as warriors or savages. In a recent analysis of Houghton Mifflin's history and social science series for kindergarten through eighth grade, Communities United, a group seeking to locate and remove "stereotypes, omissions, distortions, exaggerations, and outright lies about peoples of color" from school texts, found the series to contain "the justifications and trivializations of some of the most vicious social practices in our history."[35]

Studies of the mass media have turned up grossly exaggerated stereotypes, including widespread use of the "Indian warrior" image. One study of cartoons in the once widely read *Saturday Evening Post* found that virtually every Native American had feathers in his or her hair; one-third of the cartoons of Native Americans showed them with bows and arrows. No modern-day Native Americans were to be found in the thousands of cartoons surveyed.[36]

Some scholars have criticized the tendency of many white observers to define Native Americans and their ancient traditions in terms of eighteenth- and nineteenth-century observations. This limited basis for definition has influenced art, literature, the mass media, and the mainstream view in general and has contributed to the invisibility of contemporary Native Americans.[37] The Academy Award-winning film *Dances with Wolves* is an example of the media's focus on the past. Although this film presents a more sensitive treatment of intergroup history than most of its predecessors, it sees the historical

Native American experience, while regrettable, as proceeding to an inevitable conclusion. The film diverts attention from the present reality of Native Americans, perpetuating the notion that Native Americans are a relic of the past, to be studied only in historical context. As Ward Churchill has stated, "native people are forced to live, right now, today, in abject squalor under the heel of what may be history's most seamlessly perfected system of internal colonization, out of sight, out of mind, their rights and resources relentlessly consumed by the dominant society."[38]

Studies of white attitudes toward Native Americans have been rare. One study in the 1970s updated 1920s research conducted by E. S. Bogardus on social-distance attitudes directed at Native Americans. In the 1920s Bogardus research white college students were asked how close, on a scale from 1 ("would marry") to 7 ("would not allow them in nation"), they would allow a given racial or ethnic group to themselves. Bogardus found that white students rejected all close contact (such as friendships) with Native Americans. The 1970s study using the same social distance scale found Native Americans still being rejected by white respondents in primary-group relations, such as marriage and club membership. This study also found that white views of Native Americans mixed romantic stereotypes with traditional negative stereotypes.[39]

POLITICS

At first European settlers dealt with Native Americans as independent nations. As European communities gained strength they began to treat native nations as groups to be exterminated or as dependent wards. Many eastern groups were destroyed. Those groups remaining in the East were weak enough by the 1830s for the government to force them westward. About the same time, the Bureau of Indian Affairs (BIA) was established to coordinate federal relations with tribes, from supervision of reservations and land dealings to provision of supplies. Until the end of battles in the 1880s the BIA's role of attempting to protect Native Americans put it in direct conflict with a military policy that often sought extermination.

Under BIA domination tribal chiefs were often set aside and replaced by Courts of Indian Offenses. Tribal religions were suppressed, and large numbers of Christian missionaries were imported. BIA rations were usually provided to those who remained on reservations, while troops chased those who did not. Limited attempts were made to educate Native Americans in European ways of health and agriculture. With the termination of treaty making in 1871 and the reduction of all major groups to life on reservations by the 1890s, Native Americans entered into a unique relationship with white America: they were the only subordinate racial or ethnic group whose life was to be routinely administered directly by a bureaucratic arm of the federal government. The action of the BIA is a clear example of the role of government in shaping U.S. racial and ethnic groups, a point underscored by Omi and Winant in their theory of racial formation (see Chapter 2).[40]

From the Dawes Act to the New Deal

A major policy shift regarding land took place in the late nineteenth century. Native Americans, liberal white reformers argued, should be taught new rules of land use. The Dawes Act of 1887 provided that reservation lands be divided among individual families—even though the European tradition of private ownership and individual development of land was an alien value system for many Native American groups. White advocates of the new policy hoped that small individual allotments (40 to 160 acres) would convert Native Americans into farm entrepreneurs. Unallotted lands left over could then be sold to white outsiders. This new federal policy resulted in a large-scale land sale to white Americans; through means fair and foul the remaining 140 million acres of Native American lands were further reduced to 50 million acres by the mid-1930s.[41]

In 1884 a Native American named John Elk moved to the city (Omaha, Nebraska), adapted to white ways, and attempted to vote. Denied this right, Elk took his case to a federal court, where he argued that the Fourteenth Amendment made him a citizen and that the Fifteenth Amendment guaranteed his right to vote.[42] The court ruled that he was not an American citizen—that he was in effect a citizen of a *foreign* nation and thus not entitled to vote. However, under the 1887 Dawes Act, the "wards" of the government could become citizens if they showed themselves competent in managing their land allotments. Some Native Americans were issued "certificates of competency" by special "competency commissions," which decided if they could function well in the white world. Belatedly, in 1924 Congress passed the Indian Citizenship Act, granting citizenship, including voting rights, to all Native Americans.

The U.S. Supreme Court continued to hold that Native Americans were wards of the federal government, a status not changed by the Citizenship Act. Because of this ward status many state governments refused to provide services or allow Native Americans to vote in local elections. To make matters more confusing, the federal government on occasion tried to discontinue its services on the ground that Native Americans were officially citizens.[43]

It was not until the 1934 Indian Reorganization Act (IRA) under the New Deal that a new federal policy was developed. Designed by the liberal commissioner of Indian affairs John Collins, the law was explicitly intended to establish Native American civil and cultural rights, allow for semiautonomous tribal governments similar in legal status to counties and municipalities, and foster economic development of reservations. The changes seemed progressive. The IRA would end land allotment, require careful BIA supervision of the sale of lands, and provide for federal credit and preferential hiring of Native Americans in the BIA. Native American groups were supposed to vote on whether they wanted to come under the act.[44]

Yet as progressive as the law appeared, it had serious defects. It ignored fundamental economic problems and maintained the subordinate ward relationship to the federal government. Oklahoma tribes were excluded; the Papago tribe lost control of its mineral resources; and great power was put in the hands of the secretary of the interior, whom some called the "dictator of the Indians." The secretary made rules for elections, could veto constitutions, supervised expenditures, and made regulations for land management on the reservations.[45] One analyst has noted that "the expressed purpose of this law was finally and completely to usurp the traditional mechanisms of American Indian governance (e.g., the traditional chiefs, council of elders, etc.), replacing them with a system of federally approved and regulated 'tribal councils'...structured more along the lines of corporate boards than of governmental entities."[46]

Grassroots Native American resistance was widespread and intense; many Native Americans saw the IRA as a violation of the sovereignty guaranteed them by treaties with the U.S. government. The law was ratified only by manipulation of the voting process.

Although in several tribes the IRA lost at the ballot box, those who did not vote, including many who refused even to recognize the BIA's authority to hold an election for ratification, were counted as "yes" votes. On some reservations, dead people's votes were used to ensure passage of the act. Tribes that did not hold an election were automatically reorganized under the IRA's terms. After four years, 189 Native American nations were reorganized. Many of these groups incorporated themselves; many also developed central councils with constitutions reflecting the values of white culture. The 77 groups that succeeded in voting down the act operated under traditional customs. Numerous tribes began some self-government, managing their own property and governing their own affairs under federal supervision.[47]

Fluctuations in Federal Policies

In the 1950s House Concurrent Resolution 108, which called for the *termination* of federal supervision of Native American groups, brought yet another major shift in policy toward Native Americans. The intent of the resolution was to reject the Indian Reorganization Act and return to the policy of forced conformity to individualistic values of land use. Supporters of termination included land-hungry whites outside reservations and members of Congress seeking to cut government costs, as well as some tribal members no longer on reservations. Between 1954 and 1960 federal guardianship of several dozen groups was "terminated." Because of its negative effects, including the problems of dealing with often unfriendly local officials and white land entrepreneurs, termination came to be viewed as a failure. In the case of the Menominee tribe, which became a new political unit under Wisconsin state law, distribution payments to individual members exhausted tribal funds and thus development capital, the local hospital had to be closed because it did not meet state standards, and tribal power plants were sold to an outside company. Termination was costly for many tribes unprepared to deal with the complexity and treachery of the outside white world.[48]

Then another shift occurred. From the 1960s to the 1980s federal policy began to move away from termination. President Richard Nixon called on Congress to maintain Native Americans' tie to the federal government and to prohibit termination without consent. Following Nixon's proposals, Congress passed legislation that restored the sacred Blue Lake to the Taos Pueblo, made credit available for business purposes, settled certain land claims of Alaskan natives, and established a self-determination procedure whereby tribes would assume some administration of certain federal programs on reservations. In the late 1970s some Native American groups began to run their own schools and social-service programs.[49]

The powers of the Bureau of Indian Affairs have been far-reaching. The BIA defines who is a Native American by determining which tribes are officially acknowledged by the federal government. The bureau keeps records of "blood" lines in order to identify who is an "Indian" eligible for benefits. Official status brings a number of benefits to a tribe, including economic development aid, status as a sovereign government when dealing with the federal government, and health, education, and housing benefits for its members. To obtain federal recognition a tribe must document a continuous history and prove that its members are Native Americans, a process that many find demeaning and expensive. Several existing tribes have been denied official recognition by the BIA, an action that amounts to "administrative genocide" unless the tribe can successfully appeal its case to the courts or Congress. Some years ago an attempt by the Mohegan tribe in Connecticut to reorganize in order to acquire federal recognition was unsuccessful because the continuous tribal leadership required as proof of existence as a tribe had been outlawed by the state of Connecticut in the 1700s. In 1992 the 600-member Shinnecock tribe in New York State debated the merits of applying for recognition; it estimated the cost of doing so would be $250,000.[50] In this government-controlled definition process of who is an "Indian" and what is a "tribe" we see again evidence of the racial formation theory suggested by Omi and Winant. Governments often intrude into the process by which racial and ethnic groups are defined.

Today the BIA continues to supervise tribal government, banking, utilities, and highways, as well as millions of dollars in tribal trust funds. In the early 1990s the federal government recognized about 300 of the 500 surviving tribes and held in trust for them 52 million acres of land. The BIA supervises leasing and selling of lands, and until recently all control of social services, including education, was in the hands of the bureau or allied federal agencies. Some Native Americans have regarded the BIA as the lesser of two evils, noting that in recent decades it has to some extent protected them against predatory exploitation from the outside and has periodically expanded self-determination and community control. To terminate the BIA would be to end what protection it can provide, giving outside interests one less barrier to contend with. Under pressure from private ranching, lumbering, farming, and mineral interests, other major branches of the Interior Department have opposed the interests of Native Americans.[51]

Since the mid-1980s growing numbers of Native American leaders have called for an end to the colonialism of BIA control and have worked for recognition of their tribes as sovereign nations. In 1988 the Indian Self-Determination Act was amended to enable ten Native American nations to plan for autonomous governance. The following year government support for Native American self-government was furthered when the U.S. Senate Select Committee on Indian Affairs revealed corruption and mismanagement in the BIA. The committee recommended an end to the federal government's paternalistic control over tribal affairs and the negotiation of formal agreements with tribal governments. One Native American leader pointed out that these federal government actions "still retain the legally groundless presumption that Indian nations are somehow inherently subordinate to the United States," and that the call for negotiated agreements instead of treaties "denies Indian peoples the formal recognition of their national sovereignty implied by treaties."[52]

Growing Pressures for Political Participation

Native American political participation has been largely limited to reservation elections and service in tribal governments. With some exceptions reservations have been exempt from state control and taxation; subject to BIA approval, tribes have made their own laws and regulations. Tribal governments have often combined legislative and executive functions in one elected tribal council, and voter turnout for tribal elections has often been substantial. Political conflict has been present on reservations, as, for example, in the power struggle on the Navaho reservation in the 1980s. The chair of the tribe at the time, Peter MacDonald, was challenged by a group that considered him too assimilated and accused him of mismanaging the budget and resources of the tribe. In 1983 Peterson Zah, a leader with a more traditional approach, replaced MacDonald.[53] Numerous splits within reservations have occurred between those leaders who prefer to work with the BIA and those who support tribal sovereignty.[54]

It was not until the 1924 Indian Citizenship Act that Native Americans secured the right to vote in elections outside the reservation. Even this right required protest for its implementation in states such as Utah, Arizona, and New Mexico, where reservation Indians were barred from voting until the 1940s; as late as the 1960s and 1970s some states made voting and jury participation difficult. Discrimination in the form of state literacy tests and the gerrymandering of district lines has reduced the voting power of Native Americans in some western states. By the 1960s and 1970s the number of potential Native American voters had risen to substantial proportions in some nonreservation areas. In the 1980s and 1990s some Native American leaders referred to the Native American vote as a swing vote (a bloc that can throw close elections one way or another) and called for increased voting. Several Native American leaders participated actively in the Rainbow Coalition, which backed Jesse Jackson, a black American, for the U.S. presidency both in 1984 and in 1988.[55]

Only a handful of Native Americans have served in state and federal legislatures, most since the 1950s. About two dozen have served in state legislatures since 1900. Increased voter turnout in predominantly Navaho counties in 1964 sent the first Native Americans to the New Mexico legislature. By 1967 fifteen Native Americans served in legislatures in six western states. In 1992 thirty-five Native Americans were in 14 state legislatures, and Larry Echo Hawk was the elected attorney general in Idaho. Very few have ever served in Congress—perhaps a half dozen representatives and two senators have had some, often modest, Native American ancestry. The most famous, Charles Curtis, was born on the Kaw reservation in 1860. Said to be one-quarter Native American, Curtis was a representative for fourteen years, a senator for twenty, and vice-president under Herbert Hoover. Since 1935 only three Native Americans have served in Congress; there has not been more than one Native American representative at any one time. Ben Reifel, a Sioux, was a representative from South Dakota from 1961 to 1971. In 1992 Congress still had only one Native American member, Representative Ben Nighthorse Campbell from Colorado. However, in November 1992 five Native Americans were running for Congress, the largest number in U.S. history. Campbell was seeking to move from the House to the Senate, and two other Native Americans, one in Oklahoma and another in Alaska, were also running for the Senate. This increase in Native American political activity signaled a growing interest in off-reservation politics and a concern for federal government intervention on education and health care issues of interest to Native Americans.[56]

The slight representation in state legislatures and Congress is paralleled in town and city governments. In the 1950s and 1960s tens of thousands of Native Americans were encouraged to leave reservations for the greener employment pastures of the cities; by the 1980s about half of all Native Americans lived in metropolitan areas. Since the 1970s a few Native Americans have been elected to city councils, school boards, and county governments in these areas.[57]

The extent of representation varies by state and area. For example, the South Dakota Advisory Committee to the U.S. Commission on Civil Rights reported that few Native Americans have ever served as elected officials in that state, even though 5 percent of the population is Native American. In the early 1980s only one Native American was serving in the South Dakota legislature. Only one was mayor of a small city, and a very small number were serving on school boards, even in areas with large Native American populations.

A few studies on the role of government in the lives of Native Americans in urban areas have focused on the police system. One study in Minneapolis and St. Paul found that Native Americans were underrepresented as employees in city government, including the criminal justice system, but heavily overrepresented among those arrested. A disproportionately small percentage of the Minneapolis police force was Native American. Police harassment of Native American men in towns near reservations was a general problem, in part revealing discrimination by local white authorities. (Employment discrimination was also reported to be common in these areas.) Complaints by Native American leaders in numerous cities have focused on the lack of efforts to recruit Native Americans as police and parole officers and government attorneys, as well as unnecessarily high arrest rates.[58]

PROTEST AND CONFLICT

Native American protest against subordination has been the most sustained of any group in the history of North America. Violent resistance to Euro-American oppression between 1500 and 1900 produced some of the greatest protest leaders the continent has seen.

Yet the end of the period of armed conflict did not end protest. The character of the protest changed. By the late nineteenth century a number of protest organizations had sprung up. One of the most important was the Indian Rights Association, founded by white Quakers concerned with protecting and "civilizing" Native Americans. By exposing the corruption and oppression on reservations, such groups did lay the basis for reforms in policy. One of the first organizations formed by Native Americans was the Society of American Indians, created in the early 1900s. A major pan-Indian organization (drawing together representatives of different tribes), it was self-help-oriented; goals included developing pride and a national leadership and improving educational and job opportunities. In the decades that followed, the organization groomed a new leadership that pressed for citizenship legislation and tribal self-determination.[59]

In the 1920s a prominent white defender of Native Americans, John Collier, organized the militant American Indian Defense Association to fight attempts by Republican officials to establish "executive order reservations" not covered by treaty and accessible to exploitation by whites who wished to extract minerals. The National Congress of American Indians (NCAI) was formed in the 1940s and pressed for education, legal aid, and legislation. An influential organization, the NCAI vigorously opposed the termination policy of the 1950s and 1960s and campaigned for the War on Poverty of the 1960s and the self-determination policy of the 1970s and 1980s. As of 1992, NCAI, with 300 member tribes, was the oldest and largest Native American advocacy group. In the early 1990s the group began campaigning against Native American stereotypes after several protests against sports teams' use of Native American names and symbols. The

National Indian Youth Council, created in 1961, fought vigorously for the civil rights of Native Americans, organizing civil disobedience and developing a "Red Power" ideology. The Youth Council has been active in education and has taken up causes critical to the protection of Native American lands.[60]

Protest actions and civil disobedience movements increased in the 1960s, with at least 194 protest activities occurring between 1961 and 1970. Of these, 141 fell into the category of "facilitative tactics," such as legal suits and formal complaints. These actions continued a long tradition of coaxing institutions into concessions—the great strength of organizations such as the NCAI. Civil disobedience involved such activities as delaying dam construction, occupying offices or other government facilities, picketing, and staging sit-ins.[61] Many of the numerous Native American protest actions since the 1970s have brought changes.

In one widely publicized action, students began a long occupation of California's Alcatraz Island late in 1969; they were replaced by one hundred Native Americans claiming *unused* federal lands under provisions of an old treaty. The intent of the Native Americans was both symbolic and concrete—to dramatize the plight of their people and to establish a facility where Native Americans could preserve tribal ways. Government agents forcibly removed the occupying group in the summer of 1971. In the same period protesters made several attempts to seize other *unused* federal property, including Ellis Island in New York harbor, and occupied BIA offices in protest against BIA policies.[62]

In the spring of 1973 a large-scale occupation of Wounded Knee, South Dakota, took place under the auspices of the American Indian Movement (AIM), a group organized to address problems ranging from police brutality to housing and employment discrimination. An Indian Patrol, established by AIM to supervise contacts between Native Americans and the police, reported success in improving police behavior. AIM grew to more than a dozen groups in cities and on reservations. Some leaders and several hundred members played an important role in the seventy-one-day armed occupation of Wounded Knee, a hamlet on the Pine Ridge reservation. The protest was in response to the Justice Department's sending federal agents to Pine Ridge to support the tribal president favored by the federal government when he was challenged by Native American activists wishing to replace him with a traditional Council of Elders.[63]

In its attempts to convict AIM leaders, the federal government, with President Nixon's encouragement, behaved like a police state and used illegal wiretaps, altered evidence, and paid witnesses—which led to dismissal of the case by a federal judge. Afterward, government agents participated in a campaign to destroy the movement and were thought to be involved in a dozen suspicious murders and accidents involving AIM members. Two hundred AIM members were harassed and arrested, but only a dozen or so were ever convicted. This was an example of an open confrontation between militant Native Americans and an Indian establishment propped up by BIA and other white officials.[64]

Sometimes plagued with internal divisions, AIM has persisted in its struggle, establishing chapters in cities across the nation. AIM has organized "survival" schools for Native American children, operated a radio station in South Dakota, and participated in an encampment at Big Mountain on the Navaho reservation to prevent the forced removal of Native Americans from their land. In recent years the movement has developed relationships with liberation movements in Third World countries.[65]

In the early 1990s AIM led protests of the use of Native American names, sacred symbols, and the tomahawk chop gesture by sports teams and fans, focusing particularly on the 1991 World Series and the 1992 Super Bowl. Prior to the 1992 Super Bowl, AIM sponsored a two-day conference on racism in sports. These nationally televised sports events brought degrading caricatures into the homes of many Native Americans who otherwise have little contact with white fans' and teams' behavior. "We couldn't ignore it anymore," one Native American woman stated. "People started coming up to me at work and going, 'chop-chop' and 'woo-woo.'" Team owners and fans argued that names such as *Chiefs* and *Braves* were terms of honor, but no such claim could be made for the derogatory *Redskins*. Many Native Americans consider all such names to be offensive stereotypes. The parody of sacred chants, face paint, headdresses, and drums for entertainment purposes is viewed as a blasphemous assault on Native American religion, since all of these have spiritual significance. AIM director Clyde Bellecourt told a reporter, "We're trying to convince people we're human beings and not mascots.... Imagine if they named a team the Atlanta Bishops, and fans came to the game waving crucifixes [and] there was a guy dressed like the Pope running up and down the aisles throwing holy water on the crowd."[66]

The Native American civil rights movement and pan-Indian activism have achieved some gains in raising the consciousness of the general public and the nation's mass media leadership. In the 1970s some universities, including Dartmouth and Stanford, dropped the name *Indians* for their sports teams. In 1992, in direct response to AIM protests, the *Oregonian* became the first newspaper to discontinue using names that stereotype Native Americans. In an editorial the managing editor of this Portland daily stated that "we will not be a passive participant in perpetuating racial or cultural stereotypes."[67] Some weeks later a Washington, D.C., radio station announced a similar policy. A member of the Missouri House of Representatives introduced a bill to prohibit state financial support for the Kansas City Chiefs' stadium if the team discriminated against Native Americans or mocked their sacred symbols.[68] Films portraying Native Americans as savages and whites as heroes were less evident in the early 1990s, when films such as *Powwow Highway* and *Dances with Wolves* portrayed Native Americans in a more sympathetic if still paternalistic light.

Protests against the 1991–92 Columbus Quincentenary began in 1989 and had a noticeable impact on commemorative events planned nationwide. Native groups called for a more accurate accounting of history that presented the encounter of two old cultures rather than the discovery of a virtually uninhabited wilderness by Europeans. In addition to demonstrations at the initial Quincentenary events in October 1991, Native American leaders talked with Quincentenary planners and convinced many to include the native perspective in major events, exhibitions, and documentaries. In 1990 the National Council of Churches adopted a resolution urging their member denominations to refrain from celebrating an event that had resulted in the genocide of indigenous peoples. And in late 1991 one Native American was appointed to the National Quincentenary Commission, which had been formed in 1984. Various native groups planned mourning services or other forms of protest to coincide with 1992 Columbus Day celebrations. During the Quincentenary year, most Native American groups opted to work through mainstream organizations such as schools, museums, and the media to establish a dialogue with other Americans and to achieve the long-term goal of a greater awareness among non-Indians of the modern-day presence and problems of native peoples.[69]

Fishing Rights and Land Claims

Fishing rights and land claims have been at the heart of the conflict between Native Americans and whites. In the Pacific Northwest and the Great Lakes region Native American nations have struggled with whites for a century over fishing rights. Shootings and court battles have occurred in the state of Washington over tribal rights to catch fish, particularly salmon and trout—rights guaranteed by treaties between the nations and the federal government more than a century ago. White anglers and commercial fishing companies object because their fishing opportunities are reduced significantly when Native Americans exercise their ancient treaty rights. A major court decision, *U.S.* v. *State of Washington* (1974), ruled that the treaties did indeed reserve fishing rights for Native Americans that are different from those allowed whites. The court ordered the state of Washington to protect Native American fishers and recognized the tribal right to manage fishing resources.[70]

White fishers openly defied the court's decision, protesting that it discriminated against them, and the state of Washington appealed the decision. Native American fishers were harassed and physically assaulted, and protests were directed at the judge who had ruled in their favor. The federal government spent millions of dollars to increase the fish available in the area and to compensate whites who suffered economic hardship. In 1979 the U.S. Supreme Court upheld the lower-court ruling, and government enforcement gradually reduced illegal fishing by whites. This decision helped to revitalize reservation economies in the state of Washington. In the words of a Native American leader, "the opportunities created directly or indirectly from the legally secured right to fish are the difference between staying and leaving for many young Indian families" in more than two dozen communities.[71]

In the mid-1980s, following an agreement between Wisconsin treaty nations and state officials to honor Native American fishing rights, some Native American fishers became the targets of physical and psychological harassment by vigilante whites. By 1989 anti–Native American violence by whites in Wisconsin had escalated to include gunfire, arson, and beatings. Nonetheless, by the 1990s Native American groups in both Wisconsin and the Pacific Northwest had realized significant gains in the struggle to regain their treaty fishing rights.[72]

Historically Native American lands were taken without adequate compensation. The cause of land-claims conflict on the East Coast was stated in a report by the U.S. Commission on Civil Rights:

> The basic Eastern Indian land claim is that Indian land in the East was invalidly transferred from Indians to non-Indians in the 18th and 19th centuries because the Federal Government, although required to do so, did not supervise or approve the transactions.[73]

In recent decades many indigenous groups, such as the Oneida in New York and the Passamaquoddy in Maine, have pressed land claims in federal court. A number of tribes have won their cases, and some of the illegally taken lands have been restored. Prior to 1960 the U.S. Indian Claims Commission had denied most claims for compensation for land taken. However, pressures on the federal government since then have resulted in increases in the compensation paid by the commission.[74]

One of the land claims settled involved the return of 300,000 acres of land (to be held in trust by the federal government) plus payment of $27 million in damages to the Passamaquoddy and Penobscot nations in Maine in 1980. Also in 1980, after a lengthy court battle, the U.S. Supreme Court awarded the Lakota Sioux $122.5 million for more than 7 million acres taken illegally in the 1870s. Although the land had been guaranteed to the Sioux nation by an 1868 treaty, it was stolen in a gold rush a few years later. Significantly, this cash award was refused by the Lakota, who reiterated their position that their land was not for sale and that the land itself should be returned to them. In 1987 U.S. senator Bill Bradley from New Jersey introduced a bill to return substantial land to the Lakota and to offer the money as damages instead of as payment for stolen land. The bill gained considerable support from the Lakotas before it was withdrawn by its sponsor in 1990. The Lakotas continued working to get that same bill or a similar one reintroduced in the U.S. Senate. At the beginning of the 1990s many land claims by indigenous nations in Minnesota, Arizona, Massachusetts, Alaska, Hawaii, Nevada, New York, and South Dakota remained unsettled.[75]

White backlash against Native American land claims, fishing claims, and other militant protest led to the creation of a national organization called the Interstate Congress for Equal Rights and Responsibilities and a variety of other antitreaty organizations. Senator Mark Hatfield of Oregon publicly noted that this "very significant backlash...by any other name comes out as racism in all its ugly manifestations." Some white members of Congress, supporting the backlash, introduced bills to break treaties, overturn court decisions, and extinguish native land claims, arguing that the demands by Native Americans had soured longtime "friendly relations." Native Americans responded that they were seeking what was *legally* theirs and were not asking for special privileges. Whites had become hostile because of the expense of living up to U.S law and, as one tribal leader noted, "because of the lack of educational systems to teach anything about Indians, about treaties." White stereotypes about Native Americans and ignorance of important treaties have played a critical role in the opposition to Native American struggles for social justice.[76]

The Native American Rights Fund (NARF), a nonprofit national legal defense firm founded in 1970, has represented various tribes in lawsuits and negotiations for treaty-guaranteed land, water, and natural resource rights and for restoration of the status of tribes as separate, sovereign nations. NARF's hundreds of victories include the land returned to the Passamaquoddy and Penobscot nations in Maine. NARF has also secured tribal control over taxation, tribal courts, and tribal control of education programs and economic enterprises on reservations.[77]

THE ECONOMY

For white ethnic groups, structural assimilation at the secondary level has involved upward movement into ever higher levels of the economy. Economic mobility has been modest and uneven for Native Americans. The colonialism model best fits the way in which Native Americans have been incorporated into the U.S. economy without getting on the escalator to economic equality. Prior to being forced onto reservations, most native groups, which ranged from the Pueblo agriculturalists of the Southwest to hunting societies on the Plains to mixed agricultural-hunting societies across the continent, had self-sufficient, land-based economies.

The loss of land has meant a destruction of traditional economies. Speaking at a meeting of the Connecticut Humanities Council in March 1992, Melissa Fawcett Sayet, a Mohegan elder, explained how she put her head on her desk and cried in anguish when her high school teacher taught Manifest Destiny, the concept that the United States should expand and incorporate all of the land from the Atlantic Ocean to the Pacific. Her white audience then became defensive. By the 1880s the Native American tribes had lost millions of acres as Euro-American "civilization" proceeded westward; millions more acres were lost with the breakup of the remaining lands under the 1887 Dawes Act. Native American lands were usually reduced to areas considered the least valuable to white settlers and entrepreneurs, although in recent years some of this land has been found to be rich in natural gas, uranium, and other valuable resources. At the beginning of the 1990s only 3 percent of the land in the continental United States was under the control of Native Americans, although, as Ward Churchill notes, indigenous peoples "still retain unassailable legal title to about ten times the area now left them."[78]

More economic exploitation accompanied the growth of industrial capitalism and urbanization in the late nineteenth century. The encroachment on Native American lands by white lumbering, ranching, and railroad interests redirected resources from rural Native American lands to fuel growth in urban centers. Bison and other game were killed for skins to be sold in Eastern cities, and white ranchers and farmers took lands for cattle raising and agriculture, hastening the impoverishment of Native Americans in the West. Rural poverty increased as corporations reached out from metropolitan centers to exploit more and more land; this in turn pressured many Native Americans to migrate to the cities. Jorgensen has argued that the poverty of rural Native Americans is "not due to rural isolation [or] a tenacious hold on aboriginal ways, but results from the way in which United States' urban centers of finance, political influence, and power have grown at the expense of rural areas."[79]

Poverty and Land Theft

The poverty of many reservations is rooted in the destruction of tribal economies and in mismanagement by BIA officials. Testifying before a congressional committee on the food situation in the winter of 1883, a member of the Assiniboine tribe pointed out that tribal members were healthy until the buffalo were destroyed, and that the substitute BIA rations were not adequate:

> They gave us rations once a week, just enough to last one day, and the Indians they started to eat their pet dogs. After they ate all their dogs up they started to eat their ponies. All this time the Indian Bureau had a warehouse full of grub.... Early [the next] spring, in 1884, I saw the dead bodies of the Indians wrapped in blankets and piled up like cordwood in the village of Wolf Point, and the other Indians were so weak they could not bury their dead; what were left were nothing but skeletons.[80]

Government agents were officially responsible for supplies, instruction in farming, and supervision of lands. By the 1880s many agents were notorious for their corruption or incompetence. Many desired to make their fortunes at the expense of those for whom they were responsible. The "agency towns" growing up on the reservations developed a stratified system in which there was little equitable contact between Native Americans and paternalistic white officials. After the 1890s the BIA attempted to expand farming on some reservations. Yet white officials usually built paternalistic systems in which Native Americans had little part other than that of unskilled laborers or small farmers.[81]

The reorganization policy of the 1930s, which provided for tribal governments, put a partial brake on corruption and blatant land theft, but economic problems persisted. Federal policy fluctuated between tribal self-determination and forced individualism. Termination experiments have thrown some tribes to the "outside white wolves." Lands have been sold to pay taxes, and tribes have fallen deeper into poverty as land resources are depleted.

Native American lands have also been taken for dams, national parks, and rights-of-way for roads. The sale of lands to private lumbering and mineral interests continues. Attempts by tribes to control the use of their lands have led ranchers and other white interests to argue that self-government by Native Americans is an unreasonable threat to "rational" development. Much of the substantial money made in agriculture or ranching on reservations has flowed to whites, who lease large proportions of the usable land. Facing discrimination and often having limited technical schooling, technical assistance, and capital to buy seeds, livestock, or machinery, the Native American farmer has frequently been faced with suffering a low yield or else leasing to outsiders.[82]

Land, Minerals, and Industrial Development

In recent decades the federal government has taken some action on the economic problems of reservations. Federal antipoverty programs since the 1960s have brought some job and training benefits, mostly temporary. The BIA strategy of urban relocation and employment assistance has encouraged or facilitated the movement of thousands of Native Americans to cities. Studies have found that urbanites earn more than those on reservations but are dissatisfied with urban life. Many relocatees return to reservation areas after a few years; lack of economic success is cited as the major reason. Studies have also shown a relationship between the negative economic experiences of urban migrants, such as low wages and unemployment, and their relatively high arrest rates. Many Native Americans in cities still face poverty and discrimination in residential ghettos and in low-wage, dead-end jobs.[83]

The federal government has attempted to attract industrial plants to reservations. Yet many jobs in plants built on or near reservations have gone to workers other than Native Americans. Government funds have all too often expanded corporate profits, with modest gains for tribal members. The BIA has encouraged cottage industries, such as the revival of Native American arts and crafts, which has helped improve the economic situation on some reservations.[84]

Federal development projects on reservations, including the sixty-two resorts and fifty-five industrial parks created between the 1960s and the late 1980s, have generally been failures. Occupancy rates at the industrial parks have been 5 percent, largely because they are located in rural areas lacking the amenities many corporations desire. A *Forbes* magazine article noted that Native American "reservations do not seem fertile ground for the seeds of capitalism. Reservation resources are generally the province of the tribe rather than individuals and shared equally among the membership." The recognition in *the* magazine of American capitalism that Native American values accent the group rather than the individual and are thus alien to individualistic capitalism is noteworthy. This helps explain the limited success of attempts by the Reagan and Bush administrations in the 1980s and 1990s to foster the "entrepreneurial spirit" on reservations and to increase the number of Native Americans operating small businesses.[85]

Native American reservations in the United States encompass about one-third of all low-sulphur coal, one-fifth of oil and gas reserves, and half of all known uranium reserves. Underneath the fifteen-million-acre Navaho reservation lie an estimated 100 million barrels of oil, 25 trillion cubic feet of natural gas, 80 million pounds of uranium, and 50 billion tons of coal. Beneath the Northern Cheyenne reservation in Montana lies a huge deposit of coal, and below the Jicarilla Apache reservation there are some 154 million barrels of oil. Corporate executives have eagerly eyed these mineral resources, and a few have called for the abolition of the reservations and the Bureau of Indian Affairs so that these mineral resources can be exploited.[86]

Historically, when mineral resources have been found on Native American land, the land has frequently been taken over and exploited by white entrepreneurs and corporations. An example is the 1952 mineral extraction agreement between the Navaho Tribal Council and Kerr-McGee Nuclear Corporation. Over a period of eighteen years Kerr-McGee employed 150 Navaho men to mine uranium on Navaho land, paying them about two-thirds of the prevailing off-reservation wage. Once the easy-to-reach deposits were mined, the company closed the facility, leaving acres of radioactive debris that threatened the water supplies of downstream communities. By 1980, 38 of the miners had died of cancers related to their mining of uranium and 95 more had similar cancers.[87]

Three dozen tribes made national headlines in the 1970s when they announced the creation of the Council of Energy Resources Tribes (CERT) and hired a former Iranian oil minister to help them get better contracts with white-owned companies. Many whites worried that tribes were going to behave like OPEC and seek to be completely independent in making contracts with energy corporations. CERT was created because tribal leaders felt they were being cheated by energy companies and by the federal government. CERT provided technical assistance to tribes and worked to increase engineering and other technical skills among Native American youth. Several tribes eventually withdrew from CERT because of its support for extensive uranium mining on tribal lands, which in their view caused the "destruction of Mother Earth."[88]

Persisting Economic Problems

The urban economy has been viewed as divided into two major sectors, a primary labor market and a secondary labor market. The primary labor market, characterized by skilled jobs, high wages, highly profitable companies, and significant mobility, has been composed predominantly of white workers. The secondary labor market, characterized by instability, low wages, less profitable companies, and little job mobility, has been composed disproportionately of minority workers. Native American workers in cities have usually been concentrated in the secondary labor market.

In 1940 one-third of all Native American males were unemployed, a figure far higher than that for white males. By 1960 the rate had risen to 38 percent, compared with just 5 percent for all males. This increase reflected in part the move from agriculture to the less certain work opportunities in urban areas. By 1970 the rate had dropped to 12 percent for males, still three times the national figure. In the 1980s and 1990s the unemployment rate was more than double that of whites. These recent rates, one should note, do not include the large proportion of Native American workers who have given up looking for work. Rates for Native American women have also been high. Native Americans continue to face perhaps the longest "Great Depression" economic situation of any racial or ethnic group in the United States.[89]

Changes in the occupational distribution of Native Americans between 1940 and 1970 reflected the rural-to-urban migration. In 1940 most Native American men were poor farmers or unskilled workers. By 1960 the impact of the urban migration had become clear; the proportion of workers in farm occupations had dropped dramatically, from 68 percent in 1940 to 24 percent in 1960. Still, in 1960 both men and women were heavily concentrated in the unskilled and semiskilled labor categories. Some upward mobility was evident between 1960 and 1970 as the proportions of men and women in white-collar job categories increased.[90]

Data for 1980 combine male and female workers. In that year 18.8 percent of Native Americans were in managerial, professional, and technical jobs, compared with about one-quarter of the general work force; 21.4 percent were in clerical and sales jobs, compared with 27.3 percent of the general work force. The proportion in blue-collar jobs was generally higher than the corresponding percentage of the general work force: 14.9 percent were in craft jobs, compared with 12.9 percent of the general population. The proportion in operative and laborer positions was 22.8 percent, compared with 18.3 percent of the general population. The proportion in service jobs was higher than the corresponding proportion of the general population—18 percent versus 12.3 percent. The proportion of farmers was higher among Native Americans than in the general population—3.6 percent versus 1.5 percent. In the early 1980s more than four in ten Native Americans were in low-wage unskilled laboring jobs, factory work, service positions, or farm jobs.[91]

For decades Native Americans on reservations have had the lowest incomes of any U.S. racial or ethnic group. In 1939 the median income of males on reservations was less than one-quarter of the median income for all U.S. males. By 1970 the median income for Native American males had risen to 42 percent of the figure for all U.S. males, and Native Americans in urban areas earned about 69 percent of the national average. The median income reported in the 1980 census for all Native American families ($13,724) was 31 percent less than that for all American families.[92]

The Native American economic situation relative to that of white Americans has not changed much since 1980. In 1990 about 45 percent of Native American families on reservations fell below the official poverty line. About half of Native American workers on reservations were unemployed; most of those with work earned less than $7,000 annually. The situation for urban Native Americans was also troubling. For example, in 1990 more than one-quarter of Chicago's Native American residents lived below the poverty line. The median income of Native American families, more than half of which have only one parent present, was only three-quarters that of all Chicago families. Nationally, the picture for reservation and urban families taken together is also bleak. Native American families earn about 70 percent as much as the average American family, and about one-third live in poverty.[93]

Poverty and unemployment mean inferior living conditions. Generally speaking, Native Americans face the worst housing conditions of any group in the United States. Today Native Americans are much more likely than European Americans to have inadequate nutrition, to live in small apartments or houses, and to have inadequate water and sanitation facilities. The infant death rate is seven times the national average. Illness rates, and death rates from accidents and illness, remain very high. The suicide rate is much higher than that of European Americans, and alcoholism rates are the highest in the nation. Disease rates for flu, strep throat, hepatitis, and pneumonia are several times the national figures. Life expectancy for Native Americans on reservations is less than forty-five years for males and forty-seven years for females—far below the figure for European Americans. Inadequate medical facilities, coupled with poor nutrition resulting from low incomes, constitute a major part of the problem. Reagan administration cutbacks in federal health programs in the 1980s reduced access to medical care for Native Americans, whose medical care conditions were already among the worst in the United States.[94]

The substantial court-awarded judgments received by some tribes have brought the tribes as collective entities little benefit, in part because of the BIA's practice of dividing a large portion of these awards among individuals. The Saginaw Chippewa of Michigan, with the help of the advocacy organization First Nations, secured legislation to permit a $10 million judgment to be paid directly to the tribe. They used the funds for scholarships, health insurance, and security for home mortgages for tribe members, strategies designed to increase the tribe's self-sufficiency.[95]

In recent years a number of Native American groups have developed gambling enterprises in an attempt to improve local economies. In 1992 some 150 reservations had bingo operations and 23 operated casinos. Other tribes were planning gambling enterprises. Gambling revenues, estimated at $750 million to $1.8 billion, have paid for educational and health-care facilities, water and sewage treatment plants, job training, roads, and housing, and have reduced unemployment. For many tribes profits from gambling enterprises are their first regular, independent income. However, tribal leaders often see gambling as a short-term boon to their economies, fearing that within a few years their operations will be replaced by those of outsiders.[96]

Over the last few years many tribes have been approached to provide landfill space for out-of-state garbage; some have been urged to store nuclear waste. Reservations are attractive to waste management companies because of their low population density and because they are not subject to state environmental regulations or state taxes. Moreover, enforcement of federal pollution regulations has been virtually nonexistent on reservations. Waste management firms have expected that the prospect of substantial income would convince impoverished tribes to accept landfills. Yet most tribes have rejected the offers. One leader on the Rosebud Sioux reservation stated, "Here it is, almost the twenty-first century, and we're still fighting the invaders, only now they're trying to make us take their trash."[97]

At the beginning of the 1990s, Native Americans were more urban than rural. The Los Angeles metropolitan area has the largest urban concentration, estimated at more than 75,000. A 1986 sample reported 117 distinct tribes represented there. As a group the Native Americans in Los Angeles had experienced economic mobility in recent decades, although at least 17 percent were still very poor. Most still worked in blue-collar occupations.[98]

EDUCATION

The formal educational experience of subordinated Native Americans began early in the reservation period. Influential whites were committed to the idea of education as the channel of forced acculturation. In the white-controlled schools the "wild Indians," as whites stereotyped them, could be civilized. By 1887, 14,300 children were enrolled in 227 schools, most operated by the BIA or by religious groups with government financial aid.[99]

Yet by 1900 only a small percentage of Native American children were receiving formal schooling, most within tribal circles. In the Southwest perhaps one-quarter of the school-age children in the four decades after 1890 had experience with boarding schools; a small percentage of the rest attended public schools. From the beginning the BIA and mission schools were run according to a strict Anglo-conformity assimilationist approach. Intensive efforts were made to destroy tribal ways; students were punished for speaking native languages. The facilities and staff of most boarding schools were often inadequate either in quantity or in quality.[100]

By the mid-1930s some boarding schools were being replaced by day schools closer to home, and a bilingual educational policy was at least being discussed. Increasingly, public schools became the context for Native American education. The Johnson-O'Malley Act provided federal aid for states that developed public schools for Native Americans. Yet after World War II large proportions of Native Americans were still not enrolled in formal schools.[101]

Enforced acculturation has been an issue in public schools, where white administrators and teachers have viewed Native American cultures as a major problem. They have blamed educational problems on cultural differences and emphasized the contrast between the distinctive values of Native Americans and those of white Americans. Many teachers have attempted to make their pupils "less Indian." Little has been provided in school textbooks to help the children identify with their own culture.[102]

The decades since the 1960s have seen mounting pressure from Native Americans for social change. In part because of this pressure, government aid to primary, adult, and vocational education has expanded substantially since the 1960s. Government attention has been refocused on local public and BIA schools, and many federal schools have developed advisory boards composed of Native Americans, have added Native Americans to their staffs, and have included classes in native art, dance, and language. However, more changes are needed. In the words of an AIM member, "the curriculum taught in Indian schools [has] remained exactly the same, reaching exactly the same conclusions, indoctrinating children with exactly the same values as when the schools were staffed entirely by white people."[103]

The movement of many Native Americans to the cities has resulted in a decline in the proportion of Native American children in BIA schools in recent decades. In 1970 only 25 percent of the 204,000 Native American children enrolled in school attended BIA schools; by 1991 the proportion had dropped to 10 percent. Most of the other children now attend local public schools. In 1991 a Department of Education task force, most of whose members were Native Americans, issued a report concluding that both local and federal educational systems have failed to meet the needs of Native American students. The report cited the absence of a Native American historical perspective in the curricula, the loss of Native American language ability, the shift away from Native American spiritual values, and the overt and subtle racism of white teachers and administrators as major barriers to Native American students' educational success in school. The report called for the implementation of multicultural curricula embodying respect for Native American history and culture and for programs that would guarantee that Native American students learn standard English.[104]

In recent years a desire to increase the relevance and effectiveness of their children's education led Rosebud Sioux leaders to draw up an education code of their own to increase the tribe's authority over the public schools on their reservation. This was the first action of its kind in the nation. Tribal leaders worked to gain support from outside education officials, at both the state and federal levels, and thus to implement their plan without the need for a court battle.[105]

In 1990 about 103,000 Native Americans were enrolled in colleges nationwide. Approximately 13,000 of these attended the twenty-five colleges on reservations, where efforts are made to integrate Native American history and culture into courses and where more attention is given to Native American students' values and needs. The first reservation community college was established in 1969 on the Navaho reservation in Arizona with War on Poverty funds. Reservation colleges are typically small and poorly financed. Just fifteen are fully accredited, and all but three are two-year institutions that emphasize vocational education.[106]

The educational attainment levels of Native Americans have remained consistently below those of the general population. Some gains were made during the 1960s; the number of Native Americans with fewer than nine years of schooling decreased. Yet at the end of that decade high school graduation rates remained far below the national average. By 1980, just 57 percent of Native American males and 54 percent of Native American females were high school graduates, compared with 67 percent of all persons over twenty-five. The median years of school completed for Native Americans twenty-five and over was 12.2 years, somewhat below the national figure of 12.5 years. During the 1980s school enrollments varied greatly among reservations, with 95 percent of the children on the Pima and Papago reservations in Arizona enrolled, but only 35 percent of the Alaskan Eskimos.

The 1991 Department of Education report mentioned earlier put the proportion of Native American students who drop out after tenth grade at 36 percent, the highest of any racial or ethnic group and more than twice that of whites. The report noted that the dropout rate on some reservations is even higher.[107]

RELIGION

It was the summer of 1977. Navaho medicine men came to Sante Fe, New Mexico, to take back religious and other ceremonial "artifacts" that a museum had collected. For many white museum visitors, these prayer sticks, medicine bundles, and other items were curiosities provided to entertain and perhaps inform. But for the Navaho they were sacred objects that had been stolen from their rightful Native American owners. After holding a ceremony with chants of joy, the medicine men reclaimed the sacred objects. One said, "We will take them home and teach the younger generation what these things mean." Many sacred objects belonging to Native American tribes remain in white hands. Since the 1960s Native American groups have requested that federal museums return thousands of Native American religious and art objects, particularly those illegally acquired. In addition, many Native Americans have protested the display of Native American skeletal remains in museums and have called for the return of the remains to the appropriate tribes for proper burial ceremonies.[108]

Pressures for acculturation by Native Americans to Euro-American culture have been clear in the case of religion. The Spanish conquerors brought Roman Catholic priests to reduce southwestern tribes to a mission-centered life. Later white settlers sometimes attempted to convert what they stereotyped as the "heathen Indian" to Christianity. Some Native Americans have said that "when [the Christian missionaries] arrived they had only the Book and we had the land; now we have the Book and they have the land."[109]

With the reservation period came a jockeying among Christian denominations for control; reservations were divided up so that Episcopalians got one, Methodists another, and Catholics yet another. A dozen denominations developed "home mission" efforts. Religious boarding schools and missions were placed alongside BIA operations. For a number of reasons, including fear, many Native Americans became affiliated with a Christian denomination.[110]

Millenarian Movements as Protest

From the Pacific Islands to Africa to the United States, colonized peoples have lashed out at European oppressors by joining millenarian movements, often led by visionaries and oriented to a "golden age" in which supernatural events will change oppressive conditions. Among the most famous Native American millenarian movements were the Ghost Dance groups that emerged on the Great Plains. In the 1870s the prophet Wodziwob told of a vision in which the ancestors of Native America came on a train to Earth with explosive force, after which the Earth swallowed up the whites. Members of a number of tribes joined in the movement in the hope of salvation from white oppression. The movement declined when no cataclysm came, but experienced a resurgence in the late 1880s when the new prophet Wovoka experienced a vision ordering him to found another Ghost Dance religion. Religious fervor spread through the Plains tribes. Trancelike dances were a central part of the ritual; whites, it was said, could be driven out by means of the circle dance. The cooperation among all Native Americans preached by this movement did increase intertribal relations. Disturbed at the resurgence of millenarianism, white officials tried to suppress it. The Sioux who were massacred at Wounded Knee in 1890 were fleeing the reservations in order to hold Ghost Dance ceremonies.[111]

Peyotism, reflecting another way of protesting white cultural pressures, surfaced as the Ghost Dance movement was being destroyed. Long used by individual practitioners to treat sickness, peyotism became a group religion in 1880. Between 1880 and 1900 it spread throughout the Plains. The new religion reflected an ambivalence toward Christianity. Peyote rituals involved singing and praying but were distinctive in the visionary experiences induced by eating peyote. Devoted to meditation, practitioners of peyotism aspired to an intertribal religion rather than armed rebellion as a means of protest.[112]

Attacks by Christian missionaries and government officials welded believers together, and in 1918 the Native American church was formally incorporated as an association of Christian groups protecting the Sacrament of Peyote. The movement's formal status gave it some protection under the First Amendment guarantee of freedom of religion. Nonetheless, by the 1920s seven states had passed anti-peyote laws, and the BIA issued proclamations banning its use. Opposition stimulated church growth. In the 1930s the progressive commissioner of Indian affairs, John Collier, came to the defense of indigenous religions and allowed the resurgence of the old ways, although this brought charges that the government was fostering "paganism."[113]

Attempts to restrict peyotism had little effect. The period after World War II saw another resurgence of tribal religions, and membership continued to increase. By the 1960s 40 percent of Native Americans on some Sioux reservations were Native American church members. In 1992 the Native American church had about 250,000 members in twenty-seven affiliated chapters composed of hundreds of tribes across the country. Today the U.S. government exempts Native Americans from prosecution under anti-peyote laws that apply to other Americans. However, twenty-seven states do not exempt Native Americans from anti-peyote state laws, and in 1990 the Supreme Court denied constitutional protection to the sacred peyote sacrament. This decision and a 1988 decision upholding the right of the U.S. Forest Service to construct a logging road across a mountaintop sacred to three tribes have generated an organized effort to amend the American Indian Freedom Act to protect sacred religious sites and the sacred peyote sacrament.[114]

In contrast to Christianity, most of the traditional religious beliefs and practices of Native Americans are not exclusive; a person can be both a Christian and a traditional believer. Because of this a great variety of traditional and Christian religious practices now coexist among Native American groups.

Questioning Christianity: Oppositional Cultures

Using the standard of their own cultures, a number of Native American leaders have criticized Christianity as a crude religion stressing blood, crucifixion, and bureaucratized charity rather than true sharing and compassion for people. Closely related to this criticism is renewed opposition to the European core culture. Native leaders stress that white Europeans are newcomers who sharply accelerated war on the continent, destroying many animal species and betraying the Native Americans who aided them in becoming established here. Europeans also destroyed the ecosystem and polluted the environment. Respect for land and nature is a common theme in many Native American cultures. In 1970 a Hopi wrote to President Richard Nixon protesting strip mining and other forms of destruction of the western aboriginal lands: "The white man, through his insensitivity to the way of Nature, has desecrated the face of Mother Earth. The white man's advanced technological capacity has occurred as a result of his lack of regard for the spiritual path and for the way of all living things."[115]

Today many Native Americans argue that the solution to problems of environmental damage lies in recognizing the superiority of Native American values, including a respect for the environment and a strong sense of community. This is an example of oppositional cultures in U.S. society. Native American respect for land and ecology is strongly rooted in ancient cultures and has long been a basis for opposition to the dominant Euro-American culture's land-use values.

ASSIMILATION AND COLONIALISM

Theoretical analysis in the field of race and ethnic relations has neglected Native Americans. Native Americans are distinct among U.S. racial and ethnic groups in that the classical external colonialism model is relevant to many of their contacts with Europeans. In the earliest period Native American tribes on the Atlantic Coast saw their lands seized and their members driven off or killed by outsiders. For some tribes it was clear that the European strategy was to kill off indigenous peoples who stood in the way of settlement by Europeans. This process would recur as European Americans moved westward from the Atlantic in the next several centuries. The policy of genocide coexisted with a reservation policy. Even in the earliest periods some whites felt that subordinating Native Americans and restricting them to certain areas, later called reservations, was a better government policy. With the reservation period of the nineteenth century came new oppression for Native Americans. The Native American "race," as Native Americans were termed by whites, was now a subordinate group at the very bottom of the U.S. stratification system.

Assimilation Perspectives

Some white observers have argued that the opportunity to assimilate is more open for Native Americans than for other minorities.[116] In the 1920s and 1930s even a few Native American professionals argued that Native Americans should voluntarily follow the lead of the white immigrant groups and blend quietly into the dominant Euro-American culture.

How might assimilation theorists view the past and present adaptations of Native Americans? Applying an assimilation model to Native Americans, one might accent the extent to which traditional cultures have undergone Europeanization. Schools and missions in the nineteenth century brought changes in religion, language, and dress styles to many Native American groups. Other changes, such as in land-ownership orientations, have also been substantial. Assimilationists have argued that Native American cultural traditions are the major barriers to further acculturation. These analysts seize on the cultural adaptations that many Native Americans have already made and cite them as evidence of movement toward inclusion in the Euro-American culture.[117]

Living patterns and tribal identity among the Native American tribes today vary widely. The Sioux and Navaho have a strong tribal identity, while certain other groups have for the most part lost their old ways and identities. Some groups, such as the western Pueblos, the Navaho, and the Sioux, confine their social contacts substantially to people of their tribe; other groups, such as a significant segment of the Blackfeet in Montana, have intermarried with whites and substantially acculturated to European American ways. Olson and Wilson note that some of the small California tribes, such as the Nomlaki and the Yuki, have "forgotten ancient customs, abandoned the native language, and look upon themselves more as extended families than as members of any particular tribe."[118]

The persistence of Native American languages has been significant. Several dozen Native American languages are still spoken in the United States in the 1990s. Intensive, often forced, acculturation has not necessarily resulted in the demise of Native American cultures. Many tribal cultures have survived extremely unfavorable conditions.

Structural assimilation at other than the lowest-paid job levels in the economy has come slowly for Native Americans. Not until the urban migration of the last few decades could many Native Americans be viewed as moving into the mainstream of the U.S. economy. Urban integration has often involved less well paid blue-collar positions and poor housing conditions. Political integration has also been limited in towns and cities.

Limited structural assimilation at the primary-group level has come slowly, although it is greater in urban areas than on the reservation. One study in Spokane, Washington, found little social integration of Native Americans into Euro-American voluntary associations in that area. Some shift can be seen in urban family patterns, which involve less emphasis on extended families. Increases in marriage with whites have occurred in cities. One Los Angeles study found that one-third of the married Native American respondents had white spouses. Census data have shown a similar pattern among urban Native Americans nationwide, although the rural rate of intermarriage is about half that in urban areas. Intermarriages between members of different tribes have become more common in towns and cities.[119]

An assimilationist theorist might argue that some adaptation has occurred on other dimensions of assimilation suggested by Milton Gordon (attitude-receptional, behavior-receptional, and identificational assimilation). Some movement can be glimpsed in the area of white attitudes; the traditional stereotyping of Native Americans by whites appears to have declined. Blatant discrimination too has probably decreased. As we have seen in the sections on economy, education, and politics, however, many types of direct and indirect discrimination still restrict Native Americans.

Attachment to tribal identity seems particularly strong among most of those who have predominantly Native American ancestry. Some West Coast tribes have exemplified perhaps the weakest sense of identification. A study of the Spokane tribe in the late 1960s found over half identifying themselves in interviews as definitely Native American, while a third identified themselves as definitely more white. Many Native American tribes persist as cultural islands. A number of organizations, including the National Congress of American Indians and the National Indian Education Association, have tried to build a pan-Indian identity and promote unity across the many tribes. In the 1980s and 1990s regular pan-Indian conferences, often called "powwows," have been held in all regions of the United States. But this effort has been only partially successful. There have been conflicts within these organizations among members of various tribal groups—as well as in the BIA schools among students. Tribal membership remains very important for many Native Americans, and most Native Americans on tribal lands see themselves as Navaho or Sioux, rather than as pan-Indian.[120]

The greatest pan-Indian identity has developed in urban areas, where tribal interaction and intermarriage are more common. One study found that Native Americans in Los Angeles have experienced a degree of spatial assimilation as evidenced by some residential dispersion within predominantly white neighborhoods. Most have maintained their cultural ties by means of occasional participation in traditional Native American rituals and performances. Joan Weibel-Orlando has noted that "tribal identity is still strongly felt and voiced." The pan-Indian identity of many urban Native Americans can be seen when they commonly identify themselves to nonnatives as "American Indians."[121]

Power–Conflict Perspectives

Because of the relatively low level of structural assimilation of Native Americans, some theorists have persuasively argued that power–conflict models have greater relevance to the Native American experience. Analysts such as Robert Blauner cite Native Americans as a clear case of an externally colonized minority.[122]

Power–conflict analysis accents the deception and force involved in the subordination process. Much assimilation rhetoric—"civilizing the Indians"—was a cover for exploitation by land-hungry settlers. There was great pressure, even force, involved in treaties and laws providing for individual Native Americans to become "citizens" only after meeting such criteria as accepting individual land allotments. Unlike assimilation analysts, power–conflict analysts would look at the broad sweep of the acculturation process and see the *force* behind much of it. This theme is evident, for example, in the statement by the commissioner of Indian affairs in 1879:

> Indians are essentially conservative, and cling tenaciously to old customs and hate all changes: therefore the government should *force* them to scatter out on farms, break up their tribal organizations, dances, ceremonies, and tomfoolery; take from them their hundreds of useless ponies, which afford the means of indulging in their wandering, nomadic habits, and give them cattle in exchange; and compel them to labor or to *accept the alternative of starvation.*[123]

On the reservations forced acculturation was often the rule in missions and boarding schools, where children were isolated from their families. In recent decades the acculturation pressures in BIA and public schools have been less brutal but still intense.

Since the 1970s one major problem has been the removal of Native American children from their homes to white foster homes or institutions. White social workers sometimes argue that the homes of poor Native Americans are not "fit" places for children and place the children in white homes. According to anthropologist Shirley Hill Witt, one Mormon child-placement program has aggressively sought the placement of these children. The president of the Mormon church reportedly commented in this way:

> When you go down on the reservations and see these hundreds of thousands of Indians living in the dirt and without culture or refinement of any kind, you can hardly believe it. Then you see these boys and girls [placed in Mormon homes] playing the flute, the piano. All these things bring about a normal culture.[124]

Here we see the white culture held up as the normal culture against which Native Americans are judged. This is ironic, for the poverty in the lives of Native Americans is substantially the result of the destruction of Native American resources, the taking away of land, and discrimination by whites.

Power–conflict analysts accent the one-way character of assimilation pressures. A study of Native American college students at the University of Oklahoma found that success in college was linked with two different sets of factors. Those who had done well in high school and on college entrance tests tended to do well at the university. Those with a strong Native American identity were more likely than assimilated Native Americans to fail and drop out, regardless of their academic ability. One major problem is the white-oriented university context. The expected changes are unidirectional: the Native

American student is expected to conform to the white college environment. White institutions do not change significantly to reflect the cultures and needs of Native American and other minority students.[125]

At all educational levels Native American children face great acculturation pressures; many capitulate, frequently adopting white stereotypes of themselves and dressing and behaving in Anglo-preferred ways. This behavior, notes Witt, damages "the inner self" and creates great stress for many. Caught between their native culture and Anglo pressures, some even commit suicide. An Oklahoma study found that suicide rates among young males have been increasing; those with the highest rate were those who were the most assimilated to white culture. Historically, suicide has been rare among young Native Americans. Now it is at epidemic levels. A 1992 study reported that the suicide rate for Native American high school students on reservations was four times that of their white counterparts; 17 percent of these teenagers had attempted suicide.[126]

A colonialism analyst might stress that many Native Americans remain isolated politically and geographically—on the reservations, in rural areas, or in segregated urban areas. Many remain colonized on their own lands. Whites are often ignorant of Native American conditions. In Oklahoma there has been a prevalent white misconception that the reservation Cherokee tribe is dying out. Yet the tribe is one of the largest in the nation, clinging tenaciously to its language and values. Wahrhaftig and Thomas have suggested that this white "fiction serves to keep the Cherokees in place as a docile and exploitable minority population."[127] In effect, by denying the existence of viable and enduring Native American communities, whites can ignore their Native American neighbors and their problems.

Perhaps the strongest argument for the relevance of a colonialism model can be found in the data we examined on Native American income, employment, housing, education, and political participation. Although there have been some gains, Native Americans as a group remain on the lower rungs of the socioeconomic ladder. Poverty characterizes life for many in rural areas and many in cities. Since the late 1970s many reservations have had effective unemployment rates of more than 40 percent. On the Rosebud Sioux reservation in the early 1990s, 90 percent of adults were jobless. In urban areas, Native Americans have had to face to a disproportionate degree low-wage jobs, absentee landlords, and racial discrimination. Native Americans are relative latecomers to the cities, and many have found their "place" to be defined by whites as the secondary labor market and urban ghettos. In the 1980s President Ronald Reagan's supply-side economic policy brought significant cutbacks in social programs for Native Americans on the reservations. As a result, many tribes began gambling operations or negotiated with corporations wishing to develop tribal mineral resources for outside whites to utilize. The image of an internal colony remains highly appropriate for Native Americans on reservations.

Many Native Americans are fighting back aggressively against the vestiges of colonialism. A renaissance of Native American cultures can be seen in the many protest movements in recent decades. Power–conflict analysts are the most likely to emphasize the importance of this struggle against white pressures and oppression. This resistance is rooted in the historical cultures of Native American tribes, the oppositional cultures that have placed great emphasis on harmony with the world and nature and on the foolishness of Euro-American materialism. The oppositional cultures of Native American groups provide a valuable source of the fundamentally humanitarian, earth-centered values that many Native Americans see as on the decline in the larger society.

SUMMARY

Native Americans today remain a highly diverse group of many tribes and urban groups, most of whom are subordinated to whites with greater economic and political power. They are the descendants of the only groups that did *not* immigrate to North America in the last five hundred years. They were brought into the European American sphere over a long period, during which many tribes fought bloody battles with the invaders. After the battles came the reservation era with a long line of white bureaucrats and officials seeking to dominate or exploit them. Even white social scientists got into the act of exploitation for research purposes. This is illustrated by the Native American quip "What is a Navaho family?" Answer: "Three matrilineal generations and one white anthropologist living together in an extended family."

Often stereotyped by whites as culturally inferior, Native American tribes have suffered exploitation and discrimination in the economic, political, religious, and educational spheres. In the economic sphere they have seen their lands taken, their young forced by job circumstances to relocate to often inhospitable cities, and their upward mobility limited by continuing racial discrimination. Recent decades have seen some economic gains. Yet progress has been slow, and has yet to be matched by substantial political progress, particularly off the reservations. The BIA, although more progressive and "Indianized," remains an outside governmental bureaucracy.

Protest organizations, secular and religious, have underscored the strengths and the discontent of Native Americans. In recent years Native American activists have emphasized the cultural uniqueness of the Native American respect for human community and for ecology. Groups have organized to regain fishing rights and lands that were stolen. Calls for maintaining cultural distinctiveness and recognizing the superiority of Native American oppositional cultures have been heard. Vigorously opposing celebrations of Columbus's "discovery of America," Native Americans have accented the uniqueness and brutality of their colonization. Native Americans have a unique position in regard to citizenship, since they existed in America prior to any European settlement or government. Indeed, some in groups such as the Iroquois have argued that they are not citizens of the United States, nor do they want to be. They predate the European invasions, so they are citizens of their own nations.

The desire for full recognition of their sovereignty is strong among many Native American nations. While the federal government has made progress in recent years in returning land and control of various aspects of life to many tribes, most tribes still have a colonialist relationship with the federal government. This can be seen, for example, in the reservation-based colleges. Although these colleges do much to meet the needs of Native American students, Native Americans lack full control of them since their accreditation and a large part of their funding remain in the hands of federal agencies. In recent years many Native American nations have pressed for a government-to-government relationship, rather than an internal colonial relationship, with the federal government of the United States.[128]

NOTES

1. "Counter-Quincentenary Protesters Encounter Celebrators at Kickoff of Quincentenary Year," *Indigenous Thought* 1, nos. 4 and 5 (October 1991): 1–3.
2. "We Have No Reason to Celebrate an Invasion," *Rethinking Columbus* (Milwaukee, Wisc.: Rethinking Schools, 1991), p. 4.
3. For a discussion of the development of the designations *white* and *red*, see David R. Roediger, *The Wages of Whiteness* (New York: Verso, 1991), pp. 21–23.
4. Henry F. Dobyns, "Estimating Aboriginal American Population," *Current Anthropology* 7 (October 1960): 395–416; Kirkpatrick Sale, *The Conquest of Paradise* (New York: Knopf, 1990); Lenore A. Stiffarm and Phil Lane, Jr., "The Demography of Native North America," in *The State of Native America*, ed. M. Annette Jaimes (Boston: South End Press, 1992), pp. 23–28; see also Russell Thornton, *American Indian Holocaust and Survival* (Norman: University of Oklahoma Press, 1987).
5. Stiffarm and Lane, "The Demography of Native North America," pp. 34–38; U.S. Bureau of the Census, *The Census and You* (Washington, 1991), p. 3.
6. Edward H. Spicer, *Cycles of Conquest* (Tucson: University of Arizona Press, 1962), pp. 20–23; Clyde Kluckhohn and Dorothy Leighton, *The Navaho*, rev. ed. (Garden City, N.Y.: Doubleday, Anchor Books, 1962), pp. 23–27 et passim.
7. U.S. Bureau of Indian Affairs, *The American Indians: Answers to 101 Questions* (Washington, 1974), pp. 2–3.
8. Howard M. Bahr, "An End to Invisibility," in *Native Americans Today*, ed. Howard M. Bahr, Bruce A. Chadwick, and Robert C. Day (New York: Harper & Row, Pub., 1972), pp. 407–9; James E. Officer, "The American Indian and Federal Policy," in *The American Indian in Urban Society*, ed. Jack O. Waddell and O. Michael Watson (Boston: Little, Brown, 1971), pp. 45–60.
9. Donald L. Fixico, *Termination and Relocation* (Albuquerque: University of New Mexico Press, 1986), pp. 7–10.
10. Spicer, *Cycles of Conquest*, pp. 5, 306–7; Murray L. Wax, *Indian Americans* (Englewood Cliffs, N.J.: Prentice-Hall, 1971), pp. 6–7; Lynn R. Bailey, *Indian Slave Trade in the Southwest* (Los Angeles: Westernlore Press, 1966), pp. 73–140.
11. Leo Grebler, Joan W. Moore, and Ralph C. Guzman, *The Mexican-American People* (New York: Free Press, 1970), pp. 320–21; Spicer, *Cycles of Conquest*, pp. 4–5; Carey McWilliams, *North from Mexico* (New York: Greenwood Press, 1968), pp. 20–33; Herbert Blatchford, "Historical Survey of American Indians," Appendix H in Stan Steiner, *The New Indians* (New York: Harper & Row, Pub., 1968), pp. 314–15.
12. D'Arcy McNickle, *The Indian Tribes of the United States* (London: Oxford University Press, 1962), pp. 13–17; Alice Marriott and Carol K. Rachlin, *American Epic* (New York: Mentor Books, 1969), pp. 104–8; John Collier, *Indians of the Americas* (New York: Mentor Books, 1947), p. 115.
13. William T. Hagan, *American Indians* (Chicago: University of Chicago Press, 1961), p. 14. The discussion of these wars is taken from ibid., pp. 12–15.
14. Almon W. Lauber, *Indian Slavery in Colonial Times within the Present Limits of the United States* (New York: Columbia University Press, 1913), pp. 107–69.
15. McNickle, *The Indian Tribes of the United States*, pp. 23–28; Ruth M. Underhill, *Red Man's America* (Chicago: University of Chicago Press, 1953), pp. 321–22; Wax, *Indian Americans*, p. 13.
16. Quoted on the title page of Vine Deloria, Jr., *Of Utmost Good Faith* (New York: Bantam, 1972).
17. McNickle, *The Indian Tribes of the United States*, pp. 32–35; National Indian Youth Council, "Chronology of Indian History, 1492–1955," in Steiner, *The New Indians*, pp. 318–19.
18. Blatchford, "Historical Survey of American Indians," pp. 316–18; Hagan, *American Indians*, pp. 41–44.
19. Alexis de Tocqueville, *Democracy in America* (New York: Random House, Vintage Books, 1945), 1:364.
20. Virgil J. Vogel, "The Indian in American History, 1968," in *This Country Was Ours*, ed. Virgil J. Vogel (New York: Harper & Row, Pub., 1972), pp. 284–87; McNickle, *The Indian Tribes of the United States*, pp. 40–41.
21. Ralph K. Andrist, *The Long Death* (London: Collier-Macmillan, 1964), p. 3.
22. John D. Unruh, *The Plains Across* (Urbana: University of Illinois Press, 1979), p. 185 and elsewhere.
23. Vogel, "The Indian in American History, 1968," p. 285; Wendell H. Oswalt, *This Land Was Theirs* (New York: John Wiley, 1966), pp. 501–2.
24. Andrist, *The Long Death*, pp. 31–68, 78–91.
25. William Meyer, *Native Americans* (New York: International Publishers, 1971), p. 32. See also Thornton, *American Indian Holocaust and Survival*.
26. Andrist, *The Long Death*, pp. 140–48.
27. Ibid., pp. 240–50, 350–53; Alvin M. Josephy, *The Indian Heritage of America* (New York: Bantam, 1968), pp. 284–342; Theodora Kroeber and Robert F. Heizer, *Almost Ancestors* (San Francisco: Sierra Club, 1968), pp. 14–20.
28. Spicer, *Cycles of Conquest*, pp. 216–21, 247–70.
29. Jack Weatherford, *Indian Givers: How the Indians of the Americas Transformed the World* (New York: Ballantine, 1988), pp. 39–133.
30. Robert F. Spencer, Jesse D. Jennings, et al., *The Native Americans* (New York: Harper & Row, Pub., 1965), pp. 495–96; David Miller, "The Fur Men and Explorers View the Indians," in *Red Men and Hat Wearers*, ed. Daniel Tyler (Fort Collins, Colo.: Pruett Publishing Co., 1976), pp. 26–28; Roediger, *The Wages of Whiteness*, pp. 21–23.
31. Peter Farb, *Man's Rise to Civilization as Shown by the Indians of North America from Primeval Times to the Coming of the Industrial State* (New York: Dutton, 1968), pp. 246–49; Tyler, ed., *Red Men and Hat Wearers*, passim.
32. Lewis H. Carlson and George A. Colburn, "Introduction," in *In Their Place*, ed. Lewis H. Carlson and George A. Colburn (New York: John Wiley, 1972), p. 44.
33. Vogel, "The Indian in American History, 1968," pp. 288–89; Tocqueville, *Democracy in America*, 1:355–57.

34. Rayna Green, "The Pocahontas Perplex: The Image of Indian Women in American Culture," in *Unequal Sisters*, ed. Ellen Carol DuBois and Vicki L. Ruiz (New York: Routledge, 1990), pp. 15–21, quotation from p. 17.
35. "Children's Secret Lessons," *Indigenous Thought* 1, nos. 4 and 5 (October 1991): 24.
36. U.S. Senate Subcommittee on Indian Education, *Hearings on Indian Education* (Washington, 1969), passim; Jeanette Henry, "Text Book Distortion of the Indian," *Civil Rights Digest* 1 (Summer 1968): 4–8; Kathleen C. Houts and Rosemary S. Bahr, "Stereotyping of Indians and Blacks in Magazine Cartoons," in *Native Americans Today*, ed. Bahr, Chadwick, and Day, pp. 112–13; see also p. 49.
37. C. Matthew Snipp, *American Indians: The First of This Land* (New York: Russell Sage Foundation, 1989), pp. 23–25; Jimmie Durham, "Cowboys and…," in *The State of Native America*, ed. Jaimes, pp. 423–25.
38. Ward Churchill, *Fantasies of the Master Race* (Monroe, Maine: Common Courage Press, 1992), pp. 243–47, quotation from p. 246.
39. Howard M. Bahr, Bruce A. Chadwick, and Robert C. Day, "Introduction: Patterns of Prejudice and Discrimination," in *Native Americans Today*, ed. Bahr, Chadwick, and Day, pp. 44–45; Emory S. Bogardus, *Immigration and Race Attitudes* (Boston: Heath, 1928); Beverly Brandon Sweeney, "Native American: Stereotypes and Ideologies of an Adult Anglo Population in Texas" (M.A. thesis, University of Texas at Austin, 1976), pp. 125–33.
40. U.S. Bureau of Indian Affairs, *Federal Indian Policies* (Washington, 1975), p. 6.
41. Ibid., p. 7; Spicer, *Cycles of Conquest*, p. 348.
42. *Elk v. Wilkins*, 112 U.S. 94 (1884), See also Deloria, *Of Utmost Good Faith*, pp. 130–32.
43. U.S. Bureau of Indian Affairs, *Federal Indian Policies*, p. 7; S. Lyman Tyler, *A History of Indian Policy* (Washington, 1973), pp. 95–107 and elsewhere; Jack Forbes, *Native Americans of California and Nevada* (Berkeley, Calif.: Far West Laboratory for Educational Research and Development, 1968), pp. 79–80.
44. Spicer, *Cycles of Conquest*, pp. 351–53; McNickle, *The Indian Tribes of the United States*, p. 59; Alison R. Bernstein, *American Indians and World War II* (Norman: University of Oklahoma Press, 1991), pp. 4–10.
45. Virgil J. Vogel, "Introduction," in *This Country Was Ours*, ed. Vogel, pp. 196–97.
46. M. Annette Jaimes, "Federal Indian Identification Policy: A Usurpation of Indigenous Sovereignty in North America," in *The State of Native America*, ed. Jaimes, p. 124.
47. Ibid., pp. 95–98; U.S. Bureau of Indian Affairs, *Federal Indian Policy*, p. 9.
48. W. A. Brophy and S. D. Aberle, *The Indian* (Norman: University of Oklahoma Press, 1966), pp. 179–93; Rebecca L. Robbins, "Self-Determination and Subordination: The Past, Present, and Future of American Indian Governance," in *The State of Native America*, ed. Jaimes, pp. 98–100.
49. U.S. Bureau of Indian Affairs, *Federal Indian Policy*, p. 12.
50. Jaimes, "Federal Indian Identification Policy," pp. 123–37; Susan Campbell, "A Mohegan Family," *Hartford Courant*, March 1, 1992, p. 10; Anne Fullam, "Tribe Seeks U.S. Recognition," *Newsday*, February 11, 1992, p. 20.
51. Forbes, *Native Americans of California and Nevada*, pp. 80–82; Alan L. Sorkin, *American Indians and Federal Aid* (Washington, D.C.: Brookings Institution, 1971), pp. 48–65; Vogel, "Introduction," p. 205; James S. Olson and Raymond Wilson, *Native Americans in the Twentieth Century* (Provo, Utah: Brigham Young University Press, 1984), p. 209; E. S. Cahn, *Our Brother's Keeper* (New York: World Publishing, 1969), pp. 157–58.
52. Robbins, "Self-Determination and Subordination," pp. 98–112, quotation from p. 109.
53. Brophy and Aberle, *The Indian*, pp. 33–44; Olson and Wilson, *Native Americans in the Twentieth Century*, p. 189.
54. Olson and Wilson, *Native Americans in the Twentieth Century*, p. 191.
55. Steiner, *The New Indians*, pp. 235–36.
56. Ibid., pp. 232–34; Virgil J. Vogel, "Famous Americans of Indian Descent," in *This Country Was Ours*, ed. Vogel, pp. 310–51; "Indians Stepping Up Political Role as 5 Run for Congress," *Star Tribune*, June 11, 1992, p. A7.
57. Theodore W. Taylor, *The States and Their Indian Citizens* (Washington, 1972), pp. 82–84.
58. U.S. Commission on Civil Rights, Minnesota Advisory Committee, *Bridging the Gap: The Twin Cities Native American Community* (Washington, 1975), pp. 65–67; Olson and Wilson, *Native Americans in the Twentieth Century*, p. 186.
59. Hazel W. Hertzberg, *The Search for an American Indian Identity* (Syracuse: Syracuse University Press, 1971), pp. 20–21, 42–76, 180–200.
60. Ibid., pp. 200–208, 291–93; Isabel Wilkerson, "Indignant Indians Seeking Changes," *New York Times*, January 26, 1992, p. 14.
61. Robert C. Day, "The Emergence of Activism as a Social Movement," in *Native Americans Today*, ed. Bahr, Chadwick, and Day, pp. 516–17.
62. Vogel, "Famous Americans of Indian Descent," pp. 310–51.
63. Robbins, "Self-Determination and Subordination," p. 103.
64. Meyer, *Native Americans*, p. 88; "Pine Ridge after Wounded Knee: The Terror Goes on," *Akwesasne Notes* 7 (Summer 1975): 8–10.
65. Glenn T. Morris, "Resistance to Radioactive Colonialism: A Reply to the Churchill/La Duke Indictment," *Insurgent Sociologist* 13 (Spring 1986): 82.
66. Richard Meryhew, "Be It Redskins, Chiefs, or Lions, Indians to Protest," *St. Paul Star Tribune*, January 3, 1992, p. 1B; Wilkerson, "Indignant Indians Seeking Changes," p. 14.
67. Quoted in "Newspaper Defends Dropping Native American Names from Teams," Reuters News Service, February 19, 1992.
68. Joe Olivera, "We Can All Change Attitudes," Gannett News Service, February 20, 1992.
69. Rochelle L. Stanfield, "Cultural Collision," *National Journal*, January 25, 1992, p. 206.
70. U.S. Commission on Civil Rights, *Indian Tribes: A Continuing Quest for Survival* (Washington, 1981), pp. 61–99; Institute for Natural Progress, "In Usual and Accustomed Places," in *The State of Native America*, ed. Jaimes, pp. 223–26.
71. Institute for Natural Progress, "In Usual and Accustomed Places," pp. 224–26; quotation from pp. 224–26.

72. Ibid., pp. 231–35.
73. U.S. Commission on Civil Rights, *Indian Tribes*, p. 103.
74. Olson and Wilson, *Native Americans in the Twentieth Century*, p. 195.
75. Ward Churchill, "The Earth Is Our Mother," in *The State of Native America*, ed. Jaimes, pp. 151–69.
76. U.S. Commission on Civil Rights, *Indian Tribes*, pp. 1–2 (Mansfield quotation from p. 1; quotation from tribal leader from p. 2); Institute for Natural Progress, "In Usual and Accustomed Places," pp. 223, 231, 233–34.
77. "Shattering the Myth of the Vanishing American," *Ford Foundation Letter* 22, no. 3 (Winter 1991): 1–5.
78. Churchill, *Fantasies of the Master Race*, pp. 5–7 (quotation from p. 5); Ward Churchill and Winona LaDuke, "Native North America: The Political Economy of Radioactive Colonialism," in *The State of Native America*, ed. Jaimes, pp. 241–62; Susan Campbell, "A Mohegan Family," *Hartford Courant*, March 1, 1992, p. 10. See also Sar A. Levitan, Garth L. Mangum, and Ray Marshall, *Human Resources and Labor Markets*, 2d ed. (New York: Harper & Row, Pub., 1976), p. 441.
79. Joseph G. Jorgensen, "Indians and the Metropolis," in *The American Indian in Urban Society*, ed. Waddell and Watson, p. 85. This paragraph draws on Jorgensen's theory.
80. Quoted in Deloria, *Of Utmost Good Faith*, pp. 380–81.
81. Hagan, *American Indians*, pp. 126–27; Spicer, *Cycles of Conquest*, pp. 349–56.
82. Cahn, *Our Brother's Keeper*, pp. 69–110; Rupert Costo, "Speaking Freely," *Wassaja* 4 (November–December 1976): 2; Sorkin, *American Indians and Federal Aid*, pp. 70–71; Jorgensen, "Indians and the Metropolis," pp. 96–99.
83. Sorkin, *American Indians and Federal Aid*, pp. 105, 136–39, 201; Levitan, Mangum, and Marshall, *Human Resources and Labor Markets*, p. 443; Theodore D. Graves, "Drinking and Drunkenness among Urban Indians," in *The American Indian in Urban Society*, ed. Waddell and Watson, pp. 292–95.
84. Levitan, Mangum, and Marshall, *Human Resources and Labor Markets*, p. 443; Jorgensen, "Indians and the Metropolis," p. 83; Brophy and Aberle, *The Indian*, p. 99.
85. James Cook, "Help Wanted—Work, Not Handouts," *Forbes*, May 4, 1987, pp. 68–71.
86. Olson and Wilson, *Native Americans in the Twentieth Century*, p. 181.
87. Churchill and LaDuke, "Native North America," pp. 247–48.
88. Michael Parfit, "Keeping the Big Sky Pure," *Perspectives* 13 (Spring 1981): 44; Jeff Gillenkirk and Mark Dowie, "The Great Indian Land Power Grab," *Mother Jones*, January 1982, pp. 47–48.
89. U.S. Department of Health, Education and Welfare, *A Study of Selected Socio-economic Characteristics of Ethnic Minorities Based on the 1970 Census*, vol. 3, *American Indians* (Washington, 1974), p. 49; Sorkin, *American Indians and Federal Aid*, p. 12. The 1970 figures are for males sixteen and over; earlier figures are for those fourteen and older.
90. U.S. Bureau of the Census, *1970 Census: American Indians* (Washington, 1973); U.S. Bureau of the Census, *Population, 1960: Nonwhite Population by Race* (Washington, 1963), p. 104; U.S. Bureau of the Census, *Population, 1940: Characteristics of the Nonwhite Population by Race* (Washington, 1943), pp. 83–84. The data do not include those not reporting and, in 1960, states with less than 25,000 Native Americans.
91. U.S. Bureau of the Census, *U.S. Census of Population, 1980: General Social and Economic Characteristics*, PC80-1 (Washington, 1981), p. 102.
92. U.S. Department of Health, Education and Welfare, *A Study of Selected Socio-economic Characteristics*, pp. 59–78; U.S. Bureau of the Census, *U.S. Census of Population, 1980*, p. 112.
93. W. Richard West and Jana Walker, "Native American Study Draws Poor Conclusions from Poor Conditions," *Legal Times*, June 4, 1990, p. 30; Andrew Fegelman, "Native Americans Lose Out When City Awards Contracts," *Chicago Tribune*, p. C7.
94. U.S. Department of Health and Human Services, *Chart Series Book: Public Health Services* (Washington, 1988); Olson and Wilson, *Native Americans in the Twentieth Century*, p. 187.
95. "Reviving Native Economies," *Dollars and Sense*, no. 170 (October 1991): 18–20.
96. Paul Lieberman, "Indians See Battle Ahead over Future of Gambling," *Los Angeles Times*, October 10, 1991, p. A1; Pat Doyle, "Mille Lacs Casino Profits to Go to Band," *St. Paul Star Tribune*, January 15, 1992, p. 1B; Marilyn Yaquinto, "U.S. Says It Won't Pursue Indian Gambling Cases Yet," *Los Angeles Times*, February 6, 1992, p. B8; Josephine Marcotty, "Indians Deal Themselves In," *St. Paul Star Tribune*, February 17, 1992, p. 1D.
97. Quoted in Bob von Sternberg, "Tribe Fights Storage of Reactor's Spent Fuel," *St. Paul Star Tribune*, November 27, 1991, p. 2B. See also Dan Fagin, "Badlands in Demand," *Newsday*, October 21, 1991, p. 5; David Seals, "Sacred Ground Must Not Be Abused," *Newsday*, October 31, 1991, p. 129.
98. Joan Weibel-Orlando, *Indian Country, L.A.* (Chicago: University of Illinois Press, 1991), pp. 22–43.
99. U.S. Bureau of Indian Affairs, *Federal Indian Policies*, p. 5; Jorge Noriega, "American Indian Education in the United States," in *The State of Native America*, ed. Jaimes, pp. 371–83.
100. U.S. Bureau of Indian Affairs, *Federal Indian Policies*, pp. 5–6; Spicer, *Cycles of Conquest*, p. 349; Noriega, "American Indian Education in the United States," pp. 381–83.
101. U.S. Bureau of Indian Affairs, *Federal Indian Policies*, p. 9.
102. Noriega, "American Indian Education in the United States," pp. 384–85.
103. Interview with Phyllis Young, quoted in ibid., p. 387.
104. *Indian Nations at Risk: An Educational Strategy for Change*, report of U.S. Department of Education Task Force (Washington, 1991), cited in Kenneth Cooper, "Multicultural Focus Recommended for Education of Native Americans," *Washington Post*, December 27, 1991, p. A19.
105. "Shattering the Myth of the Vanishing American," pp. 1–3.
106. Noriega, "American Indian Education in the United States," pp. 391–92; Michel Marriott, "Indians Turning to Tribal Colleges for Opportunity and Cultural Values," *New York Times*, February 26, 1992, p. B6.
107. Olson and Wilson, *Native Americans in the Twentieth Century*, p. 186; U.S. Bureau of the Census, *U.S. Census of Population, 1980: General Social and Economic Characteristics*, PC80-1-C1 (Washington, 1983), p. 98; *Indian Nations at Risk*.

108. Stan Steiner, "Sacred Objects, Secular Laws," *Perspectives* 13 (Summer–Fall, 1981): 13.
109. Quoted in Vine Deloria, Jr., *Custer Died for Your Sins* (London: Collier-Macmillan, 1969), p. 101.
110. Ibid., pp. 108–16.
111. Vittorio Lanternari, *The Religion of the Oppressed* (New York: Mentor Books, 1963), pp. 110–32; Spencer, Jennings, et al., *The Native Americans*, pp. 498–99; Wax, *Indian Americans*, p. 141.
112. Lanternari, *The Religions of the Oppressed*, pp. 99–100; Hertzberg, *The Search for an American Indian Identity*, pp. 239–40, 251, 280.
113. Hertzbrg, *The Search for an American Indian Identity*, pp. 246, 257, 271–74, 280–84; Elaine G. Eastman, "Does Uncle Sam Foster Paganism?" in *In Their Place*, ed. Carlson and Colburn, pp. 29ff.
114. Deloria, *Of Utmost Good Faith*, pp. 177ff; idem, *Custer Died for Your Sins*, pp. 110–15; Brad Knickerbocker, "Indians Fight for Religious Freedom," *Christian Science Monitor*, April 1, 1992, p. 14.
115. Quoted in Olson and Wilson, *Native Americans in the Twentieth Century*, p. 219. See also Deloria, *Custer Died for Your Sins*, pp. 122–24; and Cahn, *Our Brother's Keeper*, pp. 175–90.
116. For example, Lurie, as quoted in John A. Price, "Migration and Adaptation of American Indians to Los Angeles," *Human Organization* 27 (Summer 1968): 168–75.
117. Snipp, *American Indians*, pp. 23–25.
118. Olson and Wilson, *Native Americans in the Twentieth Century*, p. 212; see also pp. 210–11.
119. Prodipto Roy, "The Measurement of Assimilation: The Spokane Indians," *American Journal of Sociology* 67 (March 1962): 541–51; Price, "Migration and Adaptation of American Indians to Los Angeles," pp. 169–74; U.S. Department of Health, Education and Welfare, A Study of Selected Socio-economic Characteristics, p. 35; Oswalt, *This Land Was Theirs*, pp. 513–14.
120. Lynn C. White and Bruce A. Chadwick, "Urban Residence, Assimilation, and Identity of the Spokane Indian," in *Native Americans Today*, ed. Bahr, Chadwick, and Day, p. 243; Brophy and Aberle, *The Indian*, p. 10; Spicer, *Cycles of Conquest*, p. 577.
121. Weibel-Orlando, *Indian Country, L.A.*, pp. 22–43.
122. Robert Blauner, *Racial Oppression in America* (New York: Harper & Row, Pub., 1972), p. 54; Spicer, *Cycles of Conquest*, pp. 573–74.
123. Quoted in Francis McKinley, Stephen Bayne, and Glen Nimnicht, *Who Should Control Indian Education?* (Berkeley, Calif.: Far West Laboratory for Educational Research and Development, 1969), p. 13 (italics added).
124. Quoted in Shirley Hill Witt, "Pressure Points in Growing Up Indian," *Perspectives* 12 (Spring 1980): 31.
125. Wilbur J. Scott, "Attachment to Indian Culture," *Youth and Society* 17 (June 1986): 392–94.
126. Witt, "Pressure Points in Growing Up Indian," pp. 28–31; Robert W. Blum, et al., "American Indian—Alaska Native Youth Health," *Journal of the American Medical Association* 267 (March 25, 1992): 1637–44.
127. Albert l. Wahrhaftig and Robert K. Thomas, "Renaissance and Repression: The Oklahoma Cherokee," in *Native Americans Today*, ed. Bahr, Chadwick, and Day, p. 81.
128. Institute for Natural Progress, "In Usual and Accustomed Places," pp. 228–36.

Chapter 8

African Americans

Martin Luther King Jr., Selma, Alabama
Photo Coutresy of United Press International

In May 1984 one of this country's most talented young journalists, Leanita McClain, committed suicide. Just thirty-two years old, she had won several major journalism awards and was the first African American to serve on the Chicago *Tribune*'s editorial board. Why did such a talented black woman commit suicide? The answer is doubtless complex, but one factor looms large: the problem of coping with a culturally different, often racist and discriminatory white world. Reviewing McClain's life, one writer has analyzed the conformity to white ways that is faced by middle-class black employees in historically white workplaces: "Black women consciously choose their speech, their laughter, their walk, their mode of dress and car. They trim and straighten their hair.... They learn to wear a mask."[1] Black Americans in the corporate world not only face blatant discrimination but also suffer greatly from the subtle pressures to adapt to the values and ways of that white world.

African Americans have family trees in the United States extending back to the 1600s, well before the American Revolution. They are among the oldest settlers in North America, far older as a group than many prominent white immigrant groups. There is a tragic irony here. That a people who have been here as long as the first European settlers should still find themselves so discriminated against, so unwelcome in many traditionally white institutions and places, is a fact of life that is problematical both for the assimilation theory discussed in Chapter 2 and for the future of this ostensibly democratic nation.

FORCED MIGRATION AND SLAVERY

White immigrants, for the most part, came to North America voluntarily. Most Africans had no choice; they came in chains. African Americans exemplify the slave-importation end of the migration continuum we have discussed. Their destinations were determined by slave traders and buyers. The enslavement of black Africans was seen by whites as a solution to their need for cheap agricultural labor in the South and elsewhere.

The Slave Trade

Dutch and French companies early dominated the forcible importation of Africans; England came into the trade in the late 1600s. Fed by European piracy, the slave trade soon saw the institutionalization of trading alliances between certain African chiefs, who wanted horses and manufactured goods, and white slavers, who wanted human beings to sell. Some African coastal chiefs, probably out of greed or fear, succumbed to the slave-trade pressure and established themselves as go-betweens serving European slave traders.[2]

Once captured, slaves were often chained in corrals called barracoons, where they were branded and held for transportation. The voyage was a living hell. Slaves were chained together in close quarters, with little room for movement. The horror was summed up by a young slave:

> I was soon put down under the decks, and there I received such a salutation in my nostrils as I had never experienced in my life: so that with the loathsomeness of the stench, and crying together, I became so sick and low that I was not able to eat, nor had I the least desire to taste any thing.... On my refusing to eat, one of them held me fast by the hands, and laid me across, I think the windlass, and tied my feet, while the other flogged me severely.... One day, when we had a smooth sea and moderate wind, two of my wearied countrymen who were chained

together (I was near them at the time), preferring death to such a life of misery, somehow made through the nettings and jumped into the sea.[3]

Slave suicides were common, and uprisings brought death to slaves and sailors alike. The widely believed white myth that Africans passively endured their fate was contradicted by the 155 recorded shipboard uprisings by slaves between 1699 and 1845; many other attacks on whites went unrecorded.[4]

In 1619 twenty Africans were brought to Jamestown by a Dutch ship, and by the mid-1600s the slave status of Africans had been fully institutionalized in colonial laws. For the next two and half centuries virtually all African immigrants were imported for involuntary servitude. Curtin estimates the number of slaves in the Western Hemisphere to have been 9.6 million for this period; most were brought to the West Indies and South America, only 5 percent to North America. Prior to 1790 an estimated 275,000 African slaves were brought into all the colonies; between 1790 and the end of the legal slave trade in 1808 another 70,000 were imported. The total for the entire slave period was approximately half a million.[5]

A number of prominent European Americans in the early period of this nation were slaveholders, including George Washington, James Madison, and Thomas Jefferson. In an early draft of the Declaration of Independence, the young Jefferson went so far as to attack slavery, but was careful to blame it on England's King George. As a result of southern slave owners' opposition, Jefferson's antislavery language was not included in the final version of that founding document. One of the greatest democratic manifestos in world history was severely compromised by the unwillingness of white Americans to include African Americans within its framework.[6]

Slaveholding interests forced recognition of slavery in several provisions of the U.S. Constitution. Slavery was recognized in a section that provided for each slave to be counted as three-fifths of a person; in a fugitive-slave section; and in a section postponing prohibition of slave importation to 1808. Although the slave trade was officially abolished as of 1808, the ban was not enforced. Thousands of African slaves continued to be imported illegally.[7]

In 1860 only one-quarter of the 1.6 million white families in the South owned 3.8 million black slaves. Most slave owners had fewer than ten slaves; only 46,000 white families owned twenty or more. Most white farmers had no slaves. A majority of the slaves were chained to the larger farms or plantations, where they performed most of the daily labor and produced surplus agricultural products to be marketed to the profit of white slaveholders. Most plantation owners, tied to trade with the North and England, can be viewed as agrarian capitalists attuned to commercial trade and a money profit. The wealth, as well as power, of the slaveholding gentry rose as a result of slave agriculture. This plantation gentry dominated the U.S. economy and the federal government from 1800 to the Civil War.[8]

Slave Life

There has long been a magnolias-and-mint-julep mystique about the slave system, which lingers on, particularly in the South and in Hollywood movies such as *Gone with the Wind*. According to this white imagery, centered in a big, white plantation house with multiple columns surrounded by magnolia trees, a paternalistic white master cared kindly for contented, happy slaves. Black house servants were treated like members of the family. Popular writers and some scholars have sugar-coated slavery, downplaying the brutality and oppression as well as the violent rebellions.

Slave autobiographies describe the oppressiveness of living conditions. Most slaves rose before dawn, then worked in the house or the fields until dark. Food was often insufficient. Clothing and housing were crude and inadequate. The whip and chains were mechanisms in the control system. Some masters were extremely cruel, such as the owner of this slave, who told about moving from Georgia to Texas: "Then he chains all the slaves round the necks and fastens the chains to the hosses and makes them walk all the way to Texas. My mother and my sister had to walk. Emma was my sister. Somewhere on the road it went to snowing, and Massa wouldn't let us wrap anything round our feet. We had to sleep on the ground, too, in all that snow."[9] Some white owners earned a reputation for kindness; they provided better material conditions and were less likely to use the whip. But most fell between the two extremes, caring somewhat for what they saw as their "property" but resorting to cruel punishment when necessary to prevent African Americans from resisting or fleeing. Indeed, white slaveholders generally controlled the state militias and the courts.[10]

Many historical accounts of slavery do not specifically discuss the special plight of black women. African American women were at the center of southern slavery. The research of Jacqueline Jones has demonstrated that under slavery most black women, as one slave put it, "worked in the fields every day from 'fore daylight to almost plumb dark."[11] The brutality of the slaveholders was not tempered when it came to the women: "Beat women! Why sure he [master] beat women. Beat women just like men. Beat women naked and wash them down in brine."[12]

Historian Eugene Genovese has argued that slavery was a "paternalistic" system. For the white masters, paternalism rationalized the subordination of other human beings considered to be in need of the care of whites. For the slaves, paternalism meant some recognition of material needs. Yet a paternalistic system can be dangerous for the oppressed, for it tends to foster divisions in terms of master-granted privilege (for example, house slaves versus field slaves) and thus can make organization for resistance difficult. Genovese has been criticized for exaggerating the paternalistic aspects of slavery, but many researchers consider his view important. Both accommodation and violent resistance were among the slaves' reactions to an alternately brutal and paternalistic system.[13]

African American families have long been a preoccupation of whites, including white social scientists; even the contemporary problems of poverty and "broken" families have been traced back to the assumed constant breakup of black families in slave days. Until recently, supportive family life was viewed as nonexistent for the majority of slaves. Yet there is now considerable evidence of paternalistic slave owners fostering families and, most significantly, of slaves themselves working hard to preserve and protect their families to the greatest extent possible under difficult conditions. Research has shown that typical slave families were protective, supportive environments that helped slaves as individuals to survive. African American slaves frequently deserted brutal masters in family units, and a common cause of desertion was the desire to find lost loved ones. In an extensive analysis of families on large plantations, Gutman found that enslaved African American women were expected to have their children by one man; that the names of fathers were given to sons; that adoption was used to ease the disruption caused by death within and breakup of families; and that many African American families persisted over several generations. The threat to the slave family was great. Slave marriages were likely to be broken up at some point, most often by death but frequently by the white slaveholders. An accurate picture of the slave family must include both aspects, the attempts at stability and the frequent disruption.[14]

Historically, whites systematically attacked the African culture of the slaves. Without parallel in North American history, this cultural attack was seen as necessary by the slaveholding oppressors to root out the strong oppositional possibilities of an alternative culture. Williams has underscored the dramatic difference between the oppression faced by the enslaved immigrants and that faced by white immigrants: "The black slave experience was that of lost languages, cultures, tribal ties, kinship bonds, and even of the power to procreate in the image of oneself and not that of an alien master."[15]

Nonetheless, in the face of physical torture and white attempts to eradicate their cultures, the many peoples of Africa among the slaves—the Yorubas, Akans, Ibos, Angolans, and dozens of other groups—became a single African American people and forged their own oppositional culture, an African American culture. Drawing on deep African spiritual roots, these new Americans shaped their own religion, their own art and music, their distinctive versions of Afro-English, and their own philosophical and political thinking about racial oppression, liberation, and social justice. In the colonies and later in the United States the pressures on black Americans to conform to the white core culture forced them to become bicultural, to know both the dominant Euro-American culture and their own culture as well. Since the days of slavery there has been a centuries-long struggle for the maintenance of this oppositional culture, a culture part African and part an African American adaptation to the concrete history of white oppression. This culture has provided the foundation for active black resistance to oppression since the seventeenth century.

Active Slave Resistance

Apologists for slavery have emphasized the submissive slave response, often picturing a docile black "Sambo." A similar theme has received attention in scholarly debates over slavery. Numerous scholars have underscored the severe impact of slavery on personality. Elkins argues that the major personality type created by this oppressive "total institution" was the childlike, docile one.[16]

Yet submissiveness was only one response. An assertive reaction grounded in African and African American culture was also common. Both responses are likely to have been important components of a given slave's repertoire for coping with the savagery of slavery. Depending on the circumstances, one or the other might come to the forefront. Many slaves used their wits to escape as much forced work and punishment as possible and observed the servile etiquette when necessary, but many also rebelled in dozens of small and large ways, or even attacked whites violently when that seemed necessary.[17]

Antislavery action took several forms, including flight, suicide, and psychological withdrawal. Fugitive slaves were a serious problem for slave owners, serious enough to prompt inclusion of a fugitive-slave provision in the U.S. Constitution. Perhaps the most famous route of escape was the Underground Railroad, the network of former slaves and other antislavery citizens, black and white, who secreted and passed along tens of thousands of slaves to the North between the 1830s and the Civil War. One of the famous "conductors" on this railroad was the slave Harriet Tubman, one of the greatest of American heroes. She reportedly went back south nineteen times, risking her life to deliver more than three hundred slaves to freedom. Southerners committed to the "happy Sambo" view of their slaves sometimes went to absurd lengths to explain the fugitive-slave problem. The physician Samuel Cartwright, incredibly, attributed the problem to a strange black disease, "drapetomania," by which he meant the unhealthy tendency to flee one's owner![18]

Nonviolent slave resistance also took the form of a slow working pace, feigned illness, and strikes. Violent resistance was directed at the property and persons of slave owners or overseers. Tools, livestock, fields, and farmhouses were destroyed; white masters and overseers were killed. Collective resistance included revolts and conspiracies to revolt. Aptheker found evidence of 250 slave revolts or conspiracies to revolt, a count that did not include the numerous mutinies aboard slave ships. Newspapers of the day provide considerable evidence of extensive white fear of uprisings.[19]

In 1800 a group of slaves led by Gabriel Prosser in Henrico County, Virginia, gathered weapons and planned to march on Richmond. The Virginia governor took immediate action to protect the state capital from the rebels. A thousand armed slaves rendezvoused, but a heavy rain cut them off from the city and they disbanded. Betrayed, the leaders were quickly arrested; at least thirty-five, including Prosser, were put to death. Perhaps the most serious slave revolt took place in 1811 near New Orleans. After several hundred armed slaves attacked whites on local plantations, white troops suppressed the rebellion. Several dozen slaves were killed during the encounter; others were executed later by a firing squad and their heads displayed along the route to New Orleans.[20]

The most famous rebellion took place in Southampton County, Virginia, in 1831. The leader and hero of this brave rebellion, Nat Turner, was a self-taught slave with religious leanings. Turner recruited seventy slaves in a single day; his revolutionaries attacked, and dozens of whites were killed. The black revolutionaries were eventually attacked and defeated by hundreds of white soldiers. Turner, who had escaped, was executed later. It would seem that these leaders of black slave revolts should be included among the greatest of American heroes, for they took seriously the new American principle of "liberty and justice for all." In his analysis of slave revolts Stuckey has shown that African culture and religion were one source of the revolutionaries' philosophy and inclination to rebellion.[21]

Slave revolts intensified the fears of whites, many of whom were near panic following a revolt. Revolts contradicted the apologists' notion of happy slaves; given the opportunity, slaves would resist violently. Slavery, and the fears surrounding it, had a severe impact on whites in the South. Southern whites lost much of their own humanity and morality, as well as much of their own freedom of speech and press, because of the requirements of the slave system.

Many black Americans played an important role in liberating their brothers and sisters from oppression by joining the movement to abolish slavery. Frederick Douglass, a former slave, was one of the most powerful speakers among the abolitionists. In a July

4, 1852, speech in Rochester, New York, Douglass spoke eloquently: "What, to the American slave, is your Fourth of July? I answer: A day that reveals to him, more than all other days of the year, the gross injustices and cruelty to which he is the constant victim. To him your celebration is a sham."[22] Another influential African American abolitionist was the former slave Isabella Van Wagener, better known as Sojourner Truth, who was born a slave in New York in the 1790s; in the mid-1800s she became an influential lecturer against slavery and also an early advocate of women's rights across the United States.

Outside the Rural South

Between the 1600s and the early 1800s many northern whites either had slaves or thought slavery to be legitimate. Significant numbers of slaves could be found in some northern states. The North was built in part on forced black labor and in part on the labor of European immigrants. As Ringer puts it, "despite the early emancipation of slaves in the North [slavery] remained there, not merely as fossilized remains but as a deeply ingrained coding for the future."[23] Consider Massachusetts, for example, where slavery was legalized in 1641, three years after slaves were brought in. Massachusetts merchants and shippers played a central role in the North American slave trade. It was not until the 1780s that public opinion and court cases came together to effectively abolish slavery in New England. Even then, it was not recognition of the rights of African Americans that ended slavery, but rather pressure from the growing number of white working people who objected to having to compete with slave labor. In New York, slaves made up 7 percent of the population by 1786. Not until 1799 was a statute of emancipation passed there—and one providing for only partial emancipation at that. Understanding that slavery was entrenched in the North's legal system is important for understanding the internal colonialism that black Americans still face today in the urban North.[24]

Even before the Civil War, Jim Crow laws in the North enforced the segregation of free blacks in public transportation, hospitals, jails, schools, churches, and cemeteries. Jim Crow railroad cars were established early on in Massachusetts. All northern cities had severe antiblack housing discrimination and segregated housing areas at a time when there were no comparable ghettos in southern cities because black slaves lived in the same general areas as the slave masters.

STEREOTYPING AND RACIST IDEOLOGIES

Dominant racial groups, including white Americans, develop beliefs to rationalize their domination. White theologians, intellectuals, and other southern leaders devised racial theories of biological, mental, and moral inferiority to rationalize the exploitation of Africans as slaves. Negative views of African peoples existed in Europe before the founding of the North American colonies, but these did not develop into full-blown racist ideologies until the 1700s. Thomas Jefferson personified the moral dilemma of whites in the eighteenth century: He wrote a stinging indictment of slavery in the original draft of the Declaration of Independence, yet he was a slave owner. He wrote vigorously of his opposition to interracial sex and miscegenation, yet he is reported to have had a black mistress who bore him children. He wrote of the inferiority of black men and women, but he also argued that they should be free. Writing in his 1786 *Notes on Virginia* as a white ideologue, Jefferson argued that what he saw as the ugly color, offensive odor, and ugly hair of black slaves indicated their physical inferiority and that what he alleged to be their inability to create was a sign of mental inferiority.[25]

Seeing African Americans as Inferior: White Stereotypes

At an early date, the dark color of the African and African American slaves was singled out by many white Americans as unusual and ugly. By the mid-1800s racist defenders of slavery were portraying African Americans as an inferior human group and as "apelike," a stereotyped image applied earlier by Anglo-Protestants to Irish Americans.[26] Since the days of slavery whites have often depicted black Americans in negative terms. Black men and women have been alleged to have an offensive odor. Black women have been stereotyped as immoral, black men as oversexed potential rapists. Absurd white images of black sexuality may reflect deep white psychological problems with the idea and reality of racial mixing, or miscegenation. White guilt and anger may well be linked to the historical fact that much interracial intercourse before 1865 involved the forcible rape of black slave women by white men, particularly slave owners. Legal scholar Patricia Williams has illustrated this point by relating the story of Austin Miller, her great-great-grandfather, a thirty-five-year-old white lawyer who bought Williams's eleven-year-old black great-great-grandmother Sophie and her parents. Miller soon forced the child Sophie to become the mother of Williams's great-grandmother Mary. Like many African Americans, Williams reports that her white ancestor was a *rapist* and *child molester.*[27]

Early on, black Americans were stereotyped as mentally inferior by white oppressors. Slavery advocates tried hard to depict slaves as childlike "Sambos." This white stereotype did not die with slavery. Between 1900 and World War II, prominent white scientists at leading universities, such as geneticist Edward East of Harvard University, bought into the pseudoscientific notion that "mentally the African negro [sic] is childlike, normally affable and cheerful, but subject to fits of fierce passion."[28]

A burst of renewed interest in "scientific racism" occurred around 1900, when a number of U.S. scientists argued for the inferiority of certain racial groups, including Americans of southern European and African descent. As we noted in Chapter 5, many observers, relying heavily on the so-called IQ tests, attempted to prove that southern and eastern Europeans were mentally inferior; others used the tests to the same end with black Americans. Antiblack thought was coupled with theories of northern European racial superiority to other groups, southern European as well as African. From the last decades of the nineteenth century to the 1960s, major white political leaders, including U.S. presidents, adopted some of these crude racial theories.[29]

"IQ": The Pseudoscience of Testing and Race

The theme of intellectual inferiority along racial lines has received some attention since World War II.[30] In recent decades white social scientists Arthur Jensen and Richard Herrnstein, among others, have alleged that racial groups exhibit inherited IQ differences that can be measured by conventional paper-and-pencil and object-manipulation tests. In their view groups at the lower social and economic levels are intellectually and genetically inferior to those at higher levels because they score lower on a few such tests. In the past this perspective was applied to white immigrant groups considered inferior to the Anglo-Protestant group; in the last few decades the focus has been on Americans of color. For instance, Jensen has alleged that differences in IQ test scores are not just environmentally determined but reflect genetic differences in mental ability between black and white groups, and that the two groups have different types of intelligence, perhaps requiring different educational techniques. Citing earlier studies by "scientific" racists, Jensen critical of high black birth rates. In the 1990s Jensen has continued his research on race and intelligence, focusing on the speed of the brain's nerve signals and on myopia as measures of intelligence allegedly favoring groups such as Jewish and Asian Americans over black Americans.[31]

Although the reactionary views of Jensen and Herrnstein have been successfully critiqued by many other social scientists, especially for leaving out environmental and cultural variables, their notions about black intelligence have spread to some conservative academics and journalists in the United States and to politicians around the globe. For example, in the early 1990s Michael Levin, a philosophy professor at a New York college, argued that "on average, black Americans are significantly less intelligent than whites" and that the research of Jensen on white and black IQs backed up his own arguments against affirmative action programs. While white professors who openly advocate racial inferiority are very few, they have received considerable publicity in a nation whose commitment to remedying ancient racial wrongs has vacillated.[32]

The Jensen and Herrnstein arguments have occasionally been reiterated by influential politicians in the United States and elsewhere. In 1971 Patrick Buchanan, an adviser to President Richard Nixon who was himself to become a Republican presidential candidate in 1992, picked up on Herrnstein's arguments. In a memo to Nixon, Buchanan alleged that "every study" showed black groups had lower IQs than white groups and that Herrnstein's views about race and IQ provided "an intellectual basis" for reviewing and perhaps cutting back certain government social programs.[33] This "scientific" racism has spread to other countries. In 1986 Japanese prime minister Yasuhiro Nakasone commented that "the United States is lower [in intelligence scores] because of a considerable number of blacks, Puerto Ricans, and Mexicans."[34]

In the 1930s a number of social psychologists began questioning whether IQ test results could be used as evidence of genetically determined racial differentials. Citing data on the extremely oppressive conditions suffered by black people, they argued that black–white differences in IQ test scores reflected education and income differences. A number of studies showed that IQ test scores of black children improved with better economic and learning environments, as when black children from segregated southern schools attended integrated northern schools. Most strikingly, results from large-scale IQ testing in earlier decades showed black children and adults in some northern states scoring *higher* than whites in some southern states.[35] Using the logic of analysts such as Jensen, one would be forced to conclude that white southerners were mentally and "racially" inferior to black northerners. White analysts such as Jensen would avoid this interpretation; obviously they, as defenders of black inferiority, do not wish to argue that data on IQ might actually show black intellectual superiority. Not even the "scientific" racists would argue for the racial inferiority of certain groups of white Americans. Rather, they would accept the environmental explanation for uncomplimentary regional IQ-score differentials for whites. Similarly, differentials favoring whites can most reasonably be interpreted as reflecting environment.

Some analysts have focused on the cultural bias—specifically, the white middle-class bias—inherent in traditional U.S. achievement and other psychometric tests (including IQ tests), most of which measure only certain types of learned skills and acquired knowledge (such as linguistic, literary, or geographic subjects)—skills and knowledge not equally available to all racial groups because of discrimination and inadequate educational facilities. Researchers have found that achievement-test taking itself is a skill white middle-class children are more likely to possess, because they and their parents are most familiar with such testing. White middle-class children take many such tests and in doing so they enjoy a built-in advantage over most minority children.[36]

The basic problem with conventional IQ testing is the equation of intelligence test results with intelligence. From the beginning, "intelligence" tests have been misnamed. All these tests measure are certain selected verbal, mathematical, and/or manipulative skills considered important by the white middle-class test makers. A number of scholars have argued that intelligence is something much broader than what paper-and-pencil or other conventional IQ tests can measure. More broadly, intelligence can be viewed as a complex set of abilities to deal creatively with one's social and physical environments. In reality, intelligence includes, for example, a potter's skill in pottery making or a farmer's skill in growing foodstuffs, intelligence not measured by the usual IQ tests. Only a small and highly selective portion of any person's intelligence can be revealed, even under the best testing conditions, on the typical IQ test.[37]

Antiblack Prejudices and Stereotypes

To what extent does the white public still accept negative stereotypes of black Americans? In a 1966 opinion survey half of a national white sample felt that black Americans had a different odor, were morally inferior, and laughed a lot. To our knowledge no recent national polls have asked white Americans about biological-inferiority or similar stereotypes. However, when whites in a 1990 survey were asked to evaluate on a scale of 1 to 7 how violence-prone blacks were, 51 percent chose the violent end (ranks 1–3) of the spectrum. When asked the same question about whites, only 16 percent placed whites as a group in the same ranks. When asked to rank blacks and whites on preference for welfare (versus being self-supporting), 55 percent of the white respondents ranked blacks toward the welfare end of the spectrum, while only 4 percent ranked whites as a group in that same direction. Moreover, when asked to rank blacks and whites on whether they tended to be hardworking or lazy, 17 percent ranked blacks at the hardworking end of the spectrum, compared with 55 percent ranking whites similarly. Asked to rank blacks and whites on "intelligence," 29 percent of whites placed blacks toward the unintelligent end of the continuum, while only 6 percent ranked whites in this manner. A majority of white Americans still stereotype black Americans as violence-prone, inclined to welfare, and disinclined to hard work, and a substantial minority still stereotype black Americans as unintelligent.[38]

Other surveys of white opinion have found a type of racial hostility that John McConahay has called "modern racism": the view that black Americans have illegitimately challenged cherished white values and are making illegitimate demands for changes in race relations. This hostility is reflected in negative views of certain black actions and achievements. McConahay and his associates have argued that the most extreme antiblack stereotypes and white opposition to all desegregation have to some extent been replaced by new prejudices and stereotypes. They have found strong support among whites for such statements as "Blacks, over the last few years, have gotten more economically than they deserve."[39] Most whites today publicly state their support for freedom of opportunity, unlike older racists who believed in across-the-board legal segregation. Modern racists, however, feel that blacks are too demanding, paranoid, and pushy. The ideological position of many white Americans is one of vigorous opposition to any government programs that would aggressively end racial discrimination in employment or housing. Desegregation defined as a few black employees at work, a few black students in the schoolroom, or a few black families in the larger residential community is acceptable to a majority of whites. But more substantial desegregation and thoroughgoing integration brought about by vigorous government action are not acceptable.[40]

In surveys from 1973 to 1990 the proportion of whites supporting a law prohibiting racial discrimination by a homeowner increased from 34 percent to 51 percent. In a 1990 national survey a slight majority supported this open housing law, but fully 44 percent of whites nationwide, and more than half in some parts of the South, did *not,* preferring instead a law that would give a white homeowner the right to refuse to sell to a black person. In the same survey a majority of white Americans expressed a negative view of intermarriage: two-thirds were opposed to a close relative marrying a black person, and another 28 percent said they would be neutral. Only five percent said they would have a *favorable* response. In addition, 20 percent of the whites interviewed nationwide (and more than 50 percent in the Deep South) favored a law actually banning all marriages between blacks and whites.[41] It is clear from these recent survey data that some 20–40 percent of whites still favor legal segregation, and the overwhelming majority of whites are still opposed to marital assimilation along racial lines. The American ideal of equality remains, at best, a remote abstraction when it comes to the racial attitudes of many white Americans.

INTERRACIAL CONFLICT

Antiblack Violence

Just behind the slave system's veneer of civility were the bloody instruments of social control—the whip and the guns. Free blacks also suffered at the hands of whites. Before the Civil War, white-dominated race riots directed at free blacks occurred a dozen times in northern cities. The most serious race riot in U.S. history in terms of casualties was the 1863 antidraft riot in New York City, during the Civil War. The rioters were working-class whites, including many Irish Americans, who were angry at being drafted to fight a war to which they were not committed. The white rioters were also angry that black workers were being used by employers to replace white workers on strike on the waterfront.

The end of the Civil War brought an increased threat of violence, including lynching, against the former slaves. Lynching is one of the most brutal forms of collective violence that human beings engage in. It is a group killing carried out by vigilantes seeking revenge for an actual or imagined crime by the victim. Before the Civil War most lynchings in the United States were carried out by white mobs against whites. African American slaves, as valuable white "property," could not be lynched without the lynchers being obligated to pay the slave owners. After the Civil War and Reconstruction, lynching became a means of keeping black Americans subordinated, or "in their place," as white southerners often said. Recorded lynchings show the following racial pattern:[42]

	White Victims	Black Victims
1882–1891	751	732
1892–1901	381	1,124
1902–1911	76	707
1912–1921	53	533
1922–1931	23	201
1932–1941	10	95
1942–1951	2	25
1952–1956	0	3

These numbers represent only recorded lynchings; the actual number has been estimated as at least 6,000. Most killings took place in the South. Between 1892 and 1921, the peak period of segregation, nearly 2,400 black Americans were murdered in this way. Cash points out that there was a growing "inclination to abandon such relatively mild and decent ways of dispatching the [lynch] mob's victim as hanging and shooting in favor of burning, often roasting over slow fires, after preliminary mutilations and tortures...a disposition to revel in the infliction of the most devilish and prolonged agonies."[43]

Lynchings were a show of force and brutality by whites usually fearful of black assertiveness and protest. Brutal lynchings, many whites expected, would make black residents afraid to challenge repressive segregation laws. White lynchers were seldom punished for their outrageous crimes. The decrease since World War II is somewhat misleading, since "legal" and secret lynchings had by then replaced many public lynchings. These included unnecessary killings by police officers, which took many black lives. Secret attacks resulted in hundreds of deaths of black citizens and some white civil rights workers in the South between the 1940s and the 1960s.[44]

Many black southerners moved to northern cities to escape oppressive conditions, but in the north they often met more violence. Clashes with whites became frequent as black workers and their families moved into the centers of border and northern cities. In a white riot in 1900 in New York City, a substantially Irish American police force encouraged working-class whites to attack black men, women, and children wherever they could be found. A similar riot occurred in 1917 in East St. Louis, one of the most serious white-dominated race riots of the twentieth century. East St. Louis's white workers, who saw black workers as a threat, pressed government for action. Union organizers placed a newspaper advertisement announcing that black labor was being brought into the community by local industries to reduce white wages. In the resulting attack on the black community, thirty-nine black residents and nine white attackers were killed; the ghetto residents had fought back, killing some attackers. This riot was followed in 1919 by a string of white riots from Chicago to Charleston, South Carolina.[45]

Opposition to black workers searching for better jobs has long been a cause of white violence. A glance at U.S. history books reveals that black workers often become scapegoats whenever a serious economic downturn threatens white livelihoods. African Americans, together with other groups such as Asian, Mexican, and Jewish Americans, have regularly been singled out as targets of anger, even though they have little or nothing to do with the troubles facing whites. Many white workers have little understanding of how our capitalist system now works. Many do not understand, for example, that job cutbacks and job displacement are often the result of policies of (mostly white) employers seeking better investments and profits in what is now a world economy.

In recent decades white supremacy groups have been in the forefront of those blaming black Americans for problems rooted elsewhere. The Ku Klux Klan, the leading white supremacy group for most of the twentieth century, gained strength in the 1920s and again in the 1970s and 1980s. In 1990 the number of white Americans in various Klan factions was estimated at about 10,000. Newspaper reports have documented Klan activities, including violence against minorities and paramilitary training camps where Klan members are reportedly preparing for a "race war." From the 1970s to the 1990s Klan and other white supremacy group members have been involved in hundreds of antiblack and anti-Jewish attacks; several have been convicted of murdering or assaulting black men and women. In 1979 Klan and Nazi party members in North Carolina were accused of the murders of five demonstrators who were protesting the Klan. TV cameras captured the killings on film, but a local jury acquitted the accused. In 1981 in Mobile, Alabama, Michael Donald was lynched by Klan members, who later testified they selected him at random. Donald's family sued the United Klans of America, the oldest of the KKK groups, and in 1987 won a $7 million award. This was the first time in history that a KKK group had been found guilty of such violence.[46]

Other racist groups, such as the White Aryan Resistance (WAR), headed by white supremacist Tom Metzger, have emerged in recent years. One count found 346 hate groups active in 1992, ranging from "skinheads" to a variety of neo-Nazi and white supremacy organizations. In Portland, Oregon, three whites, members of a skinhead gang, beat a black man to death. After the skinheads were convicted of the racially motivated killing, the Southern Poverty Law Center and the Anti-Defamation League made legal history by taking the WAR leaders to court in a related civil case. Late in 1991 the jury decided that by sending recruiters to Portland to agitate against black and Jewish residents, WAR had helped stimulate the growth of racist skinhead groups. The jury proceeded to hand down a $12.5 million judgment against WAR's leader and his associates for their role in laying the foundation for the violence against the black man.[47]

During the 1980s and 1990s hundreds of acts of vandalism and intimidation were directed at black and other minority Americans. One of the most notorious incidents occurred in 1986 in the Howard Beach area of New York City, when three black men were beaten and chased by white youths. One of the men died when he was chased into the path of a car. A few days later 5,000 people, black and white, marched through Howard Beach to protest the attack.[48]

In 1991 alone 25 hate-motivated murders and 110 hate-inspired assaults of minority group members, including black Americans, by whites were recorded in the United States—three times as many as in 1990. In one incident, two white men in a Washington,

D.C., suburb went on a rampage hunting down black pedestrians. They ended their night by tearing the clothes off a black woman, spraying her with lighter fluid, and calling her "nigger" while threatening to set her on fire.[49] White violence against black Americans has been a major concern of civil rights organizations from the nineteenth century to the present, a topic to which we turn in a later section.

Black Rioting: Protest against Oppression

As with other groups we have examined, it is important to distinguish violence used to oppress black Americans from violence used by black victims to *resist* oppression. Since the 1930s black urbanites have periodically rioted against the oppressive economic, political, and policing conditions they face. Historically, white violence to enforce discrimination and oppression preceded black violence against white oppression.

A few riots involving pitched battles between black residents and white police officers, often sparked by a police incident, occurred in the 1930s and 1940s, particularly in New York City. Underlying causes of these riots involved antiblack discrimination by whites. Job discrimination and restrictions on political participation have periodically prompted black Americans to lash out in violent riots. In the 1960s and early 1970s many northern cities experienced ghetto uprisings against local symbols of white oppression: especially white police officers, businesses, and landlords. Large-scale uprisings occurred in Los Angeles (Watts) in 1965, in Detroit and Newark in 1967, and in Washington, D.C., in 1968. As late as 1970–71 approximately 250 race-related riots took place in the United States. An angry new generation of black Americans showed their willingness to engage in violent protest, and the impact was felt across the nation.[50]

Riots over oppressive conditions continued into the 1980s and 1990s. In the spring of 1980 black anger over local economic and political conditions exploded in a major riot in Miami. Black residents lashed out at white and Cuban American police officers and the larger white society, burning and looting stores. The three days of rioting cost sixteen lives, caused 400 injuries, and resulted in $100 million in property damage. A *Newsweek* magazine poll conducted after the riot asked a nationwide sample of black Americans if they thought the rioting was justified. Twenty-seven percent said "yes" and another 25 percent were unsure. Half said that whites don't care about what happens to blacks or that whites want to "keep blacks down."[51] Black anger at the reality and effects of racism broke out in other cities as well in the early 1980s, from Chattanooga, Tennessee, to Washington, D.C.

Three more black riots occurred in Miami between 1982 and 1991, all triggered by incidents involving white or Latino police officers shooting to death an African American or being acquitted for such a killing. As recently as June 1991 the shooting of a black man by Latino police officers again touched off a major riot. Tensions between the black and white and black and Cuban American communities remained high in south Florida throughout this period. In Los Angeles in the spring of 1992 the acquittal (on charges of police brutality) of four white officers who had been videotaped in the process of beating an unarmed black man, Rodney King, triggered the most serious riot in the twentieth century. After several days of rioting in South Central Los Angeles, more than 10,000 blacks and Latinos had been arrested, and more than 50 people had been killed. Property damage, mostly to non-black businesses in the area, exceeded a billion dollars. At one point 20,000 police officers and soldiers patrolled large areas of Los Angeles. Rioting also broke out in other cities. As in the 1960s riots, the underlying conditions included poverty, unemployment, and poor housing conditions.[52]

Since the 1930s, white media analysts, police officials, and politicians have interpreted rioting by black Americans as a rampage by ghetto "riffraff" and blamed criminals, teenage delinquents, and recent migrants from outside a given city. Yet research has shown this view to be inaccurate. Although rioters are typically under thirty, they are not for the most part young teenagers. The majority are native-born or long-term residents of the areas in which they rioted, and most are not convicted criminals. The role of white officials and the police in generating and accelerating rioting, while overlooked by most white Americans, has been very significant; police malpractice, especially the commonplace brutality against black men and women, has often precipitated or accelerated rioting.

Police malpractice and brutality targeting black Americans remain a major problem in cities across the United States. In one nationwide poll, nearly 80 percent of the black respondents said that in most cities the police did not treat black residents as fairly as white residents. Sociologist James Blackwell's research suggests that upwards of three-quarters of white officers in many black precincts have some type of antipathy to black residents.[53] Many black communities have reported similar "mysterious" deaths of black youths in police custody. For example, *Time* magazine ran a major news report about two black men killed while in police custody in Los Angeles and Milwaukee. Under pressure from black citizens, officials in both cities decided to prosecute the police officers involved. Occasionally, secret police violence becomes public. In 1991 a white photographer in Los Angeles captured on videotape the brutal beating of Rodney King by white police officers, while more than a dozen other officers watched. Initially the white Los Angeles police chief did not condemn the officers, saying only that the beating was an "aberration." Given this background of police brutality and malpractice, most black men—including middle-class black men—see white police officers as a possible source of danger and death.[54]

THE ECONOMY

As we saw in Chapter 2, assimilation theory can be expanded to include the idea of secondary-structural assimilation in the U.S. economy, one aspect of which is the progressive movement of most individuals in a particular racial or ethnic group into higher levels of employment. Whether this optimistic interpretation can be applied to black Americans has been disputed by power–conflict theorists and analysts. A test of optimistic assimilation theories is the extent of African Americans' economic progress since their emancipation from slavery in the 1860s.

By any measure, over the course of nearly 400 years of American history African Americans have been critical to the building of this society's wealth and prosperity. From the 1600s to the 1990s they have provided much hard labor for American development. Their painful labor was stolen as they toiled in fields and houses or in the craft shops of the southern cities, building up the great wealth of the southern white slaveholding class. Put into southern and northern banks, which then loaned it out, that slave-generated wealth helped to fuel the nation's industrial and commercial development, South and North.

Prior to the Civil War the relatively few free blacks found themselves sometimes competing with white immigrants, such as the Irish, for jobs in the northern cities, and sometimes displaced from unskilled and skilled jobs by the new white immigrants. These discriminatory patterns continued after the Civil War released a large number of African Americans for the free labor market. Free black workers began to compete directly with whites in the South. Black workers were increasingly segregated in unskilled "Negro jobs" and prohibited from taking skilled employment in the newly expanding industrial sectors in the South.

With no major land reform accompanying their emancipation, most former slaves were forced to sell their labor to those controlling the agricultural system—often their old slave masters. Exploitative, semislave farm labor became the lot of many. Sharecroppers and farm laborers in particular were tied to one farm or one area because of the debts they built up in a white-controlled system. Having less money and less legal protection than whites and facing discrimination in land and consumer-product transactions, most freed slaves were unable to become independent farmers of means in the South. Those living in cities fared little better. A black physician made this comment about the high rate of still-births among black mothers: "Why should we be surprised at the great number of still-births among our women?…they do heavy washing, make beds, turn heavy mattresses, and climb the stairs several times during the day, while their more favored white sister is seated in her big armchair, and not allowed to move, even if she wanted to."[55]

The black population in 1900 was still centered in the South: nine black Americans in ten lived there. But the bustling economy developing in the northern and border cities, especially by World War I, the declining significance of "King Cotton" in the South, and southern oppression in the form of segregation stimulated black individuals and families to move to northern cities. With the anti-immigrant legislation and the cessation of massive foreign immigration discussed in earlier chapters, the demand for black laborers in northern industries increased. Thousands of poor black farmers, unable to finance the technological innovations necessary to circumvent the pestilence of the boll weevil, were driven from their farms to the cities. The major push factors, then, were segregation and the declining importance of cotton; the major pull factor was industrial employment.[56]

The Great Migration North

The migration north began in earnest around World War I; it accelerated again during World War II. By the mid-twentieth century millions of black Americans had migrated to what many saw as the economic "promised land." What were their destinations? Large cities in the Northeast, Midwest, and West. These migrants generally were forced to settle in low-income areas already occupied by black families, swelling their size. A traditional view of this migration, one fostered by assimilation theorists, is that it brought great opportunities for economic mobility: according to these theorists, black Americans were just another in a line of immigrant groups (such as the Irish and the Italians) successfully seeking their fortunes in the city. If we accept this view, we would expect that black economic gains between 1900 and 1990 would have dramatically closed the black–white gap. The reality, however, has been quite different, as we will see.[57]

A racial division of labor was established in the cities, enforced at first by coercion and discriminatory law, then by informal mechanisms. As we noted in previous chapters, the urban economy can be divided into at least two major employment sectors. The primary labor market, composed mostly of privileged white workers, is characterized by skilled jobs, high wages, and job ladders offering significant upward mobility. In recent decades the secondary labor market has been composed disproportionately of minority workers and is characterized by instability, low wages, and little upward mobility. The dramatic rise of corporate capitalism after 1900 resulted not only in large workplaces but in union organizing to expand worker rights. One method white employers used to counter the organized expression of white workers' discontent was to make concessions to the white workers, separating them from less privileged minority workers. Positions in the secondary labor market would be for minorities. We see in this arrangement the split labor market described by Edna Bonacich (see Chapter 2).[58]

The increasingly numerous black workers moving out of farm occupations found themselves channeled into urban secondary labor markets. There was a steady shift away from tenant farming and sharecropping to relatively unskilled jobs in the industrial sector. In cities the principal occupations of black men became porter, truck driver, janitor, and cook; black women served as maids, restaurant workers, and dressmakers. By 1930 the dominance of agricultural and domestic service jobs could still be seen in Census Bureau figures. Of every 1,000 black workers, 648 were in agricultural or domestic service jobs, compared with 280 of every 1,000 whites. Most of the remainder were in other unskilled blue-collar positions. Highly educated black men and women were frequently forced to do menial jobs. For example, a black woman graduate of the Cambridge Latin and High School who met the requirements for civil service positions was forced to take a factory job. Most black Americans in the small professional category were teachers, ministers, and physicians serving the black community; likewise, black business people usually served a black clientele. Black incomes were sharply lower than those of whites.[59]

Most labor unions had traditionally been segregated. By the late 1930s black pressure and federal legislation had forced many American Federation of Labor (AFL) unions to begin to reduce discrimination in recruiting black workers. The new Congress of Industrial Organizations (CIO) began with an official nondiscriminatory policy in order to attract black workers in the automobile, steel, and packing industries. In 1930 at least twenty-six major unions had officially barred black workers from membership; by 1943 the number had dropped to fourteen. Nonetheless, official discrimination was usually replaced by widespread informal discrimination.[60]

Economic Progress: From the 1940s to the 1990s

The 1940 census revealed a concentration of black workers in agriculture and the secondary labor market of cities. Seventy-three percent of black male workers were in blue-collar jobs, with a heavy concentration in unskilled and semiskilled positions or farming. Sixty percent of black women were employed in domestic service, and most of the rest were in other service, laborer, or farming positions. During World War II industries with severe labor needs were forced to make significant concessions to black demands for better job opportunities. The proportion of black employees in war-related industries increased from 3 to 8 percent over the war years. Under pressure from black civil rights and union leaders, President Franklin Roosevelt issued executive orders that reduced racial discrimination. At the end of the war this interlude came to an abrupt end: layoffs hit black workers much harder than whites.[61]

Black Americans have made occupational gains over the last few decades. U.S. government data for "nonwhite" (mostly black) employed workers in 1955 and 1972 showed increases in the nonwhite proportions in professional, managerial, sales, clerical, crafts, and operatives categories, and decreases in urban unskilled and service categories. The largest increase was in the Census Bureau's "clerical" category. The growth in the proportion of black employees in better-paid job categories was most rapid in the 1960s, but had slowed by the 1980s and 1990s. The most recent (1989) Bureau of Labor Statistics data show that black men are still less likely than white men to be in the top five better-paying job categories for men: managerial, professional, technician, sales, and crafts. For example, in 1989 about 13 percent of black men were employed in managerial and professional jobs, compared with 27 percent of white men. In contrast, black men were much more likely than white men to be in blue-collar jobs in the service, operative, transportation, and handler-laborer categories (altogether 51 percent versus 28 percent). Black women seemed to have made more occupational progress, although they too had a less favorable job distribution than whites. About 18 percent of black women were employed in managerial and professional jobs, compared with 27 percent of white women. Like black men, black women were more likely than their white counterparts to be in jobs in the service, operative, transportation, and handler-laborer categories (altogether 40 percent compared with 25 percent).[62]

In addition, black workers within the broad white-collar categories tend to be in subcategories with lower pay and job status. For example, within the professional–technical category, black employees today are most commonly found in such fields as social work, kindergarten teaching, vocational counseling, personnel, dietetics, and health care. They are less often found among lawyers and judges, dentists, artists, engineers, and professors at historically white universities.

Persisting Discrimination in the Workplace

In a 1988 *Business Week* national opinion poll 80 percent of the black respondents, compared with only 32 percent of the whites, felt that if an equally qualified black and white were competing for the same job, the black applicant would be less likely to be hired.[63] And in a 1989 ABC News/*Washington Post* survey more than half of the black respondents agreed that black workers generally faced discrimination in getting skilled jobs; 61 percent replied in a similar way in regard to managerial jobs. On the same questions whites generally saw far less discrimination than black respondents.[64]

The four types of discrimination discussed in Chapter 1 have been documented in recent research and in court cases dealing with the workplace. Discrimination confronts black employees and African Americans trying to succeed in business on their own. An example of isolate discrimination is the white manager in a company who expresses stereotyped views by discriminating against black employees without the support of fellow workers or a discriminatory company policy. In a recent research study the senior author supervised interviews with 210 middle-class black Americans in more than a dozen cities. Many told stories of discrimination in employment or business. For example, the successful owner of a small consulting firm in a southwestern city described her experiences in the business world:

> I have a contract right now with a southwestern city government; and I practically gave my services away. I had to become very creative, you know. I wanted the contract because I know I could do the work, and I have the background and the track record to do it. However, in negotiating the contract, they wanted to give it to all these other people who never had any experience...simply because they're a big eight accounting firm, or they're some big-time institution. So, I had to compete against those people. But it was good because it proved that I could be competitive, I could give a competitive price, and I could finally win a contract. But it was a struggle.

She then explained that a professional panel evaluating the bids gave her the highest rating because of her track record. But a barrier was thrown up, because

> the director of their department made a very racial statement, that "they were very sick and tired of these niggers and these other minorities because what they think is that they can come in here and run a business. None of them are qualified to run a business, especially the niggers." (Now, a white person, female, heard this statement, and because they had some confrontational problems—I think the only reason she really told me was because of that.) He was going to use that, not overtly, but in his mind that was going to be his reason for rejection.... Even though they [the panel] all recommended me (I got all five consensus votes), he was going to throw it out.... I had to really, really do some internalizing to keep myself from being very bitter. Because bitterness can make you lose your perspective about what you want to accomplish. Because you know there are so many roadblocks out there—it's just stressful trying to do these kinds of things—but I really had to do that just to keep from going off the deep end.[65]

The discrimination here took the form of a white man's blatant attempt to restrict a talented black person's advancement, apparently without the overt support of other whites in the organization. This black woman was unusual in having proof of the white man's attempt at exclusion. This type of discrimination is common; the motivation is grounded in racial prejudices and stereotyping.

Small-group discrimination is also common, North and South. Small-group conspiracies, arranged by prejudiced white supervisors or union officials wishing to subvert company or union regulations that require the hiring or promotion of qualified black employees, continue to be omnipresent if sometimes hard to document.[66]

Direct institutional discrimination consists of organizationally prescribed actions carried out routinely by whites in companies and businesses. Today this typically takes an informal, sometimes even covert, form. Examples include routinely relegating black employees to special job categories or retarding the job mobility of black employees beyond the entry level. Researcher Beth Anne Shelton examined a southern university and found that despite years of "equal opportunity" as an official government policy, occupational classifications were mostly segregated, with most black employees in service or maintenance positions. And in these sectors black employees were concentrated in custodial, food, and grounds-keeping jobs while white employees were clustered in different and better-paying positions. There was some racial diversity in occupational classifications, but black workers had only token representation in the professional, managerial, and technical sectors. Shelton found that the interview and hiring process favored whites for better-paying jobs.[67]

A 1991 Urban Institute report presented a study in which comparable white and black applicants were sent to the same employers to apply for jobs. A significant proportion of the black applicants suffered discrimination at the entry stage.[68] Even if a black person is hired, other barriers are common. Having reluctantly torn down traditional exclusion barriers in the 1960s and 1970s, many white managers have retreated to a second line of defense: hiring black workers for nontraditional jobs and putting them in conspicuous or powerless positions. Management consultant Kenneth Clark has noted that black Americans moving into nontraditional jobs in corporations have frequently found themselves tracked into "ghettos" such as a department of affirmative action, "community affairs," or "special markets." Many black professionals and managers end up in staff jobs such as "equal opportunity officer" rather than in more powerful line-manager positions. Clark notes that "they are rarely found in line positions concerned with developing or controlling production, supervising the work of large numbers of whites or competing with their white 'peers' for significant positions."[69]

Indirect institutional discrimination can be found in workplace practices that harm black employees because they perpetuate the effects of racial discrimination in the past, even though they are carried out with no discriminatory intent by the whites involved. For example, many black workers have suffered during economic recessions because of seniority rules in their places of employment, rules usually established with no racial intent. In companies that excluded black applicants in the recent past—and where as a result more recently hired black workers have been unable to build up as much seniority as whites—the use of seniority rules favors white employees over black employees in times of economic recession by perpetuating the effects of past discrimination.

There are many examples today of passing along white privilege and black harm from one era to the next. We sometimes hear younger whites saying that they "have not discriminated against blacks and have not participated in racism" and thus that they as innocents "should not have to pay any price through programs like affirmative action." But, this argument misses the many ways in which young whites benefit today from the fact that their parents, grandparents, or great-grandparents secured land, jobs, and wealth at a time when black parents, grandparents, or great-grandparents were excluded from or severely restricted in access to the same land, jobs, and wealth. It is clear that several hundreds of years of white oppression and ill-gotten wealth will take more than a few years of antidiscrimination laws and affirmative action programs to undo.

Government Action and Inaction on Discrimination

Government action on discrimination has been a hotly debated issue. Some argue it has gone too far, even to the point of large-scale "reverse discrimination" favoring people of color. Other analysts, with much more evidence, argue that federal government policies have always been modest and since the early 1980s have had a lessening impact on racial discrimination in such spheres as employment and housing because of the weakening of federal civil rights enforcement by conservative Republican administrations.

The pathbreaking 1964 Civil Rights Act and its later amendments prohibit discrimination in employment. The federal Equal Employment Opportunity Commission (EEOC) was created to enforce the 1964 act, primarily by investigating complaints, seeking conciliation, and—since 1972—filing suit to end employment discrimination by labor unions, private employers, state and local governments, and educational institutions. A major Supreme Court decision, *Griggs* v. *Duke Power Co.* (1971), defined remediable discrimination to include white practices that were "neutral in terms of intent" but that disadvantaged black employees. Until the 1980s the federal courts and the EEOC played a major role in reducing racial barriers in traditionally white employment arenas.

Under the conservative Reagan and Bush administrations in the 1980s and 1990s, however, the EEOC became less active in attacking racial discrimination in U.S. workplaces. During the Reagan era the EEOC reduced the number of field investigations of the critical class-action complaints of discrimination, as well as other broad, institutionally focused investigations of employment discrimination. In addition, Presidents Reagan and Bush appointed several conservative justices to the U.S. Supreme Court, which has subsequently handed down a number of conservative decisions on employment and other civil rights issues. The Court, for example, has backed off from the *Griggs* decision. Statistical evidence of a policy's discriminatory effects is no longer sufficient to judge that policy illegal. The Court now requires proof that a particular discriminatory employment policy was intentionally established to discriminate. This standard is difficult and expensive to meet, and it generally requires evidence that white discriminators in a particular situation actually expressed their prejudices openly. As a result, much less progress in fighting racial discrimination has been made in the 1980s and 1990s. Indeed, in a 1989 decision one of the few liberal justices remaining on the Supreme Court, Harry Blackmun, asked rhetorically whether the conservative white majority "still believes that race discrimination—or, more accurately, race discrimination against nonwhites—is a problem in our society, or even remembers that it ever was."[70] In the 1980s and 1990s many victims of discrimination have given up on help from the federal government and the courts in dealing with discrimination.

Unemployment, Income, and Poverty

The black unemployment rate has consistently been about twice the white unemployment rate:[71]

	Black (or Nonwhite)	White	Ratio
1949	8.9%	5.6%	1.6
1959	10.7	4.8	2.2
1964	9.6	4.6	2.1
1969	6.4	3.1	2.1
1975	13.8	7.8	1.8
1980	13.0	5.9	2.2
1982	20.4	9.5	2.1
1986	15.0	6.6	2.3
1992 (Feb.)	13.8	6.5	2.1

In 1986 the black–white unemployment ratio reached a record high of 2.3, and in 1992 it was still above 2.0. Related to the high unemployment rate is the fact that in recent recessions black workers have lost jobs at twice the rate of white workers, and have generally been recalled at a slower rate. In some cities the situation has been much worse.

For example, in 1989 the unemployment rate for blacks in Chicago was 17.5 percent, more than four times the white rate. One major reason for this racial inequality is the movement of capital and jobs to suburbs and overseas. The majority of new jobs in the last two decades in metropolitan areas such as Chicago have been created outside the central-city areas where most African Americans live.

Much higher than the unemployment rate for black Americans is the underemployment rate, which includes those with no jobs, those working part time, and those making poverty wages. One nationwide study found that many black workers had part-time work but wanted full-time work, received very low wages, or were discouraged workers (workers who had given up looking for work). One 1980s study found that one-third of black workers fell into these subemployment categories; the figure for whites was much lower. In 1991, Janet Norwood, head of the U.S. Bureau of Labor Statistics, criticized the Bush administration for not paying attention to this widespread underemployment. She pointed out that if underemployed workers were included, the official jobless rate would be at least 10 percent of all U.S. workers, rather than 6.7 percent. This estimate would translate into about 20 percent of black Americans. During the Great Depression of the 1930s the national jobless rate reached that high level; black workers in the early 1990s were clearly in an economic depression.[72]

Since the 1950s black family income has remained at about 55 to 60 percent of white family income. Black (or nonwhite) family income as a percentage of white family income fluctuated slightly during the 1950s, rose significantly in the late 1960s, then dropped over the 1970s; since the mid-1970s the figure has hovered just below 60 percent:[73]

Black (or Nonwhite) Income as a Percentage of White Income

1950	54%
1954	56
1959	52
1964	54
1969	61
1974	58
1980	58
1985	58
1990	58

Families headed by single, separated, or divorced mothers tend to be poorer than those with both parents present. The proportion of black families headed by women increased from 18 percent in 1950 to 44 percent in the early 1990s. Like black men, black women have faced major employment problems because of direct discrimination and because of the indirect discrimination of inadequate educational and job training programs. As Robert B. Hill has concluded, "families headed by black women are primarily poor, not because they do not have husbands, but because they do not have jobs."[74]

Whatever the type of family, black Americans generally pull in significantly fewer dollars than whites and are much more likely to live in poverty. In 1990 about 32 percent of all black Americans, and 45 percent of black children, fell below the government poverty line. The extent of black poverty grew between 1980 and 1990. Moreover, the most recent (1984) study of wealth in the United States found that the average white family, with $39,135, had ten times the wealth of the average black family ($3,397). Thirty percent of black families had no wealth, or negative net worth because of debts; the comparable figure for whites was only 8.4 percent. Recent studies have found that the wealth of black families is, on the average, still about one-tenth that of white families. For African Americans, the long history of discrimination in employment has meant little money for savings and thus for building up wealth.[75]

Since the 1970s there has been much discussion by scholars and media commentators of poor black Americans, some of whom have been regularly labeled the *underclass*. For instance, in a widely discussed book, *The Declining Significance of Race* (1978), University of Chicago sociologist William J. Wilson argues that the underclass is the most serious problem for black Americans. He also argues that the rise of the black middle class since the 1960s has resulted from shifting economic conditions and new government policies, such as affirmative action. In the view of Wilson and many other commentators equal employment legislation virtually eliminated the split labor market in which black labor suffered direct racial discrimination. The central problem now is not discrimination but the underclass. In a more recent book, *The Truly Disadvantaged,* Wilson has argued that the black underclass's major problem is unemployment, a structural condition that must be eradicated by massive governmental job training and job creation programs. Similarly, in *The Underclass* Ken Auletta has argued that racism has played little direct part in the formation of the poor black underclass; rather it is a matter of class culture. Scholars such as Auletta and Wilson contend that the black community is being polarized into a growing, affluent middle class and a poor underclass. Since discrimination has mostly been eradicated for middle-class black Americans, they argue, there is less need for affirmative action programs that primarily benefit those individuals.[76]

In scholarly books such as these and in much popular commentary in the mass media, the plight of the underclass is discussed as though racial discrimination had little to do with its high unemployment and underemployment, low incomes, and poor housing conditions. From this perspective poor black Americans have gotten locked into a lower-class "culture of poverty," with its allegedly deviant values, immorality, broken families, juvenile delinquency, and lack of emphasis on the work ethic. These stereotype-based arguments are simply more recent versions of the culture-of-poverty arguments that have been made since the 1960s. If this notion of the irrelevance of racial discrimination were true, poor black Americans should face roughly the same social, economic, political, and housing conditions as poor white Americans. But this is not the case. For example, because of past and present discrimination poor black families do *not* live in integrated neighborhoods with poor white families. Poor black Americans are less likely than comparably poor whites to get unemployment compensation when they are unemployed. They tend to hold lower-paying and less secure jobs than even poor whites. And they face much more discrimination at the hands of the police and other white officials than poor whites.

The role of past and present racial discrimination—such as that documented in earlier sections—in the "tangles of underclass poverty" must be recognized. Past discrimination, coupled with blatant, subtle, and covert racial discrimination today, is the likely reason for most black poverty, unemployment, and underemployment.[77]

POLITICS AND PROTEST

Before 1865 African Americans, whether slaves in the South or "free" men and women in the North, were not allowed to participate as equals with whites in the political system. Most were disenfranchised, and only in a few places (for example, Maine), did they have any substantial political rights. Between the 1660s and 1860s some black Americans petitioned legislatures and executive officials for redress of grievances; as a rule their petitions were ignored. The Civil War brought an end to slavery and increased black participation in electoral politics. The 1866 Civil Rights Act made black men full citizens, at least in principle. The Thirteenth Amendment to the U.S. Constitution abolished slavery, the Fourteenth Amendment stated that the civil rights of black Americans could not be denied by the states, and the Fifteenth Amendment guaranteed black men (but not black women) the right to vote.

From Reconstruction to the 1920s

The Reconstruction period that followed the Civil War came to the South as a breath of fresh air. This federally enforced policy was precipitated by southern unwillingness to make major changes in the treatment of freed slaves or to prevent the white leaders of the defeated Confederacy from resuming power. A brief period of limited federal military occupation resulted. During Reconstruction, blacks made some political gains, although these were not nearly as great as southern white apologists have suggested. Black men gained the right to vote in all states. New state constitutional conventions included black delegates, although in most states white southerners were the majority of all delegates.[78]

Between 1870 and 1901 twenty black men served in the House of Representatives and two in the U.S. Senate. African Americans Hiram R. Revel and Blanche K. Bruce were U.S. senators from Mississippi between 1870 and 1881, the first two to serve in the Senate and two of only three blacks that as of 1992 had ever served there.[79]

The overthrow of the Reconstruction governments by conservative forces came swiftly. The so-called Redemption period began with the Hayes Compromise of 1877, which removed the few remaining federal troops from southern states and thereby federal protection of freed slaves. Reconstruction was the first period in U.S. history in which black Americans gained a significant measure of freedom and justice. Although considerable racial segregation remained, the system was not nearly as all-encompassing as it would become from the early 1900s to the 1960s. In many political jurisdictions black voters were able to participate in elections and hold public office. Sometimes public accommodations, such as hotels, were open to freed slaves as well as whites on a more or less equal basis. Freedom here, racial segregation there, mixing here, racial exclusion there—such was the fluidity of the Reconstruction era.

Subsequent years witnessed the rise of agrarian populist movements that brought together poor blacks and poor whites, reflecting an awareness of common problems. The threat of a black–white coalition of farmers became too great for the conservative white gentry in the South to ignore, and its members roared an ugly response. Wealthy white conservatives appealed to poor whites' sense of racial superiority; populist voters were intimidated by the violence of the Ku Klux Klan; election fraud by white conservatives was common. The white populist was attacked as a traitor to the "white race."[80]

Enforced racial segregation became the rule in the South as Supreme Court decisions nailed the lid on the coffin of southern racial progress. The decision in *Plessy* v. *Ferguson* (1896), a case involving the racial segregation of railroad cars, was the major blow, with its doctrine of "separate but equal" facilities for blacks. The Court reasoned that racism was natural, that "legislation is powerless to eradicate racial instincts or to abolish distinctions based upon physical differences, and the attempt to do so can only result in accentuating the difficulties of the present situation."[81]

In 1922 the state of Mississippi went so far as to pass a law requiring segregated taxicabs; in 1932 Atlanta passed a law requiring black and white baseball teams to play at least two blocks apart; and Birmingham, Alabama, even prohibited interracial domino playing![82] Disenfranchisement of black voters was achieved by the rigorous enforcement of discriminatory literacy test laws, poll tax laws, and "grandfather clause" laws—the last of which limited the vote to those who had voted prior to 1861 and their (usually white) descendants. As a result, between 1896 and 1900 the number of black voters in Louisiana decreased from 130,000 to 5,300. All other southern states followed this lead.[83]

The white hypocrisy in enforcing public segregation was pointed out in the late nineteenth century by a South Carolina newspaper, which noted that the blackest woman domestic could "cook the food for prejudiced [white] throats" and hold "the whitest, cleanest baby,...but the angry passions rise when a well-dressed, educated, refined negro [sic] pays his own fare and seats himself quietly in a public conveyance."[84]

In 1915 the Supreme Court began a slow swing back to the protection of civil rights by declaring grandfather clauses unconstitutional. Voter registration increased very slowly. By the 1920s the movement to the cities had brought a few black Americans to the political forefront, particularly in the North. Independent political organizations were established in a few cities, but the only major success was that of Adam Clayton Powell, Jr., in New York City. In 1945 Powell became the first black member of Congress from outside the city of Chicago in several decades. In the North the black vote was at first strongly tied to the Republican party, but by the 1930s it had begun to shift to the Democratic party.[85]

The Limits of Black Progress: Political Discrimination

In 1940 only 90,000 of the 3.7 million adult blacks in the Deep South voted in the general election. In 1942 there were only a dozen black state legislators in the entire country, and a few black officials on school and tax boards; none served in the South, except for a few in small all-black towns. Black southerners benefited little from new government programs; schools, hospitals, parks, and other public facilities for black citizens were inadequate or nonexistent, a situation that would hold true in the South for several more decades. Black voter registration increased sharply in the South between 1940 and the 1970s, from 250,000 to four million voters.

A big jump came after passage of the Voting Rights Act in 1965, an act with a demonstrable impact on black political participation. Some social scientists suggested that inadequate civic training and less education would render blacks unable to organize effectively. Yet since their new enfranchisement in 1965 black southerners have developed effective political organizations and campaigns. In 1965 there were approximately

70 black elected officials in the South. By February 1968 the figure was 248; by the 1990s it was several thousand. Even so, black officials have attained proportional equality in very few areas of the South.[86]

Black voters still face attempts to reduce the efficacy of their political participation. Research by Chandler Davidson and by Frank Parker demonstrates that electoral discrimination persists in such forms as vote dilution, gerrymandering, the changing of elective offices into appointive offices, and unnecessary revisions in qualifications for office. A major example of vote dilution is the at-large electoral system, whereby candidates are elected citywide rather than from smaller districts. In cities across the nation this system has been demonstrated to reduce sharply the participation of black candidates and voters in local campaigns. As long as blacks constitute well under half of the voters in a city, black candidates are unlikely to win elected office in an at-large system, because many whites will never vote for a black candidate. The Supreme Court, in *City of Mobile* v. *Bolden* (1980), required minority plaintiffs to prove that at-large electoral systems were intentionally set up to discriminate. The Court ruled that evidence of the severe negative racial impact of such systems was not enough. The Court argued in effect that indirect or subtle direct discrimination is constitutionally permissible.[87]

Minority voters also face discrimination in the form of purges of voter-registration rolls, unannounced changes in polling places, intentionally difficult registration procedures, and threats of retaliation. These practices have been documented from Alabama to Texas. Davidson has noted these examples: changing an office from elective to appointive when a minority candidate has a chance to win (Georgia, Alabama); setting high filing and bonding fees (Georgia); abolishing party primaries (Mississippi); and intimidating candidates with threats of violence or of credit cutoffs (Alabama, North Carolina, South Carolina, Georgia). In the early 1980s the Reagan administration, responding to conservative white supporters, tried to weaken the Voting Rights Act. However, in 1982, after a long battle, Congress approved a twenty-five-year extension of key provisions of the act.[88]

Have black officials in the South been able to accomplish anything? Some argue that black votes and elected officials can accomplish much for black voters. Others see black citizens as unable to gain much through the electoral process. Mack Jones has argued that black elected officials have not been able to significantly reorder white priorities in employment, housing, and education. So far the accomplishments of black officeholders in the South have been more than the pessimists would expect, although much less than justice would require. Black officials have often increased public services and expanded economic opportunities for their constituents. Even where they are in the minority, most have been able to improve government services as well as increase the number of blacks hired in local government.[89]

The number of black elected officials in the nation increased sharply between 1964 and the early 1990s, from about 100 to more than 7,400. The proportion of women among these officials has grown dramatically, from less than one in twelve in 1970 to more than 25 percent in the early 1990s.[90] Since the 1960s blacks have won mayoral elections in a number of major cities with large black populations: Washington, Newark, Philadelphia, Detroit, Chicago, Cleveland, New York City, Los Angeles, Atlanta, Birmingham, and Gary, Indiana. A few predominantly white cities, such as Seattle and Kansas City, have also elected black mayors. In 1990 the state of Virginia, once home to the capital of the

Confederacy, saw L. Douglas Wilder, the grandson of a slave, become the first African American elected governor of any state. In 1991 Wilder was mentioned as a possible candidate for the Democratic party's presidential nomination the next year.

The Federal Government

The New Deal (1933–40) was the first period since Reconstruction in which the federal government gave any serious attention to the needs of its black citizens. Breaking with the exclusionary practices of previous presidents, Franklin Roosevelt appointed more than one hundred African Americans to important governmental positions. New Deal programs helped black Americans survive the rigors of the Great Depression, but benefited whites considerably more than blacks. New Deal agencies such as the Agricultural Adjustment Administration (AAA) and the National Recovery Administration (NRA) did little to ensure black citizens their fair share of government aid. Black Americans did receive aid from agencies offering temporary relief, but the more important federal recovery agencies discriminated in favor of their white constituents.[91]

Since World War II black voters have had a significant impact on the legislative, executive, and judicial branches of the federal government. In the 1950s a third African American was elected to Congress, joining the two from New York and Chicago. With the registration of new voters in the 1960s and 1970s came more gains. By 1992 there were twenty-six black representatives, including four women, in the U.S. House, but no black men or women in the Senate.

The first black person ever to serve in a presidential cabinet was Robert Weaver, who in 1967 became secretary of housing and urban development. In the 1960s Lyndon Johnson appointed Andrew Brimmer the first black member of the Federal Reserve, Thurgood Marshall the first black Supreme Court justice, and Patricia Harris the first black ambassador. Yet even in the Johnson administration few black Americans ever served at the top of a major executive department or on federal commissions other than the civil rights agencies.[92] From the 1970s to the 1990s this pattern has persisted under both Republican and Democratic presidents—a token black person in the cabinet and on the Supreme Court but no black heads of the major executive branch departments, such as state, defense, and the treasury. The overall pattern in federal legislative, executive, and judicial positions can still be described as one of serious and continuing underrepresentation for black Americans.

In federal elections the black vote has from time to time loomed large. In 1944 black voters played a role in Roosevelt's election; in the late 1940s they were important to Truman's election.[93] And the black vote in a few key states reportedly decided the 1960 presidential election in favor of Kennedy. Black voters also played a key role in electing Lyndon Johnson in 1964 and Jimmy Carter in 1976. When Ronald Reagan was elected in 1980 with a majority of the white vote and very little of the black vote, black voters kept liberal white members of Congress in office, enabling them to survive the conservative trend among their white constituents. Moreover, in congressional elections from 1982 to 1990 black voters helped elect a Congress more sympathetic to civil rights and other progressive issues, offsetting the conservative inclinations of the majority of white voters. In election after election black voters have been especially important in pressing the nation in the direction of its basic political ideal of "liberty and justice for all."

The Republican Party's Appeal to White Voters

There is a good reason why most black voters have found themselves voting for losing presidential candidates since 1980—the prowhite political strategy of the Republican party. Developed by Barry Goldwater and other Republican conservatives in the early 1960s, this strategy was effectively used by Richard Nixon in winning the 1968 election. The prowhite approach was celebrated in Kevin Phillips's *The Emerging Republican Majority,* for a while the "Bible" of many Republicans. Phillips explicitly suggested that Republicans did not need "urban Negroes" and other "vested interests" to win.[94] Republican targeting of white southern and suburban voters was effective in the 1980 and 1984 Reagan campaigns and took an even more aggressive form in the 1988 Bush campaign. In the Bush campaign, decisions made by the candidate and his campaign manager, Lee Atwater, led to a dramatic TV advertisement centered in the person of a black rapist (Willie Horton); no comparable white criminal was shown. This ad was employed to scare and recruit white voters. Bush initially stood behind the ad, and Atwater admitted its underlying prowhite southern strategy in commenting that "the Horton case is one of those gut issues that are value issues, particularly in the South."[95]

In recent decades the Republican party has moved from the position of a party linked to Abraham Lincoln and expanded civil rights for black Americans, one that long captured most black voters, to a party opposed in practice to expansion of civil rights enforcement and aggressive affirmative action to redress the legacy of racism, and thus one that captures few black voters. The Republican national conventions of the 1980s had very few black delegates—69 in 1984, and just 61 of 2,277 delegates in 1988. In 1988 half of the fifty state delegations of the party of Lincoln had *not one* black delegate. In contrast, 962 of the 4,162 delegates to the 1988 Democratic convention were black. As a percentage of the total number of delegates, black representation at the Democratic convention was almost nine times greater than black representation at that year's Republican convention.[96]

The Republican orientation toward black America did not improve in the 1990s. Speeches and ads containing President Bush's comments and those of other Republican candidates for election or reelection (for example, Senator Jesse Helms in North Carolina) frequently included racially loaded code words such as "racial quotas" and "unqualified minorities" in attempts to get whites to vote for Republican candidates. As a result of these racial appeals to whites, the overwhelming majority of black voters have continued to support Democratic candidates.

Nonviolent Protest

The fundamental values and oppositional culture of African Americans have not only provided a source of resistance to discrimination but have also infused significant elements into the evolving cultural mix that has become the U.S. core culture. A fundamental part of black oppositional culture is a deep respect for civil rights and liberty. This value commitment is one of the greatest sources of support for civil rights and civil liberties in the United States today. Over the centuries black resistance to racism has ranged from legal strategies, to the ballot, to nonviolent civil disobedience, to violent attacks on the system.[97]

In the twentieth century the goals of black protest movements have included not only the desegregation of public accommodations and educational institutions but also the opening of housing and employment arenas formerly limited to whites. Criticizing the accommodationist position of such leaders as Booker T. Washington, W. E. B. Du Bois and other black and white liberals formed the Niagara movement in 1905. Legal and voting rights, as well as economic issues, were the focus of their activities. Not long thereafter, some of these leaders helped create the National Association for the Advancement of Colored People (NAACP).

Organizations directed at self-help and philanthropic activity, such as the Urban League, were also created in the early twentieth century. The efforts of the new black organizations began to pay off in terms of more philanthropic aid for the urban poor and erosion of the legal edifice of segregation. One of the first major NAACP legal victories was a 1917 Supreme Court decision, *Buchanan* v. *Warley,* which knocked down a Louisville law requiring residential segregation—one of the first steps in reversing the segregationist position the Court had taken since the late 1800s. Most other Court decisions until the 1930s, however, hurt the cause of black rights, reinforcing segregation in schools, transportation, and the jury system.[98]

Black resistance to discrimination was obvious in the new organizations—the civil rights groups, educational organizations, and a new press. Against fierce resistance the NAACP began a large-scale attack on segregation in schools, voting, transportation, and jury selection. Beginning in the 1930s NAACP and other lawyers won a series of cases that over the next several decades expanded the legal rights of black defendants, eliminated the all-white political primary, protected the voting rights of black citizens, reduced job discrimination by unions, voided restrictive housing covenants, and desegregated schools and public accommodations. The separate-but-equal doctrine of *Plessy* v. *Ferguson* increasingly came under attack. Dramatically reversing its position in that 1896 case, the Supreme Court in a famous decision in *Brown* v. *Board of Education* (1954) ruled that "in the field of public education the doctrine of 'separate but equal' has no place."[99]

By the 1940s and 1950s more militant strategies were being generated in black communities. During World War II a threatened large-scale march on Washington, D.C., to be led by A. Philip Randolph and other black leaders, forced President Roosevelt to issue an order desegregating employment. After World War II, Randolph and other leaders organized against the peacetime draft on the basis that black citizens should not serve in a segregated army. After unsuccessful attempts to get black leaders to back down on this issue, President Harry Truman set up an agency to rid federal employment of discrimination and a committee to oversee desegregation of the U.S. armed forces. Today the military is by far the most desegregated of major U.S. institutions.[100]

The 1950s and 1960s brought a major increase in black protest against discrimination. First came major boycotts, such as that of segregated buses in Montgomery, Alabama in the mid-1950s. There a tired black seamstress and NAACP member, Rosa Parks, refused to give up her seat on a segregated bus to a white person. Her arrest triggered a boycott by the local black community, a successful movement that brought the local minister and boycott leader, Martin Luther King, Jr., into national prominence. Growing black resistance to southern segregation in the mid-1950s spurred the creation in 1957 of a group soon known as the Southern Christian Leadership Conference (SCLC), led by Dr. King.

In 1960 black students began the sit-in movement at a white-only lunch counter in Greensboro, North Carolina, touching off a long series of sit-ins throughout the South by thousands of black southerners and their white allies. The Freedom Rides on interstate buses came in 1961; blacks and whites tested federal court orders desegregating public transportation and demonstrated a lack of compliance throughout the South. Near Anniston, Alabama, the first bus of Freedom Riders was burned; in Birmingham the riders were attacked by a white mob.

In the spring of 1963 Dr. King and his associates launched a series of demonstrations against discrimination in Birmingham, Alabama. Fire hoses and police dogs were used against the demonstrators, many of whom were young children, gaining the demonstration movement much national publicity. An agreement desegregating businesses and employment ended the protests, but another round of demonstrations was touched off when a black home and motel were bombed. Then came the massive 1963 March on Washington, in which King dramatized rising black aspirations in his famous "I have a dream" speech before thousands of white and black demonstrators.[101]

Direct action against segregation in the North began in earnest in the 1960s with boycotts in Harlem, sit-ins in Chicago, school sit-ins in New Jersey, and mass demonstrations in Cairo, Illinois. The Nation of Islam ("Black Muslims") aggressively pressed for black pride and black-controlled businesses. The Congress of Racial Equality (CORE) accelerated protest campaigns against discrimination in housing and employment. School boycotts, picketing at construction sites, and rent strikes became commonplace. In 1964 black protestors in New York tried to stop traffic by staging a sit-in on a bridge, and threatened a stall-in to disrupt the opening of the World's Fair. New organizations sprang up. Led by Stokely Carmichael, the Student Nonviolent Coordinating Committee (SNCC) germinated the Black Power movement. There was a growing group of militant organizations oriented toward black nationalism and black self-help enterprises, including the Black Panthers, a group of young black men who started breakfast programs for children and engaged in surveillance of white police officers to prevent police brutality in cities across the United States. Pride and consciousness grew in all segments of the black community in the North, particularly among the young.[102]

There have been suggestions by white commentators on the nonviolent civil rights era that Martin Luther King was mostly a media creation or that the civil rights movement was mostly a middle-class movement. Neither is true. Many local demonstrations included large-scale participation by black Americans of all income backgrounds. Research on the history and development of recent black resistance movements has shown that they were grounded in organized activism that was in turn rooted in what Aldon Morris calls "a well-developed indigenous base."[103] This base was broad and deep, and included community churches, social clubs, and other voluntary organizations whose role in providing money and communications and mobilizing people enabled activists in organizations such as the SCLC and SNCC to be so successful in fighting racism and segregation.

Progress and Retreat

During the Johnson administration in the 1960s the civil rights movement played an important role in pressuring Congress to pass three major pieces of legislation prohibiting discrimination in employment, voting, and housing—the Voting Rights Act of 1965 and the Civil Rights Acts of 1964 and 1968. In the 1970s these important acts were amended and expanded, and some effort was put into enforcing them. Yet many of these advances were threatened in the 1980s and 1990s under conservative Republican administrations. From 1981 to 1989 the conservative president Reagan radically increased military spending, but cut back federal social programs, such as job training and food stamps. In addition, he cut funding for, and otherwise weakened, several federal agencies that enforce civil rights laws. As a result, major civil rights agencies were forced to reduce their enforcement activities, such as class-action suits aimed at discriminatory employers and compliance reviews of government contractors. The Reagan administration even tried to cut back the Voting Rights Act and federal programs for increasing minority employment. In a January 1989 interview the outgoing president played down the significance of racism in the United States. He argued that black leaders such as Coretta Scott King were intentionally exaggerating the magnitude of racism and were "doing very well leading organizations based on keeping alive the feeling that they're victims of prejudice."[104]

As we have noted, the subsequent Bush administration (1989–93) continued the negative approach to the interests of black Americans, who responded by pressing their fight to improve civil rights laws and enforcement. Like Reagan, Bush appointed conservative justices to the Supreme Court. In the 1980s and early 1990s this Court limited the right of victims of discrimination to sue. A new civil rights bill was proposed in the early 1990s, one designed to overcome the limitations of this and other Court decisions. Initially, President Bush rejected the bill, calling it a "quota" bill. But after a long political struggle and some watering down of the legislation, the 1991 Civil Rights Act was passed and signed into law by Bush. Because of these events, and the Willie Horton ad campaign, most black citizens understandably felt that the federal government in the 1980s and early 1990s had turned its back on them. A professor at a West Coast university, interviewed in a recent study of middle-class black Americans, put it this way: one sees "in the Reagan and Bush administration a dismantling of…Civil Rights acts that says racism is alive and well and kicking, and we will allow it to flourish."[105]

Responding to this retrenchment, civil rights organizations continued protesting on behalf of minority rights. Washington, D.C., and other cities saw demonstrations against the conservative cutbacks and the weakening of civil rights enforcement. From time to time the NAACP Legal Defense Fund, the Leadership Conference on Civil Rights, and other civil rights organizations mounted enough public pressure to stop the Reagan and Bush administrations from achieving conservative goals. Among other things they helped block appointments to federal judgeships, including Supreme Court positions, of some white conservatives insensitive to civil rights and helped defeat an attempt to abolish minority-hiring goals for federal contractors.

Political Organizations with Civil Rights Roots

In 1983 Jesse Jackson, a black minister and prominent civil rights leader, announced his candidacy for president of the United States. Jackson and many of his supporters learned their political skills in various civil rights efforts. Despite little money, no wealthy business backers, and insufficient staff, Jackson put together a strong grassroots campaign grounded in a diverse organization called the Rainbow Coalition, which included black, white, Latino, and Native American volunteers and activists concerned with a progressive political agenda. By the end of his campaign in 1984 Jackson had registered two million new voters and had won nearly four million votes in Democratic party primaries, a fifth of all the votes cast. Jackson went to the Democratic national convention in the summer of 1984 with many delegates. Although a descendant of immigrants who had come to the United States several centuries before the ancestors of some of the white Democratic and Republican candidates, he was the first African American to reach that level in politics. He lost the nomination, but succeeded in creating multiracial organizations in many states. The voters he registered helped elect numerous moderate whites to the U.S. Congress, people who subsequently voted against some of the efforts of the Reagan administration to roll back civil rights.[106]

In 1988 Jesse Jackson again campaigned for the Democratic presidential nomination with the Rainbow Coalition as his base, and again took many delegates to the 1988 Democratic national convention. Two million Americans voted for him in the primaries. He was strongly supported by black voters, receiving 90 percent or more of their votes in primaries. Many black supporters became hopeful that an African American had a shot at the White House. However, a problem for any black candidate is that a significant proportion of white voters will not vote for a black person under any circumstances. In a 1988 *New York Times* opinion poll 43 percent of white voters said they had an unfavorable view of Jackson. Margot Kidder, a white actress, reported that her daughter was harassed by fellow students at a private school in New York after they heard the actress was a Jackson supporter.[107]

Jesse Jackson stirred many Americans to participate in U.S. politics for the first time, especially people of color and those committed to a progressive political platform. He was the first presidential candidate in U.S. history to develop a strong public position on issues of great concern to black and other women of color. He and the Rainbow Coalition took public positions in favor of the Equal Rights Amendment, choice on the abortion issue, the principle of equal pay for equal worth, and a woman as a vice-presidential candidate.

Sociologist Patricia Hill Collins has demonstrated that black women were an integral part of the 1960s' civil rights movement, even though leadership roles were generally reserved for men. Collins criticizes black male leaders for not addressing issues relevant to black women, as distinct from the general issue of racial discrimination, until the 1980s. Today black women have gained more leadership positions in the civil rights movement and are pressing for a central consideration of the joint effects of sexism and racism on black women.[108]

EDUCATION

Reconstruction brought former slaves access to numerous schools sponsored by the federal government or private organizations. Religious organizations, black and white, and white philanthropists took up the slack when federal aid subsided. In the late nineteenth and early twentieth centuries many schools and colleges for young black people were set up by black communities, North and South. However, by 1900 public school segregation was in place across the South, and grossly inferior public educational facilities and programs for black students were the rule. All southern states had legally segregated schools operating under the "separate but equal" doctrine.

Yet these schools were anything but equal. For many decades little public money was spent on black children. In 1900 some counties in the South were spending ten times as much per capita for the education of white children as for that of black children. One study found that as late as the 1930s the average expenditure per pupil in elementary and secondary schools in ten southern states was $49.30 for white children but only $17.04 for blacks.[109]

In spite of discrimination, African Americans pressed on toward their dream of education. By the early 1900s a million and a half black children were enrolled in schools. There were thirty-four black colleges in the South. In the late nineteenth century, the nationally known black leader Booker T. Washington advocated vocational education for black youth in the South. Although he operated within the limits of a racist system, he played a significant role in expanding schooling opportunities. Specialized education became a dominant tradition, focusing on skills suitable for an agricultural economy, which, unfortunately, was declining. Washington was criticized by some black leaders, especially W. E. B. Du Bois, as too conservative.[110]

The proportion of black children attending school in the South continued to increase after 1900. Between the 1940s and the 1990s blacks made significant progress. Median educational attainment for those over twenty-five went from 5.7 years in 1940 to 9.8 years in 1970 and 12.4 in 1989. The black–white differential narrowed significantly over this period. In 1940 whites on the average had almost 3 years more education than blacks. By 1970 the difference was 2.3 years, but by 1989 the average black person had almost as much formal education as the average white person.[111] The educational gap between blacks and whites has narrowed more than the economic gap.

Yet educational opportunities for blacks are still not equal to those for whites. A 1991 Census Bureau report showed that 65 percent of blacks over the age of twenty-five had completed high school, compared with 78 percent of whites; about 12 percent of blacks had completed four years of college, compared with 22 percent of whites.[112]

The Desegregation Struggle

Early-twentieth-century civil rights activity was directed at improving education. The slow movement toward school desegregation began in earnest in the 1930s with an NAACP legal attack. Lawsuits attacking discrimination in graduate schools were the first to spotlight the "separate-but-equal" doctrine for the racist sham it was. In the 1930s and 1940s a series of federal court decisions forced the desegregation of the University of Missouri, University of Oklahoma, University of Maryland, and University of Texas law schools. A suit against the University of Oklahoma forced the dismantling of a segregated graduate program there. Then in 1954 black parents won the most famous school decision of all, *Brown* v. *Board of Education of Topeka*. Nonetheless, because of the fear among white judges of violent reactions by white southerners, school desegregation was allowed to proceed at a snail's pace; most white-dominated school systems ignored or circumvented the desegregation precedent set by the *Brown* decision. Some whites wishing to avoid desegregation set up private white schools. Others resorted to defiant resistance and violence. In 1956 President Dwight Eisenhower was forced to federalize the Arkansas National Guard to protect the black children who were braving white mobs to desegregate a Little Rock, Arkansas, high school.[113]

A series of court cases after *Brown* expanded the attack on segregated schooling. In *Swann* v. *Charlotte-Mecklenburg Board of Education* (1971) the Supreme Court upheld the use of limited pupil transportation (busing) as a legal means of disestablishing a dual school system. In *Keyes* v. *Denver School District No. 1* (1973) the Court, for the first time in a northern case, ruled that evidence of government-imposed segregation in part of a school district, such as selective attendance zones and school-site choice, is sufficient to prove segregation and to require desegregation. Segregated schools included those created by local authorities' efforts to keep black and white children separate, such as by gerrymandering districts or by locating new schools so as to reinforce existing patterns of segregation. However, in the 1970s the Supreme Court began to back off from the implications of school desegregation and as a rule rejected the inclusion of suburban districts in central-city desegregation plans. In the 1974 *Milliken* decision the Court overturned a lower-court order requiring the substantially black Detroit city school system and the surrounding white suburban school systems to combine according to one metro-politan-wide plan. Since then, few metropolitan-wide desegregation plans have cleared this Court hurdle. The *Milliken* decision has played a role in the slowing of school desegregation since the 1970s.[114]

During the first decade after the *Brown* decision little was done to desegregate most of the nation's racially segregated schools; most black children remained in segregated schools. The 1960s and early 1970s brought widespread desegregation, and throughout the South today large numbers of black children attend school with whites. Desegregation remains more extensive in the South than in the North. Northern school systems, such as that in Boston, have also come under court order to desegregate, and resistance—includ-ing white violence—has sometimes resulted. By the late 1970s, some white social scientists and politicians who had advocated desegregation were arguing that desegrega-tion was accelerating the suburbanization of whites and thus re-creating de facto dual systems, with blacks in the central city and whites on the suburban periphery. A common conclusion was that school desegregation policy was a failure. Actually, the suburbaniza-tion of whites had been taking place for several decades prior to the attempts at school desegregation; much of it has to do with economic mobility and housing upgrading, not with desegregation.[115]

Today, in many large cities it is not possible to desegregate schools without involving the suburbs. However, in the smaller cities, those with populations of less than 200,000, desegregating public schools usually involves much less in the way of new organization and extensive busing. Many school boards could do a great deal more to desegregate their schools without engaging in large-scale busing. For example, they could redraw gerrymandered districts or locate all new schools on the boundaries of segregated residential areas so as to maximize natural desegregation. Or they could develop more central learning centers, which would draw children from all over the city. Furthermore, the desegregation of a school's staff, extracurricular activities, or curriculum would not require the feared "massive busing."[116]

The failure of many school systems to make these changes suggests that much of the debate over busing is calculated to obscure the real issue—white opposition to white and black children attending the same school. School busing dates back long before the desegregation of schools—in fact, to the beginning of public schools.[117]

One result of school desegregation may be housing desegregation. Diana Pearce has reported that cities with metropolitan-area school desegregation plans experienced much more rapid desegregation of housing patterns than cities without such plans. Cities of similar size and racial mix differed greatly in the extent of housing desegregation as a result of differences in the scope of their school desegregation programs. Cities with school desegregation plans only for central cities had less housing desegregation than cities that desegregated both central cities and suburban areas. Pearce concluded from this that busing for school desegregation need not be a long-term program, since metropolitan desegregation of schools may eventually reduce housing segregation—which in turn would mean that schools could eventually be naturally desegregated without busing. Important too is the way in which desegregation is implemented. Much school desegregation has taken place in the face of a hostile white community and school administration, a situation that might in the short term reduce positive results. Perhaps most important, Pearce found that in virtually all schools comprehensive desegregation is a long way from being achieved.[118]

Russell Irvine and Jacqueline Jordan Irvine have suggested that school desegregation has had effects not only on black achievement but also on the relationships between black children and their teachers, on schools as black community institutions, and on black communities more generally. In many areas school desegregation has significantly reduced the number of black teachers with whom a black child comes in contact. One reason for this is that it is often the white schools rather than the black schools that are desegregated. Another reason, following from the first, is that the number of black teachers and principals may be significantly reduced.[119] Fewer black teachers means fewer role models for black children. A number of studies have shown that black teachers tend to expect greater educational achievement from black pupils than white teachers do, both in schools with high average levels of academic achievement and in schools with lower levels of achievement. The absence of black teachers means not only an absence of role models but also decreased expectations for achievement from black children.[120]

Since the late 1970s some black leaders in numerous major cities have shifted away from an emphasis on racial balance in local schools, in part for the reasons just noted. For example, in Atlanta, where the school population is mostly black, black groups settled their desegregation lawsuit without a racial-balance plan in exchange for complete desegregation of the faculty and administration. Similar compromises have been made in other cities with predominantly black school systems. Many local black leaders have given up on comprehensive school desegregation plans, although civil rights organizations continue to press for them. There is, moreover, an increasing awareness that housing desegregation is essential to educational goals.[121]

The Current School Situation

In the early 1990s the majority of black students went to schools that were mostly minority, often in central-city districts where substantial desegregation is not possible without involving the white suburbs. As we have seen, since the mid-1970s the U.S. Supreme Court has required minority plaintiffs in desegregation cases to prove that school officials intentionally acted to segregate a school system; only then can dramatic remedies such as busing be used to desegregate the schools. White support for desegregation has declined at all levels.

At a 1992 press conference marking the release of a report by the National School Boards Association, school expert Gary Orfield noted that between the early 1970s and the early 1990s no U.S. president was a strong supporter of urban desegregation orders and that Congress did nothing substantial to further encourage school desegregation. During the Republican administrations of the 1980s and 1990s government policy moved toward voluntary desegregation and neighborhood schools and away from mandatory desegregation. Many programs designed to aid black and other minority schoolchildren were cut back by the Reagan administration. The same administration supported private schools by such actions as providing tax deductions for parents who pay private-school tuition.[122]

Government reports have documented the generally poor conditions of public school systems in many central cities. One major reason for the poor funding of such systems is the movement of affluent whites to the suburbs. This movement has taken place in cities with school desegregation plans and in those without such plans. In both situations it has meant a loss of tax revenues and thus a growing financial crisis in central-city school systems, where minority proportions are increasing. A new problem is the racial segregation of suburban schools. Since the 1980s black and other minority populations in suburban areas have grown rapidly. Suburban school boards are now facing the challenge of desegregating their own schools.[123]

College Attendance

Since the 1950s black students have gone to college in significant numbers. For many decades black students in the South were restricted to all-black colleges. By the 1970s three-quarters of black college students nationwide were in predominantly white colleges. Students were encouraged by the outreach and affirmative action programs of many historically white colleges. The dream of a college education in a desegregated environment seemed to have come true. Still, many black students attend historically black colleges, campuses usually more hospitable to black students than traditionally white campuses. The proportion of black high school graduates going to college hovered around 25 percent from 1980 to 1988, then increased to 33 percent in 1990—still below the 39 percent of white high school graduates. The proportion of black faculty members on college campuses increased slightly from 1980 to 1990, moving from 4.3 to 4.5 percent. Significantly, the majority of black faculty members teach at historically black colleges.[124]

Black students face serious racial problems on white campuses. Walter Allen has reported that black students establish their own social networks because of their exclusion from white networks. In a University of Michigan study, half the black students questioned said they did not feel they were part of campus life. Many reported they were disenchanted with their college environments. Most black students come to white campuses having already been victims of racial discrimination. And, as Allen has noted, this does not disappear on campus. In the same survey 85 percent of the students reported that they had experienced discrimination on campus, including comments by professors that "black students aren't very bright" and blatant acts such as "KKK" and "nigger" being painted on a house owned by a black organization. In the late 1980s white students in KKK-like sheets burned a cross in a black student's room at the Citadel. Many anti-minority incidents have been reported on college and university campuses since 1980. Into the 1990s black students at white colleges often felt isolated and targeted for discrimination.[125]

RELIGION AND CULTURE

The first major white stereotyping of Africans was in terms of what Europeans saw as their savagery. The irony of militaristic, slave-trading, warring Europeans seeing Africans as "savage" was lost on white Europeans at the time and has been lost on most of their descendants. The slaves imported into the colonies brought African religions with them. At first slave owners feared that "Christianizing" the Africans would put notions of freedom into their heads—as if slaves did not already have the idea of freedom. Protestant missionaries were instructed, and laws were passed making it clear, that conversion to Christianity did not bring freedom along with it. Actually, many slave owners encouraged white missionaries, particularly Baptists and Methodists, to convert slaves in order that they might be better controlled.[126]

Conversion to Christianity did not eradicate African religions and culture. Historian Sterling Stuckey has noted that the religion of the slaves mixed African and European elements, yet the African values prevailed over the European.[127] As some slaveholders had feared, the Afro-Christianity of the slaves sometimes became linked to protest. The view of God that many slaves held—for example, the emphasis on God's having led the Israelites out of slavery—was different from what slaveholders had hoped for. In slave spirituals there was, hidden by the Christian symbolism, a deeper yearning to be free. Regular religious meetings were part of Afro-Christianity, and some gatherings hatched conspiracies to revolt. Black slaves were often permitted to preach to gatherings, and some of these preachers became resistance leaders, including leaders of slave revolts. As James Scott points out in his book *Domination and the Arts of Resistance,* the freedom discourse the slaves developed in private was quite different from the religious discourse they used in the presence of their masters.[128]

Formal church organizations grew among slaves and free blacks in the cities—a result of their exclusion from white churches. In Philadelphia Absalom Jones and Richard Allen, after being mistreated at a white Methodist church, established their own Free African Society in 1787. Later, Jones established the first Negro Episcopal church and Allen played a role in the emergence of the African Methodist Episcopal church.[129]

After the Civil War, churches played an important role in black communities. Churches were mutual-aid societies, ministering to those facing sickness and death, and they played a role in the pooling of economic resources. Education often came as religious education. New schools were established after the war, many under religious auspices, and some trained ministers as black leaders. Black churches continued to function as community and schooling centers, since few such centers were provided by local or state governments.

With the migration to the cities came a shift for some to a less otherworldly religious style. Urban social welfare groups and civil rights activity became increasing parts of black religious life. In addition, new urban groups became religious and political forces. One is the Nation of Islam, popularly known as the Black Muslims, a group that broke with the Christian background of black Americans. Nation of Islam leaders have pressed hard for a black-oriented theology suffused with black pride and a self-help philosophy. Prominent black leaders have arisen from this non-Christian movement, including Malcolm X and, more recently, Louis Farrakhan.[130]

Today the protestant churches still predominate among African Americans. They include a great diversity of groups, from the older Methodist and Baptist denominations to newer evangelical groups. Whatever its form, however, the church is, as a black minister recently put it, "the hub of existence in the black community," a "holistic ministry," and a "social center."[131]

Religion and Protest Movements

As we just noted, organizations committed to change and to protesting oppressive conditions have been rooted in African American religion from the beginning; religious gatherings and leaders have played a role in spreading protests against racism since the early days of slavery. In the twentieth century ministers have often been political leaders. The nonviolent civil disobedience movement that was prominent from the mid-1950s to the 1970s had religious underpinnings.[132] As we have seen, prominent among the minister-leaders was Dr. Martin Luther King, Jr. Raised in an intensely religious family with a record of fighting for civil rights, King came naturally to his essentially religious view of the legitimacy of nonviolent protests as a way of winning concessions and at the same time healing the wounds of oppressed and oppressor. He led black citizens in effective protests, for which he earned a Nobel Peace Prize, and died a hero whose example today inspires both black and white Americans.[133]

The effectiveness of black churches in providing political leadership, as in mobilizing millions of formerly disenfranchised voters, is deeply rooted in African American culture. Ministers and congregations in many black churches are more likely to openly express religious emotions than their white counterparts. The call-and-response format of many black religious services allows the congregation to provide the minister with direct feedback on the sermon. Thus in Dr. Martin Luther King's or the Reverend Jesse Jackson's civil rights speeches, with their calls to register to vote or to participate in other political activities, the African American religious tradition has provided a context for response. Black political leaders have harnessed the religious sentiments of an oppressed people to mobilize support for political action. Moreover, from the days of the slave spirituals to more recent blues, jazz, and gospel traditions, African American music and singing have reflected a strong element of protest against racial discrimination.[134]

ASSIMILATION FOR BLACK AMERICANS?

Assimilation Theories

Milton Gordon argues that his theory of assimilation is applicable to both ethnic and racial groups. He briefly applies his scheme to black Americans, whom he sees as assimilated at the cultural level in terms of language and the Protestant religion, with some black–white cultural differences remaining because of "lower-class subculture." Beyond acculturation Gordon sees little integration at the structural level, little intermarriage, little erosion of prejudice or discrimination, and no demise of group identity.[135]

As we noted in Chapter 2, Gordon has written optimistically about the assimilation of black Americans, a trend he sees in the growing black middle class. For that reason, Gordon and other assimilationist scholars sometimes call for an end to remedial programs such as affirmative action. Optimistic assimilation-oriented analysts have often under-scored black progress in terms of cultural, economic, and social integration. Sociologist Talcott Parsons argued that racial and ethnic inclusion is basic to U.S. society and that this process encompasses black Americans. But inclusion for Parsons did not mean slavish Anglo-conformity assimilation. In his view even white ethnic groups have not been prevented by inclusion from maintaining a distinct ethnic identity. Given the basic egalitarian values of the United States, "the only tolerable solution to the enormous [racial] tensions lies in constituting a single community with full membership for all."[136]

Sociologists such as Nathan Glazer have argued that there has been a major collapse in traditional racial discrimination, that assimilation of black Americans into the core economy and society is well under way. What these scholars view as dramatic economic progress for the black middle class is cited as proof of ongoing black assimilation. The major problem is the troubled black underclass, whose difficulties are not primarily questions of current discrimination. While recognizing discrimination as a barrier for black Americans, some assimilationists have in effect blamed black Americans for their slower economic and social mobility, particularly in the last few decades. In a famous report in the 1960s, Daniel P. Moynihan viewed black families headed by females as a serious retardant to progress. These arguments have been resurrected in the 1980s and 1990s, and some scholars have again pointed to a subculture of poverty among low-in-come black families as a major barrier to progress. A theme of certain white scholars and mass media analysts sometimes boils down to "Why can't black people be like us?" The suggestion is that black individuals, like the white immigrant groups before them, should be able to assimilate, to move up gradually through the various levels of the economy, society, and polity—if they will only work hard and address their own subcultural and value problems.[137]

Power–Conflict Perspectives: The Continuing Significance of Racism

Power–conflict analysts reject the optimistic assimilationist view of African American mobility and assimilation, which from their perspective often amounts to a denial of the pervasiveness and persistence of racial barriers. The current condition of black Americans is much more rigidly hemmed in and resistant to change than that of white ethnic groups because of the extreme character of Africans' incorporation into and oppression within this country. Once the system of racial subordination was established, those whites in the superior position, and their descendants, have continued to monopolize the lion's share of economic and social resources. Legal segregation in employment, education, and housing has been since the 1960s replaced by extensive, informal discrimination.

In his theory of internal colonialism Robert Blauner, for example, convincingly argues that there are major differences between black Americans and white ethnic groups in regard to social and economic oppression.[138] Africans were enslaved and brought across the Atlantic Ocean in chains. Incorporated into the economy against their will, they provided hard labor at the lowest occupational levels, first as slaves, later as tenant farmers, then as urban laborers. Even with the northward migration their lesser economic and social position and status relative to whites were not altered. Black Americans became a subordinate part of the growing urban economic system; they were incorporated at the bottom of the economy. This point underscores a major problem in traditional assimilation theory: incorporation into the society and economy has occurred mostly at the lower economic levels, those offering only modest chances of upward mobility. African slaves suffered attempts to destroy their cultures and were often forced to give up many of their traditional ways as part of their incorporation into slavery. The Protestant religion and the English language were forced upon them. Africans were forced to give up control of their own bodies, which became the property of whites; miscegenation was frequently forced on them by white slaveholders. In contrast with the assimilation view, there is an emphasis among power–conflict theorists on the *forced* acculturation and secondary-structural assimilation of African Americans.

Power–conflict perspectives also take a different view of the lack of full assimilation of black Americans into the economy and society in recent decades. They assign little importance to matriarchal families or a subculture of poverty, but instead emphasize all types of racial discrimination. For example, when white ethnic groups such as the Irish began arriving, they did not gain socioeconomic equality only on the basis of fair competition. Rather they sometimes displaced free blacks, who were then relegated to the lowest-paying jobs. By the mid-nineteenth century white immigrant workers were crowding black workers out of numerous occupations. Black workers were forbidden by law to enter such crafts as blacksmithing and mechanics, and Irish and German immigrants began to fill jobs once held by black workers.[139]

After the Civil War most black families in the South remained where they were and became poor tenant farmers and sharecroppers, for the new industrial machine mostly drew workers from southern and eastern Europe, not from the South. Discrimination prevented African Americans' structural assimilation into the economy on an equal-status basis. After 1900, with the trek northward, black southerners moved into low-level jobs in U.S. industries; not until World War II did a large proportion of black workers find better-paying jobs in industry. By the end of that war a decline in demand for black labor had begun, and with it a growing urban unemployment problem that persists to this day. Black migrants found that the opportunity awaiting them in the northern cities was much paler than the promised-land image that had drawn them. Discrimination severely limited opportunities in jobs and housing. Since World War II the demand for black labor in cities has been reduced not only by racial discrimination but also by automation and capital flight to the suburbs and overseas.[140]

Irish, Italian, and other nineteenth- and twentieth-century European immigrants benefited from urban political organizations, which played an important role in providing them jobs and thus in facilitating their upward mobility in the first decades of the twentieth century. When black workers came into northern cities during World War II, the period of great public construction in the cities was over. In most cities black communities were never able to benefit as much as "white ethnics" from the urban political patronage system.[141]

As we have documented, racial discrimination continues to handicap black Americans today in all major institutional arenas, from public accommodations to employment to schooling to housing. The power–conflict theorists are thus pessimistic about the further assimilation of black Americans into these critical institutional arenas unless there is a major change in the racist attitudes and discriminatory actions of the majority of white Americans.

SUMMARY

The social, economic, and political progress of African Americans was severely restricted by slavery and subsequent legal segregation. Even at the time of the first great waves of white European immigrants in the early 1900s, African Americans, many of whom were "old" (tenth-generation) Americans, were still sharply segregated and oppressed. Jim Crow frustrated the lives of freed slaves and several generations of their descendants. The northward trek reflected protests against southern oppression, protests "by the feet." Other types of black protest against subordination, nonviolent and violent, have punctuated the long course of black–white relations. The segregation period was followed by a long epoch, not yet ended, of informal racial discrimination.

In the early 1990s most black citizens were living in cities, North and South. The migration of black Americans had changed; more were moving to the South than were leaving the region. Yet wherever they live, black Americans face continuing racial discrimination and economic inequality. The Civil Rights Acts of 1964, 1965, and 1968 have made many formal acts of discrimination illegal, but they have not ended the array of blatant, subtle, and covert discrimination in business, jobs, housing, and education. The spectacle of "slavery unwilling to die" can be seen today: informal barriers to voting continue in the South; most black children still attend de facto segregated schools; most black families live in segregated residential areas; most blacks in all income classes face informal discrimination by banks, real estate people, landlords, and homeowners; most black defendants are tried by juries in which black citizens are underrepresented if not absent; and most black workers face some discrimination in employment.

The impact of racial discrimination remains painful, stifling, and cumulative. Reflecting on the costs of racism, a successful black entrepreneur has recently commented on what it is like to be black in a predominantly white business world:

> *One step from suicide!* What I'm saying is—the psychological warfare games that we have to play everyday just to survive. We have to be one way in our communities and one way in the [white] workplace or in the business sector. We can never be ourselves all around. I think that may be a given for all people, but [for] us particularly, it's really a mental health problem. It's a wonder we haven't all gone out and killed somebody or killed ourselves.[142]

NOTES

1. Bebe Moore Campbell, "To Be Black, Gifted, and Alone," *Savvy* 5 (December 1984): 69.
2. James H. Dorman and Robert R. Jones, *The Afro-American Experience* (New York: John Wiley, 1974), pp. 72–74; Thomas R. Frazier, preface to Chapter 1, in *Afro-American History: Primary Sources*, ed. Thomas R. Frazier (New York: Harcourt, Brace, & World, 1970), pp. 3–5.
3. Olaudah Equiano, "The Interesting Narrative of the Life of Olaudah Equiano," in *Afro-American History*, ed. Frazier, pp. 18, 20.
4. Dorman and Jones, *The Afro-American Experience*, pp. 80–82.
5. Philip D. Curtin, *The Atlantic Slave Trade* (Madison: University of Wisconsin Press, 1969), pp. 87–93; U.S. Bureau of the Census, *Historical Statistics of the United States* (Washington, 1960), p. 770.
6. Carl N. Degler, *Out of Our Past* (New York: Harper, 1959), pp. 161–63; John Hope Franklin, *From Slavery to Freedom*, 4th ed. (New York: Knopf, 1984), p. 88.
7. Franklin, *From Slavery to Freedom*, pp. 132–33.
8. U.S. Bureau of the Census, *Historical Statistics of the United States*, p. 11; Degler, *Out of Our Past*, pp. 163–64; Ulrich B. Phillips, *Life and Labor in the Old South* (Boston: Little, Brown, 1929), pp. 339ff; Kenneth M. Stampp, *The Peculiar Institution* (New York: Random House, Vintage Books, 1956), pp. 383–418.
9. Ben Simpson, "Ben Simpson: Georgia and Texas," in *Lay My Burden Down*, ed. B. A. Botkin (Chicago: University of Chicago Press, 1945), p. 75.

10. John W. Blassingame, *The Slave Community* (New York: Oxford University Press, 1972), pp. 155–60.

11. Quoted in Jacqueline Jones, *Labor of Love, Labor of Sorrow: Black Women, Work, and the Family, from Slavery to the Present* (New York: Random House, Vintage Books, 1985), p.16. We have emended the quotation slightly for clarity.

12. Quoted in ibid., p.19.

13. Eugene G. Genovese, *Roll, Jordan, Roll* (New York: Random House, 1974), pp. 5, 362–64; Stanley M. Elkins, *Slavery* (Chicago: University of Chicago Press, 1959), pp. 72–127.

14. Herbert Gutman, *The Black Family in Slavery and Freedom, 1750–1925* (New York: Pantheon, 1976); Stanley Elkins, "The Slavery Debate," *Commentary* 46 (December 1975): 46–47.

15. Patricia Williams, "Alchemical Notes: Reconstructing Ideals from Deconstructed Rights," *Harvard Civil Rights and Civil Liberties Review* 22 (1987): 415.

16. Elkins, *Slavery*, pp. 84–85.

17. Blassingame, *The Slave Community*, pp. 203–14; Genovese, *Roll, Jordan, Roll*, p. 588.

18. Genovese, *Roll, Jordan, Roll*, p. 650.

19. Herbert Aptheker, *American Negro Slave Revolts* (New York: International Publishers, 1943), pp. 12–18, 162.

20. Ibid., pp. 165, 220–25, 249–50, 267–73.

21. Herbert Aptheker, *Essays in the History of the American Negro* (New York: International Publishers, 1945), pp. 39, 49–51; Sterling Stuckey, *Slave Culture* (New York: Oxford University Press, 1987), pp. 42-46.

22. Cited in *Bartlett's Familiar Quotations*, 15th ed., ed. Emily M. Beck (Boston: Little, Brown, 1980), p. 556.

23. Benjamin B. Ringer, *"We the People" and Others* (New York: Tavistock, 1983), p. 533.

24. A. L. Higginbotham, *In the Matter of Color* (New York: Oxford University Press, 1978), pp. 144–49.

25. Cited in Thomas F. Gossett, *Race* (New York: Schocken Books, 1965), pp. 42–43.

26. See, for example, Samuel Cartwright's infamous 1850s article "The Prognathous Species of Mankind," in *Slavery Defended*, ed. Eric L. McKitrick (Englewood Cliffs, N.J.: Prentice-Hall, 1963).

27. Williams, "Alchemical Notes," pp. 401-34. See also Duncan J. MacLeod, *Slavery, Race, and the American Revolution* (London: Cambridge University Press, 1974), p. 158.

28. Excerpt from Edward East, "Heredity and Human Affairs," in *In Their Place*, ed. Lewis H. Carlson and George A. Colburn (New York: John Wiley, 1972), p. 103.

29. I. A. Newby, *Jim Crow's Defense* (Baton Rouge: Louisiana State University Press, 1965), pp. 19–23.

30. Thomas F. Pettigrew, *A Profile of the Negro American* (Princeton, N.J.: D. Van Nostrand, 1964), p. 100ff.

31. Richard J. Herrnstein, *IQ in the Meritocracy* (Boston: Little, Brown, 1973); Arthur R. Jensen, "How Much Can We Boost IQ and Scholastic Achievement?" *Harvard Education Review* 39 (1969): 1–123; Tom Wilkie, "The American Association for the Advancement of Science: Research Revives Dispute over IQ," *Independent*, February 19, 1991, p. 7.

32. Richard Brookhiser, "Fear and Loathing at City College," *National Review*, June 11, 1990, p. 20.

33. Quoted in an unsigned editorial, "Buchanan Campaign Rhetoric," *Boston Globe*, January 12, 1992, p. 68.

34. Samuel Francis, "Out of the Mouths of Japanese," *Washington Times*, February 11, 1992, p. F1.

35. See, for example, data gathered by Otto Klinberg as cited in I. A. Newby, *Challenge to the Court* (Baton Rouge: Louisiana State University Press, 1967), p. 74. See also Pettigrew, *A Profile of the Negro American*, pp. 123–26.

36. Leon J. Kamin, *The Science and Politics of IQ* (New York: John Wiley, 1974), pp. 175–78.

37. N. J. Block and Gerald Dworkin, "IQ, Heritability, and Inequality," in *The IQ Controversy*, ed. N. J. Block and Gerald Dworkin (New York: Random House, 1976), pp. 410–540.

38. William Brink and Louis Harris, *The Negro Revolution in America* (New York: Simon & Schuster, 1964) pp. 140–41; William Brink and Louis Harris, *Black and White* (New York: Simon & Schuster, 1967), p. 136; Richard T. Morris and Vincent Jeffries, "The White Reaction Study," in *The Los Angeles Riots*, ed. Nathan Cohen (New York: Praeger, 1970), p. 510; National Opinion Research Center, *1990 General Social Survey*, tabulations by the authors.

39. John B. McConahay and Joseph C. Hough, "Symbolic Racism," *Journal of Social Issues* 32 (1976): 38.

40. Joe R. Feagin and Melvin P. Sikes, *Modern Racism: On Being Black and Middle Class* (New Haven: Yale University Press, forthcoming).

41. Howard Schuman, Charlotte Steeh, and Lawrence Bobo, *Racial Attitudes in America* (Cambridge: Harvard University Press, 1985), pp. 86–125; National Opinion Research Center, *1990 General Social Survey*.

42. U.S. Bureau of the Census, *Historical Statistics of the United States*, p. 218.

43. W. J. Cash, *The Mind of the South* (New York: Random House, Vintage Books, 1960), p. 125.

44. Note a 1940 pamphlet written by a white southerner for U.S. senators and congressmen, quoted in Gunnar Myrdal, *An America Dilemma* (New York: McGraw-Hill, 1964), 2:1198.

45. Gilbert Osofsky, *Harlem: The Making of a Ghetto* (New York: Harper & Row, Pub., 1963), pp. 45–51; Arthur I. Waskow, *From Race Riot to Sit-In, 1919 and the 1960s* (Garden City, N.Y.: Doubleday, 1966), pp. 209–10 et passim; Elliot M. Rudwick, *Race Riot at East St. Louis* (Carbondale: Southern Illinois University Press, 1964), pp. 3–30.

46. Linda Diebel, "Darkest Iowa," *Toronto Star*, February 23, 1992, p. F1; John Turner, *The Ku Klux Klan: A History of Racism and Violence* (Montgomery, Ala.: Southern Poverty Law Center, 1982), pp. 48–56; "Going after the Klan," *Newsweek*, February 23, 1987, p. 29.

47. Diebel, "Darkest Iowa."

48. "Tension Rises in New York in March over Black's Death," *Austin American-Statesman*, December 28, 1987, p. A3.

49. Bernd Debusmann, "Hate Crime Shocks Washington," Reuters News Service, March 4, 1992, n.p.

50. Joe R. Feagin and Harlan Hahn, *Ghetto Revolts* (New York: Macmillan, 1973), p. 134.

51. "The Mood of Ghetto America," *Newsweek*, June 2, 1980, pp. 32–34.

52. Lara Parker, "Violence after Police Shooting Exposes Miami Racial Tensions," *Washington Post*, June 29, 1991, p. A2.

53. James E. Blackwell, *The Black Community* (New York: Harper Collins, 1991), pp. 456-57.

54. "Accidents or Police Brutality?" *Time,* October 26, 1981, p. 70; Charles Leerhsen, "L.A.'s Violent New Video," *Newsweek,* March 18, 1991, pp. 33, 53.
55. Quoted in Jones, *Labor of Love, Labor of Sorrow,* p. 123. See also Ray Marshall, *The Negro Worker* (New York: Random House, 1967), pp. 7–12; MacLeod, *Slavery, Race, and the American Revolution,* pp. 151–53; Pete Daniel, *The Shadow of Slavery: Peonage in the South* (London: Oxford University Press, 1972); and Myrdal, *An American Dilemma,* 1:228.
56. Karl E. Taeuber and Alma F. Taeuber, *Negroes in Cities* (Chicago: Aldine, 1965), pp. 12–13.
57. Charles Tilly, "Race and Migration to the American City," in *The Urban Scene,* ed. Joe R. Feagin (New York: Random House, 1973), p. 35; Taeuber and Taeuber, *Negroes in Cities,* pp. 144ff.
58. Edna Bonacich, "Class Approaches to Ethnicity and Race," *Insurgent Sociologist* 10 (Fall 1980): 11. See also Bennett Harrison, *Education, Training, and the Urban Ghetto* (Baltimore: Johns Hopkins, 1972).
59. Jones, *Labor of Love, Labor of Sorrow,* p. 179; U.S. Bureau of the Census, *Negroes in the United States, 1920–1932* (Washington, 1935), p. 289; Myrdal, *An American Dilemma,* 1:304ff.
60. Marshall, *The Negro Worker,* pp. 23–24, 56–57.
61. U.S. Bureau of the Census, *Population,* vol. 3, *The Labor Force* (Washington, 1943). See also Sidney M. Wilhelm, *Who Needs the Negro?* (Cambridge, Mass.: Schenkman, 1970), p. 57.
62. The Bureau of Labor Statistics data, retabulated, are cited in David H. Swinton, "The Economic Status of African Americans: 'Permanent' Poverty and Inequality," in *The State of Black America, 1991,* ed. Jane Dewart (New York: Urban League, 1991), p. 63.
63. James E. Ellis, "The Black Middle Class," *Business Week,* March 14, 1988, p. 65.
64. Lee Sigelman and Susan Welch, *Black Americans' Views of Racial Inequality* (Cambridge: Cambridge University Press, 1991), pp. 55-57.
65. Feagin and Sikes, *Modern Racism.*
66. Ibid.
67. Beth Anne Shelton, "Formal and Informal Mechanisms of Discrimination: A Case Study" (Ph. D. dissertation, University of Texas at Austin, 1984).
68. Margery Austin Turner, Michael Fix, and Raymond J. Struyk, *Opportunities Denied: Discrimination in Hiring* (Washington, D.C.: Urban Institute, 1991).
69. Kenneth B. Clark, "The Role of Race," *New York Times Magazine,* October 5, 1980, p. 30.
70. *Wards Cove Packing Co.* v. *Atonio* 109 S. Ct. 2115 (1989).
71. U.S. Bureau of the Census, *The Social and Economic Status of the Black Population in the United States, 1971* (Washington, 1972), p. 52; Andrew F. Brimmer, *The Economic Position of Black Americans, 1976* (Washington, D.C.: National Commission for Manpower Policy, 1976), p. 13; U.S. Commission on Civil Rights, *Unemployment and Underemployment among Blacks, Hispanics, and Women* (Washington, 1982), p. 5; U.S. Bureau of the Census, *Statistical Abstract of the United States: 1987* (Washington, 1986), p. 390; Bureau of National Affairs, "Economic Statistics," *Daily Report for Executives,* March 9, 1992, p. N1.
72. Wilhelm, *Who Needs the Negro?* p. 155; U.S. Commission on Civil Rights, *Unemployment and Underemployment among Blacks, Hispanics, and Women,* pp. 5–8.
73. U.S. Bureau of the Census, *The Social and Economic Status of the Black Population in the United States, 1971,* p. 29; Brimmer, *The Economic Position of Black Americans, 1976,* p. 37; Spencer Rich, "New Data Show Blacks' Income Outgained Whites' in 1970s," *Washington Post,* June 3, 1982; U.S. Bureau of the Census, *Statistical Abstract of the United States: 1987,* p. 436; Paul R. Krugman, "The Painful Cost of Workplace Discrimination," *U.S. News & World Report,* November 4, 1991, p. 63. The census category *nonwhite* consists mostly of blacks.
74. Robert B. Hill, "The Economic Status of Black Americans," in *The State of Black America, 1981,* ed. J. D. Williams (New York: Urban League, 1981), pp. 5–6, 33.
75. Peter T. Kilborn, "U.S. Whites 10 Times Wealthier Than Blacks, Census Study Finds," *New York Times,* July 19, 1986, p. 1; Krugman, "The Painful Cost of Workplace Discrimination," p. 63.
76. William J. Wilson, *The Declining Significance of Race* (Chicago: University of Chicago Press, 1978); Ken Auletta, *The Underclass* (New York: Random House, 1982).
77. See Joe R. Feagin and Clairece B. Feagin, *Discrimination American Style,* 2d ed. (Malabar, Fla.: Robert Krieger Publishing Co., 1986), pp. 207–34.
78. The discussion in this subsection draws on a course given by Thomas F. Pettigrew at Harvard University.
79. Franklin, *From Slavery to Freedom,* pp. 252–53; Chuck Stone, *Black Political Power in America,* rev. ed. (New York: Deli Pub. Co., Inc., 1970), pp. 30–31.
80. Cash, *The Mind of the South,* p. 174. See also C. Vann Woodward, *The Strange Career of Jim Crow,* 2d rev. ed. (New York: Oxford University Press, 1966), pp. 31ff.
81. *Plessy* v. *Ferguson,* 163 U.S. 551–52.
82. Woodward, *The Strange Career of Jim Crow,* pp. 115–18.
83. Stone, *Black Political Power in America,* p. 35.
84. Quoted in Jones, *Labor of Love, Labor of Sorrow,* p. 150.
85. Hanes Walton, Jr., *Black Politics* (Philadelphia: Lippincott, 1972), pp. 100, 119.
86. David Campbell and Joe R. Feagin, "Black Politics in the South: A Descriptive Analysis," *Journal of Politics* 37 (February 1975): 129–62.
87. Chandler Davidson, *Minority Vote Dilution: An Overview,* Reprint 85-1 (Houston: Institute for Policy Analysis, Rice University, 1985), pp. 17–18; Frank R. Parker, *Black Votes Count* (Chapel Hill: University of North Carolina Press, 1990).
88. Davidson, *Minority Vote Dilution,* pp. 17–18.
89. Remarks by Martin Luther King, Jr., quoted in *New York Times,* February 2, 1965, p. 1; Mack Jones, "Black Office Holders in Local Governments of the South: An Overview" (paper presented at the sixty-eighth annual meeting of the American

Political Science Association, Los Angeles, September 6–12, 1972), p. 38; James E. Conyers and Walter L. Wallace, *Black Elected Officials* (New York: Russell Sage Foundation, 1976), p. 159 (see also pp. 8, 137–40); James Button, *Blacks and Social Change* (Princeton, N.J.: Princeton University Press, 1989).

90. Dele Olojede, "Progress for Black Women in Politics," *Newsday*, February 24, 1992, p. 6.

91. Myrdal, *An American Dilemma*, 1:503; Raymond Wolters, *Negroes and the Great Depression* (Westport, Conn.: Greenwood Publishing Corp., 1970), p. xi and elsewhere.

92. Stone, *Black Political Power in America*, pp. 68–72.

93. Ibid., p. 47. Stone draws here on Henry L. Moon, *Balance of Power* (Garden City, N.Y.: Doubleday, 1948).

94. Kevin Phillips, *The Emerging Republican Majority* (New Rochelle, N.Y.: Arlington House, 1969).

95. Chandler Davidson, *Race and Class in Texas Politics* (Princeton, N.J.: Princeton University Press, 1990), pp. 213-57.

96. Joe R. Feagin, "White Elephant: Race and Electoral Politics in Texas," *Texas Observer*, August 23, 1991, pp. 15-16.

97. The discussions of oppositional culture in this chapter draw on Joe R. Feagin and Bonnie L. Mitchell, "America's Non-European Cultures: The Myth of the Melting Pot" (research paper, University of Florida, 1992).

98. Feagin and Hahn, *Ghetto Revolts*, pp. 81–85; Loren Miller, *The Petitioners* (New York: Random House, 1966), pp. 250–56.

99. Miller, *The Petitioners*, pp. 260–347.

100. Lerone Bennett, Jr., *Confrontation: Black and White* (Baltimore: Penguin, 1966), pp. 164–69.

101. Ibid., pp. 223–34; Bryan T. Downes and Stephen W. Burks, "The Historical Development of the Black Protest Movement," in *Blacks in the United States*, ed. Norval D. Glenn and Charles Bonjean (San Francisco: Chandler, 1969), pp. 322–44.

102. Feagin and Hahn, *Ghetto Revolts*, pp. 92–94; Bennett, *Confrontation*, pp. 234–37; Inge P. Bell, *CORE and the Strategy of Nonviolence* (New York: Random House, 1968), pp. 13ff.

103. Aldon Morris, *The Origins of the Civil Rights Movement* (New York: Free Press, 1984).

104. U.S. Commission on Civil Rights, *The Federal Civil Rights Enforcement Effort: Fiscal Year 1983* (Washington, 1982), pp. 5–7; Andrew Rosenthal, "Reagan Hints Rights Leaders Exaggerate Racism to Preserve Cause," *New York Times*, January 14, 1989, p. 8.

105. Feagin and Sikes, *Modern Racism*.

106. Sheila D. Collins, *The Rainbow Challenge* (New York: Monthly Review Press, 1986), pp. 128–43.

107. Michael Oreskes, "Voters and Jackson," *New York Times*, August 13, 1988, p. 1.

108. Patricia Hill Collins, *Black Feminist Thought: Knowledge, Consciousness, and the Politics of Empowerment* (Boston: Unwin Hyman, 1990).

109. Franklin, *From Slavery to Freedom*, pp. 280–81; Myrdal, *An American Dilemma*, 1:337–44; Henry A. Bullock, *A History of Negro Education in the South* (New York: Praeger, 1967), pp. 1–99.

110. Bullock, *A History of Negro Education in the South*, pp. 170–86; Franklin, *From Slavery to Freedom*, pp. 284–86.

111. U.S. Bureau of the Census, *Statistical Abstract of the United States: 1991* (Washington, 1991), p. 138.

112. Cited in Irene Sege, "Earnings Gap for Women Found to Persist," *Boston Globe*, November 14, 1991, p. 3.

113. Bullock, *A History of Negro Education in the South*, pp. 211–12, 225–30; Miller, *The Petitioners*, pp. 347–58.

114. U.S. Commission on Civil Rights, *Twenty Years after Brown* (Washington, 1975), pp. 11–41; *Milliken v. Bradley*, 418 U.S. 717.

115. Nathan Glazer, *Affirmative Discrimination* (New York: Basic Books, 1975); "Busing Backfired" (interview with James Coleman), *National Observer*, June 7, 1975.

116. See the numerous articles on innovative desegregation strategies in the 1966–1976 issues of the journal *Integrated Education*.

117. Nicolaus Mills, "Busing: Who's Being Taken for a Ride," in *The Great School Bus Controversy*, ed. Nicolaus Mills (New York: Teachers College Press, Columbia University, 1973), p. 7. See also U.S. Commission on Civil Rights, *Your Child and Busing* (Washington, 1972).

118. Diana Pearce, "Breaking Down Barriers: New Evidence on the Impact of Metropolitan School Desegregation on Housing Patterns" (research report, School of Law, Catholic University, 1980), pp. 48–53.

119. Russell W. Irvine and Jacqueline Jordan Irvine, "The Impact of the Desegregation Process on the Education of Black Students: Key Variables," *Journal of Negro Education* 53 (1983): 410–21.

120. R. Picott, *A Quarter Century of Elementary and Secondary Education* (Washington, D.C.: Association for the Study of Negro Life and History, 1976).

121. Feagin and Feagin, *Discrimination American Style*, pp. 201–4.

122. Gary Orfield, *National School Boards Association Press Conference, National Press Club*, Federal News Service, January 8, 1992.

123. Ibid.

124. Mary Jordan, "Black College Enrollment Up," *Washington Post*, January 20, 1992, p. A14; "Is the Dream Over?" *Newsweek on Campus*, February 1987, pp. 10–14.

125. Walter R. Allen, "Correlates of Black Student Adjustment, Achievement, and Aspirations at a Predominantly White Southern University," in *Black Students in Higher Education*, ed. Gail E. Thomas, (Westport, Conn.: Greenwood Press, 1981), pp. 128–37; Walter R. Allen, "Black and Blue: Black Students at the University of Michigan" (research report, University of Michigan, n.d.), pp. 8–12.

126. Stampp, *The Peculiar Institution*, pp. 156–62; Aptheker, *American Negro Slave Revolts*, pp. 56–60.

127. Stuckey, *Slave Culture*, p. 27.

128. James Scott, *Domination and the Arts of Resistance* (New Haven: Yale University Press, 1990).

129. Richard C. Wade, *Slavery in the Cities* (New York: Oxford University Press, 1964), pp. 161–63; Winthrop Jordan, *White over Black* (Baltimore: Penguin, 1969), pp. 422–25.

130. E. Franklin Frazier, *The Negro Church in America* (New York: Schocken Books, 1964), pp. 35–39; Myrdal, *An American Dilemma*, 2:938–39; E. U. Essien-Udom, *Black Nationalism* (New York: Dell Pub. Co., Inc., 1964).

131. Quoted in Michael Hirsley, "Churches Are Sources of Power," *Chicago Tribune*, February 5, 1992, p. C6.
132. Frazier, *The Negro Church in America*, p. 44; Joseph R. Washington, Jr., *Black Religion* (Boston: Beacon Press, 1964), pp. 2–29.
133. David L. Lewis, *King* (Baltimore: Penguin, 1970), p. 390.
134. This paragraph draws heavily on contributions by Bonnie Mitchell to Feagin and Mitchell, "America's Non-European Cultures."
135. Milton Gordon, *Assimilation in American Life* (New York: Oxford University Press, 1964), p. 78.
136. Talcott Parsons, "Full Citizenship for the Negro American? A Sociological Problem," in *The Negro American*, ed. Talcott Parsons and Kenneth B. Clark (Boston: Houghton Mifflin, 1965), p. 740; see also pp. 714–15.
137. Glazer, *Affirmative Discrimination*, pp. 40–76; Daniel P. Moynihan, *The Negro Family* (Washington, 1965); Frazier, *The Negro Church in America*; Myrdal, *An American Dilemma*.
138. Robert Blauner, *Racial Oppression in America* (New York: Harper & Row, Pub., 1972), pp. 51–110.
139. Wade, *Slavery in the Cities*, pp. 273–75; Herman D. Bloch, *The Circle of Discrimination* (New York: New York University Press, 1969), pp. ix–xiii.
140. Wilhelm, *Who Needs the Negro?*; Robert L. Allen, *Black Awakening in Capitalist America* (Garden City, N.Y.: Doubleday, Anchor Books, 1970), pp. 4–6; *Report of the National Advisory Commission on Civil Disorders* (New York: Bantam, 1968), pp. 278–79.
141. *Report of the National Advisory Commission on Civil Disorders*, pp. 279–80.
142. Feagin and Sikes, *Modern Racism*.

Chapter 9

Mexican Americans

Latino Festival of Cinco De Mayo
Photo by Robert Fried/Stock Boston (conversion)

In recent years the term *Hispanic* has been widely used to designate persons of Mexican, Puerto Rican, Dominican, Cuban, and Central and South American heritage. *Hispanic* is an English-language word derived from *Hispania,* the Roman name for Spain. This term emphasizes the Spanish heritage of these groups while ignoring the other (for example, Native American and African) components. *Latino,* an alternative collective designation, which recognizes the Latin American origins of these groups, is a Spanish-language word and therefore more acceptable to many Spanish-speaking Americans. As Edward Múrguía has pointed out, these collective terms suggest different attitudes toward incorporation into or separation from the core culture. *Hispanic* emphasizes assimilation, or aspirations toward assimilation. *Latino* emphasizes cultural pluralism and cultural maintenance, such as the continued use of the Spanish language.[1]

Múrguía goes on to discuss the advantages and weaknesses of the one-group issue. Both on a national level and more particularly in large cities such as Chicago and San Francisco whose Latino populations contain substantial segments of more than one national-origin group, a collective identity helps create a broader sense of community. It may help the various subgroups to achieve the collective strength to address common problems of education, bilingualism, jobs, and discrimination, among other things. In addition, smaller national-origin groups, especially new entrants from Central and South America, may derive some advantage from a collective identity. Still, combining these diverse national-origin groups into one category masks their diversity behind an implied homogeneity. As we will see in this and the following chapter, Latino groups differ on many socioeconomic indicators; combining data on individual groups to describe all Latinos does not accurately describe any one group. The various groups also differ in certain cultural forms—for example, in food, religious shrines, and music. Geographic distinctiveness also remains: Mexican Americans are concentrated in the Southwest, mainland Puerto Ricans in the Northeast, Cuban Americans in the Southeast. In many areas, members of one Latino group have little contact with members of other Latino groups. Múrguía foresees the development of a "dual ethnicity" based primarily on national origin and secondarily on a collective identity in the context of broader national issues.

Latinos are currently the fastest-growing segment of the U.S. population, numbering almost 25 million in 1991. The pride Latinos feel in their national heritages can be seen in their desire to maintain the Spanish language as well as certain other cultural patterns. The growing numbers of Latinos in the United States provide support for both goals. Recent years have seen an increase in Spanish-language media, Latino religious, charitable, and social organizations, and the commercial availability of Latino products and services.

Latinos maintain strong communities. In a 1991 nationwide survey of Latinos, nine out of ten adults identified themselves as very Latino and more than eight in ten projected that they would be very Latino ten years in the future. Eight in ten reported that their close friends were very Latino, and seven in ten identified their neighborhood as very Latino. Most were more comfortable speaking Spanish than English and spent more time watching and listening to Spanish media than English media. Based on language use and behavioral, attitudinal, and aspirational measures, the survey ranked the assimilation level of these respondents. Half of all Latino adults were classified as relatively unassimilated; only one in ten was ranked highly assimilated and four in ten partially assimilated.

Although Latino youth (ages six through seventeen) were more than three times as likely to be highly assimilated as their adult counterparts, fully two-thirds of them identified themselves as very Latino and projected that they would remain so ten years in the future.[2]

In this and the following chapter we examine the three largest Latino groups in the United States, Mexican Americans, mainland Puerto Ricans, and Cuban Americans—groups with diverse histories and heritages as well as different experiences in U.S. society. Mexican Americans make up 60 percent of the U.S. Latino population, mainland Puerto Ricans 12 percent, and Cuban Americans almost 5 percent. Other Latino groups, such as Central Americans, many of whom are refugees from political turmoil and persecution, make up the rest. This chapter focuses on the experiences and situation of Mexican Americans.

Among many European Americans* the stereotypical view of Mexicans is of sleepy farmers under big sombreros, mustachioed banditos, a diet of tortillas, and folk Catholicism. Such popular images are often supplemented by negative treatments of Mexicans and Mexican Americans in schoolbooks that distort the history of the Southwest,** as in the myths that glorify freedom-loving, heroic (white) Texans confronting a backward Mexican people. Typical too in popular and scholarly accounts of life in the Southwest is the omission of significant references to Mexican American contributions to the development of the United States.

THE CONQUEST PERIOD, 1500–1853

Early European expansion touched not only the Atlantic coast of North America but also the West. Beginning in 1519 Spaniards conquered, colonized, and sought to Catholicize the native population in what is now Mexico and the southwestern United States and to concentrate it in agricultural and mining communities in this area for exploitation. Since few Spanish women migrated to the Americas, sexual liaisons, often forced, between Spanish men and indigenous women were common. Amott and Matthaei classify forced sexual liaisons as a key aspect of Spanish domination along with colonization and conversion to Christianity under duress. Offspring of these unions, sometimes called *mestizos* ("mixed peoples"), came to outnumber the Spanish and to occupy a middle social position below them but above Native Americans, persons of mixed Native American and African heritage, and African slaves. Mexican legend considers the Native American mistress of the Spanish conqueror Cortés to be the mother of *La Raza,* the Mexican people.[3] Mexico finally won its independence from Spain in 1821.

Prior to the 1830s Mexicans had established numerous communities in what is now the southwestern United States. Along the Rio Grande in what would become southern Texas several thousand people with a Mexican way of life and a self-sufficient economy lived on Mexican land grants. An estimated four thousand Mexican settlers lived in the Texas area in 1821. Soon thousands of European American settlers from the United States flooded the area, and in a few years the new settlers outnumbered the indigenous Mexican population.[4]

*The terms *European American, Euro-American,* and *Anglo* are used to designate persons whose ancestry is European. The common term *Anglo* is not fully satisfactory here, because many of those involved in subordinating Mexican Americans had non-English European ancestry.

**The Southwest* refers here to California, Arizona, New Mexico, Colorado, and Texas.

The Texas Revolt: Myth and Reality

The Texas province, both its Mexican population and its new U.S. immigrants, strongly supported a decentralized system of Mexican government. By 1830 some Mexican residents there had joined the new settlers to protest actions by the central government. Mexican government actions, including freeing slaves and placing restrictions on U.S. immigration, angered the European American settlers. The causes of the Texas revolt are complex, including not only government policies in Mexico City but also the racist attitudes of the Euro-American immigrants toward Mexicans, the resentment of white slaveholders toward Mexican antislavery laws, and the growing number of U.S. immigrants coming in illegally from the north. Until recently, few analysts have been inclined to see the 1836 Texas revolt as territorial aggression by U.S. citizens against another sovereign nation, which in the end it was, but rather have excused the behavior of the Texans and blamed an oppressive Mexican government.[5]

The Texas revolt has been portrayed in terms of persisting myths about heroic Texans. The legend of the Alamo portrays about 180 principled native-born Texans courageously fighting thousands of Mexican troops. But most of the men at the Alamo mission, in the center of what is now the city of San Antonio, were not native Texans but newcomers. Many were not men of principle defending their homes but adventurers such as James Bowie and Davy Crockett. The Alamo was one of the best-fortified sites in the West: the defenders had twice as many cannons, much better rifles, and much better training in riflery than the poorly equipped Mexican recruits. Another part of the myth suggests that all the defenders died fighting heroically. In fact, several surrendered. After a series of further skirmishes General Sam Houston managed a surprise attack that wiped out much of the Mexican army in the north.[6]

The Texas rebellion was a case of U.S. settlers going beyond an existing boundary and intentionally trying to incorporate new territory into the United States. The annexation of Texas in 1845 precipitated the Mexican War. Provocative U.S. troop actions in a disputed boundary area generated a Mexican attack and then a declaration of war by the United States. The poorly equipped Mexican army lost. Some historians have questioned the view of this war as honorable, citing evidence that Mexico fell victim to a U.S. conspiracy to seize territory by force. U.S. soldiers and Texas Rangers murdered civilians and committed other atrocities in Mexico. In 1848 the Mexican government was forced to cede the Southwest area for $15 million. Mexican residents had the choice of remaining there or moving south; most stayed, assured on paper of protection by Article IX of the Treaty of Guadalupe Hidalgo.[7]

By the 1850s the population of Texas had grown to 200,000, most of whom were Euro-American in-migrants. Gradually these new settlers, particularly ranchers and farmers, used legal and illegal means to take much of the land owned by the existing occupants. Eventually most major Mexican landowners lost their lands.

California and New Mexico

In the early 1800s the 7,500 non-Native American residents of California lived on Mexican-run ranches and missions. After gold was discovered in 1849, huge numbers of Euro-Americans poured into California, taking over lands and political control from the Mexicans. The means of takeover ranged from lynching to armed theft to legal action.[8]

In New Mexico, villages provided the organization to withstand some of the Euro-American onslaught. The villages there are quite old—Sante Fe was established in 1598. The fifty thousand New Mexicans had long maintained their own traditions. The richest 2 percent owned most of the land; the poor held the rest. Many landholders did fairly well under U.S. rule, continuing to play an important role in commerce and politics in the region. Nonetheless, most Mexicans eventually suffered great losses of private and communal lands.[9]

By the mid-nineteenth century the U.S. system of private land ownership was replacing the Mexican system of communal lands. In spite of treaty promises, old land grants were ignored and treated as U.S. government land; Mexican landholders ultimately lost most of the land. The invasion of the Southwest was not a heroic period in which U.S. settlers liberated unused land. It was in fact a period of imperialistic expansion and the colonization of a communal people who already lived in the area.[10]

THE IMMIGRATION PERIOD

Estimates of the number of Mexicans within the new territorial limits of the expanding United States range up to 118,000 for the 1850s. In the decades to follow, millions of Mexican migrants entered the United States. Two major push factors shaped this immigration: political upheavals and economic conditions. On the pull side were expanding opportunities and the demand for unskilled labor in the fields and factories north of the border. On the pull side too were family ties to what was once old Mexico.

The peak periods have been between 1910 and 1930 and since 1950. There have been five major categories of immigrants: (1) those with official visas ("legals"); (2) undocumented immigrants ("illegals"); (3) braceros (seasonal farm workers on contract); (4) commuters (those with official alien visas who live in Mexico but work in the United States); and (5) "border crossers" (those with short-term permits, many of whom become domestics).[11] The exclusion of Asian immigrants by federal action (see Chapter 11) and the industrialization of the World War I era brought a sharp decline in the number of laborers available for agricultural work. Mexican labor was drawn into the Southwest by the demand for low-wage labor. Under pressure from U.S. employers federal authorities waived immigration restrictions, allowing more than seventy thousand Mexican workers to be legally brought in during World War I.[12]

This Mexican migration increased in the 1920s, with 500,000 workers and their families entering the United States. Improved canning and shipping technologies had opened new markets for agricultural produce. Business interests intensely opposed restrictions on Mexican immigration. Agencies in cities such as San Antonio specialized in recruiting Mexican workers for agriculture as well as for jobs in urban industries—in the North as well as the Southwest. Programs involving temporary work-permits were periodically expanded. Mexicans were not excluded by the Immigration Act of 1924, which did bar most southern and eastern Europeans. Mexico had become a main source of cheap labor for the Southwest and the Midwest.[13]

In the 1920s the Border Patrol of the Immigration and Naturalization Service was created, and in 1929 legislation made it a felony to enter the United States illegally. The Border Patrol has played a major role in the lives of Mexicans and Mexican Americans. Although it has had the formal authority to keep out all undocumented workers, it has instead regulated the flow of undocumented Mexican workers, allowing enough to come in to meet the work demand but not enough to cause political problems. In times of economic depression and recession between the 1920s and the 1990s, the Border Patrol has conducted exclusion and deportation campaigns; in better times restrictive activity has often been less rigorous.[14]

During the Great Depression of the 1930s federal enforcement of literacy tests and local government hostility greatly reduced the flow of immigrants. In addition, there was considerable pressure to get Mexicans already here, whether citizens or not, to leave the country. Some left voluntarily; many workers were forcibly deported in massive border campaigns; thousands of others, including U.S. citizens, were expelled in organized caravans by social agencies eager to reduce their costs.[15]

Braceros and Undocumented Workers

World War II changed the situation. In 1942 an Emergency Farm Labor ("Bracero") agreement between the United States and Mexico provided more Mexican workers for U.S. agriculture. Seasonal workers were brought in temporarily to work in the fields. In two decades nearly five million braceros were brought in. This program stimulated the migration of undocumented workers, and many Anglo employers became eager for these cheaper workers. Approximately 3.3 million documented migrants have come in between 1821 and 1991; since the 1920s somewhere between six and nine million undocumented migrants have also entered. Many of these were temporary immigrants who returned to Mexico.[16]

Considerable opposition to this migration has been generated, particularly since World War II. Union officials have called for restrictions that will protect jobs of citizens. But the issue is a very difficult one. The Mexican government has made little effort to stop the undocumented migration, for it relieves severe poverty and population pressures on that side of the border. One study of 493 workers in three detention centers in Texas and California provides a profile of the "illegals." Most had come in without papers. Most were males under thirty with less-than-sixth-grade educations and poverty backgrounds that had driven many of them to desperate measures. Many had come in under the auspices of labor smugglers, who charge $300 to $1,100 per person for their services. Some research has also revealed that a significant number of those who cross the border are women and children.[17]

Growing opposition led to the inclusion of restrictions on legal immigration from Mexico in the 1965 Immigration Act, which incorporated a new annual limit of 120,000 persons from the Western Hemisphere while removing older quotas directed at southern and eastern Europeans. Later, a limit of 20,000 persons per year was placed on legal Mexican immigration. Attempts to deal with undocumented Mexican immigrants have focused on intensified Border Patrol policing and legislation concerning visas.[18]

Because of poverty and unemployment in Mexico, a substantial flow of workers into the United States has continued into the 1990s. The best estimates for the number of undocumented immigrants in the United States at the end of the 1980s was 1.9 million; 1.1 million of these were thought to be from Mexico. Numerous studies have shown that, contrary to some stereotypes, undocumented workers actually have low rates of use of welfare, food stamps, and unemployment compensation programs. They pay out more in income and other taxes than they receive in benefits and thus are not a net burden on the citizen taxpayers.[19]

The 1986 Immigration Act and Undocumented Immigrants

Mexican and other non-European immigrants have long been seen as a problem by nativist Euro-Americans. Nativist attempts to limit this immigration were successful in 1986. The 1986 Immigration Reform and Control Act has five provisions: (1) legalization of undocumented immigrants resident continuously since 1982; (2) sanctions for employers who hire undocumented aliens; (3) reimbursement of governments for the added costs of legalization; (4) screening of welfare applicants for migration status; and (5) special programs to bring in agricultural laborers. In short, the law established penalties for employers who hire undocumented workers, as well as an identification system and an amnesty program for undocumented workers who have resided in the United States for some time. Just over 3 million undocumented immigrants applied for legalization by the January 30, 1989, deadline, representing approximately two-thirds of those eligible for the program. Mexican immigrants made up 70 percent of those applying in the general legalization program.[20]

The congressional and public debates over this legislation revived many anti-immigration arguments of the past. Many native-born residents were worried about the character and values of the new immigrants. Native-born European Americans were concerned that the United States could not absorb so many immigrants, even though the ratio of immigrants to the native-born population was much higher in earlier decades than in the late twentieth century. In 1910 the foreign-born constituted 14.6 percent of the U.S. population; in the late 1980s the figure was only 6.5 percent, giving the United States a smaller percentage of foreign-born than many other nations, including England, Germany, and Switzerland. Indeed, Australia, Canada, and New Zealand have two to three times as large a proportion of foreign-born as the United States. Given its long history of successful absorption of immigrants, it is unlikely that the United States will be overwhelmed by these new immigrants. Implicit in many Euro-American discussions of the new immigrants seemed to be a concern that most of them were from Latin America and Asia—that is, that they were not white or European.[21]

Population and Location

Official census estimates of the Mexican-origin population in the United States show an increase from 1.3 million in 1930 to 13.5 million in 1990. By the early 1990s most Mexican Americans were native-born. (Resident aliens constituted one-third of all Latin American adults in the United States.) More than 90 percent of all Mexican Americans live in urban areas, especially in the southwestern states, although many reside in other regions, particularly the Midwest.[22]

STEREOTYPING

Early Images

While competing with and subordinating the Mexican residents of the Southwest, European Americans came to hold stereotypes about the alleged laziness, backwardness, and poverty they attributed to the Mexican "race." The white slaveholders who came to the Southwest had a well-developed race prejudice rationalizing the subordination of African Americans; for them it was easy to stigmatize dark-skinned Mexican Americans as inferior.

"Greaser" has been a contemptuous term applied to Mexican Americans since the Mexican War, perhaps deriving from the activities of Mexicans who greased wagon axles. Cowardice was a stereotype that grew after the defeat of the Mexican army in the 1840s. In the 1850s John Monroe reported to Washington that the people of New Mexico "are thoroughly debased and totally incapable of self-government, and there is no latent quality about them that can ever make them respectable."[23] Ironically, it was these Mexicans whose knowledge of ranching, agriculture, and mining had laid the foundation for development of the Southwest.

The heavy Mexican immigration after 1900 triggered attacks on Mexicans by whites. Mexican labor camps were raided by the Ku Klux Klan and similar white supremacist groups and the workers beaten. The 1911 federal Dillingham Commission on immigration alleged that Mexicans were unskilled and undesirable. In the 1920s a prominent white member of Congress stereotyped Mexicans as a mixture of Spanish and "low-grade Indians," plus some slave "blood," a mongrelized people. In 1928 an "expert" witness appearing before the House Immigration Committee testified to the racial inferiority of Mexicans, branding the "Mexican race" a threat to the "white race."[24] Nativist scholars and popular writers alike expressed fear of "race mongrelization" as a result of contact with Mexicans. In 1925 a Princeton economics professor even spoke fearfully of the future elimination of Anglo-Saxons through interbreeding in "favor of the progeny of Mexican peons who will continue to afflict us with an embarrassing race problem."[25]

Much Euro-American commentary since the 1920s has stereotyped the Mexican American male as a crime-oriented villain with a knife in his pocket. For example, a report by a lieutenant in the Los Angeles Sheriff's Department after the 1943 Zoot Suit Riots (discussed in the following section) alleged that the Mexicans' desire to spill blood was an "inborn characteristic," a view endorsed by his Euro-American police chief. Much racist stereotyping linked alleged social traits to genetic inferiority: "The Mexican was 'lawless' and 'violent' because he had Indian blood; he was 'shiftless' and 'improvident' because that was his nature."[26]

Since the 1920s the results of so-called IQ testing have been used to argue for the intellectual and racial inferiority of Mexican Americans. As in the cases of Jewish, Italian, and black Americans, from time to time a few conservative commentators and academics have argued on the basis of paper-and-pencil tests that Mexican American children are of lower intelligence.[27] This view has often been linked to nativist sentiments that oppose immigration from Mexico.

Modern Stereotypes

Over the last few decades some of the harshest stereotypes have begun to fade from public view, but prejudicial attitudes have still been expressed. One study found that drunkenness and criminality were still being attributed to Mexican Americans. In a study in a central California city, one-quarter of Euro-American respondents reported they would find it distasteful to eat with a Mexican. The statement that "generally speaking, Mexicans are shiftless and dirty" was accepted by 37 percent of the respondents.[28]

All too often U.S. movies have cast Mexicans as banditos. Movies of Pancho Villa's raids in Texas, to take one example, have played up this criminal image and ignore the relationship of the guerilla raids to prior exploitation by U.S. settlers. Television movies and serials have presented Mexican and Mexican American men as "lazy, fat, happy, thieving, immoral creatures who make excellent sidekicks for white heroes."[29] Women have often been portrayed as flirting senoritas.

Some television comedy series have portrayed Latin American figures in terms other than the traditional stereotypes, but these attempts have not offset the negative stereotypes aired on other shows, not to mention those in movie reruns. Media advertising, including ads by major companies, has also played a role in perpetuating stereotypes. Frito Bandito ads have suggested that Mexicans were criminals. A deodorant company used a grubby-looking Mexican bandit in an ad that said, "If it works for him, it will work for you." Tequila advertisements in college newspapers have had a "game" whose characters represented negative stereotypes of Mexicans— the lazy peon in a large sombrero sleeping on a burro, the border-town prostitute, and the thieving bandito.[30]

George Murphy, former senator from California, linked a biological characteristic of Mexicans to menial jobs, alleging that they were "ideal for 'stoop' labor—after all, they are built close to the ground."[31] A California judge, ruling against a Mexican American youngster in an incest case, echoed the racist criminality image, with its genocidal overtones, when he asserted in court:

> Mexican people, after 13 years of age, think it is perfectly all right to go out and act like an animal. We ought to send you out of the country—send you back to Mexico.... You are lower than animals and haven't the right to live in organized society—just miserable, lousy, rotten people. Maybe Hitler was right. The animals in our society probably ought to be destroyed because they have no right to live among human beings.[32]

As a result of protests from Mexican American communities and leaders stereotypical depictions of Mexican Americans in advertising and the media have decreased significantly over the past several years. For example, in 1991 such protests forced a taco restaurant chain in Houston to discontinue a TV ad that featured a stereotypical Mexican American figure. In movies and advertising today, Mexican Americans are often ignored. One Mexican American observor has noted that Mexican Americans are "basically only good for negative imaging."

Numerous Euro-Americans, including government officials, have assumed that Mexican Americans are passive and fatalistic. Such a view is based on a stereotype reinforced in social science studies that have viewed Mexican American culture as one of passivity, lack of protest, fatalism, *machismo,* and extreme family orientation. Anthropologists such as Oscar Lewis and William Madsen portrayed what they thought was a folk culture of fatalism and familism in the villages of Mexico, a view that was extended to Mexican American life.[33] Other social scientists have criticized these traditional views of Mexicans and Mexican Americans as distortions and pointed out the errors in assuming that life in villages decades ago was the same as life in Mexican American communities today. They also point out that the diversity of Mexican American culture from southern Texas to New Mexico to California has been overlooked. Researcher Lea Ybarra notes that male domination in Mexican American families varies with class and educational background, just as it does among other racial and ethnic groups.[34]

European American outsiders have seen Mexican Americans as both an ethnic group and a racial group. Some have accented their cultural characteristics as the major indicators of their distinctiveness. Others have seen them as an inferior race, accenting dark skins and "Indian" features thought to be typical of the group. Research in Texas has suggested one likely result of this racial stereotyping over time: darker-skinned Mexican Americans do not do as well in occupational and income attainments as lighter-skinned Mexican Americans, whose physical characteristics are more similar to those of European Americans.[35]

VIOLENT CONFLICT

The Early Period

Coercion was a fundamental factor in the establishment of Euro-American domination in the Southwest. Mexican land and agricultural development were taken over by deception, theft, and force. The competition for land led to a new system of inequality. Both elite and rank-and-file Mexicans became subordinate to the invaders.

The Mexicans resisted, beginning with the taking of Mexican lands in the 1830s and 1840s. Throughout history folk ballads have sung the praises of "bandits" who have been social rebels unwilling to bear quietly the burdens imposed on their people. Typically their acts are regarded as crimes by the authorities in the dominant group, but *not* by people in the subordinate group. Such men have been protected and praised by the common people, in some cases becoming legends.[36]

Among the heroes in Mexican legends are Juan Cortina and Pancho Villa. Cortina has been typed as an outlaw and cattle thief by Anglo Americans, but he became a Robin Hood figure to many Mexicans. He was certainly more than a thief, for he fought against the oppression of poor Mexicans in the Texas borderlands. In a series of guerrilla raids along the border, his followers clashed with the local militia and the Texas Rangers. In the 1850s and 1860s Cortina fought the injustices of the European American intruders, issuing formal statements of grievances detailing biased legal systems and the stealing of land. Colonel Robert E. Lee was sent to put down Cortina's rebellions, but succeeded only in limiting his activities. Between 1910 and 1925 numerous other raids and clashes occurred along the Texas border from El Paso to Brownsville in which both Mexicans and Euro-Americans were killed. Estimates of the dead range from five hundred to five thousand.[37]

Lynching and public whipping became ways of controlling Mexicans and Mexican Americans; numerous lynchings were recorded in the nineteenth century. Much of the lawlessness by Euro-Americans against Mexicans in the Southwest had an official or semiofficial status. Law enforcement officers such as the Texas Rangers terrorized Mexican Americans. The image of the Texas Rangers has been sugar-coated in exaggerated stories of heroism. The distinguished scholar Paredes has demonstrated that the myth of the heroic Rangers covers up the oppressiveness of a police force used by the dominant group to exploit the Mexican American population. European American ranchers and farmers became rich with the aid of the Texas Rangers. In New Mexico the expansion of Euro-American ranches at the expense of Mexican Americans did not come peacefully. Vigilante groups such as *La Mano Negro* (The Black Hand) used whatever means necessary to protect Mexican American livestock and land.[38]

More Attacks by European Americans

Later decades in the twentieth century also saw open conflict. The so-called Zoot Suit Riots in the summer of 1943 in Los Angeles began with attacks by Euro-American sailors on Mexican American youths, particularly those dressed in baggy "zoot suits." Groups of whites roamed Los Angeles beating up young zoot-suiters. Mexican American groups organized retaliatory attacks on the sailors. Why did these riots occur? The local media exaggerated Mexican American crime. Police harassment increased, sometimes to the point of brutality. A few biased but well-publicized court trials involving Mexican youths stirred up local prejudices. The unusual dress of these youths became a focus of attention. One study found that in the three years leading up to the riots there was a sharp decline in the *Los Angeles Times*'s use of the term *Mexican* and a corresponding increase in an unfavorable use of *zoot suit* in connection with Mexican Americans. So intense was the paranoia during the rioting that the white Los Angeles City Council seriously discussed making the wearing of zoot suits a *criminal* offense.[39]

Protests since the 1960s

During the 1960s and 1970s three dozen Mexican American protest-oriented riots took place in southwestern cities. Young Mexican Americans, including groups such as the Brown Berets, took to the streets to fight back against harassing police actions they saw as oppressive. Among the most important group actions were the East Los Angeles riots. In August 1970, police attacked demonstrators at the end of a National Chicano Moratorium on the Vietnam War march in which twenty thousand Mexican Americans took part.* Police claimed that some deputies had been attacked by Mexican American demonstrators during the march. Four hundred were arrested; dozens were injured; two dozen police cars were damaged. Another riot along the route of a Mexican Independence Day parade resulted in one hundred injuries and sixty-eight arrests.[40]

Police forces, containing few if any Mexican Americans, were used, sometimes illegally, to end legal strikes and protests by Mexican American workers. Some cases have resulted in deaths to innocent civilians. Between 1965 and 1969 the U.S. Justice Depart-

---

*The term *Chicano* was preferred to *Mexican American* by activists in the 1960s and 1970s. By the late 1970s activists were debating its use, and today it is used alongside the term *Mexican American* by many activists and researchers.

ment received 256 complaints of police malpractice from persons with Spanish surnames; in the late 1960s the American Civil Liberties Union received 174 such complaints in California alone. From the 1960s to the 1990s the common practice of preventive police patrolling in ghetto areas, with its "stop and frisk" and "arrest on suspicion" tactics, has led to unfavorable police contacts for Mexican American males. Harassment of this type in turn intensifies negative Latino attitudes toward the police. A 1991 poll found that two-thirds of Latinos in Los Angeles reported incidents of police brutality were very common in their city; 35 percent of this group said that racist attitudes were very common among law enforcement officers. At public hearings in 1991 an independent citizens' commission investigating the Los Angeles Police Department heard testimony from Mexican Americans that the department "acted like an army of occupation" treating them like the "enemy." Later that year, following the fatal shooting of a Mexican American youth, leaders from a large number of Mexican American organizations called for an independent citizens' commission to investigate the Los Angeles County Sheriff's Department as well. Witnesses said the nineteen-year-old victim yelled at officers who had struck his friend at a neighborhood birthday celebration. This was one of several controversial shootings involving Anglo police officers in the early 1990s.[41]

These police brutality incidents were part of the buildup to the spring 1992 riot in south central Los Angeles. In that riot—many call it a rebellion—a large proportion of those arrested for protesting and looting were Latino residents of Los Angeles. While the rebellion began as a protest by African American residents over a jury verdict acquitting four white officers who were accused of police brutality (see Chapter 8), many Latinos also participated in the violent protest against oppressive living conditions in the city.

THE ECONOMY

We have already discussed the incorporation of Mexicans into the U.S. economy, first by violent conquest and later by the takeover of their lands. An estimated 2 million acres of private lands and 1.7 million acres of communal lands were lost between 1854 and 1930 in New Mexico alone. In Taos County, New Mexico, for example, two-thirds of the county's private acreage had originally been land grants to Mexican communities and families, but by 1940 this land was lost by them to Euro-American settlers or the federal government. In *Stolen Heritage* Abel G. Rubio tells how his family, who settled in northern Mexico (now Texas) long before U.S. immigrants flooded the area, lost their original land grant. Rubio recounts how his great-grandfather was defrauded of his land, which is now in the middle of one of the largest Euro-American ranches in south Texas.[42]

Across the Southwest those who lost their lands often became landless laborers as did later immigrants. In the 1850s one-third of Mexican Americans in the rural labor force in south Texas were ranch and farm owners, one-third were skilled laborers or professionals, and one-third were manual laborers. By 1900 the proportion of ranch and farm owners had dropped to 16 percent, while the proportion of manual laborers—many working for large Euro-American ranches and farms—climbed to two-thirds. A similar shift took place in the cities: a predominantly skilled labor force became predominantly unskilled.[43]

By the 1880s many Mexican Americans were laborers involved in the expansion of railroads. Mexican Americans were the original vaqueros (cowboys) on the ranches across the Southwest; they still are common among agricultural workers in the Southwest. Working conditions in agricultural "stoop" labor were so severe and pay so low that few competed with Mexicans for these jobs before the Great Depression. Job opportunities were limited by overt, sometimes violent, discrimination. A Foreign Miners Act in California placed a license tax on "foreigners" to force Mexican miners out. In the 1850s a group of two thousand Euro-American miners attacked Mexicans in Sonora, killing dozens and destroying a community. Mexican American women often worked in agriculture, as domestic servants, and in manufacturing, particularly in the garment industry and in canneries. Regardless of the job, Mexican American men and women earned less than Euro-Americans and were usually assigned the more physically demanding tasks.[44]

Persisting Job Discrimination

Institutionalized discrimination has been a major problem. From the 1920s on, agricultural firms, oil companies, mining companies, and other industries paid different rates for "whites" and "nonwhites"; Mexicans and Mexican Americans were listed under the latter category. Wages could be kept low because of the constant availability of undocumented workers. Many unions have had a record of discrimination against Mexican Americans. In the 1920s and 1930s the California Federation of Labor worked for their exclusion. Numerous industrial unions excluded Mexican Americans from membership. Attempts to create farm labor unions date back several decades, but they were not successful until the 1960s.[45]

By 1930 Mexican Americans were still heavily employed in low-wage manual labor. The 1930 census revealed that out of nearly three million Mexican American residents only fifty-four hundred were in clerical positions. During the Great Depression, the fact that many poor Mexican Americans were on relief led to increasing Anglo American hostility. Forced repatriation to Mexico was tried by a number of local welfare agencies. Between one-third and one-half million persons of Mexican origin, U.S. citizens and noncitizens, had been sent back to Mexico by the mid-1930s.[46]

The 1940s saw some improvement in the employment situation, but discriminatory barriers were still severe. One study of San Bernardino, California, found rampant discrimination keeping Mexican Americans in low-wage positions: average annual incomes were still only $700 to $800. In 1943 President Roosevelt's belated antidiscrimination order and the increasingly tight labor supply finally opened up some jobs at decent wages to Mexican Americans; however, this development was short-lived. Virtually no qualified workers moved up into skilled or supervisory positions.[47] Poorly paid jobs meant inferior housing, a situation sharpened by housing discrimination. Mexican Americans were often restricted by discrimination or income to segregated urban ghettos, called *barrios,* which were often concentrations of deteriorating housing. Restrictive covenants in deeds kept Mexican Americans out of numerous housing areas in the Southwest.[48]

In the 1950s and 1960s many Mexican Americans occupied secondary-labor-market positions as farm workers, urban laborers, or service workers. Internal migrant labor streams were important for Mexican Americans (and Mexicans). The average annual wage for migrant workers in 1956 was only $1,500 in Texas and about $2,600 outside of

Texas. Even by the late 1960s the average hourly wage for seasonal farm workers was only $1.07 in Texas and $1.50 to $1.70 in the midwestern states. Not only was poverty frequently their lot; several studies found high rates of disabling work injuries among them.[49] Many were living in camps with inadequate housing and sanitation facilities. Here is one description of the life of a farm worker's family:

> I was never a happy child; in fact I never felt that I was a child since I had to work from an early age.... In 1950 my father, Gustavo, bought a little one-room shack behind his mother-in-law's house, and here my parents and eight children lived. Dad's economic situation at the time was very bad and since he worked as a farm laborer he was only paid 60 to 70 cents an hour, hardly enough to feed eight kids much less clothe them and provide for medical attention.[50]

Other Mexican Americans worked in industries in southwestern cities. A major problem in the border region has been "runaway" industries, those that have been moved by Anglo American capitalists from higher-wage areas to this low-wage region to increase profits. For example, food-processing plants have been a major industry in the Imperial Valley of California, in southern Arizona and New Mexico, and in the Rio Grande Valley. A major garment industry developed, taking advantage of unemployment in the female labor force. Beginning in 1965 the United States and other countries began building labor-intensive factories and assembly plants, called *maquiladoras,* in the northern border region of Mexico to take advantage of cheap labor and weak environmental and worker-safety standards there. In the early 1990s almost 1,800 U.S.-owned *maquiladoras* employed nearly 500,000 people in furniture, electronics, garment, food-processing, metal-refining, and other industries. Wages in the *maquiladoras* are far lower than in the United States; workers start at about $27 for a forty-nine-hour week and make as much as $47 per week with experience. Employers save an average of $16,000 per worker per year compared with U.S. wages. Worker turnover is as high as 400 percent in some plants. Large numbers of workers live in cardboard shacks without water, heat, electricity, or sanitation facilities. Some workers report that they work in the *maquiladoras* just long enough to earn money to migrate into the United States.[51]

Many employers in the Sunbelt and the Midwest have sought undocumented workers because they can be exploited more easily than U.S. workers. If they protest oppressive working conditions, an employer can turn them in to the authorities. The *Los Angeles Times* found that 99 percent of employers refused government help in trying to find U.S. workers to replace undocumented Mexican workers who had been caught. The *Times* reporter noted that these employers wanted "workers who can be exploited"—that is, who can be paid less than the minimum wage and who will not *organize.*[52]

Language discrimination in the workplace is a growing problem. In the early 1990s the Equal Employment Opportunity Commission (EEOC) reported an increase in the number of complaints received against employers who barred Spanish-speaking employees from speaking their native language in both job-related and private conversations while at work. An attorney for San Francisco's Employment Law Center noted that English-only rules were becoming common. Many legal scholars feel that such practices constitute national-origin discrimination and thus violate Title VII of the 1964 Civil Rights Act. The EEOC's regulations state that English-only rules are presumed to be discriminatory unless the employer can show a strong business necessity for the rule.[53] As of early 1992, the most recent U.S. Supreme Court precedent on this issue was *Garcia* v. *Gloor*,[54] a 1981 action that upheld an employer's right to fire employees for speaking Spanish. Hector Garcia, a Mexican American employee of a lumber company, had been fired for answering a fellow Mexican American employee's question in Spanish. The Court reasoned that Title VII of the 1964 Civil Rights Act did not equate national origin with primary language and thus that language discrimination was permissible. In a more recent case the U.S. Court of Appeals for the Ninth Circuit came to the opposite conclusion after evaluating a similar English-only rule: "The cultural identity of certain minority groups is tied to the use of their primary tongue."[55] Referring to the EEOC regulations, the court went on to state that "English-only rules...can 'create an atmosphere of inferiority, isolation, and intimidation' [and] can readily mask an intent to discriminate on the basis of national origin."[56] This case was appealed to the U.S. Supreme Court, but the parties reached a settlement before the Court considered the case.[57] In late 1991 a federal district judge in California ruled that an English-only requirement for employees in a meat-packing plant was discriminatory. Fluency in English had not been a requirement when the employees were hired.[58] It is likely that this or a similar case will be appealed to the U.S. Supreme Court during the 1990s.

Unemployment, Poverty, and Income

Unemployment rates for Mexican Americans have been high for decades. In the early 1990s the unemployment rate for Mexican Americans was 9.0 percent, almost twice the rate for Anglo whites (4.7 percent). In addition, an examination of the occupational distribution of Mexican American workers for 1990 reveals a higher concentration in low-wage job categories than the total U.S. workforce.[59]

	Men		Women	
	Total Pop.	Mexican American	Total Pop.	Mexican American
Managerial and professional specialty	26.0%	8.3%	26.4%	14.2%
Technical, sales, and administrative support	20.5	12.6	44.9	38.1
Precision production, craft, and repair	19.4	21.2	2.2	3.2
Operators, fabricators, and laborers	20.3	31.7	8.1	18.8
Service occupations	9.8	15.1	17.4	23.9
Farming, forestry, and fishing	4.0	11.2	1.0	1.8
	100.0%	100.1%	100.0%	100.0%

Notice that Mexican American men are concentrated in the operative, laborer, production, and service worker categories. Mexican American women are located primarily in sales, clerical (e.g., typists), service (e.g., maids), and operative categories.

Mexican American incomes have been consistently low compared with those of Anglo Americans. The following table compares 1989 income levels for the three largest Latino groups in the United States with that of the non-Latino population:[60]

	Puerto Rican Origin	Mexican Origin	Cuban Origin	Non-Latino Population
Median family income	$19,933	$22,245	$31,262	$35,183
Families with incomes of $50,000 or more	15%	13%	24%	30%
Percentage of families below poverty level	30	26	13	9

Notice that on family income and poverty measures, mainland Puerto Ricans ranked lowest among the three Latino groups, followed by Mexican Americans. Cuban Americans were much closer to the non-Latino population on these measures than they were to Mexican Americans or mainland Puerto Ricans.

The median income for Mexican-origin families in 1989 was $22,245, less than two-thirds that of non-Latino families ($35,183). In general Mexican American families have more workers than non-Latino white families, which translates into per capita incomes that are much lower than those of non-Latino whites. The 1989 median income was $12,527 for Mexican American males and $8,874 for Mexican American females, compared with $22,081 for non-Latino males and $11,885 for non-Latino females. A random survey of 5,000 Latino households (including individuals and families) across the nation by Strategy Research Corporation in 1991 showed substantially higher median incomes than the census data reported above. Based on that survey, the median for Mexican American households was an estimated $27,500, compared with $38,000 for the total U.S. population.[61]

In 1989 Mexican American families were more than twice as likely to be in poverty as non-Latino families. More than 37 percent of all Mexican Americans below eighteen years of age were living below the poverty line in that year.[62] The nearly 700,000 Mexican Americans who make up the majority of the population in the lower Rio Grande Valley in Texas have one of the highest poverty rates in the United States. They endure not only the absence of material goods but what writer Maril describes as a daily devaluation of their self esteem and worth. Poverty "is systematically perpetuated by political and social institutions which justify and maintain a social order premised on inequality."[63]

Researchers Telles and Múrguía have examined income differences among Mexican American males based on physical appearance, or *phenotype*. Although intragroup differences were not as great as the gap between Mexican Americans and non-Latino whites, dark and "Native American–looking" Mexican Americans were found to earn substantially less than their lighter, more "European-looking" counterparts. Most of this earning differential could not be accounted for by variations in employee qualifications but was found to be attributable to discrimination by Euro-American employers in U.S. labor markets.[64]

POLITICS

Mexican American involvement in politics has historically been limited by discrimination. Before 1910 some Mexican Americans did hold office in territorial and state legislatures; usually handpicked by Euro-Americans, they served in the governments of

California, Colorado, and New Mexico. There were no political organizations for Mexicans immigrating after 1900, as there were in northern cities to facilitate the mobility of other groups of immigrants.[65]

Euro-American ranchers and those who controlled railroads, mining interests, land companies, and other enterprises usually dominated local and state politics in the Southwest. Until recently, these interests made sure that Mexican American voting strength was kept low. Methods of discrimination varied from state to state, but common devices used to reduce voting included the poll tax, the all-white primary, and threats of violence. Between the 1910s and the 1940s few Mexican Americans voted, often because of discrimination or fear. Voting strength was expanded by legal victories in the form of the Twenty-fourth Amendment, which banned the poll tax, and a California court case knocking down an English-only literacy requirement for voting. Substantial growth in the Mexican American population also increased voting strength. In Texas, for example, the Mexican American population grew five times faster than the rest of the population during the 1980s, and the number registered to vote doubled between 1976 and 1986. In the mid-1970s fewer than one-fifth of eligible Mexican Americans were registered to vote. As of the early 1990s, Mexican Americans still had a 40 percent lower voter-registration rate and a 49 percent lower voter-turnout rate than the U.S. population as a whole.[66]

Representation

World War II brought hundreds of thousands of Mexican American workers into wartime industries and the armed forces. With this movement came an uphill fight to expand political participation. Numerous examples of slowly expanding, sometimes regressing, participation could be seen in the counties and cities of the Southwest from the late 1940s onward. For example, the Los Angeles City Council finally saw its first Mexican American representative in 1949, but between the early 1960s and the early 1970s the council included no Mexican Americans. In the late 1980s no Mexican American was an elected county representative in the Los Angeles area, even though Los Angeles had the largest Mexican American population in the United States. Fewer than 2 percent of all elected officials in the Los Angeles area were Mexican American at that time.[67]

The 1960s and 1970s saw some changes in several areas of representation. By the 1960s Mexican Americans had moved up from no representation on school boards to 470 among the 4,600 board members in the Southwest. The number of state legislators with Spanish surnames increased from 20 in 1950 to 67 in 1973. By the late 1980s, a total of 90 Mexican Americans could be counted in state legislatures. During the 1980s the number of Mexican Americans and other Latinos serving at all political levels increased significantly. For example, in Texas the number of all Latino (mostly Mexican American) officials rose from 862 in the early 1970s to 1,969 in 1991. The *National Roster of Hispanic Elected Officials* reported a 1991 total of 3,754 Latino elected officials in the five southwestern states and 4,202 nationwide. Still, the percentage of all elected officials who are Mexican American remains low. For example, in 1991 there was only one Mexican American member on Houston's City Council although 28 percent of Houston's population was Mexican American. Only three Mexican Americans have served as state governors, two in New Mexico and one in Arizona. Two major cities (San Antonio and

Denver) and several smaller ones have had Mexican American mayors. Representation at the national level has followed a similar pattern. In 1968 there were three Mexican Americans in the U.S. House of Representatives (one from California and two from Texas) and one U.S. senator (New Mexico). Since that year the maximum number of Mexican Americans at one time in the U.S. Congress has been ten representatives and one senator; the total has been fewer at most times. This level of representation is generally too low to exert major political clout in either legislative body.

Support for the Major Parties

At the presidential level, Mexican American voting has traditionally been Democratic. In 1960 Kennedy won an estimated 85 percent of Mexican American votes, which was more than enough to make the difference for him in winning the states of New Mexico and Texas. In 1964 Johnson won an estimated 90 percent, and in 1968 Humphrey won 87 percent. Mexican Americans stayed with the Democratic party in 1972, and the 1976 and 1980 elections again saw a substantial Democratic majority among these voters.

In the early 1980s there were 3.2 million Latino citizens of voting age in Texas and California; most were Mexican American. Most of these voters remained in the Democratic party. In 1980 they voted overwhelmingly for Jimmy Carter, and in the 1982 gubernatorial elections in California and Texas 70 to 80 percent of Latino voters supported the Democratic candidates. In the 1984 election 75 percent of the Latino voters in Texas supported Walter Mondale over Ronald Reagan, and in 1986, 79 percent voted for the Democratic candidate for governor of Texas. In 1986 Latino voters in California gave two-thirds of their votes to the Democratic candidate for governor—the black mayor of Los Angeles, Tom Bradley—and three-quarters of their votes to the Democratic candidate for senator. In the 1988 national election 70 percent of Latino voters again supported Democratic candidates. The majority of Mexican American voters have consistently cast their votes for the more liberal or progressive political candidates at all levels.[68]

The Courts

Underrepresentation in the judicial branch has been common. Not until the 1960s was the first Mexican American federal judge appointed. By the end of that decade, only two of the fifty-nine federal district judges in the five southwestern states, 3 percent of the nearly one thousand state judges, and 3 percent of district attorneys and public prosecutors (and assistants) in twenty-two Southwest cities had Spanish surnames. These numbers improved in the 1970s and 1980s, albeit very slowly. Many Mexican American applicants have also been denied police positions by the indirect discrimination of height and weight requirements and English-language requirements, as well as by too-low scores on conventional English-language qualifying examinations. Also, very few Mexican or other Latino Americans have served at the higher levels of the U.S. Department of Justice or other federal law enforcement agencies.[69]

Given this underrepresentation, it is not surprising that discrimination in the criminal justice system has been documented. Arizona, California, and Colorado have required jurors to be able to speak English, screening out many Spanish-speaking citizens; the pool of jurors in numerous states has until recently been selected by whatever method has suited (usually Euro-American) jury commissioners. Mexican

Americans charged with crimes have usually been judged by juries containing few if any of their peers. Courtrooms in which no one, including judges, understands Spanish present a language problem for some Mexican American defendants. Besides the absence of Spanish interpreters in courtrooms, other harmful practices have included excessive bail, poor legal counsel, and negative views by Anglo American judges of Mexican American defendants.[70]

The exclusion of jurors on the basis of race or national origin was declared unconstitutional by the U.S. Supreme Court in *Batson* v. *Kentucky* (1986). In subsequent cases, however, prosecutors have successfully excluded Latinos from juries on the basis of language. In 1989 an all-white jury convicted Jose Razo, Jr., a Mexican American youth, of armed robberies largely on the basis of a confession he had voluntarily made to the police. His defense attorneys argued that the confession was made in order to protect others and while the defendant was under the influence of drugs. One of his attorneys objected when the prosecution dismissed two potential Latino jurors, but withdrew the objection after the judge stated that California law would compel her to declare a mistrial and begin anew if the dismissal of jurors were found to be based on discrimination. In late 1991 a California appellate court refused to hear an appeal of the case; defense attorneys were considering an appeal to the U.S. Supreme Court.[71]

A 1991 U.S. Supreme Court decision upheld a prosecutor's exclusion of bilingual Latino jurors who had hesitated before agreeing to accept the official English translation of the Spanish-language testimony that they would hear in the trial. Legal scholar Juan Perea has noted that it is common for bilingual people to hesitate when answering a question in their second language (English). It is also plausible that they might want to consider carefully whether they would accept without question another's English translation of testimony they had themselves heard in their native language of Spanish. In contrast, in 1991 a judge in San Diego County, California, dismissed fifteen indictments handed down by the county's grand jury, because the pool from which the grand jurors were selected did not represent a fair racial cross-section of the county. The population of San Diego County was more than 20 percent Latino, but the grand jury pool was only 3.4 percent Latino.[72]

The Chicano Political Movement

Disenchantment with the accommodationist perspective of some middle-class Mexican American leaders led to the emergence of the Chicano movement in the 1960s and 1970s, a militant political movement that sought power and nationalist identity. Lacking influence in mainstream politics, many Mexican Americans joined the radical La Raza Unida party (LRUP) during this period. LRUP's goals included representation of all people by a local government that served the needs of individual communities as well as an end to the causes of poverty and injustice.

LRUP's major successes occurred in Crystal City, Texas, a city of 10,000 predominantly poor Mexican American people in the Winter Garden area of south Texas. A cannery had come to that area in the 1940s, followed in the mid-1950s by the Teamsters' Union. The union gave workers job security and some political resources for electoral campaigns. During the 1960s LRUP became a leading political force in the area, and by 1970 Mexican Americans had won control of the school board and city council. These new leaders hired more Mexican American teachers, teacher aides, and administrators, started bilingual programs, and added Mexican American history to the school curriculum. Mexican Americans were hired or promoted at all levels of the city bureaucracy, including the police department. Millions of dollars in new federal aid poured in to support programs in health, housing, and urban renewal.[73]

Out of power for the first time, Euro-Americans counterattacked, withdrawing their children from school, boycotting school taxes, and firing some of their Mexican American employees. Euro-American teachers resigned, complaining of a redirection of school activities toward Mexican American goals. Refusing to tolerate self-government by the Mexican American majorities, Anglo American state officials succeeded in cutting off both state and federal funding, almost bankrupting the city government, and then blamed the Mexican American leadership for failed programs.[74]

After the mid-1970s, LRUP declined rapidly. Although internal ideological divisions and personality conflicts played a part in LRUP's demise, harassment and repression, including efforts to keep LRUP off the ballot and to coopt its leaders, were the major contributing factors. By the 1980s Mexican Americans were identified no longer with LRUP but rather with the state Democratic party. Yet LRUP had brought about the democratization of many southwestern communities, raised the political consciousness of a whole generation of Mexican Americans, and prompted Mexican American political participation on an unprecedented scale, from voter registration to office seeking.[75]

Mexican American women held a wide range of important leadership roles within LRUP. In fact, women composed the vast majority of Mexican Americans elected to office in Crystal City as well as in Zavala County. In the words of Mexican American writer Marta Cotera, "Feminism has come easily for Chicanas because of the woman's traditional role and strength as center or heart of the family.... The tradition of activism inherited from women's participation in armed rebellions in Mexico and in the political life of Mexico has also strengthened the Chicanas' position."[76] Mexican American feminists have faced two major barriers. From the beginning to the present many of the issues of greatest concern to them, including poverty and racial discrimination, have not been central to the mainstream women's movement. They have also encountered sexism from some Mexican American men who resisted women moving beyond their traditional roles. Women who sought their own liberation were sometimes accused of betraying the Chicano movement and of identifying with Euro-American individualism, a concept seen as antithetical to Mexican American culture. As a result, much of the work of Mexican American feminists has had to be done in their own organizations outside the Chicano political movement.[77]

Another political victory came in San Antonio, whose politics had long been controlled by the Euro-American business elite. In 1981 Henry Cisneros was elected mayor of San Antonio, the first Mexican American mayor of a large U.S. metropolitan area. His victory was the culmination of ten years of organization. In 1977 neighborhood organizers working through Communities Organized for Public Service (COPS), an activist neighborhood organization, and other Mexican American organizations got out the Mexican American vote for a referendum on single-member districts. With this support the referendum passed. A few months later the citizenry elected a city council with a majority of Mexican American and black representatives.[78]

Other Organizations and Protest

Union organization has a long history among Mexican Americans. Several organizations of workers came and went between 1900 and 1927. The first permanent organization was the Confederacion de Uniones Obreras Mexicanas (CUOM), organized in California in 1927 with three thousand members. A 1928 strike by the CUOM was killed by deportation and arrests. Coal miners, farm workers, and factory workers struck in New Mexico, Arizona, and Texas in the 1930s, as Mexican Americans were beginning to make their way into mainstream unions. Mexican American women participated in strikes as members of the International Ladies Garment Workers Union. During this period police force was often used to break up union meetings and strikes.[79]

Mutual-benefit associations developed early among Mexican Americans. These included worker alliances that pooled resources and provided contexts for social interaction, as well as religious brotherhoods. By the 1920s a number of Mexican American newspapers were being published. The League of United Latin American Citizens (LULAC) was organized in southern Texas in the 1920s. Oriented toward civic activities, LULAC pressed for a better deal for Mexican Americans while initially refusing to call itself a protest association. Since the 1960s LULAC has worked to break down segregation and discrimination on many fronts.[80]

A number of post–World War II organizations reflected growing militancy. After a Texas cemetery refused to allow the burial of a Mexican American soldier, the American G.I. Forum was established to organize Mexican American veterans and to work for expanded civil rights. In Los Angeles the Community Service Organization worked to organize voting strength. Two groups that formed about 1960—the Mexican American Political Association, a California organization, and the Political Association of Spanish-Speaking Organizations, a Texas organization—focused more explicitly on political goals. Mexican American protest intensified in the 1960s, reflecting growing political consciousness. "Corky" Gonzales and his associates worked in Denver in support of school reform and against police brutality. New youth organizations were formed throughout the Southwest, including the Mexican American Youth Organization and the Brown Berets, a militant organization that set forth a program of better education, employment, and housing. A new ideology of *Chicanismo* was developed, espousing a philosophy of decolonization.[81]

Among the protests were those led by Reies Lopez Tijerina. The Alianza Federal de Mercedes was founded in 1963 by Tijerina after he had spent a number of years researching the old Mexican land grants in the Southwest. In July 1966 a group of Alianza members marched to Santa Fe and presented a statement of land-grant grievances. Another group camped out without a permit on Kit Carson National Forest land, once part of a communal land grant. Forest rangers who tried to stop them were seized and tried for violating the old land-grant boundaries. Tijerina and some others were arrested for this civil disobedience. In 1967 a local district attorney broke up an Alianza meeting in a small town in New Mexico. News broadcasts were made asking Mexican Americans not to attend, and motorists were stopped by the police and given a notice that alleged the meeting was illegal. Some leaders of the Alianza were arrested and taken to the Tierra Amarilla courthouse. Subsequently, armed Mexican Americans went to the courthouse to make a citizen's arrest of the district attorney for his actions. A shootout ensued. Tijerina was later arrested as a result of the Tierra Amarilla raid, but was acquitted.[82]

Since the 1980s voter registration has been a major focus of organization. The Southwest Voter Registration Education Project, located in San Antonio and Los Angeles, has participated in hundreds of voter-registration campaigns and has joined the Texas Rural Legal Aid organization to file lawsuits seeking to dismantle discriminatory election systems and thereby expand the impact of Mexican American voters. The Mexican American Legal Defense and Education Fund (MALDEF) is also an active force for change. In the redistricting that followed the 1990 census MALDEF worked to assure voting strength and more equitable representation of minorities in several states, including Texas, California, and Illinois.[83] Mothers of East Los Angeles (MELA) is an effective grass-roots organization that works to defend its community's quality of life. For example, at a neighborhood meeting MELA members confronted the representative of an oil company wishing to build a pipeline through the center of a Latino community in Los Angeles:

> "Is it going through Cielito Lindo [Reagan's ranch]?" The oil representative answered, "No." Another woman stood up and asked, "Why not place it along the coastline?" Without thinking of the implications, the representative responded, "Oh, no! If it burst, it would endanger the marine life." The woman retorted, "You value the marine life more than human beings?" His face reddened with anger and the hearing disintegrated into angry chanting.[84]

Unions for Poor Workers

Important developments in unionization also took place in the 1960s—the creation by Jessie Lopez, Dolores Huerta, and César Chávez of the Agricultural Workers Organizing Committee (AWOC) and the National Farm Workers Association (NFWA). By 1964 the NFWA had a thousand members and its own credit union. In 1965 the first big strike was organized. Workers in AWOC struck the Delano, California, growers; the NFWA met in Delano and voted to go on strike too, demanding hourly wages of $1.40. Growers refused to talk; picket lines went up; guns were fired at farmworkers. The NFWA remained nonviolent in the face of provocation. A grape boycott was also started in 1965 and gradually spread across the country. Picket lines went up wherever the grapes were sold. A massive march on Sacramento was organized. In 1966 the AWOC and the NFWA merged into the United Farm Workers Organizing Committee.[85]

Unionization was more difficult in south Texas. The attempt by the United Farm Workers to organize in the Rio Grande Valley in the 1960s and 1970s moved slowly because of imprisonment of strikers and leaders and the intervention of the hated Texas Rangers. Attempts by the Meat Cutters Union to organize Mexican Americans in south Texas also resulted in some union victories but much suffering in the process.[86]

In 1973 the largest winery in the United States, Gallo Brothers, chose not to renew its contract with the United Farm Workers and signed with the more conservative Teamsters. Other wineries followed suit. A number of newspaper and magazine articles argued that Chávez and his union were dying. Yet the struggle continued. Governor Jerry Brown of California worked for legislation to protect farm workers, and a labor board was established to run secret-ballot elections, with protection for union activities.[87]

The United Farm Workers was the most successful farm workers' union in U.S. history, one that altered the structure of power in rural California; "it did so by building a permanent membership organization that used the power of organized numbers as a basis for economic and political change." In the late 1980s the UFW and the charismatic Chávez expanded their efforts to the issue of pesticide spraying of farm products. The UFW began a nationwide campaign to force large farmers to "stop poisoning workers and consumers," to quote campaign literature. The campaign emphasized studies indicating that many farm workers have chronic skin rashes and liver abnormalities and that much produce in supermarkets has pesticide residues. The union organized a new boycott of table grapes to persuade growers to stop using the most dangerous cancer-causing pesticides and to accept expanded collective bargaining for farm workers. The UFW won a partial victory in September 1991, when the Environmental Protection Agency agreed to ban one deadly pesticide, parathion, from use on all but nine crops. Parathion has been implicated in more than seventy deaths and thousands of illnesses among farm workers. Speaking for farm workers, Chávez called the ruling inadequate because the ban was not total.[88]

In the early 1990s an increasing number of Mexican Americans are also to be found in mainstream unions representing auto workers, miners, railroad, cannery, garment, steel, and construction workers, teamsters, and dockworkers. Still, many workers remain in companies from which unions have been excluded by employers.[89]

EDUCATION

In the first three decades of the twentieth century little attention was given to the education of Mexican Americans. The agricultural economy of the Southwest pressed for low-wage labor without the expense of education. Schooling for laborers was usually minimal—only what was needed for them to learn a little arithmetic and English.[90] Prior to World War II Mexican American schoolchildren from Texas to California were often segregated, although school segregation for this group was different from that for black Americans. As a rule, Mexican Americans were segregated not by state law but either by local laws or by informal gerrymandering of school district lines. Discrimination in housing reinforced school segregation.[91]

Persisting Problems

Following World War II Mexican American communities began to press for changes in the educational system. A major conference in Texas in 1946 called for an end to segregation, the adoption of a Mexican-oriented curriculum, better teacher training, and better school facilities. A few court decisions in the late 1940s began to outlaw segregation, yet patterns of segregation have persisted to the present. In the early 1990s most Mexican American students still attended predominantly minority schools. Indeed, the proportion of Mexican American children in many of the schools of the Southwest had increased significantly; de facto school segregation was still the rule, in part because of segregated housing patterns. In addition, many of the more than one thousand predominantly Mexican American schools had inferior educational resources. Mexican Americans were underrepresented among teachers and administrators in most school systems in spite of modest increases in their numbers. In 1991 the Congressional Hispanic Caucus introduced legislation to help remedy the educational problems of Mexican American youth, proposing, among other things, early-intervention programs for elementary school students and scholarships that would encourage college students to teach in poverty areas.

In the recent past some schools with high percentages of Mexican American students rigidly prohibited manifestations of Mexican American subculture, some going so far as to enforce dress and hair codes for students. Teachers anglicized the names of children (for instance, Roberto became "Bobby"), downgrading the heritage of the children. Euro-American teachers' treatment of Mexican American children in the classroom is another persisting problem. Teacher practices have been shown to have a strong relationship to student achievement. One study of teacher behavior in classrooms found that the average teacher praised Euro-American children 35 percent more often than Mexican American children, questioned them 20 percent more often, and used their ideas 40 percent more often.[92]

For many years Mexican American children in Texas and California were over-represented in classes for the mentally retarded. Most Mexican Americans in these classes were "six-hour retarded" children—capable of functioning in the outside world yet mislabeled largely as a result of indirect discrimination in testing. Tests were usually conducted in English. A 1970s study in Riverside, California, found that all of the Euro-American children in classes for the mentally retarded showed behavior abnormality, compared with less than half of the Mexican American children. Although certain discriminatory practices, such as placement in classes for the "mentally retarded," had been eliminated from most schools by the 1980s, vestiges of bias and discrimination remained. Into the early 1990s schools still placed too many Mexican American children in learning-disabled classes, and textbooks neglected Mexican American history.[93]

Current Issues: Bilingualism and Achievement

Writing about the historical treatment of language in the interaction between the dominant culture and other U.S. cultures, Juan Perea points out that "America has always been a land of many different languages and cultures."[94] The Articles of Confederation were officially published in three languages—English, German, and French. California's first state constitution (1849), published in both Spanish and English, provided that "all laws, decrees, regulations, and provisions" be printed in both languages. From the first, the laws of the territory of New Mexico were published in both Spanish and English; this practice continued during the first forty years of New Mexico's statehood. Education in most schools in that territory was provided in Spanish. Later, nativists succeeded in having languages other than English labeled "foreign" and laws passed restricting their use (see Chapter 3). Perea identifies such actions as "attempts to exclude certain unpopular Americans from the definition of what is American."[95] We will examine the nativist attack on Spanish speakers and proposals for English as the official language in Chapter 10.

When placed in classrooms in which instruction is given only in English, children with limited English proficiency frequently become discouraged, develop low self-confidence, and fail to keep pace with their English-speaking peers. This condition affects many Latino students. Bilingual education for Puerto Rican and Cuban American students will be discussed in Chapter 10. In 1968 Congress passed the Elementary and Secondary

Education Act, which set up a mechanism for the federal government to fund bilingual programs in public schools to meet the special needs of language-minority children. By 1973, however, no southwestern state had taken more than token steps; only 5 percent of the Mexican American children in the Southwest were being affected by federally funded bilingual programs in the 1972–73 school year.

A 1974 Supreme Court decision (*Lau* v. *Nichols*) established a child's ability to understand classroom instruction as a civil right, making it illegal for school systems to ignore the English-language problems of language-minority groups. Since 1968 federal programs have provided over a billion dollars for local school district programs to increase the English proficiency of language-minority children. Yet apart from a few stellar programs in schools with sensitive principals in scattered public school systems, the overall picture of bilingual education is one of snail-like progress, if not public opposition. One federal study found that most school systems had few qualified bilingual teachers and were unable to accurately assess the English-language needs of language-minority students.[96]

Although the median education levels for Mexican Americans have increased since 1950, they remain significantly behind national figures. In 1950 the median schooling for Mexican American adults was 5.4 years. By 1976 the figure had increased to 9 years, decreasing but not closing the gap with the national median. The 1980 census reported the figure to be 9.6 years, much lower than the national median of 12.5 years. Only 37.6 percent of Mexican Americans were high school graduates. An even wider gap exists between the rate of college graduation for Mexican Americans and that for the population as a whole. Access to higher education was provided during the 1940s and 1950s by the GI bill. This access was increased during the 1960s and 1970s by federal education programs following in the wake of the civil rights movement.[97] Yet by the early 1990s, as the following table shows, the proportion of Mexican Americans lagged behind other Latino groups.[98]

	Persons 25 years and over			
	Mexican Origin	Puerto Rican Origin	Cuban Origin	Total Population
Less than 5 years of school completed	16%	10%	6%	2%
4 years of high school or more	44%	56%	64%	78%
4 years of college or more	5%	10%	20%	21%

Mexican Americans are the lowest of the three Latino groups in terms of educational attainment and are significantly below the total U.S. population in the proportions attaining high school diplomas and college degrees. Although gradually improving, the educational attainment of the Mexican-origin population at the beginning of the 1990s is evidence of decades of limited economic and educational opportunities.

In the early 1990s the dropout rate for Mexican American students remains high. Variations in reporting methods for dropout rates (annual, longitudinal, or overall) and the fact that students drop in and out of school and sometimes reenroll somewhere else make it impossible to arrive at an exact figure, but estimates of the dropout rate for all Latino groups combined range from two to more than three times that of non-Latinos; Mexican Americans rank at the low end among the various Latino groups. Poverty and the need to earn money to help support their families are major obstacles for these students. School counselors often advise those who have fallen behind to drop out. Yet a few schools have increased graduation rates for Mexican American students significantly—in at least one case to 95 percent—by providing programs to address such student concerns as jobs, substance abuse, and teen parenthood.[99]

In 1988 researchers Romo and Falbo began tracking a group of one hundred Mexican American high school sophomores who were at high risk of dropping out of school.[100] Within two years 40 percent had dropped out. Only nineteen of the original hundred graduated at the end of their senior year, and only one student remained in school the following year. Many of those who graduated did so only with the help of special programs; their skills were scarcely better than those of the students who dropped out. Interviews with the students revealed that their school experience was demeaning and demoralizing. Some expressed the feeling that someone was "always on my back." Many of the students felt they were better off after they left school. One girl remarked about her job: "At least they care whether I come or not."

Nonetheless, education was highly valued by both the students and their families; the anguish of school failure was keenly felt. "School failure involves threats to the self-esteem of the students as well as the status of the family and results in complex intra-family tensions and conflicts.... After a student dropped out, parents felt devastated and angry." In most of these Mexican American families mothers were primarily responsible for their children's education. The mothers in this study derived much of their own sense of self from the successes of their children and tended to blame themselves, or felt that school personnel blamed them, for their children's failures. These mothers' major strategies for helping their children stay in school involved giving encouragement and pointing to individual models of success. Most of the mothers had limited schooling and were unable to help their children with schoolwork. They often did not understand the school system. Few mothers had the confidence to approach the school for help; those who did felt themselves at a disadvantage in dealing with the school system. They frequently experienced frustration over the school's unwillingness or inability to provide help and some reported encountering hostility from teachers, counselors, or administrators.

In a critique of many of the explanations that have been offered for poor school performance by minority students, including Mexican American students, Walsh explains that to attribute their school problems to their individual or cultural inadequacies is to blame the victim. Blaming incompatibilities arising from the cultural differences between Latino students and the Euro-American dominated educational system is to overlook the historical and ongoing sociological, economic, and ideological significance of these differences. That all culturally different students do not perform equally poorly in school points to the relevance of additional factors. The problem is one of unequal power relationships. To locate the problem we must look to the system, not to the student. The mainstream school curriculum is built on the dominant Euro-American culture and the English language and equates success with adopting that dominant culture and language.

Minority history, culture, language, and life experiences are typically ignored. The minority culture is seen by the dominant group as a negative environment from which students need to escape. Walsh suggests that poor school performance is often a response to alienating and oppressive conditions that have robbed minority students of identity, dignity, and voice. She notes that learning or not learning can be a political statement. Walsh quotes Frederick Erickson, who states that to overcome resistance to learning one must establish

> trust in the legitimacy of the authority and in the good intentions of those exercising it, trust that one's own identity will be maintained positively in relation to the authority, and trust that one's own interests will be advanced by compliance with the exercise of authority.[101]

Including the Spanish language and Mexican American culture in the classroom, involving students' parents in the learning process, and increasing interaction between students and teachers are important steps toward improving education for Mexican American children but are inadequate by themselves. The imbalance of power can be corrected, and Mexican American students can be accorded respect and the possibility of establishing a positive identity in public schools.

In the 1970s and 1980s a debate raged over the obligation of school systems to educate the children of undocumented Mexican aliens. State officials in southwestern states complained that educating these children was a burden on U.S. citizens. At the same time, for political reasons they publicly exaggerated the number of such children in their schools. In Texas a court case arose out of officials' attempts to charge the children of undocumented aliens a special fee to attend school. After an extended struggle in the lower courts, the Supreme Court ruled in 1982 that all children had to be provided with schooling and that children could not be discriminated against on the basis of parental condition, such as immigrant status.[102]

RELIGION

Mexican immigrants to Texas were not accompanied by Catholic priests, nor were the Catholic church and its dogma major factors in the lives of migrants. What has been termed *folk Catholicism,* a blend of Catholicism and certain non-Catholic beliefs and rituals, did play an important role.[103] Many immigrants were hostile to the established church in Mexico, and most were not ready for a U.S. Catholic church dominated by Irish Americans. In the first decades little provision was made for the religious schooling of Mexican Catholics; as late as the 1930s there were only seventy parochial schools in the major dioceses of southern California, whereas there were several hundred thousand Catholics. Prior to 1940, the church provided little sustenance or aid to a population troubled by poverty and discrimination.[104]

In the 1950s and 1960s some priests took an active role in union activities. In the 1960s, War on Poverty programs were sometimes operated in connection with church projects, and a number of "lay protest" and "priest protest" groups were formed to deal with urban problems. Yet in some areas the church hierarchy prohibited priests from participating in protest organizations. The Los Angeles cardinal refused to provide priests for the Delano farm workers on strike in the 1960s. Moreover, the hierarchy of the U.S. Catholic church has discriminated against Mexican Americans. Very few Mexican Americans penetrated positions of responsibility prior to the 1960s; the first Mexican American bishop was designated, in San Antonio, in 1970. In the mid-1980s only eighteen of the nearly three hundred bishops in the United States were Mexican American.[105]

The Catholicism of most Mexican Americans has been described as somewhat similar to that of Italian Americans, with a general allegiance to the church but less active participation than for Irish Catholics. In the 1940s Tuck found that most Mexican Americans in San Bernardino, California, were baptized, married, and buried with a priest in attendance, but participated infrequently in church activities. The power of the church was found to be great in affecting attitudes on such issues as venereal disease campaigns and unionization. In recent years, however, this influence of the church on certain secular issues has appeared to be on the wane; rejection of the church position on abortion and birth control has been extensive.[106] Still, the Catholic church today creates a central place not only for Sunday mass but also for holiday celebrations and community gatherings. In cities such as Chicago some older parishes have seen large increases in their Spanish-speaking parishioners and have re-oriented their services to meet the needs of Latino members. The U.S. Catholic church has also created a number of new churches in West Coast areas where immigration from Mexico has been substantial.

In addition, there has been some shift among Mexican and other Latino Americans to Protestant churches, although the numbers are still modest. In the 1980s and early 1990s some Latinos were converting to Jehovah's Witnesses and other evangelical groups that have welcomed new immigrants and have made them feel, as one person put it, like "part of a family."[107] In many urban Latino communities dozens of evangelical and Pentecostal churches have been created, many of them in empty storefronts and old abandoned churches. In 1988 one national poll found that 6 percent of the nation's Latinos were members of such churches, about 1.2 million people, a doubling of the number in a decade.[108]

ASSIMILATION OR COLONIALISM?

An assimilation perspective has been explicit or implicit in the prominent studies of researchers such as Tuck, Sanchez, Madsen, and Grebler. A pivotal idea is that Mexican Americans will move up the mobility ladder just as the European ethnic groups did, and thus will proceed surely, if more slowly, into the mainstream at all the assimilation levels described by Milton Gordon.[109]

An assimilationist looking at Mexican American history might emphasize that only a hundred thousand Mexicans were brought into the United States as a result of military conquest. Most immigrants came later. Most have been able to improve their economic circumstances relative to their condition in Mexico. Aspects of Mexican traditional culture began disappearing as acculturation proceeded.[110] For the first generation of Mexican Americans, cultural assimilation made itself felt mainly in terms of adjustments in language and certain workplace values. Religious and other basic values were less affected; respect for Mexico remained strong. For later generations there has been increased structural assimilation into the economy and more cultural adaptation. The Mexican American family is traditionally depicted as a large, extended, patriarchal unit;

this is perhaps most descriptive of family patterns in agricultural towns in earlier decades. Urbanization and increased incomes opened up the possibility of separate residences for nuclear families and a decline in the number of large, extended families. Fertility trends and family values have increasingly become similar to those of other Americans.[111]

However, from the traditional life of rural villages to the faster-paced life of the urban barrios there has been substantial cultural persistence. Most notable has been the Spanish language, which has persisted as the primary language or as part of a bilingual pattern for most families. Closeness to Mexico has been given as an important reason for the persistence of the Spanish language. Surveys in Los Angeles and San Antonio found that most Mexican Americans wished their children to retain ties to their Mexican culture, particularly to language, customs, and religion. A 1991 survey found that most Mexican Americans were bilingual to some extent, but a significant minority had little fluency in English. Almost all the adults felt that it was very important for their children to become fluent in both Spanish and English.[112]

Structural assimilation at the economic level has come slowly even for the second and third generations; discrimination and the resultant concentration of workers at the lower wage levels persists. Problematical too has been the limited participation in political institutions, although recent progress can be seen in some areas. Milton Gordon's dimensions of behavior-receptional assimilation and attitude-receptional assimilation have varied considerably within the Mexican American group and over time. Widespread prejudice and severe discrimination faced the Mexicans who were conquered in the expansion of the United States, as well as the immigrants since 1900. With time some lighter-skinned Mexican Americans in larger cities were treated with less prejudice and discrimination. Darker-skinned persons have often been treated the same as black Americans. Today considerable prejudice and discrimination are still directed against Mexican Americans in many parts of the United States.

The Limits of Assimilation

Structural absorption at the primary-group level and marital assimilation have not yet reached the point where one can speak of moderate-to-high assimilation for Mexican Americans as a group. Some increases in interethnic friendship contacts were found in studies in the early 1970s, particularly for Mexican American children in desegregated environments, although most still had predominantly Mexican American friends. In one study, fewer than 5 percent of Mexican respondents in San Antonio had predominantly Euro-American friends; the proportion in Los Angeles was about 15 percent. Moreover, in a 1991 survey the vast majority of Latinos (mostly Mexican Americans) in the Southwest, West, and Central regions of the United States reported that their close friends (as well as their neighborhoods) were Latino.[113]

Data on intermarriage indicate that a majority of marriages are still within the Mexican American group. In San Antonio the proportion of Spanish-surname individuals marrying outside the group slowly increased from 10 percent in the 1940–55 period to 14 percent in 1964 and to 16 percent in 1973. In Los Angeles the proportion of individuals marrying outside the group increased from 9 percent in the period 1924–33 to 25 percent in 1960–61. In Texas and New Mexico in recent years the proportion of Mexican Americans marrying outside the group has stabilized from 5 to 24 percent. The one exception to these relatively low outmarriage rates appears in a study for all California counties, which found outmarriage rates to be between 34 and 36 percent for the 1970s. Outmarriage rates seemed to be stabilizing at a rate well below half.[114]

Some conservative assimilation analysts, such as Nathan Glazer, have questioned the extent of Mexican Americans' identification with things Mexican. For example, Glazer characterized the militant Chicano movement of the 1960s and 1970s as "one of extreme views espoused by a minority for a short period." This view overlooks the fact that the majority of younger Mexican Americans supported the Chicano movement, even if they did not actively participate in its activities, and that many in the older generation—that is, the families of the young activists—were quietly supportive. In addition, the perspectives and actions of the activists in the 1960s as well as the 1990s reflect themes of militancy and change rooted in their Mexican American cultural heritage.[115]

Connor has argued that the diversity of ethnic labels used by persons with ties to Mexico—designations such as *Hispano, Chicano, Mexican, Mexican American, Latino, Spanish,* and *Hispanic*—indicate a significant ethnic diversity within this community.[116] Some whose ancestry dates back before the U.S. conquest of northern Mexico have preferred terms such as *Spanish.* But other scholars have emphasized that outside oppression forced many, particularly in earlier decades, to hide their Mexican origin under the euphemism *Spanish American;* this is not necessarily a sign of identificational assimilation. Middle-income Mexican Americans in the 1920s began to use such terms to hide from prejudice. In recent years there has been a shift back to *Mexican* and *Mexican American.* In one survey the preference of respondents in Los Angeles was for *Mexican* or *Mexican American,* while in San Antonio the majority preferred *Latin American.* Few in either city wanted to be called just American. In a survey of households in the Southwest and Midwest, most respondents preferred to be called Mexican American, Mexican, or Chicano. Pride in Mexican identity thus remains strong.[117]

Múrguia has argued that the Anglo-Protestant core society is allowing substantial portions of Mexican Americans to assimilate on a more or less equal-status basis. Yet in his view assimilation cannot go as far as it has for other Catholics, such as the Irish. The differences are narrowing, but assimilation will stop short of complete absorption. Mexican Americans might slowly gain near parity at the secondary–structural level—in the economy and politics—although considerable separation would remain at the primary-group level and major cultural differences would persist.[118]

A recent study by Strategy Research Corporation (SRC) indicates a slow rate of assimilation with some regional and generational variations. The SRC study groups together various "Hispanic" groups into one general Hispanic category and then presents the data broken down by region. Since most of the Hispanic Americans in the West, Central, and Southwest regions are Mexican Americans, we will focus only on SRC data from these regions. Almost 90 percent of the Hispanic adult respondents in the West and Central regions and more than two-thirds of those in the Southwest described themselves as "very Hispanic." When asked how Hispanic-oriented they would like to be in ten years, the percentage replying "very Hispanic" remained virtually unchanged in the Southwest and dropped only a few percentage points in the other two regions. Very small percentages in each region saw themselves as minimally Hispanic (proportions ranged from less than

1 percent in the West to just over 4 percent in the Southwest). The percentage who would like to be minimally Hispanic in ten years more than doubled in the Southwest but rose only slightly in the West and Central regions. Young people below the age of eighteen in all three regions consistently rated themselves as less Hispanic and projected a lower level of Hispanic identification for themselves in the future than did their adult counterparts. But the proportions identifying themselves as minimally Hispanic were still extremely low (ranging from 2.5 percent to 10.6 percent).[119]

In addition to these self-descriptions, the SRC study ranked respondents' level of (cultural) assimilation on the basis of identification, language used, and behavioral, attitudinal, and aspirational measures. Only some 13 percent were judged to be fully assimilated; that is, they were thought to have given up most of their Latino culture. Approximately half (49 percent) were ranked partially assimilated; although reasonably comfortable in both Spanish and English, their Spanish-language skills predominated and they retained strong ties to Latino culture. The remaining 38 percent, classified relatively unassimilated, spoke very little English. Largely recent immigrants, they are the fastest-growing segment of the Latino population in the United States.[120]

Regional and generational differences were apparent in language-use patterns. A large majority of the Hispanic adults in the West and Central regions felt most comfortable speaking Spanish and spoke it more frequently than English at home and on social occasions. The use of Spanish was less dominant among adults in the Southwest. While a majority felt most comfortable speaking Spanish, fewer than half spoke it more frequently than English at home or on social occasions. More than half of the youth in the West and Central regions felt most comfortable speaking Spanish, whereas a large majority of their counterparts in the Southwest felt most comfortable with English. In all three regions, Spanish was spoken far less frequently at home and on social occasions by the youth than by adults. An overwhelming majority of the Latino adults in all regions considered it very important for their children to learn to read and write both Spanish and English well. This divergence between reality and preference suggests that if the immigration streams from Mexico and other parts of Latin America ever abate, the linguistic assimilation of the population will increase dramatically, especially as the population ages.[121]

Today, however, persisting immigration streams create problems for an assimilation analysis. The influx of significant numbers of Mexican and Central American immigrants into established Mexican American barrios in recent years has helped reproduce and perpetuate the traditional culture of Mexican American communities, has contributed to intermarriage, often between immigrant males and Mexican American females, and has encouraged the maintenance of Spanish as a primary language. In addition, Mexican American businesses have been supplied with new customers as well as a source of low-wage labor. These immigrants have furnished both the means and the reason for the growth of various Spanish-language-based enterprises such as restaurants offering authentic cuisine, spiritualist shops offering nonmedical healing, and Spanish-language media. The new immigrants have also provided a limited amount of entrepreneurial capital for ethnic enterprises in the barrios. The new immigrants have had a significant influence in the political arena. In addition to the conflicts their presence creates for non-Latino officials, they increase the population base for electoral representation and also the constituency of Mexican American officeholders. The international political concerns of many immigrants have helped to expand the political involvement of Mexican American leaders and activists into a broader political arena.[122]

Applying a Power–Conflict Perspective

Power–conflict analysts would emphasize the extent to which Mexican Americans have not moved toward incorporation in the core society. The best that assimilation analysts can argue is that the trend is toward assimilation, for substantial economic and political assimilation is not a reality for the majority of Mexican Americans.

Internal colonialism analysts accent Mexican American history, particularly its origin in the ruthless conquest of northern Mexico in the 1836–53 period. The situation for the early Mexican, whose land and person were brought into the United States by force, is one of classical colonialism. Acuña has underscored the parallels between the Mexican American experience and that of the external colonization of other Third World populations: land is taken by military force, the native population is subjugated economically and politically, the native culture is suppressed, and the colonizing power favors a small Mexican elite in order to maintain the subjugation.[123]

One problem in applying the colonialism perspective to Mexican Americans is that most entered as immigrants after the conquest. Internal colonialism analysts underscore the differences between Mexican and European migrations. Unlike Europeans, Mexican migrants did not come into a new environment. People of their background were already here. Socially and culturally, they moved within one geographical area, all of which was originally controlled by Mexicans. Moreover, little time was required to move back and forth across the border—in sharp contrast with the time of travel required of European immigrants.[124]

Perhaps the most significant difference was that the heritage of the (external) colonial situation, with its practices of subordination, shaped the receiving situation of the later Mexican immigrants. "The colonial pattern of Euro-American domination over the Mexican people was set by 1848 and carried over to those Mexicans who came later to the Southwest, a land contiguous to Mexico and once a part of it."[125] Later subordination of Mexican immigrants by force included rigorous Border Patrol searches and deportation of those immigrants deemed unworthy by Euro-American authorities.

Later Mexican immigrants were channeled into an environment in which low wages, absentee landlords, inferior schools, and discrimination severely limited their progress and mobility. For many decades residential segregation has also reflected Anglo American discrimination. Mexican Americans are not like European immigrant groups, whose level of segregation has declined significantly with length of residence in the United States. Discrimination in employment and housing persists.

In Chapter 2 we discussed the book *Race and Class in the Southwest* by Mario Barrera, who analyzes Mexican Americans using a modified internal colonialism model that emphasizes racism and capitalism as factors in inequality. Barrera argues that each of the major classes of capitalism, the capitalist class and the working class, contains important segments that are defined by characteristics such as race. Each of the major classes contains a racial–ethnic line that separates those suffering institutionalized discrimination, such as Mexican Americans, from those Euro-Americans who do not. Consider the example of the working class. While Mexican American workers share a similar class position with white workers in that both are struggling against capitalist employers for better wages and working conditions, the former are in a subordinate economic position because of structural discrimination along racial and ethnic lines. The dimensions of this discrimination include lower wages for the same or similar work, and concentration in certain lower-status occupations.[126]

Internal colonialism analysts argue that Euro-American employers have created a split labor market from which they have profited greatly; they have focused the attention of Euro-American workers on Latinos (and blacks) as the threat to Euro-American workers. Given the segmentation of the labor force by employers, it is not surprising that Euro-American workers often try to solidify their positions and keep minority workers out of the privileged jobs reserved for themselves. This is a type of internal colonialism.

Flores has underscored the cultural and psychodynamic aspects of the Mexican American situation. Mexican Americans have been subordinated much more than European immigrant groups ever were. Great psychological as well as economic benefits have accrued to the Euro-American oppressors. The acculturation of Mexican American children and adults has involved much pressure and some coercion, as in the public schools. The racial stereotyping of Mexican Americans has played a major role in establishing and preserving the racial hierarchy of the Southwest. Theories of biological inferiority have been used to justify taking land and exploiting Mexican American labor. This subordination benefits most Euro-Americans:

> [It] is a complex cultural system of racial and cultural domination which produces privileges above and beyond the surplus value generated solely by capitalism—privileges from which all members of the dominant social groups (despite their class) derive benefit directly or indirectly.[127]

Power–conflict analysts see the real hope for decreased oppression and an improved economic, political, and cultural situation in decolonization movements in the Mexican American protest movements of the past and present.

Moreover, as we noted in discussing assimilation, a distinctive aspect of Mexican American communities today is the constant infusion of undocumented workers. Particularly in the Southwest, this undocumented immigration provides renewal of ties to Mexico and reinforcement of Mexican culture, thereby undergirding Mexican communities and identity. These immigrants provide much low-wage labor for the Southwest's Euro-American-dominated corporations, farms, and ranches. And their presence has become the center of controversy over U.S. immigration laws and policies. This influx of immigrants creates serious problems for those applying the assimilation perspective to Mexican Americans, because the close ties to the traditional Mexican culture—the closest for any immigrant group in U.S. history—significantly slow cultural and social assimilation by providing an external supportive foundation.

SUMMARY

Mexican Americans have an ancient and proud ancestry, predominantly Native American ("Indian") but with some Spanish and African infusion. Their vital cultural background is partly Native American but heavily Spanish in language and religion. After the Euro-American conquest in the Southwest, Mexican Americans became part of the complex mosaic of racial and ethnic groups in the United States. They have suffered racial stereotyping similar to that of other groups of non-European ancestry, and racially motivated discrimination in economics, education, and politics has been part of their lot from the beginning.

The literature on race and ethnic relations has often compared the situations of African Americans and Mexican Americans, the largest subordinated minorities in the United States. Both groups face substantial and similar prejudice and discrimination at the hands of whites late in the twentieth century, especially in jobs and housing, although lighter-skinned, middle-income Mexican Americans probably face less discrimination than middle-income African Americans.

At the attitudinal level, African Americans and Mexican Americans are often sympathetic to each other's problems. One study of Mexican American attitudes in Texas found more positive feelings toward blacks than were found among Euro-Americans, more sensitivity to discriminatory barriers, and more support for civil rights protest. Differences between the two groups appeared in the area of protest strategies. The researchers found that black Americans were significantly more militant than Mexican Americans on selected issues, more dissatisfied with civil rights progress, and more approving of civil rights demonstrations.[128] This difference has often made it difficult for the two groups to work together politically against the dominant group. In some situations the two groups even find themselves competing for limited benefits granted by the dominant group. Nonetheless, there have been several attempts to build black–brown coalitions, including the Rainbow Coalition led by Jesse Jackson in the 1980s. The future may well see more such multiracial coalitions.

NOTES

1. This and the following paragraph draw on Edward Múrguía, "On Latino/Hispanic Ethnic Identity," *Latino Studies Journal* 2, no. 3 (September 1991): 8–18.
2. Strategy Research Corporation, *1991 U.S. Hispanic Market* (Miami, 1991), pp 78–129.
3. Teresa L. Amott and Julie A. Matthaei, *Race, Gender, and Work* (Boston: South End Press, 1991), pp. 64–67.
4. Américo Paredes, *With His Pistol in His Hand* (Austin: University of Texas Press, 1958), pp. 3–14; Roldolfo Acuña, *Occupied America* (San Francisco: Canfield Press, 1972), pp. 10–12.
5. Acuña, *Occupied America*, p. 15; S. Dale McLemore, "The Origin of Mexican American Subordination in Texas," *Social Science Quarterly* 53 (March 1973): 665–67; Rodolfo Alvarez, "The Psycho-historical and Socioeconomic Development of the Chicano Community in the United States," *Social Science Quarterly* 53 (March 1973): 925.
6. William Lord, "Myths and Realities of the Alamo," *American West* 5 (May 1968): 20–25.
7. Carl N. Degler, *Out of Our Past* (New York: Harper, 1959), pp. 109–10; Acuña, *Occupied America*, pp. 23–29.
8. Joan Moore and Harry Pachon, *Hispanics in the United States* (Englewood Cliffs, N.J.: Prentice-Hall, 1985), pp. 18, 22–23; Leo Grebler, Joan W. Moore, and Ralph G. Guzmán, *The Mexican-American People* (New York: Free Press, 1970), pp. 43–44; Acuña, *Occupied America*, p. 105; Joan W. Moore, "Colonialism: The Case of the Mexican Americans," *Social Problems* 17 (Spring 1970): 468–69.
9. Moore and Pachon, *Hispanics in the United States*, p. 21; Ellwyn R. Stoddard, *Mexican Americans* (New York: Random House, 1973), pp. 9–13; Carey McWilliams, *North from Mexico* (New York: Greenwood Press, 1968), pp. 70–76; Acuña, *Occupied America*, pp. 60–62; Grebler, Moore, and Guzmán, *The Mexican-American People*, pp. 43–44; Nancie L. Gonzales, *The Spanish-Americans of New Mexico* (Albuquerque: University of New Mexico Press, 1967), pp. 204ff.
10. Alvarez, "Psycho-historical and Socioeconomic Development," p. 925.

11. Oscar J. Martinez, "On the Size of the Chicano Population: New Estimates: 1850–1900," *Aztlán* 6 (Spring 1975): 55–56; U.S. Department of Justice, Immigration and Naturalization Service, *Annual Report* (Washington, 1975), pp. 62–64; Julian Samora, *Los Mojados: The Wetback Story* (Notre Dame, Ind.: University of Notre Dame Press, 1971), pp. 7–8.

12. Leo Grebler, *Mexican Immigration to the United States: The Record and Its Implications* (Los Angeles: UCLA Mexican-American Study Project, 1965), pp. 20–21.

13. Ibid., pp. 23–24; Manuel Gamio, *Mexican Immigration to the United States* (New York: Dover, 1971), pp. 171–74; Gilberto Cardenas, "United States Immigration Policy toward Mexico: An Historical Perspective," *Chicano Law Review* 2 (Summer 1975): 69–71.

14. Samora, *Los Mojados*, pp. 48–52.

15. Cardenas, "United States Immigration Policy toward Mexico," pp. 73–75; Grebler, *Mexican Immigration to the United States*, p. 26.

16. Samora, *Los Mojados*, pp. 18–19, 24–25, 44–46, 57; Joan Moore, *Mexican Americans*, 2d ed. (Englewood Cliffs, N.J.: Prentice-Hall, 1976), pp. 49–51; Strategy Research Corporation, *1991 U.S. Hispanic Market*, pp. 39, 51.

17. Samora, *Los Mojados*, pp. 80–92; Moore, *Mexican Americans*, pp. 49–51.

18. Cardenas, "United States Immigration Policy toward Mexico," pp. 84–85; Cheryl Anderson, "Immigration Bill under Attack on Several Fronts," *Austin American-Statesman*, December 12, 1982, p. C1.

19. Wayne A. Cornelius, "Mexican Migration to the United States," in *Crisis in American Institutions*, ed. J. Skolnick and E. Currie (Boston: Little, Brown, 1982), pp. 154–68; Jeffrey S. Passel, "Undocumented Immigrants: How Many?" in *Proceedings of the Social Statistics Section of the American Statistical Association, 1985* (Washington: American Statistical Association, 1985), pp. 65–81; Karen A. Woodrow and Jeffrey S. Passel, "Post-IRCA Undocumented Immigration to the United States" in *Undocumented Migration to the United States*, ed. Frank Bean, Barry Edmonston, and Jeffrey Passel (Santa Monica, Calif.: Rand Corporation, 1990), pp. 41, 60, 65–66.

20. Susan González Baker and Frank Bean, "The Legalization Programs of the 1986 Immigration Reform and Control Act," in *In Defense of the Alien*, ed. Lydio F. Tomasi (New York: Center for Migration Studies, 1990), pp. 3–11.

21. Woodrow and Passel, "Post-IRCA Undocumented Immigration to the United States," p. 42.

22. Strategy Research Corporation, *1991 U.S. Hispanic Market*, p. 59; U.S. Bureau of the Census, *The Census and You* (Washington, 1991), p. 3.

23. Quoted in Philip D. Ortego, "The Chicano Renaissance," in *Introduction to Chicano Studies*, ed. Livie I. Duran and H. Russell Bernard (New York: Macmillan, 1973), p. 337.

24. Cardenas, "United States Immigration Policy toward Mexico," pp. 70–71.

25. Quoted in Ralph Guzmán, "The Function of Anglo-American Racism in the Political Development of Chicanos," in *La Causa Politica*, ed. F. Chris Garcia (Notre Dame, Ind.: University of Notre Dame Press, 1974), p. 22.

26. McWilliams, *North from Mexico*, p. 213.

27. William Sheldon, "Educational Research and Statistics: The Intelligence of Mexican-American Children," in *In Their Place*, ed. Lewis H. Carlson and George A. Colburn (New York: John Wiley, 1972), pp. 149–51.

28. Ozzie G. Simmons, "The Mutual Images and Expectations of Anglo-Americans and Mexican-Americans," in *Introduction to Chicano Studies*, ed. Duran and Bernard, pp. 387–97; Robin M. Williams, *Strangers Next Door* (Englewood Cliffs, N.J.: Prentice-Hall, 1974), pp. 29–80.

29. Livie I. Duran and H. Russell Bernard, introduction to Part 2 of *Introduction to Chicano Studies*, ed. Duran and Bernard, p. 237. See also Stoddard, *Mexican Americans*, p. 6.

30. Tomás Martinez, "Advertising and Racism: The Case of the Mexican American," *El Grito* 2 (Summer 1969): 3–13. See also Stoddard, *Mexican Americans*, p. 6.

31. Quoted in Guillermo V. Flores, "Race and Culture in the Internal Colony: Keeping the Chicano in His Place," in "Structures of Dependency," ed. Frank Bonilla and Robert Girling (manuscript, research seminar, Stanford, Calif., 1973), p. 194.

32. Quoted in Armondo Morales, *Ando Sangrando* (Fair Lawn, N.J.: R. E. Burdick, 1972), p. 43.

33. Octavio Ignacio Romano, "The Anthropology and Sociology of the Mexican-Americans," *El Grito* 2 (Fall 1968): 13–19; Oscar Lewis, *Five Families* (New York: John Wiley, 1962); William Madsen, *Mexican Americans of South Texas* (New York: Holt, Rinehart & Winston, 1964).

34. Romano, "The Anthropology and Sociology of the Mexican Americans"; Stoddard, *Mexican Americans*, pp. 42–44; Lea Ybarra, "Empirical and Theoretical Developments in the Study of the Chicano Family," in *The State of Chicano Research on Family, Labor, and Migration*, ed. Armando Valdez, Albert Camarillo, and Tomás Almaguer (Stanford, Calif.: Stanford Center for Chicano Research, 1983), p. 96.

35. Edward E. Telles and Edward Múrguía, "Phenotypic Discrimination and Income Differences among Mexican Americans" (typescript, University of Texas, 1987).

36. E. J. Hobsbawm, *Primitive Rebels* (New York: W. W. Norton & Co., Inc., 1959), pp. 15–16.

37. Acuña, *Occupied America*, pp. 48–50; McWilliams, North from Mexico, pp. 110–12.

38. Paredes, *With His Pistol in His Hand*, pp. 27–32; McWilliams, North from Mexico, p. 127; Moore, "Colonialism," p. 466; Stoddard, *Mexican Americans*, p. 181.

39. Ralph H. Turner and Lewis M. Killian, *Collective Behavior* (Englewood Cliffs, N.J.: Prentice-Hall, 1957), pp. 125–28; McWilliams, *North from Mexico*, pp. 229–38.

40. Morales, *Ando Sangrando*, pp. 100–108.

41. U.S. Commission on Civil Rights, *Mexican Americans and the Administration of Justice in the Southwest* (Washington, 1970), pp. 6–10; Robert Lee Maril, *Poorest of Americans* (South Bend, Ind.: University of Notre Dame Press, 1989), p. 52; Andrea Ford and Sheryl Stolberg, "Latinos Tell Panel of Anger at Police Conduct," *Los Angeles Times*, May 21, 1991, p. A1; Louis Sahagun, "Shooting Spurs Latinos to Reassess Law Enforcement," *Los Angeles Times*, August 8, 1991, p. A1; George Ramos, "Latinos Push Demand for Sheriff's Dept. Probe," *Los Angeles Times*, September 19, 1991, p. B3.

42. Abel G. Rubio, *Stolen Heritage* (Austin, Tex.: Eakin Press, 1986).

43. Clark Knowlton, "Recommendations for the Solution of Land Tenure Problems among the Spanish Americans," in *Chicano: The Evolution of a People*, ed. Renato Rosaldo, Robert A. Calvert, and Gustav L. Seligmann (San Francisco: Rinehart Press, 1973), pp. 334–35; George I. Sanchez, *Forgotten People* (Albuquerque: University of New Mexico Press, 1940), p. 61; Arnoldo Deleón, *The Tejano Community, 1836–1900* (Albuquerque: University of New Mexico Press, 1982), pp. 63–91.

44. Tomas Almaguer, "Historical Notes on Chicano Oppression: The Dialectics of Racial and Class Domination in North America," *Atzlán* 5 (Spring–Fall 1974): 38–39; Richard del Castillo, "Myth and Reality: Chicano Economic Mobility in Los Angeles, 1850–1880," *Atzlán* 6 (Summer 1975): 153–54; McWilliams, *North from Mexico*, pp. 127–28; Gamio, *Mexican Immigration to the United States*, pp. 39–40; Charles Wollenberg, "Huelga, 1928 Style: The Imperial Valley Canteloupe Workers' Strike," in *Chicano*, ed. Rosaldo, Calvert, and Seligmann, pp. 185–88; Amott and Matthaei, *Race, Gender, and Work*, pp. 76–77.

45. Samora, *Los Mojados*, p. 130; Grebler, Moore, and Guzmán, *The Mexican-American People*, p. 91.

46. McWilliams, *North from Mexico*, pp. 193, 220; Grebler, Moore, and Guzmán, *The Mexican-American People*, p. 526; Amott and Matthaei, *Race, Gender, and Work*, p. 77.

47. Ruth H. Tuck, *Not with the Fist* (New York: Harcourt, Brace, & World, 1946), pp. 173–83.

48. McWilliams, *North from Mexico*, pp. 217–18; U.S. Commission on Civil Rights, *Mexican American Education Study*, vol. 1, *Ethnic Isolation of Mexican Americans in the Public Schools of the Southwest* (Washington, 1971), p. 11.

49. Anne Brunton, "The Chicano Migrants," in *Introduction to Chicano Studies*, ed. Duran and Bernard, pp. 489–92.

50. Jesus Luna, "Luna's Abe Lincoln Story," in *Chicano*, ed. Rosaldo, Calvert, and Selgmann, p. 348.

51. Roberto Suro, "Border Boom's Dirty Residue Imperils U.S.–Mexico Trade," *New York Times*, March 31, 1991, p. 1; Patrick McDonnell, "Foreign-Owned Companies Add to Mexico's Pollution," *Los Angeles Times*, November 18, 1991, p. A1; Richard W. Stevenson, "Economic Scene: The Hidden Costs of Mexico Plants," *New York Times*, July 19, 1991, p. D2; Judy Pasternak, "Firms Find a Haven from U.S. Environmental Rules," *Los Angeles Times*, November 19, 1991, p. A1; Patrick McDonnell, "Mexico: Progress and Promise," *Los Angeles Times*, October 22, 1991, p. 11.

52. The *Los Angeles Times* story is quoted in Mario Barrera, *Race and Class in the Southwest* (Notre Dame, Ind.: University of Notre Dame Press, 1979), p. 124. See also *Report of the Select Commission on Western Hemisphere Immigration* (Washington, 1968), p. 120.

53. Jim Doyle, "Court Curbs 'English-Only' Company Rules," *San Francisco Chronicle*, October 5, 1991, p. A12; Juan Perea, "English-Only Rules and the Right to Speak One's Primary Language in the Workplace," *University of Michigan Journal of Law Reform* 23, no. 2 (Winter 1990): 265–318.

54. 618 F.2d 264 (5th Cir. 1980), *cert. denied*, 449 U.S. 1113 (1981).

55. *Gutierrez* v. *Municipal Court*, 838 F.2d at 1039.

56. *Gutierrez* v. *Municipal Court*, 838 F.2d at 1040, quoted in Perea, "English-Only Rules," pp. 271–72.

57. *Gutierrez* v. *Municipal Court*, 838 F.2d 1031, *vacated as moot*, 109 S. Ct. 1736 (1989).

58. *Garcia* v. *Spun Steak Co.*, DC NCalif, No. C91-1949 RHS, October 14, 1991; Doyle, "Court Curbs 'English-Only' Company Rules."

59. U.S. Bureau of the Census, *The Hispanic Population in the United States: March 1990* (Washington, 1990), p. 8; Bureau of Labor Statistics, *Monthly Labor Review*, May 1991, pp. 63–64.

60. U.S. Bureau of the Census, *The Hispanic Population in the United States*, pp. 8–9, 14–15; U.S. Bureau of the Census, *Statistical Abstract of the United States* (Washington, 1991), p. 386.

61. Strategy Research Corporation, *1991 U.S. Hispanic Market*, p. 132.

62. U.S. Bureau of the Census, "Measuring the Effect of Benefits and Taxes on Income and Poverty: 1989," *Current Population Reports*, series P-60, no. 169-RD, pp. 8–9, 14; U.S. Bureau of the Census, *The Hispanic Population in the United States*, pp. 8, 10, 12.

63. Maril, *Poorest of Americans*, pp. 1–4.

64. Edward E. Telles and Edward Múrguía, "Phenotypic Discrimination and Income Differences among Mexican Americans," *Social Science Quarterly* 71, no. 4 (December 1990): 682–96.

65. Moore, *Mexican Americans*, p. 33.

66. Robert R. Brischetto, "Electoral Empowerment: The Case for Tejanos" (typescript, Southwest Voter Research Institute, San Antonio, 1987); Juan Gómez-Quiñones, *Chicano Politics: Reality and Promise, 1940–1990* (Albuquerque: University of New Mexico Press, 1990), p. 173.

67. The data on Mexican American officials in this and the following paragraph come from Gómez-Quiñones, *Chicano Politics*, pp. 167–69, 173; National Association of Latino Elected and Appointed Officials, *National Report* 11, no. 1 (Fourth Quarter 1991): 1, 3; and personal communications with Rodolfo de la Garza and Robert Brischetto.

68. Southwest Voter Registration Project, *The Hispanic Electorates* (San Antonio: Hispanic Policy Development Project, 1984), pp. 145–49; Robert R. Brischetto, "Chicano Voting and Views in the 1986 Elections" (typescript, Southwest Voter Research Institute, San Antonio, 1987); U.S. Commission on Civil Rights, *Ethnic Isolation of Mexican Americans in the Public Schools of the Southwest*, p. 55; Gómez-Quiñones, *Chicano Politics*, p. 163.

69. U.S. Commission on Civil Rights, *Mexican Americans and the Administration of Justice in the Southwest*, pp. 79–86.

70. Ibid., pp. 66–69.

71. Eric Lichtblau, "High Court Won't Hear Harvard Scholar's Plea," *Los Angeles Times*, November 14, 1991, p. B6.

72. *Hernandez* v. *New York*, 1991, 111 S. Ct. 1859; Amy Wallace, "Latinos Slighted on Grand Juries, Judge Decrees," *Los Angeles Times*, October 10, 1991, p. B1.

73. Michael V. Miller and James D. Preston, "Vertical Ties and the Redistribution of Power in Crystal City," *Social Science Quarterly* 53 (March 1973): 772–82; John S. Shockley, *Chicano Revolt in a Texas Town* (Notre Dame, Ind.: University of Notre Dame Press, 1974), pp. 28–148, 162–77.

74. Maril, *Poorest of Americans*, p. 52.

75. Armando Gutiérrez and Herbert Hirsch, "The Militant Challenge to the American Ethos: 'Chicanos' and the 'Mexican Americans,'" *Social Science Quarterly* 53 (March 1973): 844–45; Carlos Muñoz, Jr., *Youth, Identity, Power: The Chicano Movement* (New York: Verso, 1989); Ignacio M. Garcia, *United We Win* (Tuscon: University of Arizona Press, 1989), pp. 228–31.

76. Marta Cotera, "Feminism, the Chicana and Anglo Versions," in *Twice a Minority*, ed. by Margarita B. Melville (St. Louis: C.V. Mosby, 1980), p. 231.

77. Amott and Matthaei, *Race, Gender, and Work*, pp. 83–84; Cotera, "Feminism", pp. 213–33.

78. Robert R. Brischetto, *The Mexican American Electorate: Political Opinions and Behavior across Cultures in San Antonio*, Occasional Paper No. 5, Southwest Voter Registration Education Project and the Center for Mexican American Studies at the University of Texas (San Antonio and Austin, 1985).

79. McWilliams, *North from Mexico*, pp. 191–93; Grebler, Moore, and Guzmán, *The Mexican-American People*, pp. 91–92.

80. Stoddard, *Mexican Americans*, p. 180; Gamio, *Mexican Immigration to the United States*, pp. 135–38.

81. Grebler, Moore, and Guzmán, *The Mexican-American People*, pp. 543–45; Stoddard, *Mexican Americans*, p. 188; Moore, *Mexican Americans*, p. 152.

82. U.S. Commission on Civil Rights, *Mexican Americans and the Administration of Justice in the Southwest*, pp. 15–17; Rees Lloyd and Peter Montague, "Ford and La Raza: 'They Stole Our Land and Gave Us Powdered Milk,'" in *Introduction to Chicano Studies*, ed. Duran and Bernard, pp. 376–78; Frances L. Swadesh, "The Alianza Movement: Catalyst for Social Change in New Mexico," in *Chicano*, ed. Rosaldo, Calvert, and Seligmann, pp. 270–74.

83. Robert Pear, "U.S. Sues Houston to Block Election," *New York Times*, October 22, 1991, p. A16; William Grady and Thomas Hardy, "Court Orders New Remap," *Chicago Tribune*, December 14, 1991, p. 1; Kenneth Weiss, "Latinos to Challenge Court Plan," *Los Angeles Times*, December 17, 1991, p. B1.

84. Mary Pardo, "Mexican American Women Grassroots Community Activists: 'Mothers of East Los Angeles,'" *Frontiers* 9, no. 1 (1990): 4.

85. Jacques E. Levy, *César Chávez* (New York: W. W. Norton & Co., Inc., 1975), pp. 182–201; Peter Matthiessen, *Sal Si Puedes* (New York: Delta Books, 1969), pp. 59–216; John G. Dunne, *Delano* (New York: Farrar, Straus & Giroux, 1967), pp. 110–67.

86. Shockley, *Chicano Revolt in a Texas Town*, pp. 216–17.

87. Levy, *César Chávez*, pp. 495, 522–35.

88. J. Craig Jenkins, *The Politics of Insurgency* (New York: Columbia University Press, 1985), pp. x–xi; Robert Reinhold, "Environmental Agency Moves to End Most Uses of Deadly Agricultural Pesticide," *New York Times*, September 6, 1991, p. A17.

89. Gómez-Quiñones, *Chicano Politics*, p. 167; Muñoz, *Youth, Identity, Power*, p. 177.

90. Thomas P. Carter, *Mexican Americans in School* (New York: College Entrance Examination Board, 1970), pp. 204–5.

91. George I. Sánchez, "History, Culture, and Education," in *La Raza*, ed. Julian Samora (Notre Dame, Ind.: University of Notre Dame Press, 1966), pp. 1–26; Paul Taylor, *An American-Mexican Frontier* (Chapel Hill: University of North Carolina Press, 1934), pp. 196–204.

92. Carter, *Mexican Americans in School*, pp. 97–102; Thomas P. Carter, "The Negative Self-concept of Mexican-American Students," *School and Society* 96 (March 30, 1968): 217–20.

93. Jane Mercer, *Labelling the Mentally Retarded* (Berkeley: University of California Press, 1973), pp. 96–189; U.S. Commission on Civil Rights, *Mexican American Education Study*, vol. 6, *Toward Quality Education for Mexican Americans* (Washington, 1974), pp. 21–22.

94. Juan F. Perea, "Demography and Distrust: An Essay on American Languages, Cultural Pluralism, and Official English" *Minnesota Law Review* 77 (forthcoming, 1992).

95. Ibid.

96. Kenji Hakuta and Eugene E. Garcia, "Bilingualism and Education," *American Psychologist* 44 (February 1989): 374–79; Dick Kirschten, "Speaking English," *National Review*, June 17, 1989: 1556–61; Manuel Ramirez and Alfredo Castaneda, *Cultural Democracy, Bicognitive Development, and Education* (New York: Academic Press, 1974); U.S. Commission on Civil Rights, *Toward Quality Education for Mexican Americans*, pp. 6–8.

97. National Commission for Employment Policy, *Hispanics and Jobs: Barriers to Progress* (Washington, 1982), pp. 60–62, 81–82; U.S. Bureau of the Census, *U.S. Census of Population, 1980: General Social and Economic Characteristics*, PC 80-1-C1 (Washington, 1983), p. 163.

98. U.S. Bureau of the Census, "The Hispanic Population in the United States, pp. 6–7.

99. Barbara Kantrowitz with Lourdes Rosado, "Falling Further Behind," *Newsweek*, August 19, 1991, p. 60; Maril, *Poorest of Americans*, pp. 117–18.

100. The following discussion of research by Harriett Romo and Toni Falbo is based on personal correspondence with Romo in 1991 and a summary of Romo and Falbo's research findings prepared for inclusion in the Women's Studies newsletter at the University of Texas, Austin.

101. Catherine Walsh, *Pedagogy and the Struggle for Voice* (New York: Bergin and Garvey, 1991), pp. 95–113. quotation on p. 112.

102. Moore, *Mexican Americans*, pp. 67–69; Carter, *Mexican Americans in Schools*, pp. 30–31; National Commission for Employment Policy, *Hispanics and Jobs*, p. 11.

103. Edward H. Spicer, *Cycle of Conquest* (Tucson: University of Arizona Press, 1962), pp. 285–365; Patrick H. McNamara, "Bishops, Priests, and Prophecy: A Study in the Sociology of Religious Protest" (Ph.D. dissertation, UCLA, 1968).

104. Moore, *Mexican Americans*, pp. 88–89.

105. Ibid., p. 91; Stoddard, *Mexican Americans*, p. 93; Grebler, Moore, and Guzmán, *The Mexican-American People*, pp. 459–60; Gómez-Quiñones, *Chicano Politics*, p. 179.

106. Grebler, Moore, and Guzmán, *The Mexican-American People,* pp. 436–39, 473–77; Tuck, *Not with the Fist,* pp. 152–54. See also Jane M. Christian and Chester C. Christian, "Spanish Language and Loyalty in the Southwest," in *Language Loyalty in the United States,* ed. Joshua A. Fishman (London: Mouton & Co., 1966), pp. 296–97.
107. Jill Leovy, "More Hispanics Hear Call of Witnesses," *The Seattle Times,* March 25, 1991, p. E1.
108. Jorge Casuso and Michael Hirsley, "Troubled Hispanics Find Haven within Strict Pentecostal Rules," *Chicago Tribune,* June 8, 1990, p. C1.
109. Tuck, *Not with the Fist;* Sanchez, *Forgotten People;* Madsen, *Mexican Americans of South Texas;* Grebler, Moore, and Guzmán, *The Mexican-American People.*
110. Edward Múrguía, *Assimilation, Colonialism, and the Mexican American People* (Austin: University of Texas Press, 1975), pp. 4–5.
111. Rodolfo Alvarez, "The Unique Psycho-historical Experience of the Mexican-American People," *Social Science Quarterly* 52 (June 1971): 15–29; Stoddard, *Mexican Americans,* p. 103; Benjamin S. Bradshaw and Frank Bean, "Trends in the Fertility of Mexican Americans, 1950–1970," *Social Science Quarterly* 53 (March 1973): 696–97.
112. Strategy Research Corporation, *1991 U.S. Hispanic Market,* pp. 107–108.
113. Ibid., pp. 111–15.
114. Edward Múrguía, *Chicano Intermarriage: A Theoretical and Empirical Study* (San Antonio: Trinity University Press, 1982), pp. 45–51; U.S. Department of Health, Education and Welfare, *Americans of Spanish Origin* (Washington, 1984), p. 46.
115. Nathan Glazer, "The Political Distinctiveness of the Mexican Americans," in *Mexican-Americans in Comparative Perspective,* ed. Walter Connor (Washington: Urban Institute, 1985), pp. 212–16.
116. Walter Connor, "Who Are the Mexican Americans? A Note on Comparability," in *Mexican-Americans in Comparative Perspective,* ed. Connor, pp. 4–28.
117. Grebler, Moore, and Guzmán, *The Mexican-American People,* pp. 385, 558; "Maintaining a Group Culture," Institute for Survey Research Newsletter, n.d., p. 8.
118. Múrguía, *Assimilation, Colonialism, and the Mexican American People,* p. 112.
119. Strategy Research Corporation, *1991 U.S. Hispanic Market,* pp. 109–20. SRC's survey reported specific measures of assimilation by region; the majority of Latinos in the Southwest, West, and Central regions are Mexican American (89 percent, 72 percent, and 61 percent, respectively). In this survey, the Southwest region consisted of Texas, New Mexico, and Arizona; California and Colorado accounted for 93 percent of the Latinos in the eleven-state West region; 52 percent of the Latinos in the fourteen-state Central region resided in Illinois.
120. Ibid., pp. 78–120; Jim Loretta, "Latin Population Pressure Mounts," *Inside Strategy* 3, no. 2 (September 1990): 2.
121. Strategy Research Corporation, *1991 U.S. Hispanic Market,* pp. 80–94.
122. Rodolfo O. de la Garza, Nestor Rodríguez, and Harry Pachon, "The Domestic and Foreign Policy Consequences of Mexican and Central American Immigration: Mexican-American Perspectives," in *Immigration and International Relations,* ed. Georges Vernes (Santa Monica, Calif.: Rand Corporation, 1990), pp. 135–47.
123. Acuña, *Occupied America,* p. 3.
124. Alvarez, "Psycho-historical and Socioeconomic Development," pp. 928–30.
125. Múrguía, *Assimilation, Colonialism, and the Mexican American People,* pp. 8–9.
126. Barrera, *Race and Class in the Southwest,* p. 213.
127. Flores, "Race and Culture in the Internal Colony," p. 194.
128. Chandler Davidson and Charles M. Gaitz, "Ethnic Attitudes as a Basis for Minority Cooperation in a Southwestern Metropolis," *Social Science Quarterly* 53 (March 1973): 747–48.

Chapter 10

Puerto Rican
and Cuban Americans

Puerto Rican Day Parade
Photo by Marc Anderson, United Press International

Little Havana
Photo by Steve Kagan, Photos Researchers, Inc.

Two of the Spanish-speaking countries of the Antilles—Puerto Rico and Cuba—have been the points of origin for two of this nations's most important Latino groups. Once part of the Spanish empire, since 1960 Cuba has, in the words of Cuban American editor Enrique Fernandez, "oscillated between a corrupt democracy and dictatorships of both right and left, accompanied by a humiliating dependence on a superpower."[1] This political oscillation has generated important out-migrations that have contributed greatly to the development of vital Latino communities in the southeastern United States. Cuba has a heroic history of its own, replete with heroes such as Jose Martí, the nineteenth century poet and leader in the struggle for independence whose maxim for Cuba was "a nation…but no master." The struggle for independence continues to be an important theme in the present history of Cuban Americans.

Puerto Rico was also once part of the Spanish empire, but for nearly a century has been part of the U.S. empire. Today there is much debate over the political future of the island; different factions press for independence, for statehood, or for a continuation of the current commonwealth status. Unlike the Cuban case, political debates have been relatively unimportant to Puerto Rican out-migration; the migration to the U.S. mainland has been most significantly influenced by the economic pull of the U.S. economy, coupled with the ease of migration for these U.S. citizens. Many Puerto Ricans return regularly to the island nation that maintains a complex relationship to the United States. More prosperous than their Caribbean neighbors, island Puerto Ricans are still only "quasi-citizens of the United States. They can give their lives fighting for the country in U.S. forces, but they cannot vote in national elections. They have only observer status in the U.S. Congress, but they can migrate to the mainland freely."[2] Puerto Ricans are unique among Americans, since they are U.S. citizens whether they reside on the island or are migrants to mainland cities along the eastern seaboard. Today the number of expatriates and their descendants abroad is about 2.5 million, a number growing so fast that it may soon equal the island population of 3.5 million.

Both Cuban Americans and mainland Puerto Ricans today play a critical role in expanding and maintaining Latino culture in a multicultural United States. Both groups express a strong identification with their cultural traditions, and in spite of much internal discussion about return to the home islands, both groups are committed to carving out a permanent place on the U.S. mainland.

Puerto Ricans

FROM SPANISH TO U.S. RULE

Borinquén, the original native name for Puerto Rico, had a population of about 50,000 in 1493 when Spanish imperialism reached the island. Spain used the native people there (the Taino) as forced labor in mines and fields. Forced labor, disease, and violent suppression of rebellions caused a decline in the native population, so slaves were imported by the Spanish from Africa to fill the gap. The absence of women among the Spanish colonizers led to marriages between Spanish men and Native American or African women, producing a mixed-race population of significant size. The population included a growing number of free blacks, since Spanish law allowed slaves to purchase their freedom. By 1530 only 369 of Puerto Rico's 3,049 inhabitants were European-born Spaniards. During the nineteenth century immigrants and refugees from numerous countries, both European and Latin American, made their way to Puerto Rico. The census of 1827 found that the proportions of whites and people of color in Puerto Rico were almost equal. By the end of the century the island's population comprised thirty-four nationalities. Puerto Ricans today are a product of many racial and ethnic streams.[3]

In 1897 Puerto Ricans pressured the Spanish government into granting them internal autonomy, the right to negotiate their own trade agreements, and voting representation in the Spanish Congress. The following year, during the Spanish-American war, U.S. troops occupied the island. In the peace treaty that ended this brief war (1899) Spain gave Puerto Rico to the United States, whose leaders saw it as a useful station for warships and a profitable agricultural enclave. After four centuries of Spanish colonial rule, Puerto Rico came under U.S. control with no input from its local inhabitants, losing the autonomy so recently won from Spain.[4]

As a U.S. possession, Puerto Rico was headed by a governor from the mainland appointed by the U.S. president. Puerto Rican scholar Maldonado-Denis wrote the following description of Puerto Rico's governors during this period:

> The criterion used by the President of the United States to choose the colonial governor and his cabinet was, with very few exceptions, one of compensation for political favors received. Many of these men came to Puerto Rico without knowing the language or, at times, even the location of the island.... The same can be said of many of the bureaucrats sent to Puerto Rico in the colonial free-for-all: they were ignorant and prejudiced, with the feelings of superiority common to all colonizers.[5]

Acts of the locally elected legislature were subject to veto by the U.S. Congress, the president, or the governor, and English became the mandatory language in schools. In 1917 the Jones Act awarded U.S. citizenship to all Puerto Ricans. Islanders have long been divided over the character of their political ties to the United States, with the majority party (the Unionist party) favoring greater autonomy.[6]

In 1948 Puerto Ricans were permitted to elect their own governor, and in 1952 the Commonwealth of Puerto Rico, with its own constitution (approved by the U.S. Congress), was created. Considerable home rule was granted Puerto Ricans, including the right to elect their own officials, make their own civil and criminal codes, and run their own schools. In 1948 Spanish became the official language in schools, and the Puerto Rican flag was allowed to fly. However, these changes came about only with the permission of the United States, the colonial power that still oversees Puerto Rico. Puerto Ricans living in Puerto Rico have no vote in national elections and no senators or House members. Their only representation in the U.S. Congress is by a nonvoting commissioner.

When the United States took over Puerto Rico, much of the land was owned by small farmers who raised coffee, sugar, and foodstuffs. In 1899 Puerto Ricans owned 93 percent of the farms. Under U.S. control, heavy taxes and restrictions on credit forced many farmers to sell their land to U.S. companies. Independent farmers growing coffee were driven out by the U.S.-forced devaluation of the Puerto Rican peso and the closing of European markets that came with U.S. occupation. By 1930 large absentee-owned companies controlled 60 percent of sugar production and monopolized tobacco production and the shipping lines. By 1952 sugar production dominated the island's economy. The island moved from a locally controlled, diversified economy to one dominated by sugar and under external control. Many peasant farmers and their families were forced to seek jobs with the absentee-owned sugar companies. Puerto Ricans thus became low-wage labor for international corporations, and in the slack employment seasons thousands endured terrible poverty.[7]

Until the 1930s Puerto Rico was ruled as an agricultural colony under various U.S. decrees that determined life on the island, from currency exchange to the amount of land a person could own. When 1930s (New Deal) reforms came to Puerto Rico, U.S. governor Rexford Tugwell envisioned a program for the island that would include agricultural and industrial development.

After World War II, agricultural development was forgotten, and in the late 1940s a program called Operation Bootstrap, designed by Puerto Rican governor Luis Muñoz Marín to bring about economic development by attracting U.S. industrial corporations to the island, was implemented. Lured by a ten-year exemption from local taxation as well as by lower wages than on the mainland,* some 1,700 factories had come to the island by 1975, creating more than 140,000 new manufacturing jobs and bringing a boom in the construction industry. Real annual per capita income increased almost sevenfold during this twenty-five-year period, and Puerto Rico's gross domestic product tripled between 1950 and 1970. Capital investments grew to $1.4 billion in 1960 and to $24 billion in 1979. However, the tax exemptions for most of these new industries left the burden of financing the infrastructure (sewers, water, electricity) on the local population, resulting in a high personal income tax rate. Operation Bootstrap's emphasis on urban industry and neglect of agriculture tilted the island farther away from its heritage of locally owned farms. Loss of agricultural land to industrial development even forced the island to import food. In addition, the number of agricultural jobs lost was never offset by the number of manufacturing and related jobs created.

By the 1970s massive unemployment had led approximately one-third of the island's population to migrate to the mainland; since then the island's official unemployment rate has remained at least as high as 10 percent. The return of many Puerto Ricans to the island from the mainland during the mid-1970s caused even greater unemployment. In recent years recessions have brought cutbacks in Puerto Rico's petrochemical plants, increasing unemployment rates and federal payments for unemployment compensation, welfare, and food stamps. Numerous industries have left the island, some looking for cheaper labor and tax exemptions elsewhere. One Puerto Rican immigrant testified at a U.S. Commission on Civil Rights hearing that he came to the mainland because the company he worked for had used up its fifteen-year exemption from taxes, and its executives had decided to move from the island rather than pay taxes. The official unemployment rate peaked at 23 percent in 1983 and stood at almost 15 percent (17 percent for males and 11 percent for females) at the end of the decade. Some analysts have estimated the real unemployment rate to be 40 percent or higher.[8]

---

*In this chapter the term *mainland* refers to the fifty states as distinct from the U.S. territory of Puerto Rico.

MIGRATION TO THE MAINLAND

Migration Streams

The number of Puerto Ricans in the United States before the island became a U.S. possession was small and consisted largely of prosperous merchants, political activists, and tobacco workers. Some 2,000 Puerto Ricans lived on the mainland in 1900, most in New York City. Significant immigration to the mainland in response to unemployment and poverty on the island began in the late 1920s, and a somewhat smaller group came in the late 1930s. By 1940 mainland Puerto Ricans numbered almost 70,000; most continued to reside in various parts of New York City. Over the next two decades the number increased more than tenfold, to 887,000, causing this period to be called the "great migration." Between 1945 and 1970 about one in three Puerto Ricans left the island. Thousands were farm workers, forced out of work by the aforementioned changes in agriculture. Increasingly Puerto Rican communities were established in New Jersey, Connecticut, and Chicago, although the majority of new immigrants continued to settle in New York.[9]

Many a tourist who has seen Puerto Rico has probably asked, "Why would anyone want to leave such a beautiful island?" Piri Thomas answers succinctly: "Bread, money, gold, a peso to make a living.... Diggit, wasn't that the greatest reason all the other different ethnic groups came to America for, freedom from want?"[10] Another Puerto Rican writer, Jack Agueros, describes the impact of the surge of new immigration on established Puerto Rican communities on the mainland:

> [World War II] ended and the heavy Puerto Rican migration began.... Into an ancient neighborhood came pouring four to five times more people than it had been designed to hold. Men who came running at the promise of jobs were jobless as the war ended. They were confused. They could not see the economic forces that ruled their lives as they drank beer on the corners, reassuring themselves of good times to come while they were hell-bent toward alcoholism. The sudden surge in numbers caused new resentments, and prejudice was intensified. Some were forced to live in cellars, and were then characterized as cave dwellers. Kids came who were confused by the new surroundings; their Puerto Ricanness forced us against a mirror asking, "If they are Puerto Ricans, what are we?" and thus they confused us. In our confusion we were sometimes pathetically reaching out, sometimes pathologically striking out.... Education collapsed. Every classroom had ten kids who spoke no English.[11]

The relationship between the migration of Puerto Ricans to the mainland and the island's political and economic ties to the United States made possible a variety of favorable investment and trade arrangements, ultimately displacing large numbers of workers on the island and creating the need for mass emigration.[12] The Puerto Rican government encouraged migration as a safety valve to reduce the pressures of unemployment. Pull factors were also important. Many came to the mainland as contract laborers. Puerto Rican workers brought to southern New Jersey farms in the mid-1940s were

> flown up here to a strange land, in the dark of the night, and by morning some are in the farmers' fields ready to work. There is no time for any sort of adjustment. The Puerto Rican is plunged into a strange environment with not even the advantage of a common language among these strangers.[13]

Beginning in the mid-1940s corporations sent recruiters to Puerto Rico seeking cheap labor for the booming postwar economy. Workers came to textile sweatshops in New York, steel mills in Pennsylvania, Ohio, and Indiana, foundries in Wisconsin and Illinois, and electronics industries in Illinois. Many of these immigrants hoped to earn money on the mainland and then return to the island. But for the large majority marginal employment or chronic unemployment gave them little choice but to become permanent residents of mainland urban areas. Puerto Ricans who came to work in coal mines in Dover, New Jersey, in the mid-1940s stayed to work in factories in that area. Farm workers in the Philadelphia area later worked in construction industries.[14]

The decades since 1970 have been called the period of circulating, or "revolving-door," migration. During this time many Puerto Ricans fleeing declining industrialization on the island have arrived in U.S. cities that are plagued with unemployment. A series of recessions along with deteriorating neighborhoods and living conditions on the mainland combined with love for the island, family ties there, and the desire to nurture their children in Puerto Rican culture have prompted many Puerto Ricans each year to return to the island. Often these same people come back to the mainland after a time because of lower wages and poor working conditions on the island. In the early 1990s manufacturing wages on the island were only 54 percent of those on the mainland, and Puerto Rico's per capita income was half that of the poorest U.S. state. For many who came to the mainland to work, intending to accumulate enough money to start a business and begin a new life on the island, the cycle of migration and return became a pattern. Each return to the island was accompanied by the hope of success, although few have achieved that success. In recent years the number of well-educated Puerto Ricans coming to the mainland has increased because of the absence of jobs on the island. By the early 1990s some 45 percent of all Puerto Ricans, more than 2.7 million people, resided in mainland communities in virtually every state, a 35 percent increase over the 1980 census count. Puerto Ricans now make up more than 12 percent of all Latinos on the mainland.[15]

STEREOTYPING

Puerto Ricans have been stereotyped in ways similar to Mexican Americans and African Americans. The first Euro-American stereotypes were probably developed by U.S. military officials and colonial administrators. In the 1890s, for example, a U.S. captain noted that "the people seem willing to work, even at starvation wages, and they seem to be docile and grateful for anything done for them. They are emotional."[16]

Images of lazy, submissive Puerto Ricans persist, particularly among Anglo officials who deal with Puerto Rican clients. Euro-American teachers have held images of Puerto Ricans as lazy and immoral. Lopez reports being at a college meeting in New York where an experienced teacher from a poor school spoke on instilling the "middle-class values" of thrift, morality, and motivation in the children. Lopez asked the teacher about her image of Puerto Rican children:

> It was when I asked what morality was and where it was practiced among middle-class people or what motivation was lacking in our people and how she discovered this, or finally, how the hell a person could be thrifty on eighty-four dollars a week, that she began to do some thinking.[17]

Often referred to by the derogatory term *spic,* Puerto Ricans have been viewed, as were the Italians and Mexican Americans before them, as a criminal lot. An Aspen Institute conference report noted that the English-language news media exaggerate certain aspects of Puerto Rican and Mexican American life—poverty, gang violence, and illegal immigrants. Crimes by Puerto Ricans have been sensationalized in the New York City newspapers and other mass media; this has helped foster the image of Puerto Ricans as criminals. J. Edgar Hoover, a former director of the FBI, promulgated this perverse stereotype:

> We cooperate with the Secret Service on presidential trips abroad. You *never* have to bother about a President being shot by Puerto Ricans or Mexicans. They don't shoot very straight. But if they come at you with a knife, beware.[18]

Hoover's crude stereotype of Latino Americans as dumb-but-sinister knife carriers is still common in the United States.

In the 1950s, when large numbers of migrants began coming to the mainland, the Puerto Rican government circulated pamphlets trying to prepare migrants for prejudice they were likely to face. One read as follows:

> If one Puerto Rican steals, Americans who are prejudiced say that all Puerto Ricans are thieves. If one Puerto Rican doesn't work, prejudiced Americans say all of us are lazy.... We pay, because a bad opinion of us is formed, and the result may be that they discredit us, they won't give us work, or they deny us our rights.[19]

This pamphlet recognized the ways in which Euro-Americans unfairly generalize, and it clearly implied that negative stereotypes are translated into discrimination against Puerto Ricans looking for jobs. A majority of Puerto Ricans interviewed in a recent New York City survey felt that Puerto Ricans were discriminated against by non–Puerto Ricans on the mainland.[20]

Stereotypes of Puerto Rico and Puerto Ricans have been circulated by social scientists as well. For example, Nathan Glazer and Daniel Moynihan argued in their famous 1963 book *Beyond the Melting Pot* that Puerto Rican society was "sadly defective" in its culture and family system. They characterized Puerto Rican families as weak and disorganized. Glazer and Moynihan suggested that this allegedly weak family structure was the reason Puerto Ricans on the mainland did not move into better-paying jobs.[21]

Stereotypes of Puerto Ricans as drug users and criminals influence police actions in Puerto Rican communities, which are often more closely patrolled than nonminority areas. In the words of one Puerto Rican rights activist, "There is this idea that young Hispanics are all drug abusers who come here to terrorize people." However, a recent survey in New York State found that Latino teenagers actually use drugs less often than white teenagers do.[22]

Color Coding and Euro-American Prejudice

As with other non-European groups, racial prejudices and stereotyping are reflected in Euro-American discrimination against Puerto Ricans and have a negative impact on their self-images. To understand the Puerto Rican experience on the mainland we must first look at the situation in Puerto Rico, for, although prejudice and discrimination exist on the island, there is a considerable difference between the two areas. Cultural identification supersedes racial identification on the island; the opposite is true on the mainland. On the island, Puerto Ricans are first Puerto Ricans; further classifications are based on physical appearance and social definitions. On the mainland, individuals are first white or black, and this distinction is based mainly on physical appearance. The phenomenon of "passing" on the mainland, in which a light-skinned individual hides his or her African ancestry in order to pass for white, is not necessary in Puerto Rican society. A second major difference is the larger spectrum of racial categories, based on multiple physical characteristics and not just skin color, that are used in Puerto Rico. In contrast, only two classifications, black and white, are used on the mainland. Puerto Rican society is also much more racially integrated. A Puerto Rican family's members may represent a variety of colors. An individual's treatment in terms of housing, political rights, government policy, and other social institutions is usually not racially differentiated. Finally, Puerto Rican culture represents a synthesis of multiple and diverse elements whereas acculturation on the mainland is generally one-way, with minority groups adopting dominant-group cultural values rather than the reverse or a two-way sharing.[23]

Americans of European descent tend to see Puerto Ricans as a nonwhite group, lumping them with black Americans or Mexican Americans. Until they come to the mainland, most Puerto Ricans have seldom had to deal with overt color-based discrimination. Racial discrimination on the mainland comes as a shock to most immigrants. Recalling an experience in high school when a girl whom he had asked to dance turned him down, Piri Thomas writes about his confusion and anger at whites' denial of his identity as a Puerto Rican:

> "Who?" someone asked.
> "That new colored boy."...
> I couldn't see them, but I had that for-sure feeling that it was me they had in their mouths....
> "Listen, Angelo. Jus' listen," I said stonily....
> "Do you mean just like that?"...
> "Ahuh," Marcia said. "Just as if I was a black girl. *Well!* He started to talk to me and what could I do except be polite and at the same time not encourage him?"
> "Christ, first that Jerry bastard and now him. We're getting invaded by niggers."[24]

The imposition of discrete mainland categories of black and white on Puerto Ricans, whose home culture sees racial diversity on a continuum, creates confusion and anger whether the individual is called "black" or "white." The denial of personal identity inherent in such a racial identification is the issue. Statements such as "You don't look Puerto Rican," or "Are you 100 percent Puerto Rican?" commonly confront Puerto Ricans on the mainland. Faced with the task of categorizing Puerto Rican school children as either "Negro" or "Caucasian" in 1954, New York State officials were aware of the invidious divisions that would arise if Puerto Rican families were asked to divide their children. The officials proposed abandoning the racial terms and listing these children simply as Puerto Rican even though this would imply that Puerto Ricans were a distinct racial category.[25]

Martínez found a substantial difference in the self-perception of Puerto Ricans and how they thought North Americans perceived them:[26]

| | **Racial Perceptions** | | | |
	White	Tan	Black	Total
Self-perception	33%	60%	7%	100%
North American perception	58%	−0−	42%	100%

Notice that the majority bypassed the standard U.S. categories of "black" or "white," classifying themselves instead as "tan."

The 1980 census was the first to ask every individual whether he or she was Hispanic; it included subcategories for Mexicans, Puerto Ricans, Cubans, and other Hispanic persons. A separate item asked for the race of each individual. Fewer than 4 percent of the Puerto Ricans from the New York City area stated their race as black; 44 percent classified themselves as white. Almost 48 percent wrote in "Spanish" in the space labeled "Other—Specify," indicating, among other things, the conflict between the polarized U.S. racial structure and the cultural–racial continuum with which Puerto Ricans identify.[27]

ECONOMIC AND RELATED CONDITIONS: THE MAINLAND

Writing about his experiences as an early immigrant Jesús Colon explains that Puerto Ricans did the dirty work of the society and poverty was usually their lot. Jesús and his brother worked different hours, and to save money they even shared their working clothes: "we only had one pair of working pants between the two of us."[28]

Discrimination in employment was common for Puerto Rican immigrants; those with darker skin usually suffered the most. Piri Thomas, a Puerto Rican who grew up in Spanish Harlem (*El Barrio*) and eventually became well known as the author of *Down These Mean Streets,* recounts a 1945 interview for a job as a door-to-door salesperson. He was not hired; a lighter-skinned friend was. Dark-skinned Puerto Ricans, he discovered by asking other applicants, were discriminated against by the white employer:

> "Let's walk," I said. I didn't feel so much angry as I did sick, like throwing-up sick. Later, when I told this story to my buddy, a colored cat, he said, "Hell, Piri, Ah know stuff like that can sure burn a cat up, but a Negro faces that all the time."
> "I know that," I said, "but I wasn't a Negro then. I was still only a Puerto Rican."[29]

Occupation and Unemployment

Puerto Rican immigrants have brought with them a wide spectrum of skills. Some are artists and musicians; others are skilled in wood, leather, or cement crafts. Some operated their own business on the island; others held positions of responsibility in the educational, medical, legal, or political systems. On the mainland, however, the skills of many immigrants have gone largely unnoticed and unused. Regardless of their background, Puerto Ricans have been offered few choices for employment. Mainland Puerto

Ricans have often done the dirty work for Euro-Americans. Many have been forced to take low-level jobs in factories or restaurants in New York City. They have cleaned up as busboys and janitors; they have worked in garment industry sweatshops that paid low wages; they have driven taxis. And many have faced recurring unemployment.[30]

The occupational distribution for employed Puerto Ricans on the mainland from 1950 through 1979 can be seen in the following data:[31]

	MEN			WOMEN		
	1950	**1970**	**1979**	**1950**	**1970**	**1979**
Professional, technical	5.3%	4.7%	8.2%	3.4%	7.2%	10.4%
Managers, administrators	5.4	4.2	4.6	1.2	1.6	4.2
Clerical and sales	9.6	14.9	12.2	11.0	34.1	42.0
Skilled blue-collar (crafts)	11.2	15.7	14.4	1.7	2.4	2.2
Operatives	33.0	33.5	28.1	72.5	39.7	23.4
Service workers	25.1	17.5	{19.5	6.5	12.5	{16.1
Domestic work	0.2	0.1		2.3	1.0	
Nonfarm laborers	7.3	8.0	10.1	1.0	1.1	0.8
Farmers, farm workers	2.9	1.5	3.0	0.4	0.4	0.9

From 1950 through 1979, male workers were concentrated in the blue-collar sector, especially in lower-paying jobs as laborers, service workers (e.g., busboys), and assembly-line workers (operatives). A major shift of Puerto Rican women into the clerical and sales fields, particularly as lower-level typists, retail sales clerks, and keypunch operators can be seen over the 1970s.

Puerto Ricans were hit hard in the late 1960s and the 1970s by a decline in New York City's clothing industry that increased unemployment for apparel workers. Many men moved into service jobs as dishwashers, orderlies, janitors, and recreational facility attendants. Women moved into service jobs or became file clerks, typists, cashiers, and teacher aides. Puerto Ricans in professional and other white-collar jobs tend to occupy the lower-paid positions, such as teacher, librarian, or health or recreational professional. In many East Coast areas Puerto Rican laborers have done much of the low-paid field work that has put vegetables on U.S. tables. In the late 1970s, for example, 15,000 Puerto Rican farm workers in Vineland, New Jersey, were working for low wages, often seven days a week, and living in inhumane, barracks-like housing. Nearby farm workers were fired for attempting to organize to improve their working conditions. By the early 1990s Puerto Ricans were still much more likely to be employed as operatives, laborers, or service workers than the general population. Puerto Rican men were less than half as likely to hold managerial or professional positions as men in the general population (11.2 percent versus 26 percent) and more than twice as likely to be employed in service jobs (20.6 percent versus 9.8 percent).[32]

For mainland Puerto Ricans unemployment at all points has been much higher than that for white workers. Unemployment rates began to climb sharply in the mid 1970s: in 1976 over 16 percent of Puerto Rican men and 22 percent of women were unemployed. In 1986 the unemployment rate stood at 14 percent for all mainland Puerto Rican workers. Throughout the 1980s unemployment and subemployment rates for Puerto Rican men and women were among the highest of any racial and ethnic group in the northeastern cities. The 1990 unemployment rate for mainland Puerto Ricans was 9.1 percent compared with 4.7 percent for whites and 5.5 percent for the general population. Official rates are only the tip of the iceberg, for they reflect no more than half the actual number of Puerto Ricans who are either unemployed or subemployed. To find the total number of unemployed and subemployed we must add those who are discouraged from looking for work because of long-term unemployment, those who are working part-time but who want full-time work, and those who make very low wages.[33]

Employment Discrimination and Other Barriers

Institutionalized discrimination rooted in color coding and linguistic prejudice has restricted Puerto Rican access to many job categories, contributing both to the concentration of Puerto Ricans in low-level employment and to their high unemployment rates relative to other groups. In New York City, for example, Puerto Ricans have been severely underrepresented (relative to their percentage of the population) in local and state government jobs. This is at least in part because they are less integrated into the job information networks traditionally dominated by Euro-Americans. In many cases, Puerto Ricans are screened out of jobs by tests that are, unnecessarily, given only in English. Such a procedure is discriminatory when Puerto Rican applicants are capable of doing the jobs and the screening tests are not job-related. Even trash collection jobs, for example, have sometimes required screening tests, on which those who speak English and have a high school diploma score better. As with Mexican Americans, many Puerto Ricans find themselves unfairly stigmatized as being of "low intelligence" because of their limited command of English.[34]

Institutionalized discrimination can also be seen in height and weight requirements that use Euro-American males as the standard. Such requirements have sometimes disqualified Puerto Rican applicants for police and fire department jobs. Even Puerto Ricans' status as U.S. citizens has been a source of discriminatory treatment. Some have been asked by local government officials, apparently unaware that Puerto Rico is part of the United States, to prove that they as Puerto Ricans are U.S. citizens. For other jobs, citizenship status has proved to be a handicap. In a Civil Rights Commission interview a Puerto Rican woman in California said,

> I've had about six or seven jobs since I came here. What happens is that they hire you temporarily and get rid of you as soon as possible because you don't belong to the right race. I'd even say that bosses here prefer Mexicans (particularly illegals) because they know that unions don't represent them, so they can be exploited easier. At least Puerto Ricans have citizenship and can get into unions.[35]

Racial discrimination is a major factor in the employment possibilities of Puerto Ricans. Although fewer than one-tenth of Puerto Ricans classify themselves as of African ancestry or Afro-American, the majority of white Americans classify most Puerto Ricans as nonwhite and discriminate against them for the same reasons they discriminate against African Americans. Many unions, especially those representing skilled and craft workers, have excluded or restricted Puerto Ricans. Some less-skilled jobs, such as concrete laborer, have been controlled so that token numbers of blacks and Puerto Ricans are hired;

union, private, and governmental authorities have sometimes winked at these practices. "Unions did not facilitate the economic integration of Puerto Ricans as they had for other groups," writes Rodríguez; as a result "Puerto Rican pay rates and benefits were (and are) inferior to those of other workers doing the same jobs."[36]

Industrial Restructuring

A variety of changing structural factors in the U.S. economy have contributed to high unemployment rates for Puerto Ricans. Early Puerto Rican immigrants came to the mainland, especially to New York City, to fill manufacturing jobs, primarily in the garment industry. By the time of the 1946–64 migration the central cities of the United States, and especially New York City, had generally entered a period of industrial decline. As New York City moved from an industrial economy to a service-oriented economy, production jobs once open to Puerto Ricans began to disappear. Between 1960 and 1980 New York City lost some 441,000 manufacturing jobs, and this decline continued into the 1980s and 1990s. Because the availability of low-level service jobs did not keep pace with the decline in production jobs, Puerto Rican unemployment rates have remained high for decades.

Technological innovations—automation, computerization, and the use of robots—further eroded the number of low-skill blue-collar production jobs. In addition many plants moved to the suburbs, the South, or overseas, taking jobs out of the geographical reach of inner-city Puerto Ricans who did not qualify for most of the new white-collar jobs in the city. Lack of retraining and education for white-collar jobs leaves Puerto Rican and other minority workers in New York increasingly part of a large surplus labor force.[37]

In a recent discussion in the *New York Times* about the economic situation of Puerto Ricans, sociologist Marta Tienda and William Diaz, a program officer at the Ford Foundation, argued that the reasons for the sharp deterioration in the economic position of Puerto Ricans were primarily the decline of inner-city manufacturing in the northeastern cities and the continuing circular migration to Puerto Rico. The most important reason for the rising poverty and unemployment faced by Puerto Ricans between the late 1970s and the late 1980s was the "drastically reduced job opportunities in industrial Northeastern cities like New York, Newark, and Pittsburgh, as well as in Puerto Rico." In their view circular migration, the constant movement of Puerto Rican workers back and forth between Puerto Rico and the mainland in search of jobs, causes significant disruption to families and educational attainment. It exacerbates the fundamental economic problems created by economic dislocation, capital flight, and racial discrimination in northeastern cities. Robert Garcia, a member of Congress from New York, wrote a letter to the *Times* praising the accuracy of Tienda and Diaz's assessment of the social and economic problems of Puerto Ricans and pointing out that black Americans and Puerto Ricans in New York City face common problems of poverty and discrimination.[38]

Income and Poverty

Puerto Ricans are the poorest of U.S. minorities except for Native Americans. Between 1959 and 1974 Puerto Rican family incomes declined from 71 percent of the national average to only 59 percent. Puerto Ricans were the only minority group in the United States to see a decline in family incomes in the 1970s and 1980s. Strategy Research Corporation's random survey of 5,000 Latino households across the nation in 1991 estimated that the median income of mainland Puerto Rican households was $20,900, compared with $38,000 for the U.S. population as a whole. Puerto Ricans had the lowest median household income of any Latino group in the United States.[39] Poverty or near poverty was the lot of most families. Accounts of oppressive conditions are not unusual. Felipe Luciano describes life as a Puerto Rican:

> You resign yourself to poverty—my mother did this. Your face is rubbed in shit so much that you begin to accept that shit as reality...my stomach rumbling. My mother beating me when I knew it was because of my father...the welfare investigator cursing out my mother because what she wants is spring clothing for her children.[40]

"I'd rather starve than go on welfare" is a common and often stated sentiment among Puerto Ricans regardless of their poverty status. Jack Agueros wrote of his family's experience in New York City in the late 1930s. Here he quotes his mother:

> "Your father was furious when I mentioned home relief. He said he would rather starve than go on relief. But I went and filled out the papers and answered all the questions and swallowed my pride when they treated me like an intruder. I used to say to them, 'Find me a job—get my husband a better job—we don't want home relief.' But we had to take it."[41]

The economic situation became critical during the 1980s. The high level of poverty among Puerto Ricans at the beginning of the decade did not improve significantly over the 1980s. Median family income fell in real terms (adjusting for inflation) 18 percent between 1979 and 1984—more than the huge 14 percent drop for black Americans and the 9 percent decrease for Mexican Americans. In 1984 the median family income for Puerto Ricans was quite low; The per capita income for Puerto Rican workers was half that of whites. In 1990 median family income for Puerto Ricans was well below the national average; more than 30 percent fell below the federal poverty line. The desperate nature of Puerto Ricans' situation is evident in the substantial increase in the use of public assistance over the 1970s and 1980s for both couple-headed and single-parent families, especially significant in light of the hostility of most Puerto Ricans toward the welfare system. Some observers have reported resentment by Puerto Ricans toward those non-Latinos who have entered the middle class through jobs in social welfare bureaucracies and are seen as "living off our problems."[42]

Housing

Discrimination against Puerto Ricans is significant in the area of housing. A Rutgers University professor of law contended at a Civil Rights Commission hearing that Puerto Ricans have suffered more than black Americans from housing discrimination. Puerto Ricans have been excluded from most decent housing markets and get the "housing scraps" no one else wants. In the city of Lyons, New York, a large number of poor, predominantly Puerto Rican families were forced out of a residential area as part of a downtown renewal project. In Brooklyn the Puerto Rican Legal Defense and Educational Fund won a major court victory over housing discrimination in four housing developments where racial quotas limited the number of minority residents. In *Williamsburg Fair Housing Committee* v. *New York City Housing Authority* the court acknowledged housing discrimination against Puerto Ricans and provided for legal remedies that eliminated racial quotas.[43]

Compared with other groups, Puerto Ricans use a larger percentage of their income for housing and are more likely to live in dilapidated or deficient housing. In the early 1990s only approximately 28 percent of Puerto Rican households owned or were buying their own home, compared with about two-thirds of the total population. In Chicago in the early 1990s only 16 percent of Puerto Ricans lived in suburban areas; half lived in the inner city. As low-income renters most Puerto Ricans are vulnerable to the devastating impact of urban decay. Overcrowding and deteriorating housing are characteristic of many neighborhoods. The South Bronx, home to the largest and densest mainland Puerto Rican community, is a grim example. Once composed of stable communities, this area has been gutted by highway construction, redlined by bankers, and abandoned by government agencies. Since 1970 the South Bronx has lost much of its housing stock and population, with some neighborhoods showing as much as an 84 percent drop in population between 1970 and 1980. In addition to psychic stress and severed friendship and community ties, the decay of these urban neighborhoods has had a negative impact on education, resulted in the loss of jobs, and increased the distances residents must travel to shopping, services, and workplaces. Rodríguez describes the effects on residents of depopulation and commercial and industrial flight:

> Certain neighborhoods were swept with devastation, leaving local landscapes where one or two buildings were the lone survivors of an unabated process of destruction....
> It is difficult to convey the psychic despair that is felt by people who experience the daily loss of people and places that make up their world. One day there was a supermarket to shop at, the next day it is closed. Last week you had friends or relatives up the street, today they too are leaving. Your own home edges closer to the brink of decay as the buildings on the block empty. The continual reminders of surrounding decay multiply with each day.[44]

Discrimination is an omnipresent problem not only in housing but in most other areas as well. In a recent survey in New York City, 80 percent of Latinos (mostly Puerto Ricans) reported having been mistreated by the police. More than 70 percent also reported mistreatment by landlords, employers, shopkeepers, elected officials, the courts, and the schools. When asked a general question about the frequency and extent of discrimination against Latinos, a majority of the respondents felt there was substantial discrimination in all areas of life.[45]

EDUCATION

In the early 1990s one tenth of mainland Puerto Ricans twenty-five years old and over had completed less than five years of school. This was more than four times the percent for the total population at this low education level. Just over half of Puerto Ricans in the twenty-five-and-over age group had completed high school, compared with 78 percent of the total population. About 10 percent had completed college, less than half the figure for the total population.[46]

Puerto Rican students are less likely to complete high school than other groups. High dropout rates, or more accurately *pushout* rates, for Puerto Rican students are a nationwide problem, although significant variations can be found from one area to another. Dropout rates tend to be highest in central-city school districts. In spite of its very high position among the states in per-pupil expenditures and teacher salaries, New York ranks near the bottom in student retention. New York City has a particularly dismal record in educating Puerto Rican students, whose dropout rates there are higher than for any other group. Tracking the school population's ethnic composition by grade level shows a precipitous decline in Latino enrollment in New York City schools at the ninth grade. One 1983 study put the Puerto Rican dropout rate in New York City at 80 percent; a 1987 New York State study found a Latino dropout rate of 62 percent. Some observers have characterized the inferior educational opportunities of Puerto Rican youth as "premarket discrimination"—that is, discrimination that inhibits future success in the labor market.[47]

The low college graduation rate for Puerto Ricans on the mainland restricts upward mobility. The college or university setting is often an alien environment for Puerto Rican students. Morales-Nadal notes in particular the determination and struggles of Puerto Rican women, among the poorest of all minority groups, to get an education in order to secure a decent job. "It is not uncommon for some mothers to take their children with them to class in some public colleges." She concludes that within the context of higher education intercultural exchanges that respect and value the language, culture, and identity of Puerto Ricans are vital to the empowerment of Puerto Rican youth.[48]

At least since the great migration, Puerto Ricans have struggled against an educational system that has failed many of their children. Pressing first for studies to examine the problems, Puerto Rican communities have developed local organizations to work for change. When the findings and recommendations of numerous critical studies are ignored by school boards, Puerto Rican leaders and communities have sometimes turned to the courts. Yet the educational system has proved highly resistant even to court-mandated change, for school administrators' attention to the rights and needs of culturally different and limited-English-proficiency students has not been wholehearted.[49]

Barriers to Mobility

Few Puerto Ricans have moved into influential positions in the field of education, and Puerto Ricans have little control over the educational policies and curriculum decisions affecting their children. Euro-American school authorities frequently are insensitive to Puerto Rican history and culture; the standard curriculum is based on the assumption that Puerto Ricans are culturally and linguistically deficient. Much of the curriculum seems irrelevant to Puerto Rican students. Neglect of Puerto Rican history and culture by the schools contributes to a lack of self-esteem. The schools attended by most students have a high concentration of Puerto Rican and other minority students, yet both the actual number of Puerto Rican teachers and administrators and the ratio of Puerto Rican teachers and administrators to Puerto Rican students are extremely low. More than two-thirds of Latino (mostly Puerto Rican) children in New York City attend schools that are 30 percent or more Latino; at least ten districts there are between 50 percent and 80 percent Latino. One researcher found Latino students more likely than black students to be in predominantly minority classes, noting that the segregation of Latino schoolchildren has indeed increased since 1968. Segregated schooling has serious negative implications: low retention rates, a large majority of students who read below grade level, high teacher–student ratios, less-qualified teachers, and low teacher expectations. A strong correlation has been established between expectations and academic achievement. Students whose teachers expect them to achieve are much more likely to succeed.[50]

Language

As we noted in the chapter on Mexican Americans, most U.S. schools today are not structured to deal with students who do not speak English. Prior to the American Revolution, however, bilingual education (in such languages as German, for example) was common and continued to be available to many immigrants and their children in private, and sometimes publicly funded, schools in the eighteenth, nineteenth, and early twentieth centuries. It is only in the last half of the twentieth century that bilingual education has become highly politicized.

Limited English proficiency creates multiple handicaps for Puerto Rican students, as it does for other Latino groups. Children who are unable to understand English instruction fall behind native-English-speaking classmates. Puerto Rican students are sometimes assigned to low-ability groups, to "language-disabled" classes, or to lower grades. A number of New York and New Jersey studies have found racially identifiable tracking systems and placement of children in classes for the mentally retarded without sufficient justification. In New York City these classes were disproportionately made up of Latino children. A Civil Rights Commission report noted that "the rationale for such practices is that students will benefit from special instruction in low-level classes, but the correlation between such placement and improved academic performance is dubious. In fact, the lower level of curriculum and the absence of stimulation from higher-achieving students may be negative factors that further retard the student."[51]

On the average Puerto Rican students do not do as well as non-Latino white students on achievement tests, most of which are given in English. A psychologist in Philadelphia commented on the inaccuracy of English-language test scores:

> In my clinic, the average underestimation of IQ for a Puerto Rican kid is 20 points. We go through this again and again. When we test in Spanish, there is a 20 point leap immediately—20 higher than when he's tested in English.[52]

Many of the new Spanish-language achievement and "IQ" tests are only translations of English-language tests, a practice that passes along whatever cultural bias exists in the tests. The predictive validity of the standardized tests used for college and graduate school entrance (the SAT and GRE) is considerably lower for Latinos than for whites. Use of such tests has been considered discriminatory by many critical observers.[53]

Educator Henry Giroux has written that "learning [is] not merely...the acquisition of knowledge but...the production of cultural practices that offer students a sense of identity, place, and hope."[54] Puerto Rican educator Herman La Fontaine states that "our definition of cultural pluralism must include the concept that our language and our culture will be given equal status to that of the majority population."[55] Puerto Rican educators argue that children should be taught to read and write well in Spanish first, taught subjects in that language, and then taught English as a second language. Civil rights groups have pressed for bilingual education programs for Latino children. Indeed, a goal of Puerto Rican communities in their struggle against the New York City school system has been a comprehensive educational program in which the strengths and values of Puerto Rican culture and the Spanish language are recognized. However, the outcome of their struggle so far has been a bilingual program that is designed to teach English as a replacement language and that devalues biculturalism.[56]

Some researchers report that high school students in bilingual programs have higher attendance and completion rates and that such programs contribute to more positive self-concepts for students. Yet in most instances bilingual programs have not become part of the mainstream school curriculum. Viewed by conservative officials as luxuries, bilingual programs were heavily cut by the Reagan administration in the 1980s. A leader of Philadelphia's Puerto Rican Alliance argued that this showed a "blatant disregard of a right the courts have already recognized."[57]

Official English Policies and Spanish Speakers

As we have noted in Chapter 3, support for English as the official U.S. language has grown over the last decade or two. Much of this nativist movement has targeted Spanish and Spanish speakers such as Puerto Rican and Mexican Americans. An amendment to the Arizona state constitution went so far as to make English the language "of all government functions and actions," but a federal district judge ruled in February 1990 that this violated free speech as protected by the federal constitution.[58] Nativism directed at Spanish speakers can be seen in the following passage from a Council on Interamerican Security paper:

> Hispanics in America today represent a very dangerous and subversive force that is bent on taking over our nation's political institutions for the purposes of imposing Spanish as the official language of the U.S. and indeed of the entire Western Hemisphere.... They represent a serious threat to our cherished freedoms and our American traditions.... If we desire to preserve our unique culture and the primacy of the English language, then we must so declare rather than sitting idly by as a de facto nation evolves.[59]

Xenophobic nativists praise official-language and English-only policies as a means to unify diverse groups within U.S. society and promote shared cultural values. Educator Catherine Walsh reports that instead "such efforts toward linguistic cohesion resonate with a kind of colonial domination, a hegemony that threatens to silence the less powerful [and attempts] to render invisible the complex, abstract, socio-ideological nature of language."[60] Walsh identifies language as one of the ways in which people define themselves. Far from simply a set of neutral symbols, language shapes thought and thus is inseparable from identity and everyday life. In her years as a teacher and researcher, Walsh documented the daily struggle faced by language-minority students over *whose* language and therefore whose knowledge, perspectives, and experiences are recognized and accepted, and whose are omitted or belittled. She quotes a young bilingual student:

> "Sometimes I two-times think," she said. "I think like in my family and in my house. And then I think like in school and other places. Then I talk. They aren't the same, you know."

Realizing that the language context of her home was not only different but less acceptable than that of the school, this child often told her teacher, "It makes me feel funny, all alone...different."[61] The effects of limited bilingual educational experiences on Mexican American students discussed in Chapter 9 are equally significant for Puerto Rican students.

POLITICS

In Puerto Rico, voting by registered voters runs to 60 percent or more. Among mainland Puerto Ricans voting rates have been as low as 20 percent in some urban areas. The low level of political participation by and representation of Puerto Ricans on the mainland can be explained along the lines of other exploited minority communities: insufficient education, weak electoral support of Puerto Rican candidates by whites, a lack of campaign funds, and a lack of representation in Democratic party leadership, as well as a feeling of hopelessness regarding possibilities for political change. In a recent survey of Puerto Ricans in New York City who were not registered to vote, the most frequently cited reasons for not voting were "not interested in politics" (29 percent) and "voting makes no difference" (24 percent). A total of 27 percent also stated that language barriers were either somewhat important or very important in keeping them from registering to vote.[62]

Election to political office has been slow to come for Puerto Ricans on the mainland. The first Puerto Rican was elected to the New York state assembly in 1937; it would be fifteen years before another was elected. Since the early 1940s Puerto Ricans have participated in Democratic party politics in such states as New York and New Jersey, but that participation has been token. As of the early 1990s Puerto Ricans have been able to dominate only one voting seat in Congress, that originally held by Herman Badillo, who represented the South Bronx. In 1965 Badillo became the first Puerto Rican to be elected president of a New York City borough; six years later he became the first voting member of Puerto Rican background in the U.S. House. In the 1970s, however, Badillo gave up his seat in Congress to run for mayor of New York, a race he lost. Through the 1980s Robert Garcia held the House seat previously occupied by Badillo, and in 1990 Jose Serrano was elected to fill this seat. Two new congressional districts representing Latino areas were created by redistricting in the early 1990s. One was in Chicago, the first in the Midwest, and the second was in New York City, giving that area a total of two such districts. Both changes involved lawsuits by Latino activist groups.[63]

Electoral successes at the local and state levels have been more substantial. Robert Garcia played an important role in building political bridges between black Americans and Puerto Ricans in New York, noting that "blacks and Puerto Ricans are natural allies as defined by our common position on the bottom rung of the socioeconomic ladder."[64] In 1965 he and several other state legislators, including black leader Shirley Chisholm, formed a black–Puerto Rican caucus in the New York legislature. In the early 1990s that caucus was still bringing black and Puerto Rican legislators together on issues of importance to both communities. Similar coalitions have periodically appeared at Democratic party conventions.

The 1980s saw gains in political representation at the local level for Puerto Ricans, enough to create a foundation for representation in several state governments. The *National Roster of Hispanic Elected Officials* reported a 1991 total of 76 Latino elected officials in New York, 42 in New Jersey, and 139 in Illinois. As of 1992 New York had two state senators (one male and one female), four members of the state assembly, and eight members of the New York City Council who were Puerto Rican. Early in the decade the first Latinos ever (two Puerto Ricans and two Mexican Americans) were elected to the Chicago City Council. This was achieved only after a lawsuit demanding the redrawing of district lines. By 1983 the first Puerto Rican was serving in Illinois's lower house, and in 1992 Illinois had one Puerto Rican state senator and two Puerto Ricans in its lower house. In 1992 Puerto Ricans also had one member each in the lower houses of New Jersey, Massachusetts, and Pennsylvania and three, including one woman, in Connecticut's lower house.

The long-term effects of institutional discrimination can be seen in state and city government employment, in which Puerto Ricans are significantly underrepresented. As a result Puerto Ricans frequently feel they are not part of the political system; they often report that they are treated as nonpersons by government and private agencies. Government officials serving them are usually not Puerto Rican and seldom speak much Spanish. Government services have historically been less accessible to Puerto Ricans, and job training and employment services have been slow in coming to Puerto Rican communities.[65]

Starting in the 1980s, the Midwest–Northeast Voter Registration Education Project, which operates in seventeen states with significant Puerto Rican populations, has conducted some 385 voter-registration campaigns and registered more than 800,000 new voters, many of whom were Puerto Rican. Toward the end of 1987 the governor of Puerto Rico announced that he was starting a half-million-dollar campaign to register mainland Puerto Ricans to vote. At that time an estimated 400,000 eligible Latinos, mostly Puerto Ricans, in the New York City area alone were unregistered. Local leaders welcomed this unique intervention by a nonmainland Puerto Rican leader, which demonstrated the close political alliances between the mainland and island communities. One local leader pointed out the need to couple voter registration with a get-out-the-vote effort because of the low turnout of Puerto Rican voters, especially when there are no candidates articulating policies relevant to Puerto Rican socioeconomic and political needs. The project was implemented in 1988 by the Department of Puerto Rican Community Affairs in the United States, an agency that also provides information and referral for educational, employment, legal, and other social services. The agency's funding comes from the Puerto Rican government. By late 1991 the project had registered more than 84,000 new voters in New York City, and Puerto Rican voter turnout in the November 1991 city council elections was 38 percent greater than for any previous election. This, plus a change in the size of the New York City Council from thirty-five to fifty-one, resulted in an increase in the number of Puerto Rican members on the council from three to nine.[66]

PROTEST

In Puerto Rico

In Puerto Rico the period of U.S. rule has periodically been punctuated with protest against the subordinate status that colonial domination entailed. Contrary to the stereotype of Latino docility, Puerto Ricans have fought hard to retain their language and culture and to establish self-determination. In the 1930s large numbers of Puerto Ricans attacked the colonial government buildings in periodic protests, and in 1934 there were strikes in the sugarcane fields. The Nationalist party, led by a Puerto Rican hero, Harvard-educated Pedro Albizu Campos, began pushing for expanded freedom and for independence. In March 1937 Nationalist party marchers who had joined a legal march in Ponce were massacred. By bringing in two hundred heavily armed police, the U.S. colonial governor set the stage for violence. A shot was fired, probably by the police, and a pitched battle ensued, with twenty dead and one hundred injured, mostly marchers and bystanders.[67]

In the fall of 1950 police raided Nationalist party meetings and houses. This precipitated an armed revolt that spread to five cities. Hundreds of people were killed. Two thousand people were arrested for actively advocating independence. On the mainland Puerto Rican nationalists seeking independence attacked the residence of President Harry Truman and the U.S. House while it was in session.

The future of Puerto Rico is a major political issue on both the island and the mainland. The platforms of both the Republican and the Democratic parties have supported statehood for Puerto Rico. Pro-statehood sentiment is very strong on the island; "statehood for the poor" is the slogan of this movement. In late 1991 voters in Puerto Rico defeated a measure that effectively opposed statehood. But there are substantial pressures against statehood as well. A very large group on the island supports the current commonwealth status, and approximately 10 percent of the voters support a pro-independence movement. Some islanders continue to use violence against U.S. officials and military personnel in an attempt to drive the colonialists from the island.[68]

On the Mainland

Arriving for the most part desperately poor and already stigmatized as inferior, Puerto Ricans on the mainland have long had service organizations to deal with discrimination and other community problems. Some of the major organizations are the Puerto Rican Legal Project, the Puerto Rican Legal Defense Fund, the League of Puerto Rican Women, the Puerto Rican Teachers Association, the Puerto Rican Forum, and the Puerto Rican Family Institute. The Puerto Rican Teachers Association has worked to increase representation of Puerto Ricans among teachers and principals and to expand bilingual programs. Puerto Ricans have been active in labor and union organizations on the mainland since the late 1800s.[69]

Puerto Rican protest activity in the 1960s and early 1970s led to riots in some Puerto Rican ghettos. In the spring of 1969 the Young Lords, a militant protest group patterned after the Black Panthers, occupied the administration building of McCormick Theological Seminary to publicize poverty in Chicago. They took over a Methodist church, opening a day-care center and school for the community. They protested the use of urban-renewal land for a tennis club, and they set up a "people's park" on other urban-renewal land.[70] A New York group formed a Young Lords political party. In December 1969 these Young Lords occupied the First Spanish Methodist Church in New York City for eleven days and organized a day-care center, a breakfast program, and a clothing distribution program. They created a newspaper, *Palante* (Forward), and led a demonstration of two hundred Puerto Ricans protesting squalid conditions at a local hospital.[71] The Young Lords, which had begun as a Chicago street gang, developed their own protest style. Children of poor immigrants, they articulated a thirteen-point program for a democratic-socialist society. They called for "liberation and power in the hands of the people, not Puerto Rican exploiters." At the peak of their influence, the Young Lords had chapters in twenty cities. Militant Puerto Rican groups such as the Young Lords were subject to police repression, including infiltration and prosecution of some leaders, sometimes in rigged trials. Other leaders were co-opted into government antipoverty programs. Internal divisions helped splinter the militant groups as well. The Young Lords gradually disbanded in the early 1970s. In 1989 many former members celebrated the militancy of the group and the twentieth anniversary of its founding. Many former members are today influential Puerto Rican professionals and leaders or activists in community organizations.[72]

In the early 1990s many organizations in Puerto Rican communities were working for a better quality of life and increased decision making in the political process. The Puerto Rican Legal Defense and Education Fund engaged in litigation in support of civil rights; Aspira worked on improving education; the National Puerto Rican Forum focused on employment and job training. The National Puerto Rican Coalition, representing more than 115 local organizations, served as a liaison between Puerto Rican communities and federal government officials and lobbied for educational, health, economic, and civil rights programs.[73]

Community Protest

Many Puerto Rican communities have protested discrimination. For example, in Cleveland, Orlando Morales, a young man serving two life sentences, was viewed by community groups as innocent. Much evidence indicated that Morales did not commit the murder for which he was convicted. Many in the Puerto Rican community felt the twenty-two-year-old Puerto Rican had been railroaded and actively protested what they saw as discrimination in the criminal justice system. Three hundred angry Puerto Ricans engaged in a protest meeting at Cleveland's Spanish American Committee Hall. In addition, community organizations in Chicago have protested housing discrimination and police brutality. Police injustices targeting Latinos, including abusive and derogatory language, unwarranted arrests, questionings, and searches, as well as beatings and the use of excessive physical force, have been common in Chicago. A major riot involving hundreds of Puerto Ricans occurred in Miami in 1990 after six police officers were acquitted in the fatal beating of a Puerto Rican drug dealer. Residents of the extremely poor Puerto Rican neighborhood said the violence had a lot to do with the sense of alienation and powerlessness in the Miami community. They pointed to such factors as the scarcity of Puerto Ricans in powerful government and business positions and the absence of Puerto Rican music on Spanish-language radio stations. "Cubans get everything; we get nothing," one resident stated.[74]

Some protest movements have brought changes. Pressures from Puerto Rican activists led to the founding of a community college in the South Bronx and helped create an open admissions program at the City University of New York. City and state governments have provided more funds for community projects and hired more Puerto Ricans. Schools have added more Puerto Rican studies and bilingual programs and hired more Puerto Rican teachers.[75]

Coalitions of grass-roots organizations and older established groups were created in the 1980s, among them the National Congress for Puerto Rican Rights, formed in 1981. Through such mechanisms traditional and militant leaders have tried to bridge the long-standing gap between them and improve the conditions of Puerto Ricans. In the 1990s the leaders and members of several state branches of this National Congress pressed state and local governments for equal justice in the courts and for better schools for Latino children; they participated in protest demonstrations, sometimes with black organizations, against anti-minority violence and police brutality. They were also active in pressing the mass media to do better reporting on Latino communities.

RELIGION

Traditionally most Puerto Ricans have been Catholic, but on the mainland they have generally been led by non–Puerto Rican clergy. The supportive framework that parishes gave to previous Catholic immigrant groups has largely been missing. One exception to this dependence on non–Puerto Rican clergy has been the bishop of Puerto Rico, who regularly visits Puerto Rican parishes on the mainland.

Scholar Joseph Fitzpatrick has argued that Puerto Rican religion is more a religion of the community than of the parish. Community celebrations and processions are important, as is reverence for the Virgin Mary and the saints. Formal church worship is less important than communal celebrations and home ceremonies. But many remain devoutly religious whether or not they attend mass regularly. On the mainland, Puerto Ricans have shared parishes with black and other Latino parishioners. Latino caucuses have developed within the Catholic church to press for Spanish-language services and more priests of Latino background. In Fitzpatrick's words, "the principal demand of the Puerto Ricans and other Latinos is for a policy of cultural pluralism in the church that will provide for the continuation of their language and culture in their spiritual life and the appointment of Puerto Ricans and other Latinos to positions of responsibility."[76] Today the Archdiocese of New York, which covers New York City and seven counties to the north, has been estimated to be about 40 percent Latino. Yet only 4 percent of the priests are Latino, and this lack of leadership from Puerto Rican and other Latino groups is creating a serious problem for the Archdiocese. The church has made significant attempts to reach out to the Latino poor, but has not as yet developed a sensitivity to Latino language and culture.[77]

As a result, many Puerto Ricans have left the Catholic church for pentecostal and other evangelical churches, which offer a warmer reception and a community feeling. Protestant fundamentalism has made significant inroads into Puerto Rican communities, as it has in other Latino communities. Many of these communities are now full of storefront evangelical churches. New York City alone is said to have 1,400 Latino pentecostal and other Protestant churches.

ASSIMILATION OR COLONIALISM?

Assimilation Issues

In his influential book on Puerto Ricans, Fitzpatrick relies on an assimilation model to interpret Puerto Rican experiences. While in his 1964 book the assimilation theorist Gordon found little assimilation of Puerto Ricans into the core culture or society, a few years later Fitzpatrick reported a significant degree of assimilation. Fitzpatrick noted substantial cultural assimilation, particularly for many mainland-born Puerto Ricans who have identified with U.S. society and adopted English as a second language. Yet others, such as Walsh, have argued that this cultural adaptation is limited and gives a "false hope of inclusion in [the dominant] environment." Walsh found that Puerto Rican schoolchildren often deny knowing Spanish when speaking with non-Latinos, even if they use Spanish at home and in their community. In *Up from Puerto Rico*, Padilla argues that second-generation Puerto Ricans often have a different reference group, the mainland society rather than island society, and as a result many hide their Spanish-language facility in an attempt to assimilate culturally.[78]

The pressure to assimilate culturally has been intense, as Maldonado-Denis notes: "Regardless of what Glazer and Moynihan argue in *Beyond the Melting Pot*, the American ethic is a messianic one, and all ethnic groups are required to assimilate culturally as a condition for achieving a share in the material and spiritual goods of American society."[79] For Puerto Ricans these cultural assimilation pressures begin in Puerto Rico, where for decades the colonial government pressured Puerto Ricans on the island to assimilate culturally, as in requiring the use of English in the schools. Today there is evidence of cultural assimilation. In a 1991 survey, Strategy Research Corporation ranked the cultural assimilation level of Latinos on the basis of language use and behavioral, attitudinal, and aspirational measures. The majority (59 percent) of mainland Puerto Rican heads of household were classified as partially assimilated; fewer than 10 percent were ranked as highly assimilated, and 32 percent were considered relatively unassimilated.[80]

Fitzpatrick has noted significant Puerto Rican resistance to complete cultural assimilation. The Puerto Rican quest for identity "is taking the form of a strong assertion of the significance of Puerto Rican culture, including language, and also the definition of Puerto Rican interests around militant types of political and community action."[81] Among Puerto Ricans themselves, some argue that Puerto Ricans in the United States must assimilate culturally in order to find better jobs and achieve a higher position in this society; some argue that this can be done with a minimum of soul selling—that is, with a strong persistence of Puerto Rican culture. Others worry about the heavy cost of complete cultural assimilation in terms of the identities of Puerto Ricans; they worry that assimilation pressures, as with other racial and ethnic groups, will lead to rootlessness.

In the public schools Euro-American teachers are often engaged in an ongoing struggle with Latino students. The outcome of this struggle varies: students may become culturally assimilated, fully or to a lesser degree, or they may drop out. Researchers have found that favorable, or fair, treatment of Latino students in school increases as their "difference," as perceived by the non-Latino teacher, decreases. For earlier white ethnic immigrants acculturation frequently resulted in some denial of ethnicity; differences became the source of fear, even shame, as noted by the Italian immigrant Leonard Covello:

> We soon got the idea that Italian meant something inferior and a barrier was erected between [children] of Italian origin and their parents. This was the accepted process of Americanization; we were becoming Americans by learning to be ashamed of our parents.[82]

For people of color, however, full cultural assimilation and loss of ethnic identity are impossible; the differences are too visible. Rather than becoming de-racialized or de-ethnicized "Americans," Puerto Ricans and other people of color remain distinctive minorities.

While there seems to be some decline in blatant discrimination against Puerto Ricans in jobs, blatant and subtle forms continue in other areas such as housing. For the most part, the level of assimilation in this regard is relatively low. Moreover, secondary-structural assimilation at the level of higher-paying white-collar jobs has been slow; there remains a disproportionate concentration of Puerto Ricans in blue-collar and lower-wage white-collar jobs, as well as among the unemployed. Problematical too has been the low level of participation of Puerto Ricans in mainland political institutions. Here, too, there has not been dramatic assimilation.

Structural assimilation of Puerto Ricans at the primary-group level and marital assimilation have not reached levels comparable to those of the white ethnic immigrants. A New York study of four hundred Puerto Ricans found "almost incessant interaction between the parents and their married children." In spite of, or perhaps because of, their wrenching experiences of migration to the mainland and three decades there, the first generation of immigrants has maintained a high level of social integration with their children and grandchildren. The better jobs and educations of many in the second generation have not broken up this family integration. However, outmarriage seems to be more significant for the second generation. Over half of the U.S.-born Puerto Ricans who are married have a Puerto Rican spouse, compared with more than 80 percent of the island-born migrants. Outmarriages, however, are typically to other Latinos and to black Americans rather than to non-Latino whites.

Generational conflict has been a problem for Puerto Rican families. Children grow up in the mainland culture and pick up values that often conflict with traditional values. The traditional chaperoning of girls has given way to the less restrictive mainland dating patterns. The street life of boys in large ghettos is more difficult to supervise. Moreover, identificational assimilation has come slowly for Puerto Ricans. Most, whether island-born or mainland-born, still see themselves as Puerto Rican. A study of two generations of Puerto Rican families in New York City found that both had acculturated to some extent to the mainland culture, "but internally, in the symbolisms linking them to the island, they experienced less change." Even those born on the mainland retained strong symbolic ties to the island of Puerto Rico. More than half of the first generation of migrants to the mainland and 45 percent of their children saw themselves as solely Puerto Rican in terms of values. The rest saw themselves as partly Puerto Rican and partly "North American." Not one of the four hundred persons in the sample identified himself or herself as purely "North American" in terms of values. The second generation apparently had as strong an allegiance and sense of identity with Puerto Rico as the first generation.[83]

Power–Conflict Views

Power–conflict analysts would agree that there has been heavy Anglo-conformity pressure on Puerto Ricans, but they would stress how colonized Puerto Rican Americans remain. Assimilation into the economic and political mainstream has been rather slow, which suggests that non-European migrants such as Puerto Ricans are not, contrary to the views of some assimilation analysts, just like the European immigrants in earlier periods of the twentieth century.

Puerto Ricans also have the distinctive experience of external colonialism. Unemployment in Puerto Rico has often been cited as a major reason for out-migration; the prosperity of the mainland economy has been cited as an important pull factor. But unemployment and mainland prosperity would not have created the long streams of migration from this Caribbean island without the long colonial relationship. The economic history of Puerto Ricans is grounded in the history of the colonial relationship between the United States and the island of Puerto Rico. After the war with Spain the United States took the island by force as an external colony. Since that time the inhabitants have been subject to U.S. economic and political intervention. Indeed, it was the creation of a one-crop agricultural society dominated by U.S. absentee sugar companies that originally provided a large group of agricultural workers seeking other work.

With the later industrialization of Puerto Rico under the auspices of large U.S. firms, many Puerto Rican workers became part of a growing surplus labor population, one that often made its way to the industrialized northeastern cities on the mainland. These immigrants from an external colony became part of the internal colonialism of the inner cities. Puerto Ricans live, for the most part, in segregated communities. Colonialism theorists would argue that there is a co-opted Puerto Rican elite that, like colonial elites in the Third World, has a social control function.[84]

Internal colonialism can be seen in the Reagan and Bush administrations' "urban enterprise zone" proposals, which significantly reduce taxes and regulations on corporations that open plants in urban poverty areas, thus recognizing minority ghettos as areas for economic exploitation. Bonilla and Campos have compared this "puertoricanization" of central-city ghettos to the economic colonialism of Operation Bootstrap in Puerto Rico. Under Operation Bootstrap, Puerto Rico's poverty and low wages became its main assets for attracting multinational corporations. President Reagan's advisers explicitly used Puerto Rico as an example of the reindustrialization they had in mind for mainland urban enterprise zones.

In the case of Puerto Rico, corporations were encouraged by various incentives to come in and profit from exploiting cheap labor. The puertoricanization of central-city ghettos makes them corporate havens of profitability similar to the island of Puerto Rico. Bonilla and Campos have noted that various urban-renewal schemes, new and old, for exploiting Puerto Rican and black workers show the logic of capitalistic expansion, which leads "not only to the introduction of the peoples and problems of colonialism into the metropolis, but also to the transfer there of colonial 'solutions' [such as urban enterprise zones] and practices."[85]

CUBAN AMERICANS

We will now turn to the situation of Cuban Americans, the third largest Latino group in the United States. Like Puerto Ricans, this group has its roots in a Caribbean island.

PATTERNS OF IMMIGRATION

Early Immigration: 1868–1959

Virtually all migrations from Cuba to the United States have stemmed from political upheaval and economic distress on the island of Cuba. The nineteenth-century wars of Cuban independence brought the first Cuban immigrants to the United States. Most were from Cuba's middle and working classes; many were professionals and business people. Although some of these immigrants went to New York, Philadelphia, and Boston, most chose to settle in south Florida because of its proximity to Cuba and the similarity of its climate to that of the island. By 1873 Cubans were the majority of the population in Key West, Florida. Ybor City and Tampa became home to a large number of Cubans after 1885 when cigar factories located there. Considering themselves exiles and expecting to return home soon, members of these communities were highly committed to the independence of their homeland from Spain. They contributed both soldiers and financial assistance to the war in Cuba. When Cuba won its independence in 1898, many exiles returned home. However, for tens of thousands of Cubans who had lived in the United States for more than twenty years, return was not an option; the United States was the location of their homes and jobs and the birthplace of their children. Among the major contributions of these early Cuban Americans to their adopted homeland were the organization of Florida's first labor union and the establishment of Key West's first fire department and first bilingual school.[86]

These early Cuban exiles were politically active at the local level and also lobbied for a U.S. policy that would support Cuba's liberation from Spain. However, for some time the U.S. government did not share the exiles' enthusiasm for the independence of their homeland. The United States even supported Spanish colonialism over Cuban independence. Later, during the thirty-year war between Spain and Cuban rebels, the United States made several attempts to purchase the island from Spain. Finally U.S. troops were sent to Cuba, and after Spain was driven out in 1898, they occupied the island for four years. In 1902 Cuba became a U.S. protectorate. The Platt Amendment to the 1900–1901 U.S. military appropriations bill gave the United States the right to military intervention in Cuba to preserve the island's "independence" and to protect life, property, and individual liberty. During the first two decades of the twentieth century U.S. involvement in Cuban politics took the form of military intervention to settle various political disputes. After the 1920s military actions were replaced with diplomatic interference. So great was U.S. power in Cuban affairs that no elected president of the island who was opposed by the United States could remain in office long. Cuba was in effect a colony of the United States from 1898 until 1959.[87]

During this period U.S. financial domination of Cuba was no less extensive than political domination. Within fifteen years after Cuba gained independence from Spain, U.S. investments grew from an estimated $50 million to an estimated $220 million. By the late 1920s the United States controlled almost 75 percent of Cuba's sugar industry. By the end of the 1950s U.S. businesses controlled 90 percent of Cuba's mines, 80 percent of its public utilities, half of its railways, 40 percent of its sugar production, and one-quarter of its bank deposits. Cuba was clearly an economic colony.[88]

The political turbulence that accompanied a succession of corrupt and repressive dictators in Cuba during the first half of the twentieth century brought some exiles to the United States. For many, their stay in the United States was brief; returning to Cuba, they were often replaced by those from whose power they had earlier fled. During the corrupt dictatorship of former army chief Fulgencio Batista in the 1950s, the refugees numbered between 10,000 and 15,000 per year.[89]

Recent Immigration: 1959 to the Present

The migration of large numbers of Cubans to the United States occurred after Cuba's 1959 revolution. Fidel Castro, the young rebel leader of the grass-roots insurrection that overthrew Batista, came to power in that year. To the majority of Cubans, Castro's victory brought hope for social, economic, and political reforms. Land grants to tenant farmers, guaranteed compensation for small sugar growers, and the nationalization of public utility companies were among Castro's stated goals. However, such reforms were mostly not in the interests of Cuba's business, industrial, and political elites or of the island's U.S. investors. Exaggerated views of the Cuban revolution's threat to U.S. interests, suspicions that Castro was a Communist, and Castro's declarations that he would not tolerate manipulation of Cuba by the U.S. government led to U.S. hostility toward Cuba, a break in diplomatic relations between the two countries, and a U.S. policy of welcoming refugees from Cuba's "Communist oppression" to the "free world."[90]

The first major stream of immigration began with Cuba's elite—former government officials, bankers, and industrialists who had done well under the Batista dictatorship and feared Castro's Communist political orientation even before it became a reality. These were Cubans whose economic position in Cuba was directly related to Cuba's political and economic relationship with the United States. The second wave started in 1961, when large numbers of middle- and upper-income Cubans began to flee the revolution, preferring exile from their native island to life under Fidel Castro's increasingly authoritarian Communist government. This group was composed of middle-level professionals, managers, merchants, and landlords and included more than half of Cuba's doctors and teachers. Many cited loss of job, possessions, or sources of income as reasons for their departure. Others reported harassment, persecution, or temporary imprisonment or fears that they would be imprisoned. More than 14,000 children were sent alone to the United States by parents who feared having their children educated by a Communist state. Both of these waves of immigrants were very heavily white although the island's multiracial population was 27 percent black, according to the 1953 Cuban census. By 1962 almost 200,000 Cubans had entered the United States. Smaller numbers continued to arrive by small boat or by way of other countries after air travel between Cuba and the United States was suspended in 1962.[91]

As with earlier Cuban immigrants, south Florida, only ninety miles from Cuba, was the logical destination. Because they were fleeing a Communist government, they found the U.S. government a willing host. In the first years, from the point of view of both the immigrants and the U.S. government, the Cubans were refugees forced into temporary exile with the firm intention of returning home as soon as the Castro regime was overthrown. This is a major reason why most of the refugees chose to stay in the cities of south Florida.

To provide for the immediate needs of these refugees, the Eisenhower administration created the Cuban Refugee Emergency Center in Miami and allocated $1 million in federal funds. This aid was expanded by the Kennedy administration in 1961 in the form of a Cuban Refugee Program that assisted refugees with resettlement, helped them locate employment, and provided for maintenance, health services, education and training programs, aid for unaccompanied children, and surplus food distribution. The program lasted from 1961 until 1974 and provided a total of nearly a billion dollars during its lifetime. This federal government aid was a major asset in helping Cuban refugees build and sustain their own communal and economic infrastructure. Cubans are the only large group of Latin Americans who have been granted political refugee status and on that basis have been able to qualify for federal financial aid.[92]

A third stream of Cuban immigrants, totaling more than a quarter million, arrived between 1965 and the late 1970s. Almost five thousand relatives of those refugees already in the United States were allowed to leave from the Cuban port of Camarioca in late 1965 aboard hundreds of boats arriving from Miami. This flotilla exodus was followed by an airlift jointly negotiated by the U.S. and Cuban governments. Push factors for this largely white, working-class and small-business group included concern with economic scarcities and hope for a higher standard of living in the United States, in addition to disagreement with Cuba's political regime. As with earlier groups, these refugees settled mainly in south Florida, although by the late 1960s some were spread among 2,300 Cuban communities throughout the other forty-nine states. A nationwide study of three hundred immigrant families in 1968 found that relocation patterns reflected family associations: more than three-fourths of the families in this study had relatives already in the United States. The study found that familiar occupational orientation was an important criterion in selecting a relocation city. For example, some with a background in government chose Washington, while some whose background was in business or finance chose New York City.[93]

By the late 1960s increasing numbers of Cuban immigrants had begun to think of themselves as permanent residents of the United States, more interested in improving their lives and less involved in efforts to bring about the demise of Castro's government. Many owned businesses and homes and had become integrated into the social, economic, and political institutions of their community. Many became naturalized citizens.

The Mariel Immigrants

The fourth stream of immigrants, the sudden and much-publicized influx of 125,000 Cubans between April and September of 1980 generally known as the "Mariel boatlift" (after the port from which they sailed from Cuba), gave rise to a number of myths and distortions among non-Cuban Americans. Popular images characterized the Mariel refugees as undesirables—poorer and less educated than earlier waves of Cuban immigrants and containing a large percentage of criminals and the mentally ill. This group included some who left voluntarily and some, considered undesirable by the Cuban government, who were forced to leave. However, of the entire group, only a few hundred were mentally ill and required institutionalization, and fewer than one in five had been in prison in Cuba. Among this latter group, almost one quarter were political prisoners, and the offenses of an additional 70 percent consisted of some form of dissent or other acts that were not crimes in the United States. Fewer than 2 percent were subsequently imprisoned in a U.S. federal penitentiary. The education level of this Mariel group was similar to that of the Cuban immigrants of the 1970s, and most represented the mainstream of the Cuban economy and society. More than 11 percent were professionals, including many teachers; some 71 percent were blue-collar workers. However, unlike the earlier waves of Cuban immigrants, which were mostly white, approximately 40 percent of the Mariel group was black. More than half came to waiting families or sponsors, and two-thirds of the rest were easily placed in communities across the nation. By the mid-1980s most Mariel refugees had been absorbed by Cuban American communities. However, a small number did remain in detention camps several years after arrival because U.S. government officials feared they were criminals.[94]

Because their reasons for immigration were substantially economic, the Mariel immigrants were ineligible for the federal financial support available to political refugees. They were allowed to stay in the United States by the Carter administration's creation of a special immigration category, "Cuban-Haitian entrant," which included eligibility for emergency assistance, medical services, and supplemental income, most of which was paid for by the federal government. Upon arrival the Mariel immigrants were housed in tent cities in the Miami area and flown to military bases in Arkansas, Florida, Pennsylvania, and Wisconsin. Some were held in these makeshift processing centers for an extended time while the government attempted to identify refugees who might be "dangerous." Yet as noted above, the vast majority of Mariel immigrants were neither marginal nor deviant. Many Mariel immigrants soon felt betrayed by exaggerated reports from exiles visiting Cuba concerning the wealth and ease of life in the United States. Disillusionment and crowded conditions in the detention centers led to several inmate riots and violent confrontations between the refugees and the National Guard troops in charge of the centers. In addition, from August 1980 into 1983 a few Mariel immigrants participated in several airplane hijackings in an effort to return to Cuba.[95]

The 1990 census counted over one million Cuban Americans, a 30 percent increase over the number recorded in the 1980 census. More than 97 percent lived in urban areas. The estimated median age for Cuban Americans was just over thirty-nine years, older than the population as a whole, the non-Latino population, and other Latino groups. Perez notes that "the overrepresentation of the elderly among Cubans has clear origins. Dissatisfaction with socialist revolutionary change was likely to be highest among the elderly. In issuing permits, the Cuban government has given preference to the dependent elderly while restricting the emigration, for example, of males of military age."[96]

INTERGROUP CONFLICT

One major result of the Cuban migrations over the last few decades has been a change in the population mix of south Florida. By the late 1980s Latinos had become a majority of the population in the city of Miami. The 1980 Cuban migration swelled Miami welfare rolls, increased overcrowding in the schools, and created $30 million in expenses for local governments already hurting from cutbacks in federal programs. The millions of dollars paid out to care for the new influx of Cubans angered many non-Latino whites; the latter unfairly blamed all Cubans for the many local social problems.

Tensions also accelerated with Miami's black residents, many of whom argued that Cuban Americans were taking jobs away from them. The larger and more affluent Cuban American community today controls many of its own businesses, small and large, and Cubans are usually preferred in hiring there. In one 1980s mayoral election 95 percent of black voters voted against the Cuban American candidate. Since 1980 more major race riots have occurred in Miami than in any other U.S. city. Miami's 1980 Liberty City riot and 1982 Overtown riot by poor blacks were precipitated in part by police involvement in the killing of black men. The Overtown riot involved a Cuban American police officer shooting a black man who was playing a video game. More rioting took place in 1984 when the officer was acquitted of charges in connection with the killing. After the riots some white landlords and businesses that had been damaged were replaced by Latino landlords and businesses. One former black school official complained that "after a generation of being Southern slaves, blacks now face a future as Latin slaves." The shooting of an unarmed black motorist by a Latino officer in 1989 precipitated another major riot in predominantly black areas of Miami. More than 280 people were arrested in three days of rioting. After the shooting the U.S. attorney for Miami began an inquiry into complaints of police brutality by white and Latino officers toward blacks. Latino officers themselves asked not to be assigned to black areas of the city where antipolice hostility remained high after the riot. Intergroup rivalry and competition can be seen clearly in south Florida today, with a very old immigrant group (African Americans) losing a power struggle with a new immigrant group (Cuban Americans).[97]

Inconsistent U.S. treatment of the mostly white Cuban refugees and the black Haitian refugees has been another source of intergroup tension in south Florida. Since the 1970s thousands of Haitians fleeing a repressive island government have been refused entry because their government, however corrupt and brutal, is supported by the United States. In the mid-1970s the international human rights organization Amnesty International described Haitian prisons as torture and death traps. Unlike the Cuban refugees, those Haitians who between 1972 and 1980 were allowed to stay in the United States received no financial support from the government but were left to cope on their own or with the assistance of private charitable groups. This group consisted of poor, black, and unskilled immigrants who had fled a brutal dictatorship in desperation. Beginning in 1981, Haitians reaching the United States were held at several detention centers around the country; later these Haitian detainees were moved to an army base in upstate New York, an area whose severe winters differed radically from the Haitian climate. In that same year U.S. officials began to intercept Haitian immigrants at sea and return them to Haiti, a program that was still in operation in the early 1990s.[98]

The ouster in September 1991 of Haiti's democratically elected president, Jean-Bertrand Aristide, precipitated another flight of Haitians to the United States. As an example to curb further attempts by Haitians to enter the United States, the U.S. government repatriated 500 Haitians in late 1991. After a court ordered a halt to such repatriations, Haitian refugees were taken to a tent city at the U.S. naval base in

Guantanamo Bay, Cuba. A small percentage of these were granted permission to apply for political asylum, but with no guarantee that their applications would be approved. Hundreds of thousands of Salvadorans and Guatemalans have also been refused refugee status in the United States since the 1970s; many have been deported to face certain death at the hands of their own dictatorial governments. In a clearly political maneuver the Cuban immigrants have been defined as "political refugees" eligible for U.S. citizenship by friendly U.S. officials, while most Haitian and Central American immigrants have been classified as "economic refugees" ineligible even for entry into the United States. This differential government treatment of immigrants and potential immigrants lies at the heart of tensions between Miami's Cuban and Haitian communities in the 1990s.[99]

STEREOTYPING AND DISCRIMINATION

Cuban Americans are often stereotyped as a predominantly affluent group. As we will see in the following section, Cuban Americans as a group are generally more prosperous than other Latino groups. However, this relative affluence should not be exaggerated, for a significant portion of Cuban Americans live in poverty. The Children's Defense Fund recently reported that the poverty rate for Cuban American children rose by 71 percent during the 1980s, a greater increase than for any other Latino group.[100]

Non-Latino whites have expressed distaste for the Spanish language and other aspects of Cuban American culture. Cuban Americans have faced language discrimination in various places and contexts. For example, in 1988 the voters of Florida, by an 83 to 17 percent margin, approved an "official English" initiative hostile to the state's Latino population. The initiative mandated that the state government's business be conducted in English. One Cuban American leader noted that such legislation "opens the way for bigotry and discrimination."[101] In addition, some private clubs in south Florida have excluded Latinos and other minority groups. Federal district judge Kenneth Ryskamp's support for a Miami country club with such a policy was one of several ethnically insensitive actions that led the Senate Judiciary Committee to reject his nomination by the Bush administration to a U.S. court of appeals seat in the early 1990s. The country club's Euro-American members wanted a place where they did not have to hear Spanish spoken. In most regions of the United States, the Spanish that might be heard by middle- and upper-income whites is spoken primarily by working-class Latinos. In south Florida, however, Spanish speakers make up a majority of the Miami population and are to be found in every social class. Judge Ryskamp echoed the sentiments of many prejudiced Euro-Americans when he complained that his wife was annoyed because many store clerks spoke mostly Spanish and that it was difficult for her to shop because stores now mainly stocked merchandise preferred by their Spanish-speaking customers.[102] Non-Latino whites, of course, might consider the possibility of learning Spanish!

Like other Latinos, Cuban Americans have experienced ethnic discrimination at the hands of non-Latino whites. In the 1960s signs outside some apartment buildings in Miami welcomed some Cuban immigrants with the message, "No Dogs, No Kids, No Cubans." The new immigrants not only faced housing discrimination but also employment barriers erected by non-Latino whites. One Cuban American FBI agent, Fernando Mata, helped to bring a successful 1988 lawsuit against the FBI. As a result of the lawsuit the FBI was forced to eradicate patterns of employment discrimination against its Latino employees. After the lawsuit Mata, a decorated counterintelligence specialist, lost his security clearance and was suspended by the FBI because of allegations that he was spying for Cuba. However, many FBI agents and civil rights activists outside the agency saw no proof of such spying activity and argued that Mata was being harassed because he had been part of the discrimination lawsuit against the FBI.[103]

THE ECONOMIC SITUATION

Many Cuban immigrants experienced a dramatic decline in occupational status when they entered the U.S. economy. A 1966 survey of Cubans in the Miami metropolitan area found that the percentage of immigrants who were employed as professionals, proprietors, technicians, and managers dropped from just over 48 percent to just under 13 percent while the percentage of those employed as unskilled laborers doubled (32 percent in the United States compared with 16 percent in Cuba). Even though many were willing to take jobs far below their previous occupational level, unemployment was widespread in south Florida. Still most did not migrate to other regions, but preferred to remain within the Cuban community in south Florida, where the hope of returning home was kept alive.[104]

The increased Cuban presence in south Florida made Miami more important as a center for international trade. The area's economic growth brought an increase in the number of international corporations establishing headquarters for Latin America in the Miami area, as well as an increase in the volume and value of international trade. Indeed Miami has become, in the eyes of many observers, the "capital of Latin America" because of its centrality in Latin American trade and banking as well as in the underground economy of the drug trade.[105]

A 1968 nationwide survey of Cuban immigrants across the United States found that fewer than half those who had been employed as professionals in Cuba held professional positions in the United States; the proportion who held unskilled jobs had risen from 5 percent in Cuba to 25 percent in the United States. Interviews with respondents revealed that as they increased their English proficiency, their educational background and work experience often helped them climb to a position at or near their former level within a few years of resettlement.[106]

Compared with other Latino groups, Cuban Americans have enjoyed a high degree of economic upward mobility. There are several interrelated reasons for this. Some researchers have pointed to individual strengths: the high-level educational and occupational characteristics and aspirations of many Cuban immigrants, especially the earlier arrivals, prepared them for success. Other researchers have emphasized that the large numbers of immigrants in one economic community (Miami), an "ethnic enclave," make possible the development of support networks to facilitate economic adjustment. Discussing the development of the Cuban American enclave in Miami, sociologists Portes and Bach suggest that Cubans have done relatively well economically because they migrated not as poor individuals in isolated circumstances but rather as a group that had substantial resources, access to important social networks, and support from major federal governmental programs. Pedraza has suggested that these government aid programs advanced the structural assimilation of Cuban immigrants by reinforcing their initial social-class-of-origin advantage and thereby creating a cumulative advantage. The wide range of professions, occupations, and skills among the Cuban immigrants facilitated the development of a large and interdependent local economy capable of providing jobs and incomes for many members of the immigrant community in south Florida, including some from Central and South America. Once created, the ethnic enclave economy gave Cuban American entrepreneurs access to a periodic stream of labor from Cuba. Appeals to ethnic solidarity, to the Cuban identity of the laborers, sometimes helped certain business people to exploit their own laborers.[107]

While individual and group factors are important in the economic adjustment of Cuban Americans, they do not fully account for the substantial mobility displayed by this group. A third factor must be considered: the economic organization of the Cuban American family. As Perez points out, the Cuban American family is generally "organized around realizing aspirations of economic achievement." Although few Cuban women participated in the paid labor force prior to the revolution, gainful employment became an economic necessity for upward mobility in the United States; after immigration Cuban women viewed work outside the home as an opportunity to help the family advance. Cuban American women, including those who are married with husband present and those with young children, are more likely than other Latino women to be in the paid labor force; Cuban American women are also more likely to work full-time and year-round than other Latino women. On the average, Cuban American families have fewer children than other Latino families, and thus fewer disruptions for the women who participate in the paid labor force. Significantly, three-generation families under one roof are more common among Cuban Americans, providing a source of safe childcare and additional wage earners.[108]

Among Latino groups, Cuban Americans have relatively high levels of income and education. A comparison of family income and poverty rates and levels of educational attainment for Mexican Americans, Puerto Ricans, and Cuban Americans was presented in Chapter 9. Cuban Americans are much nearer the total population on all measures than they are to Mexican Americans or mainland Puerto Ricans. The rate of college completion for Cuban Americans is twice that of mainland Puerto Ricans and four times that of Mexican Americans. The 1991 median household income for Cuban Americans (estimated at $36,300 by Strategy Research Corporation's random survey of Latino households across the nation) is 96 percent that of the total population ($38,000). In contrast, the estimated median household income for mainland Puerto Ricans is 55 percent that of the total U.S. population, and for Mexican Americans it is 72 percent.[109] However, one should not overlook the possibility of discrimination in the case of Cuban Americans. Given the relatively high level of education among Cuban Americans, their median income figure is lower than it would be for comparably educated non-Latino whites. Employment discrimination at the hands of non-Latino whites has been a problem for Cuban Americans since the 1960s.

As we have already noted, the prosperity of Cuban Americans compared with other Latino groups does not mean that all Cuban Americans are affluent. A 1991 report by the Children's Defense Fund revealed that more than 28 percent of Cuban American children lived in poverty, more than double the poverty rate for non-Latino white children. The majority lived with parents who were married and employed at least part of the year, but who earned very low wages. The dramatic increase in the poverty rate for Cuban American children during the 1980s and the development of areas of chronic poverty in Miami indicate that economic success is not a reality for all Cuban American families.[110]

POLITICS

Their expectation that the Fidel Castro regime and thus their period of exile would be short-lived led most post-1959 Cuban immigrants to remain politically inactive at the local and state levels for a number of years, although from the time of their arrival they had a strong desire to influence U.S. foreign policy toward Cuba. The mid-1970s saw an increase in the number of naturalized citizens followed by an increase in voter registration and participation in local and state politics. In the 1980s the Cuban American marketing director of the *Miami News* stated, "Cuban-Americans are definitely super-conservative. Communism for us is the enemy. On domestic issues, we will be more toward the center...but the Cuban business community is still more in favor of Reaganomics than Mexicans or Puerto Ricans."[111] However, Jorge and Moncarz point out that although Cubans tend to identify with the conservative Republican party, which they consider more likely than the Democratic party to be anti-Castro, they left a legacy of progressive politics in Cuba. Some social reforms, such as an eight-hour work day, free school lunches, and a minimum wage, instituted in the 1930s, have remained in effect through a succession of dictators.[112]

Since the 1980s Cuban Americans have become more active politically than other Latino groups. Cuban Americans now hold many elective and appointive offices in south Florida. The mayor of the area's two largest cities, the manager of the Dade County government, the superintendent of the Dade County public schools, and almost half of Dade County's state legislators are Cuban American. Similar advances have been made in urban areas in other states, particularly New Jersey. As of 1992, the one Cuban American member of the U.S. House of Representatives, from Miami, is the first and only Latino female in the history of the U.S. Congress.[113] The Cuban American National Foundation, established in 1981 with offices in Miami and Washington, has become one of the most active anti-Communist organizations in the United States. It has been very influential in lobbying Congress on legislation dealing with Cuba, and a few of its leaders exercised great influence in the Republican administrations of the 1980s.

Many of the more than half a million Cuban Americans in Miami, as well as those in other parts of the nation, have remained psychologically involved in the politics of Cuba. It is sometimes said that in the so-called "Little Havana" section of Miami, the politics that matter are Cuban politics. Some Cuban exiles have been involved in paramilitary training and plans for terrorist acts against the Cuban government. Cuban exiles recruited by the CIA were involved in the unsuccessful Bay of Pigs invasion in 1961. Members of at least one of the militant anti-Castro groups in the United States, Alpha 66, continued to practice mock invasions in the early 1990s. In late 1991 three Miami Cubans entered Cuba by boat with small arms and explosives, but they were captured, tried, and convicted of sabotage. Since 1985 Cuban Americans have been active in the operation of Radio Marti, a federally funded station, and its affiliate, TV Marti, which transmit twenty-four-hour news and public affairs programming from Washington to Cuba via Florida.[114]

The collapse of the Soviet Union in the early 1990s brought severe economic hardships to Cuba, for the two countries had been closely linked by trade for three decades. Significantly, the Antonio Maceo Brigade, a progressive Cuban American organization, reported that between September 1991 and February 1992 fifteen thousand Cuban Americans in Miami signed a petition calling for the United States to lift its economic blockade of Cuba in order to ease the island's economic plight. During this same period conservative Cuban Americans sought more U.S. government support for raids designed to topple Castro's government and to introduce multiparty politics in Cuba. In January 1992 five thousand Cuban American counterdemonstrators, including several hundred from Miami, protested proposals to end sanctions against the Castro government at an international rally against the economic blockade in New York City.[115]

The involvement of Cuban Americans in the politics of Cuba is yet another example of the way in which the development and situations of U.S. racial and ethnic groups interact with and are dependent upon the world context. In this sense, U.S. racial and ethnic relations are intrinsically international.

ASSIMILATION OR COLONIALISM?

Assimilation Issues

Cuban Americans are one of the recent additions to the bubbling cauldron of the United States. Like other Latinos, they have faced prejudice and discrimination and have reacted in a number of ways. Language discrimination has been a common problem. Another current type of discrimination is exclusion from certain private clubs. But Cubans have fought back. Efforts to maintain the old Cuban culture and social order, as well as to bypass country club discrimination by Euro-Americans, led to the creation in the 1960s of the Big Five Club, a Miami social club originally composed exclusively of members of five elite Havana yacht and golf clubs. As of the early 1990s, the Big Five Club's membership included some sixteen hundred families. The Big Five Club has had an official policy of nondiscrimination on the basis of race. However, the club has no black members, even though Miami's Cuban community includes a significant number of blacks. To attract younger members, the club recently lowered its initiation fee for families with children below the age of twenty-four. As with other immigrant groups, members of the younger generation seem less interested in maintaining old ways by joining such social clubs. According to the president of Big Five, "The ones born in this country feel they are more American than Cuban."[116] Assimilation thus seems well underway.

The preservation of Cuban culture and identity in an "ethnic enclave" (a concentrated community) in south Florida has represented a crucial foundation for Cuban Americans' economic and political integration into U.S. society. Portes and Bach found that the strong ethnic enclave created by the first groups of Cuban immigrants was rooted in old kinship and friendship ties and formed the social and economic context into which later immigrants entered. In 1973–74 these researchers interviewed 590 Cuban male immigrant heads of household at the time of their arrival in Miami. The respondents were interviewed again several years later. In the initial interview 99 percent of these respondents expressed an intention to remain in Miami, and, significantly, at the time of the final interview 97 percent still resided there. Portes and Bach note that the strong ethnic enclave provided a context in which the average immigrant could partially adapt to U.S. culture and yet carry out many of life's routine activities within a Cuban setting. Six years after these respondents entered the United States, more than one in five were self-employed in the Cuban American community and almost half worked for a Cuban American business owner. For most Cuban Americans, economic assimilation was not directly to the Euro-American core economy but to the Cuban enclave economy in south Florida. Group economic integration with only modest individual assimilation at the cultural level was the pattern for the first generation.[117]

Cuban Americans are not the only immigrant group to achieve a degree of prosperity and economic power during the first generation in the United States. Like Jewish and Japanese immigrants in the first half of the twentieth century, Cuban immigrants did not follow the model of waiting their turn in the urban queue, as had Irish and Italian immigrants in an earlier period. Instead they advanced in an economic niche as small-business owners, laying a foundation for their children's educational and occupational mobility into business and professional jobs. The economic enclaves created by the first generations of Jewish and Japanese Americans did not become part of the pattern of typical urban group succession. Nor is it likely that the ethnic enclave created by Cuban Americans in south Florida will pass in turn to another immigrant group. The presence of a large and cohesive group of immigrants provides a context of social support and economic concentration for Cuban Americans that does not exist for other current immigrant groups. This economic concentration and success also provided a foundation for some political integration, at least regionally in south Florida.[118]

Cultural-assimilation pressures on Cuban immigrants have created cross-generational problems similar to those of earlier European immigrants. Language assimilation is significant for the younger generation. An early 1980s survey of Miami's Cubans revealed that the young preferred to listen to English-language programs on radio and TV, whereas their parents switched back and forth between English and Spanish programs. Like other immigrant grandparents before them, the grandparents preferred to hear and speak the mother tongue. Parents and grandparents worried about the excessive freedom and lack of parental respect of teenagers in U.S. cities. They worried that dates between Cuban American young people were not chaperoned the way they had been in Cuba. Parents and grandparents tended to emphasize Cuban traditions and food; the grandchildren often preferred things American. Moreover, the older generations were found to be more strongly committed to overthrowing Cuba's Communist government and to returning home. The less politically active youth saw the United States as their permanent home. Nevertheless, family and community ties were strong, and the young were proud of their Cuban identities.[119]

Strategy Research Corporation's 1991 study found a similar generation gap. SRC's ranking of the assimilation level of Latinos found Cuban Americans to be the least culturally assimilated of all Spanish-speaking groups based on language use and behavioral, attitudinal, and aspirational measures. Fewer than 4 percent of Cuban American heads of household were classified as highly assimilated; just over 26 percent were rated partially assimilated and 70 percent were ranked relatively unassimilated. The high density of Cuban Americans in south Florida and the older average age of this population are major factors in the lower level of assimilation. This same survey reported other measures of assimilation by region. Among Latinos in the Southeast, 57 percent of whom are Cuban Americans, the vast majority of adults felt more comfortable speaking Spanish than English and spoke Spanish more often at home and on social occasions. A majority gave Spanish as the language they spoke more frequently at work, although almost one-third answered "both Spanish and English" to this question. Fewer than one-third of these adults reported that they spoke, read, or wrote English well. A very large majority considered themselves very Hispanic and expected to be very Hispanic ten years in the future.[120]

However, the SRC survey presented a very different picture of younger Latinos (mostly Cubans) in the Southeast. Fewer than half of those under the age of eighteen classified themselves as very Hispanic, and only 40 percent felt they would be very Hispanic ten years in the future. Compared with those over eighteen, persons in this younger group were almost eight times more likely to expect that they would be only minimally Hispanic ten years in the future. Language assimilation was dramatic. Almost three-quarters of this age group spoke English at school and felt more comfortable speaking English than Spanish. A large majority reported that they spoke, read, and wrote English well, and a majority reported that their reading and writing ability in Spanish was only very poor to fair. About half reported that they used both languages on social occasions, although over half said they spoke Spanish more frequently at home. Yet without exception, the adult respondents in this region felt that it was important for their children to be able to read and write Spanish. The young are making greater strides toward cultural assimilation than their parents are eager to accept.

Cuban Americans in Miami have assimilated selectively, with the older generation especially preserving language and social and cultural traditions. In some critical cultural and social areas the younger generation seems to be moving away from the old ways, even from the ethnic enclave, and assimilating more rapidly at the cultural and social levels. This pattern is similar to earlier groups such as Italian Americans. In other areas of the nation smaller Cuban American communities are more fully integrated into the larger community. There is less research information, however, on Cuban Americans in areas other than Miami.

A Power–Conflict Perspective?

To our knowledge no one has applied a power–conflict perspective to Cuban Americans. Some might argue that the internal colonialism and other power–conflict perspectives are not relevant to interpreting the development of the predominantly white Cuban American group, which has not been victimized as much by thorough-going long-term economic and political discrimination as have most other Latino groups. Many of those who migrated to the United States before 1980 were the beneficiaries of the economic and political colonialism of Cuba at the hands of the United States prior to the 1959 revolution. And instead of becoming low-wage labor and surplus labor forces for non-Latino industrialists, as was (and is) the case for many Puerto Ricans, most Cuban Americans have become part of a Miami area niche economy that has helped speed their economic mobility in the United States.

The opportunities and accomplishments of the U.S.-born generations of Cuban Americans (at least of the white majority), which include growing numbers of professional and managerial workers, seem more similar to those of certain white ethnic groups (for example, Italian Americans) at a comparable point in time than to those of other Latino Americans. Indeed, it may be the case that over time the adaptive development of Cuban Americans may be a variation on the ethnogenesis model, much like the long-term adaptation of white ethnic groups such as Jewish and Italian Americans. This will probably be the case only if the second and later generations of Cuban Americans disperse residentially from what is now a highly concentrated and cohesive community in south Florida. Even the south Florida ethnic enclave has not been able to resist the pressures for assimilation that now are having an impact on the second and third generations of Cuban Americans. Residential dispersion may well accelerate this assimilation process.

One major obstacle, however, to full assimilation of Cuban Americans to the Anglo American core culture and society is language. As we have seen in this and previous chapters, powerful English-speaking whites have organized to fight against Spanish and Spanish speakers and to try to impose English as the dominant language. Such nativist movements mark a type of cultural colonialism that rejects cultural pluralism if it threatens the dominance of the core culture. Even though most Cuban Americans appear to be white to other white Americans, they will not be fully accepted until they reject the Spanish language and other aspects of their Cuban culture. Thus a significant Cuban sacrifice on the altar of white nativism and ethnocentrism will be required for the majority of white Americans to welcome Cuban Americans into the Anglo core culture and society. Even then, Cuban Americans who are not white, whose ancestry is African, will not be admitted into the core society. Given these problems of discrimination and hierarchy, then, some might argue that a power–conflict perspective is indeed appropriate, and in need of development, for the case of Cuban Americans.

SUMMARY

Puerto Ricans, the second largest Latino group in the United States, are a distinctive American group with an ancient heritage. Like Mexican Americans, they represent a fusion of Native American, Spanish, and African heritages. Today Puerto Ricans are a divided nation, with one foot on the mainland and one foot in Puerto Rico, a Caribbean island. The more or less external-colony situation of the island population complicates the picture. There has been a debate among Puerto Ricans as to whether they are one nation with one set of problems with a few variations or rather two nations with different sets of problems.

The issue of class also enters this debate. The island is a self-contained society with a variety of classes, including both a local capitalist class and a local working class, as well as a small elite of U.S.-based multinational capitalists. Some argue that social-class problems on the island are different from those on the mainland. On the mainland, Puerto Ricans tend to be primarily a working-class people; there are few mainland Puerto Rican capitalists. Other commentators play down the class divisions and stress that there is only one Puerto Rican nation. As one Puerto Rican social scientist puts it, "No matter how we see ourselves internally, the Yanqui always sees us and deals with us as one class and one people with the same problems. Therefore we should band together and not divide ourselves to fight for our nation against the colonizer."[121]

Puerto Ricans have the lowest median family income and the highest incidence of poverty of the three major Latino groups in the United States. By contrast, Cuban Americans, the third largest Latino group in the United States, are relatively affluent; compared with the other Latino groups they have high levels of education and income. Cuban Americans are basically an urban population concentrated in the southeastern United States. A major reason Cuban Americans have done relatively well is that most of the early immigrants migrated not as poor individuals but rather as a group that had resources and access to important networks. Smaller families and a higher level of participation of Cuban American women in the paid labor force also contributed to the economic upward mobility of this group. The achievements of Cuban Americans underscore the advantages of migrating under the auspices of strong family and friendship networks and governmental support.

A distinctive aspect of this important Latino group has been the development of a politically powerful urban community centered in Miami. The size and economic diversity of the Spanish-speaking population in south Florida have allowed this group to develop a strong ethnic enclave and economy and to maintain many Cuban cultural practices as well as use of its mother tongue. Yet as is the case with other immigrant groups, members of the younger generation are beginning to move toward the core culture in many areas, including that of language use.

NOTES

1. Enrique Fernandez, "Puerto Rican Independence: Is It a Dream?" *Newsday*, February 27, 1992, p. 94.
2. Daniel Adams, "Puerto Ricans Vote on Independence from U.S.," *The Independent*, December 9, 1991, p. 14.
3. Manuel Maldonado-Denis, *Puerto Rico: A Socio-historic Interpretation*, trans. Elena Vialo (New York: Random House, Vintage Books, 1972), pp. 13–19; Luis Antonio Cardona, *A History of the Puerto Ricans in the U.S.A.* (Rockville: Carreta Press, 1990), pp. 8–9; Eric Williams, *From Columbus to Castro: The History of the Caribbean 1492–1969* (London: André Deutsch, 1970), pp. 109, 291.
4. U.S. Commission on Civil Rights, *Puerto Ricans in the Continental United States: An Uncertain Future* (Washington, 1976), pp. 11–12; Jorge Heine, "A People Apart," *Wilson Quarterly* 4, no. 2 (Spring 1980): 119–23.
5. Maldonado-Denis, *Puerto Rico*, p. 77.
6. U.S. Commission on Civil Rights, *Puerto Ricans in the Continental United States*, p. 12.
7. Maldonado-Denis, *Puerto Rico*, pp. 305–6; Heine, "A People Apart," p. 123.
8. Maldonado-Denis, *Puerto Rico*, pp. 311–12; Heine, "A People Apart," p. 125; Jaime Santiago, "One Step Forward," *Wilson Quarterly* 4, no. 2 (Spring 1980): 132–37; Frank Bonilla and Ricardo Campos, "A Wealth of Poor: Puerto Ricans in the New Economic Order," *Daedalus* 110 (Spring 1981): 135; Thomas, "Puerto Ricans in the Promised Land," p. 19; U.S. Bureau of the Census, *Statistical Abstract of the United States: 1991* (Washington, 1991), p. 821.
9. Adalberto Lopez, "The Puerto Rican Diaspora: A Survey," in *Puerto Rico and Puerto Ricans: Studies in History and Society*, ed. Adalberto Lopez and James Petras (New York: John Wiley, 1974), p. 318; Clara E. Rodríguez, *Puerto Ricans: Born in the U.S.A.* (Boston: Unwin Hyman, 1989), pp. 1–10.
10. Piri Thomas, "Puerto Ricans in the Promised Land," *Civil Rights Digest* 6, no. 2 (n.d.): 20.
11. Jack Agueros, "Halfway to Dick and Jane," in *The Immigrant Experience: The Anguish of Becoming American*, ed. Thomas C. Wheeler (New York: Dial Press, 1971), p. 93.
12. Rodríguez, *Puerto Ricans*, pp. 11–13.
13. Cardona, *A History of the Puerto Ricans in the U.S.A.*, pp. 95–96.
14. U.S. Commission on Civil Rights, *Puerto Ricans in the Continental United States*, p. 25; Rodríguez, *Puerto Ricans*, pp. 4–13; Cardona, *A History of the Puerto Ricans in the U.S.A.*, pp. 95–112; Felix M. Padilla, *Puerto Rican Chicago* (Notre Dame, Ind.: University of Notre Dame Press, 1987), pp. 66–72.
15. U.S. Commission on Civil Rights, *Puerto Ricans in the Continental United States*, pp. 19–25; Pedro A. Rivera, "Angel and Aurea," *Wilson Quarterly* 4, no. 2 (Spring 1980): 146–52; "The Spending Power of Puerto Ricans," *American Demographics*, April 1991, pp. 46–49; Rodríguez, *Puerto Ricans*, pp. 4–8, 28; correspondence with U.S. representative Jose Serrano's staff; U.S. Bureau of the Census, *The Census and You* (Washington, 1991), p. 3.

16. Quoted in Frank Bonilla, "Beyond Survival: Porque Sequiremos Siendo Puertoriquenos," in *Puerto Rico and Puerto Ricans,* ed. Lopez, p. 439.
17. Alfredo Lopez, *The Puerto Rican Papers* (Indianapolis: Bobbs-Merrill, 1973), p. 120.
18. Quoted in ibid., p. 211.
19. This pamphlet, entitled *What Is Prejudice?* is reprinted in *The Puerto Ricans: A Documentary History,* ed. Kal Wagenheim (Garden City, N.Y.: Doubleday, Anchor Books, 1973), p. 291.
20. Migration Division, Department of Labor and Human Resources, Commonwealth of Puerto Rico, *Puerto Rican Voter Registration in New York City* (New York: 1988), p. 9.
21. Nathan Glazer and Daniel P. Moynihan, *Beyond the Melting Pot* (Cambridge: M.I.T. Press and Harvard University Press, 1963), pp. 88–90.
22. Rose Marie Arce, "Crime, Drugs, and Stereotypes," *Newsday,* December 2, 1991, p. 5.
23. Rodríguez, *Puerto Ricans,* pp. 51–56.
24. Piri Thomas, *Down These Mean Streets* (New York: Knopf, 1967), pp. 85–86.
25. Rodríguez, *Puerto Ricans,* pp. 56–59, 79.
26. Angel R. Martínez, "The Effects of Acculturation and Racial Identity on Self-Esteem and Psychological Well-Being among Young Puerto Ricans" (Ph.D. dissertation, City University of New York, 1988); cited in ibid., pp. 60–61.
27. Rodríguez, *Puerto Ricans,* pp. 61–68.
28. Jesús Colon, "The Early Days," in *The Puerto Ricans,* ed. Wagenheim, p. 286.
29. Thomas, *Down These Mean Streets,* pp. 102–104.
30. Rodríguez, *Puerto Ricans,* p. 2; U.S. Commission on Civil Rights, *Puerto Ricans in the Continental United States,* p. 54; Bonilla and Campos, "A Wealth of Poor," p. 158.
31. U.S. Bureau of the Census, *Persons of Spanish Origin in the United States: March 1979* (Washington, 1980), p. 29.
32. Juan Gonzalez, "Puerto Ricans on the Mainland," *Perspectives* 13 (Winter 1982): 16; U.S. Commission on Civil Rights, *Puerto Ricans in the Continental United States,* p. 52; Bonilla and Campos, "A Wealth of Poor," p. 160; U.S. Bureau of the Census, "The Hispanic Population in the United States: March 1990," *Current Population Reports,* series P-20, no. 449 (Washington, 1990), pp. 8–9. 1990 census definitions differ from these of earlier censuses.
33. U.S. Commission on Civil Rights, *Social Indicators of Equality for Minorities and Women* (Washington, 1978), p. 30; U.S. Bureau of the Census, *Persons of Spanish Origin in the United States,* p. 25; U.S. Bureau of the Census, *U.S. Census of Population, 1980: General Social and Economic Characteristics,* PC 80-1-C1 (Washington, 1983), p. 165; U.S. Bureau of the Census, *Statistical Abstract of the United States: 1991,* p. 386.
34. U.S. Commission on Civil Rights, *Puerto Ricans in the Continental United States,* pp. 59–62.
35. Western Regional Office, U.S. Commission on Civil Rights, *Puerto Ricans in California* (Washington, 1980), p. 17.
36. Rodríguez, *Puerto Ricans,* pp. 92–93; quotation on p. 93. See also Herbert Hill, "Guardians of the Sweatshops: The Trade Unions, Racism, and the Garment Industry," in *Puerto Rico and Puerto Ricans,* ed. Lopez, pp. 386–88.
37. U.S. Commission on Civil Rights, *Puerto Ricans in the Continental United States,* p. 60; Vilma Ortiz, "Latinos and Industrial Change in New York and Los Angeles" (paper, 1990); Clara E. Rodríguez, "Economic Factors Affecting Puerto Ricans in New York," in *Labor Migration under Capitalism: The Puerto Rican Experience,* ed. History Task Force (New York: Center for Puerto Rican Studies, 1979), pp. 208–10; Rodríguez, *Puerto Ricans,* pp. 85–91.
38. Marta Tienda and William A. Diaz, "Puerto Ricans' Special Problems," *New York Times,* August 28, 1987, p. A30; Marta Tienda and William Diaz, letter to the *New York Times,* October 10, 1987, p. A30; Robert Garcia, letter to the *New York Times,* September 17, 1987, p. A34.
39. Strategy Research Corporation, *1991 U.S. Hispanic Market* (Miami, 1991), p. 132.
40. Felipe Luciano, "America Should Never Have Taught Us to Read, She Should Have Never Given Us Eyes to See," in *Puerto Rico and Puerto Ricans,* ed. Lopez, pp. 430–31.
41. Agueros, "Halfway to Dick and Jane," pp. 96–102; quotation on p. 98.
42. Tienda and Diaz, "Puerto Ricans' Special Problems"; U.S. Bureau of the Census, "The Hispanic Population in the United States," pp. 14–15; Rivera, "Angel and Aurea," p. 148; Patrick Reardon, "Search for a Better Life Brought Different Waves of Immigrants," *Chicago Tribune,* September 11, 1991, p. 5.
43. Testimony by Jose A. Rivera, printed in "Fair Housing and the Spanish Speaking," *Civil Rights Digest* 8 (Fall 1975): 35–36; Gonzalez, "Puerto Ricans on the Mainland," pp. 15–17; Padilla, *Puerto Rican Chicago,* pp. 117–23.
44. Rodríguez, *Puerto Ricans,* pp. 106–16; quotation from pp. 109, 110.
45. Clay F. Richards, "Jobs Top Latinos' List of Concerns," *Newsday,* October 13, 1991, p. 27.
46. U.S. Bureau of the Census, "The Hispanic Population in the United States," pp. 6–7.
47. Rodríguez, *Puerto Ricans,* pp. 122–23, 127; George Borjas and Marta Tienda, eds., *Hispanics in the U.S. Economy* (New York: Academic Press, 1985), cited in Rodríguez, *Puerto Ricans,* p. 91.
48. Milga Morales-Nadal, "Puerto Rican/Latino(a) Vistas on Culture and Education" (paper, 1991), n.p.
49. Rodríguez, *Puerto Ricans,* pp. 139–40.
50. Ibid., pp. 122–23, 149–50; Lopez, *The Puerto Rican Papers,* p. 119; Gary Orfield, "School Desegregation Needed Now," *Focus,* July 1987, pp. 5–7.
51. U.S. Commission on Civil Rights, *Puerto Ricans in the Continental United States,* p. 100.
52. Quoted in ibid., p. 99.
53. Rodríguez, *Puerto Ricans,* p. 126.
54. Henry A. Giroux, Series Introduction to Catherine E. Walsh, *Pedagogy and the Struggle for Voice* (New York: Bergin and Garvey, 1991), p. xx.
55. Quoted in U.S. Commission on Civil Rights, *Puerto Ricans in the Continental United States,* p. 103.
56. Rodríguez, *Puerto Ricans,* pp. 139–40.
57. Ibid., pp. 147–48; quotation from Gonzalez, "Puerto Ricans on the Mainland," p. 11.

58. Walsh, *Pedagogy and the Struggle for Voice*, pp. 101, 127.
59. Rusty Butler, *On Creating a Hispanic America: A Nation within a Nation?* (Washington: Council for Interamerican Security, 1985), quoted in ibid., p. 100.
60. Walsh, *Pedagogy and the Struggle for Voice*, p. ix.
61. Ibid., pp. vii–xi, 1–27, 65–68, quotations from p. vii.
62. Migration Division, *Puerto Rican Voter Registration in New York City*, pp. 5–6.
63. Data in this and the following paragraphs regarding political representation are from a conversation with Luis Caban of the Midwest–Northeast Voter Registration Education Project and the National Association of Latino Elected and Appointed Officials, reprinted in the association's *National Report* 11, no. 1 (Fourth Quarter 1991): 1, 3. The Puerto Rican Legal Defense and Education Fund was primarily involved in the lawsuit in New York City; the Mexican American Legal Defense and Education Fund was primarily involved in the Chicago case.
64. Garcia, letter to the *New York Times*, p. A34. In this section on politics and the following section on protest we draw on some insights provided by Maria Merrill-Ramirez in comments on this chapter.
65. Lopez, "The Puerto Rican Diaspora," p. 329; Western Regional Office, U.S. Commission on Civil Rights, *Puerto Ricans in California*, p. 16.
66. *Building a Road Towards Tomorrow*, Midwest–Northeast Voter Registration Education Project Newsbulletin (Chicago, 1991); David E. Pitt, "Puerto Rico Expands New York Voter Drive," *New York Times*, October 14, 1987, p. A18; conversation with Carmen Ambert at the Department of Puerto Rican Community Affairs for the United States, New York City, December 23, 1991.
67. Lopez, *The Puerto Rican Papers*, pp., 55–58.
68. Bonilla and Campos, "A Wealth of Poor," pp. 166–67; "Puerto Ricans Defeat a Measure to Restrict Voting on Statehood," *New York Times*, December 9, 1991, p. A12.
69. Fitzpatrick, "Puerto Ricans," in *Harvard Encyclopedia of Ethnic Groups*, ed. Stephan Thernstrom (Cambridge: Harvard University Press, 1981), p. 866; Padilla, *Puerto Rican Chicago*, pp. 54, 99–143.
70. John Adam Moreau, "My Parents, They Cry for Joy," in *The Puerto Ricans*, ed. Wagenheim, pp. 327–30.
71. Lopez, "The Puerto Rican Diaspora," p. 331.
72. Ibid., pp. 331–32.
73. Michael Abramson, *Palante: Young Lords Party* (New York: McGraw-Hill, 1971), pp. 34–36; conversation with Luis Burguillo of the National Puerto Rican Coalition, Washington, December 23, 1991.
74. Gonzalez, "Puerto Ricans on the Mainland," p. 17; Padilla, *Puerto Rican Chicago*, pp. 117–25; Steven A. Holmes, "Puerto Ricans' Alienation Is Cited in Miami Rampage," *New York Times*, December 5, 1990, p. A24:
75. Lopez, "The Puerto Rican Diaspora," p. 332.
76. Fitzpatrick, "Puerto Ricans," p. 865.
77. Paul Moses, "Church's Challenge," *Newsday*, October 14, 1991, p. 6.
78. Joseph P. Fitzpatrick, *Puerto Rican Americans: The Meaning of Migration to the Mainland* (Englewood Cliffs, N.J.: Prentice-Hall, 1971), pp. 22–43; Milton Gordon, *Assimilation in American Life* (New York: Oxford University Press, 1964), pp. 75–77; Elena Padilla, *Up from Puerto Rico* (New York: Columbia University Press, 1958); Walsh, *Pedagogy and the Struggle for Voice*, pp. 101–02.
79. Maldonado-Denis, *Puerto Rico*, p. 319.
80. Lloyd H. Rogler and Rosemary Santana Cooney, *Puerto Rican Families in New York City: Intergenerational Processes* (Maplewood, N.J.: Waterfront Press, 1984), pp. 76–79; Strategy Research Corporation, *1991 U.S. Hispanic Market*, p. 78.
81. Fitzpatrick, *Puerto Rican Americans*, p. 43.
82. "Interview with Leonard Covello," *Urban Review* 3 (January 1969): 53–61.
83. U.S. Commission on Civil Rights, *Puerto Ricans in the Continental United States*, p. 29; Rogler and Cooney, *Puerto Rican Families in New York City*, p. 204.
84. See Lopez, "The Puerto Rican Diaspora," p. 343.
85. Bonilla and Campos, "A Wealth of Poor," p. 172.
86. Felix Robert Masud-Piloto, *With Open Arms: Cuban Migration to the U.S.* (Totowa, N.J.: Rowman and Littlefield, 1988), pp. 7–11.
87. Ibid., pp. 11–16.
88. Ibid., pp. 13, 20.
89. Ibid., p. 11.
90. Ibid., pp. 20–35.
91. Ibid., pp. 1, 32–35, 39–41; "U.S. Hispanics: Who They Are, Whence They Came, and Why," in *The Hispanic Almanac* (Washington, Hispanic Policy Development Project, 1984), pp. 17–18; Antonio Jorge and Raul Moncarz, *The Political Economy of Cubans in South Florida* (Miami: Institute of Interamerican Studies, 1987), pp. 4, 18; Hugh Thomas, *Cuba: The Pursuit of Freedom* (New York: Harper & Row, Pub., 1971), p. 117; Sylvia Pedraza-Bailey, "Cuba's Exiles: Portrait of a Refugee Migration," *International Migration Review* 19, no. 1 (Spring 1985): 9–11, 23; Sylvia Pedraza, "Cubans in Exile (1959–1989): The State of the Research," *Scholarship on the Cuban Experience: A Dialogue Among Cubanists*, ed., Damian Fernandez (Gainesville: University of Florida, 1992).
92. Masud-Piloto, *With Open Arms*, pp. 1–5, 83–87.
93. Pedraza-Bailey, "Cuba's Exiles," pp. 15–17; Michael G. Wenk, "Adjustment and Assimilation: The Cuban Refugee Experience," *International Migration Review* 3, no. 1 (Fall 1968): 44, 48.
94. Pedraza-Bailey, "Cuba's Exiles," pp. 22–26; Masud-Piloto, *With Open Arms*, pp. 92–108.
95. Masud-Piloto, *With Open Arms*, pp. 83.

96. Lisandro Perez, "Immigrant Economic Adjustment and Family Organization," *International Migration Review* 20, no. 1 (Spring 1986): 13. Other data in this paragraph are from U.S. Bureau of the Census, *The Census and You,* p. 3; and U.S. Bureau of the Census, "The Hispanic Population in the United States," pp. 6–7, 13.

97. "Trouble in Paradise," *Time,* November 23, 1981, pp. 24–32; Max J. Castro and Guillermo J. Grenier, "Black–Latino Relations under Conditions of Latino Empowerment: The Miami Case" (research proposal, Miami, 1991), pp. 3–4; Jeffrey Schmalz, "Miami Tensions Simmering 3 Months after Violence," *New York Times,* April 10, 1989, p. A8; Holmes, "Puerto Ricans' Alienation Is Cited in Miami Rampage," p. A24.

98. Masud-Piloto, *With Open Arms,* pp. 111–25.

99. "757 Haitians Cleared to Seek Refuge in U.S.," *New York Times,* December 10, 1991, p. A8.

100. "A Million More Poor U.S. Hispanic Children in 1980s," *Reuter Library Report,* August 26, 1991.

101. Matt Spetalnick, "Florida Declares English Official Language," *Reuter Library Report,* November 9, 1988, n.p.

102. Neil A. Lewis, "Committee Rejects Bush Nominee to Key Appellate Court in South," *New York Times,* April 12, 1991, pp. A1, A11.

103. Philip Shenon, "FBI Suspends Veteran Agent," *New York Times,* March 5, 1990, p. A1.

104. Jorge and Moncarz, *The Political Economy of Cubans in South Florida,* pp. 16–19.

105. Ibid., p. 9.

106. Wenk, "Adjustment and Assimilation," pp. 39–42.

107. Lisandro Perez, "Immigrant Economic Adjustment and Family Organization: The Cuban Success Story Reexamined," *International Migration Review* 20, no. 1 (Spring 1986): 4–7; Silvia Pedraza-Bailey, "Cubans and Mexicans in the United States: The Functions of Political and Economic Migration," *Cuban Studies* 11, no. 2 / 12, no. 1 (July 1981–January 1982); Alejandro Portes and Robert L. Bach, *Latin American Journey* (Berkeley: University of California Press, 1985), pp. 200–20.

108. Perez, "Immigrant Economic Adjustment and Family Organization," pp. 4–20, quotation on p. 18.

109. U.S. Bureau of the Census, "The Hispanic Population in the United States," pp. 6–9, 14–15. Statistics on median household income are from Strategy Research Corporation, *1991 U.S. Hispanic Market,* p. 132.

110. "A Million More Poor U.S. Hispanic Children in 1980s."

111. Quoted in "Widespread Political Efforts Open New Era for Hispanics," *Congressional Quarterly,* October 23, 1982, p. 2709.

112. Jorge and Moncarz, *The Political Economy of Cubans in South Florida,* p. 30; Masud-Piloto, *With Open Arms,* p. 16.

113. Castro and Grenier, "Black-Latino Relations under Conditions of Latino Empowerment," p. 3.

114. Richard Boudreaus, "Cuba Strikes Democracy Movement," *Los Angeles Times,* January 19, 1992, p. A1; Don Kowet, "Radio Marti Head," *Washington Times,* December 19, 1991, p. E1; U.S. Commerce Department 1982 report to Congress, cited in Alexander Cockburn, "Miami Vice: The Miami Herald's January 19 Editorial on Contra Aid," *Nation,* February 27, 1988, p. 260; Deborah Sharp, "Execution in Cuba," *USA Today,* January 22, 1992, p. 3A.

115. "Protesters Disrupt 'Peace for Cuba' Rally," *Los Angeles Times,* January 26, 1992, p. A5; Arun Gupta, "5,000 oppose crunching Cuba at N.Y. Rally," *Guardian,* February 5, 1992, p. 13.

116. Jon Nordheimer, "Where Old Havana Plays," *New York Times,* April 3, 1991, p. C1.

117. Portes and Bach, *Latin American Journey,* pp. 91–93, 193–99.

118. Ibid., pp. 246–47.

119. "Trouble in Paradise," pp. 30–31.

120. Data in this and the following paragraph are from Strategy Research Corporation, *1991 U.S. Hispanic Market,* pp. 78–130.

121. Private communication with Maria Merril-Ramirez, July 1982.

Chapter 11

Japanese Americans

Senator Daniel Inouye, D. Hawaii
Photo courtesy of UPI/Bettman

THE GROWTH OF THE ASIAN–PACIFIC POPULATION

Asian and Pacific Island immigrants have benefitted greatly from the changes in U.S. immigration laws that have occurred since the 1960s, especially from the elimination of racist immigration quotas and the emphasis on social justice and civil rights.[1] Numerous media commentators have suggested that over the last decade Asian–Pacific Americans have been the fastest-growing U.S. minority group. Speaking more accurately, Asian Americans are not one group. There are more than a dozen groups of Americans with roots in Asia or the Pacific Islands. In 1940 these Asian–Pacific Americans were less than half of one percent of the U.S. population. By 1980 they had increased to 1.5 percent, and by 1990 they were almost 3 percent of the total U.S. population.

The number in each of the groups, tabulated by the U.S. Bureau of the Census, can be seen in the following table:

	1980 Census	1990 Census	Change
Chinese	806,040	1,645,472	104%
Filipino	774,652	1,406,770	82%
Asian Indian	361,531	851,447	126%
Japanese	700,974	847,562	21%
Korean	354,593	798,849	125%
Vietnamese	261,729	614,547	135%
Hawaiian	166,814	211,014	27%
Samoan	41,948	62,964	50%
Guamanian	32,158	49,345	53%
Other Asian or Pacific Islander	not available	821,692	not available

Source: U.S. Bureau of the Census, *Census and You,* September 1991, p. 3.

In 1990 the largest of the Asian–Pacific groups, about 1.6 million, was Chinese American. Filipino Americans were not far behind. Japanese, Asian Indian, Korean, and Vietnamese Americans constituted the other large Asian American groups. We will examine Japanese Americans in this chapter, then turn to certain other Asian American groups in Chapter 12.

INTRODUCTION: JAPANESE AMERICANS

Japanese Americans are one of the oldest Asian American groups. At the beginning of the 1990s Japanese Americans comprised 12 percent of Asian Americans. More than half of all Asian Americans live in western states; Japanese Americans are the most heavily concentrated of all Asian American groups, with 80 percent living in this region. Among Asian American groups, Japanese Americans have the highest percentage born in the United States, an indication of the group's early entry into the United States and the small number of recent immigrants.[2]

For some non-Asian Americans, Japanese Americans conjure up stereotypes of crafty "Orientals," images of the militaristic Japanese expansionism of the 1930s and 1940s, or resentment of "unfair" Japanese economic competition today. Even in recent years, political speeches and the graffiti of vandals have included such phrases as "fat

Japs" and "little Japs," and we have seen a resurgence of vandalism and violence targeting Japanese and other Asian Americans. A *Boston Globe* writer summed up some recent anti-Japanese incidents:

> A Honda Civic is bashed in Pennsylvania; Japanese-American community centers are vandalized; an American car salesman is fired for saying on national TV that he buys what is best for his money; a Japanese offer to purchase the Seattle Mariners baseball team sets off a national outcry; writers on Japan topics feel required to state they have never been employed by the Japanese. Frighteningly, a Japanese businessman in California is killed, apparently after receiving an anti-Japanese threat.[3]

Such verbal and physical attacks have been motivated by white fears of Japanese imports or corporations in the United States or by white resentment of Japanese competition in world trade. Anti-Asian hostility has increased during economic recessions, when non-Asians seek scapegoats for problems usually rooted in the faulty decisions of non-Asian executives, investors, and workers.

MIGRATION: AN OVERVIEW

The Serial Migration of Asians

Asian Americans include many immigrant groups: the Chinese, Japanese, Koreans, Filipinos, Vietnamese, Asian Indians, Laotians, and Asian-Pacific Islanders, as well as smaller groups. In his pathbreaking book on Asian immigration to the United States, Takaki has shown that prominent white historians of immigration have often left Asian immigrants out of the epic story of U.S. migration. Takaki suggests that such a Eurocentric history serves no good purpose, that we Americans have "come from many different shores—Europe, the Americas, Africa, and also Asia."[4]

To a striking degree, the immigration of major Asian groups has proceeded in serial fashion. This has not been by chance; it is largely the result of the actions of white employers and workers, who were often motivated by racist prejudices to stop the immigration of a particular Asian group. As we will discuss in more detail in the next chapter, the first large group of Asian immigrants to the United States were the Chinese. Early Chinese immigrants came to Hawaii, where U.S. planters were becoming influential by the mid-1800s. Later on, from the 1860s to the early 1880s, the Chinese migrated in large numbers to the West Coast to do low-wage work in construction and other industries. After racist agitation and exclusionary legislation stopped most Chinese immigration to the mainland in the 1880s, Japanese workers were recruited to fill the demand for labor on farms and in construction and mining projects.

The cutoff of Japanese immigration in 1908 (to be discussed shortly) in its turn spurred Anglo American employers to recruit Filipinos to fill the continuing labor needs of farms on the mainland and in Hawaii. In addition, the recruitment by white employers of other Asian laborers, including Koreans and Asian Indians, during the first two decades of the twentieth century was designed to reduce the dominance (and ability to organize) of Japanese American workers in the labor markets of Hawaii and the United States.[5]

Early Immigration

Japan's initial contact with the United States involved gunboat diplomacy. In 1853 U.S. commodore Matthew Perry sailed warships into Tokyo Bay, and with a show of force won a treaty granting the United States trading rights with Japan. In a few decades there would be much trade between the two nations.

Hawaii was the first destination for Japanese immigrants coming within the U.S. sphere. At least 231,000 migrated there between 1868 and 1929. European planters sought low-wage laborers for their fields. At first, Chinese laborers were brought in under contract. After 1884 thousands of Japanese laborers were brought to the Hawaiian plantations, usually under contract labor agreements. There were relatively few white laborers in the islands, and the Japanese immigrants became part of a racial hierarchy headed by the European American planters. When the agreements expired in 1894, most immigrants stayed on, laying the basis for the present-day Japanese American communities in Hawaii. Propertied European Americans strove to ensure their control of the islands, many hoping for annexation by the United States. In 1898, their hopes came true: Hawaii came under the territorial control of the U.S. government.[6]

On the islands Japanese Americans were numerous and concentrated. Dependent on the plantations owned by a few big corporations, they learned they could not "advance themselves through individualism and small business," as they did on the mainland. Rather they adopted a class-based strategy of "unionization, politics, and collective action."[7]

Mainland Migration

Between the 1880s and the so-called Gentlemen's Agreement in 1908 more than 150,000 Japanese entered; between then and the 1920s another 100,000 came. The immigrants to the mainland moved into a greater diversity of economic positions—from farm labor and mining to shopkeeping and truck farming—than did immigrants to Hawaii. Some came under contract to employers, others under the auspices of relatives, and yet others on their own. The pre-1908 Issei* had a harder time than those who came afterward, since the later immigrants were able to move directly into Japanese American communities.[8]

Like the Chinese before them (see Chapter 12), the Japanese immigrants were treated to discrimination at the hands of European Americans. Many white employers favored immigration; many white workers and unions opposed it. The mayor of San Francisco campaigned against the Japanese, arguing they were "unassimilable" and a competitive threat. In 1905 California newspapers began a campaign against the so-called "yellow peril," which they saw as a threat to public schools. Both houses of the California legislature passed a resolution calling for exclusion on the grounds that the Japanese Americans would not assimilate, given their racial differences. Because of this agitation and other factors, President Theodore Roosevelt arranged for a prohibition of Japanese migrants. In negotiations in 1907–1908 Roosevelt persuaded the Japanese government to assent to the infamous Gentlemen's Agreement, whereby no passports would be given by Japan to any workers except those already in the United States and their close relatives.[9]

Issei, Nisei, Sansei, and *Yonsei* are Japanese terms for the first four generations of Japanese Americans. The Issei were born in Japan.

Unlike the Chinese, Japanese immigrants were able for a time to bring in wives and families. Between 1910 and 1919 the majority of immigrants were former U.S. residents or parents, wives, and children of residents. The number leaving the United States was significant, about one-third the total number of immigrants. In contrast with the earlier Chinese immigrants, who were virtually all male, many of the Japanese immigrants were women and children. As a result, white supremacy groups argued wildly that the Japanese Americans were taking over, that their birthrate was so high they would overpopulate California, that they were disloyal, and that they were an alien race.[10]

More Racist Agitation and Restrictions

The same writers who proclaimed the threat posed by southern and eastern Europeans to "Anglo-Saxon" superiority often expressed fear of Asian migrations as well. Organized white groups, including the American Legion and the California Farm Bureau Association, pressed for exclusion of the Japanese. By the 1920s the U.S. Congress had succumbed to this agitation. It passed the 1924 Immigration Act, which established racist quotas based on a formula giving preference to "Nordic" nations and excluded Japanese immigration with a provision prohibiting all "aliens ineligible for citizenship" from entry into the United States. In an earlier decision, *Ozawa* v. *United States* (1922), the Supreme Court had paved the way by ruling that only those immigrants of white or African origin could become citizens of the United States. One of the most striking features of these new immigration restrictions was that, unlike European immigrants, Japanese and other Asian immigrants already in the United States could not bring the wives they had left behind. The intention here was to prevent the development of Asian families. The 1922 Cable Act had been even more extreme, requiring any U.S. woman, white or Asian American, who married an alien ineligible for citizenship to lose her own citizenship. In contrast with northern European immigrants, Asian immigrants were considered undesirable and were not permitted to assimilate in important ways.[11]

Government action against Asians, spurred by labor unions and hate groups, persisted. Until after World War II much of the U.S. labor movement supported direct exclusion of Japanese immigrants. Not until 1952 did the federal government provide even a small quota for the Japanese and permit first-generation Japanese Americans to become naturalized citizens, and not until 1965 were the anti-Asian restrictions removed from U.S. immigration law.[12]

In 1880 there were only 148 Japanese Americans. By 1920 the number had grown to 111,000. Even as late as 1965 there were only about one million Asian Americans, of whom Japanese Americans were the largest group. The 1965 Immigration Act permitted new immigrants, and since the 1970s non-Japanese Asian and Pacific peoples have predominated in the migration from Asia. There were 3.7 million Asian Americans in 1980, an increase of more than 100 percent from 1970. By 1990 there were 7.3 million Asian Americans, of whom about 850,000 were Japanese.[13]

Since the abolition of the racist 1924 immigration law in 1965, it has been possible for large numbers of Japanese immigrants to enter. But relatively few have taken advantage of the 1965 law, and their numbers have been lower than those of other Asian groups (see Chapter 12). In recent years one significant, but small, migration has been that of executives of American branches of Japanese corporations and their families. This has contributed to the revitalization of some Japanese American communities by encouraging the development of schools and businesses that serve these temporary immigrants.

STEREOTYPING

Non-Asian Americans have held positive and negative stereotypes of Japanese Americans. In recent years Japanese Americans and other Asians have sometimes been seen as "model minorities"—groups who are very successful in moving up in U.S. society. At the same time, movies about the Vietnam War have portrayed Asians as devious, corrupt, or evil, and anti-Asian graffiti such as "Look out for the Asian invasion" and "Stop the Yellow Hordes" have been scrawled on college dorm walls and highway overpasses.[14]

The white mind often lumps all Asians and Asian Americans into one group that is smeared with anti-Asian stereotypes. The serial migration of Asian groups helps to explain why whites applied stereotypes of one group, such as the Chinese, to later groups such as Japanese or Korean immigrants. All groups have suffered from similar stereotypes, such as that of the "dangerous and wily Oriental." In the earliest years, the Chinese immigrants were stereotyped as "docile," "crafty," or "dirty." Initially, some whites evaluated the new Japanese migrants more positively, considering them less threatening and more family-oriented. Soon, however, white images of the Japanese came to contain the negative notions that the Japanese were docile and servile. The new immigrants also heard white cries of "Jap go home."[15]

Within a short period many Japanese laborers managed to gain some land to farm, either by contract, shares, or leasing. European American farmers and workers exaggerated this Japanese American land ownership, which was growing but never involved more than a small percentage of western farmland. Another widespread view was that the Japanese Americans were incapable of being shaped by the Anglo core culture because of their different culture. V. S. McClatchy, a Sacramento editor, argued that the Japanese were "for various reasons unassimilable, and a dangerous element."[16] The irony in this racist view was clear to anyone who understood that state or federal laws prohibited Japanese immigrants from becoming citizens, from directly owning land, and from marrying whites—and thus from even trying to assimilate along these dimensions.

Above all, the "race" of the Issei was seen as problematical: "He is brown; we are white; and this difference, they [whites] insist, carries with it such psychological, social, and civilizational differences that any attempt to live together is sure to be disastrous."[17] From U.S. presidents and senators to ordinary citizens, many whites belabored the differences. James Phelan, U.S. senator from California, argued that Japanese Americans were a great threat to the "future of the white race, American institutions, and Western civilization."[18] Another stereotype targeted the alleged Japanese American disloyalty to the United States, said to be due to a prior loyalty to the Japanese emperor.[19]

Movie images were part of a broader smearing of Japanese Americans as treacherous, villainous, and immoral. In the formative period of the movie industry, Chinese and Japanese characters were pictured as villains. Asians and Asian Americans were crudely stereotyped as "inscrutable," poor at English, and treacherous.[20] Between 1900 and the 1920s the vicious image of the forward, buck-toothed "Jap" exploded in the mass media.

In his widely circulated "Letters of a Japanese Schoolboy," Wallace Irwin stimulated stereotypes about Japanese Americans, including a mode of speech parodied with phrases such as "so sorry, please." White legislators spoke of the alleged immorality of Japanese Americans, even using the apelike image applied earlier to Irish and African Americans.[21]

Attitude surveys in the 1920s and 1930s suggested that anti-Japanese prejudices were accepted by most white Americans, especially those on the West Coast. In a survey of white students' attitudes in California in 1927 the stereotypes frequently mentioned were negative: the Japanese were thought to be dishonest, treacherous, and unfairly competitive.[22]

War Propaganda

From the 1890s to the 1930s anti-Japan sentiment grew in the United States. The Japanese people were considered an inferior race who had the unfortunate brashness to challenge European and American interests in Asia. Even before the attack on Pearl Harbor, white politicians and labor leaders on the West Coast were portraying Japanese Americans as disloyal. This image expanded after Pearl Harbor, and rumors of spying and sabotage circulated by the thousands, including wild stories about Japanese American farmers planting flowers in a pattern that would guide attacking airplanes.[23]

Major political figures repeated stereotypes to a public inclined to accept them. California's attorney general (later U.S. chief justice), Earl Warren, depicted Japanese Americans as dangerous and threatening. In 1943 General John L. DeWitt, the West Coast military commander, argued, "A Jap's a Jap.... The Japanese race is an enemy race and while many second- and third-generation Japanese born on United States soil, possessed of United States citizenship, have become 'Americanized,' the racial strains are undiluted."[24] With no evidence whatsoever, the national press argued that there were many enemy agents in this "large alien population." The reason for this alien population was the racist U.S. law that prohibited first-generation Japanese Americans from becoming citizens. In addition, no Japanese American was ever proven to have collaborated with the enemy during World War II. The alleged disloyalty was only a notion in the prejudiced minds of white Americans.

Surveys by the War Relocation Authority after the war revealed that these stereotypes continued to be commonplace. The stereotypes slowly began to change. By the 1960s new stereotypes developed, many with apparently positive aspects. Magazines and newspapers praised Japanese Americans for being highly acculturated and successful. However, Ogawa has noted that the "highly Americanized" and "successful citizens" stereotypes are not entirely positive, for they suggest that one must become "white" in order to be a good citizen. The assumption underlying these stereotypes is that since Japanese Americans have become English-speaking, work-ethic models of virtue, they can now be accepted by whites. The "superior, successful citizen" image has been used to defend the U.S. record with other minorities: those who hold this view argue that other non-European Americans can make it too if they work hard and assimilate culturally like the Japanese Americans.[25]

Recent Distortions, Stereotypes, and Omissions

One study of the images of Japanese Americans in history textbooks found not only this successful minority stereotype but also numerous distortions of Japanese American history. One prominent textbook used in public schools tiptoes around the oppressive circumstances of early Japanese American history, speaking of Japanese being "added" to the population. There is a serious omission in such textbooks—the fact that U.S. employers in Hawaii and California actively recruited and exploited Japanese laborers. Most textbooks also do not deal adequately with the character and impact of the 1924 Immigration Act. That act violated the Gentlemen's Agreement with Japan and stopped the immigration of Japanese entirely, over the objections of the Japanese government.

The internment of Japanese Americans in concentration camps during World War II (to be discussed shortly) is not adequately portrayed. Most textbooks see the camp experience as part of the "hysteria of war" and do not discuss the long history of anti-Japanese agitation that led to the illegal imprisonment of U.S. citizens of Japanese descent. Moreover, one textbook suggests that Japanese Americans "have forgiven the government for violating their rights during World War II." The fact is that the imprisonment is well remembered by Japanese Americans; they have neither forgotten nor forgiven.[26]

The stereotyping or misperception of Japanese Americans has taken place at the highest levels of U.S. society. In the mid-1980s Senator Spark M. Matsunaga of Hawaii, a Japanese American, was assisting the White House in hosting a reception for visiting Japanese officials. The U.S. secretary of state, Alexander Haig, mistook Senator Matsunaga for one of the officials and shook his hand, wishing him a nice visit! In the late 1980s Senator Daniel Inouye, a Japanese American who lost an arm fighting for the United States in World War II, received hate mail telling him that he should "go home to Japan where he belongs." Other Japanese American elected officials have reported that white Americans frequently congratulate them on how well they speak English, as though they were foreigners. Many whites seem unaware that the nation has Japanese American elected officials, that such officials' place of birth is the United States, and that their native language is English.[27]

One issue that has become central in the 1980s and 1990s is the use of ethnic and racial group symbols and caricatures as mascots for sports teams. During the 1991 World Series, for example, the use of Native American caricatures by the Atlanta "Braves" baseball team created much protest from Native Americans and others, who noted that such symbols were racist in form and content. A number of sports teams have given up these caricatures and stereotyped symbols. For example, in 1991 Shoreline Community College in Seattle abandoned its Samurai Warrior mascot, a Japanese caricature, because of its racist overtones.

An even more serious caricature of the Japanese is developed in Michael Crichton's 1991 best-selling novel, *Rising Sun*. The Japanese business people and other Japanese characters in this murder mystery set in Los Angeles are portrayed, to quote one reviewer, as "inscrutable, technologically proficient, predatory aliens who...subsist through unpalatable foods, manipulate *everything* and *everyone*, and enjoy kinky, violent sex with white women."[28] This novel encompasses many of the negative stereotypes and prejudices with which whites have targeted Asians and Asian Americans since the beginning of this century.

REPRESSION AND VIOLENT ATTACKS

Japanese Americans have suffered not only from stereotyping and misperceptions but also from discrimination and physical attacks. The first major acts of violence against the Japanese immigrants came within a decade of their arrival in large numbers. White groups, particularly on the West Coast, used a variety of means to stop Japanese migration and competition. After the 1906 San Francisco earthquake the violence directed at Japanese Americans increased. Scientists sent by Japan to help with earthquake relief were attacked by white men and boys, and local newspapers condoned the actions. Japanese American businesses were boycotted, and shopkeepers were attacked.[29]

The anti-Japanese exclusion movement sometimes turned to violence, as in California in 1921, when large numbers of Japanese farm workers were driven out of certain farm areas. In the 1930s white farmers in Arizona petitioned the governor to throw out Japanese farmers. When this failed, attempts were made to drive them out by force. The threat of such violence spreading to California led the legislature to consider a bill restricting Japanese American agricultural enterprises. At the beginning of World War II the violent attacks escalated. In 1942 alone there were dozens of attacks on Japanese Americans and their property from Seattle to San Diego.[30]

Concentration Camps in the United States

In this century only one U.S. racial or ethnic group has been imprisoned behind barbed wire —Japanese Americans. The military victories of the Japanese government in the 1930s and 1940s, including the sudden attack at Pearl Harbor, increased fears of a Japanese invasion of the mainland. Members of Congress and the mass media parroted the old anti-Japanese stereotypes and escalated fear of Japanese Americans across the United States. By January 1942 evacuation and imprisonment of Americans of Japanese ancestry was being suggested. Some whites were motivated by economic interest. White organizations such as the Western Growers Protective Association seemed committed to destroying Japanese American business competition.[31]

Police raids on Japanese aliens, which had begun directly after the Pearl Harbor attack, were intensified in a frantic search for spies; more than two thousand aliens were arrested without evidence of disloyalty. Japanese American businesses were forced to close. Citizens were illegally detained by local police, evicted by landlords, and fired by employers.[32]

In the first phase of federal action against Americans whose ancestry was linked to countries at war with the United States, a small number of Japanese, German, and Italian aliens were moved from sensitive areas and their travel was restricted. Then came the second stage. On February 19, 1942, Executive Order 9066 was issued by President Franklin Roosevelt and validated by Congress. It ordered the secretary of war to establish military areas from which any person could be excluded. The West Coast military commander established the western parts of California, Washington, and Oregon, as well as the southern part of Arizona, as areas where no Japanese, Italian, or German aliens could reside. But *only* Japanese Americans, the nonwhites in this group, were pressured to resettle outside coastal areas. The two hundred thousand Italian and German aliens were not forced to move from their homes. Only American citizens of Japanese ancestry were detained in assembly centers and later transported under guard to barbed-wire concentration camps.[33]

Japanese American businesses were sold at a loss. By the fall of 1942 inland areas in the West housed about 120,000 Japanese, more than two-thirds of them *native-born U.S. citizens* whose only crime was to be racially different.[34] The oppression took on many forms. At the Tule Lake Camp in California the white administration arranged for camp inmates to be hired out to white personnel as domestics at the low wage of thirty dollars a month. Part of this wage was taken by the camp administration and spent on recreational facilities for white personnel. Low-price barber shops and cafeterias for whites working in the concentration camps were staffed by Japanese Americans paid wages befitting slaves, such as sixteen dollars a week for waitresses. Barracks were typically bare-board buildings with few furnishings, and conditions were primitive, with whole families forced to live in small rooms or partitioned-off areas. Many camps were in areas that were very cold in winter and dusty much of the year. One author notes that conditions were especially difficult for Japanese American women, who "faced severe racism and traumatic family strain."[35]

Japanese Americans protested their treatment in the camps in numerous demonstrations; six thousand even renounced their U.S. citizenship. Gradually several thousand college students and workers on special agricultural assignments were released from the camps; others were released to the U.S. Army, where, ironically, many served with extraordinary valor in segregated units under white officers.[36]

Late in 1944 the order to evacuate was rescinded. Most of those imprisoned returned to the West Coast and found farms and businesses in ruin, household goods destroyed, and local whites hostile if not violent. The U.S. government spent about $250 million on the evacuation; Japanese American economic losses are estimated to have been at least $400 million. The psychological and other human losses are incalculable.[37]

Why the Camps Were Created

Why were Japanese Americans imprisoned? Some commentators have emphasized the military angle. Others have focused on anti-Japanese prejudice among whites and on the role of white business people in their hostile struggle with Japanese American competitors. Yet others have accented the role of West Coast politicians who sought public favor by selecting an issue supported by popular prejudices. The U.S. Supreme Court upheld the military decision without investigation—even though two-thirds of those evacuated were U.S. citizens. This evacuation was a clear violation of the civil rights guaranteed all citizens by the U.S. Constitution.[38]

President Franklin Roosevelt and other political officials held racist attitudes toward Japanese and other Asian Americans. Roosevelt believed that the Japanese had less developed skulls and were racially inferior, and he and other political and business leaders saw the emerging struggle in the Pacific as a racial war. Racist attitudes made it easier for top U.S. government officials to order the internment of American citizens of Asian descent (but not those of German or Italian descent) in barbed-wire camps.[39]

Japanese Americans fought valiantly but unsuccessfully in the courts and in demonstrations. There was a confrontation between Japanese American evacuees and authorities at the Santa Anita Assembly Center in California over the rumored appropriation of personal property. Camp property was destroyed and a police officer was attacked by a group of angry Japanese; armed military police suppressed the rioting. At the Poston camp in the fall of 1942 there was a strike over the imprisonment of two Japanese Americans.[40] In December 1942 at the Manzanar camp in California an assault on a Japanese American who had collaborated with whites and the imprisonment of the attacker led to a mass meeting of four thousand and demands for an investigation of camp conditions. The camp director, escorted by military police with machine guns, met the crowd. A crowd again formed at night and was fired upon; two Japanese Americans were killed.[41] These events occurred at a time when the U.S. government was loudly, if hypocritically, proclaiming the values of freedom and democracy to a war-torn world.

THE POLITICAL ARENA

Because of the racist naturalization laws, the Issei and other first-generation Asian Americans were not allowed to become citizens until the 1950s. Most second-generation Japanese Americans, the Nisei, did not become old enough to vote until the 1940s, and the World War II imprisonment was a severe setback in their struggle to participate in U.S. politics.[42]

Some political and civic organization occurred in the 1930s when older Nisei formed Democratic political clubs in a few West Coast cities. The Japanese American Citizens League (JACL), under Nisei leaders, advocated the accommodation strategies of self-help and individual enterprise and pressed moderately for civil rights and for citizenship for the Issei. Voter-registration campaigns were inaugurated, but attempts to get candidates to run usually stopped at the planning stage.[43]

Compensation Pressures and Political Progress

Since World War II the JACL, together with other Japanese American organizations, has won important political and legal victories. By 1946 the JACL and some newer organizations were pressing for compensation for evacuation losses, for citizenship for the first generation, and for changes in discriminatory laws. Meager compensation for business and property losses finally came in the form of the 1948 Japanese American Evacuation Act. Japanese Americans were paid less than 10 percent of their losses.[44]

Japanese American organizations pressed the U.S. government for more adequate repayment for losses suffered. One important new organization was the National Council for Japanese American Redress, headed up in the early 1990s by William Hohri, who in 1983, with other internees, had filed a class action suit accusing federal officials of conspiring to deprive Japanese Americans of their rights during the war. Belatedly, on September 17, 1987, the U.S. House passed a law including a formal apology to Japanese Americans for the internment and providing $1.2 billion in compensation. The bill contained an admission that the "basic civil liberties" of Japanese Americans were violated as a result of "racial prejudice." The Senate passed the bill, and it was signed by President Reagan. The House passed the bill after years of foot-dragging by congressional leaders and opposition from the Reagan White House.[45]

The funding of the compensation to Japanese Americans took two more years because of more foot-dragging. The first checks were not distributed until October 1990, and the last checks were scheduled for mailing in 1993. Each of the remaining internees, or his or her heirs, was to receive $20,000. President George Bush wrote each internee a letter of apology. Some, such as Representative Robert Matsui of California, refused the check but accepted the apology letter, saying, "All of us feel like we are home again." The legislation and apology signaled the public admission of discrimination against Japanese Americans by the government and provided an improved civil rights environment not only for Japanese Americans but for the many new Asian migrants to the United States. Again we see that civil rights organizations and movements of oppressed minorities have often been the strongest advocates of the "liberty and justice for all" tradition of the United States.[46]

Unfortunately, some whites were unwilling to see these Japanese Americans receive the justice due them. In a Japanese American community in Oxnard, California, for example, anti-Japanese leaflets were circulated that said, among other things, that no apology to Japanese Americans for their unconstitutional imprisonment was necessary because the Japanese government had detained U.S. soldiers in World War II. Some non-Asians are still unable to distinguish between Japanese Americans and the Japanese government.[47]

Pressure from Japanese American organizations helped win two symbolic political victories in the 1970s: the repeal of the infamous Title II of the 1950 Internal Security Act, which had permitted U.S. government imprisonment of citizens deemed potential collaborators with an enemy in time of crisis, and the rescinding of Executive Order 9066, which had ordered the wartime imprisonment of Japanese Americans.[48]

Government Officials

Political organization aimed at electoral victories has increased decade by decade. Major gains have usually come first in Hawaii. Some Nisei were registered to vote in Hawaii as early as 1917, and a few made early unsuccessful bids for office in the territorial legislature. In 1930 the first were elected to office, two as members of the territorial legislature; by the late 1930s nine Japanese American officials were among the nearly one hundred elected officials in Hawaii. Later, returning World War II veterans, intent on expanding their political participation, became active in Democratic attempts to overthrow the traditional Republican domination of the islands. Several were elected to the Hawaii legislature; in the late 1950s their efforts facilitated Congress's conferral of statehood after years of anti-Asian opposition. War hero Daniel Inouye was elected the first U.S. representative from the new state and the first Japanese American in Congress. Spark Matsunaga became the second to serve in the House, in 1962, when Inouye became a senator. In 1964 a second House seat was won by Patsy Takemoto Mink, the first Japanese American woman to serve in Congress. In the late 1980s both senators from Hawaii, Inouye and Matsunaga, were Japanese Americans, as were the two representatives to the House. Daniel Akaka, a native Hawaiian American, was elected to replace Matsunaga after his death in 1990.[49]

Political victories on the mainland have been difficult because of the dilution of Japanese American votes in the heavily European American populations of the western states. Clarence Arai campaigned unsuccessfully for the Washington legislature in the 1930s. Only one Nisei was elected to a state legislature between that time and the late 1960s. In the 1960s a few Japanese Americans were elected to city council offices in Los Angeles County, Oakland, and San Jose. In 1972 Carl Ooka was elected a county commissioner in the state of Washington, the first Japanese American elected to office in that state and one of few ever to hold office there.[50]

Since the early 1970s only a handful of mainland Japanese Americans have held elected positions at higher levels of local, state, or the federal government. In 1976 Samuel I. Hayakawa , a prominent semanticist, was elected senator from California, the first on the mainland. In the mid-1970s Norman Mineta of California became the first mainland representative of Japanese descent. Robert Matsui was elected to the California delegation a few years later. He and Mineta led the House effort in the late 1980s to pass the bill providing compensation for the World War II internees.

Political empowerment has come slowly in the West. By 1990 about one of every ten Californians was Asian American, but only 2 percent of the state's top elected officials were Asian. Only two members of the state's forty-seven-member delegation to Congress were Asian. Not one Asian American served in the state legislature. And only 1 percent of city council and school board seats were held by Asian Americans. There are signs of change, however. In the early 1990s a number of aides and assistants to elected officials are Asian American. They may in their turn seek office.[51]

Some western cities have seen pan-Asian political cooperation. For example, in the late 1980s Warren Furutani, a Japanese American, was elected to the Los Angeles school board with the help of Filipino and Asian-Pacific Americans, as well as Japanese Americans. As a result, he developed an agenda of school issues of concern to all Asian Americans. A few other western politicians have put together similar coalitions.[52]

Politics, Stereotyping, and Competition with Japan

Since the 1970s some whites have targeted Asian Americans, including Japanese Americans, for violence and vandalism. The word Jap was spray-painted on the garage of a Japanese American state legislator in California. A Chinese American woman was pushed in front of a subway train in New York City by a man who said he had a "phobia about Asians." In Flint, Michigan, an exhibit at an auto show portrayed a car with a Japanese face falling like a bomb on Detroit, recalling the classic racist view of the "Oriental hordes" threatening white America.[53]

In recent years Japan's economic development has surpassed that of the United States in a number of manufacturing areas. One U.S. media response has been buy-American cartoons featuring caricatures of "wily Japs" and "crafty Orientals." Old stereotypes have reappeared in conversations among whites and in newspaper articles. Increasing unemployment in the wake of the recessions of the 1980s and 1990s has fueled a tendency among non-Asians to blame the Japanese for U.S. economic troubles. This scapegoating has been reflected in political action. Anti-Japanese protectionist bills have been introduced in Congress. In the 1990s Democratic party leaders such as Tom Harkin and Richard Gephardt have proposed bills that would slash Japanese imports. White congressional leaders have ignored Japanese investments in the United States that have created 110,000 new jobs. Yet many observers have noted that Japan's investments and economy have not been a major cause of U.S. recessions; the real causes lie elsewhere—often in poor U.S. corporate management and overseas investments by U.S. firms.[54]

Japanese executives and investors who have come to the United States in recent years have also faced racist agitation. In February 1992 a Japanese businessperson was killed in the Los Angeles area. Police were investigating the possibility that he was murdered by a non-Asian worker who blamed him for U.S. economic troubles. Not long before his death, he had been threatened at his door by a man who blamed him for the 1990s recession. Stereotyping is evident in much recent anti-Japan agitation in the United States.[55]

Protest Organizations and Group Pride

Social science research has documented Japanese American protest against racial oppression. At the turn of the century white delegates arriving at an anti-immigrant convention were met at the door by Japanese Americans with leaflets arguing against attempts to exclude Japanese immigrants. This was the beginning of a long series of books, speeches, and pamphlets by Japanese and Japanese Americans protesting exclusion attempts. A few voluntary associations, such as the Japanese Association, were formed in the early 1900s to combat exclusion activities and other anti-Japanese discrimination.[56]

Labor actions were part of the early Japanese experience. Japanese workers in Hawaii participated in at least sixty work stoppages in the five decades after 1870. Substantial organizing took place on the mainland. There were a few strikes in the 1890s; after 1900 their number increased. Democratic-socialist groups, formed by Japanese immigrants in the early 1900s, pressed for better working conditions. In 1903 more than one thousand Japanese American and Mexican American agricultural workers struck white farmers in California. Japanese American workers were involved in agricultural and mining strikes in California, Utah, Colorado, and Washington. Up to the 1940s, Japanese American and Mexican American workers cooperated in strikes against exploitative white farmers. Unfortunately, conservative white labor leaders, such as Samuel Gompers, often blocked the admission of Japanese Americans into older unions with the racist argument that Japanese Americans were unassimilable.[57]

As we have noted, Japanese Americans also protested their incarceration in concentration camps; thousands renounced their citizenship and returned to Japan after the war. During the 1960s pan-Asian organizations and publications appeared, often headed by the younger generation. Journals such as *Amerasia Journal* urged collective action and attention to problems of Asian Americans. Sugar-coated images of Asian American success were challenged as a renewed sense of group pride developed.[58]

One sign of group pride can be seen in the development of Asian American studies programs in more than twenty colleges and universities across the United States since the late 1960s. Several campuses of the University of California, including Berkeley and Los Angeles, and the California State University, including San Franciso and Long Beach, as well as the University of Washington and the University of Hawaii, have developed important programs. Most of these programs have become institutionalized with a core of faculty and academic legitimacy. In the early 1990s some Asian American scholars urged a rethinking of these programs, with an eye to reexamining their philosophies and methodologies, encouraging more research on Asian Americans, adding courses to accommodate recent immigrants, improving relations with Asian American communities, and establishing a national network of Asian American studies programs.[59]

THE ECONOMY

Most Japanese immigrants started out at the bottom levels of the economic pyramid, filling the hard jobs on farms, mines, and construction projects. One California study in 1909 found 65 percent of Japanese American workers in agriculture, 15 percent in domestic service work, 15 percent in small businesses, and 5 percent in other lines of work.[60]

In the first decades the new residents worked for as little as fifty cents to a dollar a day in agriculture. Japanese workers received less than European Americans. For instance, while white sawmill laborers were paid $2.60 to $3.50 a day in the state of Washington, Japanese laborers received only $1.75 to $2.75. This pattern of discriminatory wage rates was true for many jobs. In cities Japanese Americans became service workers, laborers, or the domestic servants of whites.[61]

Finding an Economic Niche

Gradually many Issei began to arrange for land to farm on their own. In urban areas, where direct institutionalized discrimination kept them out of manufacturing and white-collar employment, some went into small businesses. In the view of researchers Bonacich and Modell, the Issei came to play a middleman minority role in the California economy. By 1909 there were at least 3,000 Japanese American businesses in the western states. By 1929 there were nearly 2,000 in Los Angeles alone. An estimated 30 percent of Japanese Americans were involved with Japanese American businesses as employers or employees. Operated on a small scale, some enterprises catered primarily to a Japanese American clientele, but many eventually served a non-Asian clientele. The Issei's ethnic solidarity helped them create a niche economy, and this small-business economy in turn reinforced their group solidarity. Bonacich and Modell conclude that "the Japanese minority filled a particular and specialized niche in the western economy and was important to it, providing key products and services."[62]

Most Japanese immigrants came from eleven southern prefectures in Japan, and each was represented by an association in the United States. These prefectural clubs could act as mutual-aid associations for immigrants in a hostile environment. They aided the movement of immigrants into the economy by providing training for workers and directing clients to businesses. Restaurants and cleaning operations succeeded because they could draw on prefectural networks for reliable workers and loans. Informal money-pooling organizations and credit-rotating associations called *tanomoshi* provided capital for small entrepreneurs who could not secure funds from banks.[63]

White opposition to the new immigrants built swiftly. In urban areas the labor movement often led the opposition. Boycotts and anti-Japanese advertising were used by white groups, as in the Anti-Jap Laundry League's attempt to drive Japanese Americans out of the laundry business. One problem for whites was that the Japanese immigrants were very hardworking competitors.[64]

A 1913 California Alien Land Law, passed under pressure from white farmers, stipulated that aliens could not buy land or lease it for more than three years; nor could they pass on land to their children. As we have seen, all Issei were forced to remain "aliens" because of discriminatory naturalization laws. This California land law interfered with agricultural activity, but ways were found to circumvent it, such as registering ownership of lands under the names of children. Such practices brought new laws prohibiting Issei from leasing land and from holding it in the names of children. These discriminatory land laws reduced the number of Japanese American farms from over five thousand in 1920 to four thousand in 1930. Those who remained in farming relied on tenant or truck farming. New organizations such as the Japanese

CooperativeFarm Industry organized the flow of farm products to Japanese American retailers in cities. Japanese American farmers had again demonstrated their ingenuity and knack for success. But the wartime evacuation destroyed their operations once more.[65]

Forced out of farming by land laws and attracted to the booming cities, many Japanese Americans became gardeners or nursery operators. The 1930 California census showed that half of male Japanese workers were in agriculture or gardening, one-quarter were in trade or business, 2 percent were in the professions, and a large percentage of the rest were in other urban occupations.[66]

By the beginning of World War II some Japanese Americans in cities were moving into white-collar positions. The authors of one study estimated that half the men in highly urbanized Los Angeles County in 1940 were in white-collar positions and about 40 percent were in semiskilled and unskilled blue-collar positions.[67] Then the economy collapsed. Median economic losses per family in Los Angeles from the forced wartime evacuation were estimated at about $10,000 (in 1940 dollars) in goods, property, income, and expenses. The figures were similar elsewhere. Small businesses suffered heavy losses. Many of those who could not regain their businesses and farms after 1945 went into contract gardening and private household work.

In her research on the labor of Japanese American women before World War II, Glenn found that "from the moment they arrived, Japanese American women labored alongside the men to secure their own and their families' livelihood."[68] Much of the hard work done by the women was unpaid family labor on farms and in small businesses, but some Issei women and their daughters worked as domestic servants to whites. Before World War II discrimination against these women was so strong that most were unable to move into white-collar work as did European immigrant women and their daughters. Nonetheless, the domestics often resisted their oppression, usually in covert ways such as evasion of work pressed on them by exploitative white employers. This resistance gave them a sense of self-reliance that was critical for their development and for that of their children. They sometimes struggled against husbands as well; their subordination to white women in their domestic employment was reinforced by their subordination to their husbands at home. Yet they struggled to maintain dignity, and "despite the menial nature of employment, the Issei achieved a sense of their own strength, and in some cases, superiority to employer and husband within their own area of competence."[69]

The Postwar Economy

The booming postwar economy was in need of labor, and many white employers hired Japanese American workers. Yet racial discrimination continued to affect the second generation; certain occupations were still off limits. For example, University of California education departments discouraged Japanese American students from considering the teaching profession because of the difficulty of placement.[70] Self-employment continued to be important. By 1960 there were seven thousand Japanese-owned businesses in the Los Angeles area, most of them gardening businesses. Hotels, groceries, and laundries made up the next largest categories. According to Bonacich and Modell, the middleman minority model seems to fit the Issei generation well, but the second and later generations have gradually moved away from the niche economy of small businesses to professional and other white-collar jobs. In 1960 about half the Nisei were still involved in niche businesses, but many others used the education provided by parents to move into white-collar jobs in the general economy.[71]

Occupational Mobility and Problems

In recent decades numerous books and articles have related the Japanese American experience as a remarkable story of achievement. The usual socioeconomic indicators in census data do show that Japanese American progress since the 1950s has been dramatic. For example, in 1970 Japanese American men occupied white-collar levels in somewhat larger proportions than the total U.S. male population. In 1960 about 40 percent of Japanese American men had occupied white-collar positions, a proportion that increased to nearly half by 1970. Similarly, the majority of women were in white-collar positions in both 1960 and 1970, with the percentage also increasing over that decade. However, Japanese American women were concentrated in clerical and service occupations.[72]

The 1980 census found Japanese Americans to be concentrated in white-collar jobs. About 20 percent were in professional and technical jobs, compared with 15.4 percent of the population as a whole. Managerial and administrative positions accounted for 12.8 percent, larger than the 10.4 percent of the general population. The proportion in clerical and sales jobs was 29.9 percent, again larger than the 27.3 percent of the general population in that category. Altogether, over 60 percent of Japanese American workers were in white-collar jobs, compared with half the general population. The percentages in most blue-collar categories were smaller than comparable percentages in the total population.[73]

However, one study by the U.S. Commission on Civil Rights found significant occupational segregation for Japanese American workers compared with white workers. Examining 441 major job categories, the commission found that 42 percent of Japanese American males and a third of Japanese American females would have to change occupations if Japanese American workers were to show the same occupational distribution as white workers. The occupational niches occupied by many Japanese American workers still reflect past and present exclusion from other job categories.[74]

The income picture seems to generally support the success argument as well. In 1970 the median income for Japanese American families was $12,500, compared with $9,600 for all families. By 1980 it was $27,354, substantially greater than the national figure for all families of $19,917. In addition, only a small percentage of Japanese American families (6.6 percent) fell below the federal poverty line, a figure lower than those for whites and for other Asian groups. However, these figures reflect current income and do not include property and other wealth. Note that Japanese American families average more workers per household than white families and Japanese American workers are concentrated in two states (Hawaii and California) having both high wages and a high cost of living.[75]

Perhaps the clearest indicator of continuing discrimination is the fact that the incomes of Japanese Americans are lower than they should be, given this group's high level of education. A study by the U.S. Commission on Civil Rights calculated what Japanese American workers would have been earning if they had been white. Japanese workers earned only 88 percent of the amount earned by white males with comparable characteristics. Discrimination is the likely reason.[76] Moreover, in a survey of Japanese Americans in three

California cities, the majority of the respondents *disagreed* with the statement "Currently, Japanese [Americans] do not experience job discrimination." Majorities of both the Nisei and the Sansei felt that Japanese Americans face job discrimination.[77]

In the 1980s and 1990s Japanese Americans continued to face subtle exclusion from prominent positions in most businesses, in movies and television, in politics, and in certain civil service areas, such as police and fire departments. Indirect discrimination in the form of height and weight requirements has played a role in some occupational areas. Positions at the highest administrative, managerial, and professional levels have often been closed to Japanese and other Asian Americans, particularly on the West Coast. Whites with poorer credentials or lesser ability have been promoted at a faster rate. One study of employment in private industries in the San Francisco metropolitan area found Asian Americans to be underrepresented in manufacturing, construction, and wholesale trade. Asian Americans were also underrepresented in better-paying jobs (such as managerial jobs) and overrepresented in lower-paying work (such as clerical jobs).[78]

In 1988 Kitano and Daniels reported that only 159 (0.6 percent) of the 29,000 directors and top executives of the 1,000 largest U.S. firms were Japanese or other Asian Americans, yet those groups make up about 2.6 percent of the U.S. population.[79] A *Wall Street Journal* story noted that Asian Americans have a very hard time climbing corporate ladders because "ironically, the same companies that pursue them for technical jobs often shun them when filling managerial and executive positions."[80] Top corporate executives have been quoted as saying that Asian Americans, including Japanese Americans, are best as technical workers and not as corporate executives. Because of this stereotype, they are hired as engineers and technicians but are not even considered for major management positions. In addition to cutting off important job opportunities, this white prejudice has had an effect on younger Asian Americans. They tend to seek out scientific and technical educations and to reject humanities and the social sciences in part because of the discrimination that they know is awaiting them if they depart from the white stereotype. The promotional ceiling has also been documented in higher education. A recent study at the University of California (Berkeley) found that only one of the 102 top administrators there was an Asian American, even though the university student body was 25 percent Asian American.[81]

Overall trends in the economy have also affected the employment patterns of Japanese Americans. For example, although elementary education and secondary education have been popular college majors in the postwar period, the demand for teaching jobs slackened during recessions from the 1960s to the 1990s. Past discrimination channeled Asian Americans into certain occupations, such as teaching, thus limiting the job prospects of some in times of category-specific recessions.

Business opportunities are still limited by the anti-Japanese sentiment of many European Americans. For example, Kristi Yamaguchi became the center of much public attention after she won a gold medal in figure skating at the 1991 Winter Olympics. Previous gold medal winners, European Americans such as Dorothy Hamill, had become household names as advertisers flocked to them for profitable endorsements. *Business Week* quoted corporate officials and marketing experts as saying that Yamaguchi's Japanese ancestry would probably keep her from getting as many lucrative endorsements as a European American skater. As of mid-1992, she had gotten few of the major endorsements customary for those with her achievements. Some prominent marketing people noted that there was strong anti-Japanese feeling among non-Asian workers, and that it would not be wise for advertisers to use someone who looked so Japanese. Yamaguchi herself could not understand why the anti-Japan sentiment should apply to her: "I certainly don't think it should affect me. I'm a fourth generation American. I went to the Olympics for America." Whether or not Kristi Yamaguchi eventually gets her fair share of business endorsements, she has forever been stigmatized as a "skater with Japanese ancestry." The racism here is clear; the ancestry of other recent gold medal winners is unknown to most white Americans.[82]

That Japanese Americans have achieved remarkable economic success against enormous odds is clearly indicated in statistics from the last four decades. What they could have achieved without persisting direct and indirect discrimination can only be imagined.[83]

EDUCATION

Racism and Segregation

Like certain other immigrant groups, the Issei had a strong, lasting commitment to education. Most viewed education in pragmatic terms, as a way out of the arduous jobs of the farms and nurseries and a route to better-paying positions. Issei parents sent their children to school more often than parents in most other groups, and many pursued formal education for themselves.[84]

In 1906 the mayor of San Francisco, in a move supported by local newspapers, secured a resolution from the board of education setting up a segregated public school for Asian children. There were at the time fewer than 100 Japanese American children in two dozen schools. One white member of the California legislature spoke of the danger to the "pure maids of California" posed by older Japanese students in primary grades. The Japanese government protested the segregation, and the federal government took court action to force the San Francisco Board of Education to give Japanese American children the equal rights promised them by a treaty.

Some anti-Japanese Californians were so angered by this rare federal show of support for Japanese Americans that they began to talk about secession. President Theodore Roosevelt and San Francisco officials worked out a compromise, and after three months out of school, most Japanese American children were allowed to return; overage Japanese pupils were excluded. In return, the infamous Gentlemen's Agreement, aimed at stopping migration, was executed by Roosevelt.[85]

A common stereotype was that Japanese immigrants' children were displacing other children in California schools. The fact was that in 1920 Japanese Americans outnumbered whites only in one village school in the town of Florin. Even by the late 1930s Japanese children were present in small proportions in all but two or three schools in California. The agitation over schools brought an increase in segregation pressures. California legislators made several attempts to segregate Japanese children, and by 1930 four school districts had segregated schools for Asian Americans.[86]

Language Schools and Japanese Educational Progress

Japanese Americans developed their own language schools that focused on training in the Japanese language and in traditional values such as respect for elders. The Issei established these schools as a way of strengthening community bonds. By 1928 there were more than 4,000 pupils in 118 schools. White racists vigorously attacked the language schools as centers of emperor worship and Buddhism aimed at making children disloyal to the United States. The California legislature passed a bill, vetoed by the governor, abolishing the schools. The white exclusionists' stereotyped view of these schools was sharply out of touch with reality.[87]

By the 1930s Japanese Americans were making great strides in public education, from the primary grades to the college level, in spite of entrenched discrimination. At several branches of the University of California the ratio of Japanese American students to the Japanese American population was a little greater than the figure for the total California population. A 1930 survey of a large number of Japanese Americans in California showed the average educational level for males over twenty born in the United States to be 12.5 years. The figures for females were also relatively high. The educational attainments of Japanese Americans were at least equal to those of California whites.[88]

The war evacuation interrupted these educational attainments. Second- and third-generation Japanese Americans received part of their schooling in the camps. After the war, educational discrimination against Japanese Americans was relaxed, and major gains resumed. In 1970 the median educational levels for adult Japanese American males and females were 12.6 and 12.4 years, respectively, compared with a combined national figure of 12.1 years. By 1980 the median educational level for all Japanese Americans had increased to 12.9 years, substantially greater than that for all adult Americans.[89]

The educational sphere still contains more than a few traces of discrimination. We have noted the underrepresentation of Japanese Americans in higher administrative positions in public education. And Japanese Americans continue to be underrepresented in certain graduate programs and departments at U.S. universities because of the direct and indirect impact of white stereotypes about the scientific and technical abilities of Asian Americans. Moreover, although the education levels of Japanese Americans are higher than those of the white population, as we have seen, their income levels are lower than one would predict on this basis. The financial payoffs of a college education vary according to race and ethnicity.[90]

RELIGION

Japanese immigrants brought Buddhism and Shintoism with them. These religious traditions have remained significant in the United States. Once the Japanese arrived, Protestant missionaries converted many to Christian beliefs. Some Protestant missions provided support for immigrants establishing themselves in a difficult environment. They were crucibles of acculturation in which young Japanese Americans began to absorb the language and values of the core culture. When the missions grew, they became full-scale Japanese Protestant churches segregated from other churches. By the 1920s there were thousands of practicing Japanese American Protestants.[91]

Buddhist temples were founded in major coastal cities in the decade after 1900. By 1920 there were two dozen temples in the West. Buddhist groups made significant adaptations to the new environment, with Christian-style Sunday schools and church organizations. As they did with the Japanese language schools, white exclusionists made the outrageous claim that the temples were hotbeds of emperor worship and antipatriotic teaching. Significantly, Buddhism does not involve emperor worship.[92]

A survey of Japanese Californians in the 1930s found that while three-quarters of first-generation immigrants were Buddhist, only 39 percent of the second generation were. A majority among the Nisei were Christian. Japanese Americans were becoming a Christian group. A study in Seattle found the community there roughly split between Christian churches and traditional Japanese religious groups. Yet the division was not as great as it might have appeared. Adoption of Christian practices did not usually entail a complete break with the past, for many considered themselves Christian *and* Buddhist.[93]

Before and during World War II there was jingoistic agitation branding Buddhism and Shintoism un-American. The evacuation closed churches on the mainland; Buddhist temples were closed in Hawaii and priests imprisoned. World War II brought destruction to Buddhist temples; many were vandalized. After the war Buddhist temples increased across the United States as Buddhism regained its important position in Japanese American communities.[94]

By the 1980s there were several dozen Protestant churches in the Japanese Southern California Ministerial Fellowship, with numerous others scattered up and down the West Coast and across the country. The Jodo Shinshu Buddhist Churches of America had many churches, and there were dozens of smaller Buddhist groups. One study of Japanese Americans in San Francisco found that churches were second in importance only to the family in cementing the community; two-thirds of those interviewed were at least occasional participants in church activities. Buddhist groups have tended to attract older members; younger Japanese Americans have preferred Presbyterian and Methodist churches.[95]

There has been a resurgence of interest in Buddhism in the last decade among Asian Americans. Buddhist festivals have been celebrated in Japanese and other Asian American communities. One of the astronauts who died in the space shuttle explosion in 1986 was air force lieutenant colonel Ellison Onizuka, the first Asian American in space and a member of the 93-year-old Buddhist Churches of America, an organization that in the late 1980s had 63 temples and 150,000 members from several Asian American groups. This mostly Japanese American group represents the Jodo Shinshu tradition of Buddhism. Onizuka's Buddhist funeral made many non-Asian Americans more aware of the presence of several thousand Buddhists in the U.S. armed forces. The U.S. military also permitted Buddhist chaplains in the armed forces in the late 1980s.[96]

THE ASSIMILATION PERSPECTIVE

An assimilation perspective has predominated in much recent analysis by whites of the situation of Japanese Americans. This group has been seen as the most adaptive, in cultural and certain structural terms, of the non-European immigrant groups. Today most Japanese Americans are not immigrants. One study in Los Angeles County found that 70 percent of Japanese Americans were born in the United States, and that only 14 percent had come to the United States since 1970. Among major Asian American groups, Japanese Americans have the smallest proportion of immigrants. Most were born and have grown up under the pressures and influence of Anglo-American culture and institutions.[97]

From the assimilation perspective one might argue that cultural assimilation came at an early point for most Issei, although some acculturated to the langauge and other aspects of the Anglo core culture more rapidly than others. One segment of the Issei sought to survive white discrimination by isolating themselves from the outside world and immersing themselves in things Japanese; many others sought to acculturate rapidly, at least in those areas where acculturation was permitted, while maintaining strong social and cultural ties to their relatives and friends. Assimilation analysts would also suggest that cultural assimilation, especially in regard to language, religion, and orientation to white-collar and corporate employment, has come rapidly for later generations. In one survey, although most Issei reported they could get along in English, many reported some language difficulty. The influence of the Issei in the Japanese community has been wide-ranging, but their ability to cope with the core culture was restricted by the massive discrimination they faced. The Nisei, in contrast, generally have become bicultural; that is, they operate successfully in both Japanese American communities and in mainstream institutions. Several studies of the Sansei have underscored the apparent closing of the gap with some aspects of the outside white culture. For example, one study found that Nisei and Sansei respondents showed substantial acculturation in that they spoke mostly English at home and did not often read Japanese literature. Kitano and Daniels reported in 1988 that 49 percent of all Japanese Americans in Los Angeles County speak only English, the highest proportion for any Asian American group there.[98]

Structural assimilation at secondary-group levels has been significant for Japanese Americans, particularly in the economic sphere. As we have seen, many analysts have dramatized this aspect of assimilation. Petersen, among others, has argued that Japanese Americans represent a remarkable success story in the economic progress they have made in the face of discrimination. Relatively high levels of occupational attainment, income, and education are characteristic for second- and third-generation families. Explanations for this success have tended to focus on values and community organization. Light has opted for a traditional-culture explanation in examining the development of the small-business economy among Japanese Americans, a niche economy that sets them apart, in his view, from certain other non-European Americans such as African and Mexican Americans. Light accents the role of a "culturally preferred style of economic organization," by which he means the rotating-credit associations and similar organizations set up by immigrants from Japan. On a related issue, Kitano and Daniels have shown that most Japanese American families own their own house and have strongly adhered to homeownership values, even more so than white Americans.[99]

What Milton Gordon refers to as behavior-receptional assimilation and attitude-receptional assimilation showed little change until after World War II. Intense discrimination and prejudice marred the lives of the Issei and Nisei for the first sixty years. Since World War II discrimination and prejudice directed at Japanese Americans have decreased. Some researchers have reported that white attitudes toward Japanese Americans improved dramatically between World War II and the early 1980s. For example, Spickard argues that in the early 1900s Japanese Americans were seen by whites as the "lowest of the low" and were grouped with black Americans, but that in recent years whites do "not see them as very different from themselves, and that fact is remarkable."[100] Spickard judges white attitudes from marriage rates; he is influenced by data showing that 30 to 60 percent of third-generation Japanese Americans, depending on the region and city, have married non-Japanese, as opposed to 2 percent or so among the first generation. The third-generation figures are in the same range as those of many white ethnic groups, and contrast sharply with the current 2 percent intermarriage rate for African Americans. Spickard argues in effect that whites generally do not feel hostile about Japanese–white marriages, especially those involving Japanese American women. (Further discussion of intermarriage follows shortly.)

However, Spickard is too optimistic in reading intermarriages as indicative of positive white views. As we have noted, recent years have seen renewed white hostility and discrimination toward Japanese and other Asian Americans, especially during economic recessions. In one survey a significant number of Japanese Americans reported having faced discrimination. One-fifth of those surveyed (31 percent of the Nisei and 13 percent of the Sansei) reported experiencing considerable discrimination as adults, and another 65 percent reported a little discrimination. Only 13 percent reported *never* having experienced discrimination. In addition, three-quarters of the sample felt that Japanese Americans experience discrimination, and the majority disagreed with the statement that Japanese Americans do not face job discrimination. Given the reluctance of many Japanese Americans to speak ill of their country, these responses likely underrepresent the actual amount of discrimination, especially the subtle variety, faced by Japanese Americans.[101]

Analysts such as Spickard focus on assimilation at the level of primary social ties and voluntary associations. Assimilation in these areas did not occur to any significant degree until after World War II. In earlier decades Japanese immigrants migrated under the auspices of family members already in the United States. Employment and small-business relationships were their main contacts with non-Japanese; most remained isolated socially, in part because of discrimination. Even in recent decades the Issei have tended, much more than later generations, to reside in extended families and to localize their ties within Japanese communities.

A number of researchers have found that primary-group integration with outsiders has also been limited for the Nisei but is more extensive for the Sansei. One study of 148 Japanese American men looked at the primary-group level. Two-thirds had mostly Japanese Americans as close friends; the Sansei were a little more integrated with whites than the Nisei. However, majorities in both groups reported living in neighborhoods where 50 percent or more of their neighbors were white. According to a major study of Japanese Americans by Montero and his associates, the proportion of Japanese Americans living in heavily Japanese American neighborhoods declined from 1915 to 1967. By the late 1960s over half lived in predominantly non-Japanese neighborhoods, while 40 percent lived in mixed neighborhoods. Residential integration had increased significantly for these Asian Americans.[102]

One 1960s study found that only a minority of the Nisei and Sansei respondents preferred that their children associate only with other Japanese Americans. Data since the 1960s suggest a trend toward primary-group assimilation, especially for those in the third and fourth generations who have moved away from areas with a critical mass of Japanese Americans. However, in areas where this critical mass exists, such as Los Angeles County and Seattle, primary-group assimilation and marital assimilation have not been as significant as in cities where there are fewer Japanese Americans.[103]

Until the late 1940s antimiscegenation laws in western states made Asian–European marriages *illegal.* Aside from the Japanese war brides of returning soldiers, there was almost no marriage with outsiders until the 1950s. Los Angeles data show an outmarriage rate of 2 percent in the 1924–1933 period and a rate of 11 to 20 percent for the 1950s. Surveys in the 1950s and 1960s showed strong but declining preferences among some Nisei and the Sansei for Japanese American marriage partners. In 1967 a national survey of the Sansei discovered that one-third had outmarried or were planning to outmarry. Studies of marriage licenses in California counties in the 1970s found the proportions outmarrying to be closer to half.[104]

One analysis of 1980 census data, the most recent available as of 1992, found that 34 percent of Japanese Americans in the United States had married outside their group. The importance of this study is that its sample is national and therefore larger than the western samples used by studies showing higher rates of outmarriage. For example, a study of outmarriage rates by Kitano and Daniels for Los Angeles County for the period 1975–1984 found that the proportion of Japanese Americans marrying non-Japanese increased from 55 percent to 63 percent between 1975 and 1977, then decreased to 51 percent in 1984. An estimated 5 to 10 percent of the outmarriages were to other Asians; most were to whites. Women were more likely to intermarry than men (60 percent versus 40 percent in 1984). The researchers suggested that there may be some decline in outmarriage in Los Angeles County in recent years. Still, several researchers have suggested that in the West marriage rates for those Japanese Americans in the third and fourth generations may be high enough, especially outside the larger Japanese American communities, to dilute the sense of Japanese American identity in the future. A critical issue will be how the children of these marriages view their identities.[105]

Looking at Japanese Americans in the context of Gordon's concept of identificational assimilation, it seems clear that very few have rejected their cultural heritage for a purely "American" identity. The sense of Japanese identity is still strong in all generations. Most Japanese Americans are now bicultural, with a foot in both worlds. A 1969 study found more than 60 percent of the Sansei and more than 80 percent of the Nisei saying they were very proud of their Japanese background.[106]

Substantial differences in value orientations between Japanese and white Americans have also been found. The authors of one study asked Japanese Americans whether they saw differences in Japanese American and white orientations toward social affairs, church life, and family relations. Large percentages saw significant differences, from 42 percent for social life to 65 percent for family life and 75 percent for church life. Interestingly, the Sansei were more likely to see differences than the Nisei. The authors of this study suggest that Japanese Americans do *not* see themselves as assimilating rapidly to the core culture in regard to family and church life.[107]

Developing a broad overview of the assimilation process, Kitano and Daniels argue that Japanese and other Asian Americans can be sorted into three major categories based on (1) degree of overall assimilation to the core culture and institutions and (2) strength of "ethnic identity." They argue that many in the third and later generations and those isolated from large communities are in a "high assimilation, low ethnic identity" category; that is, they have made many adaptations to the core culture in terms of language and lifestyle and retain only weak ties to the old language and culture. These Japanese Americans have strong social ties to whites or have married whites. The other large group of Japanese Americans belong to a "high assimilation, high ethnic identity" category. These people move easily in both the Japanese American community culture and the core culture. In contrast with the first group, they are more knowledgeable about Japanese American history and culture and have a stronger ethnic identity. A third and smaller group includes those who have migrated in recent decades and those who spend much of their lives within the Japanese American communities; they are said to be in a "low assimilation, high ethnic identity" category. Marriages are within the group, and ethnic identity is very important. Of course, Kitano and Daniels are careful to note that assimilation is relative even in the case of the first two subgroups because many whites in the larger society still regard Japanese Americans as racially distinct, and this visibility forces "the retention of ethnic identity, no matter how slight."[108]

Japanese Americans might conceivably be viewed as a clear-cut example of the ethnogenesis theory of Andrew Greeley—partly in but partly outside the dominant white culture and society. No analyst has yet developed this perspective on Japanese Americans, although Petersen has argued that this group has become a "subnation" in the United States, achieving integration in the economic sphere and making some cultural adaptation, but often maintaining cohesive, family-centered communities.[109]

The Power–Conflict View

Few analysts have interpreted the Japanese American experience systematically from a power–conflict point of view. One power–conflict analyst, Robert Blauner, has suggested that Japanese Americans might be viewed as a partially colonized minority. Many early Japanese immigrants worked in a position of debt servitude or migrated to the United States under pressure. This was particularly the case for thousands of contract laborers who went to Hawaii and later moved on to the mainland.

Bonacich has underscored the intimate economic relationship between the labor needs of U.S. capitalism and the streams of immigrant workers employed over the centuries. Asian labor filled the needs of a booming frontier capitalism on the West Coast. Chinese and Japanese laborers were seen by whites as "colored" labor, with fewer rights than their white counterparts. Because the United States was an imperial power in the Pacific region, U.S. agents had easy entry into Asian countries and could more or less dictate treaties and agreements benefiting employers. U.S. capitalists actively recruited Asian laborers because they could be made to work for very low wages. Employers thus had the backing of their government in securing low-wage labor from countries such as Japan and China where the United States had the greatest influence. Neither China nor Japan possessed the power that European nations had to protect immigrant workers. Moreover, Japanese immigrants could not become citizens under U.S. law, so they could easily be excluded if they later became unsuitable to West Coast employers.[110]

In the beginning Japanese Americans, much like Mexican Americans, were often forced by discrimination to become cheap laborers in the fields. The alien-labor laws barring land ownership for Issei, the complete exclusion of Japanese immigrants in 1924 on the grounds of race, and the massive imprisonment in World War II underscore the semicolonial treatment that Japanese Americans—unlike European immigrant groups— have endured. Their experiences were not the same as those of most European immigrants, on whose experiences the assimilation models are grounded.

Acculturation might also be viewed differently from a systematic power–conflict analysis. The pressures to acculturate were coercive. Commitment to some cultural assimilation in Japanese communities can be seen as a reaction to severe white discrimination. By the 1910s and 1920s numerous Japanese American leaders were exhorting their constituents to be exemplary in their hard work and deference in order to command some acceptance by dominant groups. In the public schools, acculturation pressures took the form of attacks on the Japanese cultural heritage. Japanese Americans, while in some ways the most integrated of non-Europeans, have many experiences similar to the forcible exploitation of African, Mexican, and Native Americans.

Some Asian American scholars have raised a question about the bias in the assimilation model itself. The assimilation theory of Robert Park and other early social scientists emerged in a period of intense agitation over Japanese immigration and reflected those scholars' usually racist views of the Japanese. Moreover, applying the assimilationist perspective to Japanese and other Asian Americans prior to the 1950s is very inappropriate in one fundamental respect. Asians were prevented from even trying to assimilate politically. Unlike European immigrants, Japanese and other Asian immigrants were denied the right to become naturalized citizens. As we saw, in the 1922 *Ozawa* case the Supreme Court ruled that Asian immigrants were not white and thus could not become citizens. In a similar case the next year, *U.S.* v. *Bhagat Singh Thind,* the same racist reasoning was applied to an Asian Indian seeking to become naturalized. The Court declared further that "the children of English, French, German, Italian, Scandinavian, and other European parentage, quickly merge in to the mass of our population and lose the distinctive hallmarks of their European origin."[111] This biased reasoning misses the point that at the time—and indeed into the 1950s—Asian immigrants were not even allowed political and civic assimilation in the United States.

The "Model Minority" Stereotype

Paramount among the weaknesses in the traditional assimilation perspective has been the "model minority" stereotype. During the late 1980s and early 1990s virtually ever major newsmagazine and television network carried glowing reports on the achievements of Asian Americans, especially Japanese Americans, in various occupational categories and in education.[112] The success of Japanese Americans, seen as rooted in their values and family styles, has been cited not only in the media but also by prominent white writers as a paramount reflection of U.S. opportunities and of what other nonwhites, particularly African Americans and Mexican Americans, could achieve if they would only follow the Japanese American example.[113] Stereotypes of Japanese Americans as paragons of hard work and docility carry a negative undercurrent. Suzuki has suggested that the "model minority" image of Asian groups such as Japanese Americans was created not by these groups but rather by white American outsiders, including non-Asian scholars and media analysts, for ideological reasons.[114] As black Americans protested in the streets during the 1960s, these whites created the model minority image in order to suggest that nonwhite groups could achieve the

American dream simply by working hard. The assumption underlying this idea was that Asian Americans were more like whites in their attitude toward work.

As we have noted, recent scholarship has questioned much of this imagery. Pre–World War II educational opportunities greater than those available to segregated African Americans helped prepare Japanese Americans for the white-collar jobs opening up after the war. It was not Asian values that brought success so much as access to education and white-collar jobs. Critics of the model minority notion have also noted other factors in the economic success of Japanese Americans: the early role of the Japanese government in supporting immigrants and the availability of a small-business niche on the West Coast.

Japanese Americans, at an early point, created small businesses through which they served one another and the basic needs of a frontier economy. Japanese American employers and employees saw themselves as a single group confronting the hostile outside world. Out of economic necessity employers and employees, many having kinship or regional ties, worked together against hostile white competitors. Success came at the price of being ghettoized in the small-business economy and, later, in certain professions. As with Jewish Americans, Japanese Americans have made it as a group in U.S. society by carving a distinctive niche for themselves—a process of adaptation not completely in line with the idealistic assimilation models. The long-term effects of discrimination are still reflected in the concentration of Japanese Americans in the small-business economy and in certain professional and technical occupations.

The movement of Japanese Americans into white-collar jobs does not signal emancipation from discrimination. Thus a study of Japanese American workers in the San Francisco metropolitan area found that those in white-collar jobs were clustered in such occupations as computer programming, clerical work, architecture, engineering, chemicals, dentistry, and pharmacy. The highest level white-collar personnel, such as managers, financial officers, and management analysts, still tended to be white males.[115]

Moreover, a study of minority-owned businesses found that most of those owned by Asian Americans were in retail trade (such as grocery stores and restaurants) and selected services (such as laundries). Gross annual receipts were modest for the majority of Japanese American firms. And as we have seen, research has revealed that Japanese Americans do not get as much payoff from their high levels of education as do comparably educated whites. Japanese and other Asian American families have more workers per family than whites. Higher family incomes often indicate more working family members, not higher individual incomes than those of comparably educated whites.[116]

Takagi has pointed to another bias in the traditional cultural-background explanation of Japanese American success—the idea that those racial–ethnic groups whose values are closest to those of the dominant groups are the ones who will be, and should be, successful. In other words, success is evaluated only in terms of values prized by the dominant white culture. Although Japanese Americans have acculturated in numerous ways, the price they have paid in terms of conformity, lost creativity, and lost contributions to this society has been great.[117]

One must also remember the world context of racial and ethnic relations. From the beginning Japanese immigration and Japanese American integration into the core culture and society have been shaped by U.S. intervention in the capitalist world economy. The action of the U.S. government in forcing Japan into the world economy in the nineteenth century was eventually followed by the recruitment of many low-wage laborers for U.S. enterprises. Today, as the Japanese economy vies successfully with the U.S. economy for Pacific and world dominance, the world economy still forms the backdrop. New economic alliances on the Pacific Rim, such as the Association of Southeast Asian nations, are bypassing the United States. Japan is the most powerful economy in these alliances, and that economic success is one reason there has been little recent migration from Japan to the United States, apart from the temporary migration of business executives and investors. There is unfortunately a negative side to the prosperity of Japan and other Asian nations in the world economy: white Americans, angry over domestic economic troubles, confuse Japanese Americans with the Japanese and blame both unfairly for economic troubles caused by U.S. employers and investors or the federal government. This stereotyping is yet another constant indication to Japanese Americans that somehow they have not been accepted as "true Americans" by many white Americans.

SUMMARY

Japanese Americans are an important group in U.S. racial–ethnic history. In the beginning they were a severely exploited minority. Many entered as laborers, facing violence and intense discrimination. They endured complete exclusion as a result of racist immigration legislation. They endured laws against land ownership. During World War II they suffered the only large-scale imprisonment of U.S. citizens in barbed-wire concentration camps. Against terrible odds they prospered. They constitute a non-European group whose economic mobility has been remarkable. Yet, for all their acculturation and economic assimilation, Japanese Americans have a way to go before they are fully included in the Anglo core culture and dominant Anglo institutions. Whether they will be the first non-European group to be fully included, politically and socially as well as economically, remains to be seen.

It is important for students of racial and ethnic relations to realize that the success story of Japanese and other Asian Americans is partially a myth. Japanese Americans have suffered in the past and still suffer from discrimination in the private sector. Fewer Japanese Americans than whites can fully realize earnings levels that parallel education levels. Few rise to the top of Fortune 500 corporations or government agencies.

In general, Japanese Americans have been stereotyped or misunderstood by insensitive whites, including state and federal government officials. For example, in the 1970s Lionel Van Deerlin, California representative and head of the House Subcommittee on Communications, commented that Asian Americans did not need to be considered a disadvantaged minority group because they were "more prosperous than [majority] Americans." Yet in the communications industry, as of that date, not one television or radio station was owned by a Japanese or other Asian American, and a survey of four San Francisco television stations showed that Asian American males were underrepresented, relative to their proportions in the local labor force, at three of them.[118]

More recently, this attitude has been expressed on a more or less regular basis by white officials across the United States. Japanese Americans are still considered a "model minority" with no need of special government protection against discrimination. Yet as we have seen in this chapter, there is still much anti-Japanese sentiment among white Americans, prejudice that results in discrimination and ethnoviolence. White Americans must change their attitudes and practices if Japanese Americans are ever to enjoy equality in the United States. David Mura, the author of *Turning Japanese: Memoirs of a Sansei,* has recently argued that whites must see that the "problem of race is one of giving up power." And whites must begin to take part in "dismantling racism and redistributing power."[119]

Perhaps one day the United States as a whole will be more like the members of the space shuttle Challenger's crew who through no fault of their own died in a tragic 1986 explosion. Working harmoniously together, that seven-person crew included an African American born to sharecroppers (Ronald McNair), a Jewish American of the Orthodox faith (Judith Resnik), and a Japanese American of the Buddhist faith (Ellison Onizuka). Onizuka, the grandson of Japanese laborers who immigrated to Hawaii in the 1890s to work on a coffee plantation in the 1890s, was born on a coffee farm. He worked hard, became an aerospace engineer, and participated in two space missions. As the first Asian American astronaut, Onizuka has come to symbolize for many Asian Americans the heroic character of their struggle for success and equality in the United States.

NOTES

1. U.S. Commission on Civil Rights, *Civil Rights Issues Facing Asian Americans in the 1990s,* p. 15.
2. Ibid.; Robert Daniels, *Coming to America* (New York: Harper Collins, 1990), p. 350.
3. Kathryn Tolbert, "Pacific Grim," *Boston Globe Sunday Magazine,* March 29, 1992, p. 14.
4. Ronald Takaki, *Strangers from a Different Shore: A History of Asian Americans* (New York: Penguin, 1989), p. 7.
5. Alan T. Moriyama, *Imingaisha: Japanese Immigration Companies and Hawaii, 1894–1908* (Honolulu: University of Hawaii Press, 1985); Wayne Patterson, *The Korean Frontier in America: Immigration to Hawaii, 1896–1910* (Honolulu: University of Hawaii Press, 1988).
6. Roger Daniels, *The Politics of Prejudice* (New York: Atheneum, 1969), pp. 3–6; Hilary Conroy, *The Japanese Frontier in Hawaii, 1868–1898* (Berkeley: University of California Press, 1953), passim; Moriyama, *Imingaisha,* pp. xvi–xix.
7. Takaki, *Strangers from a Different Shore,* p. 179.
8. U.S. Immigration and Naturalization Service, *1975 Annual Report* (Washington, 1975), pp. 62–66.
9. Arinori Mori, *The Japanese in America* (Japan Advertiser Press, 1926), pp. 19–21; Kaizo Naka, *Social and Economic Conditions among Japanese Farmers in California* (San Francisco: R & E Research Associates, 1974), p. 6; John Modell, "On Being an Issei: Orientations toward America" (paper presented to the American Anthropological Association, San Diego, November 1970), p. 4.
10. T. Iyenago, *Japan and the California Problem* (New York: Putnam's, 1921), pp. 100–106; Roger Daniels, "Japanese Immigrants on the Western Frontier: The Issei in California, 1890–1940," in *East across the Pacific,* ed. Hilary Conroy and T. Scott Miyakawa (Santa Barbara, Calif.: ABC–CLIO, 1972), pp. 82–86; V. S. McClatchy, *Japanese Immigration and Colonization,* reprint ed. (San Francisco: R & E Research Associates, 1970), pp. 42–44; Kiyo Sue Inui, *The Unsolved Problem of the Pacific* (Tokyo: Japan Times, 1925).
11. Jacobus tenBroek, Edward N. Barnhart, and Floyd W. Matson, *Prejudice, War, and the Constitution* (Berkeley: University of California Press, 1968), pp. 42–43; *Takao Ozawa v. United States,* 260 U.S. 178 (1922); Takaki, *Strangers from a Distant Shore,* pp. 14–15.
12. Hilary Conroy and T. Scott Miyakawa, "Foreword," in *East across the Pacific,* ed. Conroy and Miyakawa, pp. xiv–xv.
13. The statistics are from U.S. Census Bureau publications.
14. Takaki, *Strangers from a Different Shore,* pp. 479–81.
15. E. Manchester-Boddy, *Japanese in America* (San Francisco: R & E Research Associates, 1970), pp. 25–30.
16. McClatchy, *Japanese Immigration and Colonization,* p. 42.
17. Sidney L. Gulick, *The American Japanese Problem* (New York: Scribner's, 1914), p. 16.
18. Quoted in Edward K. Strong, Jr., *The Second-Generation Japanese Problem* (Stanford, Calif.: Stanford University Press, 1934), p. 133.
19. tenBroek, Barnhart, and Matson, *Prejudice, War, and the Constitution,* pp. 26–28; Carey McWilliams, *Prejudice* (Boston; Little, Brown, 1944), pp. 30–45; Dennis M. Ogawa, *From Japs to Japanese* (Berkeley: McCutchan Publishing Co., 1971), pp. 16–19.
20. tenBroek, Barnhart, and Matson, *Prejudice, War, and the Constitution,* p. 31.
21. Ogawa, *From Japs to Japanese,* p. 12; Carey McWilliams, *Brothers under the Skin,* rev. ed. (Boston: Little, Brown, 1964), pp. 148–49; Stanley Sue and Harry H. L. Kitano, "Stereotypes as a Measure of Success," *Journal of Social Issues* 29 (1973): 83–98.
22. C. N. Reynolds, "Oriental–White Race Relations in Santa Clara County, California" (Ph.D. dissertation, Stanford University, 1927); E. S. Bogardus, "Social Distance: A Measuring Stick," *Survey* 56 (1927); 169ff. Both are cited in Strong, *The Second-Generation Japanese Problem,* pp. 109, 128.
23. tenBroek, Barnhart, and Matson, *Prejudice, War, and the Constitution,* pp. 66–70.

24. Quoted in Ogawa, *From Japs to Japanese*, p. 11.
25. U.S. Department of the Interior, War Relocation Authority, *Myths and Facts about the Japanese American* (Washington, 1945), pp. 7–8; Ogawa, *From Japs to Japanese*, pp. 35–54. Survey data document attitude changes in the period 1942–1961. See also Roger Daniels, "Why It Happened Here," in *The Social Reality of Ethnic America*, ed. R. Gomez et al. (Lexington, Mass.: Heath, 1971), p. 236.
26. Council on Interracial Books for Children, *Stereotypes, Distortions and Omissions in U.S. History Textbooks* (New York: Racism and Sexism Resource Center for Educators, 1977), pp. 42–46.
27. Letta Tayler, "Dateline: Washington," States News Service, May 8, 1987, n.p.; Takaki, *Strangers from a Different Shore*, p. 6.
28. Karl Taro Greenfield, "Return of the Yellow Peril," *Nation*, May 11, 1992, p. 636; Michael Crichton, *Rising Sun* (New York: Knopf, 1991).
29. Herbert B. Johnson, *Discrimination against the Japanese in California* (Berkeley, Calif.: Courier Publishing Co., 1907), pp. 73–74; Daniels, *The Politics of Prejudice*, pp. 33–34; Howard H. Sugimoto, "The Vancouver Riots of 1907: A Canadian Episode," in *East across the Pacific*, ed. Conroy and Miyakawa, pp. 92–110.
30. Jean Pajus, *The Real Japanese California* (San Francisco: R & E Research Associates, 1971), pp. 164–66; Daniels, *The Politics of Prejudice*, p. 87; tenBroek, Barnhart, and Matson, *Prejudice, War, and the Constitution*, p. 73.
31. Lemuel F. Ignacio, *Asian Americans and Pacific Islanders* (San Jose, Calif.: Pilipino Development Associates, 1976), pp. 95–96; tenBroek, Barnhart, and Matson, *Prejudice, War, and the Constitution*, passim.
32. Dorothy Swaine Thomas and Richard S. Nishimoto, *The Spoilage* (Berkeley: University of California Press, 1946), pp. 5–10; tenBroek, Barnhart, and Matson, *Prejudice, War, and the Constitution*, pp. 82–84.
33. Thomas and Nishimoto, *The Spoilage*, pp. 8–16; tenBroek, Barnhart, and Matson, *Prejudice, War, and the Constitution*, pp. 118–20.
34. tenBroek, Barnhart, and Matson, *Prejudice, War, and the Constitution*, pp. 120, 126–29, 130; Thomas and Nishimoto, *The Spoilage*, pp. 10–20; Edward H. Spicer et al., *Impounded People* (Tucson: University of Arizona Press, 1969), pp. 141–241.
35. Richard Drinnon, *Keeper of Concentration Camps* (Berkeley: University of California Press, 1987), pp. 47, 153; quotation from Valerie Matsumoto, "Japanese American Women during World War II," in *Unequal Sisters*, ed. Ellen C. DuBois and Vicki L. Ruiz (New York: Routledge, 1990), p. 373.
36. Thomas and Nishimoto, *The Spoilage*, pp. 54–71; tenBroek, Barnhart, and Matson, *Prejudice, War, and the Constitution*, pp. 126–32; 149–55; Spicer et al., *Impounded People*, pp. 252–80.
37. Leonard Bloom and Ruth Riemer, *Removal and Return* (Berkeley; University of California Press, 1949), pp. 124–57, 198–204; tenBroek, Barnhart, and Matson, *Prejudice, War, and the Constitution*, pp. 155–77, 180–81.
38. Bradford Smith, *Americans from Japan* (New York; Lippincott, 1948), pp. 10–12, 202–76; McWilliams, *Prejudice*, p. 4; tenBroek, Barnhart, and Matson, *Prejudice, War, and the Constitution*, pp. 211–23; Harry H. L. Kitano, *Japanese Americans*, 2nd ed. (Englewood Cliffs, N.J.: Prentice-Hall, 1976), pp. 82–88; S. Frank Miyamoto, "The Forced Evacuation of the Japanese Minority during World War II," *Journal of Social Issues* 29 (1973): 11–29.
39. Drinnon, *Keeper of Concentration Camps*, pp. 255–56. See also Christopher Thorne, *Allies of a Kind* (New York: Oxford University Press, 1978).
40. Kitano, *Japanese Americans*, p. 73.
41. Gary Y. Okihiro, "Japanese Resistance in America's Concentration Camps: A Re-evaluation," *Amerasia Journal* 2 (Fall 1973): 20–34; Arthur A. Hansen and David A. Hacker, "The Manzanar Riot: An Ethnic Perspective," *Amerasia Journal* 3 (Fall 1974): 112–42. See also Roger Daniels, *Concentration Camps, U.S.A.* (New York: Holt, Rinehart & Winston, 1971).
42. Daniels, *The Politics of Prejudice*, pp. 104–5.
43. Ivan H. Light, *Ethnic Enterprise in America* (Berkeley: University of California Press, 1972), pp. 174–79; Bill Hosokawa, *The Nisei* (New York: Morrow, 1969), pp. 199–200; Kitano, *Japanese Americans*, pp. 55–58.
44. Hosokawa, *The Nisei*, pp. 439–46; Kitano, *Japanese Americans*, pp. 89–90.
45. Nathaniel C. Nash, "House Votes Payments to Japanese Americans," *New York Times*, September 18, 1987, p. A15.
46. Ken Miller, "U.S. Pays Japanese Internees $20,000—and Apologies," Gannett News Service, October 9, 1990, n.p.
47. Santiago O'Donnell and Psyche Pascual, "Kato Slaying Raises Fears of Hate Crime," *Los Angeles Times*, March 1, 1992, p. B1.
48. Rodolfo Acuña, *Occupied America* (San Francisco: Canfield Press, 1972), pp. 212–13.
49. Kitano, *Japanese Americans*, pp. 174–86; Daniel Inouye and Lawrence Elliot, *Journey to Washington* (Englewood Cliffs, N.J.: Prentice-Hall, 1967), pp. 248–50; Hosokawa, *The Nisei*, pp. 460–69.
50. Hosokawa, *The Nisei*, pp. 486–87.
51. Sonni Effron, "Politics Are Changing for Asian Americans," *Los Angeles Times*, August 16, 1990, p. A3.
52. Rob Gurwitt, "Have Asian Americans Arrived Politically? Not Quite," *Governing*, November 1990, p. 38.
53. U.S. Commission on Civil Rights, *Recent Activities against Citizens and Residents of Asian Descent* (Washington, 1986), pp. 3–6.
54. Kenneth Walsh, Gloria Borger, Susan Dentzer, and Carla A. Robbins, "The 'America First' Fallacies," *U.S. News & World Report*, February 3, 1992, p. 22.
55. O'Donnell and Pascual, "Kato Slaying Raises Fears of Hate Crime," p. B1.
56. Daniels, *The Politics of Prejudice*, pp. 23–24
57. Yuji Ichioka, "A Buried Past," *Amerasia Journal* 1 (July 1971): 1–25; Karl Yoneda, "100 Years of Japanese Labor History in the U.S.A.," in *Roots*, ed. Amy Tachiki et al. (Los Angeles: UCLA Asian American Studies Center, 1971), pp. 150–57; Takaki, *Strangers from a Different Shore*, p. 200.
58. See the various articles in *Roots*, ed. Tachiki et al.
59. Russell Endo and William Wei, "On the Development of Asian American Studies Programs," in *Reflections on Shattered Windows*, ed. Gary Y. Okihiro et al. (Pullman: Washington State University Press, 1988), pp. 6–12.
60. Cited in Gulick, *The American Japanese Problem*, p. 11.

61. Japanese Association of the Pacific Northwest, *Japanese Immigration* (San Francisco: R & E Research Associates, 1972), pp. 22–25; Daniels, *The Politics of Prejudice,* pp. 7, 10–12.
62. Edna Bonacich and John Modell, *The Economic Basis of Ethnic Solidarity* (Berkeley: University of California Press, 1980), pp. 38–47.
63. Kitano, *Japanese Americans,* pp. 19–21; Light, *Ethnic Enterprise in America,* pp. 27–29; S. Frank Miyamoto, "An Immigrant Community in America," in *East across the Pacific,* ed. Conroy and Miyakawa, pp. 223–25.
64. Gulick, *The American Japanese Problem,* pp. 11, 32–33; Light, *Ethnic Enterprise in America,* p. 71; Daniels, "Japanese Immigrants on the Western Frontier," p. 85.
65. Pajus, *The Real Japanese California,* pp. 147–51; Light, *Ethnic Enterprise in America,* p. 76.
66. Bloom and Riemer, *Removal and Return,* pp. 115–17; Strong, *The Second-Generation Japanese Problem,* pp. 209–11.
67. Bloom and Riemer, *Removal and Return,* pp. 17–20.
68. Evelyn Nakano Glenn, "The Dialectics of Wage Work: Japanese American Women and Domestic Service, 1905–1940," in *Unequal Sisters,* ed. DuBois and Ruiz, p. 345.
69. Ibid., p. 369.
70. Bloom and Riemer, *Removal and Return,* pp. 44, 144.
71. Bonacich and Modell, *The Economic Basis of Ethnic Solidarity,* pp. 256–59.
72. The 1960 data are from U.S. Bureau of the Census, *Population, 1960: Nonwhite Population by Race* (Washington, 1963), p. 108. The "occupation not reported" data have been excluded in the calculation of percentages. The 1970 data are from U.S. Department of Health, Education and Welfare, *A Study of Selected Socio-economic Characteristics of Ethnic Minorities Based on the 1970 Census* (Washington, 1974), p. 83.
73. U.S. Bureau of the Census, *U.S. Census of Population, 1980: General Social and Economic Characteristics,* PC80-1-C1 (Washington, 1983), p. 160.
74. U.S. Commission on Civil Rights, *Social Indicators of Equality for Minorities and Women* (Washington, 1978), pp. 42–45.
75. U.S. Bureau of the Census, *U.S. Census of Population, 1980,* p. 161.
76. U.S. Department of Health, Education and Welfare, *A Study of Selected Socio-economic Characteristics,* pp. 105–8; Gene N. Levine and Darrel M. Montero, "Socioeconomic Mobility among Three Generations of Japanese Americans," *Journal of Social Issues* 29 (1973): 33ff; U.S. Commission on Civil Rights, *Social Indicators of Equality for Minorities and Women,* pp. 42–45.
77. David J. O'Brien and Stephen S. Fugita, "Generational Differences in Japanese Americans' Perceptions and Feelings about Social Relationships between Themselves and Caucasian Americans," in *Culture, Ethnicity, and Identity,* ed. William McCready (New York: Academic Press, 1983), pp. 235–36.
78. U.S. Commission on Civil Rights, *Success of Asian Americans: Fact or Fiction?* (Washington, 1980), pp. 14–15.
79. Harry H. L. Kitano and Roger Daniels, *Asian Americans: Emerging Minorities* (Englewood Cliffs, N.J.: Prentice-Hall, 1988), p. 171.
80. Winfred Yu, "Asian Americans Charge Prejudice Slows Climb to Management Ranks," *Wall Street Journal,* September 11, 1985, n.p., quoted in Takaki, *Strangers from a Different Shore,* p. 476.
81. Takaki, *Strangers from a Different Shore,* pp. 475–77.
82. Quotation in John Jeansonne, "Though Tremendously Popular after the Olympics, on the Marketing Front There's No Gold for Kristi," *Newsday,* April 16, 1992, p. 160. See also Laura Zinn, "To Marketers, Kristi Yamaguchi Isn't as Good as Gold," *Business Week,* March 9, 1992, p. 40.
83. Kitano, *Japanese Americans,* pp. 92–93, 95; Levine and Montero, "Socioeconomic Mobility," pp. 45ff; Dale Minami, "Testimony to U.S. Commission on Civil Rights," in *Civil Rights Issues of Asian and Pacific Americans* (Washington, D.C.: U.S. Commission on Civil Rights, 1979), pp. 420–22. See also "Asian Americans: A 'Model Minority,'" *Newsweek,* December 6, 1982, p. 41.
84. K. K. Kawakami, *The Japanese Question* (New York: Macmillan, 1921), pp. 143–45; John Modell, "Tradition and Opportunity: The Japanese Immigrant in America," *Pacific Historical Review* 40 (May 1971): 163–82.
85. Johnson, *Discrimination against the Japanese in California,* pp. 3–20, 40–47; Franklin Hichborn, *The Story of the Session of the California Legislature of 1909* (San Francisco: James H. Barry Press, 1909), p. 207; Pajus, *The Real Japanese California,* pp. 170–78; Kawakami, *The Japanese Question,* pp. 168–69.
86. Pajus, *The Real Japanese California,* pp. 180–81; Kawakami, *The Japanese Question,* pp. 162–63.
87. William Petersen, *Japanese Americans* (New York: Random House, 1971), p. 183; Strong, *The Second-Generation Japanese Problem,* pp. 201–4; Kawakami, *The Japanese Question,* pp. 146–51; Pajus, *The Real Japanese California,* p. 181.
88. Pajus, *The Real Japanese California,* p. 183; Strong, *The Second-Generation Japanese Problem,* pp. 185–88.
89. U.S. Department of Health, Education and Welfare, *A Study of Selected Socio-economic Characteristics,* pp. 70ff; U.S. Commission on Civil Rights, *Social Indicators of Equality for Minorities and Women,* pp. 12–14; U.S. Bureau of the Census, *U.S. Census of Population, 1980,* p. 157.
90. Kitano, *Japanese Americans,* pp. 93, 174–75; U.S. Commission on Civil Rights, *Social Indicators of Equality for Minorities and Women,* pp. 24–26.
91. Manchester-Boddy, *Japanese in America,* p. 118.
92. Petersen, *Japanese Americans,* p. 177; Manchester-Boddy, *Japanese in America,* pp. 114–18.
93. Strong, *The Second-Generation Japanese Problem,* p. 229; Shotaro Frank Miyamoto, "Social Solidarity among the Japanese in Seattle," *University of Washington Publications in Social Sciences* 11 (December 1939): 99–102; Petersen, *Japanese Americans,* pp. 174–75.
94. Andrew W. Lind, *Hawaii's Japanese* (Princeton, N.J.: Princeton University Press, 1946), pp. 212–57; Petersen, *Japanese Americans,* pp. 177–78, 185.
95. Hosokawa, *The Nisei,* p. 131; Kitano, *Japanese Americans,* p. 115; Christie Kiefer, *Changing Cultures, Changing Lives* (San Francisco: Jossey-Bass, 1974), pp. 34–38; Petersen, *Japanese Americans,* p. 187.

96. John Dart, "Military Opens Chaplain Ranks to Buddhists," *Los Angeles Times,* October 27, 1987, p. 1-1.

97. Modell, "On Being an Issei," pp. 1–2, 19–20.

98. John Modell, "The Japanese American Family: A Perspective for Future Investigations," *Pacific Historical Review* 37 (February 1968): 79; Joe R. Feagin and Nancy Fujitaki, "On the Assimilation of Japanese Americans," *Amerasia Journal* 1 (February 1972): 15–17; Abe Arkoff, "Need Patterns in Two Generations of Japanese-Americans in Hawaii," *Journal of Social Psychology* 50 (1959): 75–79; Kitano and Daniels, *Asian Americans,* p. 179.

99. Petersen, *Japanese Americans,* pp. 6–7; Light, *Ethnic Enterprise in America,* passim; William Caudill, "Japanese American Personality and Acculturation," *Genetic Psychology Monographs* 45 (1952): 3–102; Kitano and Daniels, *Asian Americans,* p. 179.

100. Paul Spickard, *Mixed Blood* (Madison: University of Wisconsin Press, 1988), p. 347.

101. O'Brien and Fugita, "Generational Differences," pp. 235–360.

102. Darrel Montero, *Japanese Americans: Changing Patterns of Ethnic Affiliation over Three Generations* (Boulder, Colo.: Westview Press, 1980), p. 80; Petersen, *Japanese Americans,* pp. 220–24; Modell, "The Japanese American Family," pp. 76–79; Kitano, *Japanese Americans,* pp. 189, 196; George Kagiwada, "Assimilation of Nisei in Los Angeles," in *East Across the Pacific,* ed. Conroy and Miyakawa, p. 273.

103. Feagin and Fujitaki, "On the Assimilation of Japanese Americans," p. 23.

104. Akemi Kikumura and Harry H. L. Kitano, "Interracial Marriage: A Picture of Japanese Americans," *Journal of Social Issues* 29 (1973): 67–81; John N. Tinker, "Intermarriage and Ethnic Boundaries: The Japanese American Case," *Journal of Social Issues* 29 (1973): 55; John W. Connor, *Tradition and Change in Three Generations of Japanese Americans* (Chicago: Nelson-Hall, 1977), p. 308; Gene N. Levine and Colbert Rhodes, *The Japanese American Community* (New York: Praeger, 1981), p. 145.

105. Sharon M. Lee and Keiko Yamanaka, "Intermarriage in the Asian American Population" (typescript, Cornell University, 1987); Kitano and Daniels, *Asian Americans,* pp. 176–178.

106. Feagin and Fujitaki, "On the Assimilation of Japanese Americans," pp. 25–26.

107. O'Brien and Fugita, "Generational Differences," pp. 231–35. See also Connor, *Tradition and Change in Three Generations of Japanese Americans,* pp. 304–8.

108. Kitano and Daniels, *Asian Americans,* pp. 191–92.

109. Petersen, *Japanese Americans,* pp. 214–21.

110. Edna Bonacich, "United States Capitalist Development: A Background to Asian Immigration," in *Labor Immigration under Capitalism,* ed. Lucie Cheng and Edna Bonacich (Berkeley: University of California Press, 1984), p. 82.

111. *U.S. v. Bhagat Singh Thind,* 261 U.S. 215 (1923).

112. For a list of media presentations, see Takaki, *Strangers from a Different Shore,* p. 474.

113. This section draws on Robert Blauner, *Racial Oppression in America* (New York: Harper & Row, Pub., 1972), pp. 54–55; Paul Takagi, "The Myth of 'Assimilation in American Life,'" *Amerasia Journal* 2 (Fall 1973): 149–58; Peter Uhlenberg, "Demographic Correlates of Group Achievement: Contrasting Patterns of Mexican-Americans and Japanese-Americans," *Demography* 9 (February 1972): 119–28.

114. B. Suzuki, "Education and the Socialization of Asian Americans," in *Asian Americans: Social and Psychological Perspectives,* ed. R. Endo, S. Sue, and N. Wagner (Palo Alto, Calif.: Science & Behavior Books, 1980), 2:155–78; William Petersen, "Success Story, Japanese-American Style," *New York Times,* January 9, 1966, p. 21; "Success Story of One Minority Group in the U.S.," *U.S. News & World Report,* December 26, 1966, pp. 73–76; Thomas Sowell, Ethnic America (New York: Basic Books, 1981).

115. Amado Cabezas and Gary Kawaguchi, "Empirical Evidence for Continuing Asian American Inequality: The Human Capital Model and Labor Market Segmentation," in *Reflections on Shattered Windows,* ed. Okihiro et al.

116. Studies cited in Amado Cabezas, "Testimony to U.S. Commission on Civil Rights," in *Civil Rights Issues of Asian and Pacific Americans,* pp. 389–93. See also Takaki, *Strangers from a Different Shore,* p. 475.

117. Takagi, "The Myth of 'Assimilation in American Life,'" pp. 149–58; Ogawa, *From Jap to Japanese,* pp. 43ff.

118. U.S. Commission on Civil Rights, *Success of Asian Americans,* p. 21.

119. David Mura, "Whites: How to Face the Angry Racial Tribes," *Utne Reader,* July/August 1992, p. 80. See also David Mura, *Turning Japanese: Memoirs of a Sansei* (New York: Atlantic Monthly Press, 1991).

Chapter 12

Chinese, Filipino, Korean, and Vietnamese Americans*

Korean Shopkeeper
Photo by Eugene Gordon

*Suzanne Harper contributed to the research for this chapter.

In the spring of 1992, Elaine H. Kim, a Korean American professor at the University of California, Berkeley, wrote insightfully in a national newsmagazine about the major Los Angeles riot that had taken place a few weeks earlier. She noted how the mass media had played up visual images of violent conflict between African American rioters and Korean American merchants, while ignoring the long histories and social contexts of these two groups. She argued that both Korean Americans and African Americans have been the victims of a long tradition of racial violence and discrimination at the hands of white Americans. Recalling her own experiences, Kim noted that

> my schooling offered nothing about Chicanos or Latinos, and most of what I was taught about African-Americans was distorted to justify their oppression and vindicate the forces of that oppression.[1]

Then she added:

> Likewise, Korean-Americans have been and continue to be used for someone else's agenda and benefit, whether we are hated as foreigners who refuse to become "good Americans," stereotyped as diligent work machines or simply treated as if we do not exist. Throughout my childhood, the people who continually asked, "What are you?" knew nothing of Korea or Koreans.[2]

Proud of her Korean heritage, Professor Kim wishes Korean history and culture were better known across the United States. She tells, for example, the story of Sohn Kee-chung, a courageous Korean marathon runner in the 1936 Olympics in Germany, who won the gold medal in front of Nazi leaders who viewed Asians as an inferior race.

Korean Americans are one of four major Asian American groups—each with a strong identity and a rich history and culture—that are analyzed in detail in this chapter. The others are Chinese, Filipino, and Vietnamese Americans. Although these groups have contributed much to the dynamic development of the United States in the late twentieth century, they still suffer greatly from stereotyping and discrimination at the hands of white and other non-Asian Americans.

MIGRATION: AN OVERVIEW

In the 1980s and 1990s the fastest-growing immigrant groups were mostly Asian American, including Chinese, Filipino, Korean, and Vietnamese Americans. Table 12–1 documents the changing scale of this immigration since the early nineteenth century.

TABLE 12–1: Immigration by Country

	1820–1900	1901–1920	1921–1940	1941–1960	1961–1980	1981–1991
Chinese*	305,455	41,833	43,835	41,910	347,564	377,049
Filipino	**	**	**	19,307	453,363	558,867
Korean	**	**	**	6,231	302,164	365,390
Vietnamese	**	**	**	335	177,160	456,400

*Figures include Hong Kong after 1951.
**Data not reported before 1951.
Source: Immigration and Naturalization Service, *1985 Statistical Yearbook* (Washington, 1986), pp. 2–5; conversation with Immigration and Naturalization Service representative.

Few Filipinos, Koreans, or Vietnamese immigrated to the U.S. mainland before the 1960s. Thereafter immigration increased dramatically. In about thirty years, the number of Filipino, Korean, and Vietnamese immigrants rose from so few that records were not kept of their arrival to a total of more than two million. Chinese immigration has followed a different pattern, with two major periods. The first began about 1850 and lasted until the passage of the 1882 Chinese Exclusion Act, which prohibited direct immigration. Although some Chinese immigration occurred in the years following the act, large-scale immigration did not resume until the immigration reforms in 1965. As can be seen in Table 12–1, the majority of Chinese immigrants to the United States have come recently.

The 1924 Immigration Act excluded most persons of Asian origin from immigrating to the United States. A 1952 Immigration and Nationality Act superseded previous laws and began to eliminate some of the anti-Asian racism inherent in the 1924 act. The 1952 act established three principles for immigration policy: (1) reunification of families; (2) protection of the domestic labor force; and (3) immigration of persons with needed skills. It permitted some small-scale Asian immigration and for the first time made immigrants from Asia eligible for citizenship. Finally in 1965 Congress took a major step toward providing Asians the opportunity to immigrate on a scale similar to that of earlier European groups. The 1965 Immigration Act belatedly abolished the national-origins quota system and established an annual quota of 20,000 for individual Asian countries. Not surprisingly, the percentage of Chinese, Filipino, Korean, and Vietnamese among the total number of immigrants to this country rose from .2 percent for the years 1901–1920 to 28 percent for the years 1981–1985.[3]

Chinese Americans

The Chinese have been the largest single group of Asian immigrants to the United States. Chinese migration began in substantial numbers in the decade before the Civil War, with a quarter million coming during the three decades after 1860. Most entered as low-wage workers, brought in to do the "dirty work" along the West Coast. Many were recruited to remedy labor shortages in railroad work and service employment, to fill menial positions in such areas as laundry and restaurant work that the European American miners and settlers did not want.

As the 1870s began, the U.S. economy entered a depression; at the same time, Chinese Americans were becoming numerous and more successful. White resentment of these Asian immigrants spread throughout the country: labor leaders, newspapers, politicians, and the white public accused Chinese Americans of driving wages to a substandard level and of taking jobs away from whites. In short, whites blamed Chinese for the country's economic plight.[4] The attacks on Chinese Americans finally led to the 1882 Chinese Exclusion Act, which officially prohibited direct immigration. Over the next few decades the Exclusion Act effectively restricted the flow of Chinese immigrants, which had reached a high of 123,201 in the years 1871–1880, and in the decade 1931–1940 immigration hit a record low of 4,928. Because most early Chinese immigrants were male, the Exclusion Act also resulted in a 40 percent decline in the Chinese population in the United States between 1880 and 1920.[5] The Chinese Exclusion Act was extended for ten years in 1892 and indefinitely in 1904. In 1905 President Theodore Roosevelt affirmed his support for the act, stating that the Chinese laborer must be kept out of this country "absolutely."[6] The Exclusion Act was not repealed until 1943, when China became a wartime ally. At that time a special quota of 105 was set for Chinese immigrants.[7]

The second major period of Chinese immigration—the largest immigration—took place after the 1960s immigration reform legislation. Many Chinese Americans today are linked to this later immigrant group. Between 1961 and 1980 nearly 348,000 Chinese, mainly from Hong Kong and Taiwan, came to the United States; they were followed in the 1980s by even larger numbers. Between 1980 and 1990 the Chinese American population more than doubled, from 806,000 to more than 1.6 million.[8] In the early 1990s, Chinese Americans constituted almost one-quarter of all Asian Americans. More than one-third were born in the United States, and more than half lived in western states.[9] The recent Chinese immigration has been related in part to U.S. political and military support of the government in Taiwan as well as to the U.S. corporate presence there.

Filipino Americans

When the islands that make up the Philippines were handed over to the United States by Spain at the end of the Spanish-American War, a direct colonial relationship began. Between 1898 and 1946 the Philippines was a U.S. colony. Almost immediately after the U.S. gained possession of the islands, a commission was sent to determine how to Americanize the Philippines. Between 1901 and 1913 a U.S. form of government was established, and a new system of public education was introduced in which U.S. teachers taught Filipino children American values and attitudes.

William Howard Taft, the first civil governor of the Philippines and later a U.S. president, inspired a plan to further Americanize the colony by sending young men to college in the United States. These students were taken into U.S. homes; after they finished their studies in such fields as education, agriculture, and medicine, they were to return to the Philippines to teach. By 1938 approximately 14,000 Filipinos had enrolled in U.S. schools.

By the 1920s and 1930s the overwhelming majority of immigrants to the United States were peasant farmers who sought employment as unskilled laborers. Since the Philippines was a territory of the United States, Filipinos were exempt from the racist exclusionary provisions of the 1917 and 1924 Immigration Acts. This exemption allowed them to immigrate freely to the United States; they were recruited by white employers to work in the sugar plantations of Hawaii and along the West Coast. Few came to the mainland in these early years; by 1924 only 6,000 lived in the continental United States.[10]

After passage of the 1924 Immigration Act, employers increased the recruitment of Filipinos as laborers on the West Coast to replace the Asian and other immigrant workers excluded by the act. Between 1924 and 1929, approximately 24,000 Filipinos came to the state of California to do low-wage work. As their numbers increased, so did anti-Filipino sentiment among whites. In 1934 Congress responded to this sentiment by passing an act granting deferred independence to the Philippines and simultaneously imposing an annual immigration quota of only fifty persons per year.[11]

Although Filipinos could enter the United States without restriction until 1934, almost all advantages ended there. Filipino Americans held an ambiguous legal position that was not resolved until 1946, when they were finally declared eligible for U.S. citizenship. Most states did not allow them to practice law, medicine, or other professions. As noncitizens, Filipinos did not even qualify for federal relief funds in hard times. At the outbreak of World War II, Filipinos' status as noncitizens exempted them from the draft and prohibited them from volunteering for the U.S. armed forces. Congress began moving toward citizenship for Filipinos during the war, since it made little sense for the United States to fight for Philippine freedom from Japanese rule while denying Filipino Americans the right to citizenship.

It is also significant that during World War II some 30,000 Filipinos were recruited to fight with the U.S. armed forces battling the Japanese army in the Philippines. At the end of the war these guerilla fighters were promised by General Douglas MacArthur and President Franklin Roosevelt that they could come to the United States and become U.S. citizens if they wished. However, the U.S. government backed out of the promise nine months before the official deadline, leaving thousands of veterans stranded. It was not until the Immigration Act of 1990 that the veterans were actually granted the right to U.S. citizenship. By that time many had died.[12]

Between 1950 and 1970 the number of Filipinos residing in the United States almost doubled. Immediately after World War II, most Filipino immigrants still found themselves restricted largely to jobs as unskilled or semiskilled laborers, mostly in agriculture. Whereas most earlier immigrants had been male and had not established families in the United States, these newer immigrants were typically men and women between twenty and fifty who brought their children with them, hoping to find better job opportunities.[13] Most Filipinos have come for economic reasons. An expert on Filipino migration has noted that "most people leave the Philippines to get a job."[14] In addition, many have come to be united with family members who migrated previously.

Since 1970 Filipino immigration has continued. The 1990 census counted 1.4 million Filipino Americans, making this group the second largest in the Asian–Pacific category. Today almost two-thirds of Filipino Americans are foreign-born; 69 percent live in western states.[15] Filipinos are the largest Asian American group in California, with a 1992 population of 732,000. Significantly, the 1990 census found a quarter million Americans of Filipino ancestry in the San Francisco area, which is sometimes called the "capital of Asian America" because of its large and diverse Asian American population. In some San Francisco Bay area suburbs Filipino Americans are a majority of the population.[16] Filipinos are also numerous in some parts of the Midwest. An estimated 100,000 Filipino Americans resided in the Chicago area as of 1992.

Korean Americans

The immigration of Koreans to the United States began in the early 1900s. Approximately 7,000 emigrated to Hawaii between 1903 and 1905. By 1905 approximately a thousand lived in California. Most came seeking better living and working conditions, but they, too, were confronted with discrimination, deplorable working conditions, and low wages. They were segregated along with Mexican and African Americans, refused housing in all but the worst areas, and denied service in restaurants and other public facilities. After learning of these conditions, Japan, which occupied Korea beginning in 1910, pressured the Korean government to ban emigration. This ban effectively restricted the entry of Koreans into the United States for many years.[17]

Even after these restrictions were imposed a small number of Koreans—mainly "picture brides" and students—were able to emigrate to the United States. Since most who arrived before the 1910 restrictions were single men, and since interracial marriage was not an option because of white prejudice and antimiscegenation laws, the picture bride system was developed. Korean men sent pictures of themselves to prospective brides in their homeland. From 1910 to 1924, more than one thousand brides came to the United States, with the largest number settling in Hawaii. In addition, several hundred students entered between 1899 and 1940, some as refugees from Japanese oppression.[18]

During World War II the U.S. government classified Korean immigrants as subjects of Japan. Thus Korean Americans living in Hawaii were classified as "enemy aliens," and those with jobs on defense projects were, to their chagrin, classified as Japanese and required to wear badges of identification. Korean American workers were understandably outraged, since Japan had been Korea's enemy and colonizer for so long. However, their protests only gained them the right to print the words "I am Korean" on their identification badges.[19]

During the heavy U.S. involvement in the Korean War in the 1950s, the people of South Korea saw prosperous Americans up close and came to regard the United States as a place to be admired. Strong U.S. support for the South Korean government, which allowed little domestic political freedom, built strong ties between the two countries. Most Koreans who immigrated from 1950 to 1965 were wives of U.S. soldiers; as such they escaped the immigration quota system. These wives continued to migrate after 1965, since the United States has maintained troops in Korea to the present. The changes in the immigration laws in 1965 opened new possibilities for immigration. The lack of economic or educational opportunities in Korea compared with those in the United States has regularly stimulated emigration. Moreover, some immigrants have been political dissidents opposed to the dictatorial regimes that dominated South Korea for decades. Others have been students who completed their education and stayed. Once established, the first immigrants sometimes used the family reunification clause of the immigration laws to bring in others. Between 1960 and 1965 only a few thousand Koreans entered each year, but by 1969 the number had reached 6,000. By 1977 annual Korean immigration exceeded 30,000. In the decade after the 1965 act, the number of Korean immigrants increased dramatically to 160,000, and between 1981 and 1991, 365,390 Koreans immigrated to this country.[20] The growing economic and political power of South Korea in Asia, especially in the 1980s and 1990s, has also increased the temporary migration of business people and students to the United States.

Over the 1980s the Korean American population more than doubled. The 1990 census counted almost 800,000 Korean Americans, about 11 percent of the Asian American population. Just under a fifth of Korean Americans were born in the United States; 43 percent lived in the western states.[21]

Vietnamese Americans

The Vietnamese do not have a long history of immigration to the United States. Most immigrants arrived after 1975, when U.S. involvement in the Vietnam War ended abruptly. The United States first became involved in Vietnam in an attempt to help French military forces maintain French colonial control in the area. When the French forces withdrew in 1954 and Vietnam was divided in two, the United States became a military ally of the South Vietnamese government, a non-Communist dictatorship. U.S. troops and dollars flowed to a war that gradually became very unpopular in the United States. In

Saigon, the capital of South Vietnam, U.S. military and civilian authorities made plans to evacuate a great number of South Vietnamese in the face of the advancing enemy forces. Included in the evacuation were family members of U.S. citizens and those Vietnamese and their families employed by the U.S. government or U.S. businesses, those at risk of losing their lives when a Communist government took over. As Communist troops approached Saigon in April 1975, the controlled evacuation that had been planned became instead a confused and tragic event. In one week, thousands of Vietnamese left their country. People jammed the airport and the U.S. embassy, climbing fences and clinging to helicopters. Those who could not get on airplanes fled by sea.[22]

In the spring of 1975 large numbers of refugees from Southeast Asia began to enter the United States. The Vietnamese were admitted outside the usual immigration process because they were considered political refugees.[23] As Table 12–1 shows, very few Vietnamese immigrated prior to 1961, in part because of the restrictive immigration laws. Changes in immigration laws, U.S. military involvement in Vietnam, and the precipitous fall of Saigon in 1975 contributed to the increase in immigrants. Between 1975 and 1980, 166,470 Vietnamese entered the United States.

Between 1980 and 1990 the number of Vietnamese Americans grew 134.8 percent—the largest percentage increase of any Asian group. More than 90 percent of Vietnamese Americans are foreign-born; more than 46 percent live in western states, even though most originally located in the South, East, and Midwest. At the beginning of the 1990s, the nation's largest Vietnamese community was in Orange County, California, where more than 100,000 live.[24]

STEREOTYPES

As we noted in Chapter 11, anti-Asian sentiment has a long history in the United States. A number of stereotypes are widely held, although they are not supported by empirical evidence. One common misconception about Asian Americans is that they are essentially the same physically and culturally. Japanese Americans are often mistaken by whites for Chinese Americans, who in turn may be mistaken for Vietnamese or Korean Americans. Asian Americans are often viewed by whites as "foreigners" rather than as Americans because of their non-European appearance. Films and television programs have sometimes portrayed Asians as faceless, fanatic, maniacal, or willing to die because they do not value life. Stereotyped white images such as the "evil Jap" of World War II and the "Communist gook" in China, Korea, and Vietnam have been recycled as U.S. foreign policy has changed from decade to decade. This uninformed and stereotypical way of thinking, sometimes called *Orientalism,* is common among white European Americans and shapes the discrimination directed at Asian Americans.[25]

Another stereotype of Asian Americans, or of particular Asian American groups, one especially emphasized by the mass media, is that they are "model minorities." We noted this image in our discussion of Japanese Americans (Chapter 11). According to this stereotype, Asian Americans have moved ahead rapidly in U.S. society, generally unhindered by prejudice or discrimination, mainly by applying the traditional Anglo values of hard work, thrift, and morality. They are also seen as especially ambitious. *Fortune* magazine, in an article entitled "America's Super Minority," went so far as to assert that

Asian Americans are "smarter and better educated and make more money than everyone else." There are indeed many exemplary individuals in Asian American communities, but the *Fortune* article overstates the situation, as we will see later in this chapter. One unfortunate result of what is seemingly a positive stereotype is that, in addition to misrepresenting Asian Americans, it may create resentment and jealousy among other Americans, both white and nonwhite.[26]

Specific Images

The first Chinese laborers on the West Coast became subjects of white derision and suspicion. They were called "coolies" and were often stereotyped as dirty and immoral. They were maligned by whites as "heathen," "mice-eaters," and "Chinks." Some of these stereotyped images have persisted for more than a century. One source of change, however, came in the 1940s. After the United States declared war on Japan in 1941, China and the United States became allies against Japan. Chinese Americans were suddenly friends. Soon after the United States entered World War II *Time* magazine printed the following explanation of the "differences" between the Chinese and the Japanese:

> HOW TO TELL YOUR FRIENDS FROM THE JAPS: Virtually all Japanese are short. Japanese are likely to be stockier and broader-hipped than short Chinese. Japanese are seldom fat; they often dry up and grow lean as they age. Although both have the typical epicanthic fold on the upper eyelid, Japanese eyes are usually set closer together. The Chinese expression is likely to be more placid, kindly, open; the Japanese more positive, dogmatic, arrogant. Japanese are hesitant, nervous in conversation, laugh loudly at the wrong time. Japanese walk stiffly erect, hard heeled. Chinese, more relaxed, have an easy gait, sometimes shuffle.[27]

The whites who put together this outrageously stereotyped statement thought they were writing something positive about their new "friends," the Chinese Americans. Yet it is in fact an example of the crude and negative stereotyping of Asian Americans that has long been part of white thinking in the United States.

The stereotypes of Filipino immigrants have sometimes fluctuated according to this group's usefulness to the capitalists recruiting them as low-wage labor, especially for the plantations of Hawaii. When European American employers were recruiting young single men, they characterized them as "not too intelligent" and "docile." But when the workers were no longer needed by white employers, they were stereotyped as "lazy, shiftless, and unmanageable."[28]

The Vietnamese arrived in the United States at a time when unemployment was high, and many non-Asian Americans feared that the new refugees would take jobs from them or drain sources of public assistance. During the mid-1970s this anti-Vietnamese sentiment was reflected in a Gallup poll in which 54 percent of the respondents felt that Vietnamese refugees should not be permitted to stay in the United States.[29] Many whites seemed to wish they could forget Vietnam and its people. Some whites still see all Vietnamese as "the enemy" because of the U.S. experience in Vietnam, and still use the racist term *gooks*. Vietnamese Americans represent a very different culture to a large segment of U.S. society, and many non-Asians have regarded them as strange, clannish, and hard to approach.[30] A 1989 survey of the 100,000 Vietnamese residents of Orange County, California, found that six in ten thought anti-Vietnamese prejudice was a problem there.[31]

In 1990 the musical *Miss Saigon*, produced in London and New York, was sharply criticized by Vietnamese Americans for its stereotyping. Critics argued that the central character, a Vietnamese "bar girl" abandoned by a GI, is a stereotype. Vietnamese and other Asian American leaders called on Asian American theatergoers and actors to boycott the play.[32]

DISCRIMINATION AND CONFLICT

"Hate Crimes"*

Violence, harassment, and vandalism directed against Americans of Asian descent have occurred across the United States since the earliest days of Asian immigration. Reports of such attacks increased over the 1980s, and the number of cases reported is only a small portion of the actual number. The U.S. Commission on Civil Rights has stated that ethnoviolence is in general underreported, especially in the case of Asian Americans, many of whom are recent immigrants who distrust the police and may have a limited knowledge of English.[33]

Until recently, few cities have collected data on ethnoviolence. In cities that have, Asian Americans are often disproportionately represented among victims. For example, Philadelphia statistics for 1988 show that 20 percent of the ethnoviolence victims were Asian American, although this group made up only 4 percent of the population. Asian Americans were the victims of one-quarter of the ethnoviolence reported in Boston during the period 1983–1987 and about 15 percent of such attacks in Los Angeles during the 1980s. One-third of the anti-Asian attacks in Los Angeles in 1988 and 1989 were directed against businesses and about two-thirds against the victim's home.[34]

The U.S. Civil Rights Commission has found that adequate police protection is not provided to many Asian American communities. Many police departments are insensitive to Asian American cultures, and some are overtly hostile. Limited English proficiency makes some Asian Americans reluctant to seek help. When Asian Americans do have contact with white police officers, their rights are often jeopardized by language barriers. Few police departments have adequate interpretive services for Asian Americans. The California attorney general's office has estimated that fewer than half the crimes against Asian Americans are reported. When Asian Americans do report a crime, they frequently do not receive justice. The Asian and Pacific Islander Advisory Committee of the California attorney general's office stated that "one of the most commonly repeated experiences is one in which the perpetrator is allowed to go free and the victim [an Asian American] is arrested."[35]

Chinese Americans

During the 1860s and 1870s anti-Chinese sentiments were common in union policies and political platforms as well as in the press. Chinese immigrants were violently attacked by whites in California and other western states.[36] Immigrants arriving since the 1960s have not been immune from such attacks. In the 1980s, the inability of non-Asians to differentiate among individuals of different Asian backgrounds has been a factor in the murder of at least two Chinese Americans. Careful monitoring of racially motivated

*The widely used term *hate crimes* is inaccurate, because many such attacks are generated not by hate but by fear or other emotions. Also many are not crimes. The National Institute against Prejudice and Violence has suggested the more accurate term *ethnoviolence*.

actions against Asian Americans began in 1982 with the death of Vincent Chin, a Chinese American, in Detroit. Two laid-off white auto workers, apparently believing Chin was Japanese and therefore to blame for the problems of the auto industry, started an argument with him in a bar and then used a baseball bat to beat him to death. A Michigan judge sentenced each man to only three years' probation and a fine of $3,780. Asian and other Americans expressed outrage at the extraordinarily lenient punishment. The U.S. Commission on Civil Rights concluded that the leniency of sentencing in this case was "suggestive of very little value being placed on an Asian American life."[37] The U.S. Department of Justice investigated the case and recommended bringing federal charges against the two assailants for civil rights violations. On June 28, 1984, a U.S. district court jury found one of the defendants guilty of violating Chin's civil rights, underscoring the racial motivation of the attack. The other defendant, apparently not directly involved in the beating, was acquitted. The guilty defendant was sentenced to twenty-five years in prison, although his conviction was later overturned by an appellate court for technical reasons. In his retrial, he was acquitted.[38]

A similar incident took place in Raleigh, North Carolina, in 1989. This time the Chinese American victim, Ming Hai Loo, who was in the company of several Vietnamese friends, was thought to be Vietnamese. He was killed by two white brothers angry about U.S. battle deaths in Vietnam. In 1990 the brother who struck the fatal blow was sentenced by a North Carolina court to thirty-seven years in prison for second-degree murder and simple assault, but with the possibility of parole after serving four and a half years. The maximum penalty for such crimes under that state's law is life in prison. The other white assailant, who made hostile racist remarks, received a six-month misdemeanor sentence. The following year he was found guilty in federal court of violating the victim's civil rights and received a four-year sentence, which was shorter than the minimum sentence specified by federal guidelines. This case was the first successful federal prosecution of a civil rights case in which the victim was Asian American. It received almost no mass media attention, a neglect that perpetuates non-Asian Americans' lack of awareness of ethnoviolence and makes such incidents likely to occur again. A report of the U.S. Commission on Civil Rights stated that "many Americans view racial hatred purely as a black–white problem and are unaware that Asian Americans are also frequent targets of hate crimes."[39]

Anti-Asian attacks are examples not only of racist violence but of the confusion of whites about Asian Americans. Many whites are not aware that there are more than a dozen major groups among Asian–Pacific Americans and often mistake a person from one group for someone from another such group. This "all Asians look alike" response points up a dimension of stereotyping that is part of the experience of other racial and ethnic groups examined in this book.

Filipino Americans

Filipino Americans, among the oldest of Asian immigrants, have also endured violent attacks. In the early period of immigration there were many clashes in California between Filipino and white farm laborers. In 1929 the Imperial Valley, the Sacramento Valley, and the San Joaquin Valley depended heavily on migratory Filipino labor; by 1930 Filipinos represented 42 percent of all non-European labor working on California farms. Filipino wages were considerably lower than the wages of whites. As a consequence of the heavy use of Filipino labor from 1924 to 1929, intense competition developed between native white and immigrant laborers over menial farm work when the Great Depression hit California.[40]

On October 24, 1929, the first anti-Filipino riot by whites took place in Exeter, a small farming community in the San Joaquin Valley. The riot resulted from white workers' long-standing bitterness over the use of Filipino labor for harvesting crops. It began at a local carnival where whites were shooting young Filipinos with rubber bands as the Filipinos walked with local girls. After a few days of harassment, a young Filipino farm laborer knifed a white man and slashed at a white group attempting to corner him. He escaped, but a white mob formed. The mob went to a nearby labor camp that housed Filipino workers, ordered all Filipinos out, then burned the camp to the ground. The local police chief refused to take action against the mob despite the destruction.

The most highly publicized and prolonged anti-Filipino riot in California occurred near Watsonville in early 1930. This riot reflected a decade of increasing tension between white and Filipino American workers. The tension in Watsonville was exacerbated by an interview in the local newspaper with a white official who blamed the Filipinos for the tensions. A series of anti-Filipino demonstrations then erupted. At one point, a vigilante mob of five hundred white youths marched on a Filipino dance hall. In this case, however, police stepped in to curtail the violence. Not surprisingly, the white-dominated press misreported the incident as Filipinos marching and rioting in the streets.

On January 22, 1930, the anti-Filipino attacks reached a peak when four hundred white vigilantes attacked the Northern Monterey Filipino Club. One person was killed in the scuffle, and a large number of Filipino Americans were severely beaten. Law enforcement officials who tried to protect them were taunted with cries of "Goo Goo Lovers." The local paper added to the tension by printing stories that condemned the dance halls frequented by Filipino Americans and the practice of socializing with white women. After this massive white attack, such incidents subsided.

Racial hostility has sometimes been a recent problem as well. Early in 1991 white guests at a party at Chicago mayor Richard Daley's Grand Beach, Michigan, estate reportedly called two Filipino American youths racist names and threw them out. The youths came back with some white friends, and there was a violent brawl. In this case whites both attacked and defended Filipino youths.[41]

Korean Americans

Koreans are relatively recent immigrants, yet they have also been hit hard by anti-Asian violence. Korean American businesses in predominantly black neighborhoods in a few cities have been primary targets of violence. Like white ethnic merchants in some black communities, Korean merchants have faced hostility. Local residents have charged that Korean merchants treat black customers rudely and refuse to hire black employees or to extend credit. Another source of black bitterness is the largely unfounded belief that the federal government helps Korean Americans start businesses; in fact Korean Americans usually pool their personal and family resources to purchase businesses in low-income neighborhoods.[42]

During the 1980s black New Yorkers boycotted Korean businesses. In Los Angeles Korean and black community leaders debated whether the killings of four Korean business people in three separate incidents were racially motivated. In 1990 a year-long boycott of two Korean stores in New York City began with a dispute between a Korean merchant and a black customer and eventually involved demonstrations.[43] In the early 1990s several serious incidents in Los Angeles involved African and Korean Americans. In December 1991 a Korean American grocer in Hawthorne, California, was charged by police with assaulting a young girl he thought was stealing candy from his store. After a boycott of the store, and talks between the Korean American Grocers Association and local black leaders, the owner apologized. Tensions remained high, however, and the authorities pressed their attempt to convict the grocer of assault.[44]

In 1991 another Korean American storekeeper accused a fifteen-year-old black customer, Latasha Harlins, of attempted shoplifting because she had placed a bottle of orange juice in her knapsack. Yet the girl was walking toward the cash register with money in her hand. The storekeeper grabbed the girl, and a scuffle ensued. Harlins threw the bottle of juice on the counter and turned to leave the store. The storekeeper got out her gun and shot Harlins in the back of the head, killing her. The lenient sentence given the merchant by a white judge—a $500 fine and community service—intensified black hostility toward Korean American merchants and played a role in the 1992 Los Angeles riot.[45]

Like Jewish American and other white ethnic merchants in similar situations, Korean Americans have become middleman minorities, groups that Bonacich has described as "the footsoldiers of internal colonialism."[46] Korean American merchants are both exploiters and exploited. They generally operate family businesses, must charge high prices to survive, and make a modest to excellent profit in low-income and working-class communities whose black residents often do not have the transportation to shop elsewhere. The high prices are resented by black residents, who also may harbor anti-Asian stereotypes. At the same time, many Korean American merchants have become fearful of all young blacks because they have been robbed by a few. The Korean immigrants' stereotyping of young blacks is made worse if they viewed American movies in Korea before they emigrated. Because those movies often portray black (and Latino) Americans in a negative light—as criminals for instance—Korean immigrants may be predisposed to view them negatively once in the United States.

Social historian Mike Davis has described the looting and burning of 2,000 Korean-owned businesses (about 40 percent of all businesses damaged) during the 1992 Los Angeles riots (see Chapter 8) as the direct product of "the black community's unassuaged grief over Harlins's murder."[47] Walking the streets during the rioting, he was repeatedly told, "This is for our baby sister. This is for Latasha." L.A.'s half million Korean Americans, however, felt betrayed by the U.S. justice system as they saw white police officers protecting large shopping centers owned by wealthy whites while smaller, Korean-owned stores were being destroyed. A Korean American university student told Davis, "Maybe this is what we get for uncritically buying into the white middle class's attitude toward blacks and its faith in the police."[48] Social scientist Elaine Kim has commented that "the so-called black–Korean problem masks a deeper racism in this country.... When the Los Angeles Police Department and the state government failed to respond to the initial outbreak of violence in South Central, I suspected that Korean-Americans were being used as human shields to protect the real source of rage."[49]

Vietnamese Americans

Many recent Vietnamese immigrants fished as a livelihood in their homeland, and it has thus seemed natural for them to do so in their new country. To pursue this dream, some moved to fishing communities on the Texas Gulf Coast. In the late 1970s they had been encouraged to move to that area because of its labor shortage. They generally took the low-paying jobs, such as cleaning fish or working in restaurant kitchens, and in that capacity they were tolerated by the white community. But as they began to buy shrimp boats and offer considerable competition to the other fishers, Anglo and Latino attitudes toward them changed. Many European American natives of the area resented the success of the Vietnamese Americans and blamed them for the economic recession along the Gulf Coast.

These Vietnamese Americans have experienced open hostility from their Anglo and Latino counterparts since they began fishing. A 1979 conflict between Vietnamese Americans and local fishers in Seadrift, Texas, culminated in the shooting death of a white fisher. Two Vietnamese refugees were arrested for the shooting, which followed an argument over the placement of crab traps. Within hours of the death, three Vietnamese boats were burned, one house was fire-bombed, and an attempt was made to bomb a packing plant where many Vietnamese Americans worked. The attacks caused most of the Vietnamese refugees to flee to another town. The Vietnamese Americans were eventually acquitted of the shooting. In response to this verdict, some white fishers turned to the local Ku Klux Klan for "protection of their industrial interest."[50]

Since the late 1970s Vietnamese Americans have faced racial violence in a number of cities across the country. For example, Boston had 339 civil rights crimes reported in 1980, a number of them targeting Vietnamese immigrants. Between 1983 and 1987 the Boston police department reported that nearly a quarter of the racial violence in the city was directed at Vietnamese and other Asian Americans. In 1989 five Indochinese children were killed in Stockton, California, by a white man partially motivated by racial hostility.[51]

THE POLITICAL ARENA

As we mentioned in the chapter on Japanese Americans, a number of Asian Americans have distinguished themselves politically, including U.S. senators Daniel Inouye and Samuel I. Hayakawa, in spite of anti-Asian prejudices. These senators, elected from states having a larger proportion of Asian American voters than the nation as a whole, are rare examples of Asian American political success. In general, Asian Americans have been significantly underrepresented in the U.S. political system, especially in the western states where large numbers reside. This underrepresentation became conspicuous in the early 1990s when Asian American leaders in California protested a court redistricting plan. Federally mandated redistricting in California, based on the 1990 census, had created seven new congressional districts, but the new districts, as they appeared in the court plan, did not increase the likelihood of new Asian American lawmakers in this key state. At that time, moveover, no Asian American was serving in the California state senate or assembly.[52]

As of the early 1990s, Asian Americans had achieved extremely limited political representation except in Hawaii. Federal appointed offices have also been inaccessible. Even the U.S. Congress has not set a good example. In the early 1990s only 45 of the

8,200 important staff positions in Congress were held by Asian Americans.[53] Moreover, California had only two Asian American members of Congress (Robert Matsui and Norman Mineta) and only one Asian American (Secretary of State March Fong Eu) in an elected position at the state level. A serious lack of representation existed at the local level as well. For example, one California city with a 42 percent Asian American population has never had an Asian American elected to its council. And no Asian American has ever served on New York City's council even though that city's Asian American population now exceeds 400,000. A large proportion of Asian Americans in these cities have immigrated too recently to be eligible to vote, and the voting rate of eligible Asian Americans is low. For example, while 80 percent of non-Latino white and black citizens voted in California in the mid-1980s, only 69 percent of Asian American citizens voted. White prejudice and discrimination also play a role in Asian American political involvement.[54] Participants in recent Civil Rights Commission conferences have pointed to several barriers to Asian American political participation:

1. apportionment policies that dilute the voting strength of Asian American voting blocks;
2. the unavailability of Asian-language ballots and other election materials;
3. problems with the implementation of the Census of Population; and
4. anti-Asian sentiments among non-Asian voters and the media and the consequent dearth of Asian American political candidates.[55]

Until the 1980s there was no national political organization specifically addressing the concerns of recent Asian American immigrants. In 1986 the first major pan-Asian political effort began with the founding of the Asian-American Voters Coalition. The coalition includes twelve national and seven local organizations representing Japanese, Chinese, Asian-Indian, Filipino, Korean, Vietnamese, and Thai Americans. Today the organization seeks to consolidate Asian American citizens into a more effective bloc of voters—a bloc that could have an especially significant impact on elections in the large states of California, Texas, New York, and Illinois. According to the president of the organization, Jane Hu, the group's most important issues are protecting the civil rights of Asian Americans and fighting anti-Asian legislation, distorted media images, racial violence, and employment discrimination.[56]

In the spring of 1992 the Multicultural Association for Voter Registration was created by Latino, African, Vietnamese, Korean, Chinese, and other Asian American leaders in the Los Angeles area. Their intent was to encourage all people of color to register to vote and to become more active politically in southern California. Such coalitions reflect an awareness among many minority Americans that political power can be gained through cooperation and coordination.[57] These organizations also signal a new active resistance to the dominant white group.

Chinese Americans

Perhaps because Chinese Americans have had the longest history of immigration of the four groups studied in this chapter, they also have been the most politically active of these groups. Chinese American political activity increased in the period 1917–1920, shortly after the revolution in China. Chinese Americans became involved in a wide variety of political organizations and spent much time discussing political developments in China. A number of labor-oriented organizations were created and tried to organize laborers in New York's Chinese American communities, where the largest concentration of Chinese Americans lived. These attempts proved unsuccessful, however, because much of the labor there was organized along family networks.[58] Between 1900 and 1930 the Chinese language newspaper *Chung Sai Yat Po* (CSYP) was an important advocate of civil and political rights for Chinese Americans, including the rights of Chinese American women. The paper's emphasis on political events in China, where the role and status of women were progressing toward equality, contributed to the social and political awakening of Chinese American women.[59]

The second period of major Chinese immigration, which occurred after the immigration reforms of 1965, revived political activity among Chinese Americans. Explaining barriers to expanded political activity, Michael Woo, one of the few Chinese Americans in city government, has noted that "cultural traits" are a major challenge to the "Asian community in getting out the vote" because Chinese and other Asian Americans "traditionally view all political activity as suspect." Woo added, however, that more and more Asian Americans are breaking with tradition and contributing to election campaigns.[60] Some Chinese Americans have begun to explain these political problems to the U.S. Congress. Irving Chin, chair of the Chinatown Advisory Committee to the Borough President of Manhattan, told a U.S. Senate committee in the 1960s that Chinese protest had been limited because of Chinese Americans' problems with English, their fear of and lack of familiarity with government, and a traditional reluctance to engage in political activity. In addition, Professor Ling-chi Wang, a San Francisco community activist and later chair of the Asian American studies department of the University of California, Berkeley, spoke to the same committee in support of government social programs, which he said were sorely needed. Wang testified that the unemployment rate in San Francisco's Chinatown was almost double the citywide average, that available housing was substandard, and that the incidence of tuberculosis was far above the national average. This testimony to Congress signaled a growing willingness to speak openly of Chinese American problems.[61] The growth of the Chinese American population has coincided with a movement in behalf of civil rights for all Asian American minorities and a demand for self-government by oppressed Asian American groups.

As the number of Chinese American immigrants in the United States continues to increase and as many of these immigrants and their children concentrate in particular geographic areas, they are becoming more influential in U.S. politics. Chinese and other Asian immigrants are involving themselves politically to try to influence events in their communities. One example is Monterey Park, California, a Los Angeles suburb of 60,000 people, three-fourths of them Asian and Latino Americans. After New York's Chinese American communities this is the largest place of Chinese immigrant settlement in the United States, particularly for those from Taiwan and Hong Kong. Although Chinese Americans are the most numerous in Monterey Park, a number of other Asian American groups are well represented. When white city council members passed a resolution saying that Monterey Park did not consider itself a sanctuary for "illegal aliens" and that English should be the official language of the United States, many Asian Americans in the community were outraged. No fewer than 4,000 people signed petitions demanding that the city council rescind the resolution, which it did. The controversy over the resolution indicated a serious rift within the community between fearful whites, who often contend that the Asian Americans are not trying "to assimilate" and are "taking over," and Asian Americans, many of whom are politically concerned suburbanites with successful businesses.[62]

In the early 1990s Chinese American candidates ran for the city councils in several Los Angeles area communities. In the fall of 1992 Monterey Park's city council was expected to elect its first Chinese American majority.[63] Chinese Americans have also become increasingly active in national politics. For example, in May 1992 Chinese Americans organized a boycott of an Asian American community dinner for President George Bush, who while visiting Los Angeles after the 1992 riot had ignored Chinese Americans and their significant losses in the riot. In addition, many Chinese Americans have pressed both major political parties to select Chinese American candidates, for no Chinese American has ever served in the U.S. Congress.

Filipino Americans

In the chapter on Mexican Americans we discussed César Chávez and the United Farm Workers Union. This union was the result of a merger between a Mexican American organizing drive and a Filipino labor organization, the Agricultural Workers' Organizing Committee (AWOC). The head of AWOC was Larry Itliong, an energetic Filipino American activist.[64] A number of other Filipino American labor and political organizations have been created in the United States. In the 1970s the Filipino Organizing Committee was created in the San Francisco area to address issues of concern to Filipino Americans seeking greater political participation.[65]

New resistance tactics have emerged in the 1980s and 1990s. The National Filipino-American Council, a group of 3,000 Filipino social, community, and civil rights groups across the nation, has fought for fair immigration laws. In April 1992 Filipino Americans held a national empowerment conference to generate a political strategy and a movement to secure political positions in cities where they make up a significant percentage of the population.[66] In spite of their large numbers, Filipino Americans have rarely been elected or appointed to political offices. In the early 1990s the California legislature had no Filipino American members, even though Filipinos have the highest naturalization and citizenship rate of any California immigrant group. Few Filipino Americans held any elective offices at other government levels. One exception was in the Los Angeles area. In 1992 the first Filipino American was elected to the city council in Carson, a community near Los Angeles.

Perhaps one reason Filipino Americans have not been more active in U.S. politics in this country is that they represent such cultural diversity—several religious groups, for example. Filipino Americans are also divided by language differences and subgroup cultures. Because of the strength of local community groups and their competing loyalties, large-scale organizations are difficult to sustain. But international political events seem to be pulling Filipino Americans into more political organizing. For example, a number of Filipino American organizations have responded to the Philippine government's appeal for investment in the islands to help overcome the Philippine economic crisis. This is further evidence of the global influence on racial and ethnic groups in the United States. In addition, the overthrow of the Ferdinand Marcos dictatorship and the coming to power of Corazon Aquino in the Philippines in the late

1980s boosted Filipino American pride. Filipino identity was strengthened by the advent of democracy in the Philippines. This trend in the homeland seems to have reinforced the commitment of Filipino Americans to greater political participation in the United States.[67]

Korean Americans

Korean American political actions, like those of Chinese and Filipino Americans, have sometimes been inspired by events in the homeland. For example, during the years 1905–1919 many Korean Americans were active in the fight for Korean independence from Japan. Japan, however, maintained its military dominance over Korea, and after 1919 the Korean independence movement began to decline. Korean Americans who had devoted energy to the cause of independence could not sustain the political movement, and many organizations reemerged as nonpolitical associations.[68]

In recent years Korean Americans have had little political visibility. None has held a major political office in the western states. However, Korean Americans have been active in the Asian-American Voters Coalition, discussed earlier. After the April 1992 riot in Los Angeles the local Korean-American Coalition became more active. Jerry Yu of the coalition commented that during the riot "Korean Americans really saw with their own eyes the lack of political strength that we as a community have."[69]

Korean Americans typically maintain very close ties to Korea. After the urban riots of 1992 (an election year in the United States) officials from Korea promptly visited the riot areas of Los Angeles, arriving before President Bush or the Democratic presidential candidate. Some Korean Americans have expressed much uneasiness about their new home. Approximately 7,000 Korean Americans moved back to Korea during 1991; following the Los Angeles riots many more indicated their intention to do so.[70]

Vietnamese Americans

The home country context has also been important for Vietnamese Americans. In recent years the icy relationship between Vietnam and the United States has begun to thaw. In a 1989 survey of the Vietnamese residents in Orange County, California, about half felt that establishing diplomatic ties with Communist Vietnam would be a good idea for the United States, and that they might return home for a visit under such conditions.[71] The issue of reestablishing ties to a Communist homeland has been a heated topic of debate within Vietnamese American communities since the 1980s, just as it has for Cuban American communities (see Chapter 10).

In 1989 a white city council member in Orange County told a group of Vietnamese Americans wishing to parade that "if they want to be South Vietnamese, go back to South Vietnam." The permit was turned down by the city council because the parade to honor the Vietnamese war dead was not seen by local whites as truly "American." Vietnamese stores and signs were defaced by white vandals. After political protest from the Asian American community, however, the white council member backed down and apologized for his comments. Although the protest indicated growing political activity, by 1991 no Vietnamese American sat on any city council in Orange County, even though the county had a very large Vietnamese American population. Even so, by early 1992 the county had an active Vietnamese-American Political Action Committee working for expanded political participation and influence for Vietnamese Americans.[72]

THE ECONOMY

In a recent report, the U.S. Civil Rights Commission documented the exploitation of Asian immigrants unaware of their rights by white employers who violate laws regarding safe working conditions, wages, and hours. The commission noted that Supreme Court decisions in the late 1980s had failed to protect Asian American workers from racial harassment. As we have noted previously, the Civil Rights Act of 1991 was designed to undo the effects of some of these conservative Court decisions. Well-educated Asian Americans with professional experience in their homelands have also faced employment barriers in the United States. Many find that their experience and credentials are discounted or ignored by white employers. Some have been hired for research, engineering, or other technical positions, but they are generally underrepresented at all levels of management in most large U.S. companies. A Civil Rights Commission study found that U.S.-born Asian American males with English proficiency were less likely to hold managerial positions than white males with comparable qualifications. Asian Americans were even less likely to hold top executive positions. For example, in 1990 they made up only .3 percent of the top executives in Fortune 500 companies—about one-tenth of their percentage in the total population. Moreover, a large majority of Chinese and Filipino American professionals and managers responding to a recent survey in San Francisco felt that racism blocked them from advancing in their jobs.[73]

The Civil Rights Commission study found racially based employment discrimination to be more severe for Asian American women. These workers are vulnerable to sexual harassment and gender discrimination on the job, and most have little knowledge of their legal rights. They are frequently excluded from the critical informal networks of their co-workers, and hence enjoy few sources of support when confronted with racial or sexual harassment. In one instance cited by the commission, an Asian American woman working at a military base in San Francisco encountered severe retaliation after reporting sexual harassment. In addition, after she reported the retaliation her working conditions became so intolerable that she suffered a nervous breakdown. The Civil Rights Commission report noted that "because of the stereotypic expectation of compliance and docility, a formal complaint from an Asian American woman might have been considered as a personal affront or challenge. Her notification of the alleged retaliation to the base authorities was to no avail: it aggravated an already bad situation."[74]

Discrimination based on language proficiency or accent is also common. In one 1990 case the Ninth Circuit Court of Appeals upheld an employer's right to consider an applicant's verbal skills when these were relevant to job performance, although the court cautioned employers not to misuse language proficiency to discriminate on the basis of national origin. Recent Asian immigrants are adversely affected by English-only rules in the workplace, many of which have been found by the courts to be inappropriate because no business necessity for such language requirements can be demonstrated.[75]

Chinese Americans

In the nineteenth century Chinese immigrants were recruited to fill the lower rungs of the occupational ladder in the United States. Some were small merchants and crafts workers, but most were unskilled laborers. Chinese workers were employed to build railroads in

California as early as the 1850s, but the first large-scale use of Chinese labor—more than 12,000 workers—was in the construction of the transcontinental railroad, finally completed in 1869. By 1880 there were at least 135,000 Chinese Americans. Most lived in California, and there they became an important factor in the economy. They converted swampland in California to rich farmland; their skills in planting, cultivating, and harvesting were used extensively at white-owned vineyards, orchards, and ranches. Some farmed as sharecroppers; others raised their own vegetables for the market.

Chinese factory workers were an important part of the California economy after the Civil War. By the early 1870s, Chinese workers made up most of the labor force in woolen mills and most of the cigar makers in San Francisco; by the mid-1870s they were a majority of the shoemakers and garment makers. Chinese American entrepreneurs developed shrimp fisheries, which by the 1880s were exporting a million pounds annually; they were leaders in developing abalone fisheries. Chinese American workers were a mainstay of canneries in the Pacific Northwest. Thousands more operated or worked in laundries and served as cooks or domestic servants. Most labored long hours in poor working conditions for very low wages.[76]

The need for large numbers of factory workers in defense plants during World War II opened employment opportunities for thousands who had previously been confined to laundry and restaurant jobs. An estimated 30 percent of young Chinese American men in New York City found jobs in defense plants. Between 1940 and 1950 more than one-third of Chinese American men remained in service occupations, but the percentages in craft, technical, and professional occupations more than doubled. War industries also provided employment opportunities for Chinese American women in clerical and technical jobs in defense plants.[77]

The prospects for many recent Chinese immigrants have not been much better than those for the early immigrants, because many lack money, skills, and the ability to speak English. Most have settled in Chinese American communities in large cities such as New York and San Francisco, where many of the men work long hours in restaurants or other service jobs and thousands of women labor in the hundreds of nonunion garment factories in or near the Chinese residential areas. Conditions in these sweatshops are substandard or dangerous, and pay is often below the minimum wage.[78]

Some postwar immigrants have been well educated; among them there have been engineers, doctors, mathematicians, and scientists. Some were trained in China and fled after the Communist victory in 1949; others received their education in Taiwan, where schools prepared them for emigration to the United States. Still others completed their advanced studies in the United States and found employment in U.S. industries and universities. Members of this elite group of immigrants have found better jobs and generally have had an easier time adjusting to their new country than the large number of poorer immigrants.[79]

The 1980 census revealed that Chinese Americans were heavily concentrated in white-collar jobs, with 39 percent in professional, technical, and managerial jobs, compared with 26 percent of the population as a whole. This was the highest concentration in white-collar jobs among the four Asian American groups considered in this chapter. The proportion in clerical and sales jobs was 24 percent, compared with 27 percent of the population as a whole. The proportion in blue-collar jobs was only 19 percent, compared with about one-third of the general population. Chinese Americans are underrepresented in blue-collar jobs other than service jobs.[80] In 1980 the median family income for Chinese Americans was $22,559, higher than the $19,917 average for the general population.

However, considering that 39 percent of Chinese Americans held white-collar occupations in 1980, compared with only 26 percent of the general population, one would have expected to find a greater difference in median income.[81] (1990 Census data on income and occupations are not available as of this writing.)

The Chinese American community is represented at both extremes of the economic spectrum. An Wang, the former head of Wang Laboratories computer firm who died in 1990, became a billionaire. He was fifth on Forbes's 1983 list of the wealthiest Americans and was still on the Forbes Four Hundred list of richest Americans in 1989. One of the nation's leading architects, I. M. Pei, may well be the most famous Chinese American, at least to non-Chinese. Several Chinese American women, including Amy Tan and Jade Snow Wong, are prominent novelists.[82] At the other extreme, the 1980 census estimated that 14.8 percent of Chinese Americans lived below the poverty line. One reason for this economic diversity may be the length of the immigrants' stay in this country. The U.S.-born Chinese tend to be better educated, to hold managerial or professional jobs, and to live outside the "Chinatowns" of the larger cities. The more recent immigrants tend to have less education, to be unemployed or hold low-wage jobs, and to live in inner-city communities.[83]

Filipino Americans

Filipinos were first recruited as farm workers for the sugar plantations in Hawaii and farms along the West Coast. The vast majority of these workers were single men who endured a grueling schedule and meager wages. Their typical day began at 4 A.M.; with one fifteen-minute break for breakfast and a half hour for lunch, the men worked until three or four in the afternoon. The wage for this labor remained the same from 1915 to 1933—an incredibly low eighteen to twenty dollars a month.[84]

In the early 1930s thousands of Filipino American workers, a group that constituted 40 percent of the agricultural work force in the Salinas Valley of California, formed the Filipino Labor Union (FLU). An FLU-led strike of lettuce workers in 1934 met with violent opposition from white growers supported by local law enforcement officers. The strikers eventually won wages of forty cents an hour and recognition of the union. Subsequent actions by the FLU led to a Mexican-Filipino union chartered by the American Federation of Labor. "The FLU represented...the entrance of Filipinos into the labor movement in America.... The involvement of the Filipinos in the labor movement reflected a changing consciousness—a sober recognition of shattered dreams and a new sense of ethnic unity."[85]

In the 1950s and 1960s many Filipinos entered the U.S. work force when the U.S. armed forces, especially the navy, began recruiting Philippines residents. This continuing process has created military-related Filipino communities on the West Coast. Filipinos are the only "foreigners" recruited into the U.S. armed forces. In addition, in recent years hospitals in California have actively recruited Filipino nurses, who later have become U.S. citizens. Many Filipino scientists, engineers, and other professionals have emigrated because of political turmoil and economic crises at home, creating a serious shortage of such professionals in the Philippines.[86]

One analysis of 1980 census data for Filipino Americans in California found considerable occupational and economic inequality between Filipino Americans and white Americans. Filipino men, whether U.S.-born or foreign-born, had only about two-thirds the income of white men. Filipino women had only about half the income of white men. The study also revealed inequality in the occupational distribution of Filipino Americans compared with that of the white population. In the managerial and professional ranks, Filipino men were mostly accountants, civil engineers, and electrical engineers, while women were mostly registered nurses, elementary school teachers, and accountants. Few Filipino Americans were found among public administrators, financial managers, marketing managers, physicians, attorneys, architects, aerospace, industrial, and mechanical engineers, and social scientists—occupations that showed high concentrations of native white men.[87]

According to the 1980 census, the proportion of Filipino Americans in upper-tier white-collar jobs was 31 percent, higher than the national average of 26 percent. At least half of the most recent Filipino immigrants have been professionals, such as nurses and other health-care workers. The proportion of Filipino Americans in clerical and sales work was roughly the same as the national average of 27 percent. Twenty-five percent of Filipino Americans were blue-collar workers, lower than the national average of 33 percent. The proportion of service workers among Filipino Americans was 17 percent, higher than the 12 percent of the population as a whole. The median family income for Filipino Americans was the highest among the four Asian groups, at $23,687. This was also higher than the average for the general population, which was $19,917.[88]

A 1989 study of the New York region found the per capita income of Filipino Americans to be higher than that of non-Asians.[89] As with Japanese and Chinese Americans, Filipino family income in many areas now exceeds the income of white American families. But again this is misleading, because on the average more family members work among Filipino Americans than among whites and most Filipino Americans work and live on the West Coast, where both wages and living costs are higher.

Job discrimination, however, remains a serious problem. In 1974 two thousand workers, many of them Filipino Americans, at a Ward Cove Packing Company factory in Alaska sued the firm over exclusion from white-collar jobs. Almost all white-collar jobs were held by whites, and most blue-collar jobs by Filipino and Native Americans. In 1989 the conservative Supreme Court decided against the workers, ruling that their clear statistical evidence of great disparities in hiring and employment was not enough to prove "intentional discrimination." As we have noted, the 1991 Civil Rights Act was an attempt to remedy the adverse effects of this and similar Supreme Court decisions.[90]

Filipino Americans have also fought discrimination, including language discrimination, in other West Coast areas. For example, in 1988 a class action lawsuit filed with the Equal Employment Opportunity Commission charged that the San Francisco city government systematically discriminated against Filipino Americans. The suit cited statistical data that Filipino Americans held only 1 percent of the city's administrative and supervisory positions although they made up 12 percent of the city's professional workers. The Filipino American organizations behind the lawsuit charged that Filipino professionals were stereotyped by many whites in the city government as incapable of leadership, and that they were penalized because of their accent.[91] In October 1991 a federal judge upheld a Los Angeles area hospital's ban on Tagalog, the native language of many Filipinos. The hospital prohibited its Filipino nurses from speaking Tagalog, even while on breaks. And a Filipino American in Hawaii unsuccessfully sued city officials who discriminated by turning him down for a white-collar job because of his heavy Filipino accent.[92]

Korean Americans

Language barriers and racial discrimination kept early Korean immigrants, most of whom were in Hawaii, from obtaining employment in accordance with their abilities and skills. The early-twentieth century immigrants engaged in hard physical labor for extremely low wages. Many, including professionals, worked as agricultural laborers or as dishwashers, kitchen helpers, houseboys, or janitors in urban areas. During World War I, a few Korean Americans began to open small, family-operated shops—laundries, shoe-repair shops, and used-furniture stores, mainly in Hawaii. By World War II, Korean Americans owned about fifty small and medium-sized businesses on the mainland. But among the total Korean population of ten thousand, only 5 percent were engaged in business.[93]

Koreans arriving after the 1965 immigration reforms have included mathematicians, scientists, and other professionals. A significant percentage of recent immigrants have become entrepreneurs, starting small grocery and other retail stores, often in low-income black and Latino areas. Korean Americans have filled an important small-business niche in cities, such as New York, Philadelphia, and Los Angeles. In the mid-1970s, 34 percent of Korean American householders in New York owned small businesses. Most of these arrived in the United States with some capital. Only 6 percent had been small-business owners in Korea; most had held white-collar jobs in Korea's modern economy.[94] A study in Los Angeles found that 40 percent of Korean American heads of household were self-employed in 1978, compared with only 8 percent of the general population of Los Angeles County. An additional 40 percent were employed by these Korean entrepreneurs, so that fully 80 percent of employed Korean Americans in Los Angeles County worked in Korean-owned firms, mostly service and retail proprietorships.[95]

Many Korean immigrants have been forced into self-employment because of exclusion from the professions for which they were trained. Limited English proficiency is one factor, but more significant is discrimination in the labor market. Moreover, Korean Americans in white-collar jobs are often passed over for promotions, regardless of their language skills. Many prefer the freedom and dignity afforded by self-employment. Most Korean immigrants have arrived at a time when earlier white immigrant groups are moving out of the inner-city small-business niche into the professions and other white-collar jobs. Most Korean women have little knowledge of spoken English, and thus their main employment option is a family business where the entire family may work long hours for a modest income. Many first-generation Korean Americans say they accept the idea that "the first generation must be sacrificed" in order to provide education and a brighter future for the children. Some small businesses are highly profitable, although in order to succeed many proprietors have exploited other Korean immigrants, who are paid low wages because they have few options in the labor market.[96]

Light and Bonacich found a high degree of geographic mobility among Korean immigrants in Los Angeles. Many lived for only a short time in a heavily Korean inner-city area before moving to a suburb. Korean American businesses were dispersed throughout most of the postal districts in the county; only one-third of Korean American businesses were located in the Los Angeles area locally called Koreatown.[97]

Many Korean immigrants arrive with capital or have collateral, and thus are able to borrow money to start a business. They often have the support of a large Asian American community and of Asian American banks. An L.A. survey found that Korean American merchants whose customers are primarily black or Latino earn more than those whose customers are primarily white. Many of these Korean American merchants take the money they earn in low-income black or Latino communities and move to middle-class areas. Black resentment over Korean merchants taking money out of the black community has contributed to the hostility many black urbanites feel toward Korean Americans.[98]

The 1980 census statistics for Korean Americans were similar to the statistics for the general population. The proportion of Korean Americans in professional, technical, and managerial jobs was 29 percent, compared with 26 percent of the general population. Twenty-four percent of the general population were in clerical and sales work, while 27 percent of Korean Americans pursued such occupations. Thirty-one percent of Korean Americans were in blue-collar occupations, compared with approximately 33 percent of the population as a whole. The proportion of the general population in service occupations was 12 percent, compared with 16 percent of Korean Americans. The 1980 median family income for Korean Americans, $20,459, was close to the national average of $19,917.[99]

Vietnamese Americans

Because the Vietnamese are such recent immigrants to this country, they do not have a long economic history. Most have arrived since 1974. Those immigrants who came immediately after the fall of Saigon in 1975 were often more affluent and better educated than those who came later. Many knew English and had adopted some aspects of Western culture. Some of these immigrants had been in business in their home country. Their contact with Western trade in Vietnam made it somewhat easier to adjust to the business milieu in the United States. However, the information available for the late 1970s shows a pattern of downward mobility for many immigrants. A 1977 study found considerable downward occupational mobility for Vietnamese American heads of household. Of the 319 Vietnamese in the survey who had held white-collar jobs in Vietnam, more than six in ten held blue-collar jobs at the time of the study. The remainder held white-collar jobs, with the largest category being in clerical and sales positions. This downward mobility was true for professionals as well. Of the 142 Vietnamese Americans surveyed who were employed as professionals in Vietnam, fewer than one in five had been able to find similar work in the United States.[100]

The 1975 refugees make up a minority of Vietnamese Americans. Most Vietnamese immigrants have come since the late 1970s, and many have remained poor. They and their children have not had as much economic success as earlier arrivals.[101] Census data for Vietnamese Americans reveal that in 1980 they lagged far behind other Asian immigrants in occupational attainment. Only 21 percent were in upper-tier white-collar occupations, compared with the national average of 26 percent; only 19 percent were in clerical and sales work, compared with 27 percent of the general population. The proportion of Vietnamese Americans in blue-collar work, 44 percent, was substantially higher than the national figure of 33 percent. And the proportion in service work was 15 percent, also higher than the national figure of 12 percent. Vietnamese Americans were concentrated at the lower end of the occupational ladder, with almost 60 percent in blue-collar and service work. This was reflected in the median family income for Vietnamese Americans—$12,840—which was substantially below both the national average of just under $20,000 and the median incomes of the other Asian groups.[102]

During the late 1980s the labor-force participation of Vietnamese Americans was only slightly more than half that of the total population, and their unemployment rates were more than twice the national average. A large percentage still hold jobs that are lower in status than their positions before immigration.[103]

EDUCATION

High Achievement and Persisting Problems

A stress on educational success has been a central part of Asian American cultures. In 1987, for the first time, the top five of the ten scholarships awarded in the prestigious Westinghouse Science Talent Search were won by teenagers of Asian American parentage.[104] In 1990 nineteen of the forty Westinghouse scholars were Asian Americans.[105] However welcome these prizes were to the student winners, they were a mixed blessing for Asian Americans as a group. Winning the national science competition has served to reinforce popular stereotypes of Asian Americans as "naturally" gifted in science and as "model minorities." Asian Americans have been critical of these stereotypes, for many excel in areas other than the natural sciences. Even more important, many Asian American children, especially immigrant children, are in great need of strong and supportive educational environments. Yet the "model minorities" stereotype reduces the likelihood of government action to meet their educational needs.[106]

As was the case with earlier immigrant groups, many recently immigrated Asian children, along with the American-born children of recent Asian immigrants, face problems of limited English proficiency and the shock of an unfamiliar Anglo-Protestant culture when they enter the public school system. Non-Asian teachers and administrators are often ignorant of Asian cultures and indifferent or insensitive to the needs of these students. Some are even unwilling to protect Asian American students from mistreatment by non-Asian students. In addition, many recent arrivals from Southeast Asia have vivid memories of the horrors of war in their homeland; their high incidence of post-traumatic stress syndrome interferes with their success in school.

The U.S. Civil Rights Commission reported in 1992 that only a small proportion of limited-English-proficiency Asian American students had teachers who spoke their native languages, in spite of the legal obligation of the public schools to help these students develop English proficiency. Recent immigrants not proficient in English frequently have low grades and high dropout rates. A study of San Diego high school students found that Vietnamese, Cambodian, and Pacific Islander students had higher dropout rates than white students.[107]

Many schools have witnessed substantial white hostility and even violence against Asian Americans. One 1990s study quoted a female Chinese immigrant high school student:

> Before I came to America I had a beautiful dream about this country. At that time I didn't know the first word I learned in this country would be a dirty word. American students always picked on us, frightened us, made fun of us, and laughed at our English. They broke our lockers, threw food on us in cafeteria, said dirty words to us, pushed us on the campus. Many times they shouted at me, "Get out of here, you Chink, go back to your country." Many times they pushed me and yell on me. I've been pushed, I had gum thrown on my hair. I've been hit by stones.[108]

Educational Attainment

In 1980 the median years of school completed by Chinese Americans was 13.4, higher than the median of 12.5 years for the general population. Seventy-one percent of Chinese Americans were high school graduates. Filipino Americans' median years of school completed was 14.1, the highest of the Asian groups discussed in this chapter and well above the national average. Three quarters of Filipino Americans had completed high school. Close to the Chinese Americans were Korean Americans, with a median of thirteen years of school completed; 78 percent were high school graduates.[109]

In 1980 Vietnamese Americans ranked the lowest among the Asian groups in educational attainment, yet they were still close to the national average. Vietnamese Americans had completed a median of 12.4 years of school in 1980, barely under the national average of 12.5; 62 percent had graduated from high school.[110] (1990 census data on education are not yet available.) Studies of Vietnamese American students in San Diego and Orange County in the mid-1980s found a bipolar situation. The Vietnamese were a high proportion of the straight-A students, but a somewhat higher proportion of Vietnamese than of white students dropped out of high school.[111] Vietnamese Americans present a picture of high achievement against great odds, mixed with a significant dropout rate.

The reasons for Asian American success in education have been the subject of considerable discussion. Some observers say the success is rooted in a traditional reverence for learning in Asian cultures, the strong support of family, or in some cases a head start gained in schools in the homeland. Others point to those Asians who have learned English at a young age and argue that they have gained educational benefits from their bilingualism.[112] Education has also been used as a weapon against the prejudices of white Americans; in one sense it has become part of an oppositional culture in which education is seen as part of family rather than individual achievement.

One writer also points out that Asian Americans often have access to educational institutions, such as those in California, that facilitate economic and educational mobility better than the schools attended by many black and Latino students in southern states. Even though Asian American students reside in large metropolitan areas, they are usually not segregated from the mainstream of the educational system. Asian American students, unlike black and Latino students, are typically better integrated into public schools having white majorities.[113]

Controversy in Higher Education

Asian Americans, who make up about 2 percent of the college-age population, accounted for 11 percent of first-year classes at the nation's top universities in the mid- to late 1980s. Asian American leaders, however, have suggested that discrimination against Asian American students still exists. Some colleges have apparently imposed measures to reduce their numbers. For example, Ivy League universities began admitting a large percentage of Asian American applicants in the mid-1970s, but the acceptance rates often dropped as the number of Asian American applications increased. At Yale, the acceptance rate for Asian Americans fell from 39 percent to 17 percent between 1977 and 1986.[114] Critics have accused the universities of using such nonacademic pretexts as lack of alumni parents and regional distribution to exclude Asian American students.

The proportion of Asian Americans among the students admitted at Brown University rose from 2.6 percent for the class of 1979 to 14.8 percent for the class of 1993, although the proportion of Asian-American applicants admitted fluctuated between 14 percent and 47 percent during this period. When the proportion of Asian applicants admitted dropped sharply between 1982 and 1983, Brown's Asian American Student Association voiced its concern to the administration. Investigators reported that the admissions staff had assigned comparatively low nonacademic ratings to Asian American applicants and had sought to hold steady the number of Asian American students admitted, even though their applicant pool applicants had more than tripled between 1979 and 1983. As a result, the Brown administration took action to ensure that the percentage of qualified Asian American applicants admitted would not fall below the percentage of qualified non-Asian applicants admitted.[115]

Between 1983 and 1992 the proportion of Asian American students at Harvard University increased from 5.5 percent to 14.2 percent. However, in each of these years the admissions rate for Asian Americans, which fluctuated between 11 percent and 15 percent, was lower than Harvard's admissions rate for non-Asians. An investigation found the major cause of this disparity to be the special preference given to children of alumni and to recruited athletes. Alumni preferences are recognized as legal under Title VI of the Civil Rights Act of 1964. This discriminatory practice, which puts Asian Americans and other minority groups without alumni parents at a disadvantage, has not been tested in court, however.[116]

A note on Asian-Indian Americans

Of all the major Asian–Pacific groups in the United States, the least well known and least researched by social scientists is the group the census bureau now calls "Asian Indians"—those who come from India. Asian Indians have immigrated in increasingly large numbers since the 1965 Immigration Act abolished racist quotas. Many Asian Indians are former students here who decided to make the United States their permanent home. More than 850,000 Asian Indians now live in the United States. Unlike other Asian Americans the majority do not live on the West Coast. Many reside in midwestern and eastern cities. About 120,000 live in the greater Chicago area. Another 100,000 live throughout New York City, and about 80,000 in New Jersey cities. In many metropolitan areas they have had the money to move directly into suburbs rather than settling first in central-city areas, as did other Asian immigrants. As a result, Asian Indian Americans are more scattered geographically than other immigrant groups. There are no large urban concentrations, as there are for other Asian American groups. Rather, Asian Indians are dispersed widely throughout the metropolitan areas in which they have settled. Even so, wherever there is a substantial Asian Indian population, there is usually an Indian house of worship.

The majority of Asian-Indian Americans are professionals and business people. Asian Indians have by far the largest proportion of college graduates (52 percent) and professional and managerial employees (49 percent) of all Asian–Pacific American groups. In the early 1980s they had the second highest (after Japanese Americans) median family income among Asian Americans.[117]

In the early 1990s Asian-Indian Americans formed a number of organizations and networks to increase their political influence. In Hartford, Connecticut, one such group began pressing for expanded U.S. aid for India and for changes in discriminatory state licensing requirements for foreign-born physicians. The lobbying for aid to India is yet another example of the close relationship between the international context and the political orientations of U.S. racial and ethnic groups. Asian-Indian Americans have also organized to fight racial hostility and discrimination in several cities. Anti-Indian leaflets have been circulated in several New Jersey cities; attempts to include Indians as Asians in affirmative action programs designed to help minority businesses have been opposed by non-Asians in San Francisco.[118]

ASSIMILATION FOR ASIAN AMERICANS?

An Optimistic Assimilation View

Milton Gordon has argued that his theory of assimilation is applicable to a wide range of ethnic and racial groups. However, Gordon has not explicitly applied the stages of his assimilation scheme to Asian American groups, groups whom other assimilation-oriented analysts have viewed as well on their way to integration at the core-cultural level in terms of language and at the secondary–structural level in terms of job placement. Yet for most of the Asian American groups examined in this chapter, there appears to be modest integration with the European American core society at the primary-group and marriage levels. Substantial acculturation in language and core-culture values has taken place, but assimilation at the other levels has come slowly. Still, assimilation-oriented analysts tend to be optimistic about the assimilation of Asian Americans, including the trend toward a large middle class among these groups.

Some optimistic assimilation-oriented analysts have underscored Asian American progress in terms of cultural and economic integration. Sociologist Talcott Parsons argued that racial and ethnic inclusion is a basic process in U.S. society; one aspect of this process is the increasing inclusion of various racial and ethnic groups in the institutions of the society. Analysts such as Thomas Sowell and Nathan Glazer have argued that traditional discrimination is collapsing and that assimilation of nonwhite Americans, such as Asians, into the core society is well under way. Some recent media analysts of Asian Americans have argued in a similar vein: "with a command of English, light brown skin, and Spanish-sounding names, Filipinos have few problems assimilating into American society," asserted James T. Madore, a reporter for the *Christian Science Monitor.*[119] It is true that Filipino immigrants find the United States a reasonably comfortable point of destination because they have been influenced by the somewhat Americanized culture of their own country, which was a U.S. colony for half a century. Even today English is the language used in schools in the Philippines. Yet the ease of adaptation can easily be exaggerated, as the discrimination we have discussed indicates.

Numerous assimilation scholars and other analysts see not only Japanese Americans but also other Asian Americans as "model minorities." In their view, a minority has succeeded when it attains certain economic privileges comparable or superior to those of the dominant white group, attainments measured by quantitative socioeconomic indicators such as education, occupation, and income. This message is used by some white analysts to affirm that the United States is a just and fair society in which any minority group can succeed if its members are willing to work hard enough. As a result, some argue that government programs such as affirmative action are counterproductive.[120] The National Asian Pacific Bar Association (NAPBA) opposed Supreme Court nominee Clarence Thomas at the 1991 Senate confirmation hearings, challenging Thomas's publicly asserted image of Asian–Pacific Americans as model minorities. Judge Thomas has argued that Asian–Pacific Americans have "transcended the ravages caused even by harsh legal and social discrimination" and should not be the beneficiaries of affirmative action because they are "overrepresented in key institutions." The NAPBA pointed out the actual conditions of racial hostility and discrimination faced by Asian Americans.[121]

As we noted in Chapter 11, Kitano and Daniels have applied a version of the assimilation model to Asian Americans. They have developed a complex model of assimilation and ethnic identity that distinguishes three major types of adaptation: (1) high assimilation, low ethnic identity; (2) high assimilation, high ethnic identity; and (3) low assimilation, high ethnic identity. Asian Americans who fall into the category of high assimilation and low ethnic identity are more core American than Asian. Their language, lifestyle, and expectations are core American, and their traditional culture and language are mostly forgotten. High rates of marriage to non-Asians occur in this group. While a significant proportion of Japanese Americans seem to fall into this category of assimilation, the proportions for the groups examined in this chapter are smaller.

Those Asian Americans in the category of high assimilation and high ethnic identity differ from those in the previous category by retaining a strong ethnic identity. They move easily in and out of both cultures, and their friendship patterns and interests reflect a bicultural perspective. They tend to be comfortable with their group identity, and they question persisting racial prejudice and discrimination. A significant proportion of Filipino and Asian-Indian Americans appear to fall into this category of adaptation. The proportions of Korean and Vietnamese Americans who are thus assimilated are much smaller."[122]

Asian Americans in the third major category, low assimilation and high ethnic identity, are often recent immigrants or those who have spent most of their lives in ethnic enclaves in cities. Most have attained some level of adaptation to the dominant culture, but they prefer their own communities. These individuals tend to form friendship and marriage bonds with people in their own ethnic group.[123] Most recent Korean and Vietnamese immigrants fall into this category. A significant proportion of recent Filipino and Chinese immigrants also appear to be modestly assimilated at the cultural level but firmly rooted culturally and socially in their own communities. Takaki has noted that Korean, Chinese, and Vietnamese immigrants over the last three decades "have concentrated their economic resources in their own ethnic communities."[124]

A 1989 survey of Vietnamese Americans in Orange County found that the Vietnamese language was still dominant in 83 percent of households. Two-thirds said that their families remained strongly Vietnamese in customs and traditions, and most of the rest said they were somewhat involved in Vietnamese culture. There is dependence on a type of oppositional culture in the face of white antagonism. Three-quarters reported regular contact with relatives and friends in Vietnam. And six in ten reported spending their dollars in Vietnamese businesses.[125] On the other hand, research by Roberts and Starr has found "a slow change toward a more Americanized reference group and away from traditional Vietnamese beliefs and values" among Vietnamese refugees as a group. Yet they too found that refugees with close Vietnamese friends were more likely to maintain Vietnamese customs and thus were slower to assimilate.[126] Gold found the large, extended family, which discourages individualism and prescribes rights and duties to its many members, to be the "most basic, enduring, and self-consciously acknowledged form of national culture among refugees."[127] A former Vietnamese professor explained the Vietnamese family's function of mutual aid:

> To Vietnamese culture, family is everything. There are aspects which help us re-adjust to this society. It is easy for us because of tradition of helping in the family. We solve problems because the family institution is a bank. If I need money—and my brother and my two sisters are working—I tell them I need to buy a house. I need priority in this case. They say "okay," and they give money to me.[128]

Vietnamese Americans are mostly first generation immigrants, and what the future holds in terms of further assimilation is not clear. Among the respondents to the 1989 Orange County survey, one-third said that the greatest community need was more English classes—the largest percentage for any community need listed. These Vietnamese Americans expressed a strong desire for mastering English in order to acculturate and advance economically. Moreover, nearly half the adults interviewed did not expect their children to marry a Vietnamese American.[129]

Korean immigrants also seem committed to their language, culture, and relatives and have built strong institutions within their own communities. For example, in the Koreatown area of Los Angeles, Korean Americans have created many important community institutions, including newspapers, schools, a symphony orchestra, and many Korean Christian churches.[130] Religion has sometimes facilitated the adjustment of Koreans in the United States. Korea has one of the largest Protestant populations of any Asian nation, and many Korean immigrants come in as Christians. These immigrants have established new churches here. For example, in Chicago in the early 1980s Korean Americans supported as many as a hundred Christian churches, which typically combined Western practices with Korean ceremonies and Korean-language services.[131]

Korean Americans who operate businesses in non-Korean areas of large cities, such as Los Angeles, come into contact with non-Asians on a daily basis. Their children are likely to have much contact with white children in public schools. Over time this interaction may facilitate greater assimilation to the core culture and society, as it has for Japanese Americans.

One sign of the slower assimilation of the Asian–Pacific groups in this chapter, compared with that of Japanese Americans, is their lower outmarriage rates. For Japanese Americans, as we saw in Chapter 11, outmarriage rates are high—between 30 and 50 percent for the younger generations—with most of these marriages involving whites. Although the rates have been lower for the groups considered in this chapter, intermarriage between Asian and white Americans is increasing. In California in 1980 the rate of marriage to whites was 24 percent for Filipinos, 19 percent for Koreans, 15 percent for Vietnamese, and 14 percent for Chinese.[132] In 1991 the rate of marriage to whites for all Asian groups taken together was estimated to be about 17 percent, well above the 3 percent rate for African Americans but still much lower than the rate for third-generation Japanese Americans.[133]

Some Questions from a Power–Conflict Perspective

Power–conflict analysts of Asian Americans reject the optimistic assimilationist perspectives, including the model minorities stereotype. They argue that the model minority view exaggerates Asian Americans' progress and downplays the problems of racial prejudice and discrimination.[134] As we noted in the chapter on Japanese Americans, the model minority image of Asian groups was created not by those groups but rather by outsiders, including white scholars and media analysts, usually for conservative ideological reasons. In response to black and Latino American protesting, some whites broadcast this image to suggest that non-European groups could achieve the American dream not by protesting but simply by working as hard as Asian Americans. For example, in the 1960s the term *model minority* was used in a speech by Democratic politician Hubert Humphrey at a Chinese American high school, during which Humphrey praised Chinese Americans for *not* rioting and demonstrating. An article in *U.S. News & World Report*, entitled "Success Story of One Minority Group in U.S.," compared Chinese and African Americans. The tone of the article was negative toward black Americans: in praising the hard work, thrift, and morality of Chinese Americans, the article clearly implied that if black Americans possessed these virtues it would not be necessary to spend "hundreds of billions [of dollars] to uplift" them. ("Billions" was, of course, a gross exaggeration.) The article omitted any mention of the extreme racial discrimination suffered by African Americans. The model minority stereotype also obscures the problems and needs of the many poor and uneducated Asian Americans. Recent studies have shown that many Southeast Asian immigrants, especially those from rural backgrounds with little education, have experienced severe economic strain in the economically troubled 1980s and 1990s.[135]

A power–conflict analyst would point out that the secondary–structural integration of Asian Americans into the U.S. economy is not as untroubled as some assimilation analysts suggest. For example, one study of the income differentials among Asian Americans, whites, and blacks demonstrates that the Asian American success story is overstated. In examining 1980 census data for California, researchers found that Asian Americans earned an average of $20,790, compared with $19,552 for whites and $12,534 for blacks. However, this differential should be considered in relation to the number of workers per household. Asian American families had 1.70 workers per household, compared with only 1.28 for whites and 1.20 for blacks. Therefore, Asian Americans earned only $12,229 per worker, while whites received $15,275. Asian American income per worker was only 80 percent of white income. This gap was wider in urban areas, where most Asian Americans reside. There is also a regional bias inherent in these figures. Most Asian Americans live in New York and California, two states that have higher pay rates than most other states.[136] Anecdotal reports for the 1990s suggest that this economics of disparity still holds.

Asian Americans suffer discrimination in educational institutions. We have noted the informal quotas used to reduce Asian American penetration of some universities. In addition, many Asian Americans who have excelled in the U.S. educational system are finding employment discrimination barriers once they finish school. As we have seen, many get white-collar jobs that are not as good as what their credentials should have secured them. In other words, although Asian Americans tend to excel in their college studies, they often receive a lower rate of return on their investment in higher education than whites do.[137] Moreover, although many Asian Americans are hired by major companies, most find that promotions into upper management are unlikely.[138]

Assimilation analysts often do not discuss the problem of anti-Asian violence. Kitano and Daniels's approach to assimilation, for example, indicates the complexity in patterns of adaptation, which depend on length of stay in the United States and strength of ethnic identity. But it does not pay sufficient attention to such external factors as continuing prejudice and discrimination, which handicap Asian Americans and affect long-term assimilation probabilities. Asian Americans may be experiencing some backlash born of their success—or the media image of their success. As the section in this chapter on discrimination and conflict has demonstrated, Asian Americans have been the victims of vicious violence, such as the killing of Vincent Chin and the attack on Vietnamese Americans by whites in Texas. Japan-bashing was on the increase in the early 1990s, and all Asian American groups suffered because of anti-Japanese sentiment on the part of non-Asian Americans. In addition, Asian Americans have found themselves struggling to protect their civil rights and growing political power. For example, in the spring of 1992 the Asian American Legal Defense Fund had to fight for an extension of the 1965 Voting Rights Act in order to protect the right of non-English speakers to bilingual ballots and other election materials. A number of white members of the U.S. Senate argued that Asian American voters did not need such protection, even though the Senate had no Asian Americans from mainland states. From the perspective of most Asian Americans, the struggle over power and resources goes on, and full assimilation is a long way from being realized. For that reason new organizations fighting against anti-Asian racism and for Asian American rights have been formed in recent years.[139]

SUMMARY

Korean, Filipino, and Vietnamese Americans—and the newest Chinese Americans—are among the most recent of the immigrant additions to the bubbling cauldron. Yet, as with immigrants before them, they have been the targets of much prejudice and hostility, and not a little violence. In general, their educational success has been so dramatic that they have often been stereotyped, like the Japanese Americans, as model minorities. Some who portray Asian Americans in this way have had the ulterior motive of critiquing non-Asian minority groups. Moreover, assimilation-oriented social scientists have been inclined to accent Asian American progress in the U.S. economy, but to downplay the persisting problems of discrimination.

We have documented the problems that confront Asian Americans today. From a power–conflict perspective, a non-European minority group has not achieved success until it can participate fully in the mainstream of the economy and society without paying higher material or psychological costs than the dominant white group. No Asian American group has attained that comfortable equality with the oldest white immigrant groups, such as Scottish and English Americans. Physically distinct groups, Asian Americans have remained disadvantaged minorities experiencing some economic mobility problems, recurrent hostility and discrimination, and only modest gains in political power—so far at least.[140]

During the 1980s and 1990s, as Daniels has emphasized, "immigration took up a central position on the American social agenda" and there was much talk about regaining "control of U.S. borders."[141] In 1981 Congress set up a Select Commission on Immigration and Refugee Policy to investigate the so-called "immigration crisis." The commission presented an ambiguous set of recommendations, including on the one hand a continuing liberal policy on immigration and on the other hand strict border control to reduce illegal immigration. In earlier chapters we examined the restrictive immigration legislation that was passed in the 1980s. Much of the current white opposition to immigration goes beyond the question of immigrants taking jobs to the issue of racial characteristics, since most recent immigrants have been Asian and Latin American. Recent Asian immigrants have often been the victims of anti-Asian stereotyping, much of it suggesting they are a new "yellow peril." They have also suffered from anti-Japan sentiment among non-Asian Americans.

However, it is the hard work and vigor of these new immigrants, like those of earlier immigrants, that have made the United States a great nation. Nathan Glazer has spoken of the United States as being "a permanently unfinished country."[142] It is the immigrant dimension of the "unfinishedness" that has made this nation capable time and again of surging out of stagnation into development and creativity.

NOTES

1. Elaine H. Kim, "They Armed in Self-Defense," *Newsweek*, May 18, 1992, p. 10.
2. Ibid.
3. Immigration and Naturalization Service, *1985 Statistical Yearbook* (Washington, 1986), pp. 2–5; U.S. Commission on Civil Rights, *Civil Rights Issues Facing Asian Americans in the 1990s* (Washington, 1992), pp. 2–5.
4. U.S. Commission on Civil Rights, *Recent Activities against Citizens and Residents of Asian Descent* (Washington, 1986), p. 7.
5. Immigration and Naturalization Service, *1985 Statistical Yearbook*, pp. 2–5; Ronald Takaki, *Strangers from a Different Shore: A History of Asian Americans* (Boston: Little, Brown, 1989), pp. 111–12.
6. U.S. Commission on Civil Rights, *Recent Activities against Citizens and Residents of Asian Descent*, p. 8.
7. U.S. Commission on Civil Rights, *The Tarnished Golden Door: Civil Rights Issues in Immigration* (Washington, 1980), p. 10.
8. Immigration and Naturalization Service, *1985 Statistical Yearbook*, pp. 2–5; U.S. Bureau of the Census, *The Census and You* (Washington, 1991), p. 3.
9. U.S. Commission on Civil Rights, *Civil Rights Issues Facing Asian Americans in the 1990s*, p. 15.
10. Stephan Thernstrom, ed., *Harvard Encyclopedia of American Ethnic Groups* (Cambridge: Harvard University Press, 1981), pp. 357–59.
11. U.S. Commission on Civil Rights, *Recent Activities against Citizens and Residents of Asian Descent*, p. 9.
12. Vanessa Ho, "Filipinos' American Dream Comes True," *Seattle Times*, April 29, 1992, p. B1.
13. *Harvard Encyclopedia of American Ethnic Groups*, ed. Thernstrom, p. 359.
14. Tim Schreiner, "Philippine Brain Drain," *American Demographics* 8 (December 1986): 14.
15. U.S. Bureau of the Census, *The Census and You*, p. 3; U.S. Commission on Civil Rights, *Civil Rights Issues Facing Asian Americans in the 1990s*, p. 15.
16. Frank Viviano, "Asian Population Booming in U.S.," *San Francisco Chronicle*, February 27, 1991, p. A7; L. A. Chung, "State's Asian Americans Push for Unity," *San Francisco Chronicle*, May 7, 1992, p. A1.
17. Wayne Patterson, *The Korean Frontier in America: Immigration to Hawaii, 1896–1910* (Honolulu: University of Hawaii Press, 1988), p. 177; Takaki, *Strangers from a Different Shore*, pp. 270–71; U.S. Commission on Civil Rights, *Recent Activities against Citizens and Residents of Asian Descent*, p. 9.
18. Warren Y. Kim, *Koreans in America* (Seoul: Po Chin Chai Printing Co., 1971), pp. 22–25.
19. Takaki, *Strangers from a Different Shore*, pp. 365–66.
20. David M. Reimers, *Still the Golden Door: The Third World Comes to America* (New York: Columbia University Press, 1985), pp. 110–11; Immigration and Naturalization Service, *1985 Statistical Yearbook*, pp. 4–5; conversation with Immigration and Naturalization Service representative, Washington, D.C., June 3, 1992.
21. U.S. Commission on Civil Rights, *Civil Rights Issues Facing Asian Americans in the 1990s*, p. 15.
22. Darrel Montero, *Vietnamese Americans: Patterns of Resettlement and Socioeconomic Adaptation in the United States* (Boulder, Colo.: Westview Press, 1979), pp. 1–3.
23. Morrison G. Wong and Charles Hirschman, "The New Asian Immigrants," in *Culture, Ethnicity, and Identity*, ed. William C. McCready (New York: Academic Press, 1983), p. 381.

24. U.S. Commission on Civil Rights, *Civil Rights Issues Facing Asian Americans in the 1990s*, p. 15; Sonni Efron, "Few Viet Exiles Find U.S. Riches," *Los Angeles Times*, April 29, 1990, p. A1.

25. Harry H. L. Kitano and Roger Daniels, *Asian Americans: Emerging Minorities* (Englewood Cliffs, N. J.: Prentice-Hall, 1988), p. 176.

26. U.S. Commission on Civil Rights, *Recent Activities against Citizens and Residents of Asian Descent*, pp. 32–33; Anthony Ramirez, "America's Super Minority," *Fortune*, November 24, 1986, p. 148; David J. Hellwig, "Black Reactions to Chinese Immigration and the Anti-Chinese Movement: 1850–1910," *Amerasia Journal* 6 (Fall 1979): 26.

27. Quoted in Takaki, *Strangers from a Different Shore*, p. 370.

28. Miriam Sharma, "Labor Migration and Class Formation among the Filipinos in Hawaii, 1940–1946," in *Labor Immigration under Capitalism*, ed. Lucie Cheng and Edna Bonacich (Berkeley: University of California Press, 1984), pp. 583, 593.

29. Montero, *Vietnamese Americans*, pp. 3–4.

30. Paul Sweeney, "Tolerance in a Texas Town," *Texas Observer*, September 17, 1982, pp. 7–9.

31. Steve Emmons and David Reyes, "Gangs, Crime Top Fears of Vietnamese in Orange County," *Los Angeles Times*, February 5, 1989, p. 3.

32. Sonni Efron, "'Saigon' Is under Fire Once More," *Los Angeles Times*, September 7, 1990, p. F1.

33. U.S. Commission on Civil Rights, *Civil Rights Issues Facing Asian Americans in the 1990s*, pp. 22–48.

34. Ibid., pp. 45–47.

35. Ibid., pp. 49–69, quotation from p. 52.

36. Ibid., pp. 5–6.

37. U.S. Commission on Civil Rights, *Recent Activities against Citizens and Residents of Asian Descent*, pp. 43–44; U.S. Commission on Civil Rights, *Civil Rights Issues Facing Asian Americans in the 1990s*, pp. 25–26 quotation from p. 28.

38. U.S. Commission on Civil Rights, *Civil Rights Issues Facing Asian Americans in the 1990s*, pp. 25–26.

39. Ibid., pp. 26–28, quotation from p. 28.

40. Howard A. DeWitt, *Anti-Filipino Movements in California: A History, Bibliography and Study Guide* (San Francisco: R & E Research Associates, 1976), pp. 27–66.

41. David Ibata, "Asians Seek Spot in America's Melting Pot," *Chicago Tribune*, April 26, 1992, p. 1.

42. Terry E. Johnson et al., "Immigrants: New Victims," *Newsweek*, May 12, 1986, p. 57.

43. U.S. Commission on Civil Rights, *Civil Rights Issues Facing Asian Americans in the 1990s*, pp. 34–40.

44. Greg Krikorian, "Grocer Says He's Sorry," *Los Angeles Times*, December 20, 1991, p. B3.

45. Andrea Ford, "Slain Girl Was Not Stealing Juice, Police Say," *Los Angeles Times*, March 19, 1991, p. B1; Itabari Njeri, "Perspectives on Race Relations," *Los Angeles Times*, November 29, 1991, p. B5; Mike Davis, "In L.A., Burning All Illusions," *Nation* 254, no. 21 (June 1, 1992): 743–46.

46. Quoted in Njeri, "Perspectives on Race Relations," p. B5.

47. Davis, "In L.A., Burning All Illusions," p. 745.

48. Quoted in ibid., p. 746.

49. Kim, "They Armed in Self-Defense," p. 10.

50. U.S. Commission on Civil Rights, *Recent Activities against Citizens and Residents of Asian Descent*, pp. 50–52; Sweeney, "Tolerance in a Texas Town," pp. 7–10.

51. Michael McCabe, "U.S. Leaders Urged to Fight Hate Crimes," *San Francisco Chronicle*, February 29, 1992, p. A1.

52. Tim Schreiner, "Asians, Hispanics Upset about Reapportionment Boundaries," *San Francisco Chronicle*, December 4, 1991, p. A18.

53. Miles Benson, "Washington's Top Positions Seldom Go to Minorities," *Houston Chronicle*, December 13, 1991, p. 1.

54. U.S. Commission on Civil Rights, *Civil Rights Issues Facing Asian Americans in the 1990s*, pp.157–63.

55. Ibid., p. 159.

56. Paul Sweeney, "Asian Americans Gain Clout," *American Demographics* 8 (February 1986): 18–19.

57. Carla Rivera, "Orange County Focus," *Los Angeles Times*, April 28, 1992, p. B3.

58. Peter Kwong, *Chinatown, N.Y.: Labor and Politics, 1930–1950* (New York: Monthly Review Press, 1979), pp. 45–67.

59. Judy Yung, "The Social Awakening of Chinese American Women," in *Unequal Sisters*, ed. Ellen Carol DuBois and Vicki L. Ruiz (New York: Routledge, 1990), p. 196.

60. Martin F. Nolan, "California Confronts the Politics of Growth," *Boston Globe*, October 23, 1991, p. 1.

61. Kitano and Daniels, *Asian Americans*, p. 49.

62. Nicholas Lemann, "Growing Pains," *Atlantic Monthly*, January 1988, pp. 57–62.

63. James Rainey, "Minorities Poised for Gains at Ballot Box," *Los Angeles Times*, April 14, 1992, p. B8.

64. John Gregory Dunne, *Delano: The Story of the California Grape Strike* (New York: Farrar, Straus & Giroux, 1967), p. 77.

65. Lemuel F. Ignacio, *Asian Americans and Pacific Islanders* (San Jose, Calif.: Pilipino Development Associates, 1976), pp. 11–56; Kitano and Daniels, *Asian Americans*, p. 86.

66. Chung, "State's Asian Americans Push for Unity," p. A1.

67. James T. Madore, "Long-quiet Asian Group Starts to Mobilize," *Christian Science Monitor*, May 20, 1988, p. 7.

68. Bong-youn Choy, *Koreans in America* (Chicago: Nelson-Hall, 1979), pp. 141–89.

69. Quoted in Grey La Motte, "Asian Americans: A Diverse Voting Block," Cable News Network, June 1, 1992, transcript no. 76–5.

70. Survey by Eui-Young Yu, cited in Emily MacFarquhar, "Fighting over the Dream," *U.S. News & World Report*, May 18, 1992, p. 34.

71. Steve Emmons and David Reyes, "The Orange County Poll," *Los Angeles Times*, February 5, 1989, p. 1.

72. Ibid.

73. U.S. Commission on Civil Rights, *Civil Rights Issues Facing Asian Americans in the 1990s*, pp. 131–36, 145–48.

74. Ibid, pp. 131–36, 153–56, quotation from pp. 155–56.

75. Ibid., pp. 136–48.
76. *Harvard Encyclopedia of American Ethnic Groups,* ed. Thernstrom, pp. 218–20.
77. Takaki, *Strangers from a Different Shore,* pp. 374–75.
78. Reimers, *Still the Golden Door,* p. 107.
79. Ibid.
80. U.S. Bureau of the Census, *U.S. Census of Population, 1980: General Social and Economic Characteristics,* PC80-1-C1 (Washington, 1983), p. 160.
81. Ibid., pp. 157, 162.
82. Roger Daniels, *Coming to America* (New York: Harper Collins, 1990), p. 355.
83. Kitano and Daniels, *Asian Americans,* pp. 48–50.
84. Sharma, "Labor Migration and Class Formation among the Filipinos in Hawaii, 1906–1946," p. 589.
85. Takaki, *Strangers from a Different Shore,* pp. 322–23, quotation from p. 323.
86. Steve Lohr, "Filipinos Flocking to the U.S. as Manila's Troubles Grow," *New York Times,* June 6, 1985, p. A14.
87. Amado Cabezas, Larry Hajime Shinagawa, and Gary Kawaguchi, "New Inquiries into the Socioeconomic Status of Pilipino Americans in California," *Amerasia Journal* 13 (1986–87): 3–7.
88. Data cited in ibid.
89. Marvine Howe, "Asians in New York Region," *New York Times,* April 17, 1989, p. B4.
90. "Justice for Cannery Workers," *Seattle Times,* May 4, 1992, p. A10.
91. United Press International, March 30, 1988, n.p.
92. Irene Chang, "Ruling on Foreign Language Ban Criticized," *Los Angeles Times,* October 26, 1991, p. B3.
93. Choy, *Koreans in America,* pp. 123–33.
94. Takaki, *Strangers from a Different Shore,* pp. 441–44.
95. Reimers, *Still the Golden Door,* pp. 111–12; Ivan Light, "Immigrant Entrepreneurs in America: Koreans in Los Angles," in *Clamor at the Gates,* ed. Nathan Glazer (San Francisco: ICS Press, 1985), p. 162.
96. Takaki, *Strangers from a Different Shore,* pp. 441–42.
97. Ivan Light and Edna Bonacich, *Immigrant Entrepreneurs* (Berkeley: University of California Press, 1988).
98. Survey by Eui-Young Yu, cited in MacFarquhar, "Fighting over the Dream," p. 34.
99. U.S. Bureau of the Census, *U.S. Census of Population, 1980,* p. 160.
100. Montero, *Vietnamese Americans,* p. 39.
101. Dennis McLellan, "Writer Urges the U.S. to See 'A Hidden Treasure of Talents,'" *Los Angeles Times,* February 7, 1992, p. E3; Efron, "Few Viet Exiles Find U.S. Riches," p. A1.
102. Montero, *Vietnamese Americans,* p. 39.
103. Steven J. Gold, *Refugee Communities: A Comparative Field Study* (Newbury Park, Calif.: Sage Publications, Inc., 1992), pp. 64–65.
104. Sam Howe Verhovek, "Two Girls Win Westinghouse Competition," *New York Times,* March 3, 1987, p. C1.
105. Guy Halverson, "Indicators of U.S. Prospects," *Christian Science Monitor,* January 31, 1991, p. 13.
106. Dennis A. Williams et al., "A Formula for Success," *Newsweek,* April 23, 1984, pp. 77–78.
107. U.S. Commission on Civil Rights, *Civil Rights Issues Facing Asian Americans in the 1990s,* pp. 68–99.
108. Laurie Olsen, *Crossing the Schoolhouse Border: Immigrant Students and the California Public Schools* (San Francisco: California Tomorrow, 1988), p. 90; see also p. 34.
109. U.S. Bureau of the Census, *U.S. Census of Population, 1980,* p. 160.
110. Ibid.
111. Efron, "Few Viet Exiles Find U.S. Riches," p. A1.
112. Williams et al., "A Formula for Success," p. 78.
113. Gary Orfield, Franklin Monfort, and Rosemary George, "School Segregation in the 1980s," *International Development Research Association Newsletter,* November 1987, p. 5.
114. Eloise Salholz et al., "Do Colleges Set Asian Quotas?" *Newsweek,* February 9, 1987, p. 60.
115. U.S. Commission on Civil Rights, *Civil Rights Issues Facing Asian Americans in the 1990s,* pp. 109–12.
116. Ibid., pp. 120–29.
117. Ibid., p. 17.
118. Arlene Newman, "Festival Reflects Indians' Growth," *New York Times,* August 18, 1991, sec. 12NJ, p. 1; Joel Kotkin, "Asian Indians in California Spotlight after Years in Shadows," *Washington Post,* May 6, 1990, p. H2.
119. Madore, "Long-quiet Asian Group Starts to Mobilize," p. 7.
120. Ronald Takaki, "Is Race Surmountable? Thomas Sowell's Celebration of Japanese-American 'Success,'" in *Ethnicity and the Work Force,* ed. Winston A. Van Horne (Madison: University of Wisconsin Press, 1985), pp. 218–20.
121. Senate Judiciary Committee, "Capitol Hill Hearings," *LEXIS,* September 20, 1991, n.p.
122. Takaki, *Strangers from a Different Shore,* p. 473.
123. Kitano and Daniels, *Asian Americans,* pp. 190–92.
124. Takaki, *Strangers from a Different Shore,* p. 473.
125. Emmons and Reyes, "Gangs, Crime Top Fears of Vietnamese in Orange County," p. 3.
126. Alden E. Roberts and Paul D. Starr, "Differential Reference Group Assimilation among Vietnamese Refugees," in *Refugees as Immigrants: Cambodians, Laotians, and Vietnamese in America,* ed. David W. Haines (Totowa, N.J.: Rowman & Littlefield, 1989), p. 51.
127. Gold, *Refugee Communities,* pp. 54–56, quotation from p. 54.
128. Quoted in ibid., p. 56.
129. Emmons and Reyes, "The Orange County Poll," p. 1.
130. Daniels, *Coming to America,* p. 367.

131. Reimers, *Still the Golden Door*, p. 111.

132. Takaki, *Strangers from a Different Shore*, p. 473.

133. John Dillin, "More Blacks Enter Middle Class," *Christian Science Monitor*, August 9, 1991, p. 7.

134. B. Suzuki, "Education and the Socialization of Asian Americans," in *Asian Americans: Social and Psychological Perspectives*, ed. R. Endo, S. Sue, and N. Wagner (Palo Alto, Calif.: Science & Behavior Books, 1980), 2:155–78.

135. Ishmael Reed, "America's Color Bind: The Modeling of Minorities," *San Francisco Examiner*, November 19, 1987, p. A20; "Success Story of One Minority Group in the U.S.," *U.S. News & World Report*, December 26, 1966, pp. 73–76.

136. For summaries of this research, see Patricia A. Roos and Joyce Hennessy, "Assimilation or Exclusion? Attainment Processes of Japanese, Mexican Americans, and Anglos in California" (paper presented at the American Sociological Association meetings, San Antonio, 1984); and Ronald Takaki, *From Different Shores* (New York: Oxford University Press, 1987).

137. Gloria Luz R. Martinez and Wayne J. Villemez, "Assimilation in the United States: Occupational Attainment of Asian Americans, 1980" (paper presented at the American Sociological Association meetings, Chicago, 1987), pp. 31–32.

138. U.S. Commission on Civil Rights, *Civil Rights Issues Facing Asian Americans in the 1990s*, pp. 103–36.

139. Wendy Lin, "Asians, Latinos Rip Voting Plan," *Newsday*, May 29, 1992, p. 4.

140. Kwang Chung Kim and Won Moo Hurh, "Korean Americans and the 'Success' Image: A Critique," *Amerasia* 10 (Fall/Winter 1983): 15.

141. Daniels, *Coming to America*, pp. 388–89.

142. Nathan Glazer, "Introduction," in *Clamor at the Gates*, ed. Nathan Glazer, p. 3.

Chapter 13

The Boiling Cauldron:
The Future
of Racial and Ethnic Relations

Jesse Jackson and the Rainbow Coalition
Photo courtesy of Associated Press/Wide World Photos

INTRODUCTION

Numerous articles in the mass media have noted that if current population trends continue, by the middle of the twenty-first century the typical U.S. resident will not be a European American but rather a Native American or a person who traces her or his ancestry to Asia, Latin America, Africa, or the Middle East. The 1990 census found that one in four Americans is rooted in non-European areas or is a Native American. Non-Latino whites are now a minority in areas such as southern California. Unfortunately, however, much of the private and public discussion of these demographic changes, especially among Americans of European descent, has an alarmist tone, doubtless because many non-Latino whites fear a loss of power and privilege to people of color. Such discussion again raises the old nativist fear of immigrant and nonwhite challenges to the Anglo core culture and society.[1]

THE NATION OF IMMIGRANTS

The United States has always been a nation of immigrants. Immigration is its foundation, its uniqueness, and its great strength. Tens of millions of immigrants have come to these shores from all corners of the globe, in numbers and diversity unparalleled in the rest of the world. Dozens of languages, scores of cultures, a great diversity of resources, and an array of physical characteristics have characterized these millions of immigrants. This diversity can be seen in something as simple as the array of Asian, African, European, Middle Eastern, Indian, and South American restaurants, or something as complex as voting patterns in California and debates over multicultural education in U.S. schools.

A 1990 national survey by the National Opinion Research Center (NORC) revealed the countries of origin of immigrants to the United States. The NORC researchers asked a random sample of 1,372 adults, "From what countries or part of the world did your ancestors come?" Countries cited by at least 1 percent of those mentioning only one country of origin were:

Africa	Germany	Poland
Canada	Ireland	Russia
Czechoslovakia	Italy	Scotland
Denmark	Mexico	Sweden
England and Wales	The Netherlands	
France	Norway	

Dozens of other countries were mentioned in proportions of less than 1 percent. The list shows that the major infusions of immigrants to this country originated in Africa, Mexico, Canada, and certain areas of Europe, particularly Great Britain and the rest of northern Europe.[2] Conspicuously absent in this 1990 list are countries in the Middle East and Asia.

Certain peculiarities in this list of countries, as well as the total number of immigrants from each, have been shaped by the distinctive economic and political conditions that characterized the United States and the sending countries in particular historical periods of immigration, a point we have explored in earlier chapters. The economic and political situations in the immigrants' homelands were often distressing or inhospitable to personal and family development. While variable, the U.S. economy, often a booming one with many low-wage jobs, attracted poor immigrants, such as the Irish, the Jews, the Koreans, and the Italians—all studied in this book. Most came more or less voluntarily. Only the Africans came in chains.

The political situation in the United States has been important in shaping immigration. Whites, usually Anglo Protestants, controlled national institutions and the government, including the power to launch military invasions overseas or to draft restrictive immigration laws at home. Imperialism overseas, as in the Philippines or Puerto Rico in the late nineteenth century, has clearly shaped immigration to the United States. Tough, often discriminatory immigration laws have been used to control the streams of migration to the United States. Historically, white Protestant leaders, including employers and politicians, have permitted or restricted immigration according to their racial and ethnic preferences and prejudices.

Particularly important have been the discriminatory restrictions in U.S. immigration laws, such as the Chinese Exclusion Act and the 1924 Immigration Act with its restrictive national-origin quotas. These laws were constructed by white Protestant Americans and thus guaranteed that by the late twentieth century the population mix of the United States would include fewer Asian Americans and Americans from southern and eastern Europe than would otherwise have been the case. The discriminatory 1924 law, for example, sharply reduced the number of Catholic immigrants from Italy and Poland, as well as the number of Jews from eastern Europe. As a result, the United States is today overwhelmingly Protestant; only a quarter of the population is Catholic or Jewish. The provisions excluding Asians insured that the United States would have fewer than 8 million Asian Americans in a population of more than 250 million by the late twentieth century. It is ironic that those responsible for anti-immigrant discrimination in one period have always included descendants of immigrants to the United States of a *previous* period. Only the Native Americans can accurately claim that they are the real natives and that all others are intruders.

Recent U.S. immigration acts, those passed in 1965, 1986, and 1990, have no exclusionary racial or national-origin quotas, yet they limit the number of immigrants who can come to the United States from any one country. The 1990 Immigration Act set the annual limit of all immigrants at 700,000 for the early 1990s and 675,000 after 1994. This limit most affects immigrants from those countries, such as certain Asian countries, in which many people now wish to come to the United States. This limited immigration contrasts with the generally unlimited immigration allowed from Europe before the 1910s.

Two recent restrictive acts reflect dominant concerns about immigration. The 1986 Immigration Reform and Control Act was intended to restrict the flow of immigrants from south of the U.S. border, particularly from Mexico. As we have seen in Chapter 9, Latino and other Americans are troubled by several provisions of that act, including intrusive governmental documentation of legal work status, sanctions for businesses that employ undocumented aliens, a program screening welfare applicants for migration status, and programs to bring in low-wage agricultural workers.

The 1990 Immigration Act made several additional changes in the law, including an expansion of the total number of immigrants allowed annually. The act set up several special visa categories. While most of the immigrant visas available are reserved for family members of legal U.S. residents, with an eye to family reunification, the employment-based category is now much larger, at 140,000. The latter visas are now mostly reserved for highly skilled workers, such as professionals. Visas for unskilled workers are virtually unavailable. A special category of 40,000 visas is reserved to provide legalization for certain illegal immigrants from 34 (mostly European) countries, and 10,000 visas are reserved for wealthy immigrants willing to invest at least one million dollars to create jobs in the United States.[3]

There has been much congressional and public debate over these new immigration laws. Many native-born (especially white) business leaders, politicians, and immigration activists have publicly expressed concern about the character and values of the new Latino and Asian immigrants who make up most of the current immigration stream. These native-born leaders are concerned, like earlier nativists, about whether the United States can absorb even the legally permitted number of new immigrants. They worry about the impact of this immigration on public schools, public social programs, and workplaces. Expressing concern over excessive population growth and overcrowding, Dan Stein, head of the Federation for American Immigration Reform, has charged that the new laws and regulations will allow at least 15 million new immigrants into the United States in the 1990s. Using exaggerated figures, Stein and other advocates of restriction have suggested that these new immigrants are a threat to the jobs of those already here, especially during recessions, and that they are likely to become public charges—two arguments made by nativists in the late nineteenth and early twentieth centuries against European immigrants.[4]

In fact, the new immigration from Asia and Latin America is not fueling a great population expansion in the United States. The 1980s saw a population increase of about 10 percent, the second-lowest rate of increase for any decade in U.S. history. Moreover, the ratio of immigrants to the native-born population is much lower today than in earlier decades of the twentieth century. Today the United States has not only a smaller percentage of foreign-born than it did in the 1920s, but also a smaller percentage of foreign-born than several European nations. Given its long history of successful absorption of immigrants and its geographical size, the United States is not likely to be overwhelmed by new immigrants.

In contrast to opponents of current immigration levels, demographer Ben Wattenberg has argued that immigrants make mostly positive contributions to this country: As a group immigrants are "upwardly mobile, ambitious, saving; they have traditional values, care about their children, all that sort of stuff. They've done something very dramatic to upgrade themselves." In his view immigrants are generally hardworking and honest and seek to make a good life for themselves and their families.[5]

Wattenberg and other pro-immigration scholars also point out that immigrants create jobs, as well as take them, because they create new demands for housing and other commodities. Wattenberg sees immigration as the force that has made the United States a great nation: "The United States is the first truly pluralist nation; it's no accident that we're also the only world superpower."[6]

Implicit in many discussions of restricting immigrants is a concern that the new immigrants from Asia and Latin America are not compatible with, or assimilable to, a core culture and society that has been substantially white and European American. Popular magazines have run major stories asking "What will America be like when whites are no longer the majority?" But what does color have to do with immigration and population growth, unless one has racist concerns? Concern with new immigrants is an old worry of nativists. But today nativists are also concerned about the physical characteristics of immigrants. The agenda of many in the anti-immigration groups appears to be the protection of the white European American core culture and structural dominance of the immigrants. In the view of many anti-immigrant groups, the U.S. experiment as a "nation of immigrants" should be stopped. However, the outcome of their efforts is unclear, because of strong opposition from Americans whose pro-immigration sentiments tap the deepest values of this society.

As we have emphasized throughout this book, the United States is still seen overseas as a "golden land"—a land of opportunity and freedom for the poor and oppressed peoples of the world. Recent immigrants, like their predecessors from Europe, bring intelligence, hard work, and cultural invigoration to the United States. An understanding of these contributions and the recognition that most of us are ourselves immigrants or the descendants of immigrants should make us welcome these and subsequent streams of immigrants to U.S. shores. Such hospitality will make the inscription on the Statue of Liberty, the words of Jewish American poet Emma Lazarus, ring true:

> Give me your tired, your poor,
> Your huddled masses, yearning to breathe free,
> The wretched refuse of your teeming shore,
> Send these, the homeless, tempest-tost to me:
> I lift my lamp beside the golden door.

THE MELTING POT: EARLY IMAGES OF IMMIGRANT INCORPORATION

There is still much debate as to how the immigrants, once ashore, are to be incorporated into the larger society. As we have seen throughout this book, pressures for assimilation are often matched by the desire of immigrants to maintain their own cultures and values. For nearly a century the most prominent image of the incorporation of immigrants has been that of the "melting pot." In the early 1900s the writer Israel Zangwill made an influential statement of this optimistic idea in his popular play *The Melting Pot.* In that play a struggling Russian immigrant argues that

> America is God's Crucible, the great Melting-Pot where all races of Europe are melting and re-forming! Here you stand, good folks, think I, when I see them at Ellis Island, here you stand in your fifty groups, with your fifty languages and histories, and your fifty blood hatreds and rivalries. But you won't be long like that, brothers, for these are the fires of God.... A fig for your feuds and vendettas! Germans and Frenchmen, Irishmen and Englishmen, Jews and Russians—into the Crucible with you all! God is making the American.[7]

Zangwill's idealistic image of a great crucible that melts fifty divergent groups to form a truly new "American blend" symbolizes a mutual adaptation process in which old and new groups freely blend together on a more or less equal basis. As we have seen throughout this book, actual intergroup adaptation has often involved more conflict than is suggested here. Also conspicuously absent from this image are Americans of color, such as African, Asian, Latino, and Native Americans.

In the early twentieth century the nation's most famous capitalist, Henry Ford, also had a vision of the melting pot, but one that was less of a blended pot than of an Anglo-conformity transmuting pot. Ford and his managers actively recruited the new southern and eastern European immigrants as auto workers. They set up a "Sociological

Department" in the company, complete with investigators who visited workers' homes and gave advice on family budgets, personal morality, and living arrangements. Immigrant workers attended a "melting pot school" where they learned not only English but also Anglo-Protestant values. At graduation ceremonies Ford's employees, dressed as in the old country, walked through a big pot labeled "melting pot" and emerged in business suits holding American flags.[8] Although he labeled this socialization process the melting pot, Ford's actual model was one of Anglo-conformity assimilation. Ford's schooling is a major example of the mostly one-way adaptation pressures faced by non-English immigrants from the nineteenth century to the present.

In Chapter 2 we saw that assimilation theorists such as Milton Gordon argue that in practice the U.S. melting pot has diverged greatly from Zangwill's ideal. The trend of immigrant adaptation has typically been in the direction of Anglo-conformity; each new stream of immigrants have given up much of their cultural heritage for the Anglo-Protestant core culture. As Gordon notes, "If there is anything in American life which can be described as an overall American culture which serves as a reference point for immigrants and their children, it can best be described, it seems to us, as the middle-class cultural patterns of, largely, white Protestant, Anglo-Saxon origins."[9]

CURRENT DEBATES OVER MULTICULTURALISM

In recent years the melting pot imagery has again become common. Modern-day pluralists and assimilationists have expressed great concern over the racial and ethnic groups formed by recent immigrants from Asia and Latin America. Popular and scholarly analysts vigorously debate the meaning of the melting pot for the United States today. These debates have reached corporate boardrooms, the U.S. Congress, and the White House. Recent discussions are centered in newer terms such as *multiculturalism* and *cultural diversity*—terms that stress the importance of respecting the many racial and ethnic groups and subcultures that have contributed to U.S. development, especially the contributions of non-European groups.

Multiculturalism is a variation of the cultural pluralism perspective. It emerged out of the racial and ethnic protest movements of the 1960s, and has spread across the United States. Hundreds of U.S. colleges and universities, as well as many public and private elementary and secondary schools, have developed multicultural courses and study programs in order to give voice to the people of color (and sometimes white women) who have done much of the hard work that built this society. In the late 1980s and early 1990s universities from Stanford and the University of California at Irvine to the University of Florida and Tufts University implemented new B.A. requirements that included courses dealing centrally with cultural diversity. And teachers at the New Utrecht High School in Brooklyn's predominantly white Bensonhurst section, where a black man shopping for a used car was killed by whites, pioneered a successful multicultural class that was soon added to the curriculum in other high schools. Their goal was to shatter racial and ethnic stereotypes and provide students with an opportunity to discuss the causes of intergroup strife.[10] Publishers and voluntary organizations have made multicultural teaching materials more readily available to colleges and public schools. In the early 1990s the Southern Poverty Law Center in

Montgomery, Alabama, developed a program for public schools that provides a biannual high-quality teaching resources magazine, called *Teaching Tolerance,* and other curriculum materials for multicultural programs.

Multiculturalism has been enthusiastically embraced by scholars and other Americans with roots in Africa, Asia, and Latin America. Other scholars and analysts, mostly white Americans, have viewed multiculturalism as an attack on the Anglo core culture and institutions. In recent books and speeches the prominent historian Arthur Schlesinger, Jr., has called the multiculturalism perspective "an astonishing repudiation" of the idea of the melting pot: "The contemporary ideal is not assimilation but ethnicity. We used to say *e pluribus unum.* Now we glorify *pluribus* and belittle *unum.* The melting pot yields to the Tower of Babel."[11]

Social scientists and popular writers who make such arguments fall into the "order theory" framework we have discussed. These critics of multiculturalism, seemingly fearful of losing the centripetal forces of the Anglo core culture, argue that some type of Anglo-conformity is still the best assimilation model for non-Anglo groups in the United States. Their "melting pot" is not so much a mutual blending of diverse groups as a melting of newcomers (and some older groups) into the Anglo core culture. While they sometimes recognize the contributions of non-Europeans to U.S. culture, these critics of multiculturalism emphasize a version of the Anglo-conformity assimilation theory when they assert that the United States is founded on the Eurocentric philosophy of individualism, not on a philosophy of ethnic and racial pluralism. The Eurocentric bias is clear in Schlesinger's argument: "It is not that the Western cultures are superior to other cultures as much as it is, for better or worse—our culture."[12] He adds that "our public schools, in particular, have been along with the workplace a great agency of assimilation, a great means of transforming newcomers into Americans."[13]

The bias and parochialism of the "Western culture" generally dominant in U.S. schools and other institutions are seen not as problematic but rather as essential for the integration of diverse racial and ethnic groups into one workable societal whole. Eurocentric observers are concerned that non-Europeans, including those in recent immigrant groups, assimilate to the core culture in order to prevent a cultural and structural "Balkanization" of the United States. They worry that this country will not survive with a vibrant pluralism of racial and ethnic groups. As a result, they usually oppose the teaching of multiculturalism and the creation of most multicultural courses and programs in public schools, colleges, and universities. For example, in a prominently discussed book Dinesh D'Souza, a recent immigrant from India who has served as a fellow at the conservative American Enterprise Institute, argues that multiculturalism represents an "academic and cultural revolution" on college campuses that is "revising the rules by which students are admitted to college, and by which they pay for college. It is changing what students learn in the classroom, and how they are taught." In his view the modest programs of multiculturalism, which he stigmatizes as "illiberal education," represent a serious threat to education in the United States.[14]

Other analysts and scholars have responded that multiculturalism and cultural diversity programs provide a necessary corrective to the dominance of the Anglo core culture. Such programs protect those subcultures and values repressed or excluded by Euro-Americans holding the reigns of power in educational, economic, and political institutions. Multicultural studies, University of Delaware sociologist Margaret Anderson suggests, "have encouraged us to look at traditionally excluded cultures and study them on their own terms rather than seeing them through the eyes of the dominant class." From this point of view multiculturalism is not separatist, as Schlesinger argues, but rather encourages "people to see in plural ways, so that they are not seeing through the lens of any single culture, but understanding the relationships of cultures to each other."[15]

For many, multiculturalism not only accents repressed or excluded subcultures but also challenges white (male) dominance in many institutions. Harvard literary critic Henry Louis Gates, an African American, has argued for setting aside the "antebellum aesthetic position" articulated by such authors as Schlesinger, an approach "where men were men and men were white, when scholar-critics were white men, and when women and persons of color were voiceless, faceless servants and laborers, pouring tea and filling brandy snifters in the boardrooms of old boys' clubs."[16]

Debates over multiculturalism and cultural diversity programs are about more than the creation of a few new courses focusing on racial and ethnic issues. The controversy becomes heated because it involves issues of white power and racial and ethnic inequalities. Some see multicultural courses as simply exposing students to diverse racial and ethnic cultures, but others also want the courses to critique the power imbalance and stratification of U.S. racial and ethnic relations. The latter concern is more generally an issue of power inequality and major social change, as it is for the power–conflict theorists we have examined throughout this book. Power–conflict analysts argue that multiculturalism means not only including the perspectives of nondominant groups but also scrutinizing and changing the core curricula in all college disciplines so that they "fairly represent the variegated nature of American culture."[17] From this viewpoint multiculturalism also means changing the hierarchies of colleges and universities so that minority people are represented at all levels of the administrative chain of command and are an empowered presence in policy making on such matters as the hiring of administrators and faculty, the drafting of curricula, and the makeup of college investments.[18]

RACE, ETHNICITY, AND EQUALITY

An Egalitarian Society?

The equality and justice often sought by subordinated racial and ethnic groups have been viewed in changing ways since 1776. The philosophy that "all men are created equal" held by the founders of this nation initially meant equality of social and political participation for white, European, Protestant, male immigrants and their male descendants, especially those with property. This limited equality of access to political institutions was certainly a dramatic step forward in an autocratic era, but it excluded such groups as women, African American slaves, Native Americans, and to some extent Jewish and Catholic Americans.

Over the next two centuries conceptions of equality would become more inclusive, so much so that numerous commentators have seen equality as an ideal whose driving force has been extraordinarily great in U.S. history and society. From this perspective the historical process has been a progressive egalitarianization of the U.S. social, economic, and political systems. The concept of equality has evolved to include equality of worth among individuals, equality of opportunity for all individuals, and equality before the law (civil rights). Many scholars and popular analysts, as well as politicians and business leaders, have praised the egalitarian trend they see over the course of U.S. history. Over time poor and subordinated ethnic and racial groups have achieved greater equality in some or all of these categories. Between the early 1800s and the early 1900s economic development and prosperity came dramatically to the United States, giving substantial opportunity to the many millions of white immigrants from Europe. Although they suffered discrimination, white ethnic Americans or their children eventually succeeded. From this optimistic perspective, the white ethnics soon "made it." Many assimilation-oriented analysts view non-European groups from the same perspective, arguing that these groups too are moving, albeit more slowly, toward full equality in the social, economic, and political institutions of this society.

Yet the rosy view of a society committed to "liberty and justice for all" is problematical. Substantial movement up the economic and political ladders did indeed come for most white ethnic groups. But an overly optimistic view ignores the great poverty and misery that white ethnics endured, for a generation at least, as poorly paid laborers, servants, or peddlers in an exploitative economic system. In this book we have documented capitalistic exploitation of groups such as Italian, Irish, and Jewish Americans. The racist immigration law that existed until 1965, restricting the entry of allegedly inferior white "races" from southern and eastern Europe, presented serious obstacles for immigrant families trying to reunite. White ethnics faced racist stereotyping for several decades; for some, such as Jewish and Italian Americans, the stereotyping persists, resulting in discrimination. One should not overlook the significant discrimination that still takes place, particularly for Jewish Americans, who are often the target of ethnoviolence and of institutionalized discrimination, such as in elite Anglo-Protestant clubs and in the executive suites of some large corporations.

The optimistic picture of equality and freedom in the United States also glosses over the continuing subordination and discrimination faced by Americans with roots outside of Europe. To some extent, Asian, African, Latino, and Native Americans have benefited from the trend toward expanded equality, especially in regard to formal legal rights and opportunities. Today's problems are centered in the *informal* operation of our economic, social, educational, and political institutions, where prejudiced whites discriminate, usually without fear of severe penalties.

Racial Discrimination: The 1990s and Beyond

The early 1990s marked the 500th anniversary of the landing of Christopher Columbus in the Americas. In the United States many celebrations were planned. But as we have seen, the Quincentenary celebrations generated protests from many Americans, especially Native Americans, who worked hard to counter the traditional images of brave and beneficent European explorers "discovering" America. They showed how foolish it was of Europeans to claim to "discover" a land that had already been occupied by millions of people for thousands of years. The European invasion benefited Europe, but it created major new problems for Native Americans, who were forced into a long and continuing struggle to maintain their lands, cultures, and institutions in the face of land theft, attempted genocide, and omnipresent discrimination.

"Liberty and justice for all" has bypassed the *original* Americans, who remain the forgotten Americans. As Native American leader LaDonna Harris has put it, "How do our children feel when they read the textbooks and they're not included? What does it do to their psyche?" Harris has emphasized the vital pluralism of the Native American tribes that survived white attempts to destroy them. Respect for this non-European pluralism could help white Americans prepare for a future of diversity that seems to frighten many. "The browning of America is coming whether or not we like it. It's coming and we're not prepared for it, because we haven't incorporated it into our thinking."[19]

Asian Americans too have long provided lessons in cultural pluralism. In the broad category of Asian Americans one finds many diverse groups, including Japanese Americans, who today must struggle with renewed anti-Japanese (and thus anti-Asian) sentiment among whites concerned and confused about job losses and economic restructuring in the United States. Some observers have noted that Japan has replaced the Soviet Union as the latest "enemy" of the United States, an enemy seen by whites as responsible for U.S. economic decline. Yet recent Japan loathing has targeted not only the country but also the character and color of the people, a racist aspect that did not characterize U.S. fear of the former Soviet Union.[20]

Anti-Asian sentiment has recently generated ethnoviolence by whites against Asian Americans in cities across the nation. We have noted the recent report of the U.S. Commission on Civil Rights citing the killing in Detroit of Vincent Chin by two jobless white autoworkers who thought him to be Japanese, and the murders of five Indochinese children at a Stockton, California, school in 1989 by a white man who harbored racial hatred.[21] "Liberty and justice" for Asian Americans is frustrated today by bias in the justice system. In the spring of 1992 a group of Asian Californians testified before a distinguished panel of state judges and lawyers about problems in the state justice system. Dennis Hayashi, director of the Japanese American Citizens League, testified before the panel that the courts must become tougher on hate criminals: "Hate violence is at an all-time high in America. But acts of racial violence are assigned a low priority [by the courts]."[22]

Latino Americans continue to face many problems in securing justice and equality. Reading through newspapers across the country recently, the authors found much evidence that anti-Latino discrimination continues to be a serious problem. One newspaper story in the spring of 1992 reported that the chief executive of a health insurance firm in the Southwest had publicly defended discrimination against Latinos by insurance companies, noting that people "who cannot speak, understand or read English are considered ineligible for coverage."[23] Other media stories reported Latino leaders protesting the absence of Latino actors in major roles on television and the portrayal of Latinos in the media as drug dealers, maids, and "Latin lovers." One article cited a 1992 research study that found discrimination by white Anglo employers against Latinos. Today Latinos continue to find their progress toward equality and justice limited by racial stereotyping and discrimination.[24]

African Americans too face obstacles in securing the equality and justice promised by the American creed. It was only a century ago that Reconstruction, a period of great progress in opportunities for African Americans (circa 1865–1885), was followed all too soon by a dramatic resurgence of reaction, the so-called Redemption period. And in this century, only two decades or so after public policy shifted significantly in favor of expanded opportunities for black and other non-European Americans in the 1960s, this society again moved in a reactionary direction. Powerful political leaders such as Ronald Reagan and George Bush have eliminated, or kept ineffective, various affirmative action, equal opportunity, and other civil rights programs benefiting minority Americans. Decades after these programs were established, no fundamental or lasting changes can be seen at the top levels in most major institutions in the United States. White males, mostly of Anglo-Protestant heritage, overwhelmingly dominate upper-level and middle-level positions in most major organizations, from the executive branch of the U.S. government, to Fortune 500 corporations, to state legislatures, to local banks and supermarket chains.

Since the 1970s the dominant white concern has shifted away from eradicating discrimination against black and other minority Americans. Indeed, in recent years a majority of whites have denied that white racism is still a major and widespread problem in all regions of the United States. Yet the reality and pain of racial discrimination can be seen if white Americans wish to see it. For example, when asked in a recent study what it is like being black in America, a retired professor who has lived in several regions of the country replied:

> I feel angry. I feel betrayed. Sometimes I feel very cynical. Most of the time I feel that I live in a country where I'm still not respected as a person. I lived at a time when I was told that if I got a good education, did all the right things, that I could be anything I wanted to be. I got a good education. I did all the right things, but even today I run into situations where my opportunity structure is limited because I am black. So I found that all along that no matter what I did, no matter how hard I tried, limitations were placed on me strictly because of the color of my skin. So I feel betrayed by the Constitution that guaranteed me certain rights. I feel betrayed by the Pledge of Allegiance to the flag, which says "liberty and justice for all."

When asked, on a scale from one to ten, how angry he gets at whites, he replied:

> Ten! I think that there are many blacks whose anger is at that level. Mine has had time to grow over the years more and more and more, until now I feel that my grasp on handling myself is tenuous. I think that now I would strike out to the point of killing, and not think anything about it. I really wouldn't care. Like many blacks you get tired, and you don't know which straw would break the camel's back. But you do know that there is a straw that might, and you don't try to prepare yourself not to do it any longer. You allow yourself the luxury of doing that. And I think that I'm at that point in my life where I avoid as many situations as I can. But if I'm forced and pushed into a corner, I'm going to strike out blindly. I will strike out blindly. I know that now, and I really don't care. Because it gets to a point where your life isn't worth it if you don't have some sense of respect and freedom. I don't mean license. I simply mean freedom to be like anybody else, to be treated like anybody else. And I'm angry at what's happening to our young people. I call it impotent rage, because it's more than anger. It's a rage reaction, but something that you can't do something about and that makes it even more dangerous when you do strike out.[25]

These comments were prophetic. They were made a bit more than three years before the twentieth century's most severe racial riot—the explosion that rocked poverty-stricken South-Central Los Angeles for several days in the spring of 1992. The acquittal of four white police officers of police brutality in beating up a black man—an incident captured in a widely viewed videotape—sparked the rebellion. Angry at the verdict, some poor blacks and Latinos took to the streets and burned or looted hundreds of local businesses. By the time the rebellion was over, more than fifty people had died. Los Angeles was not the only city to explode along its racial and ethnic fault lines. Other cities have experienced similar protests in the 1990s. The underlying conditions have included racism, poverty, unemployment, and poor housing conditions.[26]

In the aftermath of these recent urban riots many white Americans have asked why black Americans rebelled. As they did in earlier decades, many white officials in the 1990s have asserted that urban riots are not about protest, racism, or civil rights; instead they talk mostly of wild youngsters, criminal rioters, and the need for more police and, sometimes, for one-shot economic programs of a modest sort for the troubled central cities. Across the country black Americans in all income groups, however, have spoken of their great frustration, disillusionment, anger, and rage. Angry black and other nonwhite reactions to discrimination signal that the equality-and-justice agenda remains unfinished in the United States. Contrary to white conclusions, the black rebellions *are* usually about protest, equality, and civil rights. They are about inequality in a justice system that acquits white police officers who engage in brutal and excessive force against blacks and other minorities. They are about the persistence of racial discrimination that keeps many minority men and women from having jobs at decent wages. And they are about the racial discrimination that many black and other minority Americans routinely encounter on the streets and in restaurants, department stores, workplaces, and white neighborhoods.

CONCLUSION

Racial and ethnic equality and justice have long been part of an authentic American dream. The roots of that dream lie in the Declaration of Independence and the U.S. Constitution, pathbreaking documents that reflect this nation's centuries-old movement in the direction of expanded equality. However, both documents were marred by a capitulation to the supporters of slavery. After the Civil War the Constitution was amended to abolish slavery and expand the liberties of African Americans. Later, in the mid- and late-twentieth century, Supreme Court decisions and civil rights laws brought *formal* equality and justice to Americans of all racial and ethnic backgrounds. Yet anti-discrimination laws have often gone unenforced, and such laws cannot eradicate many informal types of racial and ethnic discrimination. Whether equality and justice can ever be a reality in the sphere of racial and ethnic relations in the United States remains to be seen. The likelihood of realizing this equality and justice is conditioned on successful political action and organization by those Americans, of all colors and creeds, who are committed to the ideals of equality and justice.

NOTES

1. David Gergen, "The Future of the Melting Pot," *U.S. News & World Report*, April 8, 1991, p. 35.
2. National Opinion Research Center, *1990 General Social Survey* (Chicago, 1991). Tabulation by authors.
3. Wendy Lin, "Stakes Are High in Lottery for U.S. Green Cards," *Newsday*, October 13, 1991, p. 19.
4. Transcript of press conference with Dan Stein held by the National Press Club, Federal News Service, January 7, 1992, n.p.
5. Quoted in Keith Henderson, "Immigration as an Economic Engine," *Christian Science Monitor*, March 27, 1992, p. 9. See also Ben Wattenberg, *The First Universal Nation* (New York: Free Press, 1990).
6. Quoted in Gergen, "The Future of the Melting Pot," p. 35.
7. Israel Zangwill, *The Melting Pot* (New York: Macmillan, 1925), p. 33.

8. James J. Fink, *The Car Culture* (Cambridge: MIT Press, 1975), pp. 88–90; Itabari Njeri, "Beyond the Melting Pot: In America, Blending in Was Once the Ideal," *Los Angeles Times,* January 13, 1991, p. E1.
9. Milton M. Gordon, *Assimilation in American Life* (New York: Oxford University Press, 1964), pp. 72–73.
10. Terry Lefton, "Building Bridges in the Big Apple," *Teaching Tolerance* 1, no. 1 (Spring 1992): 8–13.
11. Quoted in Njeri, "Beyond the Melting Pot," p. E1.
12. Arthur Schlesinger, Jr., "Speaking Up: A Look at Noteworthy Addresses in the Southland," *Los Angeles Times,* February 7, 1992, p. B2.
13. Ibid. See also Arthur Schlesinger, Jr., *The Disuniting of America: Reflections on a Multicultural Society* (New York: W. W. Norton, Co., Inc., 1991).
14. Dinesh D'Souza, *Illiberal Education* (New York: Random House, Vintage Books, 1991), p. 13.
15. Quoted in Njeri, "Beyond the Melting Pot," p. E1.
16. Henry Louis Gates, Jr., "Whose Canon Is It Anyway?" in *Debating P.C.,* ed. Paul Berman (New York: Bantam, 1992), pp. 190–91.
17. Ted Gordon and Wahneema Lubiano, "The Statement of the Black Faculty Caucus," in *Debating P.C.,* ed. Berman, p. 251.
18. Ibid., pp. 251–53.
19. LaDonna Harris, "Rediscovering Native Americans," *Forum,* Spring 1992, p. 8.
20. Robert J. Samuelson, "The Loathing of Japan," *Washington Post,* February 19, 1992, p. A19.
21. "Asian-Americans: Growing Racism; Major New Report Warns against the Vile Danger," *Los Angeles Times,* March 3, 1992, p. B6.
22. Quoted in Reynolds Holding, "Panel of Judges, Lawyers Chided for Courts' Toleration of Racism," *San Francisco Chronicle,* May 9, 1992, p. A15.
23. Scott Rothschild and Debra Beachy, "Insurance Bias Probe Requested," *Houston Chronicle,* February 14, 1992, p. 1.
24. Reuben Blades, "The Politics behind the Latino's Legacy," *New York Times,* April 19, 1992, sec. 2, p. 31.
25. Quoted in Joe R. Feagin and Melvin P. Sikes, *Modern Racism* (New Haven: Yale University Press, forthcoming).
26. Tom Mathews et al., "Fire and Fury," *Newsweek,* May 11, 1992, pp. 30–37.

INDEX